And Now My Soul Is Hardened

And Now My Soul Is Hardened

Abandoned Children in Soviet Russia, 1918–1930

Alan M. Ball

UNIVERSITY OF CALIFORNIA PRESS
Berkeley · Los Angeles · London

University of California Press
Berkeley and Los Angeles, California

University of California Press, Ltd.
London, England

Library of Congress Cataloging-in-Publication Data

Ball, Alan M.
    And now my soul is hardened : abandoned children in Soviet Russia,
1918–1930 / Alan M. Ball.
        p.   cm.
    Includes bibliographical references and index.
    ISBN 0-520-08010-6 (alk. paper)
    1. Abandoned children—Soviet Union—History.   I. Title.
HV887.S58B35   1994
362.7 ′6 ′094709041—dc20   92-46236
                                                               CIP

Printed in the United States of America

9 8 7 6 5 4 3 2 1

For my mother and father

Contents

List of Tables and Illustrations

Tables

Maps

Photographs follow p. 126

Preface

This is our own Russia tramping along the road, our own
Russia, as young and orphaned as these abandoned children,
as visionary and embittered, without a corner of her own,
with never a caress, with no one to look after her. Our own
Russia—that strange child who has already experienced
everything.

Ilya Ehrenburg

No spectacle in Soviet cities more troubled Russian and foreign observers during the first postrevolutionary decade than the millions of orphaned and abandoned children known as *besprizornye*.[1] Whether portrayed as pitiable victims of war and famine or as devious wolf-children
preying on the surrounding population to support cocaine and gambling
habits, they haunted the works of journalists, travelers, and Party members alike. "Every visitor sees it first," noted an American correspondent,
"and is so shocked by the sight that the most widely known Russian
youth are the . . . homeless children flapping along the main streets of
cities and the main routes of travel like ragged flocks of animated scare-
crows."[2] Averell Harriman recalled them as "a particular tragedy of the
time . . . , begging or stealing and living as wild animals unconnected
with the normal community life."[3] The very fact that no one could remain indifferent to their travail made them tempting ammunition in the
ideological charges and countercharges exchanged in these years. On
one side of the battle lines, critics of the Bolsheviks featured the children
as "proof" that the new regime had failed even to care for its own young.
In reply, Soviet officials pointed to the problem's origin in disasters
largely beyond their control and insisted that the Party had assigned far
higher priority to rehabilitating homeless juveniles than "bourgeois"
governments allocated to the care of their own downtrodden.

In other ways as well, these children meant different things to different people. Government officials, for instance, set out to rescue them

with widely varying understandings of who belonged in the category of *besprizornye*.[4] Translated literally, the singular *besprizornyi* means "unattended" or "neglected," though "homeless" or "waif" would be closer to the meaning intended by most Russians.[5] While everyone agreed that the label fit children orphaned or jettisoned by their parents and left to the streets, numerous educators, scholars, and social workers applied the word to a broader range of candidates. Their capacious definitions often encompassed minors still living with parents or relatives but not receiving a proper upbringing. Any number of factors—parental destitution, neglect, cruelty, or debauchery—could deprive offspring of a healthy adult influence and place them, advocates maintained, in the category of *besprizornye*. According to the principal Soviet encyclopedia of the time, "One must not restrict the term *besprizornye* to children who have lost their parents (or guardians) and homes. If parents (or guardians) deprive children of food, treat them crudely, steer them to crime, or set a harmful personal example—children of such parents are also *besprizornye*."[6]

We will focus primarily on youths who spent all, or at least most, of their time in the street. Our gaze thus takes in juveniles who drifted out of families, as well as the more obvious millions orphaned, discarded, or otherwise separated involuntarily from parents. Those who remained at home will not be included, regardless of the abuse or neglect they may have experienced there. Soviet administrators responsible for raising indigent children inclined toward a similar sense of their mission's scope, for even the narrowest definition of the *besprizornye* yielded more candidates than state institutions could absorb. The time when other youths, living with parents in unsatisfactory settings, could be lodged in children's homes together with the nation's orphans—a goal often avowed immediately following the Revolution—quickly receded far over the horizon.

Thus defined, the *besprizornye* represented first and foremost a stubborn challenge remaining to confront the Bolsheviks after their victory in the Civil War. The dismaying presence of countless young beggars and thieves underscored how deeply war and famine plague a society long after guns fall silent and crops return to fields. Even a wealthier and more experienced government than the one newly ensconced in Moscow would have been hard pressed to overcome rapidly the adversity bequeathed by nearly a decade of catastrophes. Later in the 1920s, though the street children's ranks diminished considerably, factors such as rural poverty and the unraveling of traditional families spawned additional urchins at a rate that frustrated the government's attempts to rid the country of their misfortune. As a result, in Alexander Solzhenitsyn's estimation, any description of Soviet urban life in this period remains incomplete without attention to abandoned juveniles, so common were they in train stations, markets, and other public places.[7]

Meanwhile, the government's desire to create a new socialist generation touched homeless boys and girls in a manner that revealed the new regime's hopes and fears. As banners unfurled to proclaim children "the flowers of the future," ubiquitous *besprizornye* prompted many to worry that weeds choked the country's flower beds, portending numerous thistles among the roses. Others, more optimistic, saw an opportunity to employ various theories of education and upbringing that competed for acceptance in the years following the Revolution. In their view, the Commissariat of Enlightenment's long-term boarding institutions possessed a seemingly unsurpassed opportunity to orchestrate the training of adolescent bodies and minds. What better facility, visionaries asserted, than a children's home in which to nurture the country's flowers—and the ragged crowds in the street insured that institutions would not lack seedlings to cultivate.

Despite their significance as a massive social problem and the many parallels between their predicament and that of the world's growing number of homeless juveniles today, the Soviet Union's abandoned children have eluded thorough investigation in Western scholarship. They find spotlights in only a few recent articles and figure peripherally in a handful of other works on education, the family, and crime.[8] Though useful, these studies' nature limits them to an overview—mainly of policies adopted to cope with the affliction—with little on the lives of the youths themselves. A lengthier treatment of the subject did appear in English translation some sixty years ago, but it consisted primarily of quotations from several Soviet newspapers, a minuscule sampling of the sources available.[9] The only extensive English-language work on the topic to surface in the decades since is a dissertation unnourished by published and archival materials accessible exclusively in the former Soviet Union.[10] Beyond this, one must look principally to memoirs and travel accounts if Western volumes mark a search's limits.

Meanwhile, a much larger body of sources evolved in the Soviet Union during the 1920s. Scholars, social workers, educators, and journalists published books, articles, collections of laws, and statistical information on the plight of waifs and the measures taken to save them.[11] National and provincial branches of the Commissariat of Enlightenment issued many of these works (and generated numerous internal documents that archives have recently been willing to provide), though other government agencies, notably the Commissariat of Health, contributed as well. So, too, did citizens' "volunteer" organizations, especially the "Friend of Children" Society (*Obshchestvo "Drug detei"* or ODD). ODD cells in several cities published periodicals (sometimes with the participation of government agencies) that carried reports from around the country. Two of these journals, composed in Moscow and Khar'kov and both titled *Drug detei*, are particularly rewarding vehicles for an often unflinching look at the street habitat of abandoned children. Similarly forthright reports appeared in newspapers—national papers with their far-flung staffs and local gazettes concentrating on a single city or region—as correspondents explored derelict buildings, train station basements, and other entrances to a harsher world. The dispatches carried by their papers displayed a frankness unmatched in the Soviet press until the ascendance of Mikhail Gorbachev.

Once the 1920s gave way to decades of more regimented tone, Soviet scholars added comparatively little to these earlier publications. Prolonged interest in tragedies that accompanied the nation's infancy seemed out of place, indeed undesirable, on a stage featuring triumphant remembrances of the Revolution and pageants of "socialist construction." The most helpful exceptions have been scattered regional studies of the *besprizornye*, a few essays on juvenile delinquency, and biographical material on such personages as Feliks Dzerzhinskii and Anton Makarenko who strove to rehabilitate difficult youths. As with Western historians, the emphasis here rests invariably on official responses to the problem (rather than on the children's street experiences), though Soviet authors naturally view the policies more favorably.

Taken as a whole, the array of Western and Soviet sources now available suggests two broad avenues of investigation: the children themselves and the government's reaction to their presence. Following an introductory chapter on the origins of the youths' distress, the remainder of the work adopts this dual approach. Chapters 1–3 examine the lives of juveniles on the street and provide a glimpse into corners of the urban underworld. Principal topics include the forms of shelter sought by waifs, the measures they adopted to secure sustenance, and their mores, amusements, and views of the surrounding society. Illegal activities and the ties many children acquired with adult criminals appear throughout.

This survey of the street then yields in chapters 4–7 to an analysis of the government's response. How serious a problem, for example, did authorities regard the tattered figures of tender years? Did confidence prevail that the *besprizornye* could be recast as builders of socialism? In what ways did official assumptions and remedies change during the period under consideration? Looking beyond policy to its implementation, how were children actually captured or otherwise channeled into orphanages? What was the nature of these facilities, and did they succeed in clearing the streets? Finally, what happened to adolescents after their discharge from institutions? Did their paths lead back into the mainstream of Soviet society, or did other fates await them?

Many people have assisted me generously during various stages of this project, and I am pleased to acknowledge my debt to them. Samuel Baron read a draft of the entire manuscript, while Richard Stites and Lynne Viola each scrutinized portions. Their comments both encouraged me to continue with the endeavor and suggested numerous improvements. In addition, I would like to thank Bill Creech and Dane Hartgrove at the National Archives for steering me reliably to documents of the American Red Cross, Wendy Goldman for alerting me to certain archival *fondy* prior to my departure for the Soviet Union, and Don Raleigh for kindly sharing materials he acquired while conducting his own research in Saratov. Professor V. M. Selunskaia of Moscow State University was most congenial and accommodating during my stay there in 1987–88 as a participant on the US-USSR Long-term Exchange of Advanced Researchers administered by the International Research and Exchanges Board (IREX). Needless to say, I am grateful to IREX for supporting this year of research in the Soviet Union. Numerous Soviet archivists and librarians aided me as well, but the staff at the Central State Archive of Literature and Art (TsGALI) deserve special mention for their willing help in obtaining copies of several archival photographs. They made work in TsGALI more rewarding than I could ever have anticipated. Closer to home, at the University of California Press, Sheila Levine's sure-footed combination of encouragement and advice served the project well. She, with able assistance from Monica McCormick, Dore Brown, and Anne Canright, brought the book into this world with a deftness that required no recourse to the profession's equivalent of forceps or general anesthesia. Finally, excerpts from earlier versions of some chapters have appeared as the core of articles in *Slavic Review*, *Russian Review*, and *Jahrbücher für Geschichte Osteuropas*. I thank the editors of these journals for allowing me to draw on that material here.

Terms and Abbreviations

ARA (American Relief Administration). In the years after World War I, this agency (under the direction of Herbert Hoover) provided relief for famine victims in a number of countries. It was by far the largest of the numerous Western organizations so engaged in the Soviet Union during the early 1920s.

Artel'. A producers' collective composed of handicraftsmen.

Besprizornost'. The condition of abandonment and homelessness.

Besprizornyi (pronounced bespreeZORnee, with the *e* in the first syllable sounding like the "ye" in "yes"). A single orphaned or otherwise homeless and abandoned child (pl., *besprizornye*, pronounced bespreeZORneeye). Also used as an adjective. The variant *besprizornik* (pl., *besprizorniki*) is used only as a noun.

Central Commission for the Assistance of Children (*Tsentral'naia komissiia pomoshchi detiam*, or TsKPomdet). The Ukrainian equivalent of the Children's Commission.

Cheka. The secret police. During the 1920s the Cheka became first the GPU (*Gosudarstvennoe politicheskoe upravlenie*) and then the OGPU (*Ob"edinennoe gosudarstvennoe politicheskoe upravlenie*).

Children's Commission (full name: Commission for the Improvement of Children's Life; *Komissiia po uluchsheniiu zhizni detei*, or Detkomissiia). An interagency body formed in 1921 on the initiative of Feliks Dzerzhinskii, head of the secret police. The commission was active in the campaign against *besprizornost'* throughout the decade.

Children's Extraordinary Commission (full name: Extraordinary Commission in the Struggle with Juvenile *Besprizornost'* and Juvenile Crime; *Chrezvychainaia komissiia po bor'be s detskoi besprizornost'iu i pravonarusheniiami nesovershennoletnikh*, or DChK). A division of MONO formed to combat *besprizornost'* and its consequences. Combined with another body to form a SPON unit in 1925.

Children's Social Inspection (*Detskaia Sotsial'naia Inspektsiia*, or DSI). A corps of social workers administered by Narkompros and intended to replace the police in most dealings with minors. Among other duties, they were to search out *besprizornye* and steer them into institutions.

Council for the Defense of Children (*Sovet Zashchity Detei*). An ineffective interagency body formed in 1919 and headed by Narkompros with the goal of coordinating the provision of aid to juveniles. Supplanted by the Children's Commission in 1921.

Detdom (contraction of *detskii dom*; pl., *detdoma*). Children's home. The most common long-term boarding institution for raising homeless juveniles. The vast majority of *detdoma* were administered by Narkompros.

Detskie gorodki. Children's towns. Usually large units composed of several (occasionally dozens) of individual institutions; sometimes a loose collection of formerly independent *detdoma* or, in other instances, a colony of more tightly integrated buildings.

Ermakovka (*Ermakovskii nochlezhnyi dom*). A flophouse in Moscow.

Factory-apprenticeship schools (*shkoly fabrichno-zavodskogo uchenichestva*, or FZU schools). Programs combining postprimary education with industrial training in a host factory.

Glavsotsvos (*Glavnoe upravlenie sotsial'nogo vospitaniia i politekhnicheskogo obrazovaniia detei*; Main Administration of Social Upbringing and Polytechnic Education of Children). The central branch of Narkompros most responsible for responding to the problem of *besprizornost'*.

GPU. See Cheka.

GubONO (*Gubernskii otdel narodnogo obrazovaniia*; Province-level Division of Education). Province-level branch office of Narkompros.

Gubsotsvos (*Gubernskoe upravlenie sotsial'nogo vospitaniia i politekhnicheskogo obrazovaniia detei*; Province-level Administration of Social Upbringing and Polytechnic Education of Children). Province-level equivalent of Glavsotsvos.

Investigators-upbringers (*obsledovateli-vospitateli*). Social workers intended primarily to assist Juvenile Affairs Commissions.

Juvenile Affairs Commission (*Komissiia po delam o nesovershennoletnikh*, or Komones). A board, administered by Narkompros, established to resolve the cases of juvenile delinquents.

Khitrovka (*Khitrovskii rynok*). A large outdoor market in Moscow.

Kitaigorod (literally, "Chinatown"). A district in Moscow, just east of the Kremlin.

Komsomol (*Kommunisticheskii soiuz molodezhi*; Communist Union of Youth). Communist youth organization intended mainly for those in their teens and twenties.

Kulak. A wealthy peasant (literally, "fist"). The term has a negative connotation suggesting that the kulak exploited other peasants.

Kvass. A lightly fermented beverage, somewhat similar to beer.

Labor commune (trudovaia kommuna). Facilities intended to rehabilitate "difficult" juveniles with a variety of "enlightened" measures, rather than through imprisonment and punishment.

Labor home (trudovoi dom). Facilities run by the Commissariat of Justice until 1922 (and through the rest of the decade by the Commissariat of Internal Affairs) for juvenile offenders sentenced by courts to terms of confinement.

MONO (Moskovskii otdel narodnogo obrazovaniia; Moscow Division of Education). The Moscow branch of Narkompros.

Narkompros (Narodnyi komissariat prosveshcheniia). The People's Commissariat of Enlightenment.

NEP. The New Economic Policy (in force from 1921 until the decade's close) that permitted considerable private commerce and manufacturing, small-scale peasant agriculture, and free trade of grain.

Nochlezhnyi dom (often shortened to nochlezhka). A flophouse.

Observation-distribution point (nabliudatel'no-raspredelitel'nyi punkt, or raspredelitel'). Facilities designed to examine children for an extended period in order to determine their mental and physical condition and thus establish the most suitable type of boarding institution for their rehabilitation.

ODD (Obshchestvo "Drug detei"). "Friend of Children" Society. Composed of volunteer groups expected to contribute time and money to various endeavors benefiting children—in particular the campaign to rescue and raise besprizornye.

OGPU. See Cheka.

Patronirovanie. Foster care. In the case of besprizornye, generally implemented by transferring children from detdoma to peasant families.

Pioneers. Communist youth organization intended mainly for those of primary-school age.

Receiver (priemnik). A facility designed to receive children directly from the street and tend to their immediate needs before passing them on to other institutions.

Samoobsluzhivanie. "Self-service." A program in which youths in children's institutions assumed wide responsibility for daily chores.

Samoupravlenie. "Self-government." A program in which youths in children's institutions participated to one degree or another in the administration of their facilities.

Sovnarkom (Sovet narodnykh komissarov). The Council of People's Commissars.

SPON (Otdel sotsial'no-pravovoi okhrany nesovershennoletnykh; Division of Social and Legal Protection of Minors). The subsection of Glavsotsvos most responsible for rehabilitating besprizornye.

Sukharevka (Sukharevskii rynok). A large outdoor market in Moscow.

Teplushka (also called a *vagon-priemnik*).   Train cars designed to range over principal lines, stopping at stations to collect *besprizornye* for initial processing before transfer to stationary receivers.

uezd.   A district within a province.

VTsIK (*Vserossiiskii tsentral'nyi ispolnitel'nyi komitet*).   The All-Russian Central Executive Committee elected by the All-Russian Congress of Soviets.

War Communism.   A turbulent period (1918–1920) of civil war, foreign intervention, widespread starvation, frequent epidemics, sweeping nationalization decrees, grain requisitioning, and zeal in Bolshevik ranks about building a communist society. Followed in 1921 by NEP.

A Note on Conventions

1. This work employs the Library of Congress system of transliteration, with the following minor modifications: (a) diacritical marks are omitted; (b) certain familiar names (e.g., Trotsky, Mayakovsky, Zinoviev) are spelled as they customarily appear in English.

2. Fiscal years (i.e., twelve-month periods beginning on October 1) are designated with a "/" between the two years in question: thus "1926/27" stands for the period October 1, 1926–September 30, 1927. If the reference is to consecutive calendar years, a "–" is employed (e.g., 1926–1927).

3. When quotations are presented from sources with Russian titles, the translations are my own.

A Note on Renamed Cities

During the period covered by this book, the Soviet government changed the names of several cities present on the maps included here. The older or newer designations for some municipalities turn up from time to time in the following pages, and the list below supplies these names accompanied (on the right) by the maps' alternatives. Names bestowed after 1930 do not appear.

Dnepropetrovsk—Ekaterinoslav to 1926

Ekaterinburg—Sverdlovsk from 1924

Ekaterinodar—Krasnodar from December 1920

Novo-Nikolaevsk—Novosibirsk from 1925

Petrograd—(St. Petersburg to 1914), Leningrad from 1924

St. Petersburg—(Petrograd from 1914 to 1924), Leningrad from 1924

Simbirsk—Ul'ianovsk from 1924

Stalingrad—Tsaritsyn to 1926

Map 1. Soviet Central Asia and Siberia, 1925

Map 2. Western Soviet Union, 1925

Introduction: Tragedy's Offspring

Inasmuch as revolution is the destruction of the old outdated order, of old family and social relations, it is also one of the causes of *besprizornost'*.

Nadezhda Krupskaia

We are thrown out like puppies born blind.

A besprizornyi

Orphaned and abandoned children have been a source of misery from earliest times. They apparently accounted for most of the boy prostitutes in Augustan Rome and, a few centuries later, moved a church council of 442 in southern Gaul to declare: "Concerning abandoned children: there is general complaint that they are nowadays exposed more to dogs than to kindness."[1] In tsarist Russia, seventeenth-century sources described destitute youths roaming the streets, and the phenomenon survived every attempt at eradication thereafter. Long before the Russian Revolution, the term *besprizornye* had gained wide currency.[2] What, then, distinguished vagrant juveniles of the nation's first postrevolutionary decade? To some extent it was their privation, though taken individually the children's experiences knew precedent enough in Russia. Much more shocking was their vast number. By 1922 the twentieth century's relentless opening sequence of warfare, epidemics, and famine had left the new Bolshevik government at least seven million waifs. Even to observers well aware of social problems under the tsarist regime, homeless youths now inundated Russian cities to a degree unimaginable only ten years earlier.

To be sure, few imaginations accurately forecast horrors of unusual dimension. The exuberant demonstrations that attended the march of tsarist troops to the front, for instance, appear now as exultation around an unquenchable inferno. Those shouting for blood in August 1914 did not anticipate the scale of impending havoc that would extinguish some sixteen million lives within the nation's borders by 1922.[3] Yet this was the reckoning which commenced that summer—and hardly the Great War's sole measure of grief. Along with its slaughter in the trenches, the conflict administered a variety of blows that severed contact between millions of children and their parents.[4]

From the beginning, mobilization of adult males deprived numerous families of their primary breadwinners and compelled mothers to work outside the home. Sons and daughters sought subsistence in any way possible, with little or no supervision. Whatever their choice—begging, peddling, prostitution, or theft—they spent an ever larger portion of their time on the street, drifting out of shattered families that could no longer support them. Those who turned to relatives often discovered these havens to be just as precarious, for if wartime adversity overcame their adoptive guardians, the newcomers' weak claim on household re-sources saw them first out the door. By summer's end in 1917, a Pro-visional Government ministry noted the presence in Petrograd of "5,000 children without parents and absolutely homeless. According to the es-timates of the city there are about 150,000 children who are partly destitute, their fathers being in the army and their mothers at work."[5]

One family shredded by the conflict included a boy named Aleksei, born in the city of Ekaterinburg. His father, who had worked as a cob-bler in a factory before the war, perished in the fighting, leaving his mother, a washerwoman, to support five children. After making ends meet for a time through the sale of household property, she fell ill, suf-fered a mental breakdown, and was taken to a hospital. Testimony is silent on the children's fate, but at some point they lost their dwelling, for on their mother's discharge the family sought refuge in a crude dug-out shelter. Soon, another breakdown returned the woman to the hos-pital, and she appears no more in the account. After an unspecified interval, her sons and daughters were placed in children's homes—from which Aleksei escaped repeatedly to spend ever longer periods stealing from traders in local markets.[6]

Meanwhile, as the Russian army suffered one defeat after another, the combat moved eastward, pushing residents out of villages and towns in the western portion of the country. A stream of over three million refugees issued from four provinces in Belorussia alone by early 1917, as people left on orders from officials or fled independently.[7] Those evac-uated at the bidding of authorities were generally informed that they would be conveyed by train or other means to safe regions deep inside the country. Inevitably, youths lost contact with their parents during these wartime relocations. Mothers and fathers (and, of course, some juveniles as well) died of starvation or disease as periods of travel in packed train cars alternated with endless waiting at stations. Looking back a few years later to describe their abandonment, children sometimes recounted that while they were off searching for food during such stops, the trains—with their parents aboard—were ordered to depart. Here and there, local officials sorted minors from adults, sending them to different, often remote, destinations. Inadequate coordination and record keeping commonly accompanied the shunting of citizens from place to place and made it difficult to reunite families later on. The government, in short, handled millions of refugees with the same lumbering confusion that it displayed in conducting other aspects of the war.[8]

Many evacuees washed up as far east as the Urals, particularly the area around Cheliabinsk. Children whose parents had perished or disappeared en route could rarely hope for anything more than refuge in squalid orphanages or temporary shelters. As the months dragged by, they were joined by others whose parents had died after reaching evacuation regions—often carried away by outbreaks of cholera and typhus that also claimed many juveniles. The brief autobiography of an orphan, identified only by the surname Korneliuk, reports that World War I forced his family to flee their village. With hardship and illness ever at hand, he and his parents covered thousands of miles (presumably part of an evacuation managed by the government) to reach a village in Cheliabinsk province, where he worked five years as a hired laborer for a prosperous peasant. After the war, his family joined others in the province petitioning to return to their native region, now part of Poland. When the passage of time brought no response, they journeyed to Cheliabinsk to take up the matter with authorities there. The city thronged with refugees, many of whom clogged a barracks previously stocked with Austrian prisoners of war. In this setting the boy survived a bout with typhus but discovered upon recovery that his parents had died. Some time thereafter, his name appeared on a list of orphans collected in the barracks and transported westward back across the country to the town of Velikii Ustiug, where he worked on a state farm. Six months later, local officials dispatched him to Poland, a trek destined to lead instead to a children's home in Moscow.[9]

Juveniles routinely fended for themselves after overcrowded shelters denied them entry. Others vanished from official sight in the shuffle from one institution to another or fled facilities whose conditions seemed more wretched than life on the street. Even families that survived intact the long journey to the Urals or one of the cities in the middle Volga region did not always withstand the trials that lay ahead. After a lifetime of misery compressed into less than a decade, they faced in 1921 a famine that desolated the territory to which manmade ruin had flung them.[10] This sequence of events forms the heart of an autobiographical sketch left by an orphan from the city of Grodno. His family numbered among the millions pouring from western districts to the interior during World War I, in this case again to a village in Cheliabinsk province. Here the boy quit school and found work with local peasants in order to help support the family, his father having died in 1914. For six years they managed in this fashion, until famine arrived to eliminate the village's food and drive them in desperation to Cheliabinsk. Five people in a starving multitude, they were swept into a cold, typhus-ridden barracks that soon claimed the boy's mother and a sister. Three days later his other sister died, leaving him alone with an ailing brother. "There were many like us."[11]

But before the scourge of famine descended on the country, civil war between the Bolsheviks and diverse adversaries beset a society already bled pale by World War I. From 1918 through 1920 families continued to disintegrate under the assault of combat, flight, hunger, and disease, casting adrift still more children. Every contested province revealed them in abundance. As the fighting approached its last summer in southern Russia, for example, American Red Cross personnel in the vicinity told of "1,000,000 Russian children separated from their parents and needing food and clothing."[12]

With warfare spread across much of the country, refugees streamed in huge numbers and in all directions. A Red Cross document titled "The Agony of Western Siberia" portrayed scenes by no means unique to the Siberian front: "The whole of the towns in this region are over-crowded in an incredible manner, and the congestion is indescribable. To quote one example, in Omsk where the population prior to the war was about 180,000 souls, it is estimated that there are at the present time 700,000 herded in and around this town."[13] City after city near the ever-shifting front lines teemed with people on the run. By 1920, over three hundred thousand refugees jammed the Crimean city of Sevastopol', normally home to only seventy-five thousand. In the Northern Caucasus sector, as Bolshevik troops approached Rostov-on-the-Don during the winter of 1919–1920, "trains went out with refugees clinging all night to the platforms, bumpers and huddling on the roof. This is not unusual in the summer," commented a Red Cross official, but it was then "bitter winter weather." No doubt many of these people made for the neighboring Kuban' region—where they joined five hundred thousand to one million other uprooted adults and children.[14] With even less guidance than that provided by the tsarist government for evacuations during World War I, the Civil War's refugees plodded blindly into chaos and death that stripped innumerable children from their parents.[15]

As casualties from battles, reprisals, and executions grew, so did the number of households deprived of their principal source of economic support. Most of those killed in military operations were men, of course, and the tragedy of newly widowed mothers unable to support their offspring remained the fecund source of homeless youths that it had become after 1914. Furthermore, the collapse of government authority in numerous areas left armed bands to roam the countryside, seizing whatever they could, killing whomever they pleased, and strewing additional orphans in their wake.[16] Such was the experience of the Aleichenko family in the village of Fliugovka, Voronezh province. A few months after the father departed for the trenches of the First World War, notification arrived that he had sacrificed his life "for the faith, tsar, and fatherland." Then, after a yearlong illness, the mother died, leaving five children with their grandfather, Anton. One of the five, a boy named Vasilii, recalled that in 1919 or 1920 groups of armed men began to raid their village. As the peasants scrambled to bury their grain and conceal their livestock, Anton sought to hide his only horse. In the process, the animal kicked him in the chest, a fatal blow that deprived the children of their guardian. Vasilii's older brother took the youngest of the three boys to live in the Northern Caucasus region with distant relatives and managed to find refuge for his two sisters with compassionate neighbors. Then he and Vasilii set out for the Northern Caucasus, hoping to survive in any manner possible. Along the way they were separated, not destined to meet again until 1964, and Vasilii began a vagrant life that would take him throughout the Crimea, Northern Caucasus, and beyond. Eventually he entered an orphanage, from which his path led to school, the communist youth organization, factory work, action in World War II, and service in the Cheliabinsk police force.[17]

Behind the Civil War's violence trailed a retinue of hunger and disease, tearing untold thousands of youths from their guardians. Years of fighting had bequeathed the population severe shortages of food and other essentials, thereby inviting epidemics and starvation for lengthy stays. Perhaps typhus or cholera arrived to gut a child's village, or a father journeyed off in search of food and never returned. Entire families left home, fleeing privation or soldiers, only to be decimated by disease along the rails, roads, or waterways.[18] In Omsk, for instance, the American Red Cross opened an orphanage for children whose parents had succumbed to typhus and other maladies—often spread by soldiers, as described in the following report:

> [In the rail yards across the Irtysh River from Omsk] the congestion of trains of soldiers coming from the West ahead of the advancing Bolsheviks soon led to a frightful situation. Hundreds upon hundreds of patients in the height of typhus fever arrived from the West and many of them wandered delirious in and out among the other trains and among the refugee families, spreading the disease. Lacking water, lacking food, lacking fuel, lacking every facility for decent living, the railway yards at Kolumzino became a [sic] inferno of suffering.[19]

Hunger, too, pried children from households that could no longer sustain them, including a boy named Andrei growing up in the industrialized core of the Donets basin. One day in 1917, after news of the tsar's fall reached the area, unrest broke out at an iron mill. Policemen responded, and the ensuing battle claimed among its casualties a worker from Orlov province—Andrei's father. His mother had died years before, so the children were sent back to their home region to live with an uncle. Here they managed to get by until hunger overcame the area in 1919, prompting the beleaguered uncle to evict one of the boys, Andrei, to forage on his own. "I cried, not knowing what to do, and set off with no idea of a destination. I got on a train and left without knowing where I was going. I wanted to eat, but I was afraid to beg and afraid to steal . . ."[20]

While Andrei groped for survival among the homeless, conditions also deteriorated in Petrograd, Moscow, and other large cities. Desperate officials even evacuated children to colonies in Ufa province, the Caucasus, Ukraine, and Crimea, where they hoped for more abundant food and fuel. Some evacuees subsequently lost contact with their parents when the ebb and flow of fighting cut off regions temporarily from Soviet Russia, as the American Red Cross observed: "Poltava was the centre of a district selected by the Bolsheviki where the children from the northern cities were to be sent, consequently, with their [the Bolsheviks'] forced evacuation, some 8000 children were left to be taken care of by the new [White] government. Conditions in this respect were very bad and unless some outside assistance is given this winter much suffering will result."[21] Colonies left in such straits frequently crumbled, and their inhabitants dispersed to fend for themselves.[22]

Thus it was that by 1920, as combat finally diminished, local officials noted an alarming number of orphans and abandoned children, growing ever more primitive and dissolute as they swelled the contingent of delinquents, prostitutes, and hawkers clinging to life on the street.[23] More would soon join them.

Within a matter of months, in the second half of 1921, the bony hand of famine strangled countless villages in the nation's heartland. The territory devastated most completely stretched along the Volga basin all the way from the Chuvash Autonomous Region and the Tatar Republic through Simbirsk, Samara, Saratov, and Tsaritsyn provinces down to Astrakhan' at the river's mouth. It extended as far north as Viatka province, as far east as Cheliabinsk and the Bashkir and Kirghiz republics, including Orenburg, Ufa, and Perm' provinces, and west as far as southern Ukraine. The long period of war had removed hundreds of thousands of peasants from the soil and cut sharply into the number of draft animals available, reducing acreage under cultivation. Also, the Bolsheviks' policy of grain requisitioning (not to mention similar measures taken by their opponents), while possibly necessary for victory in the Civil War, diminished the peasantry's grain reserves and rendered them more vulnerable to unfavorable conditions that might subsequently arise.[24] And arise they did, for a severe drought blighted the crops of the Volga basin by the summer of 1921, inaugurating a catastrophe destined to claim at least five million lives.[25]

For nearly two years, chilling accounts surfaced from the famine region, describing a population driven to ever more wretched extremes by hunger. Investigators found village after village where people had abandoned hope in exchange for numbing apathy. They lay in their huts with changeless, blank expressions—after having dug their own graves on occasion—and waited quietly to die.[26] Others committed the most brazen thefts from homes, mills, storehouses, and similar facilities thought to contain food. Newspaper articles and telegrams from local officials reported a huge increase in such offenses, though in some localities they were so common that no one bothered to count them or even view them as crimes.[27] As starvation and disease spread in the second half of 1921, millions resolved to flee their villages. Many thronged to provincial capitals or more distant sites rumored to be better supplied, including Central Asia, Siberia, and Ukraine. Some wandered aimlessly down the roads, passing forlorn figures trudging just as blindly in the opposite direction. For a long time thereafter, human remains dotted these routes, marking the end of refugees' ordeals.[28]

In Orenburg, a former waif recalled, hunger reduced his family to such misery that he and his father boarded a train for Tashkent, said to harbor substantial grain stores. Day by day, the journey took one frightening turn after another. First, illness overcame his father. Then, at a station, other passengers ordered the boy to take a bucket and steal some oil for the stove in the crowded car. They promised to throw him and his father out if he failed, but the terrified boy managed to pilfer the oil and preserve his place among the travelers. On another occasion he narrowly escaped a fire that destroyed much of the car. Later, when he and his father were searching for tea in a station, the train departed, stranding them until accommodations turned up in a freight car. Eventually his father died, leaving the boy to push on alone to Tashkent and then Samarkand before returning to Orenburg. He supported himself along the way by selling his clothing and begging, with adversity continuing to overshadow good fortune.[29]

As food supplies disappeared from the Volga provinces, ravenous inhabitants turned for sustenance to leaves, bark, acorns, roots, weeds, grass, chaff, straw, and sunflower stalks. Peasants hunted dogs, cats, mice, rats, and crows until none remained in their villages. A delegation from Samara reported that "people deranged from hunger are wandering about like packs of wolves, tearing apart the burrows of rodents, digging up the carcasses of diseased cattle, and grinding their half-decayed bones into flour." Others vainly sought nourishment in carrion, manure, leather, and clay.[30] Numerous dispatches told of suicides and of parents resolved to end the anguish of their emaciated offspring by suffocating the children or throwing them into wells and rivers.[31]

Even this did not mark the limit of ghastliness inflicted by the famine. When references to cannibalism first reached Moscow and Petrograd, they seemed wild exaggerations, inconceivable in twentieth-century Europe. But with each passing month, cases multiplied, reaching into the thousands by 1922. In the town of Nikopol', two American relief workers sought confirmation from local officials: "Comrade Titov, the ruler of the town, verified these reports and even showed us official photographs of two children picking the meat from the head of their dead mother; and another where the members of the family, father, mother and several children, were satisfying their insane appetite on the cooked remains of one of the members of the family."[32] The practice occurred frequently enough in some districts that local inhabitants ceased to regard it as remarkable. Here and there people plundered graves and morgues in search of corpses, and human flesh even appeared for sale.[33]

The famine's wrath added legions of abandoned juveniles to the millions already at large. Clad in filthy, lice-infested rags and staggering from exhaustion and hunger, they began to appear on the streets of Moscow by late summer of 1921. From Kazan' came word that every ship and train arriving in the city brought waifs from the surrounding area. With the onset of cold weather and the ever-worsening supply of food in their home districts, they flooded numerous cities, both in and out of the famine region. Reports described "whole armies of children— grimy, starving vagrants"—who jammed train stations, docks, and bazaars.[34] Armand Hammer, traveling on business in 1921, was shocked by the spectacle surrounding his train at the station in Ekaterinburg:

> Children with their limbs shrivelled to the size of sticks and their bellies horribly bloated by eating grass and herbs, which they were unable to digest, clustered 'round our windows begging piteously for bread—for life itself— in a dreadful ceaseless whine. We could not help them. Here and there it was possible to give one youngster a meal, but if we had distributed every scrap of food on our train, it would have been as nothing to feed this multitude.[35]

A telegraph from Simbirsk province sketched some victims as "little wild animals" living in the woods and fields, where they fed on roots and avoided adults. As late as the end of 1923, well after the drought had passed, approximately 70 percent of the youths still roaming Moscow were originally from the Volga famine territory.[36]

Simply put, the famine played a greater role in depriving children of their homes than did any other single cause. Proof abounded in city streets and welfare institutions, overrun with juveniles in 1921–1922.[37] While it is impossible to be certain how many boys and girls lost parents during the famine, the total certainly reached into the millions.[38] By May 1922, each *day* saw three to four hundred newly forsaken children accumulate in most principal municipalities of the middle-Volga basin. Cities located at rail hubs in the famine region found themselves overwhelmed with as many as 50,000 young refugees—36,000 in Simbirsk, 50,000 to 60,000 in Ufa, 48,000 in Cheliabinsk, and 55,000 in Orenburg.[39] As early as the autumn of 1921 a Soviet journalist discovered "many children around the Ufa train station. Their bodies are filthy; their faces deathly pale, skin and bones. In the rain and slush they sit and silently watch passersby and travelers. The fortunate among them receive alms on rare occasions. On every street, wherever one turns, there are children starving, homeless, and even dying in the dirt and dampness."[40] In Ufa province, the number of *besprizornye* grew from 100,000 in June 1921 to 280,000 just four months later. Figures from the Kirghiz Republic jumped from 129,000 in December 1921 to 408,000 the following March, while the Workers' and Peasants' Inspectorate reported a total of nearly 800,000 waifs in the Tatar Republic well before the end of 1921.[41] Clearly, the tragedy's scope had reached catastrophic proportions.

The famine severed children from parents in a variety of ways. Juveniles typically received priority over adults where relief supplies existed, and in such cases—as in families where parents ate less in order to continue feeding their offspring—children could elude death more successfully than did their elders.[42] Others lost parents during flight from famine areas or on long expeditions by the family (or some of its members) in search of food. Numerous variations on this theme occurred as hunger and disease took their toll. Parents also disappeared during chaotic layovers at train stations, as in the evacuations forced earlier by World War I. "There were sad scenes," a traveler observed, "when the trains came into stations. People rushed to the doors of the third-class carriages. Every place was soon taken, every space filled, corridors packed, the platform full. Children were separated from their parents, never to see them again." After languishing several days, refugees could be herded unexpectedly onto a departing train and torn from relatives who happened to be off foraging for food or otherwise temporarily engaged away from the station. Parents or children who fell ill, as many did, might be taken from trains to hospitals or barred from continuing with the other passengers. Adults thus stripped of dependents often learned upon recovering that their progeny's trail had grown cold in the streets or the maze of overcrowded relief institutions.[43]

One boy recalled that World War I forced the evacuation of his family to a village in Kazan' province, where they lived tolerably well until the famine arrived in 1921. As hunger and death closed in, they headed for Kazan', some eighty miles away, hoping to secure passage to their native Grodnensk province. But the appalling conditions around Kazan' crushed the health and morale of the boy's parents. Bloated from hunger, they lay inert, four or five miles outside the city. After supporting the family for a time through begging and stealing, the boy could no longer endure his parents' hopeless condition. Bidding them and his elder sister farewell, he departed for Kazan' with his two younger sisters,

Vavara (age eight) and Anna (ten). Hardly had they begun when Vavara sobbed that she could go no further. Drivers of passing carts ignored their pleas for a ride, so they supported Vavara by the arms and even dragged her along the ground for much of the way. It was a cold Christmas Day. On they walked, crying and hitting Vavara in the back with their fists because she was not bearing her weight. People coming from the city shed tears when they encountered the trio, and two travelers gave them a little bread. At last they reached Kazan' and found a children's home willing to admit them. Relief appeared at hand, until Vavara contracted typhus and died. The journey of her brother and sister had only begun.[44]

Sources commonly include accounts of children jettisoned by parents. With hunger paramount, any number of motives—a sense of helplessness to ease a child's torment or, alternatively, a desire to shed a burden and save oneself—prompted adults to abandon youths. As noted earlier, such feelings provoked some parents to kill offspring, but much more frequently they elected to part company with their children and entrust the outcome to providence.[45] In some cases, parents simply thrust them out of the home to wander hungry, swollen, and undressed through the village, filling the road with their sobbing. Others decided to take youths to neighboring settlements and forsake them there (or leave them at home and ply the roads themselves). So many peasants chose to desert children at urban bazaars that market days doubled or tripled the flow of minors to relief institutions in some cities.[46] From Rostov-on-the-Don, a journalist reported that parents regularly stranded dependents in the large square outside a train station, telling them to wait there just a minute until they returned from some minor undertaking. As time passed and the adults did not reappear, children around the square began to wail helplessly. Rarely did anyone respond to their grief, merely a drop in a sea of misery.[47]

Adults also discarded children after joining the throngs of refugees. Sometimes this had been the parents' intent from the moment they left home, though often the decision was reached only after considerable travail in an increasingly bleak odyssey. In Samara, a young peasant girl sat in a temporary facility for homeless children and asked all who passed if they had seen her mother. Earlier, as the famine drove her parents toward this provincial capital on the Volga, she and her mother lost contact with her father. One day, after further wandering, her mother set the child outside a house, telling her to wait until she returned with an egg. There the little girl remained, all through the night. When she was found the next morning and taken away, she protested desperately that she had to wait there for her mother.[48]

Other parents, drained by the famine to the point where they could no longer support their young, brought them to the nearest orphanage or government agency that administered these institutions. If told by officials that no resources or space remained in a facility, they frequently deposited offspring in the hallways and stairwells of the building or on the street outside. In Samara, the local head of the Commissariat of Enlightenment (Narkompros) discovered some children dumped at the door of his apartment.[49] Here and there, adults no longer able to care for dependents would engage an unusual type of unscrupulous entrepreneur who made the rounds of famine-stricken villages, collecting payments from peasants in return for promises to place their children in urban institutions. Having assembled a batch of perhaps twenty to thirty youths, he or she herded them off to town and then disappeared after disposing of the group in the street.[50]

The millions of abandoned juveniles scattered across the country by war and famine diminished in following years to the range of several hundred thousand halfway through the decade. Such a sharp drop inspired the view that remaining waifs were merely a fading inheritance from the old "capitalist" order and the calamities of 1914–1922—a comforting suggestion that time would soon eliminate the problem altogether. But the assumption withered under scrutiny in studies at a variety of children's institutions, where investigations revealed that many residents—sometimes 50 percent or more—had first landed on the street in the years *after* the famine.[51] "I myself wrote previously that *besprizornost'* is the legacy of war and devastation," admitted Nadezhda Krupskaia, Lenin's widow and a figure active in Narkompros from its foundation. "But, having observed *besprizornye*, I see that we must cease such talk. We must state that the roots of *besprizornost'* are not only in the past but in the present."[52] In short, a variety of factors continued to generate homeless youths throughout the 1920s—not in the vast quantities of 1921–1922, but enough to prevent the government from realizing its goal of clearing them from the streets.[53]

The countryside, home to some three-quarters of the population, long supplied reinforcements. Partial crop failures that plagued one region or another did not have to approach the nightmare of 1921–1922 to foster additional street urchins. Through much of the decade, in other words, an experienced urban eye had no difficulty spotting quaintly clad peasant children gazing around in bewilderment at train stations or walking nearby with the hesitant gait of newcomers. Though they soon sank into the unsavory world around them, new arrivals from the villages followed fast on their heels.[54] Even a good harvest failed to halt the flow of rural youths to cities, for most villages contained landless or at least impoverished families, often headed by widows. Sooner or later, the absence of adequate support or employment pushed many children of such households, along with village orphans, to seek life's necessities in cities or towns. These themes echo throughout the sources, time and again accounting for the departure from a village of juveniles who could not be fed or employed.[55]

In some cases, youths worked in the countryside for several months each year, from spring until the autumn harvest brought the agricultural season to an end. With the onset of winter, the village could no longer support them, and they decided—or were ordered by parents and relatives—to migrate to cities in hopes of eking out a living. While they generally intended to return to their villages in the spring or at least at the end of summer for the harvest, some found life in the city's stations and marketplaces more appealing than the rural alternative. Wedded to the bustle of urban thoroughfares, they did not set out for the countryside when the sun had melted the snow and warmed the fields.[56]

Abandoned youths emerged as well from urban homes whose adults lacked the means to raise offspring, a predicament that gripped with special tenacity families headed by single parents, usually widowed or divorced women.[57] Heavy male casualties from World War I and the Civil War created many such households, and new developments in the 1920s added more. The Family Codes of 1918 and 1926, for example, made divorce much easier to obtain than before the Revolution, contributing to a dramatic increase in the number of marriages dissolved. The Soviet divorce rate climbed to almost three times that of Germany and twenty-six times that of England and Wales. As one might expect, urban areas far outstripped the countryside in this regard, with Moscow leading the way at a pace of almost one divorce for every two marriage "ceremonies" in 1926. The new laws—intended to promote equality between the sexes—had the effect of encouraging men to leave their spouses (at a time when the numerical imbalance between the sexes due to war losses increased the "competition" among women for those men who remained). The difficulty women met in vying with men for jobs outside the home meant that a woman abandoned by her spouse could face an extended period of poverty—especially if she had dependents. Soviet law provided for the payment of alimony in such cases, but in amounts insufficient for adequate support and, in any event, frequently not delivered by ex-husbands.[58] Mothers deserted in this fashion (or by men they had not married) often could not sustain their sons and daughters. Whether a child's route to the street thereafter proved direct or passed through intermediate stops in relatives' homes, the broken families of the 1920s represented a fertile seedbed for waifs.[59]

Along with families headed by single parents, numerous other domestic arrangements funneled children—through poverty, abuse, or neglect—into the ranks of the *besprizornye*. Much as in other eras and countries, harsh treatment at home, especially when combined with penury, could accelerate a child's exit. Blows from a drunken father, for example, presented the street in a different light—that of refuge—to the victim of the thrashing. In addition, adults reduced to rage by drink or by dependents' demands on scant family resources might lash out and banish youths without waiting for them to run away. A child's failure to perform a chore properly could also spark parental fury and lead to expulsion, as could exasperation at offspring continually under foot in a crowded hovel.[60]

Juveniles ignored (rather than ejected) by parents were likewise free to occupy themselves in nearby lanes and market squares, where they might encounter street children and learn the ways of a new world.[61] Meager supervision often stemmed directly from poverty, which inclined adults to send children out to beg, steal, or engage in petty hawking to help support the family. Thus deployed, they absorbed the street's mores along with techniques for scratching a living from a difficult environment. This knowledge, accompanied by dire poverty at home, prodded them to loosen family bonds and spend more time in the company of other roving juveniles.[62] A group based on Khar'kov's Sumskaia Street contained several members whose passage to vagrancy included a stretch of work as bootblacks. One boy, who had lost his father years before, experienced a childhood of relentless but scarcely unusual privation. Eventually, he and his mother moved in with his married sister, a sickly, impoverished woman burdened with a large family. Both newcomers were regarded by the others as parasites, which goes far to explain the youth's appearance with polish and rag on the sidewalk and his preference for life there with footloose friends.[63]

Neglect also occurred as a by-product of parental employment outside the home. The absence of a comprehensive system of day care institutions compelled adults lacking assistance from their own parents or other stand-ins to lock offspring in rooms each day or, more likely, abandon them to the street's tutelage. Left to forage like stray animals, some youngsters soon passed their time with full-fledged waifs and took up petty thievery. In households with just one parent, the odds in favor of this outcome climbed even higher, for only the most fortunate individual could support a family and supervise it at the same time.[64]

Two other factors deserve mention as well. First, the unemployment rate among teenagers remained high after the introduction of the New Economic Policy (NEP) in 1921. NEP itself bore some responsibility for the problem, because it required numerous state organizations to operate profitably. This new discipline stirred such enterprises to cut expenses by dismissing staff—with women and adolescents representing a disproportionate number of the layoffs. In many types of production, labor laws stipulated that juveniles work fewer hours per day than adults, with lower output norms but at the same wage scale as their older coworkers. Moreover, the preceding years' turmoil deprived youths of adequate schooling and labor training, and thus of qualifications needed to compete for jobs.[65] Under these conditions, supervisors had little incentive to hire minors as long as capable adults remained available—as they did in considerable number until the industrialization drive at decade's end. In the meantime, teenagers forced to support themselves found the labor market a difficult nut to crack, closing for many a gateway that might have saved them from indigence.[66]

While unemployment blocked an escape route for the homeless, the ineffective work of welfare institutions *returned* juveniles to the street. Countless thousands over the years fled the abysmal conditions in orphanages and headed for their former stamping grounds. Even among those who remained, many did not receive adequate training to secure steady work upon discharge into a glutted labor market and thus replenished the ranks of abandoned youths after failing to find employment.[67] In addition, local officials struggled throughout the decade to reduce the strain on their budgets caused by orphanages—sometimes disbanding institutions altogether, even in defiance of orders from Moscow to maintain the existing network. Residents discharged early for budgetary reasons often landed on the street, either directly or after transfer to the families of relatives or strangers who could not support them and did not relish the financial burden any more than did local officials.[68]

The homeless wave crested during the famine of 1921–1922, with estimates ranging typically from four to seven and a half million orphaned and forsaken youths.[69] Lists compiled around the country commonly identified 75 to over 90 percent as Great Russians, reflecting both their numerical predominance in the nation and the famine's devastation of several Great Russian provinces. The catastrophe, of course, spared no one in its path and thus accounted as well for sizable pockets of Chuvash and Tatar waifs, both in their home territories along the Volga and as refugees elsewhere. Many young Ukrainians also appeared in the totals, after famine in the south followed years of warfare in much of the republic. Other street children sprang from smaller ethnic groups—Jews, Volga Germans, Poles, Bashkirs, Armenians, Georgians, and Moldavians, to name a few—typically emanating from regions scourged by violence, disease, and hunger.[70]

While the quantity of street children clearly declined in the years following the famine, sources continued to offer widely varying assessments of their number in any given year. Estimates for 1923 generally fell between one and four million, though a few ranged even higher, or as low as 800,000.[71] In 1924, figures from local offices of Narkompros prompted tabulations for the Russian Republic that ran from 125,000 to 300,000 youths. But totals of this order could not have convinced the author of an article in *Komsomol'skaia pravda*, who warned that "before us stands the fact of the insignificant reduction in the number of *besprizornye* in 1924 compared to 1922 and 1923." Earlier, in the spring of 1924, an article in *Izvestiia* placed the total at "over one million."[72] Estimates for 1925, 1926, and 1927 covered a span from the neighborhood of 300,000 to less than 100,000.[73] Even as late as 1930, when most sources trumpeted the virtual elimination of the problem, an article in a provincial journal maintained that 200,000 abandoned children continued to inhabit the Russian Republic alone.[74]

It bears stressing that accurate data eluded officials throughout the decade, a fact acknowledged by nearly everyone from Anatolii Lunacharskii, head of Narkompros, to provincial investigators.[75] The youths' very nature—streetwise and wary of outsiders—rendered futile all attempts to count them precisely. Furthermore, local officials worked with differing understandings of the term *besprizornye* and diverse methods for determining their number. The results proved difficult to compare with one another and unreliable in combination as a national total.[76] More often than not, the numbers relayed from the provinces to Moscow were far too low. In fact, the slippery street children left some investigators able to count nothing more than those already in institutions.[77] Even special efforts to tally homeless juveniles during the national census of 1926 produced results widely judged as well below the actual total. Substantial numbers evaded the census takers with ease, on occasion greeting them with a hail of stones before fleeing.[78]

Statistical difficulties, however, cannot obscure the massive nature of the problem, evident to anyone touring Russian streets, markets, and train stations in the 1920s. Nor can there be any doubt that a majority of these youths issued from nearly a decade of calamities—wars, epidemics, and famine—that had battered the land since 1914. Thereafter, while the number of victims dropped sharply, other types of misfortune replenished their ranks at a rate exceeding the government's ability to respond as rural poverty, unemployment, and numerous single-parent families stubbornly continued to restock the streets. To be sure, the adversity faced in mid-decade paled before that of preceding years and therefore offered hope of satisfactory control before long. But that day arrived much later than anyone could have imagined at the time, for new upheavals—collectivization, dekulakization, the famine of 1933, and World War II—cast fresh waves of homeless children adrift in a country that had already seen far too many.

PART ONE

CHAPTER ONE

Children of the Street

Who has not seen them, sleeping in caldrons and garbage
bins, traveling under train cars, singing songs and begging in
every station?

Mikhail Kalinin

. . . waifs in drab tatters who scurried hither and thither
thieving and warming themselves at asphalt caldrons on the
streets, without whom one could not picture the urban life of
the twenties . . .

Alexander Solzhenitsyn

By the early 1920s, abandoned children crowded cities and towns across
much of the new Soviet state. Their wretched appearance advertised
misery already endured, and an untold number, weakened by hunger
and disease, soon perished as anonymously as they had arrived. Survi-
vors were left to confront a world in which sustenance issued from practices both alien and disagreeable, for little in their lives had prepared
most to face the street alone. Their responses, shaped to some extent by
age and other personal characteristics, reflected in a broader sense the
imperatives of this harsh environment—a setting that must be explored
to understand the conduct of *besprizornye*.

Waifs did not scatter evenly over the Soviet Union. Nor did they
always congregate in areas with the greatest population densities. Efforts
to account for clusters of them in various regions focused time and again
on the following questions: Had a province recently experienced famine
or some other misfortune? Did the territory contain a major rail junction
or sit astride an important waterway? Was the district's climate mild?
If not, was refuge accessible? Just as important, did the area, if not a
goal itself of vagrants and refugees, lie along a main route to popular
destinations? The more closely a locale met such criteria, the more homeless children it drew.[1]

Within these general limits, cities exerted a far more powerful attraction than did the countryside. During the famine, starving children poured from villages to the capitals of their provinces, and subsequent years did not reverse the current. To a homeless youth, the train stations, markets, crowded streets, and derelict buildings of a city offered a more promising field for begging and shelter than did a rural hamlet. For those seeking escape from the street, the concentration of government assistance in urban areas further enhanced their appeal. Others of more incorrigible bent also preferred cities, where amusements and thieving opportunities eclipsed anything the countryside could offer.[2]

Cities situated at major railroad junctions or along important waterways often acquired throngs of abandoned offspring—not just from their own environs but from throughout the country—while towns well removed from these arteries generally tempted fewer.[3] In Nizhnii Novgorod, for example, the number of young visitors began to increase each spring with the opening of navigation on the Volga and Oka rivers, and before long the waterfront quarters teemed with dirty, barefoot children. This homeless host continued to expand through the summer months, peaking at the time of the city's famous fair, which summoned youths from all parts of the nation. During opening day alone in 1925, authorities apprehended over a hundred inside the fair's boundaries in a largely futile effort to preserve the premises from depredation.[4]

Numerous cities, not destinations themselves, nevertheless accumulated sizable populations of nomadic children during certain times of the year, owing to their location along well-traveled routes. Orenburg, for instance, found itself the first extended stop for many venturing in early summer from their winter quarters in Tashkent or Samarkand to resort towns of the Northern Caucasus or Crimea. Along the Volga, cities such as Samara did not maintain their large homeless populations solely with local victims of the famine. By linking the river with rail lines leading to and from Siberia and Central Asia, Samara collected year after year a considerable transient community of juveniles, especially during navigation season on the Volga.[5]

No city, however, could match the potent attraction exerted by Moscow. "It would be difficult," wrote secret police chief Feliks Dzerzhinskii, "to find in the entire republic a city or town from which there has not been a pilgrimage to Moscow of abandoned children. . . . [Moscow] has become the national refuge to which *besprizornye* stream from all ends of the country." Only the most reclusive resident of the capital could fail to notice the bedraggled flocks in central squares, train stations, and markets—a multitude twenty thousand strong according to an estimate for the beginning of 1923. Leningrad, because of its location in the far northwest corner of the country, did not share Moscow's magnetism.[6] Asked why they journeyed to Moscow, youths often responded simply, "Moscow is the center," "Here is the power," "They say food is given out in Moscow." Peasant children, traveling to the metropolis to obtain food through begging, stealing, or petty street trade, sometimes described the trip as "going to pasture." Rumors and reports of better conditions in the center—more food or easier access to welfare institutions, for example—passed among homeless juveniles in all corners of the country, even prompting some to flee remote orphanages and set out for the capital.[7] This allure produced such an influx that native Muscovites numbered no more than 10–20 percent of the city's waifs in the middle of the decade, earning Moscow the informal title "All-Russian Receiver" of *besprizornye.*[8]

In years following the famine, the Northern Caucasus region possibly contained more street children than any other section of the country, and its principal city, Rostov-on-the-Don, probably absorbed more than any site but Moscow. Many gathered in Rostov with much the same expectations that propelled others to the nation's capital. Here, they thought, waited opportunities to acquire food, shelter, and perhaps admission to government boarding institutions. In one estimate the Northern Caucasus, with a mere thirteenth of the Russian Republic's total population, accommodated fully a seventh of all abandoned youths in the republic midway through the decade.[9] Only a third of these were indigenous. Early in the 1920s, most came as refugees from neighboring famine provinces of the Volga basin, but Rostov continued to woo others long after. The city's relatively warm climate and location at the hub of a rail network—with tracks leading south to the Caucasus, north to Moscow, and west to the Crimea—insured for years a steady stream of new arrivals.[10]

One day, on just such a line to the Crimea, a passenger noticed that the railroad bed was covered in sand along stretches near the sea. Well-scrubbed boys and girls, traveling on vacation, jumped out at a stop and plunged under the cars to gather seashells from the sand. No less abruptly they recoiled from the train as if stung, crying to their parents in fright, "*Besprizornye! besprizornye!*" They had discovered other young passengers ensconced in the undercarriage, as determined as anyone else on the train to reach the sunny resorts.[11] Hospitable weather and the food it nurtured lured thousands of urchins to the Crimea and

Black Sea coast, augmenting the ranks of native youths left adrift by the Civil War and, in southern Ukraine, famine. As word spread among homeless children elsewhere in the country, cities such as Krasnodar, Simferopol', Sevastopol', Feodosiia, Kerch', and Odessa mustered large crowds. In particular, when pale citizens headed south in the summer to Black Sea sanatoriums, waifs followed close behind, hoping to secure a living during the resort season by begging or stealing directly from the crowds of vacationers or from the stores, markets, and restaurants they frequented.[12]

Many other regions and cities also hosted considerable numbers of *besprizornye*. In Ukraine, Khar'kov deserves special mention, while along the Volga, in addition to Samara, cities such as Kazan', Simbirsk, and Saratov retained sizable homeless populations well after the famine. The quest for food and shelter (or warm weather) even carried youths over the frontiers of European Russia. During the famine, they followed the rails to the Urals and often far beyond—to cities in Siberia (such as Omsk and Novosibirsk) and Central Asia (notably Tashkent and Samarkand). In the years thereafter, the prospect of accessible food and a mild climate continued to attract them to Central Asia—and through the Caucasus to Baku and Tiflis. They made these treks in surprising numbers, so large in fact that Tashkent's population of abandoned juveniles reportedly ranked third among all Soviet cities in the middle of the decade.[13]

A city's complement of street children fluctuated considerably during the course of a year, even in the absence of such misfortunes as an epidemic or poor harvest that always produced a local proliferation of homeless minors. More than anything else, apart from famine and war, seasonal changes dictated their travel. As chilly nights heralded the approach of autumn, major cities found their streets sheltering larger numbers of youths. They crowded into train stations, abandoned buildings, and any crevice affording protection from the wind. Some had spent the warm season living on the outskirts of cities or deeper in the countryside, perhaps engaged by peasants for agricultural work.[14] Others, typically the more experienced and adventurous, had departed in the spring or summer to journey around the country, often south to the resorts of the Northern Caucasus and Crimea. At the end of the season, beaches and mineral baths lost much of their clientele, prompting markets, restaurants, and hotels to close or scale back their activity. Because dormant resort towns could not support large numbers of young beggars and thieves, many left until the following summer. Some remained in the general area of the Black Sea's mild temperatures, but more headed north again to major cities.[15]

Veterans of the circuit often entered a city in the fall intending to gain admission to a children's institution, live there through the winter, and then run away with the return of warm weather. Some repeated this pattern year after year, returning each winter to one city or another like migratory birds. These "seasonals" (*sezonniki*) effectively transformed certain orphanages into way stations providing food and shelter (but not rehabilitation) to juveniles waiting for the spring thaws to trigger their escape. On occasion, as winter approached, streetwise youths even committed intentionally clumsy crimes, planning to be apprehended and placed in institutions—from which departure in the spring, experience taught, would be a minor challenge.[16]

Winter survival, then, required that street children avoid exposure to frigid weather in one of two ways. They could seek shelter, or they could attempt to outrun the approaching frost by traveling south to such havens as Odessa or even farther to Transcaucasia or Central Asia. Though the number journeying to remote ranges for the winter did not equal the total remaining in European Russia, southbound traffic of diminutive stowaways on the railroads did strike observers each autumn, as did the swollen numbers of tattered youths in cities as distant as Baku and Samarkand.[17]

While most homeless juveniles settled in one area or another for at least a few months, some (approximately 10 percent, according to one estimate) traveled incessantly. Whether lodged aboard ships or clinging to trains, they roamed the length and breadth of the land. Astonishing odysseys took them across Siberia, Central Asia, and to every important municipality in European Russia. "They discuss Khar'kov, Moscow, Baku, and Sverdlovsk," marveled an observer, "as if they were talking about the streets of a single large city." One boy, hidden on a ship, even reached Marseille and thereafter several other cities in France, Belgium, and Germany before he was evacuated back to Russia along with former prisoners of war.[18] These travels often amounted to a quest for more favorable living conditions, inspired by rumors of greener pastures down the line. But other youths remained on the move because they enjoyed it or at least felt restless staying long in any one location. Years after reentering society, some reported that, come spring, they still sensed the call of the road.[19]

Such instincts guided Vasilii G——shev, a thirteen-year-old boy dispatched to a children's colony at the beginning of 1923. Information gathered during the handling of his case portrayed a difficult life at home. His father, who worked for the postal service and then in a railroad telegraph office, drank heavily and beat the rest of the family. In 1915 he moved in with another woman, leaving his former wife and eight children with nothing but a modest monthly payment, which he cut off two years later. Vasilii's mother, prematurely aged by her travail, worked as a messenger for wages insufficient to lift the family from poverty. At some point, probably the early 1920s, Vasilii began to disappear from home for periods of a few days. He would return hungry, dirty, and emaciated, refusing sullenly to disclose his itinerary. This pattern continued until he was sent to the colony for examination by personnel from the Commissariat of Health. His mother did not conceal her skepticism and asserted (with Vasilii's affirmation) that he would not remain long in any institution. He seemed to have a passion for travel and yearned to journey as far as America. According to the colony's log book, the slender boy with sparkling eyes did not adjust well to the facility's regimen or the other youths. An entry for January 16, 1923, reads: "Vasilii does not get along with the other children; he fights with them and is always beaten. Even Vitia D——kov, who is always beaten when he fights others, manages to pummel Vasilii and celebrate a victory. Whether as a result of this abuse, as Vasilii claims, or because of his own insurmountable urge to roam, he has already tried to flee the colony three times." Four days later he escaped. At the end of the month his mother arrived to declare that he had come home and would not be returning to the colony. When questioned later, he spoke with contempt of the institution's residents, who he felt had surrendered their freedom for life in a "stone sack." Before long his wanderings commenced again. At first the forays consumed no more than a week, but in the middle of April he departed for two months, apparently turning back only after failing to breach the Romanian border. Shortly thereafter he bolted once more, and his family concluded as the months passed that he had perished. Eventually, word arrived through one of Vasilii's friends that he had reached the Siberian city of Chita, beyond Lake Baikal, and would not be returning to Moscow.[20]

Official documents, journalists' reports, and children's autobiographical sketches portray rail journeys as routine among homeless youths.[21] A handful traveled legally, using money they had stolen or begged to purchase tickets.²² But far more concealed themselves on board, in a wide variety of locations accessible to slight physiques. Coal bins, storage boxes, footsteps, bumpers, roofs, recesses inside the cars, rods underneath, and cavities deep among the pipes and moving parts of the engine all served as accommodations. At the station in Tashkent, Langston Hughes encountered an insouciant waif who indicated that his destination was Moscow. " 'Have you got your ticket?' we asked. 'Sure, ten of 'em,' he said, and held up his hands," revealing the fingers with which he intended to grasp his perch on the train.²³

Many factors—including body size, experience, weather, vigilance of conductors, and availability of spots not already claimed by other young stowaways—influenced the choice of "berths." Each presented drawbacks that an experienced vagabond knew all too well. Clambering into coal bins was difficult, for instance, and, once inside, lack of oxygen posed a serious threat. Some children carried nails with which to claw air holes in the walls and thus avoid suffocation amid the coal dust.²⁴ Nooks in the bowels of a steam engine were hot, grimy, and cramped— not to mention dangerous if located near moving parts. Mechanics tending engines gaped at the dexterity and hardiness of creatures, completely blackened by grease and dirt, who crawled out of the machinery like imps before their eyes.²⁵ A boy who traveled to Khar'kov from the Kuban' described just such a niche under the engine: "It was like a bathhouse there, but I didn't climb out [at stops]. You can't do this because you may return too late and find new passengers in your place. In Khar'kov I climbed out and everyone looked at me wondering whether I was a human or a devil. I ran around the station and people hurried out of my way."²⁶

Those who chose to ride in one of the small storage compartments, or "dog's box" (*sobachii iashchik*), underneath a car did not face coal dust, grease, or a boiler's heat, but they often had to remain curled up in the tiny, dark chambers for long intervals—prepared to defend their quarters from challenges at stations by other would-be squatters, all the while hoping to escape the eye of railroad personnel. *Izvestiia* reported that, on occasion, conductors who noticed children in these boxes locked the covers and left the victims trapped inside for hours or even days. Farther underneath a car, axles and beams offered billets less cramped but more exposed to cold temperatures. They were also more precarious as the tracks whizzed by inches below, ending suddenly the lives of many a careless or clumsy traveler. Those who hid inside cars sidestepped these problems but risked discovery by conductors, who might administer a beating and hand them over to the police at the next station.[27]

Hardships associated with the various toeholds aboard trains did not exhaust the list of a young vagrant's concerns. Simply reaching the train (or ship) was itself often a challenge. Conductors and policemen kept a close eye on children loitering at stations and guarded the cars waiting to take on passengers. If faced with such obstacles, hopeful stowaways usually concealed themselves as close to the tracks as possible and waited for the sound of two bells, signaling the train's imminent departure. At that moment (or even later, as the train lurched into motion and the conductors climbed into the cars), they darted across the tracks and slipped aboard. Some waited inside a station for the two bells to summon a crowd of passengers pushing toward the train. Inserting themselves into this human tide, they attempted to evade a policeman or conductor at the station door and then disappear into or under the cars.[28]

Not all boarded successfully, as Theodore Dreiser noticed while on a ship docked at the Black Sea port of Novorossiisk. A girl discovered on the vessel and placed ashore tried repeatedly to dodge sailors and dart back up the gangplank.

> But regularly one of the large, genial sailors is picking her up and carrying her a little way down the dock; shooing her off, as it were. But always as he releases her she eludes him and runs screaming toward the plank. And now the other sailor repeats the process. Only, like so much of all that one comes upon in Russia, it is all so casual. No real excitement in so far as any one else is concerned, passengers or sailors or officers all going their several ways. Some soldiers conversing indifferently on the dock. Stevedores taking up hay, crates of geese, boxes of canned goods. Altogether quite a brisk industrial scene. But here is the child, still screaming and kicking. And the sailors always heading her off or carrying her away again, her ragged little skirts far above her waist, her naked legs exposed to the cold. And one sailor carrying her far down the dock to a gate guarded by soldiers.[29]

No one mourned the passing of summer more deeply than did abandoned children, and no one waited more impatiently for its return. The icebound months racked them so severely that people in Dnepropetrovsk dubbed the unseasonably warm weather of early December 1923 an "orphan's winter."[30] Across most of the country, as the temperature fell along with the leaves, a source of protection from the icy winds became a matter of survival. Indeed, whatever the season, virtually any location offering concealment and protection from the elements did not long escape attention. Youths slept under boats upturned on river banks, in forests on the edge of towns, under bridges, in discarded trunks and barrels, under or along fences, inside wooden columns set up for displaying posters, and in stalls vacated overnight in bazaars and markets.[31] The entryways to apartment complexes (and sheds in the yards of these buildings) provided warmth and thus attracted many. Custodians often drove the waifs away, but only the most closely watched or securely locked structures did not acquire new complements of squatters.[32] Public toilets and garbage bins also served as domiciles. An investigator in Odessa reported that one could walk the streets at night opening trash bins and find in most of them clusters of young lodgers sleeping on top of the litter. In parts of Moscow, during warm weather, there appeared to be something of a rule among them that no more than six could sleep in a single bin. "This is not a tram!" one lad proudly informed an inquirer, meaning that the youths did not wish to duplicate the crowding prevalent in public transportation.[33] A few turned up in the most unlikely places—on board ships anchored overnight, for example, and even on the roof of a building in the Kremlin.[34]

The search for shelter sent children burrowing into woodpiles, haystacks, reserves of coal at train stations, drainage pipes, mountains of industrial waste products, and even a cemetery's burial vaults.[35] Garbage dumps, in particular, served as refuge for considerable numbers. Here, social workers, newspaper correspondents, and others seeking homeless youths found them living like nests of insects in rotting waste amid an overpowering stench.[36] Juveniles also fashioned shelters by tunneling directly into the earth. Their warrens ranged from the simple and temporary—a shallow dugout or a cavity scraped out under the edge of a sidewalk—to quite elaborate subterranean chambers. Hillocks, sides of ditches, and river banks engaged these excavators, who sometimes produced extensive networks of tunnels or caverns large enough to accommodate dozens, along with campfires and watchdogs. A group living in a cave near a rail depot in Tashkent even planned to run electrical wires from the station into their dwelling. (They had to abandon the scheme when one of their number, a boy claiming to possess the expertise required for the project, was taken into a reformatory.) Natural grottoes, too, in parks or in hills and cliffs on the outskirts of cities, harbored waifs and highlighted most vividly their animal-like existence.[37]

Ruined or otherwise abandoned buildings, frequently in slums or on the fringes of town, beckoned irresistibly to the homeless. Virtually any unutilized structure, including cellars, old bathhouses, storage facilities, and buildings destroyed by fire, could provide at least a wisp of shelter—and to far more people than the casual eye imagined. In Odessa, large groups of children lived in the skeletons of buildings destroyed by French naval bombardment and the explosion of German ammunition dumps. The remnants of an edifice in the center of Dnepropetrovsk housed youths in such number that it was dubbed their "headquarters" for the city. Abandoned structures that remained comparatively intact sometimes drew so many new inhabitants (adults as well as juveniles) that investigators entering at night had difficulty proceeding without stepping on the dark shapes sprawled at every turn.[38] A newspaper correspondent, exploring a large cement granary in the "Rostov slums," encountered the following scene in 1925:

> Snoring, moaning, and delirious babbling can be heard from all corners of the building. We strike a light and behold a scene recalling our train stations during the years of ruin and civil war. Human beings, shivering from the advancing predawn cold, lie along the walls and in the corners in "heaps," pressing close to each other. . . . Disturbed by the light and our voices, they begin to stir, poking their heads out from under the rags that cover their bodies, and regarding their night visitors with fright.

Half an hour later, as the light of early dawn struggled through cracks in the building, they arose and set off "to fill the streets and bazaars" in their daily search for food.[39]

Many cities retained ramshackle portions of walls and towers built in earlier centuries as fortifications or embellishments. Often constructed by filling a stone or brick shell with a softer core of dirt and debris, these walls developed large cavities as time erased their original function. But if municipalities no longer valued the protection they afforded, street children had a different view. Just east of Moscow's Kremlin, stretches of the *kitaigorod* wall housed a hundred or more at a time, prompting some Muscovites to dub it "the dormitory." The wall's inhabitants dragged in junk to serve as furniture, cooked food and warmed themselves over campfires, and, in the case of one group, deployed a watchdog to warn of outsiders approaching. Youths also slept in old structures such as the famous tower at Moscow's Sukharevskii Market and the watchtower at the Red Gates. Over a period of a few months in 1922/23, the police removed several hundred from the second tower alone, netting up to forty in a night.[40]

As Soviet cities recovered in the 1920s from the turmoil of the previous decade, repair and construction projects dotted the urban landscape. Pedestrians passing these sites after the working day often noticed
strange noises emanating from large tanks used to heat asphalt or tar.
If curiosity prompted closer investigation, they discovered children prat-
tling inside. The caldrons, heated during the day, did not surrender their
warmth until long after the workers departed, thus attracting those seeking shelter for the night. In Moscow, to cite one instance, city officials
decided to remove streetcar rails from the Arbat and repave the thor-
oughfare with asphalt. During the project, immense boilers for the asphalt stood on each block and soon acquired flocks of urchins. "There
were dozens and scores of them there," recalled a resident of the street,
"tattered, half-famished, dirty, all of them sneaking about these big
warm boilers like little animals."[41] Residue in caldrons, which left inhabitants black and sticky, seemed a small discomfort to endure in return for sanctuary. Even as the night wore on and the vats cooled, they
continued to offer some protection from the wind (and the rain or snow,
if tenants devised a means to cover them). The tanks could generally
accommodate half a dozen occupants, though the bottom of the caldron—the choicest spot in winter because it retained heat longest—
could typically hold no more than three or four. In some cases, fights
determined the distribution of places, with losers relegated to the vessel's
sides. Once in their vats, youths remained vulnerable to eviction by
watchmen and the police—though one group managed to secure a
watchman's indifference by supplying him with stolen food.[42] In any
case, such hazards were routine on the street and did not diminish significantly the caldrons' appeal.

Almost any other source of heat also enticed waifs. Institutional garbage incinerators, for example, remained warm long after their fires had
died, and children often tried to slip onto the premises and crawl into
the openings of furnaces. One could sometimes see their rag-covered
legs protruding from the brick burrows where they lay asleep. Electric-
power generators, too, resembled oases to shivering figures who spared
no effort to approach the buildings. Even if unable to secure places near
boilers and steam pipes, they might find warmth huddled next to reservoirs of hot water discharged by the plants.[43] In the absence of shelter
and heat produced by other sources, youths sometimes resorted to sleeping on the ashes of their own campfires after lighting second fires along-
side. Others, frequently the weakest or most inexperienced and thus the
most helpless and exposed, tore down posters tacked up around every

city and used them as blankets.[44] Even those able to secure a niche in a train station or derelict building did not entirely escape the frigid winter temperatures. They often slept—like their less fortunate brethren bunched on the sidewalk under posters—pressed tightly together, resembling a nest of shivering mice. In some cases, these grimy piles clutched live dogs for additional warmth.[45]

Street children who gained a few coins by the end of the day might opt, especially in the winter, to spend the night in a flophouse (*nochlezhka*). Moscow's *Ermakovskii nochlezhnyi dom* (located near the Riazan' Station and dubbed the Ermakovka) was the best known, but the capital contained several, as did other major cities. A relatively modest fee, typically ten to twenty kopecks, secured entry and thus a night's protection from the elements. Adults—thieves, prostitutes, drunks, drifters, the unemployed, and other people down on their luck (including a sixty-two-year-old Princess Viazemskaia, reduced to begging in Leningrad)—made up most of the clientele, but youths were admitted too, as long as they could pay.[46]

Each day unruly crowds formed outside the institutions, waiting noisily for the doors to open in the late afternoon or early evening. If the "line" contained more people than could possibly be admitted, the pushing, cursing, and pleading grew energetic. Policemen helped restrain the crowds at some locations, but in their absence, fights broke out periodically. At the Ermakovka one afternoon, over twenty men reportedly raped a drunken woman without intervention by the building's administration. People lacking enough money for admission sometimes tried to beg a few kopecks from others in line or sold pitiful possessions to entrepreneurs on hand for such opportunities. More brazen individuals simply seized money from the docile and weak who waited along with them to purchase admission tickets.[47]

Some flophouses accepted only adult men or only women and juveniles, but others designated sections for a variety of people. Those who could afford to pay more than the regular entry fee had the option in certain institutions of sleeping in comparatively clean portions of the building. In any case, when the doors opened, children entered along with unsavory company. Thieves tutored them in the underworld's values and diversions (including cocaine, hashish, and other drugs) and drew them into their gangs. The Ermakovka contained six floors, and as people purchased their tickets, the cashier sized them up and assigned them to one or another of the levels. Women went to the second floor (food was sold on the first), while men able to pay a bit more—and judged by the cashier not to be criminals or unacceptably rank—were directed to one of the three upper floors. Urchins found themselves steered to the third floor, reserved for the most unpalatable lodgers.[48]

Flophouses commonly sold tickets in numbers far exceeding their legal capacities. An investigation of two institutions in Khar'kov, for instance, found that in 1925 approximately one thousand people occupied space suitable for no more than two hundred. Reports from many cities described rooms so crowded that only the most fortunate lay on bare plank beds. Many slept side by side on the floor—under the beds, in the halls and stairways, and on windowsills.[49] As one would expect, the level of sanitation left much to be desired. In some facilities people relieved themselves wherever they pleased, but even in the absence of this practice, putrid air remained the rule. Marauding armies of bedbugs, typically reinforced by lice and other vermin, held sway throughout the buildings, and numerous infectious ailments flourished. As the years passed, establishments began to set aside rooms for disinfecting clothing, which improved conditions somewhat. These efforts reportedly purged so many lice from garments in Leningrad's flophouses that the creatures had to be removed from the floor with scoops and shovels. In fact, lice infested some of this clothing so thoroughly that officials included samples of the apparel in an exhibition at the Pasteur Museum in Paris.[50]

Unlike flophouses, which few abandoned children could regularly afford, train stations and their immediate environs sheltered more youths than any other area of comparable size in most cities. During the Volga famine, when people fled the stricken provinces in droves, juveniles traveled along the rails in such force that scores might crowd even a minor provincial station. In the years thereafter, while the number of waifs diminished, stations lured many who remained. Several of Moscow's terminals, none more notorious than the Kursk Station, long bore reputations as their dens. Far to the east, in the Siberian city of Omsk, an investigation of the local station in February 1924 turned up fifty children ranging from eight to seventeen years of age. Repeatedly apprehended in the past and turned over to the police, many reappeared before long at the depot and set about supporting themselves through begging and thievery.[51]

Railroad stations of ample size commonly housed a wide variety of youths. These included vagabonds who arrived in cities by train, stayed for a time, and then set off again. Newly homeless juveniles, too, fresh from the countryside and completely at sea in the urban environment, typically remained, at least initially, in or near the stations at which they arrived. Conspicuous in their peasant clothing and palpably intimidated by the stations' noise, they made a painful impression on many observers. They also served as prey for more experienced street children, who beat newcomers and stripped them of their possessions. A lad who arrived at a station wearing relatively serviceable clothes likely found himself forced at knife point in a dark corner to surrender his garments or footwear—in return, perhaps, for foul lice-infested attire.[52]

Many others as well, neither transients nor novices, spent much of their time at stations. The ever-changing crowds of travelers attracted youths intent on begging or such endeavors as shining shoes, carrying baggage, and selling water in the summer. The bolder or more desperate among them found stations rewarding areas in which to steal from passengers, vendors, or freight shipments. Terminals also sustained those, primarily girls, who had turned to prostitution, for the buildings furnished both customers and secluded nooks. Others went out into the city during the day to beg or steal, returning "home" most evenings to sleep in or around the station. Some clambered aboard local trains to solicit or rob the passengers, ending the day back at the depot to await the next morning's tide of commuters.[53]

Children sought refuge in even the most squalid or uncomfortable corners of stations. In Saratov, a census of abandoned juveniles conducted in 1924 found twenty-seven, from six to seventeen years of age, living in a derelict lavatory. Though emaciated and covered with filthy rags, they stubbornly refused to enter an orphanage.[54] In Omsk, the departure of the last passenger train each evening left the terminal almost deserted. Officials must then have closed the building, for a crowd of youths departed to spend the night in a dilapidated empty barracks behind train cars on the siding. Adopting the station's language, they referred to their quarters as "first class." Those with venereal diseases were compelled by the others to sleep "second class" in the station's latrine—a fetid series of outdoor pits covered by a few boards encrusted with excrement. Here they huddled, soaked by the rain and covered with sores, beseeching investigators for access to "first class." One even complained that two boys in the barracks had gonorrhea but were not expelled because they stood watch and ran errands for the others.[55]

Many stations, especially the larger ones in major cities, contained basement cavities and underground passages for heating pipes and other equipment. Offering a measure of security from outsiders as well as shelter from severe weather, these caverns enticed throngs. The maze under the station in Khar'kov, known locally as the catacombs, housed over a hundred youths as late as the second half of the decade. Eerie whistles from invisible children, signaling to their comrades the approach of strangers, greeted census takers (escorted by policemen) descending the dark spiral staircase into the catacombs at the end of 1926. Upon reaching the bottom and electing to push on, the officials negotiated long, narrow corridors lined with burning-hot steam pipes that produced a stifling atmosphere. When the passageway widened at last, they found themselves in a chamber packed with scores of juveniles.[56]

Others lived above ground in the recesses of main terminal buildings. Here, of course, they were generally more visible and thus more likely to be driven out periodically by policemen and station officials. In this event, they often departed for a few hours, or all night, and then returned. Upon eviction from their train-station home in Khar'kov, two young girls—described as having the faces of children and the voices of old prostitutes—commonly spent the night in a public lavatory across the street but soon slipped back to the terminal. In Moscow, early in the decade, youths (along with adult criminals and tramps) moved from the Riazan' Station when it closed at 2:00 A.M. to the Kursk Station, which opened at 4:00 A.M., where they lounged in the corridors and waiting rooms.[57] Investigators choosing to search outside the main buildings could expect to find juveniles living in empty train cars, especially in derelict rolling stock on the fringes of rail yards. At Moscow's Kursk Station alone, the 1926 census recorded 131 children so sheltered.[58] Here and at other depots a single car might house an entire colony, as described in an article titled "How I Lived Free," written for a newspaper issued by a children's colony:

> There were about 30 of us living on the railroad. In the summer we slept wherever we pleased, out in the open on the ground. Winter was a different matter. We did not go into the station building because another group of kids, hostile to us, lived there. If someone from our group appeared at the station, he was driven away immediately with kicks and blows. In turn, if we caught an outsider on our turf, he, too, got it hot. And so came the rainy days of a long autumn. We chose an empty train car with warm boarding and occupied it as our own fine dwelling, feeling ourselves the masters. We worked in the following manner: at daybreak we took sacks to the park where the steam engines were kept. We knew some mechanics there, and they gave us coal in return for cigarettes. Each of us got nearly a sack full of coal, which we carried away and sold. This was what the older boys did. The younger kids, whom we called "*patsany*," had their own duties and work. One remained in the train car, swept it out, and kept it warm until evening. The rest went out after food. Into the station came the Minsk-Khar'kov train. Before the passengers had even climbed out of the cars, the "*patsany*" were

scouring the train, looking for bread. On the tables they found pieces of fat, sausage, apples, and the like. We lived on this. It also happened on occasion that a passenger would leave in too great a hurry and forget to take along a bundle, suitcase, or basket. Ten minutes later he would run back to the car—too late. His possessions had long since disappeared. In the evening, after such a success, we enjoyed cocaine, cards, liquor, and all sorts of bread. When the watchmen came by, they were treated royally, given cigarettes, and good-bye! Only by morning did it grow quiet in the car as everyone fell asleep. That is how I lived free.[59]

Case histories and autobiographical sketches of homeless youths indicate that many, after arriving at city stations, sooner or later shifted the focus of their activity to bazaars. Some discovered the markets rapidly and on their own; others were introduced to these bustling sites only after coming under the influence of those more experienced.[60] In any case, whether or not their paths had previously taken them through train stations, numerous street children spent their days (and often nights) in and around markets. Moscow's Zemlianyi Val—a large bazaar located in the relative vicinity of six stations—contained thousands of petty entrepreneurs and a sea of shoppers that beckoned temptingly to abandoned juveniles early in the decade. Of all the city's markets, however, none matched the fame and notoriety of the Sukharevskii and the Khitrovskii. Known popularly as the Sukharevka and Khitrovka (or Sushka and Khiva in the jargon of the street), these bazaars drew so many waifs that a survey of the Sukharevka in 1925 counted 123 in a matter of two or three hours.[61]

As sites containing large concentrations of food in accessible booths and stands—as well as numerous customers carrying cash, handbags, and bundles—markets attracted forsaken children all across the country. Hungry young thieves on the prowl found them fertile stalking grounds, and the terrain also offered opportunities to beg scraps of food, perform odd jobs, or engage in petty trade oneself. If nothing else, a youth could wander the rows of stalls, gathering meals from discarded peelings, apple cores, and similar garbage. When policemen or vendors chased them away, they often scattered for an hour or two and then returned to their former activities.[62]

Wherever they lived, street children frequently did so in groups. Typically numbering under a dozen members (though occasionally much larger), bands developed customs and rules of conduct that were often quite similar from one region of the country to another. In many cases, they patterned their behavior after the example set by gangs of adult thieves, whose domain overlapped their own.[63] Seasoned toughs predominated, of course, but the very nature of street life often prompted novices as well to join forces. A group could seize and defend more effectively a desirable location to spend the night or lay claim to a section of street or market square. Teamwork, such as the participation of a lookout or decoy, made possible various thefts beyond the capability of loners.[64] Gangs, in short, enjoyed advantages in most areas vital to homeless youths.

The longer the members of a band remained on the street, the more likely they were to develop a sense of their group as removed or isolated from the society around them. Outsiders came to represent a threat from whom the group's secrets and turf had to be protected. Whether a non-member appeared to the gang as a menace or as their intended victim, the person could expect no restraint or pity. The most cohesive, tightly knit bands were those in which a sense of separation and alienation had fully matured. At the other end of the spectrum, clusters of juveniles who still returned occasionally to the homes of relatives for sleep or a meal tended to display a less wary or hostile outlook.[65]

The suspicion and enmity brandished by gangs toward the outside world often extended to other abandoned children, especially to green youths newly on their own. Regarded as outside the pale (*ne svoi*) by hardened adolescents, many a novice found himself stripped of his clothing and beaten by a group whose path he crossed while groping about in a harsh, unfamiliar environment. The outcome was grimmer for sixteen-year-old Vasilii Riabov, fresh on the street in November 1924. Facing ever colder nights, he sought shelter in the ruined basement complex of a large building on Moscow's Tverskaia Street, a frequent refuge of the homeless. As he entered the cellars, other pairs of eyes noted the comparatively good condition of his apparel, and after he had fallen asleep a group of four (three *besprizornye* and a twenty-three-year-old man) sprung to action. Grabbing his arms and legs, they suffocated him by stuffing ashes into his mouth and then removed his clothing. The corpse they buried in the cellar.[66]

Recently a Russian student of organized crime pointed to underworld slang as an indication that the nation's criminal stratum amounted to a subculture distinct from the rest of society.[67] Much the same could be said of experienced *besprizornye* in the 1920s. The argot developed in their groups, with hundreds of words and expressions unintelligible to ordinary citizens, underscored the gulf between the street and the surrounding population. In Moscow, for example, a committee investigating the case of a fourteen-year-old girl found her testimony so studded with this jargon as to be nearly inaccessible, and youths conspiring among themselves sometimes took advantage of the language barrier to confound adults within earshot. There were even reports that veterans employed their patois as a test to determine whether others just arrived in the area were "genuine"—that is, experienced members of their world. Those unfamiliar with the language of the street found themselves regarded as informers or novices—and thus targets of abuse.[68]

Waifs acquired much of their slang from the lexicon of adult thieves, testimony again to the close contact between the two groups. However, they also added words of their own and altered the meaning of some terms borrowed from their older neighbors in the underworld, which resulted in a new dialect.[69] While a thorough study of the language lies beyond this book's scope, a few examples will provide a sense of the flavor and subjects commonly encountered:

psy: a derogatory term used to denote children new to the street and unfamiliar with its ways. Sometimes applied contemptuously to youths who supported themselves by begging rather than stealing.

shpana: a streetwise, veteran *besprizornyi*.

fraier (sometimes rendered *fraer*): a person having no understanding of the street world. Often applied to the victim of a theft.

liagavyi: a betrayer or informer. Used by some as a strong term of reproach for almost any occasion.

ban: a train station.

maidan: a train.

shalman: a den or haunt.

chinar: a cigarette butt.

stirki (or *stirochki*): playing cards.

marafet: cocaine.

shmara: a street girl taken as a lover by a *besprizornyi*.

puliat': to beg.

kanai: go away!

shirmach: a pickpocket.

mil'ton or *ment*: a policeman.

kicha: a prison.[70]

Among a minority of youths, the influence of the criminal world also appeared in the form of tattoos, which urchins as young as nine sought to acquire in imitation of the adornments sported by older thieves around them. Prisons, the street, and even orphanages here and there all sheltered practitioners able to oblige. A study of 146 juveniles in the Moscow Labor Home discovered 37 with at least one tattoo in 1924, and a later investigation reported such decorations on "nearly all" the residents. Popular motifs included nude figures, the sex organs, and emblems signifying membership in a gang. Nearly any part of the body might carry a design, including locations chosen to allow the characters a semblance of animation. A naked man on one shoulder blade, for example, and a naked woman on the other, or a cat and mouse on the buttocks, could be moved in provocative or amusing fashion.[71]

Some adolescents, including a sixteen-year-old orphan dubbed Odessit, managed as well to ape adult criminals' lusty, unbridled lifestyle. In Odessit's case, the models who swayed him inhabited Ukraine and the port that inspired his nickname. Since 1922, this bold and resourceful boy had ranged through all the republic's principal cities, imbibing the underworld's habits and vocabulary. Eventually his travels brought him to Khar'kov, where he joined the Sumskaia Street group mentioned in the Introduction and turned the boys more resolutely to crime. Apart from facilitating thefts, membership in the group provided Odessit with a setting for his favorite amusements. He had a passion for gambling, drink, and ostentatious displays of money when treating comrades—among whom he developed a reputation for strictly honoring obligations. A rough-edged dandy, he dressed well by the standards of the street and rarely stood in need of cash.[72]

Like Odessit, most experienced waifs—and especially those in groups—went by nicknames. In fact, with the passage of time, many forgot their original surnames and identified themselves *only* with street names.[73] This evolution, too, symbolized and further emphasized the void between them and the surrounding society. Nicknames often sprang from a youth's physical appearance—hence appellations such as Krivoi (one-eyed), Kosoi (cross-eyed), Riaboi (pock-marked), and Ryzhii (redhead). Those with a countenance wasted by heavy consumption of cocaine or vodka might answer to Starik (old man). One pale thin lad acquired the name Monashka (nun), and another, whose blanched, oblong face suggested an icon figure, became known on the street as Bogomaz (icon dauber). In addition to physical features, children's special skills or experiences provided inspiration for names. The moniker Sevastopol'skii (from the Crimean city Sevastopol'), for example, referred to a youth who had traveled extensively in the southern part of the country, while the leader of a gang in Odessa received the name Simuliator because of his ability to assume a variety of roles in order to escape capture.[74] Diminutive forms of girls' names, applied to boys, also enjoyed circulation, as did names of animals such as Medvezhenok (bear cub), Lebed' (swan), and Krysa (rat). In at least a few instances, girls' nicknames stuck to boys who worked as prostitutes.[75]

With the passage of months, a group's Krysa or Kosoi would fall into the hands of the police or depart for other reasons. The band's core of veterans therefore took in new boys now and then, typically from among recent arrivals at a station, market, or other location that served as the gang's base. An initiate often underwent a trying, sometimes brutal, probationary period of beatings and orders to perform difficult tasks. If he proved himself by enduring these tests, which could last for weeks, the group accepted him as a reliable member. Those who ran away to escape the torment were dismissed by the others as sniveling babies or worse.[76]

According to some observers in the 1920s, many gangs divided stolen goods among all members equally or, failing that, in proportion to their involvement in the theft.[77] No doubt something of the sort occurred here and there, though the true extent of the practice remains difficult to determine. One sometimes senses in these accounts an author's eagerness to emphasize the cooperative nature of street children, even to the point of suggesting that they harbored embryonic collectivist qualities that educators could cultivate to transform them into builders of a communist society. Other reports, while noting that youths on occasion displayed considerable unity inside their groups, stressed as well that dominant members often tormented the rank and file. This abuse—which included beatings, appropriation of the most desirable portions of food, and sexual exploitation of other boys or girls in the gang—stood in vivid contrast to any custom of communal disposition of spoils.[78]

However sharply the conduct of groups might differ in some respects, certain rules of behavior and discipline gained wide currency, especially among adolescents experienced on the street. Loyalty to comrades, for example, was embedded deeply enough to prevent many, when questioned by police or social workers, from informing on the gang. "Betrayal" represented a sin of such proportions that young boys raped by older residents of the Moscow Labor Home complained to the staff only with great reluctance, fearing the merciless retribution likely to follow. Also, while respecting those of their world most adept at deceiving outsiders, vagrant children typically regarded cheating at cards or other games played among themselves—not to mention failing to pay debts incurred—as a grave transgression. Offenders risked savage reprisals, usually in the form of beatings, though the authors of one study witnessed instances of gang rape of group members considered guilty of such offenses. In a few reported cases the exaction of vengeance resulted in the victim's death.[79]

A youth who fled his group after violating one of its rules might well find that word of his act followed in short order. Gangs sometimes maintained connections with groups in other markets and train stations— even other cities—and could pass information along regarding the misdeeds of former members. In one such case, a boy who had fled from Tula to Moscow was eventually tracked down and dragged out of an institution. Only the staff's intervention saved him.[80] In a few instances, children arriving at shelters requested permission for a brief visit to the street in order to "earn" some money with which to settle their obligations before entering the institution. Among other things, they apparently felt that a safe return to the street in the future hinged on paying their debts.[81]

Most groups featured a leader (sometimes more than one), known in the youths' slang as a *vozhak*, *glot*, or *glavar'*. In some cases, leaders reportedly attained their preeminence by exercising such qualities as resourcefulness, intelligence, and strength of will, but this seems to have been the exception. Usually the oldest and strongest members (who might also possess the traits just mentioned) employed their physical attributes to intimidate others in the gang and thereby assume the dominant position.[82] A leader made the group's important decisions, enforced discipline as he saw fit, and in some cases demanded payment of tribute (cigarettes, perhaps, or something similarly desirable) from other members. While he might experience a challenge periodically, observers were more often struck by the unhesitating obedience his commands received.[83] Some groups depended so entirely on a leader's initiative that they crumbled when arrest or other misfortune removed him from the scene. Cohesiveness returned only with the emergence of a new *vozhak* from the ranks or the arrival of a strong figure from outside. The most submissive and dependent members followed their leaders with blind determination, whether to commit a risky crime or to enter an orphanage.[84]

One day, a man looking over the waifs gathered in the reception room of Narkompros's Moscow branch found his eye drawn to an older lad who sat smoking cigarettes and spitting frequently on the floor. There could be no mistake; it was Chainik. As the boy haughtily surveyed the room's other ragged children, the adult recalled their previous encounter in Moscow's Alexander Station. Like other large railway terminals, the station sat above a basement labyrinth of tunnels and steam pipes that sheltered many homeless youths from winter's frost. When Narkompros officials learned of this lair, they organized a foray to collect its urchins and place them in institutions. The man in the reception room had been among those in the search party that descended with quivering nerves into the station's basement. Aided by a single lantern, they groped down a long passage, clambering over pipes and turning several corners. With each step, oxygen seemed to grow scarcer, until one of the group lost consciousness. After carrying her from the basement, the others retraced their steps and arrived at an oval aperture in the wall—the mouth of a steam-pipe conduit so narrow that it could be negotiated only by crawling. A few minutes of this squirming sapped two members' resolve, leaving the party's leader to continue down the channel alone, his lantern now extinguished. The others backed out of the duct and crouched at its entrance, where they could hear muffled cries of *besprizornye* awakened in their chambers. The expedition had penetrated Chainik's winter home, and before long he stood among a score of cohorts herded out of the basement and assembled in the station for processing.

Years before, as it happened, his mother had brought the seven-year-old boy to this same hall with the apparent intention of deserting him. She placed her son on a bench and then lingered to watch from a distance, perhaps reluctant to take the final parting step. In any case, as evening approached, she told him that she would go out for a minute to buy a roll in the bazaar—and disappeared. That night, when the station closed, someone noticed the boy asleep under the bench with a raw carrot protruding from his mouth like a pacifier. He stuck to the premises for weeks, living on handouts from passengers, until he overcame his shyness and adjusted to the city's bustle. His nickname derived from the ploy of carrying a teakettle (*chainik*) to impersonate passengers, who often took pots and kettles into stations to obtain hot water. Under this cover he ran less risk of challenge while stealing baggage for his group to sell in the Sukharevskii Market. Come spring he migrated to the Crimea and did not return to Moscow until autumn, when stinging temperatures drove him into the caverns underneath "his" station.[85]

Chainik's experience illustrates the challenge faced by all children thrust out on their own, for even the most Spartan set of requirements included shelter from winter and other perils. The very young, weak, or ailing—those most handicapped on the street—could often hope for nothing beyond garbage piles, ditches, and the like. Unless admitted to institutions, few survived long. Others, more experienced or fortunate, managed to sniff out and cling to niches in structures that afforded securer refuge. But sanctuary lay not only in the basement of a train station or an abandoned building; it also resided in numbers. Like an irresistible force, the advantage of teamwork in activities essential for survival drew many into groups. With life a matter of competition reduced to its most unvarnished form, those who could not defend their dens soon lost them. Under these stark rules, gangs wielded the upper hand. This applied not only to the apportionment of shelter, but to all other matters of importance in an environment that prompted more than one observer to recall the name of Charles Darwin.

CHAPTER TWO

Beggars, Peddlers, and Prostitutes

What the *besprizornis* live on I do not know.

André Gide

Besprizornost', often appearing in the most twisted,
horrifying forms—such as juvenile crime and prostitution—
threatens the young generation with the most severe and
alarming consequences.

Feliks Dzerzhinskii

Whereas the need for shelter waxed and waned with the seasons, other
difficulties confronted waifs throughout the year. Disease, harassment,
and drug addiction numbered among the predicaments that tormented
many, but a far more widespread challenge lay in the unremitting urgency of procuring food. Death in short order faced those unable to
wrest provisions from the street. No abandoned child, from the greenest
beggar to the sliest gang member, was immune, and some spent nearly
every waking hour in search of bread. Techniques ranged from the passive to the criminally aggressive, with the choice influenced by a multitude of factors including age, health, gender, location, level of desperation, and degree of experience with street life. As among wild animals—
with whom they frequently found themselves compared—the strongest
and cleverest extracted the most food and clung to life with the securest
grip.

Youths neither strong nor clever could often do no more than pick
through garbage piles. Here they encountered minimal competition for
their wretched bits of "food" and ran little risk of punishment from
policemen or other citizens. Because this activity required no special
skills or experience, it attracted children only recently thrown onto the

street and those otherwise desperate and helpless. During the famine, when an observer recorded the following scene in a town along the Volga, similar cases appeared numberless:

> Three men were sitting on the top of a low shed eating water-melon. The side of the shed was filthy with dirt and excrement. As they ate their slices of melon they threw the rind into the dirt, and, unseen by them, a little boy would come and pick it out and chew it ravenously. Not far away were women selling rolls of bread and large but unpleasant-looking sausages; the hungry child looked at them, and they at him, but at such a time nobody can help anybody else. Besides, such sights as these are commonplaces all through the vast famine area.[1]

Discarded scraps—whether fish heads and peelings thrown in the dirt of market squares or the daily trash generated by apartment dwellers—enticed juveniles in later years as well.[2] Some tried to intercept unwanted food even before it reached the refuse heap. A man who pushed away his plate at a restaurant in Kherson was startled by the events his action triggered:

> No sooner had I shoved the plate aside than a boy of about seven, attired in nondescript rags, rushed in like a fury, grabbed a piece of meat from my plate and as quickly rushed out again. The whole scene transpired in the twinkle of an eye. It gave me the creeps. But there was still more to come. A minute later, a tiny tot crept in, almost naked, except for a skimpy dirty shirt which he lifted and cupped apronwise. Suddenly he seized a piece of meat and threw it in his shirt, where it found congenial company among bones, bread crusts, and other refuse.[3]

In Saratov, youths known as *tarelochniki* (from *tarelka*, plate) lingered around cafeterias and snack bars, waiting for patrons to finish their meals. As soon as a diner departed, they scurried to the table and devoured anything left on the plate. Every cafeteria in town had a contingent of *tarelochniki*, most of whom remained throughout the day.[4]

In a manner of speaking, begging represented a step up from the practice of rummaging through garbage, because it required a youth to make an impression on another citizen. The rewards, too, while often modest compared to those of other activities undertaken by homeless adolescents, generally exceeded anything available in piles of trash—especially for skilled practitioners. According to a number of accounts, juvenile begging did not assume mass proportions in most of the country immediately following the Revolution. Its scale doubtless increased during the Civil War, but not until the famine of 1921–1922 did young beggars inundate cities and towns across much of the nation.[5] A report

from Saratov province told of tattered, starving boys and girls roaming
the bazaars and streets in the summer of 1921, beseeching passersby,
"Uncle, give a bit of bread." Others could manage nothing more than
to approach silently, with outstretched hands and tear-stained faces.[6]
Rail passengers at major stations in famine districts and neighboring
regions described a continuous wail produced by multitudes—often
hundreds or even thousands—of children's voices clamoring for food
from travelers. Variously described as flocks of sparrows and ravenous
locusts, they swarmed instantly over any scraps of food or garbage
thrown to them from the cars, fighting for every crumb. The scene re-
curred at station after station, testifying graphically to the scale of destitution produced by the famine.[7]

For years thereafter juvenile beggars remained a common sight.[8] Indeed, most studies concluded that a majority of abandoned children
took up begging during a portion of their time on the street. A survey
of 1,183 youths passing through one institution found that 952 had
previously solicited alms.[9] While a child newly arrived among the homeless rarely shunned thievery if a safe opportunity presented itself, most
novices did not possess the experience or resolve to plunge immediately
into such a career. Instead they commonly clung at first to begging. Only
when steeled by the street and schooled in crime did they graduate to
bolder illegal pursuits.[10] Youths with physical or mental disabilities
found few alternatives to begging. Their infirmities rendered them unlikely even to contemplate an active life of robbery, let alone pursue it
successfully. Tests of physical adroitness administered in a children's
institution during the second half of the decade revealed that those who
had supported themselves only with begging scored considerably lower
than their counterparts who had left begging for crime.[11]

Young beggars naturally assembled in public locations crowded with
citizens carrying money or provisions. Thus, train stations and markets,
favorite sites for other reasons as well, lured many bent on panhandling.
So, too, did stores, nightclubs, cinemas, and theaters, around whose
doors children congregated to implore patrons for a few coins or a piece
of bread. Some did not wait for people to venture forth to these establishments, choosing instead to make the rounds of apartments to beg
from the occupants. Churches and cemeteries also drew them, especially
on Saturdays, Sundays, and holidays—when youths could hope for
larger, more philanthropic crowds.[12] Competition for favorable locations flared frequently, with those who had established their positions
resisting newcomers vigorously. One lad, who sang for money on a train

each day, was expected by other beggars not to continue past a certain station. Eventually he pushed beyond this limit—and fell victim to knives, according to the boy who soon replaced him.[13]

Children often haunted entrances to restaurants, cafeterias, snack bars, taverns, and the like—in many cases entering the premises to seek money or a portion of the repast directly from diners.[14] They were not always greeted warmly, as Ilya Ehrenburg noticed in the refreshment room of the train station in Gomel': "Here, too, wandered homeless children in the hope of scraps. A passenger handed one girl his plate with some bits of meat and gravy: 'Here, gobble it up!' A waiter (or as they used to say then a 'serving citizen') ran up, tore the plate out of the child's hands and threw the pieces of meat and potatoes all over the rags she was wearing. I was revolted, but nobody backed me up. The little girl cried and ate hastily."[15] Another observer described mentally deficient juveniles begging in taverns whose coarse clientele made them the butt of crude jokes and abuse. Before receiving food or money, they might be required to clown, recite obscene verses, or down considerable amounts of liquor. Some youths recognized the tone of these establishments and developed their own acts of ribald tomfoolery to perform in return for sustenance.[16] Indeed, alert minds soon learned that success hinged on adjusting an approach to suit the nature of one's prospective benefactor. According to several children, the following "rules" had guided them in begging from patrons in dining facilities:

1. Never approach a diner who has just sat down to the table, because his hunger leaves him disinclined to give anything. Wait for a break in the meal, such as between the first and second courses. Do not wait to approach him after the second course, because he will likely be hurrying and therefore unreceptive to appeals.

2. Do not approach a diner from behind and surprise him with a request. The reflex response of a person startled in this way will probably be a refusal, and then he will not want to appear to change his mind.

3. Try to determine in advance what sort of person the diner is. Do this by noticing how he is dressed, what type of luggage he has, what brand of cigarette he is smoking, and so on. Then one can adopt the physical carriage and deportment most likely to appeal to the patron.

4. Beg in a cheerful manner (*veselo*) from a fat person—unless he appears short-winded, because then he will be cross. With a thin person, adopt a sad, whining voice.

5. If the diner is sitting with a woman and does not talk with her during the meal, beg from him, because the woman is his wife and probably will not give anything. If he speaks and jokes with the woman during the meal, beg from her—and the man will more quickly give something.

6. If there is a group of people at the table, approach the person who first places his order with the waiter. He will be the one who pays for the meal, which means that he has money.[17]

Youths appealed for charity with a wide variety of techniques, ranging from the passive to the energetic and deceitful. Some did nothing more than sit or stand in place for hours on end, often mute, with upturned palms and vacant expressions. A girl begging in the Sukharevskii Market stood barefoot, clad in a torn dress and jacket, silently watching the traders. Her swollen face, its dull eyes encased in dark circles, appeared set in a listless expression, divorced from nearby arguments and the market's other pungent qualities. Finally, she approached a row of booths and rooted herself before them without a word, never diverting her worn gaze from the broiling sausages. Sedentary methods of this sort, involving little effort to seize the attention of prospective donors, were adopted most often by the frightened and inexperienced, along with those in poor physical and mental health or otherwise reduced to apathy. A doctor in the Crimea during the famine noted that hunger had so weakened some children that they lay crying softly on the side-walks of busy streets, no longer able to make any overt effort to beg.[18]

Bolder urchins selected individual pedestrians and scampered along with them, appealing relentlessly for a few kopecks. *Pravda* reported from Odessa that "on warm days, no one on the boulevards can avoid them. Their badgering is tenacious, and the pedestrian simply cannot drive them off." Others performed little services—such as brushing the snow or dust off people or opening a shop door for customers—as part of their appeal for alms.[19] Some fabricated stories to exploit their con-clusion that adults would respond more sympathetically to the tempo-rary distress of "ordinary" children than to requests from waifs. Tales included variations on a claim that the juvenile, arriving in the city to visit relatives, had been unable to find them. Now, with his money and documents allegedly lost or stolen, he begged for funds to purchase a train ticket home. In addition to the pitch itself, youths employed "props" (such as a knapsack) to bolster their credibility. Several roamed the bazaars of Rostov-on-the-Don in 1922 carrying coffin lids, pleading for money to bury their parents, said to be just deceased. Children also claimed, with tears in their eyes, that they had lost coins given them by parents to buy food for the family. How could they return home, they lamented, without recovering the sum in question? Whatever the entreaty, polished supplicants adjusted the contents, delivery, and form of address—from the familiar *bratishka* (roughly, pal, buddy, or brother) to the deferential *gospodin* (mister or sir)—to suit the targets of their appeals.[20]

Rather than concoct stories, others feigned illness or injury to win sympathy. This tactic commonly involved simulating blindness, convulsive fits, or the loss of a limb (by doubling it up under clothing). One cold winter day, a fourteen-year-old boy noticed that he received more money when he shivered visibly, and thereafter he resolved to quiver whatever the temperature. When spring finally arrived, he found that this trembling, initially a ploy, had become involuntary. Some children even equipped themselves with festering sores. Dirty needles stuck under the skin, for example, and left there for a few days, produced wounds to help stir the hearts of potential benefactors.[21]

The most conspicuous young beggars relied on songs to elicit contributions. "On any day in Moscow you can hear and see some *besprizorni* 'perform,' " a visitor to the capital wrote in 1926, and the experiences of many citizens prompted similar observations. Trams, for instance, stopped at certain points along their routes for five or ten minutes, presenting children opportunities to climb aboard and sing to people awaiting the vehicles' departure. A passenger recalled one such youth, about seven years old, clad in shredded garments revealing much of his body, which was blue from the cold. When the conductor ordered him out, he jumped to the sidewalk, pulled out a cigarette, and hurled abuse at his evictor—then slipped onto the next tram approaching the stop.[22] Juveniles (including Chainik) also dodged conductors to ply their songs on the railways. Some worked the same suburban lines so frequently that commuters gave them nicknames, as in the case of a lad dubbed Solovei (nightingale). While his voice bore no resemblance to a songbird's, the sole selection in his repertoire lamented that after his death, no one save a nightingale would visit his grave. He introduced some new material at the beginning of the year but soon returned to his lachrymose standby,

explaining that the mournful song drew more money. Another boy re-
galed passengers on local trains with a few short tunes and then always
ended his performance with the appeal: "Help a future Shaliapin!" After
making his rounds among the audience, during which he collected as
much as thirty kopecks on a good day, he proceeded to the next car for
another performance.[23]

In addition to targeting mass transportation, street children aimed
their songs at citizens in other busy public sites.[24] The lyrics (sung for
entertainment or solace, as well as to solicit donations) most often featured some aspect of a vagrant, thieving life. Frequently, as in the nightingale lament, the singer described an adolescent at turns neglected and
abused—ultimately dying anonymously and unnoticed in a cold land.
Konstantin Paustovsky heard the following verse from a homeless boy
in 1924.

> Forgotten, neglected
> In my youthful state
> I was born an orphan
> And misery's my fate.[25]

Some songs focused on the transformation of an artless pup into a petty
thief and ultimately a hardened criminal.[26] In one, the protagonist re-
proached citizens who had refused to offer him any assistance and
thereby turned him to crime. "Because of you, I suffer. Because of you,
I will find my grave."[27] In other selections, lyrics featured portrayals of
life in prison—including debilitating idleness, abuses, and even death—
or descriptions of Dickensian children's institutions.[28] While most songs
presented a rough-edged world, a number praised at the same time the
vagabond "freedom" of life on the street.[29] Some even adopted a saucy
air, such as a tune in which a thief secured his freedom by bribing a
policeman; thus enriched, the officer proceeded to the Khitrovskii Market and purchased cocaine.[30] Finally, many songs depicted romances—
affairs generally doomed to misfortune as one partner forsook the other
or was caught committing a crime. In a composition set to the melody
of a well-known lullaby, a mother sings her baby to sleep with the pre-
diction that he will grow up to become a pickpocket and abandon her
for a hussy. With this lass, and cocaine in his pocket, the prophesy
continued, he would spend his evenings on the town. In the end, while
stealing for his lover, capture by the authorities awaited him.[31]

Along with singing, youths staged other performances in public locations—simple acrobatics, dancing, or juggling, for example—as part

of their appeal to passing citizens.[32] Reports from a number of cities described groups that roamed thoroughfares, markets, and apartment courtyards accompanying their songs with primitive instruments fashioned from pans, plates, and the like.[33] Vasilii Aleichenko, the orphan whose grandfather died trying to conceal a horse during the Civil War, joined forces on the road with a boy skilled at mimicking the sounds of machinery and animals. Once the pair learned to evade policemen, they found that spectators would reward them for these imitations.[34] Others practiced more unusual forms of begging. Passengers on board a ship in Sevastopol' harbor noticed several waifs who had undressed and swum out to the ship as it prepared to depart for Yalta. Treading water, the boys called to people on deck to throw them kopecks—which some travelers did to amuse themselves, watching the swimmers dive far to the bottom in search of the coins.[35] A handful of children earned money from onlookers by humiliating themselves in grotesque fashion. In Omsk, a boy who lived at the train station clowned oafishly for money and let people do anything they pleased to him in return for a kopeck. For five kopecks he smeared his face with his own excrement. At the Nikolaev Station in Moscow, a child covered himself with oil from a steam engine and then rolled in the dirt to win a few kopecks from petty traders nearby.[36] More coercive juveniles, claiming to have syphilis or other venereal diseases with which to afflict hesitant donors, transformed the art of pleading into extortion. They threatened to bite or spit on passersby, hoping that purses would open to ward off the alleged risk of infection.[37]

Finally, some homeless youths begged together with one or more adults. According to numerous accounts, the latter took all the money earned by children, generally in return for providing food and a corner in which to sleep. In some cases adults sent juveniles out to beg alone, while in others they worked as a team. A grownup might pretend to be blind or crippled, for instance, hoping that the child's presence would enhance the pathos of his spectacle and melt the indifference of passersby. Adult beggars who did not shrink from thefts to augment their income introduced their assistants to a darker side of street life and another means of support. Other youths participated in the acts of older street performers (musicians, conjurers, or acrobats), sometimes running away eventually to continue routines on their own.[38]

The question remains, how did juveniles fare when they approached the surrounding population for assistance? There seems little doubt that a majority of citizens regarded abandoned children as nuisances, quite

possibly thieves, and rebuffed their appeals for alms.[39] But the plight of
the homeless did move some people to offer them money, food, cigarettes, and other items without hesitation. In response, books, articles,
letters to editors, and slogans of official campaigns implored the Soviet
population throughout the 1920s not to contribute anything to young
mendicants. Such gifts, some contended, contributed to the ruin of children in the grip of vodka and cocaine by encouraging them to continue
begging rather than enter institutions. Those wishing to assist were advised to donate money or time to the various organizations formed to
rescue youths from the street.[40]

While such recommendations may well have diminished the contributions citizens made to beggars, the flow certainly did not dwindle to
the point where it no longer behooved hungry urchins to pursue charity.
Handouts supported many indefinitely. Langston Hughes learned of an
old woman who had placed bread on her windowsill each day all winter
for a group of boys living in a nearby train station. When the warm
weather of spring finally summoned them to the rails for another season
of travel, they presented her in parting with an attractive handbag stolen
from a foreigner at the station. Most full-time beggars, of course, could
not hope for a constant source of generosity and depended on passing,
anonymous benefactors for a few coins and morsels. A day's take rarely
exceeded one ruble. Two boys interviewed in 1925 received a total of
1.05 rubles (30 kopecks and 75 kopecks, respectively), which they spent
as follows: 14 kopecks for two hundred grams of sausage, 28 kopecks
for two rolls, 16 kopecks for two hundred grams of sugar, and 7 kopecks
for candy. The youth who had brought in the larger amount claimed 40
kopecks to attend the movies. This budget, similar to those of other
juveniles in the same study, indicates that beggars could survive on the
street for well under 30 rubles per month. A handful of the most talented
or fortunate exceeded this sum three or four times over, prompting a
few to reject any thought of learning a craft in an institution. Begging,
they felt, promised a better income.[41]

Children also sought money from the surrounding population by offering something in return—that is, through trade. To be sure, the bound-
ary between begging and trade was indistinct on occasion, as when
youths played primitive instruments or opened doors for shoppers. In
some cases, too, when the items offered for sale by a peddler were particularly meager, trade could serve as a mask or a means for begging.

But such qualifications aside, numerous observers remarked in the 1920s on the clusters of waifs roaming markets and other crowded locations, trying to interest people in their modest inventories. Even before the 1920s, during the War Communism years when the state attempted to ban private trade, youths were much in evidence on the streets carrying small quantities of food and other goods for sale. The elimination of large private enterprises and the inability of the state to supply more than a trickle of consumer products compelled the population to rely heavily on petty, itinerant traders. Some in the corps of vendors were dispatched by parents to help support families during these years of privation, while others sprang from the burgeoning ranks of homeless children and traded anything they could steal or otherwise acquire. With no adequate alternative to small-scale private trade, officials in many cities watched the proceedings through their fingers and cracked down only intermittently—even then rarely focusing their energies effectively on juveniles.[42]

The legalization of private trade by the New Economic Policy in 1921 nudged authorities in most regions to adopt a still more indulgent attitude toward young street entrepreneurs. While the law required that traders possess licenses and stipulated that only people at least sixteen years of age could obtain them, these provisions were frequently ignored. Numerous unlicensed juveniles worked the streets and markets openly, often without any interference from the police. Even if apprehended, youths generally faced nothing more than a reprimand, after which they could return to hawking their wares.[43] Eventually, the government's diminished opposition to private trade amounted to a mixed blessing for small-scale peddlers, because the New Economic Policy also spawned larger shops and stalls that presented stiff competition to petty vendors. But the millions of abandoned children created at the same time by the famine insured that ragged young hawkers would remain a common sight in cities for years to come.[44]

Waifs often worked in groups when conducting trade. A need to defend themselves from plunder by gangs, and to assemble enough eyes to watch in all directions for the approach of the occasional zealous policeman, frequently inspired this clustering.[45] Early-warning functions aside, some groups operated much like guilds. They attempted to restrict competition by driving away others displaying similar wares in what they regarded as their own territory.[46] At the very least they sought to prevent outsiders from offering merchandise at lower prices. Studies of street children reported a few groups that regulated their own activities to an even greater degree. The leader of several boys selling candies in the Sukharevskii Market made the rounds of the members periodically to collect their take and later divided the receipts among them. A second group of young candy peddlers in the market pooled and redistributed their receipts with those of a youth who shined shoes and two who sold kvass.[47]

The means employed to acquire merchandise varied as widely as the goods themselves. Some children stole the items they sold, or hawked commodities purloined by others. One boy described how he pilfered apples, marketed them, and used the money to purchase cigarettes, which he resold.[48] Youths occasionally captured animals—pigeons, for example—intending to sell them to consumers. Some hunted rats to eat the flesh and peddle the skins. A group of about thirty homeless people (adults and children) living in an abandoned building in Leningrad specialized in trapping cats, skinning them, and dying the pelts to resemble other furs more desired in the markets.[49] Another illegal, but rarely prevented method of obtaining goods involved waiting in lines at movie theaters to buy tickets for resale later at higher prices.[50]

Juvenile traders secured some products from state agencies unable to market all of their stock through the rudimentary and ponderous official distribution network. Thus tobacco trusts recruited children to sell a portion of the trusts' merchandise in the streets.[51] But no other state-supplied commodity attracted as many young hawkers as did newspapers. According to an extensive study conducted over a period of months, Moscow contained several hundred such peddlers (less than 500 in the winter and about 750 in the summer) in 1926/27, and their counterparts were visible (and audible) at major intersections, stations, and tram stops in other cities as well.[52] Responding to the question of why a large number of juveniles engaged in selling newspapers, the study stressed the activity's accessibility. It required neither registration with the labor exchange nor special training. Anyone with the small sum necessary to purchase a few papers could join the others waiting at distribution locations. Also, while the earnings were not lavish, most youths could count on garnering from one to one and a half rubles per day—enough to survive on the street.[53]

As described in the study, morning newspapers (*Rabochaia gazeta*, *Rabochaia moskva*, *Pravda*, and *Izvestiia*) were distributed to vendors (adults as well as children) at many points around Moscow between 5:30 and 7:00 A.M. Some hawkers lined up earlier, seeking to be among the first to reach the public with their papers and thereby sell them more rapidly. Out on the street, the work still included an element of competition. Who would infiltrate most successfully such places as tram cars and dining halls, where the sale of newspapers was forbidden but lucrative? Who could yell most convincingly and loudly the sensational news supposedly—but not always in fact—contained in the papers? A majority of vendors sold all their morning papers by 10:00 or 11:00 and returned to distribution points by 1:00 P.M. to await the evening paper, *Vecherniaia moskva*—handed out between 2:00 and 2:30, if it appeared on time. Roughly five hours later, most youths had exhausted their second stock and their bodies.[54]

Rather than ply stolen wares or merchandise purchased from state agencies, some street children sold products easily procured at no charge, notably water. During the summer months in many cities, youths traversed market squares carrying large containers from which they dispensed drinks. After obtaining water from a variety of sources close to the market, including faucets in public lavatories, they often tried to enhance the liquid's appeal by coloring it with powders or other fluids. One child, under observation for a few hours in the Sukharevskii Market, changed the tint of his water three times before arriving at a hue that tempted customers. This study found that, unlike juveniles purveying other goods, those selling water generally did so on their own rather than in groups. As a result, prices varied considerably around the market, ranging from two kopecks per glass to two glasses for one kopeck. The lack of organization may have been due to the temporary, seasonal nature of this trade and to the likelihood that those selling such commodities as water had just begun their trading careers.[55]

The inventory hawked by unsupervised children also featured other types of food (including fruit, seeds, rolls, and fish), flowers (often near the entrances to theaters), programs (near theaters, race tracks, and the like), and cheap haberdashery. A newspaper article describing the situation in Leningrad near the middle of the decade reported numerous abandoned boys and girls on the street selling homemade cigarettes, chocolate, matches, seeds, rotten apples, and "in general anything that comes to hand." Young bootblacks, too, graced the sidewalks, with little more than a box, a rag, and a tin or two of polish. Some youths changed lines of trade repeatedly, peddling whatever seemed profitable and in reach.[56] A few in Odessa worked as guides, though not to sights customarily visited by city tours. They led sailors from foreign ships to the city's prostitutes. Because they navigated this terrain on a daily basis, they knew "where is better and where is worse," as *Pravda* put it, and could

make expert recommendations.[57] In the absence of merchandise and special knowledge, adolescents sometimes sold raw labor—hauling loads
at train stations and markets or holding places for people waiting in
long lines. According to a report in the middle of the decade, such un-
skilled work typically netted a child no more than forty to seventy kopecks per day. Nevertheless, youths continued to seek out this employment, a fact that testified to both the difficult conditions on the street
and the steady appearance, year after year, of new, inexperienced
waifs.[58]

Thousands of children, unable to support themselves through other
means, turned sooner or later to prostitution. "Who among the inhabitants of Moscow," an author inquired, "is not familiar with the figures
of rouged and curled adolescents, flooding every evening the sidewalks
of the Tverskaia [Moscow's main street]? Who has not seen the dishev-
eled, ragged inhabitants of the Smolenskii, Trubnyi, and other markets?
They are all a juvenile 'commodity,' awaiting its consumer."[59] While
very little statistical information exists concerning prostitution, especially during the chaotic years immediately following the Revolution, a
wide variety of sources stressed the direct link between homelessness
and the multitude of juvenile prostitutes in evidence by the beginning of
the 1920s.[60] As abandoned children proliferated during the years of War
Communism—that is, even before the famine of 1921–1922—several
studies and reports warned of an enormous increase in the number of
young prostitutes. "The results of my investigation are horrifying," a
professor informed his colleagues. "They show that child prostitution,
which formerly was only an isolated phenomenon, is now very widespread." According to one estimate, the number of juveniles engaged in
prostitution had increased twentyfold since 1917. Whatever the preci-
sion of this figure, it would not have astounded a woman who operated
a brothel near Moscow's Khitrovskii Market. She disclosed that the
problem of finding enough young girls, previously a difficult task, no
longer plagued her establishment.[61]

     Not until the famine triggered a new deluge of castaways, however,
did the tide of juvenile prostitutes reach its crest—a "catastrophic" increase, according to the editor of a recent Soviet work.[62] Relief officials
and others noted that among the millions of destitute youths, many
clung to life, at least for a time, by selling their bodies for as little as a
piece of bread.[63] By the middle of the decade the number had decreased,

but the variety of forces that continued to generate street children insured that young prostitutes would remain visible and very much a cause
of concern.[64]

A considerable proportion of homeless girls supported themselves, at
least in part, through prostitution—in contrast to boys long at large,
most of whom depended primarily on theft. At the beginning of life on
their own, some girls (probably most) tried to acquire sustenance
through begging or petty trade. If these endeavors proved fruitless—and
often after being raped by denizens of the underworld or even passersby—they undertook prostitution. Reports also told of juveniles,
trading without licenses, who obtained the forbearance of policemen in
return for sexual favors and eventually dropped their original enterprises
to sell themselves.[65] Though prostitutes' income was far from steady, a
number divulged earnings as high as three to five rubles in a single day.
This amounted to more than they could realize through the other dismal
alternatives available to them and thus was incentive enough to begin.[66]

While there can be no precise estimate of the percentage of all abandoned girls who tried to survive by marketing their bodies, local investigations suggested a high figure—quite possibly a sizable majority, at
least among those who had been homeless for more than a few months.
In 1920, for instance, a survey of 5,300 street girls up to the age of
fifteen found that 88 percent had engaged in prostitution. Among a
smaller assortment of children (mostly boys) removed from the Northern Caucasus railroad at the end of the decade, *every one* of the girls
had worked as a prostitute.[67] Though nearly all young prostitutes were
girls, a few investigators also discovered boys who were similarly experienced. The latter, according to an article describing the situation in
Khar'kov in the middle of the decade, tended to be very young—often
no more than seven to nine years of age—and frequently turned to prostitution after first finding shelter with adult males. Their number increased in the winter, as harsh conditions made survival by other means
more difficult.[68]

The boys' tender age did not distinguish them greatly from their much
more abundant female counterparts. In fact, nothing struck observers
more sharply than the girls' youth. By their middle teens, many ranked
as veterans, and reports of prostitutes no more than eight to ten years
of age appear in numerous sources.[69] When asked how old girls had to
be in order to work for her, the proprietress of the previously mentioned
Moscow brothel replied: "It doesn't matter. We take whoever comes
along. The younger the better." Her visitor noticed a prostitute there

who appeared to be eight or nine years old.[70] The engagement of a young girl in such activity (and much the same could be said to a lesser degree of street life in general) often produced a child bearing vividly incongruous personality traits—cynical, sexually experienced, and accustomed to alcohol and cocaine on the one hand, but eager to play with dolls and listen to stories on the other.[71]

A city's juvenile prostitutes worked in a variety of districts and facilities—some, as just indicated, in brothels. Girls alone and without shelter quickly caught the attention of "aunties" (teten'ki) or pimps (koty), who lured them to prostitution in return for a corner in a room.[72] In 1920 a girl named L, who could not have been much older than ten, ran away from a children's shelter. She had lost her mother shortly after birth and did not know her father, so she joined some other youths climbing aboard a train bound for Moscow. Along the way she was separated from her companions and found herself groping alone in one of Moscow's stations. Suddenly, it seemed, fortune smiled on her, for a woman approached, offering food and clothing if L would come to her apartment. Off they went, but their destination proved to be a tearoom near the station where L was sold (prodana) to a "well-dressed man." He proceeded to intoxicate his new acquisition and then led her to his apartment. L regained consciousness the next day in a hospital. Upon discharge from the facility two weeks later, she was evidently left to her own devices, for she made her way back to the man and lived with him for a few weeks. When, at the end of this period, he announced plans to leave Moscow for his native Khar'kov, he bought her some dresses and shoes and returned her to the street.[73]

Most juvenile streetwalkers, however, did not reside in brothels or settings similar to that of L. They sought customers on their own, frequently in large urban markets (the Smolenskii, Trubnyi, Tsvetnoi, Khitrovskii, and Sukharevskii in Moscow, for example, and the Nevskii, Ligovka, and Aleksandrovskii in Leningrad).[74] Among the waifs in Moscow lived an eight-year-old girl whose parents had divorced in 1918. Her father moved into another household, and her mother was imprisoned for concealing stolen property, leaving the girl and her brother alone on the street. They soon made their way to the Khitrovskii Market, which became their new home and school. Here the girl not only took up prostitution but also discovered a rich underworld lexicon, the art of stealing, and cocaine. The children returned to their mother after her release from prison, and a social worker managed to interest the girl for a time in literacy. She gave up cocaine but not prostitution.[75]

Train stations, too, supported contingents of young prostitutes, who utilized lavatories, dark corners in the terminals, empty train cars, outbuildings, and secluded spots around the rail yards to conduct their business. Clients included passengers, depot employees, and members of train crews.[76] While markets and stations may have been their points of greatest concentration, homeless children also worked as prostitutes in other sites, including abandoned buildings, vacant lots, taverns, restaurants, squares, public baths (such as the Sandunovskie and Samotechnye in Moscow), movie theaters, parks, and other outdoor locations, especially in the summer. A teenager apprehended in a public bathroom at Moscow's Strastnaia Square indicated that her sexual activities with customers—as many as five or six in an evening—took place in their apartments or the entryways of buildings.[77]

This general habitat, combined with the nature of the youths' work, insured close contact between them and the criminal underworld. Much of their sexual activity transpired with the unsavory individuals who frequented the same parts of town as they, and girls sometimes moved in with petty thieves while continuing to work as prostitutes.[78] Little wonder, then, that many in this position—with criminals as customers, lovers, and acquaintances—soon began to combine prostitution with thievery. Some even worked to funnel victims to adult thieves by luring unsuspecting clients to dens where bandits could later prey on them.[79]

Children long exposed to these influences naturally developed personalities lacking common ground with societal norms. An eleven-year-old girl in Khar'kov, for example, already a prostitute for three years, considered the street her home and resisted all efforts to dislodge her. When placed in a family, she ran away. She smoked, used cocaine, and decorated her body with tattoos in the style of the underworld. After falling under a tram—which tore the skin from one side of her face and head, leaving her terribly disfigured—she was taken to a hospital. There she lay, swearing wildly, demanding to be released to the street.[80] In children's institutions, former prostitutes were among the most difficult cases. Many flew into fits of rage or tears at the slightest provocation, while others appeared completely indifferent to everything around them.[81] Well after leaving the street for an institution or a job, their experiences as prostitutes continued to torment some in their dreams, prompting them to wake up screaming in the night.[82]

Thus, numerous youths adrift on the street relied on begging, petty trade, or prostitution to maintain an often precarious existence. Of the three endeavors, begging attracted the most practitioners, especially during years of widespread misfortune, when destitution left countless juveniles too broken to do more than appeal with extended hand. Later in the decade, the "advantages" of begging remained compelling. It demanded no experience or inventory and could be practiced almost anywhere. Indignant rejection—not beatings or arrest—represented the most disagreeable outcome normally endured. For these reasons, homeless children tended to try begging first. Later, if alms grew scarce, or when experience revealed more lucrative options, their energies might shift elsewhere. In the case of girls, a deeply worn path led abruptly to prostitution. But the large majority (roughly two-thirds to three-fourths) of street children were boys, and when they looked beyond begging or trading, it was rarely to prostitution.[83] Instead, they turned to stealing, the activity most indelibly associated with *besprizornye* in the popular mind.

CHAPTER THREE

From You
I Can Expect No Pity

To those who are used to angels' twitter,
I say: ponder the words of *besprizornye* bitter.
                    Vladimir Mayakovsky

We're against you, and you're against us!
                    From a street children's song

"Rarely does one encounter two phenomena so closely linked, one proceeding so directly from the other," asserted a provincial author, "as the
phenomena of 'juvenile *besprizornost'*' and 'juvenile crime.'" Certainly no one should have been surprised that the creation of millions
of homeless youths led year by year to extensive juvenile delinquency.
"*Besprizornost'*," the saying went, "is the mother of crime."[1] Reports
from around the country—especially at the beginning of the 1920s, but
also later in some cities—spotlighted waifs, far too numerous for institutions to absorb, as the source of sharp local surges in thefts by minors.[2]
A number of authors observed that abandoned children did not merely
expand the ranks of young offenders; they represented the large *majority*
in the first half of the decade, with the most incorrigible hoodlums the
most likely to have spent time on the street.[3]

As more youths found themselves deprived or neglected during the
course of World War I, juvenile crime assumed ever larger proportions
in Russia—and hardship associated with the Civil War and War Communism only furthered the trend. According to one source, while the
number of residents five to eighteen years of age in St. Petersburg/Petro-
grad plunged from 400,000 in 1910 to 175,000 in 1920, property offenses committed by minors more than tripled in the city during the same
interval.[4] By all accounts, though, the volume of juvenile crime grew
most rapidly—and reached its peak—during the period 1921–1922,
when the famine created additional millions of bereft children.[5] In the

Russian Republic (excluding Moscow, Petrograd, and certain other regions), during a six-month period in 1921, the number of youths appearing before Juvenile Affairs Commissions (boards that determined what to do with most delinquents) soared 161 percent compared to a similar period the previous year. In Krasnodar, Moscow, and Rostov-on-the-Don, the volume of cases handled by commissions in 1921 swelled by 27 percent in the first two cities and by 143 percent in Rostov.[6] Juvenile crime may well have increased not only in absolute terms but also more rapidly than adult crime. Minors arrested by the Russian Republic's police in the first quarter of 1920 reportedly amounted to 6 percent of all people apprehended; a year later the total jumped to 8 percent, and by the first quarter of 1922 it stood at 10 percent. The juvenile share of arrests in Moscow approached 20 percent in 1920, 15 percent in 1921, and 13 percent in 1922. By contrast, national figures for the period 1911–1913 ranged between 3 and 5 percent.[7]

One sign of homeless children's central role in the juvenile crime wave lay in statistics showing a much higher percentage of orphans among delinquents by 1921–1922 than before 1914. According to an estimate for Moscow, only 3.5 percent of the delinquents surveyed in 1909 were orphans, compared to 28.8 percent in 1921. In St. Petersburg/Petrograd the figure sprang from 5.7 percent in 1914–1916 to 31 percent in 1920.[8] Thereafter, cities that attracted large numbers of waifs, such as Moscow and Rostov-on-the-Don, maintained an extremely high percentage of orphans among their underage offenders. According to data for 1925, approximately 22 percent of the youths appearing before Juvenile Affairs Commissions in the Russian Republic (excluding Moscow) were orphans, while for Moscow the number doubled to 44 percent—and reached 59 percent in Rostov.[9] Most studies of young lawbreakers in various regions throughout the 1920s revealed that approximately 60–70 percent lacked one or both parents, with the highest percentages generally found among recidivists.[10]

Statistics naturally present certain problems of interpretation. The growing volume of cases heard by Juvenile Affairs Commissions, for example, followed in part from an increase in the number and efficiency of the commissions themselves. Moreover, the actual dimensions of juvenile crime in famine regions exceeded official figures by a large margin. "In the atmosphere of 'famine life,' " one author observed, "they [juvenile crimes] became so commonplace that it was not worth reporting them or even reacting to them."[11] Data showing a significant decrease in the number of adolescents appearing before commissions in 1922 also create confusion. This drop appears to result largely from a change made to the Criminal Code in June 1922, which sent the cases of most youths sixteen to eighteen years of age directly to the courts, rather than to commissions.[12] Statistics aside, however, no one would dispute that juvenile crime reached unprecedented levels during the famine and that homeless children accounted for the lion's share.

After an improved harvest in 1922, the volume of juvenile offenses moderated by 1923–1924.[13] But hunger continued to prompt remaining and newly spawned waifs, still far more numerous than in the prewar era, to seize the necessities of life in any way possible. Clearly, the pressing requirement of food (and, to a lesser extent, clothing) underlay most thefts. Autobiographical sketches of street children describe the turn to these crimes prosaically, as a natural feature of their world, requiring no special explanation or justification. Many undertook their first robberies with nerves tingling and even trembling with fright, but before long the forays became routine.[14] This said, and without refuting the statement that most stole to satisfy basic needs, other motives appeared from time to time. Thefts provided the funds to acquire narcotics, stylish clothes, movie tickets, and similar items well outside the category of necessities. They also served as a form of amusement or adventure—and as a means of proving one's reliability and prowess to the rest of a gang.[15]

Many youths did not plunge into crime immediately after landing on the street. Any number of factors contributed to the hesitation, including a lingering inhibition carried over from the society a child had departed, fear of capture and beatings, sufficient earnings produced by begging or petty trade, and lack of experience in the realm of illegal undertakings. On this issue, a study conducted over the period 1925–1928 of more than a thousand "difficult" children concluded that those who had engaged in begging only briefly before moving on to stealing came much more often from urban families than from the peasantry. By the same token, youths who had clung to begging longer revealed a greater tendency to have arrived from the countryside. Other things being equal, the author concluded, a peasant lad's inexperience with city life made him less likely than a homeless boy of urban background to embrace thievery rapidly.[16]

Some indigent juveniles, of course, never became criminals, certainly not habitual bandits. But in general, the longer a child remained adrift, the more likely he was to join the corps of petty thieves. Probably a large majority of boys on their own for at least several months supported

themselves to a significant extent by stealing.[17] Aside from level of desperation and tenure on the street, several additional considerations encouraged or retarded the turn to crime. Older children, for example,
those at least fourteen years of age, generally took up stealing with less
hesitation. Doubtless their greater speed and strength emboldened them,
as did, perhaps, the reported adverse relationship between one's age and
begging receipts. Conversely, according to the study just mentioned,
youths hampered by physical or mental deficiencies remained beggars
longer than their healthier comrades. Finally, whatever a waif's personal
qualities, the sooner he joined a gang, the shorter his path to crime under
the tutelage and prodding of the group's veterans.[18]

The immediate circumstances that convinced a child to exchange
other means of support for thefts varied considerably. Perhaps a beggar
or vendor saw his customary flow of coins dry up for a few days or
simply tired of the work's monotony. Maybe he stumbled upon an un-
expected opportunity to steal with impunity—goods left temporarily
unguarded outside a store or restaurant, for example. Having profited
from the chance to acquire far more than he could hope to earn begging
or trading, he kept an eye peeled for new openings. In some cases, gambling debts or an introduction to narcotics prompted robberies. So too
might a desire for other "luxuries," such as the better food and clothing
enjoyed by experienced thieves.[19] In any event, when a boy replaced (or
supplemented) begging or peddling with stealing, the thefts often bore
a relationship to his previous occupation. A former beggar on trains, for
instance, might specialize in burglarizing railroad cars and their passengers. Children who made the rounds begging in apartments began sometimes to enter antechambers, communal kitchens, and other rooms sur-
reptitiously, no longer intent on soliciting. Similarly, those accustomed
to begging or trading amid crowds in streets and markets recognized
opportunities to raid vendors and snatch purses.[20]

Indeed, few inhabitants of Soviet cities in the 1920s had not heard
startled cries to seize small ragged figures darting off with handbags or
parcels.[21] Before long, the image of a waif probably coincided in most
minds with that of a petty thief. Unfair though it may have been to
regard all street children in this light, persons in crowded public places
were well advised to guard their bundles and pockets, especially in the
decade's early years. "More and more often," an author from Kazan'
observed at this time, "one hears complaints from citizens about the
extraordinary boldness and brazenness of juvenile delinquents" working
the streets, stations, wharves, and markets of large cities. According to

a report from the famine-stricken Crimea, attacks by bands of hungry youths grew so frequent that many women ceased venturing to bazaars without escorts.[22]

Groups as large as ten to thirty children swooped in lightning fashion on individuals, knocking them down and making off with their purses, bags, or packages. While gangs generally preferred to ambush women and the elderly, even healthy men, stunned by the suddenness of an assault and swarmed over as if by a school of piranhas, found themselves stripped of belongings on occasion. A doctor, strolling through a bazaar in Simferopol' with another man of substantial height and strength, described the following scene. His friend paused to purchase some bread, while the doctor went on ahead to a cigarette vendor. As he paid for the cigarettes, he noticed a group of children dash by and, a second later, heard a cry.

> My companion was literally enveloped by a pile of boys: some hung on his arms; others clambered up his legs, trying to reach a parcel that he held high above him in his hand. The bread had already vanished; they seized it first of all. One lad managed to grab the parcel, which turned out to be a box of cigarette wrappers, and tore it open. The wrappers fell out, but the boys did not pay any further attention to them and dashed off. All of this happened so quickly that I did not have time to run to my companion's assistance.

As a result of such attacks, officials increased patrols in the bazaars— to which some youths responded by carrying tobacco to throw in the eyes of resolute policemen.[23] Other reports described boys who waited for passengers to pull out money to pay cab drivers and then made a grab for the funds before dashing off. Even toward the end of the 1920s, back pages of newspapers contained reports of street children surrounding a pedestrian, seizing her purse, handbag, or other possessions, and then scattering. Their familiarity with the neighborhood's escape routes and hiding places made them difficult to apprehend. If people nearby caught one or more of the culprits, the latter had often managed already to relay the stolen goods to others in the group.[24]

Rather than rush at their targets or overwhelm them with sheer numbers, many children preferred to steal more discreetly from passing citizens. Hence the legions of young pickpockets in the nation's cities.[25] These thieves naturally selected such locations as squares, bazaars, and train stations, where the press of bodies facilitated their probes. One observer watched for an hour as a boy took advantage of the crowds struggling to board trams at a stop near the Sukharevskii Market. Carefully gauging a group's flow, he reached into pockets just as people grabbed for the rail at the tram's entrance—and rarely emerged empty-handed. Far to the south, on the busy thoroughfares of Sevastopol', a visitor noticed many filthy, half-naked street children, their long hair bleached by the sun, worming in and out of the sidewalk traffic. Few paid them attention until a man grabbed at his pocket and turned to pursue one of the boys. Like a rabbit reaching a thicket, the lad darted into the crowd, leaving the victim to gesture in resignation and continue on his way.[26] Other youths exploited opportunities presented not by the jostling of torsos but by temporary distractions. Street singers, jugglers, contraptions set up in market squares to test one's strength—anything would do that drew the curious and diverted their attention momentarily from belongings. In the case of inebriated citizens sprawled unconscious outdoors, adroit fingers required no artifice at all to relieve the dormant revelers of boots and other possessions.[27]

Witnesses noted that some juveniles maneuvered in teams to concoct distractions for their prey. Two children in a market, for example, approached a woman from different directions. One occupied her vigilance by creating the impression that he sought an opening to snatch her basket, while his companion moved in from the side and put his hand in her pocket under the cover of a little board he held.[28] At a train station, another pair employed a strategy in which one diverted a woman by begging persistently, even tugging her sleeve, despite her threats to call for the police. Meanwhile the other slipped in unnoticed and deftly removed parcels from her basket.[29] A group of four prowling the Sukharevskii Market concerted their efforts somewhat differently. The lead youth scrutinized a line of shoppers until a promising target caught his eye. He then wormed his way into the densest portion of the line, seeking to position himself to explore the quarry's pockets. Following this move, his three comrades pushed vigorously into the line behind him, trying to magnify the jostling and thus avail the group's undertaking. On this occasion, however, their efforts bore no fruit, as the intended victim turned quickly and left.[30]

After committing thefts of one sort or another, the perpetrators did not always make good their escape. Victims or others nearby managed now and then to seize some of the culprits, and youths so detained did not expect or generally receive mercy. Before ceding a boy to the police, those robbed—and even groups of onlookers—often expressed their exasperation by administering beatings that could leave arms, legs, ribs, jaws, or skulls broken. A survey of the Moscow Labor Home's residents reported that 85 percent had received drubbings from citizens who apprehended them.[31] Aleksei P——iaev, the boy whose father's death in World War I and mother's mental breakdown lay behind his arrival on the street, carried scars on his head from such batterings. "When you are caught stealing," he confided, "it is good if they send you straight to the police station. Many people, when they catch you, begin beating you so hard that you go away scarcely alive."[32] Even so, hungry juveniles resigned themselves to the blows, a routine feature of their struggle for survival that could not be avoided. A scene in a market square brought this point home to an observer, who marveled at a ravenous lad devouring bread during the course of a thrashing:

> I myself saw a boy of about 10–12 years of age reach out, while being beaten with a cane, for a piece of bread already covered with grime and voraciously cram it into his mouth. Blows rained on his back, but the boy, on hands and knees, continued hurriedly to bite off piece after piece so as not to lose the bread. This was near the bread row at the bazaar. Adults—women—gathered around and shouted: "That's what the scoundrel deserves; beat him some more! We get no peace from these lice."[33]

Bantam thieves focused as much attention on street hawkers and market vendors as on pedestrians and shoppers. Most days, a line of petty traders (adults and children) stretched along Moscow's Strastnoi Boulevard near the statue of Pushkin, where they sold cigarettes, apples, rolls, and the like. From time to time one of their number, sighting a gang bearing down on them at full speed, let out a warning cry, prompting the vendors to gather up their baskets or trays and scamper off in all directions. Encumbered with their wares, they did not always manage to escape. The *New York Times* correspondent in Moscow was struck by the raids' explosive nature. "Suddenly there materializes beside you a group of children, seven, ten, and twelve years old. . . . They shuffle together, taking counsel, then swift as swallows make one after another a leap for the counter, grabbing anything, running like the wind." Such attacks—everyday occurrences early in the 1920s—remained common throughout the decade. Nowhere could waifs expect to find food so accessibly displayed day after day as on street traders' stands and in the market stalls of any large city.[34]

Inexperienced juveniles, reduced by their circumstances to desperation, sometimes stalked vendors alone. But traders faced a more serious threat from thieves who struck in groups—occasionally numbering as many as thirty to forty youths—intent on overwhelming an entrepreneur and stripping her (less often his) stand of its goods.[35] A long-term study of street children in Khar'kov yielded an unusually detailed description of such a raid on a woman selling cigarettes. The group's leader deployed members with instructions to play one of four roles. Some were to distract the woman by asking about the prices she charged, while others, apparently as another diversion, pretended to look for lost coins nearby. Taking advantage of the opportunity thus created, the remaining participants were either to snatch cigarettes from her stand or seize bags hanging underneath. Once set in motion, however, the plan immediately ran into difficulty. The woman paid no attention to the youths pretending to look for coins and stared instead at the "assault troops" fidgeting nearby. Rather than abort the venture, the group's leader took matters into his own hands by suddenly shoving the woman into her stand. During the resulting turmoil, those assigned to the task rushed in and grabbed cigarettes and bags.[36]

Whatever the target, this organized approach typified a large number of thefts carried out by experienced children. One or more often stood watch to warn of approaching danger, especially if the crime involved surreptitious entry of an apartment, warehouse, or other facility. Depending on the undertaking's nature, a decoy might also be stationed to distract the attention of a policeman, passersby, or owner of the item to be stolen—perhaps by feigning a fit or in the manner just described. Apart from those who actually seized the goods, others frequently positioned themselves in preparation to receive the loot and relay it instantly to a safe hiding place, especially if the group anticipated that the crime would be detected immediately.[37] These support roles commonly fell to younger or less experienced participants, including a boy who had fled a children's home in Khar'kov and traveled to Moscow. Youths with whom he became acquainted in a train station introduced him to the Khitrovskii market, where he received lessons in stealing from apartments. As a first step, his friends left him just outside the targeted building, poised to dash away with the stolen goods. Despite the operation's success (celebrated with a drinking binge), teamwork did not strike him as essential, for he soon attempted a robbery on his own—resulting in a six-month prison sentence. As he headed back to the market following his confinement, he noticed an open door and crept in to steal whatever lay at hand. Once again, prison rather than riches ensued.[38]

As this impulsive attempt indicated, not all raids germinated from careful planning. Sometimes a group simply rushed down the street— "like a pack of young wolves," according to an observer in Moscow— with one member or another snatching on the run any exposed item that caught his eye in the booths or stands they passed.[39] On occasion, children undertook these dashes as much for the adventure as for the spoils. In Khar'kov one day, the same leader who planned the attack on the cigarette vendor proposed two options for his followers to consider while loitering outside a movie theater: sneak into the theater or launch a thieving spree. Opting for the latter, the group set out immediately in unorganized fashion down the street, accompanied by a few school children caught up in the excitement of the impending escapade. Descending on the first cigarette trader to appear in their path, they seized some of his cigarettes and his cash box. The money fell out onto the ground, but the band did not break stride to gather it up and sped on, as if to outrun the vendor's cries. Reaching the end of the street, they grabbed more cigarettes from another tray (at which point the police managed to apprehend two of the youngest, most passive participants) and rounded the corner. This new tack soon brought them upon snack bars, which surrendered a few bottles of mineral water to the passing raiders. As they approached a pharmacy, one of the boldest darted in and, a moment later, leaped out carrying a vessel extracted from a tank of boiling water. The group then made for the sanctuary afforded by back lanes, where they consumed the mineral water before returning to their home street.[40]

Rather than harry vendors and pedestrians, some children preferred to steal from apartments. To this end they devised a variety of techniques for entering rooms, ranging from picking locks and crawling through windows to masquerading as laundresses or delivery boys.[41] The strategies often entailed considerable risk, as suggested in the youths' songs:

> Stealing, too, I learned the practice,
> And to vodka my love did give.
> Among apartments I took up prowling,
> And to prison I went to live.[42]

One night, just such a figure wriggled through an apartment window intending to open the doors for his confederates after the tenants had left in the morning. He wormed into a cupboard to hide until daybreak and soon fell asleep. The scheme collapsed when a resident surprised the unfamiliar lodger and shook him awake in a manner that betrayed no admiration for his dexterity.[43]

D. Sergeev, who lived in the Gor'ky colony administered for years by Anton Makarenko, described a similarly bold robbery he had earlier attempted. Under night's cover, he and some friends escaped from a children's home and hopped aboard a train that reached Taganrog the next morning. After carousing much of the day in this southern city, just down the line from Rostov-on-the-Don, they decided to break into a dwelling. When darkness fell, the group set to work on the chosen structure and silently removed a window pane. Sergeev climbed inside, threw some linen out to the others, and turned to a dresser in search of money. As he probed for the key, it fell to the floor with a clatter that sent him scrambling for cover behind the piece of furniture. Almost at once a woman appeared with a light and walked around the room, while Sergeev crouched motionless, afraid to breathe. Then she approached another bed to wake a man who arose and noticed the broken window. Alarmed by the discovery, he came over to inspect the dresser, where his startled gaze fell on the intruder. Sergeev made a dash for the window, but the man seized his legs and beat the boy severely before turning him over to the police.[44]

Warier urchins stole from apartments by reaching inside the outer door for galoshes or a coat. Only as their experience and nerve developed did they penetrate further in search of more valuable items—forays that often took place under the cover of begging. A boy who found the door to an apartment or communal kitchen open, and with no sign of people within, would slip inside. If the occupants or someone in the hall noticed him, he began begging for food or money as if that had been his intent all along.[45] Aleksei P——iaev stumbled upon this tactic by chance, after escaping from a children's home. His travels took him through Viatka and Vologda to Moscow's Iaroslavl' Station, where hunger or some other motive drove him to beg at a nearby block of apartments. Inside the building, an unattended pair of boots changed his plans. With footwear in hand, he sped away and later resold his plunder in the Sukharevskii Market. Here he chanced upon a boy he had met in Vologda, and the two decided to join forces stealing from apartments in the guise of beggars. For a time, they mainly pilfered Primus stoves— so many, in fact, that Aleksei could not pass the market without middlemen shouting to inquire if he had more stoves to sell.

Before long the boys began to seize anything of value that opportunity presented. Nor did they confine themselves to rooms with doors ajar. Aleksei later offered the following tip on breaking windows to a staff member of a children's colony: "You smear honey on the glass and break it with a rag. All the splinters will stick to the rag without making any noise." During the pair's last successful robbery, in a building near the Arbat, they entered a corridor lined with several locked doors.

Scarcely discouraged, the "beggars" broke into four apartments using a piece of iron and a skeleton key without attracting other residents' attention. Their exploits yielded two large sacks of loot, including men's suits and a fur coat, which they sold in the Novo-Spasskii Market for more than enough money to outfit themselves with boots, leather jackets, and other clothes well beyond the reach of most street children.[46]

Thefts from individuals and apartments, while accounting for the majority of robberies committed by homeless juveniles, did not exhaust the list of their targets. They pillaged storage facilities, workshops, and stores—sometimes smashing the glass to reach goods in window displays—and preyed on deliverymen's vehicles and the carts of peasants bringing food to markets.[47] Some who obtained work carrying loads at wharves, markets, and similar locations took advantage of opportunities to divert goods to destinations unintended by their employers.[48] On the railways, precocious thieves stole baggage so frequently that travelers were well advised to close carriage windows as stations neared, however hot the weather. "One day this past summer," a foreigner recounted, "as the train slowed up for a station, one of my friends saw a ragged little arm insinuate itself into the compartment through the window and gracefully appropriate his valise; four *besprizorni* fled with the booty, thumbing their noses at the despoiled."[49] During the unloading of fruit and vegetables, youths became a common sight in rail yards, maneuvering for opportunities to slink under cars and snatch produce. One boy even bored holes in cars and then filled up bags with the grain that poured out.[50]

These illegal activities, not to mention the street setting that encompassed every aspect of waifs' lives, insured contact between them and the underworld of adults. Locations in which children sought refuge often sheltered older vagabonds and criminals as well, thereby serving as schools for newcomers in the occupations and diversions of the street.[51] Little wonder, then, that numerous groups quickly developed ties with grownups and conducted thefts under their direction.[52] Many sources told of adolescents living in thieves' dens, sometimes as camp followers, but frequently as active participants in the bands' activities.[53] From a youth's point of view, membership in an adult gang offered multiple advantages—not the least of which were food, shelter, and protection from threats that menaced one alone on the street.[54] He in turn performed a variety of tasks to earn his keep. Even a relatively inexperienced boy could soon be trained to stand watch at a lair or during robberies, and children were likewise deployed to observe buildings—

in order to determine the residents' daily schedules, for example—or
gather other information.[55] The underworld also utilized juveniles to
spirit away stolen goods and serve as couriers if messages or parcels had
to be delivered around town. Purveyors of bootleg liquor and cocaine
sometimes marketed their products through street urchins, who might
also be instructed to take orders for new deliveries.[56] Finally, echoing
Bill Sikes's manipulation of Oliver Twist, thieves on occasion dispatched
diminutive accomplices through narrow apertures or up drainpipes
toward destinations inaccessible to larger bodies.[57] Lacking Charles
Dickens to rescue them, youths who fell in with this company stood
the greatest chance of entering adulthood as proficient and habitual
criminals.

That prospect appealed to a boy named Alexander as he served a
sentence in the Moscow Labor Home. A few years earlier, after the death
of his widowed mother, his older brothers had placed him in school,
where nothing engaged his interest. Deserting the classroom to romp
with street children, he began to commit petty thefts and eventually
gravitated into the orbit of an adult criminal. This man, an Estonian
who had fled his native land, fed and clothed Alexander and trained him
as an assistant. Over a span of two years they succeeded in several large
thefts and lived comfortably on the proceeds. But one day Alexander
decided his schooling was complete and undertook a robbery alone,
without his mentor's knowledge. Capture and imprisonment were the
result, and Alexander expressed regret in the Moscow Labor Home over
venturing forth without the master's guidance. He continued to idealize
the Estonian as an "invincible thief" and dreamed of achieving similar
standing. The opportunity may have arisen, for the Estonian promised
to take him in again upon his release.[58]

Abandoned children vexed many people around them even when not
stealing. To the fastidious eye, their mere appearance represented an
affront and caused numerous pens to shudder when describing lice-
ridden creatures encountered about town. Caked with grime and clad in
filthy garments, their sooty feet often bare or wrapped in newspaper,
they inspired revulsion as often as pity. Some wore shoes and clothing
of outlandish size, stolen from adults or retrieved from garbage, as a
traveler noticed in Batum. There, a boy begging in the train station
flopped about inside pants so big that he could pull them over his head.
The man who noticed Chainik in Narkompros's waiting room described

the other youths present as "clad just in underwear, blackened by dirt, with rags hanging down to the knees; or barefoot, with the remains of a coat over an otherwise bare body. Some wore sacks in place of outer clothes, with immense galoshes on their feet."[59] A sympathetic Konstantin Paustovsky came upon a group in similarly mangy dress:

> These jackets obtained from some grown-up man or woman were long, reaching below the knee, with dangling sleeves. Time, dust and dirt had given them a uniformly mouse-grey colour and made them shine as if covered with oil. In the torn and battered pockets of these jackets the *besprizorniki* kept all their belongings—bits of broken combs, knives, cigarettes, crusts of bread, matches, greasy cards, and bits of dirty bandages. They did not even have shirts, however old or decayed, under their jackets—just their frozen, dirty, greenish-yellow bodies, covered with bleeding streaks which they got from scratching.[60]

Youths in need of warm clothing donned whatever came to hand, turning themselves into strange spectacles, as when boys sported both men's and women's apparel. *Pravda* described a girl in Moscow wearing meager tatters through which appeared her naked body, bluish from the cold—by itself, scarcely an exceptional sight among the homeless. But on her feet glistened new, fur-trimmed overshoes, evidently stolen. The juxtaposition of these foppish boots with the rest of her attire jarred the eye.[61]

Such children stood out everywhere—splashing in mud puddles, loitering in public areas, riding on the bumpers of trams, and dashing through crowds, lacing the air with vulgar observations.[62] Their recreation filled many with the aversion registered by a woman watching a group playing cards on the sidewalk: "Dirty, infested rags hung in shreds over them, and it was difficult to say which looked dirtier and more revolting, the rags or the bare parts of the body that could be seen through the rags." Before long a stray cat walked by. "Immediately a boy jumped up, threw his cap over its head and began to choke it. A minute later he removed the cap and started on a run, pulling the wretched animal by the tail amid a chorus of screams and oaths."[63]

While some citizens might dismiss these antics as mild annoyances at worst, other pastimes of vagrant youths displayed more destructiveness, frequently taking the form of vandalism. "*Besprizornye*," one official emphasized, "are the breeding grounds of hooliganism."[64] At railroad terminals, on occasion, they broke windows in cars and buildings, showered station personnel and passengers with rocks, and threw objects under passing trains. From the provinces came word that street children in the town of Podol'sk broke windows in the women's section of the bathhouse on Fridays and Saturdays, its period of operation.[65] Spiteful waifs also molested pedestrians—tripping passersby, setting dogs on them, staining their coats with various substances, and cutting off women's braids. In at least a few instances, they abducted other youths and stripped them of their clothing.[66]

Among the more private indulgences of homeless juveniles, none surpassed the allure of gambling. Cards apparently captured the largest number of enthusiasts across the country, but many other vehicles for betting, such as guessing which side of a thrown coin would land up, enjoyed popularity as well. Aside from children only recently orphaned, most youths whose lives centered on the street—from newspaper vendors and other petty traders to thieves—were well acquainted with games of chance. In the absence of commercially produced playing cards, they manufactured their own by such methods as laminating a few sheets of paper together with glue made from bread, cutting out blank rectangles from this stock, and adding the appropriate designs and numbers.[67] Some groups even made gambling their full-time occupation and supported themselves for the most part with their winnings. Roaming a city's seedy districts, they stirred up games with other lads, whom their expertise and trickery often relieved of coins and possessions.[68]

Passionate gamblers added their clothing to the stakes frequently enough that the appearance of a half-naked child amid a group of urchins could well testify to the youth's recent setback at cards.[69] Rather than play for cash or goods—or lacking such items—some elected to gamble for the right to inflict blows of one sort or another on the loser. At the train station in Omsk, a boy nicknamed Baldy (*Lysyi*) preferred to gamble *na volosianku*: that is, the winner gained the right to yank out a tuft of hair from the head of the loser. His half-bald head, covered with bloody wounds, suggested that good fortune had not been his steadfast companion.[70] Card players at the Moscow Labor Home, after losing everything else, occasionally stayed in the game by agreeing to undergo sodomy if their reversals continued. One who lost "himself" in this fashion avoided the penalty by slashing his body with glass splinters to secure admission to a hospital.[71]

In games demanding the wager of money or goods, youths without either might gamble on credit. They promised to cover any losses with future income generated by begging, trading, or stealing—in some cases an amount requiring several days' work. Such debts inspired a verse heard among juvenile newspaper vendors in Moscow: "For aces and jacks, I traded all summer" (*Za tuza i za valeta, torgoval ia tselo leto*).[72] On occasion, a boy gambled away to others in his group a promise of everything that he could beg or steal the next day (or several days), rather than a fixed amount of money or food.[73] Those who ran up debts far larger than they could ever hope to pay might be required to perform services desired by creditors. In Odessa, a group of children prowling the streets came upon a cluster of youths singing in public for money. As it happened, one of the performers was deeply in debt to the leader of the first band, a boy named Kolia. Recognizing the debtor, Kolia instructed him to sing for his group, forgiving anywhere from fifty kopecks to one ruble of the debt for each song. Even as his voice grew hoarse, the child acknowledged his obligation and sang on endlessly as ordered.[74]

Though hardly as popular as gambling, motion pictures also occupied the time of juveniles on their own. Large cities contained numerous movie houses by the 1920s, and these enticed homeless youths along with the rest of the population. To be sure, part of the cinema's appeal had little to do with the films themselves. The bright lights, nearby vendors of cigarettes and candy, and (in some cases) prostitutes lured street children whose intentions did not include an evening inside the theater. Even those actually seeking to enter the buildings often viewed the facilities as more than purveyors of gripping tales. Cinemas offered shelter from the cold and a dark hall in which other viewers, absorbed in the screen's story, did not always pay sufficient attention to their pockets and handbags.[75]

That said, numerous abandoned youths did enjoy the movies. According to reports from several cities, they—like many others then and now—preferred fast-paced adventure films with vivid plots, bold stunts, and exotic settings. Their favorites included several American productions, such as *The Mark of Zorro*, as well as various Soviet sagas of action and peril, among them *The Battleship Potemkin*. When asked in an anonymous survey which actor they would most like to emulate, thirty of thirty-three named Americans, with Douglas Fairbanks alone garnering eighteen votes.[76]

Homeless children seeking to enter cinemas generally faced obstacles. Certain theaters did not admit them—even those with tickets in hand—because of their soiled appearance and no doubt their reputation as thieves. Even at less immaculate movie houses, many waifs did not possess sufficient money for tickets and therefore developed a number of techniques for entering free of charge. Some slipped in past the door attendant by taking advantage of distractions. A few stole tickets purchased by others. On occasion, crowds of juveniles overwhelmed ticket takers and burst into theaters. At least one group pooled their coins to buy a single ticket, enabling a member to enter the building. Once inside, he waited for the lights to dim and then admitted his comrades through a back door. In some neighborhoods, gangs defended "their" cinemas from other groups based along nearby thoroughfares, insisting that only they had the right to sneak into the building in question.[77]

Among the other diversions pursued by street children, tobacco figured prominently. More than one investigator concluded that "almost all" homeless youths smoked, and this assessment struck close to the mark, at least in the case of those long at large.[78] Reports from numerous children's institutions listed anywhere from 50 to 100 percent of the residents as smokers—some of whom had consumed twenty-five to thirty cigarettes per day on the street when only six years old. Efforts to eradicate the practice encountered tenacious resistance and prompted one boy to shout defiantly: "Down with Soviet power, not cigarettes!"[79] Alcoholic beverages, too, attracted *besprizornye* (though not in numbers to match tobacco's devotees).[80] Despite restrictions on the sale of liquor, juveniles had little difficulty locating willing vendors. Some acquired enough money to purchase comparatively palatable spirits and cigarettes, but most consumed tobacco and alcohol of a sort unlikely to tempt connoisseurs. Unless they could steal alternatives, they made do with *makhorka* (coarse, acrid tobacco), discarded cigarette butts, homebrewed drinks, or even substitutes such as varnish.[81]

Investigators who scarcely regarded it a revelation to find urchins familiar with tobacco and alcohol were struck by the number using cocaine, for only a decade earlier few adolescents knew of the drug. The first half of the 1920s witnessed a dramatic change, owing both to the larger supply of cocaine in general and the newly deserted multitudes living in close proximity to dealers and consumers of narcotics.[82] Thus, forms listing information to be gathered by Juvenile Affairs Commissions incorporated a question on cocaine, and many sources mentioned street children who had acquired the substance.[83] Some youths tried other narcotics as well, notably opium, morphine, and hashish (especially in Central Asia). But none approached cocaine's popularity, probably in large part because of its wider availability and ease of use, with no special facilities or equipment required.[84]

For obvious reasons, precise information is unavailable regarding the number of juveniles introduced to narcotics. In the realm of estimates, a publication of the Commissariat of Health in 1923 mentioned young cocaine users as totaling "in the thousands," and other sources surmised that 10 to 15 percent of homeless children in large cities consumed drugs (which included heavy drinking).[85] Among institutions, those stocked with the street's veterans naturally recorded the highest percentages of these *narkomany*. A group of doctors investigating three of Moscow's labor communes in 1924 established that every one of the residents in a compound for the most "difficult" had used cocaine, while no one in the other two facilities gave indication of this experience. The previous year, an examination of juvenile delinquents in the Moscow Labor Home found 28 percent to have taken cocaine (some starting as early as seven to ten years of age), and results from another study published in 1926 put the figure at 85–90 percent.[86] A boy's physical appearance alone might advertise his drug habit to investigators. As previously noted, waifs sometimes bestowed telling names on heavy users of cocaine and alcohol—youths whose wasted, shriveled cast stood out even in their rough surroundings.[87]

Such was the drug's effect on Grigorii Valentinov. He had parted with his parents in Samara during the famine and traveled to Moscow, where officials placed him in a shelter. After learning from some of the other children how to steal, he escaped.

> I began to hang around train stations and markets, looking with dark thieving eyes for something to swipe. When evening comes there is nowhere to sleep. You have to sleep somewhere on the street, on the cold dirty grit. In the morning you get up filthy and go about business. Sometimes, when you are unable to steal anything, you go around hungry, mean, and depressed.
>
> In this way I lived two years—in cold and hunger. One day I went to see some of the guys at the train station. They were snorting some sort of white powder. I asked with surprise what this was. They answered: "This is *marafet*," that is, cocaine. They gave me some to take, and I became like a madman, unable to say a word.
>
> From that time on, I began to take cocaine. Whatever I stole went to get cocaine. I took cocaine for two and a half years and became thin and pale, hardly able to walk. Eventually I landed in a clinic and began to recover.[88]

Cocaine and other narcotics were most readily available in the nation's principal metropolises, but lesser cities also included drugs among their underworlds' distractions. A study in 1925 of the links between cocaine and crime ascertained that a "significant number" of the criminals under consideration had first encountered cocaine in the provinces.[89] Whether in the capitals or far removed, street children were often introduced to cocaine by older thieves and prostitutes. Some hoodlums drew juveniles to their gangs and kept them loyal by periodically supplying the boys with drugs. On occasion, criminals gave doses of cocaine to youths in order to render them less reluctant to perform such harrowing tasks as climbing a drainpipe to enter a second-floor window.[90] Whoever first acquainted them with narcotics, though, most underage users had to obtain the drugs themselves. As with addicts of other ages and countries, the habit's expense inspired thefts.[91]

Cocaine could be purchased in a variety of urban quarters. Large outdoor markets and the lanes around them often proved abundant sources, as did certain bars, cafes, flophouses, restaurants, and theaters. Derelict buildings and labyrinthine alleys of rundown neighborhoods also provided suitable cover for transactions and soon acquired a corresponding reputation. Among the purveyors, newspaper accounts listed several dens operated by Chinese and Koreans, who sold morphine, opium, and cocaine.[92] Those at home on the street knew of convenient buildings where they could buy cocaine and stay to consume it. A proprietor generally did not charge for use of the room—in which dozens of youths sometimes gathered—making his money instead by selling the drug. In Moscow, a group of formerly homeless boys showed authorities a lair where children (and others) could exchange stolen goods for cocaine. The author of another account visited an urban wasteland of debris, pits, and ramshackle structures, not far from the Sukharevskii Market, where he watched youths and prostitutes purchase cocaine openly. An even brisker trade transpired there at night, he was told, but it would be dangerous to return then for a look.[93]

In addition to tobacco, alcohol, and cocaine, the street introduced many of its inhabitants to sexual activity without delay. A study in 1925 of ninety-four former waifs in Odessa determined that 40 percent had begun their sex lives by the age of fourteen. Sources are filled with accounts of sexually active children only ten or twelve years old, and some began even earlier. Investigation at an institute for girls (many of them former prostitutes) revealed that 3 percent first had intercourse by the age of seven.[94] One way or another, abandoned juveniles commonly learned sexual practices from the adults who shared their seedy domain. In this respect, as with underworld jargon and criminal skills, thieves and prostitutes served as tutors readily emulated.[95] Of course, the first

sexual encounters of many youths, especially girls, were entirely involuntary, the product of rape. Those newly on their own fell to the mercy
of experienced street children, adult thieves, railway workers, and others, with rape time and again a result.[96] According to a report presented
at a conference on juvenile problems in the summer of 1920, one reason
for the extensive sexual experience among a sample of institutionalized
girls lay in the long period of warfare the country had just endured.
World War I and the Civil War spread large numbers of soldiers as well
as refugees throughout the country, and sexual contact between the
troops and homeless girls (either as prostitutes or rape victims) was apparently substantial.[97]

   As in attempts to gauge drug use, confidence shuns efforts to estimate
the number of sexually active juveniles. No doubt initiation was routine
among those long on the street—not just prostitutes, but others who
engaged in sex with fellow orphans, adult prostitutes, and thieves. A
report that lists fully three-fourths of the Moscow Labor Home's delinquents as experienced in this regard provides some idea of the practice's
extent among boys accustomed to the underworld. Sexual relations frequently appear to have been casual and fleeting, though a few accounts
describe instances of a girl and boy living together, or sometimes one
girl and several boys, imitating arrangements chosen by adult thieves
and drifters.[98] A handful of observers noted boys who engaged in sex
among themselves—by means of rape, for example, or prostitution
within institutions.[99]

   Before long, some sexually active youths contracted venereal diseases,
usually syphilis or gonorrhea.[100] Investigations of children in Khar'kov,
Odessa, and Tashkent found that from 4 to 12 percent of the sample
(some straight from the street, others by then in institutions) had at least
one such disease. These figures may apply accurately to the country as
a whole, but the small number (several hundred) involved in the studies
renders such a conclusion difficult to embrace with confidence. If this
extrapolation proved reasonably accurate, however, it would challenge
the conclusion, shared widely in the general population, that waifs as a
group were saturated with sexually transmitted diseases.[101] Among
street girls alone, the percentage almost certainly was higher. While here,
too, fragmentary data do not permit precise calculations, the numerous
girls who worked as prostitutes or suffered rapes doubtless resulted in
a larger portion—30 percent of a thousand girls in one study—contract-
ing venereal diseases.[102] In any case, it seems safe to accept the conclusion of a medical journal in Khar'kov that homeless youths accounted

for the lion's share of juveniles who acquired syphilis through sexual contact. As another author put it in 1921, the surge in the number of boys and girls treated for venereal diseases stemmed directly from the high tide of *besprizornye*.[103]

Life as described in the preceding pages naturally left a deep imprint on those who experienced it. Few could endure this existence for long without developing characteristics regarded as undesirable by much of society. To be sure, a big difference existed between a starving village youth, newly arrived in a strange city, and an adolescent tempered by years in the street. The huge contingent of homeless children produced by war and famine struck observers most often as exhausted and helpless, not wicked and perverted. As the years passed, many died, returned to relatives, or entered state institutions. But others remained at large and learned to cope in ways that inclined few to view them as pitiable victims. Similar differences existed among juveniles who replenished their ranks in the middle and later years of the decade. A boy long accustomed to train stations and markets as a result of parental neglect joined the homeless with an outlook far different from that of a child thrown suddenly into the same milieu by unanticipated adversity. Whatever their route to the street, though, the longer they remained there, the more vividly they displayed qualities considered twisted and threatening by society beyond the underworld.[104]

Some authors argued that the rigors of independent life nurtured certain *positive* attributes rarely exhibited so prominently by "normal" children. Boys and girls struggling to survive, in other words, allegedly developed impressive resourcefulness, adaptability, boldness, and similar qualities.[105] No doubt something of the sort did occur, at least among youths not reduced by their plight to illness or apathy. Occasionally, though, the claims went further, suggesting against most evidence that a Spartan life in groups on the street rendered juveniles collectivists at heart, hostile to "bourgeois materialism." Forced by their harsh environment to work together, the argument went, they developed an unspoiled, cooperative outlook, which social workers were urged to utilize in reclaiming them as part of a new generation of communists.[106]

For the most part, however, observers acknowledged the obvious: homelessness yielded bitter fruit. Time and again, studies revealed a wide range of personality problems among waifs, ranging from abysmal hygiene habits to severe psychopathic disorders. Reports frequently described veterans among them as emotionally volatile, vengeful, unreliable, disinclined to work, and devoted to any number of underworld vices.[107] Whatever qualms a Bolshevik might harbor regarding traditional schools, only the most naive could fail to prefer their work over lessons taught in the alleys outside. Anyone who argued that vagrancy helped groom countrymen for socialism betrayed either a fanciful view of street life or an alarming image of the Party's goal.

Little effort is required to imagine that forsaken youths, miserable in their wretched habitat, clamored for escape into relief institutions. Many certainly did, sometimes besieging government buildings in large numbers to press their desire.[108] Investigators often discovered groups in whose midst appeared individuals pleading desperately for admittance to already overcrowded facilities.[109] Nevertheless, such scenes should not obscure the fact that numerous juveniles adjusted to the street in one way or another and displayed no desire to change their way of life. Greater success in begging, crime, or prostitution—*not* entrance to a school or boarding institution—occupied their concern. A teenage girl, working as a prostitute since the age of thirteen, stated bluntly: "When I have money, I like to take a little cocaine and smoke a bit. I like this life and will never change it." A twelve-year-old boy, living on his own, declared: "It's better to live free like this. I eat what I please and don't starve. It's cold here, yes, but I like it better than in an orphanage. I can go wherever I please."[110] Children rounded up and placed in institutions fled by the thousand and returned to the markets and rails. Many repeated this cycle for years, driven in part by the facilities' deplorable conditions, but just as powerfully by a desire, as they often put it, "to be free."[111]

Out on the street, they typically regarded the society beyond their world with emotions that ran from wariness to loathing. Probably a majority of the population viewed them with much the same feelings—as thieves and degenerates. This produced a chasm between the two camps that appeared in the youths' songs:

> Spit at me and throw your stones,
> It's nothing new, I will endure.
> From you I can expect no pity,
> There's none to help me, I am sure.

Or

> Other kids are treated fondly,
> And from time to time caressed.

> But for me the handling's cruel,
> I to none at all am blessed.[112]

This animosity flared into view one summer's day on a Black Sea beach, where several waifs startled a group of sunbathers. Cursing all the while, the children plunged into the waves and then dashed around the beach, splashing water to and fro. People nearby fired verbal abuse and threats at the swirling figures and ordered them to leave. Not the least intimidated, the newcomers mocked and swore at the bathers, who soon departed themselves. A witness who recorded the incident recalled most vividly the hatred and contempt that burned in the juveniles' eyes.[113]

Nor was this an isolated incident. Time and again, in their actions, interviews, and reminiscences, homeless youths expressed aversion for a surrounding citizenry that represented to them only potential victims or persecutors.[114] At a station near the Black Sea, a young passenger leaned out of his train car and spat in the face of an adolescent vagabond below. The latter riveted his gaze on the window from which the offense had come and picked up a rock. But at that moment a whistle sounded, and the train lumbered into motion. He slipped back into his spot under the carriage, still clutching the stone and muttering that he would yet pay back the little *burzhui*. At another station, near Saratov, a peasant recounted to a traveling companion how street children had robbed him on several occasions. Warming to the topic, he promised a thrashing to the next one he caught and punctuated the vow with a menacing gesture out the window to a group of his antagonists standing near the train. They responded with their own threats, assuring him in turn that they would find an opportunity to carry them out.[115]

Youths such as these did not view stealing as a transgression. Questioned on the point, they responded along the following lines: "Some people have things. We don't. So why shouldn't we steal from them?" and "Since I don't have it, why shouldn't I take it?" Some did not hesitate to blame their deeds on the callousness of society, in the process abandoning pity for any but themselves. "And now my soul is hardened," proclaimed one of their songs—a reproach to those whose refusals of assistance had steered many to crime.[116] An investigator in Saratov described the alienation in stark terms:

> People fear the *besprizornyi*, shun him, sometimes avoid him. And he, this juvenile delinquent, learns early to pay back this cold society in the same coin. Feelings of sympathy for people are removed from him; people become hateful to him. It is a pleasure for him to cause them any sort of unpleasantness. Thus, crime in his eyes amounts to a violation of the laws only of

these well fed, clothed, and complacent people—not something to trouble his conscience. Anything may be done when it comes to these alien, hostile people.[117]

Little wonder, then, that many considered waifs depraved and malignant to an extent that precluded any prospect of rehabilitation. An investigator in Omsk, distressed by the conditions in which children were living in the city's train station, approached a police official to see if something could be done. The policeman revealed no enthusiasm for the topic and cut short the conversation with an emphatic assessment: "Here's how it is, comrade. Officially, I have nothing to say to you. Unofficially, my opinion is this: the sooner all your *besprizorniki* die, the better. I have to deal with them daily, and I tell you sincerely that they are a hopeless bunch, soon to be bandits. And we have enough bandits without them. Is that clear?"[118] Even the chairman of the Baku Juvenile Affairs Commission—whose organization was entrusted with the very task of placing delinquents on the road to recovery—once remarked: "When all is said and done, you will not make a human being out of a *besprizornyi*. They are all toughs, thieves, hooligans, and murderers."[119] The youths themselves sometimes expressed doubt that they would ever be able to change their ways, even if they so desired. "A thief I have been, and a thief I will remain," declared one on his dispatch to an institution. Said another to a social worker: "I will put it to you this way, sister. Half of us are such that nothing will work with us now."[120] In the face of such pessimistic assessments, the young Soviet government set out not merely to save the *besprizornye*, but to transform them into builders of a new, communist society.

PART TWO

CHAPTER FOUR

Children of the State

Children in orphanages are state children.
Their father is the state and their mother is the whole of
worker-peasant society.
Anatolii Lunacharskii

Prison, prison! What a word,
Shameful, frightful to the ear.
But for me it's all familiar,
I have long since lost my fear.
From a street children's song

In the heady days of revolutionary triumph, the new Bolshevik government sought to take upon itself the task of feeding, clothing, and even
raising a large share of the country's children. Decrees instructed central
and local agencies in 1918 and 1919 to arrange the distribution of food
to juveniles—free of charge—from schools, special dining halls, and
other outlets.[1] As late as July 1921 the Council of People's Commissars
(Sovnarkom) noted that while the rest of the population was expected
to provide for itself, the state would continue to assume responsibility
for supplying food to minors.[2] More ambitious still, Narkompros and
other government agencies anticipated the development of a network of
children's homes that would be capable before long of raising the nation's offspring.[3] Enthusiasts viewed the institutions as far better
equipped than the "bourgeois" family to fashion youths into productive,
devoted members of a communist society. What task could be more
important, they asked, than replacing the traditional family environment—often steeped in ignorance, coarseness, and hostility toward the
Bolsheviks—with homes administered by the government itself?[4] "The
faculty of educating children is far more rarely encountered than the
faculty of begetting them," observed *The ABC of Communism.* "Of one
hundred mothers, we shall perhaps find one or two who are competent
educators. The future belongs to social education."[5]

87

Ambitious in the best of times, these plans were deflated by the dire reality of the Soviet regime's early years. As millions of waifs overwhelmed government institutions and budgets, Bolshevik hopes of rearing most other youths appeared practical only to unflinching visionaries. Children's homes may have been intended originally for all juveniles, but they soon acquired a reputation as refuges for the multitude of young vagabonds bred by war and famine. Even this restricted clientele proved so vast that most facilities could long do little more than struggle to prevent their charges from dying or running away. The goal of a socialist upbringing retreated to await more auspicious days.[6]

As commissariats of the Soviet government took shape following the Revolution, rivalry soon developed among three of them—Narkompros, the Commissariat of Health, and the Commissariat of Social Security—over responsibility for child welfare. Each pressed claims to administer a variety of institutions entrusted with aiding abandoned juveniles.[7] At first, early in 1918, decrees specified that care of homeless youths (including the operation of children's homes) belonged in the Commissariat of Social Security's hands.[8] But Narkompros, undaunted, continued to lobby Sovnarkom for a greater share of responsibility in this area and gradually prevailed. As early as June 1918, Sovnarkom ordered the transfer to Narkompros of institutions for delinquents, and the following month Narkompros sent circulars to provincial agencies, instructing them to turn over Juvenile Affairs Commissions (which handled the cases of delinquents) to Narkompros offices on the scene. Unimpressed by these instructions, some local branches of the Commissariat of Social Security refused to relinquish control, and the matter lay unresolved for months. As a result, from province to province, one found commissions run by each of the two commissariats and even, in a few instances, by the Commissariat of Health.[9] Finally, in February 1919, Sovnarkom ordered the Commissariat of Social Security to transfer its remaining children's institutions to Narkompros by year's end, thereby terminating the former's brief tenure in the vanguard of the campaign to rescue street urchins.[10]

Narkompros also bickered with the Commissariat of Health, for each claimed a larger role in the care of indigent children than the other deemed appropriate.[11] Champions of Narkompros naturally stressed the importance of providing a proper education and general upbringing, while health officials emphasized the need for medical care. Beset by these competing appeals, Sovnarkom issued a series of decrees beginning in the autumn of 1919, spelling out the domain of each agency. In general, the Commissariat of Health retained control of children's clinics, sanatoriums, and similar institutions where medical treatment and physical therapy represented the principal activity, while pedagogic facilities remained under the administration of Narkompros. According to a decree issued by Sovnarkom in September 1921, doctors chosen and paid by the Commissariat of Health would provide medical treatment for youths in Narkompros's establishments. At the same time, local Narkompros branches received the right to nominate candidates for these positions and to dismiss individual physicians.[12] Jurisdictional rivalries flared now and then during the remainder of the decade, but they were not so severe as to prevent the two agencies from reaching an accommodation. Health officials operated homes for juveniles up to age three (as well as medical facilities for older youths), and Narkompros administered institutions for residents three years of age and older.[13]

Thus Narkompros emerged with primary responsibility for the rehabilitation of street children. By the beginning of 1923, after a series of internal reorganizations, the agency had evolved the following departments and subsections to undertake the mission: At the highest level, in Moscow, the commissariat's branches (covering such bailiwicks as publishing, the fine arts, censorship, propaganda, higher education, and vocational training) included one titled Main Administration of Social Upbringing and Polytechnic Education of Children (Glavsotsvos). Glavsotsvos in turn contained a number of subsections with responsibilities that included preschool and primary school education, teacher training, and experimental educational institutions. The subsection of central importance in the attempt to reclaim abandoned youths bore the name Social and Legal Protection of Minors (SPON).[14]

SPON's four subdivisions focused their attention respectively on (1) the struggle against juvenile homelessness and delinquency; (2) the establishment of guardianships for youths; (3) the rearing of "defective" children (which included delinquents); and (4) the provision of legal assistance and information of benefit to juveniles (such as locating lost dependents and reuniting them with relatives). SPON thus administered most of Narkompros's orphanages, supervised its Juvenile Affairs Commissions, and dispatched social workers to approach young inhabitants of the street.[15] Throughout the Russian Republic, each province maintained its own Narkompros office (GubONO), generally organized to resemble the basic blueprint of Narkompros in Moscow. Among the branches of a GubONO, therefore, one customarily found a Gubsotsvos (the provincial equivalent of Glavsotsvos) with its own SPON subsection shouldering assignments similar to those of SPON in Moscow. Even smaller administrative units, such as districts (*uezdy*) and cities, sometimes opened their own Narkompros offices, which commonly retained a structure close to that described above.[16] In Moscow, the thousands of tattered youths thronging the capital by 1922 prompted formation of an Extraordinary Commission in the Struggle with Juvenile *Besprizornost'* and Juvenile Crime (the Children's Extraordinary Commission, for short)—a division of the Moscow City Narkompros organization (MONO). Thereafter the Children's Extraordinary Commission sought out Moscow's homeless, handled cases of juvenile delinquents, and administered welfare institutions until it was combined at the beginning of 1925 with another unit of MONO to produce a new division bearing the SPON title.[17]

In January 1919, amid the commissariats' wrangling, Sovnarkom decreed the formation of a Council for the Defense of Children. Headed by a representative from Narkompros and including members from the commissariats of labor, food, social security, and health, the council received instructions to coordinate the work of individual government agencies to improve the supply of food and other essentials to juveniles.[18] However, as it lacked the leverage to command respect from even the commissariats represented in its own offices, the council made little headway promoting bureaucratic cooperation and played an insignificant role in providing relief to destitute youths.[19] Before long, it gave way to a more imposing interagency body, a commission driven initially by the zeal and clout of the secret police.

To some, the name Feliks Dzerzhinskii, head of the Cheka (secret police), suggested dry-eyed ruthlessness—an image that Dzerzhinskii himself scarcely shunned. But when conversation turned to the plight of waifs, his expressions of dismay at their misery struck more than one interlocutor.[20] In just such a conversation he told Anatolii Lunacharskii, head of Narkompros:

> In this matter we must rush directly to help, as if we saw children drowning. Narkompros alone has not the strength to cope. It needs the broad help of all Soviet society. A broad commission under VTsIK [the All-Russian Central Executive Committee]—of course with the closest participation of Narkompros—must be created, including within it all institutions and organizations which may be useful. I have already said something of this to a few people.

I would like to stand at the head of that commission, and I want to include the Cheka apparatus directly in the work.[21]

Pursuing this goal, Dzerzhinskii took the lead in establishing, on February 10, 1921, a Commission for the Improvement of Children's Life attached to the All-Russian Central Executive Committee.[22] Apart from Dzerzhinskii as chairman, the commission included six other representatives, one each from the Cheka, Narkompros, the commissariats of health and food, the Workers' and Peasants' Inspectorate, and the Central Trade Union Council. In some respects their duties differed little from those of the earlier Council for the Defense of Children. They were to facilitate the flow of supplies to agencies responsible for juveniles' welfare and oversee implementation of decrees (as well as suggest new legislation) to protect minors. But the Children's Commission, more than the council, focused its energy and resources on the problem of homelessness, underscoring the government's growing concern with this phenomenon. The order creating the council in January 1919 had called for aid to needy youths in general, without referring specifically to those abandoned. Two years later, in February 1921, the All-Russian Central Executive Committee directed the newborn Children's Commission to assist "first of all" agencies caring for boys and girls of the street.

The same decree of February 10 instructed province and district executive committees to designate officials for children's commissions at these levels in the Russian Republic, and similar organizational structures took shape in other republics. In Ukraine, for example, the equivalent of the Children's Commission bore the title Central Commission for the Assistance of Children and was attached to the All-Ukrainian Central Executive Committee.[23] The primary role of the commission in the Russian Republic, and of analogous bodies elsewhere, was to assist *other* government agencies, most notably Narkompros, rather than operate their own orphanages and schools. Nevertheless, Lunacharskii and his lieutenants at Narkompros displayed little enthusiasm for the commission and proposed the creation of interagency bodies featuring a more prominent role for Narkompros and none for the Cheka.[24] But the commission weathered these early challenges (it survived for nearly two decades), and other agencies eventually accepted it as a partner in their labors.

Meanwhile, the number of homeless juveniles steadily increased. As the government struggled to assign general responsibility on this front to such bodies as Narkompros and the Children's Commission, the question remained: *how* should they go about aiding millions of beggars and thieves? Everyone desired that prerevolutionary shelters be replaced, but many social workers and educators had no idea—others a bewildering variety of utopian theories—how to organize and operate new institutions.[25] Ilya Ehrenburg described the chaos that reigned among facilities for "morally defective" youths in Kiev during the months of Bolshevik control in 1919. Though he possessed no experience or even any connection with such work—and thus much to his surprise—he received an assignment to help rehabilitate children.

> We spent a long time working out a project for an "experimental pilot colony" where juvenile law-breakers would be educated in a spirit of "creative work" and "all-round development." It was a great time for projects. In every institution in Kiev, it seemed, grey-haired eccentrics and young enthusiasts were drafting projects for a heavenly life on earth. We discussed the effect of excessively bright colours on excessively nervous children and wondered whether choral declamation influenced the collective consciousness and whether eurhythmics could be helpful in the suppression of juvenile prostitution.
>
> The discrepancy between our discussions and reality was staggering. I began investigating reform schools, orphanages and dosshouses where the *besprizornye* (lost children) were to be found. The reports I drafted spoke not of eurhythmics but of bread and cloth. The boys ran away to join various "Fathers"; the girls solicited prisoners of war returning from Germany.[26]

The approach developed at Narkompros by the early 1920s called for three stages of institutions: one to remove a child from the street and tend to his or her immediate needs; a second to observe and evaluate the youth; and a third to achieve rehabilitation. Closest to the street in this system were the receivers (*priemniki*), facilities generally administered by SPON personnel and often located near markets, train stations, and other settings frequented by the homeless.[27] Narkompros planned for receivers in all cities and towns down to the district level and intended that they admit waifs twenty-four hours a day for emergency shelter, care, and questioning.[28] In addition to youths who arrived on their own, receivers were to accept children dispatched by social workers, the police, and private citizens. This included juveniles apprehended for begging, prostitution, street trade, and thefts, as well as those who appeared to have lost contact with their parents only temporarily. In the case of delinquents, Narkompros hoped that receivers would provide a less pernicious environment than police-station cells and issued instructions in 1920 that staff members greet all entrants with warm attention.[29]

Upon arrival, a youth was to be questioned (in an effort to establish identity, recent activities, place of residence, reason for entering the facility, and so on), then taken to receive a bath, haircut, medical exam, and disinfected clothes, followed by isolation for those with infectious diseases. Narkompros intended that children remain in receivers no more than two or three days and therefore did not foresee extensive pedagogic activity at this stage—nothing more than exercise, crafts, singing, readings by the staff, domestic chores, and attempts to nurture better personal hygiene.[30] The plan stipulated that inhabitants be sorted and housed separately according to age, sex, and other characteristics to prevent contact between a practiced young criminal, for instance, and a lad new to the street.[31] Finally, after a few days of observation, a child faced discharge to a destination deemed appropriate by the staff. This might be to parents or relatives if they could be located, to a Juvenile Affairs Commission in most cases involving crimes, to a children's home to begin rehabilitation, to a hospital, or to an intermediary institution for additional observation.[32]

The last option routed a child to an "observation-distribution point." Here ensued an extended period of examination designed to establish the subject's mental and physical condition—and thus the type of institution likely to provide suitable upbringing. Narkompros considered observation-distribution points particularly appropriate for difficult or troubled youths and intended that information assembled at this stage be passed on to assist Juvenile Affairs Commissions in deciding the means of rehabilitation for delinquents.[33] According to a circular prepared by a division of SPON in Moscow, the normal length of stay in an observation-distribution point was to range from one to three months, though it could reach "six months or more" if necessary. Under these conditions, regular school classes still made little sense, but SPON recommended that some form of rudimentary instruction take place—making a start toward literacy, for example—in addition to the sorts of activities suggested for a receiver.[34] Given the resources and staff required to maintain observation-distribution points, Narkompros must have expected them only in large cities, a pattern of concentration that soon developed in any case.[35] As the years passed, so few such facilities appeared that the vast majority of Narkompros's wards never entered their doors, moving instead from receivers (or the street) directly to institutions of rehabilitation.

Lunacharskii's commissariat intended the children's home (*detskii dom*, often shortened to *detdom*, pl. *detdoma*) to be the most common site of extended rehabilitation. A model charter for *detdoma* sent by Narkompros in 1921 to its provincial branches presumed an extensive array of these institutions—some for preschool candidates, some for older youths, some for delinquents, some for the physically handicapped, and so on.[36] Narkompros emphasized repeatedly that the network's success hinged on *detdoma* admitting only children who had already undergone preliminary sorting in a receiver and, ideally, an observation-distribution point. In addition, *detdoma* were to conduct periodic evaluations of their residents' mental and physical health so that those with problems rendering them unsuitable for a particular *detdom* could be identified and sent to a more appropriate institution or to an observation-distribution point for further appraisal.[37]

As spelled out in the charter, a model *detdom* maintained the following facilities: ample sleeping quarters, kitchen, dining room, laundry, bath, storerooms, quarantine, separate rooms for the staff, rooms for special projects, and a few workshops for activities such as carpentry, leather work, and sewing. Narkompros also desired the children to receive a standard education, either inside the *detdom* or at a nearby public school. To supplement traditional classroom instruction and fill free time productively, *detdoma* received strong encouragement to organize clubs and circles. Suggested activities included drama, music, handicrafts, sports, animal and plant raising, investigations of nature in the surrounding area, and studies of local folklore.[38] In addition, every *detdom* was to have at its disposal sufficient land for a kitchen garden and, if possible, a larger field to provide food and labor training for the inhabitants. An order from Narkompros and the Commissariat of Land in December 1923 specified that a *detdom* receive approximately one-quarter of an acre per child.[39] Finally, institutions were urged to implement a program of "self-service" or "self-government" (*samoobsluzhivanie* or *samoupravlenie*), which, broadly speaking, meant that youths assumed responsibility for daily chores and some administrative decisions.[40] Such measures, designed to imbue residents with a sense of control over their lives and an instinct for collective responsibility, were destined to receive considerable attention in years to come.

While the government anticipated that most homeless children would follow the path just described, from receiver to *detdom*, it made additional provisions for youths charged with crimes. Shortly after the Revolution, in January 1918, Sovnarkom and the Commissariat of Justice directed that juvenile delinquents not appear before courts or receive prison sentences. Instead, the decree ordered the formation of Juvenile

Affairs Commissions to handle cases of all offenders less than seventeen years of age.[41] Originally placed under the Commissariat of Social Security, but transferred to Narkompros in 1920, each commission comprised three members from local offices of Narkompros and the commissariats of health and justice, with the first serving as head.[42] Soviet authors proclaimed at the time (some noting the contrast with the treatment of delinquents in tsarist Russia and Western countries) that youths would now be rehabilitated, not punished.[43] At the beginning of the 1920s, plans called for commissions in virtually every city down to the level of district towns, a network as dense as that envisioned for receivers. Indeed, Narkompros intended the closest cooperation between commissions and receivers, with the latter (or observation-distribution points, where these existed) holding delinquents temporarily and providing commissions with information on their mental and physical condition.[44]

Commissions were instructed to conclude cases by selecting one of numerous options, among them a simple conversation or reprimand, the dispatch of children to parents or relatives (if these could be located and appeared capable of providing a satisfactory upbringing), or placement in a job, school, *detdom*, or medical facility. By 1920, however, instructions recognized that such measures might not be appropriate for inveterate young criminals (who were proliferating along with homeless adolescents in general) and therefore granted commissions the choice of passing particularly difficult offenders on to the courts.[45] In March, Sovnarkom increased by one year the maximum age of juveniles whose cases were to be handled by commissions—but at the same time allowed these bodies to transfer intractable youths at least fourteen years old to the courts. Because such decisions required the establishment of a child's age, often difficult under the circumstances, additional directives advised commissions to rely, if necessary, on estimates derived from medical examinations. The Commissariat of Justice received orders to hold teenage defendants apart from adult criminals in all stages of the judicial process and place those sentenced by the courts in special reformatories.[46]

When commissions (as opposed to the courts) channeled delinquents into institutions, the destination was generally a facility operated by Narkompros. Here and there around the country, officials inaugurated establishments bearing a variety of names—*detdoma*, colonies, communes, institutes—intended exclusively for a "difficult" or "morally defective" clientele. Narkompros issued detailed instructions for the proper operation of these institutions, accompanied by articles in its journals stressing the wisdom (and economy) of reclaiming youths before crime became their adult profession.[47] According to reports and resolutions at the First All-Russian Congress of Participants in the Struggle with Juvenile Defectiveness, *Besprizornost'*, and Crime (held in the summer of 1920 in Moscow) and instructions issued later by Narkompros, facilities for difficult children were to resemble regular *detdoma* in many respects. Officials stressed, for example, that an institution contain residents of the same sex, age, and level of development (or degradation). Also, activities in schools, clubs, and workshops had to fill the inhabitants' lives, eliminating unsupervised idleness. In particular, guidelines emphasized labor training, whether on the land or in workshops, as essential in nurturing desirable work habits and good character—besides preparing trainees to help build a new society.[48]

At the same time, Narkompros's resolutions and instructions indicated a number of ways in which institutions for delinquents should differ from ordinary *detdoma*. Discipline, for instance, had to be stricter, though never vindictive. If a violation of the rules seemed to warrant sanction stiffer than a reprimand, additional punishments could include extra chores, temporary deprivation of recreation and other pleasures, or even isolation in a separate room (under staff supervision). Corporal punishment was not permitted.[49] Narkompros also advised that facilities for difficult children operate on the principle of "closed doors" (*zakrytye dveri*), meaning that instruction take place on the premises and youths not be permitted to leave the grounds on their own.[50] Institutions themselves belonged mainly in the countryside, far removed from temptations afforded by train stations, markets, and other bustling urban sites.[51]

Commissariats other than Narkompros (and the Commissariat of Health) also administered facilities for delinquents—in particular, for teenagers whose cases Juvenile Affairs Commissions had transferred to the courts. Once before a court, a youthful offender faced sentence to a labor home (*trudovoi dom*) run by the Commissariat of Justice until 1922, and through the rest of the decade by the Commissariat of Internal Affairs.[52] Activities favored here resembled those expected in Narkompros's *detdoma* for difficult children—school, workshops, agriculture, sports, even a form of "self-government"—but with still more emphasis on rehabilitation through labor.[53] Guidelines for operating labor homes appeared in the Russian Republic's Correctional Labor Code rather than Narkompros's publications. Also, while labor homes shared many of the pedagogic methods of *detdoma*, they were to employ stricter discipline together with window bars and guards to restrain their charges.[54] As in other "institutions for the deprivation of freedom," those assigned to labor homes served *sentences*, which a court could extend to an inmate's twentieth birthday.[55]

This, in broad strokes, completed the array of facilities intended at the beginning of the 1920s for most abandoned and other abused or delinquent children. To guide them into such institutions, Narkompros set about deploying a corps of social workers. In September 1921, Sovnarkom ordered the formation of a Children's Social Inspection, under the administration of Narkompros, to spearhead the battle against juvenile homelessness, delinquency, begging, prostitution, and speculation (a term often applied to street trade). The inspectors were intended to replace the police in most dealings with minors, and their duties included patrolling markets, stations, and other locations that attracted waifs. They could call on the police for assistance but did not carry weapons or wear uniforms themselves. Narkompros hoped they would manage to establish contact with youths, draw them out of places exercising an unhealthy influence, and direct those lacking homes to receivers.[56]

The doorstep of a receiver or Juvenile Affairs Commission did not mark the end of the Social Inspection's beat. Sovnarkom noted in its September decree that inspectors' duties included supervising youths admitted to receivers (or observation-distribution points) and assisting in their examination. Both receivers and commissions, as interested parties, held the right to submit candidates for positions in the Social Inspection.[57] Commissions themselves were to rely first on another set of social workers, known as investigators-upbringers (*obsledovateli-vospitateli*), for the following assistance: (1) investigation of offenders (their backgrounds, personalities, and crimes) scheduled to appear before commissions; (2) presentation of this information in commission hearings; and (3) implementation of decisions reached by commissions (supervising guardianship arrangements, for example, or escorting youths to institutions). The general similarity between the duties of the Children's Social Inspection and investigators-upbringers allowed commissions to call on the former for assistance in the absence of the latter.[58]

This was the plan. Almost at once, however, the problem's breadth overwhelmed officials and the institutions just described. Even during the period from 1918 to early 1921—before the Volga famine confronted the state with additional millions of starving refugees—youths roamed the country in numbers far exceeding the government's capacity to respond. At this time, investigations of children's institutions around the country revealed that shortages of food, clothing, buildings, equipment, and staff not only complicated the opening of new facilities but prevented many already in existence from meeting their charges' most basic material needs (to say nothing of education and rehabilitation). Nearly the entire population, after all, suffered privation during the gaunt years of War Communism, and *detdoma* bore no immunity to these hardships.[59] Conditions in some institutions appeared as deplorable as life on the street and left officials uncertain whether to continue packing urchins inside.[60] Despite instructions from Moscow that no effort be spared to supply orphanages (and, at a minimum, to distribute food to hungry youths left outside), stern commands could not alter the stark reality of pervasive shortage.[61]

Throughout the Civil War, the army naturally consumed a sizable portion of the government's meager resources, including materials previously earmarked for children's institutions. In many regions military authorities commandeered buildings in use or intended as juvenile facilities—and sometimes proved reluctant to surrender the structures to Narkompros or the Commissariat of Health after hostilities had ceased.[62] Government agencies besides the army, facing the same shortage of serviceable buildings, appropriated *detdoma* while shrugging away protests from provincial children's commissions and Narkompros. Ironically, given Dzerzhinskii's leading role in the Children's Commission, a report from Irkutsk told of the local Cheka requisitioning such an institution during the Civil War and refusing to relinquish it after the Bolsheviks' triumph. These difficulties left Narkompros (and the Commissariat of Social Security earlier) to enlist many substandard structures in the expanding network of *detdoma*.[63]

The torrent of waifs loosed by the Volga famine thus descended upon a makeshift network of receivers and *detdoma* already swollen with victims of previous catastrophes. From the summer of 1921 well into 1922, Narkompros offices across broad stretches of the starving heartland found themselves besieged daily by dozens and even hundreds of juveniles clamoring for admission to *detdoma*. Some beleaguered officials could scarcely stir in their own buildings, so clogged were the halls with children who had often been waiting weeks for assignment to the orphanages. Parents, too, joined this throng and thrust forth offspring they could no longer feed. Desperate appeals from provincial agencies to Moscow grew routine—and could not be satisfied, as the calamity's scope dwarfed resources at hand.[64]

Throughout the famine territory, and in many nearby provinces, children swamped *detdoma* even after officials had scrambled to open additional institutions in every conceivable structure. For each building pressed into service, thousands of homeless youths remained on the street. A Narkompros office in Simbirsk province accepted only candidates facing imminent death, so overcrowded were the facilities.[65] To ease institutions' congestion, Narkompros branches around the country ordered the discharge of low-priority inhabitants whose parents or relatives could be located.[66] Many residents shown the door had been placed in *detdoma* by parents pleading inadequate family resources or (less often) a desire that their sons and daughters receive a collectivist upbringing. Some were progeny of the institutions' own staffs. In a number of regions, local officials transferred adolescents from *detdoma* into the care of peasant families. By no means all peasants selected had volunteered—with the predictable result that "their" new children often fared poorly and soon fled to the street.[67] Narkompros hoped, of course, that these measures would free more places in *detdoma* for the genuinely homeless, which they did. But those inside the walls of institutions still represented a small fraction of the crowds on their own.

The introduction of the New Economic Policy during 1921 presented administrators of children's institutions with another set of problems. NEP forced many state enterprises and provincial government agencies to assume greater responsibility for their own finances. Unable to rely any longer on Moscow for more than a fraction of their budgets, and finding other government bodies in similar straits now unwilling to supply necessities free of charge, local Narkompros officials moved to close some *detdoma* in order to reduce expenses. By 1922–1923 they had done so in substantial numbers.[68] The children involved were squeezed into other *detdoma*, placed in families of the surrounding population, or left to fend for themselves. Whatever the economic advantages of NEP's "market discipline," they were difficult to ascertain at once from the vantage point of orphanages.

A decade later, looking back over her years of work with abandoned youths, Asya Kalinina recalled that in 1922 the task appeared nearly hopeless. She and her colleagues feared then that juvenile homelessness and delinquency, which were assuming ever more dire proportions, might eventually corrode the foundation of the Soviet state.[69] The briefest tour of famine provinces erased any thought that the boarding institutions of Narkompros and other agencies might perform as planned. How could anyone press ambitious programs for rehabilitation and upbringing on facilities buried in wraithlike children? Yet something had to be done.

As early as the summer of 1921, the number of people threatened with starvation had reached a scale sufficient to trigger planning for a variety of emergency measures, none more dramatic than mass evacuations of juveniles from afflicted provinces. The Children's Commission, Narkompros, and other bodies formed special divisions for the project, with Narkompros's Evacuation Bureau (whose members included representatives from several agencies) most directly involved in its implementation.[70] Officials in comparatively prosperous regions received telegrams instructing them to inform Moscow how many Volga youths they could accept, while evacuation procedures were devised to guide authorities in the famine zone. The ambitious plan for September–October 1921 called for removing approximately 40,000 boys and girls.[71] Not surprisingly, as soon as the policy of evacuation appeared on the government's list of options, officials in ravaged districts showered Moscow with communications emphasizing the distress in their areas and pleading that thousands of juveniles be transported to other parts of the country. Well before year's end the number claimed to require evacuation approached 175,000—exceeding by nearly 100,000 the total that other sections of the country agreed to support.[72] Authorities in some stricken cities abandoned all restraint and placed candidates—in a few cases, the entire populations of detdoma—on trains headed out of the region, without waiting for Moscow's permission.[73]

Altogether, from June 1921 to September 1922, the government evacuated approximately 150,000 children. A majority appear to have been orphans or otherwise homeless, though information is far from complete. Nearly all came from seven provinces (Samara, Saratov, Simbirsk, Ural, Ufa, Cheliabinsk, and Tsaritsyn), three Autonomous Republics (Tatar, Kirghiz, and Bashkir), and several smaller Autonomous Regions (those of the Volga Germans and Chuvash among them). Saratov and Samara provinces alone each supplied over 25,000, and the Kirghiz Republic over 20,000, in scarcely more than one year.[74] Destinations lay in every direction from the Volga basin and included Siberia (notably Omsk and Semipalatinsk), Central Asia (Samarkand, Bukhara, and Tashkent), the Transcaucasian republics, Ukraine (mainly the provinces of Podol'sk, Kiev, Poltava, Volynsk, and Chernigov), and Petrograd.

Many other cities (and their surrounding districts) also received contingents numbering in the thousands, including Vitebsk, Novgorod, Pskov, Smolensk, Gomel', Kursk, Nizhnii Novgorod, Orel, Tula, Iaroslavl', and Tver'.[75] Published plans did not designate an especially large share for Moscow, possibly because young refugees arriving on their own had already inundated the city. Finally, in the fall of 1921, the Children's Commission even approved projects for evacuating juveniles to Czechoslovakia, Germany, and England. The documents do not indicate whether any ever set out for Germany and England, but agreement was reached with Czechoslovakia on the evacuation of 600 children, at least 486 of whom arrived.[76]

While several thousand youths made their journeys by boat, commonly sailing up the Volga to Nizhnii Novgorod, well over 90 percent traveled by train.[77] Special "sanitary trains" (*sanpoezda*) often carried from 400 to 600 children, and one hauled 983.[78] Juveniles selected for these trips were to receive haircuts, baths, and disinfected clothes, along with a clean bill of health. Indeed, no one qualified for evacuation from a *detdom* if cases of any severely contagious disease had been detected at the facility during the previous two weeks. Those living outside institutions faced a two-week quarantine before departure.[79] As it turned out, in areas where the starving population lived far from rail lines, youths did not always assemble at stations in accordance with Moscow's timetable. Authorities in Saratov, for example, received instructions initially to load each arriving train only with residents of one district or another. When the intended passengers did not materialize in Saratov on time, trains had to wait, thus disrupting the evacuation schedule. Before long, new orders permitted officials to fill trains with any candidates available.[80]

Conditions on board varied considerably. Some trains were clean and warm, with ample food, medical attention, and dedicated personnel.[81] Others left a different impression. Trains deployed to pick up children were supposed to contain supplies of food, clean clothing, and bedding, but many clattered into town empty and filthy. A telegram from the Samara Children's Commission to Moscow complained on one occasion that officials had to strip clothing from juveniles left behind in order to outfit those departing. In Saratov, a local journal revealed that train crews stole shoes and clothing sent for evacuees and sold the items in bazaars. Once a trip had begun, shortages of food sometimes prompted the young passengers to slip out at stops to forage for provisions. Delays at stations could stretch on for days—as when depot authorities unhitched the trains' engines for other tasks or refused to provide fuel and similarly vital supplies. Meanwhile, poor sanitation produced illness and death. In fact, officials among the Volga Germans, after evacuating a few trainloads of the region's offspring, resolved to send out no more. Such wretched conditions obtained aboard the trains, they concluded, that youths possessed a better chance of surviving in the famine region itself.[82]

The most vociferous complaints sounded outside the famine territory—from authorities who received the deliveries. Time and again they bombarded the Children's Commission and Narkompros in Moscow with indignant reports of trains unloading boys and girls clad only in undershirts or similarly inadequate apparel. According to a Narkompros official in Poltava, "all of the children who arrived were, without exception, absolutely naked and barefoot." The Ukrainian Central Commission of Aid to the Starving protested repeatedly to the Russian Republic's Narkompros that youths evacuated from the Volga provinces to Ukraine had not been given adequate clothing for their journey. This violated Moscow's own instructions on evacuation, the Ukrainians reminded Narkompros, adding that they could not themselves supply all the arrivals with clothes.[83] Worse still, dispatches from many cities described disease as commonplace among evacuees, an indication of disregard in the famine zone for the two-week quarantine rule. Of the 578 juveniles delivered by a single "sanitary train" to Vladimir, "over 100" had to spend the first few weeks in hospitals with cases of typhus, measles, and smallpox. Narkompros's office in Novgorod reported in December 1921 to the Evacuation Bureau in Moscow that "many" on the most recent train from the Volga were sick—and a "few" dead. A health official in Novgorod telegraphed to Moscow that trains from famine provinces had saturated local hospitals with typhus cases, exhausting resources available to treat them and threatening the entire region with infection.[84]

Instructions from Moscow specified that children evacuated from famine districts be housed, upon reaching their destinations, in special facilities (such as a converted receiver, *detdom*, or clinic) for a two-week period of medical examination and quarantine. Youths routed to Smolensk province, for example, traveled initially to the town of Roslavl', where they stayed in a set of old barracks for medical processing. Only then were they deemed fit for transfer to more permanent accommodations.[85] More often than not around the country this meant *detdoma*—supported in part by trade unions, factories, military units, institutes, newspapers, cooperatives, and the Cheka. Even the involvement of these organizations did not provide sufficient resources to sustain all famine refugees, however, and officials turned to placing some children in local peasant families.[86]

Regions struggling to absorb evacuees found the task complicated by still more boys and girls, at least 100,000 strong, arriving from the famine zone on their own.[87] In December 1921 and January 1922, for instance, the Kuban–Black Sea province received 200 youths in "organized fashion" from famine districts and another 3,400 whose travel arrangements appeared in no government plans. Thousands of miles to the east, in Siberia's Eniseisk province, 967 children arrived through official channels between March and November 1922, while 280 made the journey themselves.[88] Some authorities in the Northern Caucasus and Georgia, areas that attracted many refugees, attempted to seal their borders by stationing detachments there to repulse anyone traveling without "legitimate" purpose.[89] Though the success of these measures is questionable, their extraordinary nature testifies to the difficulties that those fleeing the famine caused administrators of territories they entered.

The seemingly endless stream of refugees, "organized" and otherwise, combined with the central government's inability to provide anything approaching the resources necessary to support them, soon moved provincial officials to appeal that Moscow route no more shipments their way. On occasion these entreaties included threats to turn any future trains around and send them, still loaded, out of the region. A few district authorities eventually did refuse to unload evacuation trains and dispatched them down the line to other towns—which in turn sometimes passed them on further.[90] While open defiance did not constitute the norm, the provinces made no secret of their impatience for permission to reevacuate those who bulged their *detdoma* and exhausted their resources. By the middle of 1922, with a better harvest anticipated in the Volga basin, Moscow heeded such complaints and began the process of sending refugees home.[91]

According to guidelines developed in the capital, officials were authorized to reevacuate minors only after obtaining written confirmation of parents' consent and only if the children received shoes, clothing, food, and train tickets.[92] It often proved next to impossible, however, to locate mothers and fathers hundreds of miles away and document their agreement for the return of offspring. During the famine, parents themselves traveled far and wide as refugees, and many had left this world altogether. In response, local authorities began sending juveniles

back to home regions—or any other available province—without authorization from Moscow and without observing the guidelines they
received. Eager to reduce the financial strain imposed on them by
thousands of evacuees, they shipped them home, observed a Narkompros report, "allegedly to their parents, who almost never, incidentally,
turn out to be alive." Approximately 25 percent of the youths reevacuated to the Tatar and Bashkir republics fit this description, and close
to 30 percent of those transported "home" to Saratov and Samara provinces found neither parents nor relatives on their arrival. They either
crowded into receivers and *detdoma* just as overtaxed as those they had
departed or hunted for shelter in alleys and train stations.[93]

Among the children reevacuated into a void were the boy and his
sister, Anna, who had dragged their younger sister, Vavara, along the
road to Kazan' on Christmas Day of 1921. After Vavara succumbed to
typhus, the children's parents and elder sister arrived in Kazan' and
found room in other shelters; thus family members were reunited in the
same city if not the same building. But as each week of famine left the
region ever more desperate, officials decided to evacuate the two youngest children (and many others) by rail to Ukraine. At the end of a
month's journey, the special train reached Vinnitsa, where local authorities, already swamped with starving youths, turned it away. The
train itself became something of a *besprizornyi*, rumbling down the
tracks to the town of Mogilev-Podol'skii on the Romanian border. Here
the passengers' fortunes improved. They landed in a children's home
that provided not only ample food but also schooling and other activities. Several months later, after the famine had abated, the youths were
reevacuated to Kazan'. Anna and her brother discovered no trace of their
parents and could do nothing but enter a foul shelter for indigents. The
conditions soon prompted them to leave Kazan', bound initially for their
native Grodnensk province (by then part of Poland), but destined instead
for separate children's homes in Moscow.[94]

For years the government struggled to reassemble such families. Even
before the famine scattered its victims across the country, parents and
relatives approached officials regularly for help in determining the
whereabouts of progeny lost during World War I and the Civil War.
Toward the end of 1921, Narkompros organized a Central Children's
Address Bureau to collect information on institutionalized juveniles for
use in responding to these inquiries—which multiplied in the aftermath
of the Volga basin evacuation.[95] The Address Bureau did manage to
locate some youths sought by relatives (582 in 1923/24), but the num-

bers never exceeded a small fraction of those who had disappeared.[96] Such modest results prompted Narkompros and the Children's Commission to approach local officials and the public more directly by publishing lists of vanished offspring. These rosters appeared now and then in various periodicals by the middle of the decade and commonly included the names and ages of dozens or even a few hundred youths missing from one region or another. On occasion, the inventories produced responses that reunited families, but not at a rate sufficient to trim the homeless population perceptibly. The lists that Narkompros placed in its weekly bulletin, for example, succeeded in uncovering only four lost children.[97]

Why were tens of thousands of sons and daughters, even those transported from famine districts by the government itself, so difficult to find as conditions slowly improved after 1922? No doubt many parents whose children had embarked on "sanitary trains" shared this perplexity. Much of the frustration stemmed from the evacuation's chaotic nature. Four copies of a form (containing such information as the child's name, location of original family home, and addresses of the dispatching and receiving institutions) were to be prepared for each boy or girl shipped out of the famine zone. But all too often the records were transcribed inaccurately, lost, or not compiled in the first place. Haste and sloppiness in these desperate times corrupted data to the point where someone searching for, say, Anastasiia Shcherbakova, and finding on the list an Anastasiia Shcherbaniuk, had grounds to wonder whether the two names identified the same girl. More likely, the object of an inquiry failed to appear in government registers at all. According to an article published in 1928, the list of evacuated minors composed by the middle of the decade contained only about thirty thousand names. Even when records were filed properly, subsequent undocumented transfers of juveniles to peasant families or from one institution to another rendered the original paperwork obsolete—as did the flight of youths from foster homes and *detdoma*.[98] Many children obscured their tracks by entering relief facilities under fictitious names. Wily vagrants, with no desire for a trip home, proffered aliases with polished ease. Others, especially the very young, who could not remember their identities, received names (and even nationalities) arbitrarily from officials. Revolutionary heroes numbered among the sources of inspiration for these choices—leaving some orphanages stocked with such ersatz celebrities as Klara Tsetkin, Inessa Armand, Mikhail Kalinin, and Sof'ia Perovskaia.[99]

❖ ❖ ❖ ❖

As early as 1921, an occasional voice questioned the mass evacuations then in progress, arguing that the exercises wasted government relief funds and even harmed some of the children involved. A teacher traveling in 1921 with a train transporting youths from Saratov to Vitebsk contended that this method rescued only an insignificant percentage of those starving, far fewer than could be saved by allocating equivalent resources to the blighted provinces themselves.[100] If such objections did not sway Narkompros initially, problems beleaguering the evacuation and reevacuation campaigns convinced the government by 1923 to abandon these large-scale endeavors. In 1924, the All-Russian Central Executive Committee ordered a halt to mass transfers of children. *Individuals* might still be reevacuated, *if* parents or relatives awaited them and possessed means to provide proper care. Otherwise, juveniles qualified for transfer only by consent of the Narkompros office in the province of their destination. When partial crop failure returned to several Volga provinces in 1924, Narkompros rejected another round of mass evacuations and concentrated instead on directing aid to the stricken districts.[101]

Whatever the wisdom of evacuation in 1921–1922, the policy sprang from the sound conclusion that receivers, *detdoma*, and clinics in the region could not begin to cope with the prostrate multitudes. This same realization prompted the opening of food distribution points in the famine zone, as a socialist upbringing for residents of *detdoma* yielded to efforts aimed at keeping the starving alive wherever they huddled. To this end, the government established cafeterias and dispatched trains to traverse the famine provinces distributing meals and medical care.[102] The public, too, was pressed to donate funds for the emergency. Newspapers carried frequent articles on contributions (doubtless not always as voluntary as described) by soldiers, sailors, workers, and private entrepreneurs to bolster *detdoma* and provide assistance to other young famine victims.[103] At its peak, aid from individuals, factories, trade unions, military units, and other organizations appears to have maintained at least two hundred thousand juveniles, with trade unions responsible for over half the total.[104]

The government even opened afflicted areas to foreign relief groups.[105] By July 1922, according to Soviet figures for the Volga basin and Crimea (but not Ukraine), foreign organizations were feeding nearly 3.6 million children, with the American Relief Administration (ARA) responsible for slightly over 80 percent of the total. An American account credits the ARA in July with supplying daily nourishment to 3.6

million minors and 5.4 million adults, totals that peaked the following month at 4.2 and 6.3 million respectively. Meanwhile the state distributed food to approximately 1.3 million boys and girls (30,000 by means of the special trains), bringing the number of youths receiving at least occasional meals from these sources close to 5 million.[106] Yet despite this valiant undertaking, millions more went unfed.

The gap between these figures and the enthusiasm fostered by the Revolution for child-rearing projects could not have been greater. As Narkompros put the finishing touches on plans for a network of institutions intended to fashion waifs into a new socialist generation, the famine shifted official priorities to stark survival. Here, obscured by the overwhelming tragedy of the spectacle, resided a forlorn irony. In 1920, as it wrenched primary responsibility from the Commissariat of Social Security for the care of destitute juveniles, Narkompros justified its action by claiming preeminent expertise in educating and rehabilitating youths, as opposed merely to providing for their material well-being. But when Lunacharskii's commissariat finally turned to the mission it had won, officials found themselves facing conditions that rendered education and rehabilitation all but impossible. The new generation, its members dying by the million, had to be saved before it could be trained.

CHAPTER FIVE

Primeval Chaos

A revolution does not deserve its name if it does not take the
greatest care possible of the children—the future race for
whose benefit the revolution has been made.

Leon Trotsky

At the time the tragic problem of these children seemed
unsolvable.

W. Averell Harriman

While the famine scuttled any thought that Narkompros's receivers and
detdoma could operate as planned, it did not eliminate these institutions.
Quite the contrary. In 1921–1922 they multiplied as rapidly as the most
ardent partisan of "social education" could have dreamed three years
earlier. But the reason for the increase—the soaring number of waifs—
did not coincide at all with the expectations of euphoric revolutionaries
in 1917–1918. As the crisis deepened, officials in Narkompros and other
agencies asked ever more urgently how the network of children's institutions could absorb the deluge of abandoned girls and boys. They wondered, too, about the effort to decriminalize juvenile delinquency when
young thieves appeared at every turn. Such concerns prompted, or
stemmed from, another question: What was actually happening inside
facilities for homeless youths during these difficult years? The answer
would help shape renewed efforts to salvage a socialist generation from
the street, once the famine had run its course.

Nowhere did children's institutions proliferate more rapidly than in
the nation's capital. As early as June 1921, Narkompros acknowledged
the need to enlarge Moscow's network of receivers in order to absorb
urchins, who seemed more numerous each day. Plans called for several
additional receivers (and observation-distribution points, sometimes
combined with receivers), whose intended capacities ranged as high as
one thousand.[1] The space would not go unused. From November 15 to
December 15, with refugees pouring into Moscow from the famine zone,

the Pokrovskii receiver alone admitted 3,925 youths. Slightly under 1,000 had been evacuated by the state, while the remaining 3,000 had fled starvation on their own. During the course of 1922, the city's receivers processed approximately 1,000 juveniles per month, only 4 percent of whom were native Muscovites.[2]

In the country as a whole, the number of receivers increased steadily during the famine period, reaching 237 (along with 160 observation-distribution points) in the Russian Republic by the summer of 1922.[3] Unfortunately, this represented only a fraction of the quantity required to accommodate the homeless millions, and remained more than 300 below Narkompros's original goal of one receiver per district. Local officials, lacking resources to open hundreds of additional facilities, packed existing receivers five and even ten times over intended capacity.[4] A doctor in Simferopol' characterized the city's receivers as "dumps" into which boys and girls were crammed without attention or even count, and whose exhausted staffs simply "threw up their hands before the ceaseless influx." In one large room, roughly two hundred children covered plank beds, the floor, window sills, and a piano. Circumstances numbed them to the point where they matter-of-factly utilized as tables the bodies of others who had already died. "Corpses served as pillows for those who, tomorrow, might expect the same fate." Every evening, personnel counted the inhabitants and then placed an order for the next day's food. By morning, the census was usually obsolete: residents had died, run away, or, conversely, arrived during the night. Furthermore, a constantly changing number materialized from the bazaars each day at mealtime—and disappeared again after eating.[5] American relief officials inspecting receivers in Samara described the conditions as "heartbreaking": "The first place we visited was a 'receiving home.' Before the war this building was erected as an orphanage for fifty children; today [September 1921] it holds more than six hundred. They lie in the yard, on the floor, on wooden benches, one on top of another, sick and well together, covered with dirty, lousy rags. For this large number of children there are only ten small soup dishes and fifty wooden spoons."[6]

During the famine, youths often arrived at receivers and observation-distribution points in deplorable condition: grotesquely swollen stomachs bulged from shriveled physiques covered with excrement, dirt, and lice. Now at death's portal, many expired shortly after entering crowded rooms and sinking into vacant spaces on the floor. Figures do not exist to reveal the toll in institutions at this time, but reports from individual facilities underscore the obvious. Children succumbed in droves. At a

receiver in Orenburg, 118 (from a total of 935) perished in just two
days. Institutions in Groznyi and Vladikavkaz recorded mortality rates
as high as 30 percent in the period November 1921–early January 1922,
while in Simferopol' thirty inhabitants died every day in one receiver
during the emergency's peak. Given the shortage of buildings and the
vast quantity of victims, those with infectious diseases could not be isolated from the rest. Bodies weakened by the famine offered little resistance to myriad ailments, which thus spread rapidly in crowded rooms.
Staff members themselves sometimes contracted the maladies, a risk that
prompted a few to sever all contact with their charges and even flee the
institutions.[7]

As the famine waned in 1922–1923, receivers' primary clientele
changed gradually from emaciated, desperate refugees to juveniles adept
at fending for themselves. These vagrants, cast loose by the famine or
earlier misfortune, drifted in and out of institutions or tried to avoid
them. With time, they mastered the skills necessary to survive indefinitely on the street and absorbed its manners and recreations. Thus en-
dowed, they presented different problems to receivers than did famine
victims listing on grave's edge. Of course, some abandoned adolescents
in 1923 could not yet be classified as veterans of markets and train
stations, while numerous children at large during the famine had already
been hardened by years in such haunts. But after 1922, as fewer new
urchins appeared, inveterate waifs accounted for an increasing portion
of the remaining pool of homeless children.

These pupils of the underworld complicated greatly the work of receivers, sometimes disrupting them to such an extent that institutions
assumed the air of criminals' dens. Even when a staff managed to maintain control—by driving out, transferring, or domesticating troublemakers—the process rarely proved smooth or rapid.[8] In overcrowded
buildings, practiced young thieves could not be separated from weak or
green occupants (often dubbed *ogol'tsy*, meaning stripped or naked
ones), thereby enabling the former to prey on the latter. In receivers
where seasoned youths held sway, they greeted newly arrived *ogol'tsy*
with beatings, just as they had on the street, and commonly seized clothing, blankets, and meals from those unable to resist. At Moscow's large
Pokrovskii receiver, a staff member noticed the leader of a gang brazenly
consuming several servings of food while a newcomer in poor health sat
quietly in the corner with only a meager portion of thin soup. She demanded that the leader share his repast with the silent diner—and received an indignant refusal. Her order struck the gang member as an

affront to the institution's protocol; the idea that he be placed on the same footing as the sickly figure in the corner seemed absurd. Thus he continued his meal, rebuffing the woman with icy rudeness. Flinty aristocrats of this sort reigned throughout the Pokrovskii receiver early in the decade, reserving the best places to sleep, buying and selling others' belongings, "hiring" lads to perform chores, and collecting "tribute" from weaker neighbors. One boy extracted protection payments from a group of Tatar children who feared abuse at the hands of their Russian counterparts. In some receivers, toughs exercised more control over other residents than did the institutions' staffs.[9]

Juveniles despoiled not only each other but the receivers themselves. Food, sheets, blankets, clothing, even furniture disappeared with daily regularity at some institutions, often to be resold in nearby streets and markets. Thieves also slipped out to steal from the surrounding population, in one case filling an entire neighborhood with fear of the adjoining receiver.[10] In such conditions, the relations between adult personnel and their charges bore little resemblance to those desired by Narkompros. It took a patient, optimistic staff member not to regard experienced waifs as irretrievable hooligans, and many adolescents in turn expressed sullen mistrust toward their "upbringers." Most often, the suspicious, restless, and unhappy (including those abused by other youths) ran away before they could be sent on to an observation-distribution point or *detdom*. Some remained less than a day, long enough only to secure a set of new clothes or a meal.[11]

Narkompros had anticipated that receivers would hold children for no more than a few days of preliminary observation and processing before distributing them to Juvenile Affairs Commissions, *detdoma*, or other destinations. But the homeless tide that flooded receivers also engulfed *detdoma*, colonies, and clinics, leaving few openings to which receivers could discharge their multitudes. As a result, receivers found themselves obliged to keep youths for months rather than days, which greatly exacerbated overcrowding and related problems.[12] It also meant—for something had to be done with wards remaining indefinitely—that receivers came to assume responsibilities originally intended for *detdoma*, including the provision of classroom education and labor training.[13] In most cases the transformation took place by force of necessity and without prearrangement, as staffs contended with a situation thrust on them by reality rather than decree.[14] The outcome varied greatly. Despite setbacks and disappointments, some receivers managed to break (or at least loosen) the street's hold on their residents, even arrivals wedded to a vagabond life.[15] More often, however, sources early in the decade portrayed facilities plagued by the aforementioned deficiencies—hardly grounds for astonishment, given the magnitude of the problem facing an inexperienced government armed with modest resources.

While the process often required several months, receivers did eventually discharge children who had not already left on their own. The intended destinations included relatives' homes, hospitals, clinics, and observation-distribution points, but the route traveled far more frequently, especially by the genuinely homeless, led to *detdoma*.[16] In broad terms, the designation *detdom* referred to a facility housing children during the extended period of education and labor training considered essential for a productive life. Institutions of this sort received a wide assortment of other names in various localities—including colony or labor colony, labor institute, school-commune, and home-commune, to list a few—with a document sometimes employing first one label and then another (and perhaps a third) in reference to a single *detdom*. Some authors observed clear distinctions when using these terms, but many others interchanged them freely. As a general rule, establishments sporting "colony" in their titles were located in the countryside and occupied youths primarily with agricultural pursuits. They, along with facilities whose titles included "labor," were typically intended for the rehabilitation of "difficult" or "morally defective" juveniles. But institutions so named did not all share these characteristics, and they did not monopolize them.[17]

As local authorities scrambled to acquire buildings for expanding the network of *detdoma*, they faced the same difficulties that beset them in securing premises for receivers. With resources insufficient to construct hundreds of new facilities, they pressed the widest variety of existing structures into service, including municipal buildings and establishments used prior to the Revolution as shelters for orphans and delinquents.[18] Officials also sought the rights to houses, dachas, and estates confiscated from the prerevolutionary elite. In this event, if someone of Dzerzhinskii's stature intervened, splendid mansions opened their doors to the homeless. More often, though, the modest clout mustered by provincial offices of Narkompros (and the Commissariat of Social Security before it) yielded estates and residences in extreme disrepair. A *detdom* in Zvenigorod district, for example, appeared at first glance to be a superb facility. Standing in a large park on a bank high above the Moscow River, the manor, formerly property of the wealthy Morozov family, boasted thirty-six rooms, a marble stairway, central heating, running water, and electricity. But closer examination revealed that the local population had carried off everything movable and smashed most of what remained, including the heating, electrical, and water systems. Similarly, when a "labor school-commune" was established on a former noble's estate near Simbirsk, children and staff had to enter the building with shovels to clear it of filth deposited during the previous few years by hundreds of deserters.[19] Churches and especially monasteries also took on new roles as *detdoma*. Some had lain abandoned for months or years after 1917; others sheltered monks or nuns throughout the revolutionary period, until they were evicted to make room for waifs. A few continued ecclesiastical activities, at least for a time, even after the youths arrived.[20]

The legions of juveniles who disrupted receivers moved on to burden *detdoma* with many of the same predicaments—most obviously overcrowding. Even before the famine, the Workers' and Peasants' Inspectorate discovered that *detdoma* in numerous provinces bulged with as many as several times their intended volume of inhabitants. So, too, did shelters in sectors outside Bolshevik control during the Civil War, as American Red Cross representatives noted in Ukraine. There a local official told them of "54 orphanages in the country controlled by Petliura with 30,000 children inmates [an average of 556 youths per orphanage!]."[21] By autumn of 1921, the squalor described in these accounts paled against the horror reported routinely from the Volga basin, southern Ukraine, and nearby regions inundated with famine refugees. Skeletal forms packed every square foot of *detdoma*, while hundreds more waited outside many facilities, begging for admission and perishing in untold numbers.[22] Altogether, the *detdoma* of Ufa province took in 60 to 100 youths every day as early as June 1921. By December the total reached 150 per day—and exploded to 500 two months later. As a result, the province's *detdoma* staggered under a load estimated at 500 percent of their planned capacity at the beginning of 1922, with an additional 50,000 candidates left in the street.[23] One of Samara's *detdoma* struck a visiting journalist as nothing so much as "a 'pound' for homeless dogs":

> They picked up the wretched children, lost or abandoned by their parents, by hundreds off the streets, and parked them in these "homes." At the place I visited an attempt had been made to segregate those who were obviously sick or dying from their "healthier" fellows. The latter sat listlessly, 300 or 400 of them in a dusty court-yard, too weak and lost and sad to move or

TABLE I   INCREASE IN THE NUMBER OF
DETDOMA AND THEIR INHABITANTS, 1921

	January 1, 1921		December 31, 1921	
	Detdoma	*Children*	*Detdoma*	*Children*
Volga Germans	12	428	33	3,300
Simbirsk province	65	3,530	117	11,719
Stavropol' province	40	2,279	125	12,490
Tambov province	113	7,834	134	13,372
Tatar Republic	110	5,670	232	17,971
Ufa province	103	4,976	239	23,985
Cheliabinsk province	90	6,103	222	22,200
Tsaritsyn province	51	2,374	159[a]	14,721[a]
Samara province	294	18,000	407[b]	44,660[b]
Astrakhan' province	67[c]	2,964[c]	92	5,509
Viatka province	89[c]	3,347[c]	109	10,934
Perm' province	165[c]	7,703[c]	203	12,214
Saratov province	145[c]	—	180	18,000
Chuvash region	12[c]	489[c]	40[d]	4,500[d]

SOURCE: TsGA RSFSR, f. 1575, o. 6, ed. khr. 4, l. 25.
[a]March 28, 1922
[b]August 1, 1921
[c]July 1, 1921
[d]February 1, 1922

care. Most of them were past hunger; one child of seven with fingers no thicker than matches refused the chocolate and biscuits I offered him and just turned his head away without a sound. The inside of the house was dreadful, children in all stages of a dozen different diseases huddled together anyhow in the most noxious atmosphere I have ever known. A matron and three girls were "in charge" of this pest-house. There was nothing they could do, they said wearily; they had no food or money or soap or medicine. There were 400 children or thereabouts, they didn't know exactly, in the home already, and a hundred or more brought in daily and about the same number died; there was nothing they could do.[24]

All across the famine zone, as homeless children proliferated at a much faster rate than did institutions to house them, the populations of existing *detdoma* mounted (table 1). Many local authorities could have written the lines sent to the Children's Commission in Moscow by a Narkompros official in Baku: "I declare without exaggeration that we have,

not children's homes, but children's cemeteries and cesspools in the lit-
eral sense of the words."[25] Later, when the famine subsided, it left behind
institutions in such dismal condition that one author wondered point-
edly whether boys and girls already in *detdoma* might require aid just
as urgently as those still on their own.[26]

Inevitably, severe food shortages accompanied overcrowding. Mal-
nutrition and outright starvation occurred most routinely during the
famine, of course, but the lack of sufficient provisions crippled institutions throughout these early years—reflecting the privation faced by
much of society. Time and again, as the number of waifs increased in a
province and local officials opened additional *detdoma*, they received
ever more irregular and inadequate deliveries of food. Appeals to superiors rarely availed, because the same misfortunes that spawned a
surge of homeless juveniles often reduced a region's food supplies.[27] As
rations dwindled in *detdoma*, some children not yet incapacitated by
starvation launched forays to steal from nearby markets or peasants.
Even before the famine, girls at an institution in Petrograd engaged in
prostitution to acquire food, and desperate authorities in Beloozero
(Cherepovetsk province) sought permission to release *detdom* residents
to forage for themselves. By the end of 1921, ravenous staff members
joined youths at some institutions on expeditions to beg for sustenance.[28]

In these grim years, *detdoma* lacked not only food but adequate supplies of nearly everything else as well—furniture, clothing, utensils,
tools, books, and agricultural implements. Reports streamed in to provincial capitals and to Moscow, describing children who lapped soup
out of cupped hands (in the absence of bowls), occupied themselves with
disturbing activities learned on the street (as insufficient books, equipment, and staff thwarted more wholesome projects), and, in general,
languished in buildings devoid of the most basic conveniences.[29] Administrators of many *detdoma*, left to shift for themselves, received no
supplies for weeks and even months. Anton Makarenko explained in
1922 that when he needed kerosene to light the buildings of his colony,
the local Narkompros office instructed him to catch dogs and melt down
their fat.[30]

Most *detdoma*, overcrowded as they were, could not maintain ample
sleeping facilities. Three or four youths often shared each bed, and many
simply huddled on the bare floor, covering themselves with anything at
hand, including old curtains and rugs. An institution in Viatka, with no
blankets at all, issued sacks to sleep in.[31] Similarly meager supplies of
shoes and clothing did not stretch to outfit the ragged and half-naked

millions. Reports told of numerous institutions providing footwear for as few as a quarter of their inhabitants, and even these shoes were not always serviceable. The entire populations of some *detdoma* faced winter barefoot or with only a few pairs of boots and shoes to share. This, combined with a dearth of warm clothing, commonly required *detdoma* to keep their charges indoors all winter, which in turn prevented the children from attending school if the *detdom* did not operate one of its own.[32] Even inside, the bite of winter left its mark. Crumbling walls, broken windows, and lack of heating fuel permitted icy winds to roam buildings as master, lowering interior temperatures to the neighborhood of zero degrees Celsius. From the Kuban' came word of frostbite acquired *indoors* and floors coated with ice after a washing; in Tashkent, desks were smashed and burned as fuel; and in Iaroslavl', children slept embracing each other tightly for warmth. A report to Dzerzhinskii described certain *detdoma* in Simbirsk, Saratov, Penza, Vladimir, and other provinces as completely unheated—so vulnerable to the cold, in fact, that snow drifts developed now and then inside rooms.[33]

Shortages of food, clothing, heat, and space contributed to levels of hygiene and illness in *detdoma* that shocked investigators. Early in 1923, a health commission portrayed a *detdom* in Samarkand as "an utter cemetery of decaying, live children," and this spectacle was not restricted to Central Asia. In Samara province, health officials were brought before a revolutionary tribunal "because of the horrible, unsanitary condition of children in institutions." Many *detdoma* had no lavatories at all, so that boys and girls relieved themselves in yards, hallways, and even their own beds. Existing latrines often overflowed with filth, through which barefoot youths walked routinely. In some overburdened facilities, juveniles caked with grime and parasites received baths only at intervals of several weeks.[34] Their crowded buildings also lacked space to isolate the ailing from the relatively healthy, which further hastened the march of infections. Rare indeed was the institution at this time whose inhabitants did not suffer from a wide variety of maladies, and in some facilities nearly everyone (even the staff) was stricken. In Kazan', for instance, fully 85 percent of the residents in one *detdom* had malaria early in 1921. Throughout the country, common ailments included skin and eye infections, fungi, parasites (often lice), typhus, dysentery, tuberculosis, malaria, and scurvy. Nor were venereal diseases strangers to institutions, especially those for delinquents. Among 290 at a home for the "morally defective" in Ekaterinodar toward the end of 1920, 60 had contracted syphilis.[35]

In light of the preceding, there can be no doubt that many thousands (perhaps hundreds of thousands) died in *detdoma* during the period 1918–1923. While precise information for the country as a whole has not been published, and may well have escaped compilation in these turbulent years, a few *detdoma* reported during the famine that half or even three-fourths of their occupants had perished. "At one children's home that I visited," wrote a traveler in Buzuluk, "of 141 boys and girls received in the course of the previous week, 76 had died. This was by no means an exception." More often, however, dispatches told only of "high" or "very high" mortality, leaving details to the imagination.[36]

Along with illness and death, thefts appeared among the consequences of shortages rife in *detdoma*, for hunger stimulated much the same desperation within institutions as it did on the street. Underworld veterans, of course, might plunder any *detdom*, well supplied or not, to support habits acquired while at large or merely for the adventure. But insufficient food in a facility prompted others to join them in pilfering anything at hand—sheets, blankets, shoes, clothing, tools, utensils—and spirit the items away to the nearest market for sale. Such transactions deprived *detdoma* of essential supplies, to be replaced with great difficulty if at all. Some residents, rather than (or along with) stealing from *detdoma*, took to raiding other targets in their neighborhoods, such as peasants' storerooms and passing travelers.[37] As Makarenko put it, recalling the early years of his colony:

> In full accordance with the theories of historical materialism, it was the economic base of peasant life which interested the boys first and foremost, and to which, in the period under consideration, they came the closest. Without entering very deeply into a discussion of the various superstructures, my charges made straight for larder and cellar, disposing, to the best of their ability, of the riches contained therein.[38]

Finally, youths not disabled by hunger or disease frequently responded to woeful conditions in *detdoma* by fleeing. Though they abandoned institutions for other reasons as well—a city's lights and excitement, perhaps, or to escape beatings and gambling debts—it appears reasonable to suppose that lamentable facilities prompted most flights in these initial years. In any case, children slipped away and returned to the street in countless thousands, often absconding with clothing and other property to sell for food and entertainment.[39]

Facing so many obstacles, it must have been a rare staff member who did not succumb at least occasionally to bottomless despair.[40] Aside

from the formidable difficulties just described, gangs, gambling, drinking, brawling, anti-Semitism, rapes, vandalism, insolence, and occasional attacks on adult personnel plagued many *detdoma* that housed
streetwise youths.[41] Little wonder these institutions often failed to attract
and retain qualified educators. Those not intimidated at the outset by
the prospect of working with troubled adolescents often left their positions before long, fed up with the grueling work and monthly pay (when
it materialized at all) lower even than that of teachers in schools for
"normal" pupils.[42] Congresses of concerned officials and investigations
of *detdoma* identified a crying need for more trained staff, especially in
the growing number of institutions for "difficult" residents. *Detdoma*
did attract people of generous spirit, prepared to shoulder considerable
sacrifice to assist abandoned juveniles. But the institutions also served
as refuges for those who could not find or hold jobs elsewhere and who
viewed their positions as little more than nests in which to live off supplies intended first of all for the children.[43]

Despite the abundant and often overwhelming hardships faced by
detdoma during the Revolution's first half-decade, their portrait should
not be painted solely in black. Studies did find most institutions in miserable condition, but a minority received favorable reports. Comparatively clean and adequately equipped, they left an encouraging impression, even if they also displayed room for further improvement. Where
their histories are known, one finds almost invariably that they faced
the same problems besetting *detdoma* in general—dilapidated facilities,
few supplies, and unruly inhabitants. But eventually, sometimes not until the passage of several trying months or even a few years, signs of
progress began to reward the efforts of a dedicated staff. Workshops,
schools, clubs, kitchen gardens, and livestock came to occupy the children's energies, while flight and theft faded to occasional nuisances.
Thus nurtured, most youths in these establishments gave reason to be-
lieve that they had broken, or were breaking, their bonds with the street
and might well join society before long as productive, well-adjusted
citizens.[44]

A *detdom* for difficult juveniles in Moscow provided a vivid illustration of this transformation. Prior to the arrival in December 1920 of
new teachers and administrators, the youths did whatever they pleased,
completely intimidating the staff. Some disappeared for hours each day,
taking food and clothing along to sell in the Sukharevskii Market. Others remained in the *detdom* and engaged in such "manual labor exercises" as destroying furniture to make sleds and slamming a piano with

wet towels to frighten a teacher when she tried to "meddle" in their lives. Many were extremely volatile, quickly vexed by the slightest obstacle, and prone to fly into rages and fights on trivial grounds. They shouted from morning to night, even while conducting mundane conversations. In short, numerous obstacles greeted the new staff's effort to bring rudimentary decorum to classes, meetings, and meals. Activities requiring collective discipline and the observance of rules, such as team sports or simple theatrical productions, were completely beyond the residents at first. When rehearsing a play, for instance, some actors saw no need to wait for others to finish speeches before sounding forth with their own. Informed of the coherence yielded by the delivery of lines in proper order, they stormed from the room. Though the new group of educators had resolved initially to abjure compulsion, they soon concluded that basic rules of behavior would have to be introduced, beginning in the dining room. Here children leaped up from the table throughout the meal, screamed whenever they pleased, made obscene gestures, and ate out of their hands. It was therefore announced that no one who arrived late, left the table early, or ate sloppily would receive any more food that meal. This tactic soon diminished chaos in the dining room, though shouting was not overcome for several months.

As time passed, the staff's devotion to the *detdom* won the youths' trust. Thefts and destruction of property shrank to trivial proportions. Abusive and hysterical inhabitants, though still capable of rough moments, grew more stable and dependable. Eventually the group even received invitations to attend festivities in other institutions, something their reputation for wildness had earlier precluded. To be sure, the success did not extend to all children, a handful of whom remained immune to the adults' efforts and finally ran away or were conveyed to relatives or other facilities. But isolated setbacks notwithstanding, the *detdom* made striking progress from year to year—organizing clubs, excursions, and schooling, for example—and by 1923 bore few traces of its former seedy character.[45]

A perusal of such histories indicates that *detdoma* required nothing so much as an energetic, dedicated staff. Without instructors and administrators devoted to weaning juveniles from the street, even a well-equipped facility could achieve little. It should also be noted that the Moscow *detdom* featured here contained six teachers and only 25 to 38 children. Had the staff been swamped by 100–150 boys and girls, a common occurrence in this period, the institution's accomplishments would have remained modest. The most saintly corps of educators could not absorb an unlimited number of starving or unrepentant youths and expect, with completely inadequate supplies and facilities, to reshape their lives. In any case, ardent, skilled personnel did not represent the norm in *detdoma*. Thus, despite individual successes, these institutions taken collectively made little progress toward the goal of rehabilitating waifs in the first five years of Soviet power.

As described in the preceding chapter, Narkompros (and the Commissariat of Social Security from 1918 to 1920) intended to rely on hundreds of Juvenile Affairs Commissions to replace the courts in deciding proper treatment for young lawbreakers. No longer regarded as criminals, the children were to be spared traditional trials and incarceration. Although the plan envisioned a network of commissions reaching nearly every municipality down to the district level, implementation proceeded slowly. By March 1920, when Narkompros assumed responsibility for the commissions, only about 50 had been established, nearly all confined to the largest cities. As the ranks of homeless youths (and thus juvenile thieves) continued to increase, so too did the number of commissions. In the Russian Republic the total reached 190 by May 1921, 209 by September 1922, and 236 by December. Thereafter the figures leveled off at 273 in 1923 and 275 in 1924—in other words, roughly paralleling the opening of new receivers and still approximately three hundred short of the goal.[46]

The number of children processed by a commission in any given area depended on numerous factors, including the board's efficiency and the region's share of offenders. In Petrograd, ravaged during the War Communism years but far removed from the subsequent Volga famine, the caseload of the city's commission rose steadily from 5,888 in 1918 to 8,404 in 1919 and peaked at 9,106 in 1920. As local conditions improved, volume dropped to 7,902 in 1921 and then plunged to 4,520 the following year. Moscow's commissions, by contrast, were busiest during the famine year of 1921, handling by one account 14,307 youths (down to 7,121 in 1922).[47] Figures available for the Russian Republic as a whole must be regarded merely as rough estimates, given the incomplete compilation and reporting of information from the provinces. According to one source, commissions decided the cases of 54,424 juveniles in 1921, while a second author estimated that the actual total approached 85,000. A work published later in the decade listed the number who appeared before commissions as 50,580 in 1922, 43,484 in 1923, and 48,945 in 1924.[48]

The volume of children passing through commissions was affected not only by the country's supply of delinquents and commissions at any particular time, but also by periodic changes in the law. The decree of January 1918 had stipulated that commissions decide the cases of all minors (defined then as anyone under seventeen), stressing that adolescents no longer be sent before courts or to prisons. But the relentless increase in delinquency that accompanied the epidemic of homelessness during the next few years overwhelmed commissions and convinced the government to enact stricter measures. Thus Sovnarkom's decree of March 1920, while increasing by one year the maximum age of youths sent before commissions, permitted the transfer of those fourteen through seventeen to the courts if commissions considered inadequate the "medical-pedagogic" measures at their disposal.[49] Similar concern over a country saturated with young bandits colored the Russian Republic's new Criminal Code, issued in June 1922, which reduced from eighteen to sixteen the minimum age at which an offender's case went directly to a court. Only for those fourteen and fifteen years old did commissions retain authority to decide whether they or the courts should determine treatment.[50]

In the summer of 1922, the expansive scale and brazenness of juvenile crime prompted a series of interagency meetings to consider transferring from Narkompros to the Commissariat of Justice *all* responsibility for rehabilitating delinquents. Although Narkompros managed in the end to retain its Juvenile Affairs Commissions, an amendment to the Criminal Code approved by the All-Russian Central Executive Committee in October 1922 further reduced their competence. More specifically, the new wording granted *courts* the sole authority to decide in each instance whether they or commissions would hear cases of children fourteen and fifteen years old. These provisions of the Criminal Code and the October amendment, rather than a significant abatement of crime, appear to account for most of the sharp drop in the number of youths coming before commissions in 1922. More now traveled straight to the courts.[51]

Meanwhile, Narkompros petitioned the All-Russian Central Executive Committee to repeal the October amendment. Among the agency's arguments numbered a reminder that the courts possessed only a handful of juvenile institutions (administered at the time by the Commissariat of Internal Affairs) to which they could sentence the tens of thousands of adolescents now destined by the Criminal Code to appear before them. Either an expensive network of detention facilities would have to be constructed—a most unlikely development—or courts would sentence minors to confinement in regular prisons cheek by jowl with adult criminals. Habits and skills acquired here would likely remain beyond the ken of rehabilitation programs. Appeals along these lines may well have struck home, for in July 1923 Narkompros's commissions regained the responsibility stripped from them by the previous year's amendment to the Criminal Code.[52]

By no means every local commission, court, and police force followed nimbly, or at all, the series of legal changes sketched above. Even when agencies learned of the latest guidelines and attempted to implement them, they often lacked instructions or resources adequate to insure uniform application from one district to the next. More than a few officials regarded vagrant adolescents as hopeless criminals, "morally defective" and impossible to salvage, who deserved the same treatment as adult thieves. Authorities who shared this view sometimes refused to recognize the competence of Juvenile Affairs Commissions and locked up underage offenders in prisons and labor camps. In contrast, others flooded commissions with delinquents at the first opportunity, apparently seeking to shift the burden of feeding and supervising them onto different shoulders.[53] A minority of commissions behaved much like courts themselves and referred to their decisions—including fines, forced labor, and imprisonment—as "sentences." To mark major holidays, a few granted early release through amnesties similar to those accorded adult criminals. This, Narkompros superiors complained, made no sense if one supposed that the children had been placed in settings designed to provide a healthy upbringing.[54]

Once a boy (rarely a girl) appeared before a commission, its members were to discuss his background and the case's particulars in order to select a suitable course of rehabilitation. As shown in table 2, the action taken was often nothing more than a conversation, reprimand, or the youth's placement with relatives. Unregenerate offenders (including most veteran street children) found themselves routed to institutions or transferred to the courts.[55] The data for 1922 reveal that courts received nearly a fifth of all cases, reflecting (temporarily) the terms of the new Criminal Code and its October amendment.

The three members (representatives from Narkompros and the commissariats of health and justice) who made up a Juvenile Affairs Commission could not themselves assemble pertinent information on all cases

TABLE 2 DISPOSITION OF CASES HANDLED
BY JUVENILE AFFAIRS COMMISSIONS IN
THE RUSSIAN REPUBLIC
(% of All Cases Decided)

	1921	1922	1923	First half of 1924
Conversation or reprimand	26.5	23.9	25.4	28.6
Place under supervision of a social worker	6.2	3.3	4.5	4.6
Place under supervision of parents or relatives	14.8	11.4	13.7	16.3
Dispatch to home region	3.6	1.6	2.4	2.1
Place in a job	2.8	1.7	1.6	1.1
Place in a *detdom*	4.0	4.2	7.2	5.9
Place in a *detdom* for "morally defective" youths	5.8	7.2	12.5	8.6
Transfer case to the courts	7.1	18.8	11.9	9.7
Halt proceedings	26.6	26.4	18.4	20.1
Other measures	2.6	1.5	2.4	3.0
TOTAL	100.0	100.0	100.0	100.0

SOURCE: V. I. Kufaev, *Bor'ba s pravonarusheniiami nesovershennoletnikh* (Moscow, 1924), 13.

and supervise the implementation of decisions reached in their hearings. For support, they were expected to rely on social workers, as explained in the previous chapter. Many Narkompros offices, however, especially at the district level, lacked funds to provide such personnel, thereby reducing the number of cases commissions could handle and the effectiveness of their rulings. In these straits, commission members relied on their own efforts or cast about for assistance from the Children's Social Inspection, the police, and recruits from the ranks of schoolteachers, Komsomol members, and officials in local soviets. Most people thus enlisted had to perform their new tasks on top of prior obligations and without extra pay—not a recipe for swift, enthusiastic work.[56] Apart from this, commissions here and there were crippled by the frequent turnover and poor quality of their own members. Some provincial offices of the three commissariats ranked work with juvenile delinquents low among their responsibilities and shunted less able employees to commissions. These factors, and severe budget cutbacks brought by the New

Economic Policy to Narkompros branches, idled local commissions on occasion for weeks and even months.[57]

Nevertheless, many commissions, especially those in large cities, met regularly—roughly twice a week on average for the country as a whole and nearly every day in Moscow—hearing hundreds or thousands of cases in a year.[58] But even the most efficient, well-staffed commission sometimes found its work frustrated by the inadequate number of institutions to which offenders could be sent for rehabilitation. In fact, "inadequate" appeared too generous a characterization in numerous regions, where no *detdoma* at all existed for the "morally defective."[59] As a result, commission members frequently found themselves forced to adopt measures they regarded as inappropriate for the individual before them. If a child required placement in an institution, and no facility contained an opening, what could they do? This quandary goes far in explaining the large percentage of youths dismissed with merely a reprimand or channeled to relatives or home provinces. Some commissions also turned to the opposite extreme among their options and disposed of cases by shunting them to the courts.[60] Juveniles so transferred, in other words, included not only those deemed incorrigible but candidates considered suitable for Narkompros's custody, if only the appropriate institutions were available.

After reaching the courts, adolescents sentenced to "deprivation of freedom" were generally expected to spend this period in labor homes (*trudovye doma*) intended exclusively for minors and administered by the commissariats of justice (until 1922) and internal affairs (through the remainder of the decade).[61] There appear to have been three labor homes functioning in or near Moscow, Petrograd, and Saratov in 1921, joined by a fourth in Irkutsk the following year. The intended total capacity of these facilities—531 youths—far exceeded the number actually housed, 310, owing to shortages of equipment and supplies. By 1923, published lists included three more locations, adding the cities of Khar'kov, Kiev, and Kazan' to the four earlier sites. Thereafter the number of institutions continued to grow slowly, reaching ten by 1926–1927, with a joint capacity of 1,883.[62] This handful of structures could not begin to accommodate the thousands of delinquents nurtured by the country's misfortunes, and courts found no alternative but to send young offenders to prison. In 1922, approximately three-quarters of all children deprived of freedom landed in regular penal facilities rather than in labor homes. Even Juvenile Affairs Commissions occasionally consigned teenagers to prisons, despite legal prohibitions.[63]

Youths sentenced to prison were to remain isolated from adult inmates in order to avoid the grownups' unsavory influence. In theory, sections of prisons shielded by this quarantine might then function much like labor homes. But the reality of prison life subverted partitions in most facilities, and children mingled with other convicts.[64] Whatever else a boy acquired in this environment, it was not rehabilitation. Viewed by older prisoners as a *golets, plashketa, shket,* or *margaritka*—all underworld terms denoting an uninitiated and vulnerable individual, ripe for plucking—he likely suffered numerous rapes in their domain.[65] He also learned from a ready corps of instructors the criminal world's thieving techniques, language, and diversions. While he may have entered prison relatively unscarred, forced by hunger to take up petty thievery, he walked out of the institution in all probability a more formidable practitioner of the craft that had led originally to his confinement.[66] Thereafter, especially if he lacked relatives able and willing to support him, the imperatives of survival pulled him back among the *besprizornye.* He returned to them, however, with a new store of knowledge (and possibly venereal disease) to pass on to those less experienced, whom he beheld in much the same light as adult convicts had appraised him in prison. Regardless of his transgressions prior to incarceration, a more hardened criminal now faced society, as chronicled by street children in song.

> My first term in prison didn't last long:
> Nothing but a third of a year.
> And when I came out to freedom,
> There was no one I did fear.[67]

No impression emerges more starkly from a survey of the state's early efforts to cope with abandoned youths than a picture of agencies confronting a task far beyond their means. The plans begun in 1918 for rehabilitating the country's already considerable population of homeless juveniles were shattered and swept away by the torrent of waifs, which rose relentlessly each year. As the number of children's institutions swelled in response, conditions inside them deteriorated to a level that one journal labeled "primeval chaos."[68] Sources routinely described receivers and *detdoma* in which education and training had given way entirely to, at best, temporary survival.[69] When the crisis receded, Narkompros found itself presiding over a network of mostly squalid facilities where few activities seemed both so urgent and unpromising as rehabilitation. Scrutinizing this landscape at the beginning of 1923, an author in one of the agency's journals wondered if *any* solution existed to the problem and worried that a bleak future on the edge of society awaited Narkompros's wards.[70] In the months to come, the quest for remedies stoked a debate on how best to proceed—from which there soon arose a call for sweeping reform of *detdoma*, based in turn on a reassessment of the *besprizornye* themselves.

THE STREET WORLD

❖ ❖ ❖ ❖

1.   A waif noticed by American Red Cross personnel as she wandered through Irkutsk's freight yards in 1919.

2. American Red Cross
representatives in Siberia
during the Civil War
encountered this homeless
girl, who approached
them with the words
"Please help my brother!"

3. A homeless girl with
her infant brother in
Siberia during the Civil
War.

4–7. Homeless youths photographed at large around the Soviet Union.

8. A street girl in Moscow featured on the cover of an émigré publication.

9. Waifs seeking refuge in a vacant shed.

10. A boy discovered in a haystack outside Saratov.

11. A pair at the mouth of their burrow near Khar'kov (where they lived before entering an institution).

12. A group huddled for warmth in a garbage bin.

13. Two pictures spliced together—each showing children discovered living in a dump.

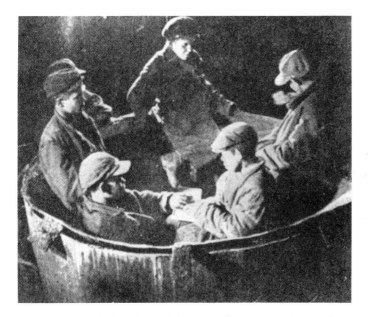

14. Accommodations in a caldron used by construction workers during the day to melt asphalt.

15. A boy observed living in a den of adult thieves in Saratov.

16–17. Four young travelers in their "berths" underneath trains.

18. A beggar.

19. A scuffle over begging receipts.

20–23. Drawings by former *besprizornye* in Khar'kov showing street children stealing luggage from a train car (fig. 20), belongings of people sleeping overnight in a station (fig. 21), produce and the contents of a pocket (fig. 22), and cigarettes (fig. 23).

24–26. Groups of waifs playing cards, a favorite pastime among those accustomed to the street. The trio in figure 24 is perched on top of a train.

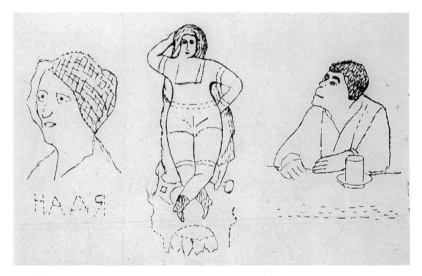

27.   Patterns for tattoos worn by children at the Moscow Labor Home.

RESPONSES TO THE PROBLEM

❖ ❖ ❖ ❖

ПОМОГИТЕ НАЙТИ ДЕТЕЙ!

1. Андрусова Анна Терентьевна 10 л. В 1921 г. была в Харькове, теперь не числится.
2. Афанасьев Василий Сергеев. 15 л. Сам. г.
3. Борисов Самошин Александр. 12 л., скрылся из Ульяновск. д-д. 14-VIII т. г.
4. Башчатов Дмитрий Павлов. 14 л.
5. Беликов Николай Мих. 15 л. - ушел из дому (г. Подольск., Моск. г.) осенью т г.
6. Великонваненко Григорий Тихонов. 12 л.
7. Гайзиенко: Матрена 12 л., Мария 8 л., Гордей 11 л. из Актюбинска.
8. Грушко (Кузьменко) Константин 13 л. Петров Исчез 3 мес. назад. Школьник. Единств. сын. Ищут родители.
9. Геренберг Александра Ив., была в Свердловск. д-д.
10. Городничевы: Иван и Прасковья, Сталингр. губ. Ищет Ком. Кр. Охр. Взаимопом.
11. Геращечко Григорий Серг. 16 л.— ушел из дому в феврале т. г. Ищут родители.
12. Град-блянские: Иван 12 л., Владимир 10 л. Семенов., из Сибири.
13. Глотов Мирон Трофим. 12 л., Сталино—ищет мать.
14. Ефимов-Жадовский Алексей Яков. В 22 г. отправл. из Самары эшал. № 13, ищет мать, потерявшая в гол. годы всех родства.
15. Зарицкий Владимир Фед. (м. б. Иван Ф.) 13 л., исчез из села. из дому родит., в августе т. г.
16. Коровин Нестор Нестор., Самарск. губ.
17. Кузнецов (Заводов), г. рожд. 1921, Михаил Адр., ищет отец, красноарм.
18. Киндяковы: Дарья 14 л., Ульяна 5 л., Илья 12 л., ищет сестра Ирина.
19. Ляхин Владимир 6 л., ушел из дому (Днепропетровск) в августе т. г.
20. Любченко Серафима 15 л. Мария 13 л. Ив., были в Киеве; в окр.ДДсе не значатся.
21. Логинов Константин 13 л.

22. Мамаев Александр, из Полтавы. ищет отец.
23. Морозов Константин Ив. (г. р. 1909), ищет отец.
24. Малюк Василий Антонович 8 л. Артемовск.
25. Мозоль Виктор 13 л., Ольга 15 л. Карпов, Николаев, ищет дед, П. Г. Данилов.
26. Петрух Евдокия Михайл. 11 л., Актюбинск.
27. Пашков Михаил Семенович 15 л., Уральск.
28. Плесюковы: Феодора 17 л., Афанасия 14 л., Ефросинья 12 л., Владимир 9 л. в 22 г. были в Харькове.
29. Петращенко Анна Ионовна 11 л., Мелитоп. окр. — ищет мать, работница Ново-Смол. рудника.
30. Славин Иван Серг. 16 л., ушел из дому 4-VIII т. г.
31. Самойловы: Анна и Максим Яковл., Пенза.
32. Собукарь: Анна (г. р. 1912), Илла Иванов (1914), Иван (1916). Анастасия (1920) Иванов. В 22 г. были в Харькове. В окр. ДДсе не числятся.
33. Толмачев Матвей Петров., Днепро-петр. р-н.
34. Тараненко Ольга Алексеевна: потер. в 21 г. в пути ст. Крым—Лозовая.
35. Уваровы: Наталия 13 л., Феофил 12 л Иванов., Гроднеиск. губ.
36. Фирсов Николай 16 л.— исчез 1 мая тек г.
37. Чельтер Иван и Дмитрий Пантел., близнецы, г. р. 1907. Днепропетровск.
38. Шпегель Емилия 11 л., Ерна 10 л., Рудольф 8 л., потерялись в 22 г. в пути Сибирь - Украина.
39. Шендюшевы: Прасковья 13 л., Ти хон 10 л., Елена 6 л.; в 1922 г. были в Харьк ве; в окр ДДсе не числятся.
40. Шехтер Борис Мотел. 8 л, в 1921 г был в Крымопольской д-д. Тульчин. окр. дом расформирован.
41. Янкова Анастасия Алексеевна 17 л потер. в 22 г. в мест. Смелы (Смелое).

ИЩУТ РОДИТЕЛЕЙ

1. Бывш. воспит. д. д., работающие в Изюмск. мастерских:
   а) Денисенко Иван Данил.—ищет мать Харитину и Николая, Василия и Евдокию Денисенковых.
   б) Дуанна Лидия Алексеев. 16 л.— ищет родных, потеряла их из виду в 1920 г., в г. Брянске

2. Гребенков Никита Тихонов. (раб. на южн. жел. дор.) ищет: мать, Дарью Аки мовну, брата Семена, сестру Евдокию Потерял связь в 1921 г. в Харьковск. губ.

3. Воспит. д-трудкол. им. Петровского Ганна Болжина ищет брата, Максима Степан. Болжина, работающ. в шахтах.

28. A published list of vanished children, similar to many other rosters issued in certain periodicals during the 1920s. The title reads: "Help Find the Children!" A much shorter list of youths searching for parents and other relatives follows at the bottom of the page.

29. A poster issued in 1922 as part of a public campaign to achieve the goal proclaimed in the placard's title: "Not a Single *Besprizornyi* in the USSR!"

30. A postage stamp sold to raise money for aiding
besprizornye. The spiraling banner proclaims:
"Children are the builders of the future."

31.   Street boys at an asphalt caldron. This drawing (with varying captions) appeared from time to time in the newspaper *Izvestiia* as part of a long-running effort to involve citizens in the struggle to eliminate juvenile homelessness. The title reads: "Remember the *besprizornye*!" The caption below adds: "Assistance to *besprizornye* is the obligation of each Soviet citizen."

32.   Policemen marching off a group of Moscow's *besprizornye* in 1918.

33–34. Groups of street children just after their roundup in Zaporozh'e
(fig. 33) and Khar'kov (fig. 34).

Сеть первичн
учреждений д
беспризорнь
на Украине в
ширится
нашем сним
группа дете
подобранн
с улицы и г
мещенных в
члежку е г
Запорожье.

35. Abandoned offspring (evidently gathered up already by officials) waiting in a train station.

36. Initial processing of boys removed from the street.

37–38. Haircuts were a common measure taken against lice. The group in figure 37 has lined up outside a train dispatched during the famine to provide medical care and food.

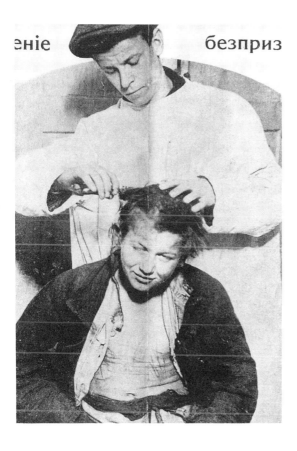

INSTITUTIONS

❖ ❖ ❖ ❖

39. Children and staff at a *detdom* established with resources from the secret police in the Kuban'.

40. A lesson in the secret police's labor commune at Bolshevo.

41.   Reading at an unidentified institution for *besprizornye*.

42.   A clinic for juvenile cocaine users from the street.

43. A carpentry workshop at an institution for "difficult" children in Ivanovo-Voznesensk.

44–45. Scenes from an excursion to the Crimea undertaken in 1930 by Anton Makarenko's Dzerzhinskii labor commune. The commune's photography club produced the pictures.

46. Another group of Makarenko's charges on excursion in the Crimea (year unspecified).

47. Residents of Makarenko's Gorky colony (at Trepke) working on a ditch used to store potatoes.

48. Members of the Dzerzhinskii commune clearing the road to their institution.

49. Residents posing in the Gorky colony's courtyard (at Kuriazh).

50. Pupils in one of the Dzerzhinskii commune's classrooms.

Florists and Professors

There must not be deprived and homeless children in the
republic. Let there be young and happy citizens.

Vladimir Lenin

If you read sometime about the condition of our "pedagogic
institutions" for *besprizornye*, your hair would stand on end.

Nikolai Bukharin

By 1923 the famine had subsided, and emergency assistance agencies set
about winding down their operations. Leaders in Moscow, and no
doubt much of the remaining population, expressed relief that the worst
of the horror had passed. But the problem of abandoned juveniles remained stubbornly at hand, both in the streets and in the teeming *detdoma*. Lunacharskii and other Narkompros officials called urgently in
1923–1924 for a drive to rescue homeless youths and joined the authors
of numerous books, articles, and hortatory slogans in prophesying calamity if the effort failed. The most ominous danger appeared to loom
in the guise of a thief, as observers pondered the prospect of desperate
adolescents acquiring instincts and skills that would steer them by the
million to lifelong crime. Campaigns to focus public attention on their
plight included such slogans as: "*Besprizornost'* in childhood means
criminals as adults" and "*Besprizornost'* begets crime." "If we do not
build schools and shelters for them," one author concluded, "we will
be forced to build prisons for them later." Even the poet Vladimir Mayakovsky, scarcely an avatar of decorum, worried that street children
represented a "limitless source of hooligans."[1] Aside from tomorrow's
criminals, young vagabonds were often portrayed as a potentially malignant cancer within the new generation expected to shape a better
society. Those pursuing the medical analogy most literally claimed that
waifs' unsanitary, itinerant existence rendered them prime transmitters
of infectious diseases. Others, fearing contamination on a different

plane, warned that the youths' adventuresome life could entice unsupervised, "normal" boys and girls. "Struggling with *besprizornost'*," proclaimed a slogan, "we save our own children."[2]

As speeches, slogans, and publications paraded the dire consequences of juvenile homelessness through Narkompros and before the public, many people both in and out of government recognized that the past five years of struggle on this front had not yielded heartening results. Something clearly had to be done, given the peril associated with failure, but what? Erect more *detdoma*? The cold reality of budgetary restrictions paralyzed such plans. In any case a chorus of voices, centered in Narkompros and broadcast most powerfully through the agency's publications, rose by 1924 to question even the existing array of institutions. It was not an issue of numbers—though more buildings, of course, would be better than fewer. Reformers demanded instead a fresh look at the *operation* of facilities, based in turn on a rejection of common assumptions about street children.[3]

In particular, they showered criticism on the concept of "moral defectiveness" (*moral'no-defektivnost'*)—the view that long-term vagrancy and delinquency resulted primarily from a child's own psychological defects rather than from outside influences.[4] The issue represented part of a larger debate that continued to ricochet through much of the 1920s among Soviet criminologists, legal theorists, and others. Controversies flared over such topics as the causes of crime and the character of offenders—questions that often boiled down to disputes over human nature. Regarding the roots of criminal behavior, for example, one school blamed genetic disorders or other innate personal qualities rather than external circumstances. Opponents insisted that deviance arose not from congenital flaws but from unfavorable living conditions. Improve a person's surroundings, they advised, and antisocial traits would no longer appear indelible.[5]

Among those concerned with the treatment of juveniles, the second, or "environmental," outlook rose to prominence. Enthusiastic applause punctuated a debate at the First Moscow Conference on the Struggle with *Besprizornost'* in March 1924, when a participant remarked that anyone who clung to the doctrine of "moral defectiveness" suffered from "scholarly defectiveness."[6] After spirited discussion, the conference rejected the theory of "moral defectiveness," though this hardly ended dispute. The theory's defenders, dubbed the "Leningrad professors" because several scholars among them were based in Leningrad, crossed swords repeatedly at conferences and in print with reformers known as

"Moscow florists" (from the slogan "Children are the flowers of life."). While "florists" gained the upper hand in the controversy—especially in central organs of Narkompros, its principal publications, and numerous provincial branches—the notion that many homeless juveniles were "morally defective" proved impossible to eradicate among teachers, scholars, and the general population.[7]

The "florists" tried, however. Time and again in the middle years of the decade they contended that grievous social and economic forces accounted for nearly all instances of children wandering at large and committing crimes. An inclination to shift blame to the youths struck them as typical of bourgeois scholarship and capitalist society, which, in their opinion, demonstrated no interest in assisting the downtrodden. The admittedly antisocial demeanor of numerous urchins sprang not from inherently twisted personalities, they asserted, but from the harsh setting into which they had been swept by currents beyond their control. Inveterate psychopaths stemmed no more frequently from the street than from the "normal" population, proclaimed a resolution adopted by the Moscow conference.[8] The very phrase "juvenile crime" was an oxymoron. Hardship might impel its young victims to violate the law, but this did not make them criminals. "There are *no* child criminals," announced a slogan prepared for public display; "there *are* sick and neglected children."[9]

Many authors went further, insisting that while street life encouraged various undesirable habits, it also nurtured virtues. As noted in chapter 3, these alleged boons included boldness, resourcefulness, perceptiveness, a collectivist spirit developed from living in groups, and even a dislike for prosperous, bourgeois elements of society. Institutional personnel who counted their charges as "morally defective" thus remained oblivious to the potential supposedly acquired in the austere arena outside. Instead, a critic fumed, they behaved as if confronting incorrigible criminals or the mentally ill, thereby rendering ineffective a "whole mass of institutions for *besprizornye*" prior to 1924. The staff of a properly run *detdom*, the argument concluded, employed an understanding of waifs' true nature to strip away their coarse veneer and cultivate the worthy qualities sprouted in hothouse fashion by their previous struggle for survival.[10] Viewed in this light, homeless youths shed the label of "lost children," immune to rehabilitation. "We regard the *besprizornyi* as a child of the Revolution," a Komsomol delegate informed the Moscow conference. "If he is approached correctly, he can become an active builder of a socialist state."[11]

Despite such revelations, reformers complained, many *detdoma* continued to treat residents as embittered, irredeemable spirits beyond the reach of pedagogy—in short, as "morally defective" inmates. Resolutions repudiating the theory of "moral defectiveness" meant little if they failed to stir these institutions—which were said in some cases to resemble prisons "still awaiting their own October Revolution."[12] Partisans of change (sounding much like today's critics of juvenile penal colonies in Russia) attacked the common practice of isolating youths from the community, the policy of "closed doors." They argued that high walls and barred windows, adopted under the assumption that those inside were "morally defective," ostracized the inhabitants and hindered their reintegration into society. Reformers also judged disciplinary measures employed in numerous *detdoma* as excessively harsh and likely to drive children further from rehabilitation. Common punishments—especially in the provinces but also encountered in Moscow and Leningrad—included deprivation of food or recreation, isolation in a separate room for as long as a few days, removal of an offender's clothes, icy showers, extra work assignments, and beatings. Consensus regarding appropriate means of discipline never emerged—as was evident at a conference of personnel from institutions for difficult juveniles, held in November 1925—and even reformers did not always agree where, short of corporal punishment, to draw the line.[13] But they did concur that severe methods yielded little but disappointment. Despite the bars, locks, and guards at institutions for hardened delinquents, thousands fled every year. Even those who remained, critics emphasized, often emerged alienated, untrained for available jobs, and destined once again for the criminal world.[14]

What, then, was to be done? Mass homelessness had transformed the nature of *detdoma*. The primary role first envisioned for these facilities following the Revolution—that of providing an upbringing for any and all children of working parents—now appeared a dream for the remote future. In the meantime, the structures bulged with indigent and sometimes hostile youths, many unintimidated by compulsion and rigid discipline.[15] Facing this reality, Narkompros reformers issued detailed instructions, both from Moscow and in provincial journals, on the proper operation of institutions engaged first and foremost in the rehabilitation of abandoned, difficult, but not "morally defective" juveniles.[16]

First of all, official documents and individual authors urged that *detdoma* encourage healthy contact between their wards and the society they were to enter upon discharge. Adolescents had to learn how to participate productively and eagerly in life, reformers declared, not glimpse it sullenly from behind bars. An institution secured only peda- gogic bankruptcy by relying on "closed doors" to retain occupants.[17] Narkompros instructed local officials to open these doors by removing schools from inside *detdoma* and sending youths to attend regular schools side by side with other pupils. Where possible, children were also to visit nearby workshops, factories, and state farms for at least a portion of their labor training. If such options did not exist, thereby requiring *detdoma* to maintain their own schools and workshops, con- tact could still be established with society by opening these facilities to boys and girls from the neighborhood.[18]

At the same time, Narkompros called with greater insistence for many other activities to supplement classroom instruction, both inside and beyond the walls of *detdoma*. These pursuits included circles and clubs (science, reading, drawing, drama, music, hobbies, and the like), in- volvement with communist youth groups, and extended summertime excursions to camps at natural attractions. The endeavors were said to provide fresh opportunities for social and political education, as well as promote the policy of "open doors." They would also spice the routine of institutional life, dissuading the restless from escape.[19] Toward the objective of maintaining *detdoma* without bars and locks, many Nar- kompros documents in the middle of the decade stressed more vigor- ously than before that residents be made to feel a part of their institu- tions through participation in "self-government." This usually meant at a minimum the organization of groups to assume responsibility for daily chores, while more ambitious efforts centered on meetings (run, at least nominally, by the children themselves) to discuss house operations, emergencies, and disciplinary matters. Reformers regarded condemna- tion of offenders by their own "collective" as preferable to punishment imposed by the staff. A firm adult hand might be necessary temporarily, when most inhabitants had just arrived from the street, but discipline maintained by youths themselves represented the goal as "collectives" matured.[20]

Of all the improvements desired for *detdoma*, none received as much emphasis as expanded labor training in workshops and fields. Work- shops in particular were often depicted as the heart and soul of *detdoma*, the feature that most distinguished them from prerevolutionary shelters and flophouses. Reformers claimed that the shops nurtured a healthy labor psychology—namely, good work habits and a respect for manual labor—essential in preparing adolescents to join the proletariat. Facilities that produced goods for sale in local markets also helped cement relations with the surrounding community while securing additional income for *detdoma*. Finally, by providing skills (metalworking, leatherworking, carpentry, and so on) with which juveniles could later support themselves as adults, workshops offered homeless children a clear hope for the future and an incentive to remain in *detdoma*.[21]

Official zeal for workshops rose in part from the reforms favored by many Bolsheviks and their supporters for schools in general. In the early postrevolutionary years, Narkompros insisted that arid, bookish rigidity—seen as characteristic of tsarist schools—give way to a curriculum featuring "socially productive labor." The nation's students would then accrue essential academic skills, including the three R's, while engaged in diverse projects that took them outside the classroom. Even theoretical fields were thought more accessible to pupils steeped in practical work than to those who remained all day behind desks. As youths progressed through their school years, they would receive broad polytechnic training to ready them for flexible and productive lives in a modern industrial society whose features could not yet be fully divined. Moreover, asserted the *ABC of Communism*, they would learn "to look upon labour, not as a disagreeable necessity or as a punishment, but as a natural and spontaneous expression of faculty. Labour should be a need, like the desire for food and drink; this need must be instilled and developed in the communist school."[22] "Indeed," explained a treatise titled *The Unified Labor School*, "the wise and experienced teacher cannot help but notice that for these three questions: how to form the child's will, how to mold character, how to develop a spirit of solidarity, the answer is one magic word—labor."[23] Such exertion, in other words, did far more than train hands; it shaped the identity of a socialist citizenry.

If so, the argument for labor training applied with special urgency to street children. The point had been made before, but reformers turned spotlights on it in the middle of the decade. Who stood more in need of labor's civilizing touch, they asked, than the *besprizornye*? Unfortunately, the difficult years just past had prevented most *detdoma* from acquiring equipment and instructors to establish proper workshops. The desperate quest for food, clothing, and medical care exhausted resources and rendered labor training a secondary concern. In the aftermath, as the flood of orphans slowly ebbed, this shortcoming proved difficult to overcome. Investigators surveying *detdoma* found the room for improvement of labor instruction to be far more substantial than resources necessary for progress. Where shops existed at all, they often lacked equipment and staffs to do anything but occupy children with the most primitive handicrafts—skills unlikely to provide passage from the street.[24]

The gap between goals and reality vexed reformers wherever they turned. Some *detdoma* appeared to be operating properly, either in response to instructions from Moscow or on the basis of methods developed independently, but more establishments persisted with minimal labor training, harsh punishments, and "closed doors."[25] When a facility with "open doors" encountered difficulty managing its charges, the setback emboldened skeptics to proclaim reform "reckless and harmful sentimentalism." At conferences and in the field, voices could still be heard insisting on stricter discipline. " 'Open doors,' " a critic asserted in 1926, "in no way give an institution any sort of special significance regarding upbringing. They lead only to corruption in every sense, if they are adopted in institutions containing youths with antisocial tendencies."[26] Thus in the middle of the decade, though instructions for change crowded conferences and publications, the desired improvements remained far less evident in *detdoma*. "Florists" found their tussle with "professors" a mere skirmish compared to the challenges beyond.

Even the most optimistic reformer likely recognized that central and local budgets would not soon relinquish funds to support accommodations for all abandoned juveniles. This reality spurred various Narkompros bodies, notably the State Scientific Council, to advocate "halfway" institutions designed to provide something short of full-time room, board, and instruction.[27] In 1923–1924 night shelters (*nochlezhki*, not to be confused with flophouses of the same name that required payment and catered mainly to adults) were established for street children in many cities, especially as the approaching winter drove larger numbers to seek asylum from the elements. If *detdoma* could not absorb all candidates, in other words, some could turn to night shelters for temporary sanctuary from the worst rigors of their environment.[28]

The shelters were envisioned not only as a less expensive alternative to other institutions, but as a means of enticing the obstinate and wary to take a first small step off the street. They could come every night, if they wished, or only intermittently. At any rate, they were not to be rounded up and brought against their will. If they violated a facility's rules, they might be denied the evening meal and expelled, but they would not be hauled to institutions for delinquents. To a degree, shelters resembled receivers in that they were designed to receive youths directly from a brutalizing world, introduce them to rudimentary education, and eventually send them (voluntarily, in the case of shelters) to permanent institutions for rehabilitation.[29] Before long, some shelters began to operate daytime divisions, hoping thereby to wean children entirely from the street by offering them each morning an alternative to train stations and markets. Activities—drama clubs, reading circles, literacy training, and simple workshops—remained voluntary, though house rules required typically that one participate for a stipulated number of hours in order to receive lunch. Where these daytime operations emerged, they further enhanced the similarity between shelters and receivers, sometimes to the point where significant differences vanished altogether.[30]

As expected, a large share of those who frequented shelters came from the street's hard core. They had escaped repeatedly from other institutions and were long accustomed to life in seamy quarters of town. According to a study of two hundred juveniles who passed through a certain Moscow shelter in 1924–1925, approximately 40 percent had already roamed the land for over three years.[31] When they entered shelters, they brought their mores with them and frustrated the facilities' work. Investigators discovered ragged, lice-covered urchins of all ages crowded together in filthy rooms, obscured by clouds of their own cigarette smoke. Many departed periodically to engage in thievery and other exploits unscheduled by Narkompros. Veterans commonly entered in groups—the same gangs in which they lived outside—and their leaders sometimes sabotaged the plans of an institution's staff. Even in the absence of gangs, experienced youths routinely beat the new or feeble and seized their clothing. In some facilities, gambling and cocaine enjoyed much wider appeal than workshops and clubs. The Moscow study found approximately one-third of the sample to be long-term cocaine users, and other accounts confirm that such children saw no reason to abandon the practice in shelters.[32]

Thus, numerous shelters resembled an extension of the street more than a stepping-stone away from it. Not all youths disrupted regimens, but even the docile could prove difficult to work with because of their physical and emotional debilitation. An observer described children in a Moscow shelter as emaciated wraiths, with sunken eyes encased in enormous black circles, gazing about with "a sort of senile expression." Shriveled black rootlets protruded from the gums of those who had already lost their teeth.[33] While some shelters managed eventually to steer 40–50 percent of their visitors to other institutions, the nature of the juveniles they courted made this an achievement that few facilities could surpass.[34] Vagrant life did not surrender readily its favorite apprentices.

Night shelters were the most ambitious "halfway" institutions of the period, but they shared some of the street's brood with others, notably daytime playgrounds set up in parks, squares, and vacant lots during the year's warm months. Much like shelters, playgrounds were intended to attract homeless and other unsupervised youths voluntarily, by offering a meal, games, excursions, and crafts. The staff hoped to gain newcomers' confidence, erode their bond with the street, and eventually convince them to enter institutions or at least to spend the night in shelters.[35] Confronting an often troublesome clientele, shelters and playgrounds deserve credit for guiding *any* children (certainly several thousand over the years) out of slums and down the road to a productive life. But it must be stressed that these facilities never multiplied to admit (let alone win over) more than a small percentage of abandoned juveniles. They remained modest projects to retrieve some of the neglected and alienated who had not settled in Narkompros's much larger network of *detdoma*.

By 1923–1924 it was clear that the solution to the problem of street children lay in something more than scooping them up for delivery to receivers and *detdoma*. Thousands had already traveled this route repeatedly, each time running away to their familiar haunts. Such discouraging results encouraged experiment with alternative approaches, and none more fully embodied the reformers' spirit than the labor commune (*trudovaia kommuna*).[36] Here was an institution organized in the belief that even the most belligerent adolescent could be rehabilitated—indeed, an institution intended *especially* for teenage delinquents, many of whom had prowled the streets for years. While some might regard prison as the only place for these ruffians, communes faced them having disavowed traditional measures of control, including "closed doors" and harsh punishments. Instead, supporters predicted, youths and staff would work together as comrades.[37]

The most striking difference between *detdom* and commune, a feature heralded tirelessly by the latter's champions, was the principle of voluntary entry and departure. Children were to join only if they so desired, and they could leave if disenchantment overcame them subsequently.[38] Ideally, they would emulate a group that formed the initial nucleus of the Rosa Luxemburg Labor Commune, established on the outskirts of Moscow in 1924. Late one night in February, a social worker (accompanied by a policeman) descended into a tunnel leading under the Alexander Station. Among the adult criminals and tramps ensconced in the basement, she found a group of nine boys, some of whom had been living on the premises for years. Several had passed more than once through Juvenile Affairs Commissions and on to *detdoma*—from which they always fled back to the station. Calming them with assurances that they did not face another roundup that night, the social worker described a labor commune and asked them merely to think about the opportunities available there. On subsequent visits in weeks thereafter, she continued the discussion with this group, suggesting that they consider such an undertaking. Eventually, after their leader and a few other lads inspected a proposed site, the group agreed to embark on the venture.[39]

In addition to voluntary entry and departure, labor communes were expected to devote particular emphasis to practices promoted by reformers for *detdoma*, most notably "self-government" and labor training. As indicated previously, "self-government" (and "self-service") meant that children were to assume responsibility for daily chores and participate in the commune's general assembly to run the institution. Treated as full-fledged partners and sustained by a sense of control over their lives, they would bear no resemblance to the bitter, unruly inmates of other facilities.[40] Nor would they lounge about the grounds, as the name *labor* commune suggests. Even more than in *detdoma*, instruction in workshops or in nearby factories and state farms represented the key to rehabilitation. Benefits thought to derive from labor in any institution—access to a profession, self-respect, and a sense of solidarity with other workers—seemed to be urgent requirements for commune members. Their difficult nature and the fact that, as teenagers, they would soon be discharged to support themselves made training for workbench and field the first priority.[41]

Communes appeared here and there in 1923 and then mushroomed to such a degree that, by the end of the following year, they had lost the quality of puzzling curiosities.[42] Some were established on the initiative of social workers and local officials before Narkompros could issue guidelines, which did not circulate in comprehensive form until 1925.[43] Viewed in a broader context, the institutions were a comparatively late, government-inspired manifestation of communal living endeavors that had flourished spontaneously among diverse segments of the population ever since the Revolution. In October's glow and the ensuing adversity of War Communism, groups of students and workers had rushed to pool resources and live in what they took to be the new socialist manner. Communes also sprouted (or were rejuvenated) among people less drawn to socialism—peasants and religious sectarians, for example—who shared nonpersonal property and organized collective living arrangements. Even in the case of sectarians, the Bolsheviks displayed remarkable sympathy for their efforts during the 1920s, often finding in them aspects of a communist lifestyle.[44] Still more attractive, then, seemed the prospect of Narkompros's communes, for they would lack religious or superstitious blemishes associated with communities conceived by sectarians and peasants.

While Narkompros administered the majority of labor communes for *besprizornye*, other agencies, most notably the secret police (OGPU), operated similar facilities of their own. The first OGPU commune (as distinct from the agency's earlier institutions for homeless children) appeared near Moscow in 1924. Dzerzhinskii and some of his colleagues hoped to demonstrate that a suitable atmosphere could salvage even the most unrepentant delinquents—though others in police circles harbored less fervor for the enterprise and referred to the project as their chief's "baby farm." At any rate, more OGPU communes soon followed, and by 1928 the total stood at thirty-five. Best known in the long run was the Dzerzhinskii Labor Commune, established near Khar'kov in 1927 and directed for several years thereafter by Anton Makarenko. In theory, the communes of Narkompros and the OGPU shared basic principles—voluntary entry, "self-government," and extensive labor training—though stricter discipline was generally expected on the part of the OGPU. Its facilities sought the most difficult youths, often recruited from jails. The Rosa Luxemburg Labor Commune, for example, after several months in Narkompros's hands, passed into the OGPU's domain late in 1924 and began to receive juveniles from Moscow's Butyrskaia Prison.[45]

Some communes, of both Narkompros and the OGPU, reportedly enjoyed considerable success. They implemented "self-government," involved members in labor training, and gradually broke the binding spell of life on the street. A number of institutions appear to have retained nearly all their recruits, including those who had previously fled countless *detdoma*.[46] But even descriptions of the most successful communes usually shrank from suggesting that rehabilitation proceeded smoothly. Thefts, gambling, drinking, cocaine use, and fights proved difficult to eradicate and flared up from time to time, especially when a large new contingent arrived from the street or prison. "Self-government" might degenerate into a charade or collapse entirely, and gang leaders could disrupt an institution by continuing to demand the deference and tribute they had customarily enjoyed.[47] Youths in communes located near markets and train stations succumbed on occasion to the lure of these locations and disappeared. Even an article endorsing labor communes as the most suitable place for difficult juveniles acknowledged that, despite the success of a few institutions in retaining their populations, the overall percentage of residents who abandoned communes was "very large."[48] Though information is sketchy, certain ventures clearly failed altogether, torn by mass brawls requiring police intervention or simply disintegrating until adolescents roamed without any supervision.[49]

No less a trademark of communes than the policy of voluntary entry faded rapidly. At a meeting in May 1925 of a subsection of Narkompros's State Scientific Council, a participant remarked: "Labor communes, as a mass institution, have not proven themselves because life has forced the violation of their basic principle—voluntary entry. Now [juveniles] are dispatched to labor communes by force." Instructions sent in October of the same year to provincial Narkompros offices praised the rule of voluntary entry, but then explained that the principle did not mean a youth could be delivered to an institution *only* if he consented. That would be "too facile and narrow" an interpretation, noted the order, because adolescents often had no desire to enter facilities. The document urged tenacious exertion to secure a child's approval, but the clear implication remained that absence of assent need not thwart the routing of new members to communes.[50]

Numerous resolutions and instructions generated by various Narkompros bodies in 1924–1925 favored the reorganization of all *detdoma* (or all institutions for difficult youths) as labor communes.[51] Articles on communes that appeared in Narkompros publications focused almost invariably on the most successful, and the positive impression left by these descriptions encouraged, sometimes explicitly, the transformation of *detdoma* along similar lines. But no such mass reorganization occurred, and it seems plausible to conclude that most, less publicized, communes experienced enough difficulties to eliminate their appeal as models. Had they consistently delivered superior results, nothing would have prevented the recasting of *detdoma* in their image. Whatever the accuracy of this speculation, labor communes never flirted with ubiquity. A work published in 1926 calculated that they housed less than 4 percent of all institutionalized street children, and this share scarcely soared as the decade waned. For better or for worse, the vast majority of these wards (roughly 90 percent, according to the account just mentioned) resided, as before, in *detdoma*.[52]

As Narkompros struggled to reform its children's institutions, many social workers, journalists, and government officials, while praising these efforts, concluded that the task of recovering abandoned boys and girls exceeded the state's capabilities. With the homeless continuing to deplete resources applied by Narkompros and other agencies, publications and official resolutions called more frequently for society as a whole to lend a hand.[53] Apart from individual citizens, the public (*obshchestvennost'*) targeted in these appeals included semiofficial bodies such as trade unions and communist youth groups (the Komsomol and Pioneers), individual factories, institutes, military units, and societies of volunteers devoted to saving destitute juveniles. During the famine, many such people and organizations had strained to provide whatever they could to rescue victims of the catastrophe, but by 1923 the sense of emergency had passed. In addition, the New Economic Policy, by requiring state agencies to support themselves with less subsidization from Moscow, helped dry up contributions from factories and other enterprises.[54] Finally, as some observers alleged, a considerable portion of society may have grown accustomed to young ragamuffins in the streets and accepted the phenomenon with less distress or even contemplation than had been the case a year or two previously. Those who found their attention drawn to the scruffy figures were more likely than during the famine to regard them as scoundrels, whose plight merited no sympathy.[55]

Hence, in the middle of the decade, Narkompros and the Children's Commission redoubled their push to secure assistance from individuals and groups. Books appeared describing the bleak street world, and rebukes stung organizations for their passivity in aiding the homeless.[56] Many newspapers carried fund-raising displays listing recent donors (individuals, Party cells, work units, editorial boards, and so on), followed by names of others who were challenged to respond. In *Izvestiia*, for instance, under the title "Help the *Besprizornyi*," a group of authors called on such colleagues as Alexei Tolstoi, Boris Pil'niak, Vladimir Mayakovsky, Andrei Belyi, and Osip Mandel'shtam to join them in contributing. Some papers ran these appeals with near daily frequency for months. During the first half of 1926, most issues of *Pravda* contained a section urging readers to donate funds for a labor commune, and by late July, when *Pravda* described the commune's opening, gifts totaled nearly 140,000 rubles. From time to time, following the death of well-known personages, the paper listed those who forwent customary wreaths and chose instead to commemorate the deceased by giving money to care for waifs.[57]

The government also encouraged special "weeks" (or, less often, other periods), with the goal of focusing public attention on abandoned children's misfortune. These undertakings—with such titles as "Week of the *Besprizornyi*," "Fortnight of the *Besprizornyi* and Ill Child," and "Week of Aid to *Besprizornye*"—were usually local operations centered in a single city and sometimes projected through the province, though drives occasionally encompassed an entire republic.[58] Bodies in and out of government might share responsibility for implementing a "week"; as a result, the exact array of sponsors varied considerably from place to place. "Society" most often contributed such partners as trade unions, teachers, the Women's Section of the Party, the Komsomol, and volunteer groups formed to aid minors. Less frequently, military units and even boys and girls from *detdoma* participated.[59]

Because promoters of a "week" could choose any number of activities, their plans differed markedly from one region to the next. But even with all the local variations, fund-raising remained a common attribute. Money was solicited from enterprises and collected through the sale of flowers, handicrafts (some made by youths in *detdoma*), special stamps, postcards, pins, emblems, and other petty objects. Slogans usually appeared in public places, rousing the population to make donations. Auctions and lotteries also generated funds, as did special shows featuring plays, movies, music, and other productions for which admission could be charged. Aside from gathering revenue, "weeks" often sought to familiarize society with the misery of street life and explain the problem's importance by means of public lectures, exhibitions, pamphlets, and newspaper articles. Here the aim might extend to recruiting citizens for voluntary organizations in which they could assist state officials. "Only with participation of the entire population," proclaimed a slogan, "can victory be achieved on the long and difficult front of *besprizornost'*." In some cases a "week" included inspections of local *detdoma* and even expeditions to round up homeless juveniles and convey them to institutions.[60]

It is difficult to gauge popular reaction to these appeals. Reports from numerous regions told of workers and officials donating small portions of their pay (either as a single gift or in regular installments over many months) and volunteering to prepare clothing for children in local receivers and *detdoma*. Some organizations, especially Pioneer and Komsomol units, staged shows and contributed extra days of work on weekends to raise money for the cause.[61] Occasionally, a factory, trade union, or military unit gave considerable sums to a nearby institution and even assumed formal responsibility for its material support. Such accords often called as well for the sponsoring organization to carry out periodic inspections of the facility and assist Narkompros with labor training and general upbringing.[62] As improbable a benefactor as the state film agency auditioned some three hundred juveniles fresh from the street and selected twenty for instruction. After a difficult start, during which several trainees fled or displayed little enduring talent, those who persevered set to work producing a children's film.[63]

The labor and resources supplied through these channels by a small minority of citizens spoke well of their devotion to a worthy cause and helped save youths from prolonged vagrancy. At the same time, critics asserted that the public's interest wandered fast on the conclusion of officially orchestrated exhortation. All fell quiet, and the problem remained much as before.[64] A few children's institutions did benefit greatly from local donations, but the overwhelming majority of facilities remained primarily dependent on funds and materiel provided (or not provided) by central and local government bodies.

Apart from money and supplies, Narkompros lacked sufficient personnel, especially social workers out in the street. Most cities, including Moscow, found their branches of the Children's Social Inspection grossly understaffed and unable to work effectively with hundreds or thousands of youths peering from the urban landscape's nooks and crannies. In response, communities around the country recruited groups of "volunteers" (*druzhinniki-dobrovol'tsy*), often from the Komsomol in general and universities in particular, along with participants from trade unions, the Women's Section of the Party, and other organizations. Large numbers were marshaled in this fashion, especially during academic vacations and for special exercises of short duration. Approximately one thousand "volunteers" worked with *besprizornye* in Moscow's streets in 1925, "over eight hundred" in Leningrad the following year, and in 1924 roughly three hundred young people helped conduct a census of homeless children in Saratov.[65]

"Volunteers" assumed, with varying degrees of training and supervision, duties that took them deep into a city's shadows. They helped tally the local street population, usually by groping through shabby sections of town at night when the search's objects were most likely to be in their "dwellings." More routinely, they patrolled markets, stations, and other prime locations, searching for lairs and keeping an eye peeled for new arrivals. Many received instructions to establish contact with veterans of this terrain, win their trust, and coax them into permanent institutions or temporary accommodations such as night shelters.[66] The work naturally entailed certain dangers, for juvenile delinquents, not to mention the adult criminals among whom they commonly lived, rarely summoned enthusiasm at the approach of social workers and census takers. Most often, youths simply vanished into the urban labyrinth they knew so well. But on several reported occasions, similar no doubt to many that went unrecorded, they greeted visitors with barrages of stones.[67]

Citizens also participated in dramatic mass roundups of homeless children conducted repeatedly in cities across the country. On the given day, scores, hundreds, and even thousands of "volunteers" were divided into small groups and assigned to search various districts known to harbor concentrations of their quarry. After receiving instructions, brigades set out—usually at night—to comb train stations, ruined buildings, flop houses, taverns, apartment entryways, dumps, and other promising habitats. In a few instances, boys recently removed from the street helped guide search parties to abodes of cohorts still at large.[68] The objects of a roundup often displayed no inclination to exchange their domiciles for an institution. Many had already fled more than one *detdom* and quickly disappeared into the night as brigades approached. If cornered, they responded with searing obscenities and even violence. The following taunts, dispensed by a youth netted one night, ranked as a comparatively mild expression of defiance.

> —"What is your name?" [asked a social worker].
> —"Ivan, or maybe Aleksei."
> —"And your last name?"
> —"I have forty. I'll say them all if you like. Choose one."
> —"How old are you?"
> —"One thousand! And then some."
> —"Where were you born?"
> —"In Peter [i.e., St. Petersburg]. In the Winter Palace."
> —"Who were your parents?"
> —"Nikolai Romanov. But perhaps someone helped him. I don't remember exactly."[69]

In turn, most brigades devoted little attention to securing the consent of those corralled. Briefings might discourage the use of force, but head-long chases after elusive urchins tended to drain pursuers' patience. Only the most pacific men and women confined themselves to persuasion when steering a struggling, abusive lad to an institution. More likely he was marched off under guard—with hands bound, according to a report from Saratov—and the frequent participation of policemen further in-sured a tone remote from the reformers' spirit.[70] Where possible, chil-dren apprehended in the sweeps were taken to receivers for processing and then dispatched to permanent institutions. But the numbers amassed in a single night, sometimes reaching into the hundreds, often far ex-ceeded the capacities of local primary facilities. In this event, the night's catch waited in any quarters available, including police stations, until they could be moved to more appropriate buildings.[71]

One of the most common vehicles by which citizens joined the effort to aid abandoned minors was the "Friend of Children" Society (*Ob-shchestvo "Drug detei"* or ODD). Formed on the initiative of the Chil-dren's Commission in Moscow and Khar'kov at the end of 1923, ODD soon grew into a nationwide network of cells, with an official member-ship of one million by October 1926.[72] Many cells functioned inside trade unions, Komsomol groups, Women's Sections of the Party, mili-tary units, and other organizations, though ODD branches also existed outside the framework of such bodies and recruited participants from society at large. With resources obtained from initiation fees, yearly dues, donations, and public fund-raising drives, cells engaged in a wide range of activities.[73] They furnished "volunteers," helped conduct "weeks" and similar campaigns, contributed money and supplies to *det-doma*, and assisted state agencies in the operation of receivers, shelters, playgrounds, workshops, and cafeterias. They also sought to place youths with guardians or, following their discharge from institutions, in jobs and decent living quarters. In addition, ODD provided aid to poor families and worked to improve the methods with which parents raised their offspring—thereby seeking to prevent children from reaching the street at all.[74]

Of course, few ODD cells managed all these endeavors. Many did little more than collect dues for occasional contributions to the cause, and in some units even fund-raising fell by the wayside. Reports often noted cells that formed and then lay dormant for want of local initiative or encouragement from above. The only sign of their members appeared on rolls of names initially filed.[75] In Moscow, Leningrad, Khar'kov, and a number of other cities, ODD did emerge as a mass organization, visibly engaged in the struggle to end juvenile homelessness. But in other regions—especially the countryside, where ODD was expected to help stem the flow of peasant youths to the cities—cells remained few and far between.[76]

In its review of the well-known motion picture *Road to Life* (which portrayed a group of delinquents led to better ways in a labor commune), ODD's Moscow journal complained in 1931 that no hint of the organization's work appeared on the screen. An individual member of ODD did materialize briefly in the film, but in a decidedly unflattering role of "a petty bourgeois beating a *besprizornyi.*" More serious, resolutions issued by various bodies early in the 1930s repeatedly characterized ODD's work as inadequate. The All-Russian Central Executive Committee went so far as to claim in 1934 that ODD had not fulfilled the mission entrusted to it and "does not play any sort of discernible role in work with children."[77] Such an assessment is too harsh, at least when characterizing ODD during the 1920s. Certainly it had problems, and the organization never lived up to the expectations that accompanied its inception. But in many cities, and even in some smaller towns, ODD cells received frequent mention as participants in charitable projects. Judging from the evidence at hand, ODD assisted thousands of youths in one way or another over the years, either helping to remove them from the street or reducing the likelihood that they would find their way there. The fact that these efforts overall generated only modest progress toward the goal of eliminating homelessness demonstrated not only ODD's shortcomings but also the imposing scope of the task.

No more direct means existed for citizens to help juveniles and reduce demand on Narkompros than to open the doors of their homes. During the years of war and famine, a multitude of young refugees—one hundred thousand according to one estimate—were placed with private citizens. Though host families came mainly from the peasantry, the nation's titular head, Mikhail Kalinin, and his wife also adopted two orphans found wandering the parched roads. Officials generally resorted to these arrangements as emergency measures, particularly when boys and girls were evacuated into districts in quantities that engulfed local institutions.[78] While results in some instances appear satisfactory, most evidence conveys a discouraging impression. Families commonly accepted wards under pressure from authorities, and this compulsion did not presage a hearty welcome for the household's newcomers, even assuming they possessed no diseases or troublesome individual qualities. At any rate, peasants living near the subsistence level found an extra mouth a considerable burden, as an American Red Cross agent discovered near Arkhangel'sk: "I enquired of [a local official] how the refugees [adults as well as children] were received by the families where they were quartered and from his reply I gathered that in the majority of cases they were not very welcome." Children regarded by their hosts in this light often lived miserably—exhausted by work, begrudged food and clothing, and made to feel every inch an affliction. Some families refused to feed their new lodgers or sought to return them to local Narkompros offices, unless the youths took matters into their own hands first and ran away. An investigator concluded that the hardships confronted by famine refugees after assignment to private homes soon drove "a huge percentage" to the street.[79]

Placement of the homeless in foster families grew far less common in 1923–1924 compared to the preceding years.[80] The famine had abated, and there seemed little reason to pursue a policy widely judged to be disappointing. Like evacuation, mass foster care appeared a crisis tactic whose time had passed. Within a year, however, Narkompros resolved to revive the practice in modified form, not as an emergency measure but for the long term. The decision represented yet another thrust at problems associated with *detdoma*. First, observed numerous journalists, officials, and Narkompros orders, the nation's overcrowded network of institutions could not possibly absorb all those still on their own. Second, not a flicker of hope existed that additional funds would be forthcoming to construct enough new facilities. Diverting children to families of peasants and artisans would diminish the financial burden on Narkompros. Properly screened, some might pass directly from the street to private households, bypassing *detdoma* altogether. In addition, many adolescents already living in institutions could be discharged to families, thereby freeing places in *detdoma* for younger candidates. It was far more cost effective, proponents of foster care maintained, to offer financial incentives to peasant families than to pay for upbringing in institutions. Furthermore, they claimed, juveniles would more likely acquire labor skills in properly selected households than in underequipped and poorly organized *detdoma*. These arguments were bolstered in 1925 by a study conducted in Samara province, indicating that youths placed previously in peasant families had flourished more than their counterparts in *detdoma*.[81]

To be sure, notes of anxiety also registered in meetings and publications. Foster care, after all, signaled a retreat from the goal of collective, institutional upbringing and promised to expose some children to religion and other influences scarcely compatible with Narkompros's curriculum.[82] But the arguments for relieving pressure on *detdoma* outweighed these objections, and decrees soon began to include foster care *(patronirovanie)* routinely in the list of options for authorities confronted with homeless juveniles. Some local officials, eager to reduce the strain *detdoma* placed on their budgets, discharged youths into families in 1924–1925 even before receiving guidelines from Moscow.[83]

When such instructions did appear in 1925–1926, they reflected an awareness of the sorry results obtained four years earlier. No family, they stressed, should be compelled to accept new members. Local Narkompros personnel were encouraged to promote foster care among the surrounding population, but the peasants themselves had to desire the arrangement and take the initiative in communicating their decision to officials.[84] Few could be expected to do so without enticements, of course, and the government offered several. Families accepting children were to receive an extra strip of land (freed of the agricultural tax for three years), a cash payment, and additional privileges regarding local taxes and fees to be worked out by officials on the scene.[85] Should a household rise to these offers, Narkompros staff in the area had instructions to initiate an investigation of the family to insure that it could provide a suitable environment. This meant that a representative of the Children's Social Inspection—or, in the unit's absence, nearly anyone else available, including a recruit from the Komsomol or ODD—had to ascertain that the prospective hosts exhibited no such disqualifying brands as infectious diseases, poverty, alcoholism, or criminal proclivities. Similarly, Narkompros reminded its provincial offices that a successful program required careful selection of youths. Those with illnesses, a disinclination for agricultural work, or objectionable habits acquired in the underworld did not make promising candidates.[86]

After screening of this sort had produced an acceptable match, representatives from the family and Narkompros drew up an agreement. It listed the promised remuneration and detailed the household's obligation to provide agricultural training and raise the child as one of its own for a certain number of years.[87] Every six months thereafter, the Children's Social Inspection or one of the substitutes just mentioned was to visit the dwelling and verify the terms' fulfillment. In some provinces, officials chose to appoint separate legal guardians as well.[88] When a boy came of age and left his foster family, the strip of land contributed previously by the state became his. In addition, the peasant household was to provide him with agricultural implements and other supplies as specified in the agreement. If both parties wished, he could continue to live with the family, which then retained the extra land. Should he run away or otherwise depart prematurely, the field reverted to the state.[89]

Narkompros also sought to transfer youths from *detdoma* to live with artisans. The rationale was much the same as when peasant families represented the intended hosts, and agreements likewise offered incentives (monetary rather than land) to participating artisan households and larger groups (*arteli*) of craftsmen. In addition to any initial outlays negotiated, Narkompros agreed to pay for the support of apprentices during the first year of instruction. The hosts in turn were to set aside funds each month to help establish their charges in *arteli* or as independent handicraftsmen upon completion of training.[90]

The total number of children transferred to peasants and, less often, artisans appears to have ranged between fifteen and twenty thousand by 1925–1926, including a few thousand placed during the famine and still living with families. According to a Narkompros report, peasant households concluded agreements in 1926 to receive approximately 4,400 inhabitants of *detdoma* in the Russian Republic, and the following year they took in an additional 7,500.[91] In certain provinces (most notably Samara), as many as several thousand juveniles lived in foster homes, while in other regions the policy failed to take root.[92] Overall, the practice gradually developed beyond a negligible scale but did not yield the volume of transfers desired by Narkompros. Even the optimistic figure of twenty thousand equaled less than 10 percent of those in the country's *detdoma*.[93]

What accounted for the population's lukewarm response? The difficulties varied from place to place, but generally included some combination of the following. Numerous local officials remained unfamiliar with foster-care legislation or did not bother to publicize the new terms and incentives. Perhaps in some cases they recoiled from the program's extra administrative work. More often, they lacked or refused to commit money and land called for in the decrees. Here and there, as before, they forced children on families—with predictably discouraging results, Narkompros pointed out to its provincial offices. Reports also told of peasants failing to receive payments after accepting new "sons" or "daughters," which cooled a village's interest in further participation.[94] Even where incentives were distributed punctually, peasants did not always evince enthusiasm for the program. Some refused candidates younger than fourteen or so, deeming the pact worthless if it did not provide a capable worker. Others wanted nothing to do with *any* child from a *detdom*—an institution, they felt, whose walls sheltered only miscreants.[95]

Testimony varied considerably regarding the fate of those placed in families. Many cities, including Moscow, registered encouraging results, and a number of sources asserted that a scant tenth of the country's foster-care arrangements collapsed. Samara province boasted a failure rate of only 2 percent.[96] But other investigations and Narkompros documents created a different impression, sometimes of the same region praised elsewhere. In an account published in 1927, for example, Irkutsk appeared on a list of cities where no more than 6 percent of host families returned to Narkompros the boys and girls they had received—in contrast to another journal's report that out of four hundred juveniles sent in 1927 from *detdoma* to families in the Irkutsk region, "about two hundred" had run away. Both figures may be accurate, but each casts the policy in a decidedly different light. Where children remained with their hosts, fragmentary evidence suggests that sooner or later they may not have received what Narkompros considered adequate food, clothing, labor training, or opportunities to attend school. Some peasants even took in youths for work during the agricultural season and then drove them out at the onset of winter.[97] Much of the difficulty in appraising mass foster care derived from Narkompros's inability to supervise those it transferred to peasant villages. The agency's staff did not approach the size necessary to bring most of the countryside into view, and many youths thus disappeared over the bureaucratic horizon when they entered new families. Some local officials, having signed an agreement with a peasant or artisan, regarded the matter as closed and severed all contact with the household. There were offices that failed even to compile a list of families receiving children. Such practices left Narkompros personnel in Moscow squinting through fog in their efforts to evaluate the program.[98]

At the end of the decade, as the Party prepared to launch its twin campaigns of collectivization and dekulakization, journal articles and Narkompros orders hearkened to the new winds blowing from the Kremlin and questioned the practice of distributing youths to individual peasant families. Warnings focused in particular on the pernicious influences allegedly awaiting boys and girls sent to prosperous kulak households—a peril best avoided in the healthy setting of collective farms expected soon to blanket the countryside.[99] Some authors dismissed the topic by contending that the surge to socialism would eliminate vagrancy and with it the need for *any* policy of foster care. As it turned out, devastation loosed on the peasants by collectivization, dekulakization, and the famine of 1933 sired new millions of street children and insured that decrees would continue to promote foster care in that turbulent era. Later still, the sea of homeless juveniles produced by the Second World War forced Soviet officials to resort as never before to foster care and such kindred measures as adoption. According to incomplete data, the end of hostilities saw some 350,000 orphans placed in families that had managed to survive the savage conflict intact.[100]

The stubborn problem of abandoned youths prompted a variety of remedies in the mid-1920s. Some were new, at least as measures vigorously promoted by the central government, while others bore a strong resemblance to previous policies. As an assortment, they represented a combination of what might be called revolutionary idealism and strategic concession—in the latter instance paralleling the concurrent New Economic Policy. Foster care, for example, did not inspire passionate endorsement as a means to implement October's dreams. Just as the New Economic Policy signaled a retreat from socialism by calling on private entrepreneurs to help revitalize the economy, the enlistment of private families to raise homeless children marked an about-face from the goal of socialist upbringing in state institutions. Foster care, in short, stemmed from the painful recognition that resources for *detdoma* were inadequate. Much the same could be said of night shelters, at least to the degree that they were promoted as an inexpensive stopgap source of minimal care. Even the call for society's assistance—whether as volunteers in the street or contributors of funds—usually appeared in official documents accompanied by an explanation that the government alone had been unable to muster sufficient resources for the task. Phrased in this way, suggesting that Narkompros and other agencies would have preferred to accomplish the undertaking on their own, participation of civilian volunteers could be seen as a bow to necessity rather than a long-desired stride toward a Bolshevik vision. At the same time, however, conviction characteristic of the revolutionary dawn found voice in the arguments of "florists" and glistened in the promotion of labor communes by directives, resolutions, and other publications. Here the dominant tone remained faith in government institutions to produce a new socialist generation, even from the most unpromising raw materials.

As the Soviet Union entered the second half of the 1920s, then, it did so having deployed a wide range of measures to eliminate the spectacle of youths roaming the streets. Difficulties remained, of course, along with differences of opinion on how best to proceed. But the nation had safely weathered the storms that attended its inception and no longer faced anything like the catastrophes that poured millions of waifs across the land five years earlier. Time at last appeared an ally in the drive to reclaim the "Revolution's children," and those involved in the effort did not consider it audacious to anticipate success by the end of the decade.

CHAPTER SEVEN

Progress and Frustration

In my view, the policy of Soviet power toward the
"*besprizornyi*" and the "socially-dangerous individual" has
yielded and is yielding results which it can proudly count as
one of the most remarkable achievements of its wise, deeply-
humane work.

Maxim Gorky

. . . those numerous homeless children for whom Russia is
always going to do something and never does . . .

Theodore Dreiser

Whatever their differences, all strategies for reclaiming street children
demanded money. Nobody realized this more acutely than central and
provincial government officials, whose treasuries provided the lion's
share of resources.[1] They also knew that their regular budgets could not
stretch to embrace every waif, and the shortfall drove them after extra
revenue from diverse sources. Most directly, they tapped the local population with additional taxes, including surcharges on specific groups
(usually private traders), on various commodities (among them playing
cards, tram fares, movie tickets, and alcoholic beverages), and on establishments (typically restaurants, taverns, theaters, and other places of
leisure). Some assessments did not outlive brief campaigns to assist the
homeless, while others remained on the books for years.[2] In either case,
the levies often revealed a desire to place more of the bill on idle, prosperous, or otherwise "bourgeois" citizens.

Another supplementary conduit of money ran through the Children's
Commission and its Ukrainian equivalent, the Central Commission for
the Assistance of Children. These bodies and their provincial branches
acquired funds through (1) government subsidies, (2) contributions from
individual citizens and ODD, (3) income from businesses operated by
commissions, and (4) proceeds from bazaars, concerts, movies, and

other shows they staged.[3] As further encouragement, the government shielded a variety of the commissions' enterprises (including dining facilities, dairies, workshops for abandoned youths, and stores that sold goods produced in the workshops) from state and local taxes.[4] Casinos, lotteries, and billiard halls opened by commissions around the country often proved especially lucrative. Indeed, the Ukrainian division planned for gaming rooms to generate fully half its budget in 1925/26.[5] The Children's Commission eventually instructed branches to cease such fund-raising practices because of their unwholesome aura, and by 1928 demanded as well that its network close taverns and other facilities selling alcoholic beverages. The appeals for reconsideration presented by a number of local offices underscored how profitable these ventures had been.[6]

Lenin's death early in 1924 inspired creation of yet another revenue channel. On January 26, in memory of the nation's father, the All-Union Congress of Soviets called for a V. I. Lenin Fund of Assistance to *Besprizornye* Children, and in July the All-Union Central Executive Committee issued a decree to this end. The All-Union Lenin Fund was set at 100 million rubles—50 million from the central government and 50 million to be provided by Lenin Funds at the republic level. The government was to make its contribution over five years, with no yearly payment less than 10 million rubles. Only the interest generated by this money could be spent, and decisions regarding distribution rested with a committee of the Central Executive Committee's Presidium.[7] In the spring of 1926, a newspaper reported that the fund had already disbursed 600,000 rubles around the country. While hardly approaching the tens of millions of rubles budgeted more directly through Narkompros for work with street children, this did represent more than trivial assistance. In certain regions with large concentrations of *detdoma*, Narkompros viewed the Lenin Fund as an essential supplement to the budgets of its local offices.[8]

These offices needed such reinforcement because the duty to maintain *detdoma* fell on their shoulders soon after the famine. By 1924/25, 80 percent of the sixty million rubles spent to run the institutions came from provincial budgets.[9] Just a few years before, when millions of homeless youths swarmed across the nation, the central government had taken the lead in funding *detdoma*. But 1923 saw Moscow busy depositing this financial obligation on the doorsteps of Narkompros branches around the country, where it represented a staggering burden. In 1923/24 *detdoma* typically swallowed a third to a half of local Narkompros budgets, roughly a quarter in 1924/25, and often a fifth or more in 1925/ 26—debilitating expenses for authorities with many other responsibilities, including regular schools.[10]

Once Narkompros offices discovered themselves obligated to support most *detdoma* in their areas, they sought not only to raise revenue but to reduce expenses. Across the country they began dismissing children from institutions and closed thousands of facilities altogether by 1925, leaving less than half the number that existed only three years before. Narkompros headquarters itself urged the discharge of older inhabitants and those whose parents or relatives had been located—but with the goal of making room for an equivalent number from among the multitude still on their own. Local officials generally required no prodding to implement the remedy's first stage, sending juveniles out to face the world, but they displayed no enthusiasm for bringing new candidates into places vacated by those departing.[11] According to data from twenty-five provinces in the Russian Republic, the number of youths discharged from *detdoma* more than doubled the total crossing institutions' thresholds in the opposite direction. During the period January–September 1926, thirty-six provinces reported bidding farewell to approximately 26,000 boys and girls from facilities that accepted only 9,800 replacements during the same interval. In Moscow province the numbers discharged and admitted were 4,334 and 1,616, respectively; in Siberia, 3,537 and 705; and in Saratov province, 1,877 and 323.[12]

This trend continued throughout the decade, impervious to frequent orders from Moscow to halt further attrition in the nation's system of *detdoma*.[13] Instructions to preserve children's facilities did not move the head of Narkompros's office for Stalingrad province, in whose view "[some district officials] are carrying out their work without sufficient vigor, often appearing too soft-hearted and trying to preserve *detdoma*. This must cease. The course of reducing the number of *detdoma* and emancipating local budgets must be pursued resolutely."[14] From one end of the country to the other, such concerns closed homes for abandoned children. In the Ural region, 311 institutions dwindled to 189 between 1925 and 1927. The Crimean Autonomous Republic's total fell from 47 to 30 over a roughly similar period, and Moscow province's network withered from 386 to 208.[15] Of course, the quantity of *detdoma* required to meet the nation's needs diminished along with the number of homeless juveniles after 1922. But financial considerations swayed local authorities to close *detdoma* at such a brisk rate that those remaining could not accommodate thousands of youths still on the street. In the summer of 1925, according to an article in the Komsomol's principal newspaper, surviving institutions could shelter little more than half the nation's waifs. Moreover, many of those hastily discharged found themselves alone, without employment or training, and soon rejoined the homeless world.[16]

Short of closing buildings, officials conceived other ways to curtail support for *detdoma*. Some shifted as much of their financial responsibility as possible to the Children's Commission or, less often, to ODD. Numerous reports and reprimands from Moscow focused on local authorities who received funds from the Children's Commission and then trimmed their own expenditures by the same amount or spent the contributions on inappropriate projects.[17] In at least a few instances, provincial Narkompros offices displayed a determination to regard labor colonies and communes as self-sufficient institutions requiring no support at all. Budgetary concerns rendered them immune to abundant evidence that few children's facilities could long flourish on their own.[18]

In some regions, especially localities that attracted large numbers of young refugees and vagrants, authorities provided aid only to those identified as natives of the province, district, or city in question. Others they simply left on the street or shipped back to areas thought to contain their original homes.[19] In addition, rural officials commonly placed local urchins they could not or would not support on trains bound for the nearest city. Thus launched, a child arrived in the metropolis with no money and only a document identifying him as an orphan requiring placement in an institution. All too often he landed on the street instead. As far back as 1924, various government agencies forbade these unsanctioned transfers, but the practice continued along with the prohibitions throughout the decade. Occasionally, the dumping of youths from one area into another (what one newspaper called the "get out of our sight" approach) assumed mass proportions. Officials in Baku, for example, decided to "cleanse" themselves of rootless juveniles in the autumn of 1930 and jettisoned eight hundred into the territory of their Georgian neighbors. One wonders how many soon headed back across the border.[20]

By the middle of the decade, then, *detdoma* were harried on multiple fronts. Local officials begrudged them funds, while others promoted alternatives such as labor communes and foster care. It may have seemed that *detdoma* faced an institutional equivalent of the abandonment experienced earlier by the children they housed. But despite these threats, the welfare of homeless youths remained primarily in the hands of Narkompros's original network of facilities. No other option caught on sufficiently to displace them. Throughout the 1920s, the overwhelming majority of orphans who left the street via officially devised channels entered receivers and *detdoma* without ever seeing communes or foster families.

Of the two institutions—receiver and *detdom*—the latter played by far the more important role. Numbers alone erase any doubt. Receivers (including observation-distribution points) never reached a total of even 300 in the Russian Republic, increasing from 175 to 284 between 1921 and 1926 according to one calculation, while *detdoma* towered above these sums by a multiple of over thirty in 1921–1922 and nearly ten in 1926.[21] Children often moved directly from the street to permanent institutions, with perhaps a visit to a night shelter enroute, in either instance never entering a receiver.[22] For that matter, many receivers themselves came to resemble *detdoma*. Originally, they had been expected to provide little more than preliminary screening and preparation (haircuts, baths, clean clothes, and the like) before passing a child along to a *detdom* for education and training. But as the number of candidates continued to exceed vacancies in *detdoma*, receivers could not place youths promptly. The average stay stretched into months, confronting facilities with upbringing duties previously reserved for *detdoma*.[23] A majority of those eventually dispatched from receivers continued on to *detdoma*, but the transition had ceased to be striking.[24]

In short, the aggressive pruning of their ranks did not challenge the position of *detdoma* as the state's principal means for rehabilitating waifs. Underscoring this point in 1926, Lunacharskii noted that the government spent forty-five million rubles per year on the struggle with juvenile homelessness—"almost exclusively on raising children in *detdoma*."[25] The Russian Republic's complement of facilities surpassed 6,000 during the famine and still topped 2,000 during the first half of 1927, as evident in the following totals.[26]

1921–1922	6,063
October 1, 1923	3,971
June 1, 1924	3,377
January 1, 1925	2,836
December 1, 1926	2,224
December 15, 1927	1,922

According to less complete information, Ukraine contained nearly 2,000 *detdoma* early in 1923 and 788 in 1925. The Soviet Union as a whole supported 5,119 *detdoma* on January 1, 1924; 3,827 a year later; 3,119 in 1925/26; and 2,493 in 1926/27.[27] The numbers of children housed in the Russian Republic's institutions are shown in the following list.[28]

1917	25,666
1918	75,000
1919	125,000
1920	400,000
1921	540,000
1922	540,000
1923 (October 1)	252,317
1924 (June 1)	239,776
1925 (January 1)	228,127
1926 (December 1)	177,000
1927 (December 15)	158,554
1927/28	136,989
1928/29	129,344

Ukrainian *detdoma* sheltered an additional 114,000 juveniles at the beginning of 1923 and approximately 72,000 by the summer of 1925. One source estimated that all *detdoma* together in the Soviet Union contained "about 1,000,000" youths in 1922/23—an immense figure compared to that of 1917, but only a fraction of those in need of care. For reasons just presented, the nation's *detdom* population plunged in the years thereafter, but it nonetheless totaled roughly 359,000 on January 1, 1924; 317,000 a year later; 293,000 in 1925/26; and 222,000 in 1926/27.[29] During this period, as officials began discharging children whose relatives could be located, two-thirds to three-fourths of those remaining in most *detdoma* were classified as full orphans, and over 90 percent had lost at least one parent.[30]

These statistics should be viewed as approximations, useful in revealing trends and the rough scale of action, but scarcely precise measures of *detdoma*. Complete information never arrived from many remote provinces and autonomous regions, especially during the period's chaotic early years. In addition, despite instructions from Moscow to standardize institutions' names (as *detdom*, agricultural colony, or labor commune, for example), numerous facilities around the country bore other titles such as "*besprizornye* shelter" or "handicraft school." Moreover, some changed their names when the concept of "moral defectiveness" came under attack in the middle of the decade. The "Saratov Home for the Morally Anomalous" continued on as a "Children's Agricultural Labor Commune," for instance, and the "Rostov Children's Home for the Morally Defective" became the "Rostov Institute for Social Rehabilitation."[31] The bewildering variety of titles contributed discrepancies to data, as some investigators were more inclined than others to regard a *detdom* by any other name as a *detdom.*

Further complicating the statistics, some sources divided institutions into numerous subcategories, with different bodies (notably Narkompros and the Central Statistical Agency) employing their own, slightly varying lists.[32] Column headings might include *detdoma* for preschool children, *detdoma* for school-age youngsters, "experimental demonstration" facilities, labor communes, agricultural colonies, agricultural *detdoma*, handicraft *detdoma*, homes for adolescents, and a variety of institutions (including *detdoma*, colonies, and communes) specifically for "difficult" inhabitants or those with physical impairments.[33] While all these categories could be maneuvered into a coherent array on paper, they acquired an air of unreality when applied to actual establishments around the country. Waifs outstripped the capacity of facilities by such a margin that local officials often had no choice but to send groups of disparate age, health, and experience to the same place. Thus a *detdom* designated for relatively unscarred youths might also contain a sizable complement of teenage delinquents for whom no other institution could be found. In similar fashion, authorities lacking more suitable options deposited emotionally disturbed and retarded wards in "normal" *detdoma* and even in colonies for unrepentant veterans of the street.[34]

Subtleties and confusion aside, most facilities bore the general characteristics and often the title of a *detdom*.[35] According to figures published in 1926 that arranged children's institutions into several categories—including three labeled *detdom*, agricultural colony, and labor commune—*detdoma* accounted for nearly 90 percent of the total.[36] The vast majority of these establishments, whatever their name, were administered by Narkompros. Other agencies (including the Children's Commission, the Central Commission for the Assistance of Children, the OGPU, and the commissariats of health and transportation) did operate their own *detdoma*, colonies, and clinics. But Narkompros's share of institutionalized street children, estimated by one account to exceed 90 percent, dwarfed the rest.[37]

The mission desired for *detdoma*, namely education and upbringing (as opposed, say, to alms, quarantine, or punishment), explains Narkompros's dominant role. From the beginning, Lunacharskii's commissariat strained to provide all residents an opportunity to attend school—though not often, as it turned out, inside *detdoma*. Fewer than 20 percent of the Russian Republic's *detdoma* contained primary schools in the spring of 1924, and fewer than 10 percent offered advanced instruction.[38] Generally, *detdoma* did not possess the resources and staff to furnish more than rudimentary education, which prompted Narkompros to order that most instruction take place in regular schools outside institutions. However numerous the shortcomings of general public schools, they seemed better able than *detdoma* to conduct the training desired by Moscow, and they also represented to reformers a means of integrating *detdoma* into the surrounding society.

But the absence of classroom activities at a *detdom* did not guarantee youths an education elsewhere. Inadequate resources that precluded instruction inside facilities also reduced the accessibility of classes "beyond the walls." Numerous accounts described children unable to walk to school during cold weather (a substantial portion of the academic year in much of the country) because they lacked coats and other outdoor attire. Although statistics listed most *detdom* inhabitants as attending school, a Narkompros report for 1923/24 added that a "majority" missed many lessons for want of shoes and warm clothing.[39] An overall assessment of the schooling provided is colored by the direction in which one gazes. Much improvement stood out compared to the desperate conditions of 1921–1922, when the struggle for survival all but eclipsed education. Who could doubt that a larger percentage of institutionalized juveniles received instruction in the second half of the decade? Still, turning to face the future, it was clear as well that a long interval remained before most teenagers who walked out the doors of *detdoma* for the last time would carry with them a secondary or even primary education.[40]

From the first years after the Revolution, and as reformers emphasized again in the middle of the decade, *detdoma* were expected to provide an upbringing much broader than instruction in traditional classroom subjects. Reading, writing, and arithmetic represented a small part of the process and could not by themselves insure employment. To survive—and contribute to the construction of socialism—adolescents required vocational preparation. Most *detdoma* (except those whose charges received training in factories and other enterprises outside the home institution) were urged year after year to open workshops, and many scrambled to comply. According to a study of approximately 1,300 workshops in the Russian Republic's *detdoma* in 1926/27, the trades most commonly taught in these settings (roughly 300 of each) were carpentry, leatherworking, and sewing. Close to 100 shops engaged in metalworking, and a similar number bound books. A variety of other handicrafts, such as basket making, were also represented, and some *detdoma* maintained smithies.[41] While training remained the workshops' primary purpose, some of the healthier operations also acted as businesses and accepted orders from state agencies and the surrounding population. Such transactions helped motivate the young craftsmen (who were allowed here and there to keep a small portion of their shops' earnings), and they also brought in revenue for the *detdoma*.[42]

Most workshops, however, appear to have sold little if anything to customers outside the institutions. In some cases the reason boiled down to competition from factories and artisans, or the failure of local Narkompros offices to purchase goods produced by their *detdoma*.[43] More often, the impediments were internal. Shortages of equipment, instructors, and raw materials, along with poor discipline and low morale, resulted in products of distressing quality or no output at all.[44] Furthermore, *detdoma* could not afford to provide proper labor training for everyone and thus frequently limited instruction to adolescents closest to discharge. While the percentage of residents with access to training in workshops increased from year to year, the figure amounted to only about 40–50 percent for teenagers as late as 1926/27, and no more than half that for children of all ages.[45] Even toward the end of the decade, then, workshops did not serve as a means of rehabilitation for many who entered institutions.

Facilities for homeless youths were also expected to introduce their wards to agricultural labor. Colonies and communes in particular, while not shunning workshops, devoted large portions of their resources to farming, as did rural *detdoma*. Even some of their urban counterparts sent children to work on state farms during the summer.[46] Each year, the agricultural season's opening moved such institutions to abridge or eliminate activity in schools and workshops in order to focus effort on the fields.[47] The scope of their projects ranged from little more than a kitchen garden to well over one hundred acres of crops and orchards. Successful undertakings also acquired dozens of pigs, horses, cows, and, in a few cases, a tractor and steam-powered mill.[48]

Some rural institutions so flourished that they could boast herds of pedigreed livestock and harvests surpassing yields obtained by neighboring peasants—a situation that occasionally stirred the latter to adopt new agricultural and animal husbandry practices. A bountiful harvest also left facilities less dependent on government agencies and permitted dietary improvements, no small matter in an institution's well-being.[49] In general, though, the work of agricultural *detdoma*, colonies, and labor communes remains difficult to evaluate. Almost by definition, they lay off the beaten track, frustrating a comparison of them with individual success stories publicized in some districts. A survey of *detdoma* in the Northern Caucasus region concluded that labor training (in workshops and fields) functioned poorly in many facilities but proceeded effectively in others, "especially in *detdoma* of an agricultural type." Less encouragingly, a second study asserted that agricultural work in a "majority" of Soviet children's institutions suffered from deficits of equipment, seeds, and funds for hired assistance with heavy tasks. In a similar vein, Narkompros estimated that *detdoma* utilized no more than 40 percent of their land in 1923/24 owing to such shortages.[50] The success of their agricultural endeavors was far from universal, in other words, but precisely how far eludes specification.

Schools, workshops, and agriculture did not exhaust the means of rehabilitation. *Detdoma* were also instructed, as previously observed, to occupy youths' leisure hours with a variety of clubs and circles.[51] Here boys and girls could work productively with others, expand their knowledge, and acquire a social and political outlook congenial to the Party. The groups, ideally several in each institution, featured activities and hobbies as diverse as sports, military drill, photography, model airplanes, singing, and drawing.[52] Most *detdoma* claimed the existence of at least a few circles by the second half of the decade, though questions surfaced regarding their vigor. Observers pointed out that personnel often formed clubs on paper in order to improve an institution's appearance in their superiors' eyes, but with little concern that the ventures thrive.[53] There were exceptions to this rule, however, and considerable evidence reveals energetic activity at scattered institutions. Some, for example, maintained libraries offering thousands of volumes and several current periodicals. These collections, and those of more modest dimensions elsewhere, attracted literary circles whose members (children and staff) read stories aloud, discussed works, and occasionally took up pens themselves.[54]

Drama circles, too, burst into view, though the young thespians' volatile nature and the rowdy audiences they sometimes faced lent additional meaning to the label "drama." Generally, a group worked under an adult's direction and staged anything from frothy, raucous pieces to classics from previous centuries. Productions with political subjects (revolutionary themes, the Civil War, or the menace of religion, for instance) also figured prominently in repertoires. In Ivanovo-Voznesensk, youths prepared a play based on Lidiia Seifullina's story "Lawbreakers," an account of street children's lives. This amounted to the cast playing themselves, which yielded a most convincing performance, a spectator recorded, except when the actors forgot their lines. At some institutions the productions developed such an appeal that they drew audiences from beyond the facilities' walls, especially in the countryside, where fewer alternative forms of entertainment existed.[55]

In Moscow, the absence of girls in Labor Commune No. 8 complicated rehearsals of a play on the Paris Commune. Evidently, none of the boys would consider a female part, and thus an invitation went out to a local Pioneer detachment. The Pioneers responded with a girl named Budkova, who filled in effectively and earned the cast's respect—so much so that cursing diminished in her presence. Later, when the drama circle embarked on a play about a fascist plot uncovered by Pioneers, the previous success with Budkova prompted the group to request that she bring a second girl to act in the new production. But unlike Budkova, the newcomer's discomfort and affectation drew laughter with every entrance, and her acting did not improve with anger. Additional harassment awaited offstage, beyond the staff's capacity to intervene. Soon the girl's mother arrived to complain of nocturnal attention shown her daughter by commune members, and the beleaguered youth withdrew from the drama circle shortly thereafter. Her departure left open the second female role and gave rise to a new problem. Some of the older boys caroused with girls still on the street, and one of these adolescents dreamed of stationing his favorite inside the commune. Was an actress needed? He knew of a lass who might be available. Unfortunately for the young couple and others that would have followed, the circle's adviser had divined the ambitions of the institution's Lotharios and scrambled to prevent the transformation of her troupe into a conduit for paramours. A quick amendment of the group's "charter" thwarted such levies of talent. In the end, the company supplemented its ranks with two more Pioneer girls, though only one managed to win the boys' acceptance.[56]

Many *detdoma*, colonies, and labor communes also issued their own wall newspapers (*stennye gazety*), which typically assumed the form of a thick paper scroll, often several yards long, on which articles and illustrations were pasted for display.[57] Literary circles and other groups of children and staff assembled the papers with a frequency ranging from every few days to a handful of times per year for official holidays.[58] Certain papers focused mainly on life in the home institution—day-to-day activities, problems, accomplishments—and contained numerous drawings, poems, and stories contributed by the youths themselves. Much of this material was lively and easy to read, no doubt more appealing to juveniles than the heavily political essays (often written by adults) that dominated other wall papers at some children's facilities. Typical articles in the paper "Young Leninist," prepared at a *detdom* in Maikop, groaned under such titles as "The Red Army," "Why There Is No Soviet Power in America," "We Set Up a Bond with the Peasants," and "Our Participation in Elections to the Rural Soviet." The contents, an investigator concluded, were too dry and required the spice of more humorous, buoyant selections.[59]

While literary circles, drama clubs, and wall newspapers did not shun themes from the world of contemporary politics, the most concentrated exposure usually occurred in another setting, the "political circle." These bodies organized an institution's most "conscious" residents to discuss articles in *Pravda* and other papers, conduct ceremonies in honor of special events and people (the October Revolution, May 1, Lenin, and local revolutionary heroes, for example), and perhaps compose their own wall newspapers.[60] Frequently, participants belonged to the Komsomol (or, in the case of the youngest, the Pioneers), sometimes in such numbers that a Komsomol cell assumed a political circle's place.[61] According to published figures, as many as three-fourths of the children in *detdoma* wore the Pioneers' red neckerchief, and approximately 60 percent of the adolescents joined the Komsomol.[62] Behind these impressive totals, however, lay a somewhat different reality. As with circles and clubs, the existence of a Komsomol cell on paper did not guarantee that it met regularly or kindled any fervor. Some groups plainly did; others clearly did not. In most cases a cell's vitality is obscure.[63]

Narkompros's array of rehabilitation measures culminated in a sense with the policies of "self-service" and "self-government."[64] Spurred on by reformers in the middle of the decade, facilities often adopted the policies' trappings. Youths attended general meetings along with the staff to assess performance and approve future courses of action. They elected representatives to various committees, councils, and brigades to oversee daily work.[65] In numerous institutions they assumed more responsibility for cleanliness and order: washing floors, sweeping the grounds, tending animals, helping to prepare food, serving meals, guarding storerooms and kitchen gardens, mending clothes, and collecting

firewood, to list jobs commonly mentioned.[66] A few establishments reportedly went far beyond increasing juveniles' involvement in routine
chores. Young voices were portrayed as decisive in resolving what to
plant and whether to take on more animals at the Perm' labor colony,
and they allegedly dominated general meetings at a *detdom* in Tobol'sk.
In some facilities, children accused of infractions were tried and sentenced by panels of their peers. More surprising, sources occasionally
described special meetings called by youths to judge *staff members* accused of misdeeds (such as striking a child). As the proceedings unfolded,
teachers and even a director humbly asked forgiveness or sought in
shame to resign.[67]

Whatever the reliability of these firsthand accounts, one can scarcely
imagine similar assemblies in the vast majority of institutions. Observers
more often described "self-service" and "self-government" as measures
implemented to enhance discipline and control rather than bestow
greater independence. Reports sent to superiors might stress the adoption of "self-government," but the actual consequences likely amounted
to a more effective harnessing of children for mundane duties. While
this sometimes trimmed reliance on hired help (cooks, cleaning ladies,
and so forth), the consequent reduction of expenses did not rank high
on the list of benefits heralded by advocates of "self-government." Far
from developing a positive attitude toward work, some argued, piling
domestic tasks on youths (without additional measures to win their enthusiasm) encouraged them to view labor as a burden or even a
punishment.[68]

At the same time that Narkompros promoted the policy of "self-government," it was "administering" some *detdoma*, colonies, and communes in which children already ran their own lives in a different fashion. They smashed windows, obstructed meetings, and crawled over
buildings and grounds at will. Ignoring or intimidating their teachers,
they roamed streets and markets during the day and cavorted with juveniles yet at large.[69] D. Sergeev, the boy discovered hiding behind a
dresser after breaking into a dwelling, had previously spent several years
in a *detdom*. He passed a good deal of this time in the bazaar, absorbing
lessons on theft and striking up an acquaintance with youths on the
street. Evenings commonly saw him slip out to spend the night playing
cards in a shed with his friends.[70] Problems such as theft, widespread at
the beginning of the decade, succumbed only slowly as residents per-

sisted in spiriting away sheets, blankets, clothes, food, and anything else that could be sold in adjacent markets. Rarely did cohabitants reveal thieves' identities, for the "law" of the street maintained its sway tenaciously.[71] Here and there, as before, seasoned adolescents greeted newcomers with beatings and tormented the defenseless, especially girls and young boys. Rival groups of occupants continued to mar institutions on occasion, transforming them into arenas of gang warfare.[72] Certainly, improvement over the years left fewer *detdoma* out of control by the mid-1920s. But many still suffered to one degree or another from the foregoing afflictions.

Narkompros had hoped that *detdoma* would be able to develop cordial relations with the surrounding population in order to ease the introduction of former waifs into society. Institutions could (and did) make encouraging progress by inviting neighbors to attend plays and festivals and by opening their schools, workshops, and reading rooms to those living nearby. Some facilities provided agricultural assistance (even electrical power in one instance) to local peasants and took part in election campaigns for rural soviets. Children also participated now and then in various civic ceremonies, notably May Day, and in municipal projects (helping to clean up a park, for example, and move a library).[73]

But incidents common in earlier years (such as thefts by *detdom* residents from neighboring apartments) did not diminish rapidly enough to win applause from much of the population.[74] Reports arrived from numerous cities attributing acts of hooliganism to aggressors from institutions. Here they attacked schoolchildren, seizing their books and caps; there they loitered menacingly around stores and movie theaters, looking for opportunities to make off with possessions briefly unattended. A group of boys ranging daily through a Siberian town amused themselves from time to time by pelting a statue of Lenin with stones.[75] In Rostov-on-the-Don, 14 percent of the delinquents processed by the Juvenile Affairs Commission in 1924 were *already* living in *detdoma*, and the figure climbed to 16 percent the next year.[76] However benign the conduct of many other "state children," boarding institutions established for them gained little popular favor as the years passed.

While *detdoma* contained fewer youths in the middle of the decade than in 1921–1922, a larger percentage of this dwindling number had spent years on the street and in relief institutions. The famine victims who had earlier flooded *detdoma* included accomplished thieves, but these crowds were more often harmless—new to their condition and crushed by hunger—than the less abundant street children of subsequent years.[77] Novices continued to appear among the latter, of course, but the passage of time left an ever more incorrigible residue of juveniles confronting Narkompros. Steeped in the ways of the underworld and scornfully familiar with receivers and *detdoma*, they resisted the government's efforts to reclaim them. Schools, workshops, and circles ran a poor second, in their view, to gambling, tobacco, alcohol, and cocaine. Indeed, a desire to obtain money for such pastimes frequently lay behind the youths' thefts from *detdoma* and other facilities.[78] Along with gambling and narcotics, they brought with them sexual experience, which forced some educators to contend with the rape of younger boys, with girls who worked as prostitutes, and even with abortions on the premises.[79]

Institutions that had managed to conceive reasonably effective programs found them disrupted temporarily by the arrival of these veterans. Thefts increased, discipline waned, and teachers despaired. Time and again, like Sisyphus, they saw hard-won progress threatened as facilities approached for a time the troubled condition that had marked their inception. Authorities responsible for apprehending urchins often sent them to any institution at hand, regardless of suitability. Thus a *detdom* for comparatively manageable youths might receive a truculent group completely unfit for activities devised by the staff. Perhaps this was unavoidable, given the shortage of *detdoma*, colonies, and labor communes; but the immediate result left instructors anything but poised to boast of their wards' rehabilitation.[80]

Leaders of street gangs represented a special challenge. In facilities where they retained (or rebuilt) a band of cohorts, they could undermine a staff's authority. Other children, fearing reprisals from the gang, dared not ignore the leader's will. If he told them to shun the classroom, perform his own chores, or turn over the best food, they did not have to think twice about obeying. Dominant figures of this sort (perhaps several at a single institution) sometimes ordered younger lads to slip out and steal money or treats.[81] At a colony near Khar'kov, Anton Makarenko encountered the following situation:

> They [the older boys] call the little ones their "pups." Each of them has several "pups." In the morning they say to them—"go where you like, but bring me this or that in the evening." Some of them steal—in trains or at the market, but most of them don't know how to steal, they just beg. They stand in the street, at the bridge, and in Ryzhov. They say they get two or three rubles a day. Churilo's "pups" are the best—they bring in as much as five

rubles. And they have their norms—three-quarters to the boss, one-quarter to the "pups."[82]

Where leaders flourished, attempts to implement "self-service" and "self-government" commonly fell under their control and enabled them to exploit others more efficiently. Thus entrenched, they could be neutralized only by deft maneuvering on the part of the staff.[83] Some administrators preferred to wash their hands quickly of troublemakers through a variety of artifices: by engineering their transfer, conveying them to the courts, or simply discharging them back to the street.[84]

Directors often strove to assert control through stern discipline—sometimes executed by monitors in rooms and guards outside buildings—even demanding absolute silence during meals, lessons, and activities. At least a few institutions (among them Makarenko's) assumed features of military schools, with uniforms, banners, and strict marching drills.[85] Despite objections from Narkompros officials, especially those opposed to the concept of "moral defectiveness," corporal punishment endured. This included not only beatings but such practices as forcing children to remain standing for long periods, driving them out into the cold clad only in shirts, and ordering them to wash their bodies with snow. At a *detdom* in Odessa, iodine smeared on a boy's tongue served as the penalty for a rude comment. The staff punished two other youths by sewing their underwear together, turning them into so-called Siamese twins.[86]

Institutions frequently maintained an "isolator" (*kartser*), a room in which disruptive youths could be held for a few hours or even days. Those in less drastic disfavor might be confined to the buildings in which they lived. In the town of Nikolaev, children guilty of infractions in a *detdom* were prohibited for a time from leaving to attend school—a restriction usually enforced by removal of an offender's outer clothing. One girl had been barred from school in this fashion for nearly a year. Administrators also employed as punishment the assignment of extra chores or particularly unpleasant duties, such as cleaning latrines. At a *detdom* in Barnaul, several residents were sent to work on a state farm as a penalty for their misdeeds.[87] Some facilities for "difficult" juveniles divided occupants into categories, with different rules applied to each. The least desirable status belonged to newcomers and others deemed especially unruly. Rarely allowed out of the buildings, they were often kept in their underwear or housed behind bars to prevent escape. Those in more advanced categories, thought to have shown progress toward rehabilitation, received such privileges as greater freedom of movement, better food and clothing, and permission to smoke.[88]

Despite all precautions, however, children continued to flee. At some poorly administered facilities they received so little attention that many vanished without ever being registered. Even strict-regime establishments failed to hold the most determined spirits.[89] Each year at the Moscow Labor Home, for instance, spring's advent germinated a flurry of escape attempts that occasionally succeeded, despite the institution's barred windows and armed guards. The most popular method required a stolen knife blade or similar object to rub on a rock until the metal developed the teeth of a primitive hacksaw. On the chosen night, with other youths deployed to warn of approaching guards or teachers, the tool's creator severed a window bar and waited. When the guard outside occupied himself in another sector of the yard, out the window flew a "rope" made from torn sheets and towels down which the fugitive slid in hopes of making his way undetected to a low point in the wall.[90] Few *detdoma* presented such a challenge. Over a period of years, many children fled up to ten times from sundry institutions, and some compiled dozens of escapes.[91] At a number of facilities for delinquents, close to half the youths ran away in 1923/24. While the rush for the road gradually diminished thereafter, escapees still accounted for a third of all departures from these sites in 1927. At "normal" *detdoma*, Lunacharskii wrote in 1928, fewer than 2 percent of the inhabitants now disappeared—a worthy achievement for Narkompros—though the total sometimes exceeded 10 percent at receivers and institutions for "difficult" juveniles.[92]

Motives for escape abound in the preceding pages. Dilapidated or crowded buildings, inadequate supplies, and harsh personnel all inspired flight. So, too, did beatings and other abuse received from stronger youths. Even gambling setbacks lay behind some exits, as losers disappeared to evade debts or obtain funds to pay them.[93] The most resolute young fugitives abandoned facilities because they felt stifled by the structured life. Long accustomed to rough freedom and mores remote from those preached by Narkompros, their restlessness seemed beyond the reach of *detdoma*.[94] Chainik, after his removal from the basement of the Alexander Station, entered a *detdom* and became a model resident. He studied diligently, and his art was soon displayed as evidence of the achievements possible in work with wayward adolescents. But time did not reinforce this progress. Chainik's inclination for travel and adventure resisted the institution's routine, which grew ever more monotonous for the boy. He ran away, returned, and fled again.[95]

Some transient residents chose to enter institutions temporarily, just to obtain food, clothing, and perhaps shelter for the winter. With no intention of staying long, they proved troublesome for teachers—who may thus have shared the boys' sense of release when spring's warmth called them back to the street.[96] Youths could avoid even the modest challenge of escape if they convinced staff members to send them "home," a technique mastered by one Grisha M——ov. After his father's death, his mother placed her son in a children's shelter in the town of Sudogda (Vladimir province), where Grisha's misbehavior began a series of transfers to institutions around Vladimir's environs. These steps finally reached a colony in which severe discipline sent Grisha fleeing to board a train for Moscow. Over the next month he wandered the capital's markets and stations amid a group of boys, supporting himself with thefts from street vendors and with begging receipts generated by acrobatics and lewd songs. When this life grew tiresome, he presented himself at Moscow's Narkompros office, whose staff decided to return him to Vladimir. Grisha had no intention of rejoining his mother—who "was always yapping at us," he maintained later, "and now she's probably glad that she doesn't know where I am"—and hopped onto another train after arriving in Vladimir. His travels eventually brought him back to the thoroughfares of Moscow and later the Pokrovskii receiver, where he requested passage "home" to Vladimir. The receiver's personnel obliged with clothes, shoes, and food for the journey, and off he went to initiate another cycle. Time and again the emaciated, lice-covered boy appeared at the "Pokrovka" to lounge in the receiver before another trip. Grisha claimed to have set out for Vladimir ten times—clothed, washed, and fed—and boasted with a smile of his ability to deceive administrators of children's institutions.[97]

As noted earlier, the pressure placed by *detdoma* on local budgets prompted provincial authorities, in defiance of orders from Moscow, to reduce sharply the ranks of *detdoma* after 1922 and to limit supplies allocated to those that survived.[98] Consequently, conditions at institutions improved less rapidly than the declining number of waifs might otherwise have permitted. Homeless juveniles continued to exceed the much-reduced capacity of the nation's network of *detdoma* in the middle of the decade, as confirmed by reports from around the country. Though congestion did not approach that of the famine period, over 40 percent of residents slept two or three to a bed, and inadequate resources long hindered elimination of other problems endemic in 1921–1922.[99] Years later, those in some establishments still greeted winter shivering in frosty rooms, barefoot and without blankets. Poor sanitation and shortages of clothing remained, as did complaints from *detdoma* forced to feed each child on five rubles (or less) per month.[100] A large majority of facilities entered the second half of the decade without medical personnel and with no clinics or rooms in which to quarantine the sick.[101] Lists of diseases encountered by investigations seemed to contain every conceivable childhood ailment as well as afflictions normally restricted to adults. A summary includes malaria, dysentery, tuberculosis, anemia, syphilis, gonorrhea, trachoma, and other eye, skin, tooth, and gum infections.[102] In the Northern Caucasus, a survey of 130 *detdoma* detected such illnesses among 45 percent of the occupants, while another investigation of several thousand youths housed in the *detdoma* of Saratov, Kazan', Simferopol', Verkhnedneprovsk, and Ekaterinoslav discovered 25 percent suffering from trachoma alone. In a few of the nation's *detdoma* fully 85–100 percent of the children had tuberculosis.[103]

Along with the inhabitants, the buildings themselves were frequently in poor condition or of otherwise dubious suitability. Many required urgent repairs, and only a few—about 13 percent in the middle of the decade—had been designed originally as boarding institutions for juveniles. Instead, approximately 8 percent of *detdoma* turned up in monastery buildings; another 9 percent on estates confiscated from nobles; 29 percent in stables, barns, and previously private quarters; and 41 percent in former schools, barracks, almshouses, infirmaries, libraries, clubs, rest homes, community buildings, and so on.[104] Whatever the structure, it rarely shined, as *detdoma* did not command high priority when local authorities allocated quarters. Even institutions fortunate enough to be situated in stout, well-appointed rooms could lose them later. Officials in search of buildings risked little by drafting instructions to move orphanages, for Narkompros was not among the most powerful of government agencies. Authorities in the Northern Caucasus, uninhibited by the irony, transferred a *detdom* to an inferior site so that the original facility could serve as an incubator for chicks. In disregard of restrictions that Moscow placed on such transfers, moves took place (from cities out to rural locations more often than not) with great regularity in the second half of the decade. Occasionally, youths and staff

ousted from a building had to live under the open sky for a time before
another dwelling materialized. Even where a new home awaited, its de-
crepitude had sometimes reached the point of broken windows, collapsed ceilings, and frigid interiors.[105]

Another chronic weakness of *detdoma*—stemming once again from
the familiar lament of insufficient resources and the prickly disposition
of many street children—centered on the quantity and quality of teachers and other personnel. A shortage of capable educators persisted, especially in the provinces and at facilities for delinquents, because work
in conditions described above struck few as appealing.[106] Turnover remained high, pay and training low. As late as 1926–1927, a Narkompros report lamented that a quarter of the teachers (*pedagogicheskie
rabotniki*) in the Russian Republic's *detdoma* possessed no more than a
primary school education, and virtually all the rest had not gone beyond
secondary school.[107] The problems of rapid turnover and low motivation
emerged vividly at a *detdom* in Kaluga province. A new director, Smirnova, was assigned in 1926 to replace a man who had scarcely bothered
to visit the institution. Though Smirnova sought at first to administer
the facility, she soon discarded the mission in favor of a love affair and
other personal pursuits, thereby triggering her removal in favor of a man
named Sedov. He, in turn, seemed primarily concerned with living comfortably on his own property and devoted no attention to the *detdom*.
On Sedov's heels came a director, Gerasimov, who swiftly made clear
his partiality for vodka. In this case, neglect of the children might have
been preferable, for he dispatched youths to purchase liquor and invited
them to share it with him. Following Gerasimov's dismissal, a sick, irritable man assumed the director's position—and soon died. Alas, concluded the account, his replacement represented no improvement over
the others.[108]

Dedicated teachers and administrators, undeterred by inadequate facilities and meager pay, still faced myriad disappointments in raising
waifs.[109] Adolescents who had embraced the criminal world's practices
over a period of several years were especially difficult, but others as well
acquired characteristics that sorely tried instructors. Only combative-
ness or cunning, the street had taught, deterred abuse at the hands of
others. Initially, and sometimes for months after entering a *detdom*,
youths remained suspicious and mistrustful—qualities ingrained by even
a comparatively short period of victimization in train stations and slums.
Numerous reports described them as high-strung, irritable, belligerent,
and coarse, ready with tears or rage at the slightest imagined provoca-

tion. All this, combined with an advanced disinclination to sit quietly, made them daunting pedagogic challenges.[110]

Grisha M——ov, the boy who had repeatedly convinced personnel at the Pokrovskii receiver to send him "home," grew so disruptive during his last stay that the staff routed him to a colony administered by the Commissariat of Health. Here, they hoped, he could be examined and then raised in a manner calculated to overcome his vagrant ways—a task that proved formidable. Grisha flouted the facility's rules and revealed no interest in classroom activities, preferring to slip away and balance on window ledges, clamber up trees, or penetrate locked rooms. Teachers who upset him became targets of the searing epithets that had served as a means of attack and defense on the street. These qualities alone were sufficient to aggrieve the colony's instructors, but Grisha undermined their efforts further with periodic escapes. The institution's daily log noted: "He often runs away from the colony to the Smolensk Market [in Moscow], where evidently he steals, because in the evenings he returns with *makhorka* [coarse tobacco], candies, and seeds." When told that further escapades would bring his transfer to another facility, he fled with a companion. A few days later they returned and secured readmittance with a promise to obey the establishment's rules (though Grisha soon disdained them much as before). Then, amid inaccurate rumors of the colony's imminent closure, he and a handful of other boys departed once again for the neighborhood of the Smolensk Market. This time, ten days elapsed before an emissary from the group appeared with a request to return. "Don't think that we are mangy," he insisted. "It is clean where we are. We cleared out a corner in a tumbledown building, piled up fresh straw, and do not let in outsiders. We always have someone on duty, just like in the colony. Each day we go to the river to bathe." The staff detected grounds for hope in this declaration and granted the runaways' desire. Shortly thereafter, Grisha allowed that he would remain in the colony "for the time being" (where he was well fed and not forced to do anything), while flatly refusing to stay "forever" or participate in classroom instruction. He did not rule out spending some time in a cobbler's workshop but never retreated from his view of stealing as an honorable occupation. More than once he stated without hesitation (or bravado), "I am a thief and will remain so."[111]

Teachers entrusted with Aleksei P——iaev (the boy who had entered apartments to steal Primus stoves under the pretense of begging) also found their hands full. Aleksei appeared unmanageable, though his impetuosity occasionally turned engaging, as during a stay in the colony's clinic for treatment of an eye ailment. The young patient refused to remain in bed and scurried around the ward looking for something to read, until a book on the meaning of dreams turned up. Armed with this manual, he pressed staff members to divulge their nighttime visions for interpretation and longed himself to dream of diamonds, said to foretell happiness and wealth. However, no sense of restraint moderated this youthful exuberance. While still in the clinic, Aleksei slipped outside to gather wood and then fired the stove so hot that emergency measures were required, much to his delight, to cool the metal. On returning to the colony's general quarters, he displayed the same troubling qualities—irritability, aloofness, and suspicion—that were evident during his first days in the facility. He rejected the institution's rules and refused to participate in schooling and other group activities. When rebuked, he fell into a rage, swore savagely, and threw nearby objects at instructors. They, in turn, despaired at his intransigence and decided to confront him with an ultimatum: either obey the colony's rules (general decorum and attendance in classes and workshops) or leave to stray wherever he pleased. Aleksei did not require time to ponder the options and, cursing everyone encountered in parting, disappeared.[112]

On top of everything else, men and women who worked with former street children doubtless wondered now and then if the adolescents would assault them. Attacks on staff members rarely erupted in most institutions, but at some, especially those for "difficult" adolescents, they arose with enough frequency to intimidate or even drive teachers away. Though abuse more often remained verbal—nevertheless unnerving and vulgar for those unaccustomed to the street's argot—beatings and even attempted rapes did take place. So did other harassment, including batches of lice dumped on instructors.[113] At a *detdom* in Leningrad, a boy threw a rock at a teacher and was sent to the director's office. Roughly twenty-five of the youth's comrades rose on his behalf and set to smashing the institution's windows and thrashing personnel. This so terrorized the latter that many tendered notice.[114] Much the same thing transpired regularly during the first few months of a clinic for juvenile drug users in Moscow. The entire staff had to be replaced several times following their mistreatment by young patients ever primed to sack the facility and escape.[115]

A compendium of problems common to *detdoma* dominated newspaper articles about a colony in the village of Pushkino, fifteen miles outside Moscow. Altogether, the site contained approximately 1,500 children housed in nearly a hundred structures—by no means the worst of which was the Voroshilov *detdom*, a coeducational facility for some 45 youths, none older than fourteen. A correspondent expressed shock upon entering this dismal, cold building whose broken windows and general dilapidation represented in large measure the occupants' own handiwork. Many of the inhabitants, dressed in rags and such accessories as torn boots of adult size worn over bare feet, appeared indistinguishable from children still on the street. Had their faces been smeared deliberately with mud and soot they could not have been dirtier. As dinnertime approached, the youths huddled together in a room lit by a single kerosene lamp to consume their "meager" fare with "black and revolting" utensils. Afterward, though it was only six o'clock, they went to bed because the home possessed no additional lamps to ward off the darkness. Underworld jargon caught the ear, and thefts occurred, as did other forms of abuse (including rape) suffered by the defenseless— among whom probably numbered several retarded children assigned inappropriately to the home. Girls in particular seemed "intimidated and absolutely cowed," some even fearing to appear at meals. The visitor expressed no surprise that people living nearby regarded their young neighbors as vandals and hoodlums.

To be sure, the colony's numerous schools and workshops suggested a model facility at first glance. "But look a little closer," advised the journalist, "and you will see that all these things remain mere devices and produce no results at all." The morning school, for instance, was well run but could accommodate only 380 pupils, while the carpentry shop fashioned its crude tools from stolen train rails. All told, fewer than 200 youths frequented the workshops, and even they generally departed "entirely untrained." In short, worried the author, "we are in danger of producing an army of useless unemployed, thieves, hooligans and prostitutes."[116]

How should one assess the condition of *detdoma* during the middle years of the decade? A case for positive appraisal would stress, quite correctly, significant gains in care and training compared to the fetid chaos that reigned at the beginning of the 1920s. In subsequent years, no matter how many shortcomings observers identified in *detdoma*, they could hardly fail to recognize that the situation had improved.[117] Disastrous institutions still caught the eye, but not on a scale to duplicate the crushing hopelessness of 1921–1922. Beyond noting a reduction of debacles, numerous accounts described institutions that had managed

to establish schools, workshops, clubs, and features of "self-government" along lines sketched earlier in the chapter. Even authors who
criticized many of the *detdoma* in one region or another commonly
identified others as respectable. Nor were the achievements limited to
facilities for docile, inexperienced street children. Some of the most
heartening successes had been little more than seedy shelters for juvenile
thieves before the arrival of devoted personnel.[118]

At the same time, contemporaries concluded with near unanimity that
most *detdoma*, especially those in the provinces, floundered in defects.
The All-Russian Conference of *Detdom* Personnel heard a report in
1927 that over 80 percent of the children's institutions in the Russian
Republic were not organized or operating properly. Many directors and
teachers misunderstood or disliked the changes advocated by Narkompros's reformers and ignored these measures where possible.[119] Furthermore, whatever one's opinion of the reforms, the actual state of affairs
in most *detdoma* hardly ignited enthusiasm. Excluding the best and the
worst facilities, life inside appears to have been drab and monotonous.
Children generally received rudimentary shelter and some food, but little
in the way of clubs, excursions, well-supplied workshops, or stimulating
instruction. No longer did they die by the thousand in the state's hands,
but the goal of a socialist upbringing had scarcely moved within reach.
In the meantime they sat idly, according to one report, with the same
bored expressions encountered among people waiting for hours in a
train station.[120]

Efforts to overcome the predicament by forming new types of facilities made little headway. Along with labor communes, the innovations
included "children's towns" (*detskie gorodki*), usually amalgamations
of a few (sometimes many) *detdoma*, similar in configuration to the
Pushkino colony. Here the goal was bigger institutions that could pool
facilities, equipment, land, and personnel to provide a more fruitful upbringing. A few children's towns took shape as early as 1918, but most
lumbered into existence after the famine. They ranged in size from undertakings equivalent to an ample *detdom* (roughly a hundred inhabitants) to sprawling ventures totaling as many as several thousand
youths.[121] In some cases all lived in close proximity, while elsewhere
they remained in what had been a series of independent *detdoma*, separated from one another by miles. As it turned out, the settlements generally suffered from the same problems as *detdoma*, though their un-
wieldy size and loose structure also saddled them with shortcomings all
their own.[122] Like labor communes, they never assumed a major role.

Less than 5 percent of all institutionalized waifs lived in them during the mid-1920s, and Narkompros soon discouraged the opening of any more.[123]

For better or for worse, then, *detdoma* continued to receive most youths removed from the street as the Soviet regime marked its first decade of existence. Authors who paused on this anniversary to assess the ten years of raising "state children" could rarely avoid misgivings. They might note certain accomplishments, but they emphasized enduring deficiencies more forcefully. An article in the journal of Narkompros's Moscow division went so far as to claim impressive progress in all areas of education save one: facilities for homeless juveniles.[124] Anxious questions thus persisted as *detdoma* began their second decade. Did their "graduates" find promising opportunities to begin independent lives upon departing the institutions? If so, how successfully did the young men and women navigate thereafter in a society that often regarded them warily? These concerns loomed large at the same time that Stalin and his supporters launched the Soviet Union on its own dramatic voyage—in the process, confronting *detdoma* with new opportunities and new obstacles.

Conclusion:
On the Road to Life?

Ten years ago, every traveler in Russia came back with
stories of the hordes of wild children who roamed the
countryside and infested the city streets. . . . After methods of
repression had failed, they gathered these children together in
collective homes; they taught them cooperation, useful work,
healthful recreation. Against great odds they succeeded.
There are today no wild children in Russia.

John Dewey

If there were old people . . . who could not adjust to Soviet
society, there were young ones, too, who could not—or
would not. My roommate, Nichan, had adjusted brilliantly
after his years of wandering, and had become an inspiring
and useful citizen under state guidance, helping others along
the path of progress. But many young vagabonds had refused
to accept—or accepted only temporarily—the aid of
institutions established for them. These determined little
hooligans were making a last stand for freedom.

Langston Hughes

Toward the end of the 1920s, as the Party set a new course for socialism,
comprehensive planning took the helm amid feverish acclaim. Zeal for
blueprints and guidelines, most prominent in fanfare surrounding the
First Five-Year Plan, spread beyond the economy to many other undertakings, including the campaign to eliminate homelessness. Narkompros
tacked to the changing winds as early as 1927, when the preface to one
of its publications announced that "the struggle with juvenile *besprizornost'*, like all other areas of Soviet construction, is taking on a
planned, systematic character."[1] In November of the same year, a report
to the All-Russian Conference of *Detdom* Personnel urged that uncoor-

dinated bursts of activity, which had failed to clear the streets, give way to a deliberate approach. Improvised emergency measures may have been unavoidable when desperate millions inundated the country, observed the report, but current conditions dictated a meticulous, studied solution. This was not an instruction to be ignored. Only a few months before, the government had unveiled a Three-Year Plan to rescue abandoned children, and the conference dutifully urged that local officials compose similar documents tailored to their own regions.[2]

The Three-Year Plan was approved by the Council of People's Commissars and the All-Russian Central Executive Committee on June 20, 1927. It followed a draft prepared by the State Planning Commission, based on an estimate that in 1925 the Russian Republic contained 125,000 homeless juveniles requiring "full maintenance." Of this total, the planners calculated that 20,000 would enter institutions by the end of 1925, leaving 105,000 in need of accommodations. Places were to be created for nearly two thirds by discharging 68,000 inhabitants from *detdoma* and other facilities over three years (23,000 in 1926/27, 22,000 in 1927/28, and 23,000 in 1928/29). Concurrently, the plan expected construction of new institutions and expansion of existing establishments to accept the remaining 37,000. As before, Narkompros figured prominently. Fully 34,000 of the 37,000 youths were earmarked for its facilities, with only 2,000 intended for the Commissariat of Internal Affairs's labor homes and 1,000 for the Commissariat of Health's sickbeds. At the same time, the decree ordered provincial officials to draft local plans following the guidelines sketched above, thus forbidding further reductions in the budgets and capacities of *detdoma* during the three-year interval.[3]

The decree of June 20 also called for a concerted effort to remove juvenile stowaways from the nation's railways, a goal promoted again five months later by Lunacharskii at the All-Russian Conference of *Detdom* Personnel.[4] While the passage of time had reduced the number of youths plying the rails, many who persisted (some 24,000, according to an estimate in 1926) now boasted years of experience on the road. In contrast to refugees from war and famine, they were skilled in the tricks of survival and familiar with the criminal subculture at stations. More comfortable in this footloose world than in children's institutions, they (along with a smaller number who traveled aboard ships on inland waterways) presented facilities with a severe challenge. Regulations and discipline struck them as chafing impositions, and they kept an eye open for opportunities to flee. It came as no surprise that a majority plucked from the rails late in the decade had already compiled records of escape from *detdoma*.[5]

Waifs on the railways confronted other government agencies and citizens with vexations, too, notably damage to train cars and equipment, frequent safety hazards, and thousands of thefts each year.[6] In 1926, well before the Three-Year Plan, the Council of People's Commissars ordered the Commissariat of Transportation to invigorate its heretofore ineffectual efforts to remove young vagrants from trains and ships. The resulting strategy required the deployment of thirty stationary receivers along routes heavily traveled by juveniles and the dispatch of sixty special train cars intended to range over principal lines, stopping at stations to collect children for preliminary processing (haircuts, disinfection, meals, questioning, and so forth). After no more than three days, youths were to be transferred from the cars to the commissariat's stationary receivers for up to sixty days of further study and rudimentary education similar to that in ordinary receivers.[7] Thereafter, most were expected to enter Narkompros's domain, following the well-worn path to *detdoma*, with a much smaller number placed directly into production work or institutions operated by other agencies. Those discovered to have parents or relatives were to be sent home.[8]

The Commissariat of Transportation's train cars and receivers removed thousands of urchins (at least temporarily) from the rails. But the procedure also encountered predictable difficulties, including the same shortages of resources and trained staff so evident in Narkompros's institutions. At the station of Armavir in the Northern Caucasus, for instance, a fire hose served to douse youths in the absence of disinfection equipment, and children had to prepare their own meals while living in a derelict freight car.[9] In addition, provincial Narkompros branches did not fling open the doors of their *detdoma* to candidates from the Commissariat of Transportation's receivers. Balking at the prospect of still more mouths to feed and bodies to clothe, they delayed or refused outright to accept juveniles gathered from the railroads by transport authorities. The string of reprimands and orders on this score, issued from Moscow into the 1930s, could not erase the defiance of officials determined to conserve their means.[10]

Fragmentary data (and the Three-Year Plan's renewed attention to the problem) suggest that the number of receivers and roving train cars never reached the totals anticipated in 1926.[11] It appears that in most regions the strategy had shifted by 1930 to one of maintaining fixed receivers at stations—often in cars on sidings—rather than moving them up and down the tracks. Some mobile receivers continued to operate, but preference grew for establishing cordons at important junctions to apprehend extra passengers as they arrived. Frequently, the stations chosen bespoke not only a desire to collar stowaways and deposit them in receivers, but also a hope to block their perennial migrations to major cities, first and foremost Moscow. To assist employees of Narkompros and the Commissariat of Transportation, members of "society" (representatives from the Komsomol, ODD, trade unions, schools, and so on) were urged to form brigades to search trains at local depots. The tiny Tikhonova-Pustyn' station, on the Moscow-Kiev-Voronezh line, fielded an effective inspection unit consisting of one person, a former waif, familiar with all the crevices on trains. Within two weeks he apprehended fifteen youths and sent them to a receiver in Kaluga.[12] Around the country, such efforts helped reduce markedly the number of homeless children riding the rails by the end of the 1920s. Optimism seemed in order—just before the next decade's upheavals in the countryside left thousands more clinging to trains in search of sustenance.

The decree of June 20, in approving the Three-Year Plan, pointed to other sore spots as well, among them an insufficient effort to prevent impoverished, abused, or neglected juveniles from landing on the street in the first place. Reiterating the complaint, a resolution of the All-Russian Conference of *Detdom* Personnel observed that three years earlier, another congress on homelessness had appealed for more attention to this very issue—with little discernible improvement. As a result of the problem's tenacity, concluded the resolution, even if all needy youths entered institutions immediately, new contingents would likely materialize to void the accomplishment.[13] This was an important point. How could the Three-Year Plan, whose arithmetic did not allow for newly abandoned offspring, retain any chance of success if the street acquired more boys and girls on the heels of those wedged into *detdoma*? Quite apart from the plan, anyone could understand that the declining number of homeless children in the second half of the decade presaged the blight's complete eradication only if reservoirs of potential replacements were drained.

Thus, while resolutions and directives prior to 1927 mentioned prevention now and then, agencies promoted this goal more frequently in the period 1927–1929.[14] Attention centered on youths thought most vulnerable, especially those whose parents or guardians left them unsupervised for extended intervals. Whatever the reason for neglect—parental disinterest, jobs far from home, or poverty (forcing dependents out to beg, trade, or steal)—it led to unattended children roaming their neighborhoods. These juveniles prompted observers and government decrees to demand action, including (1) material assistance to impoverished families and single mothers, (2) out-of-school activities to occupy the idle (similar to clubs, circles, and workshops desired in *detdoma*), and (3) employment for adolescents. Occasionally, appeals also sounded for criminal charges against comparatively prosperous parents who left offspring to grow up on their own.[15] Responses of this sort, implemented broadly, would doubtless have depleted the street's reserve army. But the massive industrialization and collectivization drives begun in 1929 eclipsed such modest programs. Industrialization did provide jobs for teenagers who might otherwise have floundered, but the concomitant traumas of collectivization and dekulakization churned a new homeless wave across the country.

Meanwhile, by no means all "new" waifs were new. Thousands on the street arrived there from *detdoma*. Some had run away; others had been discharged with minimal training and then failed to catch on in work or school. As the years passed and this "recycling" pattern developed, substandard conditions in *detdoma* gained wider recognition as a cause of "secondhand" homelessness. Here lay another reason for reform. During the years 1928 to 1930 numerous decrees from the Council of People's Commissars, the All-Russian Central Executive Committee, and the Children's Commission demanded the facilities' improvement.[16] Most of these commands, especially by 1930, did not restrict their attention to remedies indistinguishable from previous years' legislation. Breaking new ground, and also promoting certain old ideas much more insistently, they called for reorganization of institutions to bring them in line with the dramatic economic policies launched by Stalin and his supporters.

Few corners of the Soviet Union remained untouched by the industrialization and collectivization campaigns of this era, and juvenile facilities, the forges of a new generation, received their marching orders promptly. A conference on neglected and homeless minors, for example, declared it essential in 1930 "to restructure fundamentally the whole system of children's institutions to prepare cadres for industry and agriculture." Shortly afterward, a circular issued by a number of government agencies, including Narkompros, warned: "Against the background of rapidly growing industry and the socialist reconstruction of the countryside, and with the consequent huge demand for workers, it is especially intolerable that children's institutions contain adolescents who are not receiving sufficient training and who are not finding a use for their strengths and skills in a single branch of construction."[17] The new priorities even affected documents retroactively. As late as April 1928, the Council of People's Commissars had instructed Narkompros and the Commissariat of Health to prepare residents of their establishments for *handicrafts* as well as factory work in order to expand the youths' opportunities for employment. But almost as soon as these instructions appeared, the government's burgeoning appetite for industrial labor rendered them obsolete—and a collection of documents published in 1932 displayed the decree minus its offending advocacy of handicrafts.[18]

Numerous resolutions and directives sought to incorporate *detdoma* and similar facilities more fully into the transformation of Soviet life by "attaching" them to nearby factories. This could take the form of an arrangement where teenagers worked by day as apprentices in a plant and, after discharge from their *detdom*, found employment and housing at the enterprise in which they had trained. In November 1929, the Council of People's Commissars ordered Narkompros and the Supreme Council of the National Economy to establish "apprentice brigades" of *detdom* occupants to undergo instruction in factories. After their training (for which the local Narkompros office and factory shared expenses), each youth, the decree insisted, had to receive permanent employment commensurate with his qualifications. Less ambitious variants of "attachment" included a factory's agreement to supply the workshops of a *detdom* with tools, raw materials, and instructors. But whatever the details, they pointed to the same end: more adolescents with skills readily harnessed by industry.[19]

At rural institutions, the onslaught of forced collectivization generated official demands for change along analogous lines. Many of the decrees and circulars that promoted industrial "attachment" stipulated likewise that agricultural *detdoma*, colonies, and communes be "attached" to state or collective farms. Some urged the transformation of facilities into collective-farm training schools or pressed for their merger with nearby farms already in existence.[20] The policy of foster care also felt the new winds. Without ceasing immediately to place children in peasant families, Narkompros began to recommend that institutions transfer residents to collective farms instead. The general terms resembled those announced a few years earlier for private families and artisans: the child had to agree to the move, and the collective farm received a strip of land and various payments. In return, Narkompros expected, youths would be raised in a communal atmosphere more conducive to socialism. Just as decrees lauded factory apprenticeship as a means to marshal foot soldiers for the industrial front, a Narkompros order proclaimed that training in collective farms promised to "make former *besprizornye* into future fighters for economic and cultural revolution in the countryside."[21]

Many other features of the "Stalin Revolution" crowded directives on *detdoma*. The period's militant language muscled forward in some publications to attribute deficiencies in work with street children to the now ubiquitous bogies of "opportunism" and "wrecking." Official documents and journal articles recommended to *detdoma* such favorites of the season as "friendly socialist competition" and "shock brigades" of ardent workers. Grounds for "socialist competition" between institutions or inside individual facilities included the performance of workshops, the level of Pioneer/Komsomol activity, the organization of "self-government," and attendance at school. Some contests covered extensive territory—Siberia or even the entire Russian Republic—with victorious *detdoma* qualifying for prizes that could reach thousands of rubles.[22]

Labor training in factories, work on collective farms, "socialist competition," and shock brigades: these were among the endeavors desired by the government for *detdoma*—and much of the rest of society for that matter—in 1930. But staging competitions between facilities and organizing youths into "shock units" to perform their customary work could not alone erase the chronic problems of *detdoma*. If anything, resources for institutions grew scarcer by the early 1930s as the government channeled investment into industrialization with growing determination. Reports from around the country still found children's establishments dilapidated, overcrowded, poorly supplied, and hobbled by inhabitants of inappropriate age or disposition. Complaints over freezing indoor temperatures, filthy bathrooms, snow eaten in the absence of water, and schools unattended for lack of warm attire dotted newspapers and journals.[23] So, too, did allegations of wretched sanitation— "beneath all criticism," according to one article—and diseases that appeared more frequently than doctors.[24]

The shortcomings helped keep universal labor training far beyond Narkompros's reach. Though some facilities were indeed "attached" to factories or collective farms and provided vocational preparation to most of their charges, others could do so for only the oldest. In many regions, fewer than half and sometimes none of an institution's residents received labor instruction of any sort. Here and there youths loitered unattended, broke windows in nearby buildings, and threw rocks at passersby.[25] Fighting, gambling, narcotics, and sexual abuse endured at some addresses in both Moscow and the provinces.[26] These conditions and the street's lure continued to pull thousands of juveniles from facilities as escapees rather than as new workers striding forth to the factory bench.[27]

It would be incorrect, of course, to suggest that few if any institutions yielded impressive results as the decade waned. Some did, and a larger number managed to propel children into worthy occupations at least occasionally.[28] Say what one might of discipline or sanitation, the most compelling measure of a facility remained its ability to place "graduates" in productive careers. Substantial numbers participated in the test each year, as the Russian Republic's *detdoma* discharged twenty to thirty thousand youths annually in the second half of the decade.[29] A majority headed for one of four destinations: (1) relatives or parents whom authorities had located; (2) other families (generally peasants) on a foster care basis; (3) production jobs in factories, agriculture, and handicrafts; or (4) schools and apprenticeship programs.[30] In 1927, for example, inhabitants of institutions for "normal" children in urban areas of the Russian Republic departed as follows:[31]

25 percent to parents or relatives

7 percent to factories

5 percent to agricultural work

2 percent to handicraft occupations

7 percent to foster families

10 percent to schools and apprenticeship training

26 percent to other children's institutions

11 percent to other or unknown destinations

6 percent ran away

1 percent died

Parents, relatives (the latter more frequently than the former), and other households (through foster care or adoption) received the largest number of juveniles from *detdoma* during the middle of the decade. In 1926, over half those released were so earmarked.[32] As the decade drew to a close, this proportion diminished, in part because institutions contained fewer youths whose parents or relatives could be identified; most had already been removed by local officials shepherding their budgets. At the same time, new opportunities and decrees spawned by industrialization and collectivization encouraged authorities to send adolescents in other directions. Above all, this meant to factories, for the surge of industrial activity prompted by the First Five-Year Plan transformed a labor glut into a shortage.[33] Youths soon crowded the path to "production" as *detdoma* received insistent orders to turn out workers for the country's new projects. In 1928/29, for instance, 40 percent of those discharged from a large sample of *detdoma* headed for industrial work, while only 24 percent set out for relatives and peasants' families.[34]

The government had long tried to place more of its wards in industry. Early in the decade, factories and plants received instructions to reserve quotas of jobs—between 3 and 20 percent, depending on the branch of production—for minors. Youths who qualified need not have come from children's facilities, but in 1923 the All-Russian Central Executive Committee stipulated that 25 percent of the places reserved for juveniles through labor exchanges go to candidates from *detdoma*. In subsequent years provincial officials in many regions set aside even more, as much as 30–50 percent of the juvenile quota, for residents of institutions.[35] Still, the implementation of these orders remained spotty for some time. Factory administrators resented requirements that adolescents work reduced hours while receiving full pay, and trade union members tried on occasion to reserve jobs for their own offspring.[36] Only the First Five-Year Plan's boundless demand for labor overcame such obstacles by multiplying opportunities in the industrial sector for recruits from *detdoma*.

Much the same could be said about schools. Officials had sought from the beginning to reserve places in technical schools for former street children, and incomplete data suggest that increasing numbers left *detdoma* for additional education over the years.[37] Whatever progress may have been made in the mid-1920s, however, was dwarfed at the end of the decade as industrial acceleration brought with it a much greater demand for technical training. New institutions to provide this education opened their doors across the land, creating room for a larger contingent of pupils from *detdoma*. They (and other recruits) often entered programs that maintained a direct relationship with production, notably factory-apprenticeship schools. Here basic industrial training accompanied postprimary education, with students frequently supported at the host factory's expense. By 1930, *detdoma* hoped to discharge most occupants along paths of this sort, anticipating no doubt that the climate of full employment and abundant educational opportunity would ease the youths' transition into society's mainstream.[38]

What happened when an adolescent walked out the door of a *detdom* for the last time? Did a life of independent respectability commence, or were impediments forthcoming that few could surmount? While no statistics or even reasonably precise estimates indicate the number who turned their fortunes around, the undertaking clearly represented a steep climb for many. In the case of juveniles sent from *detdoma* to relatives (and, less often, to foster families), Narkompros and the Children's Commission complained throughout the decade that local officials, keen to reduce demands on their budgets, proceeded without assurances that the households could support new members. As a result, boys and girls risked landing in families that did not want them or could not feed them, with the street a likely refuge.[39]

The scarcity of effective labor training in *detdoma* also impeded juveniles' reentry into society. Accounts from around the country described institutions clogged with residents in their late teens and early twenties, still without skills needed for employment. An author from Saratov expressed amazement in 1930 that the city's nine *detdoma* contained 208 adolescents between sixteen and eighteen years of age whose lack of training prevented them from securing jobs even as the country's demand for labor soared.[40] Just as often, local officials simply discharged youths, including those with little vocational instruction, rather than house them year after year. "Unloading" children seemed the quickest way to alleviate overcrowding, reduce expenses, and dispose of troublemakers—enough to preserve the practice despite official condemnations. But in time, numerous teenagers released with slim employment prospects rejoined the homeless and later appeared again in *detdoma*.[41]

When youths left an institution for work or school, the first days and weeks were generally difficult. They entered an unfamiliar environment, perhaps without a job or stipend in hand, and encountered neighbors who viewed them askance. To reduce the jolt of the transition and help anchor juveniles in their new lives, Narkompros ordered on several occasions that *detdoma* give clothing and food (or money) to those setting out into the world. Some institutions apparently did. But the chronic poverty of many others left them unable to provision departing wards.[42] Of course, support could take forms beyond bread and shoes. As early as 1921 Narkompros directed facilities to preserve contact for two years with former occupants in order to encourage the youths with demonstrations that others shared an interest in their well-being. Correspondence, visits, or gifts could assure adolescents that they had not been abandoned once again. The effort might make the difference, Narkompros felt, in convincing some to persevere in the face of difficulties confronted while adjusting to a new life. Toward this end, a children's institution in Moscow province organized a society of "graduates," now working in factories and schools, to help those who came after them to navigate securely. Publications of the period reveal a few similar undertakings; but much more frequently, into the 1930s, they criticized *detdoma* for treating residents' farewells as deliverance from an onerous obligation best terminated with all speed.[43]

Out in the provinces, officials continued to send children on journeys to cities armed only with one-way tickets and instructions to seek employment or admission to schools. A Narkompros circular complained in 1928 that local authorities began shipping adolescents from *detdoma* to Moscow shortly before each school term—transferring their responsibilities to the capital, in other words, and hoping for the best. Without money for food and lodging, and with no advance application to the schools and factories approached, these ill-fated quests generally foundered before long. Youths had to beg or steal to survive, and all too often the street reclaimed them for its own. In short, warned the Children's Commission three years later, launching teenagers to cities under these conditions bordered on a criminal act, for which prosecution was now contemplated.[44]

Even those who stayed in *detdoma* until a school or enterprise accepted them did not always enjoy smooth sailing. Prospective students bound for educational institutions might receive their stipends only after classes began—or not until the start of a new budget year—and hence be stranded financially for weeks. To make ends meet, some turned to selling their clothes and sleeping in train stations or night shelters, establishments whose atmosphere contributed little to academic success.[45] Housing represented a particularly intractable problem. Millions of citizens suffered from a shortage of accommodations that aggravated the plight of youths discharged from *detdoma*. Factories and schools, if they provided housing at all, often placed these children in ramshackle dormitories worse than their previous abodes. A correspondent in Tula described one such building itself as a *besprizornyi*, while a report from Vladimir told of juveniles leaving primitive barracks assigned them by a factory and returning ragged and hungry to their *detdoma*.[46] At the end of the decade, Narkompros went so far as to seek control over the apartments of parents who had died and left offspring to state care. Living space previously occupied by those now entering children's facilities should be reserved, the agency argued, for others leaving.[47] Unacceptable to brawnier government bodies, the unorthodox proposition succeeded mainly in demonstrating Narkompros's difficulty in competing for scarce resources.

A long series of resolutions and decrees stipulated that adolescents from *detdoma* receive preference in the allotment of housing and jobs—often at the high level of priority extended to workers and demobilized soldiers. While this seemed encouraging, many of the same sources complained that the orders were widely ignored.[48] Part of the problem stemmed from the deficit of housing and (until the end of the decade) jobs, for laws alone could not erase the nation's shortages. But there was more to it than that. Beyond economic and bureaucratic difficulties lurked the widespread view of waifs as thieves, prostitutes, and drug addicts. "Who," asked a Siberian author, "does not speak often with annoyance, indignation, and contempt of these youths, feared by people in the bazaar, station, wharf, train, bus, and at home?!" A woman in Moscow overheard someone encourage bystanders to douse a pair with kerosene and set them on fire. In one of Leningrad's schools, a large majority of pupils, questioned on the sources of hooliganism, included street children in their lists. Around the country, many observers commented on the bitter remarks uttered by citizens who spotted urchins: "Beasts!" "Damned bandits!" "They should be destroyed!" These and similar convictions filled the air. Even the chairman of the Baku Children's Commission, as previously noted, characterized them as robbers, hooligans, and murderers, impossible to mold into human beings—an opinion shared by the head of a receiver in Moscow. She called her charges "bandits" and told them: "You will never become human beings; every one of you will end up in the Solovki [labor camp]."[49]

The unsavory reputation of homeless adolescents rubbed off on *detdoma*. Facilities that overcame initial hostility from the surrounding population and established better relations with their neighbors appear to have been the exception.[50] Most evidence suggests that people viewed *detdoma* at best as barracks where children languished in idle poverty and, at worst, as lairs of unspeakable debauchery. Some citizens feared or loathed residents of *detdoma* to the point where they refused to walk nearby.[51] As shown in preceding chapters, many institutions merited unflattering reputations, and there were indeed buildings best given a wide berth. Youths of the Lenin *detdom* in Tambov, when not engaged in such activities as burglarizing nearby apartments, amused themselves by pelting passersby with rocks. Occupants of a receiver in Saratov poured tubs of water from an upstairs window on pedestrians and showered them with stale bread, melons, and stones.[52]

In turn, the unpalatable image of *detdoma* haunted those who passed through them. According to a report from the Urals, for example, a group of peasants working the land noticed a fire in their village and rushed back to help extinguish it. Upon learning that the conflagration raged only at the local children's institution, however, they returned without further ado to the fields. Long after discharge from their facilities, wards of *detdoma* remained soiled in the public mind—for girls in particular, a possible hindrance to marriage.[53] To this day, negative opinions of *detdoma* and their charges persist, as a recent letter to *Pravda* made clear. The anonymous author, who had adopted youths from a *detdom*, implored readers not to spread word of boys and girls with this background, for those so informed tended to regard the youngsters as misfits. "People," she appealed, "have pity on me and my children. Why can't you be quiet after discovering that a neighbor has children from a *detdom*?"[54]

Thus, when former denizens of the street left institutions to enroll in schools and factories, they often encountered suspicion and even hostility from supervisors, teachers, workers, and students. Some enterprises and schools wanted nothing to do with *detdom* veterans, considering them poorly trained, wanton at heart, and likely to corrupt others. "It is important to bear in mind," Narkompros reminded its provincial offices, "the widespread (even if to a considerable extent preconceived) opinion of economic organs and enterprises that those raised in *detdoma* are unreliable and poorly suited for systematic work." In short order, complaints from schools, dormitories, and factories piled up at the youths' doorstep, alleging thefts, hooliganism, laziness, and absenteeism. Even if a former inhabitant of a *detdom* did not deserve to be viewed in this light, at some point after leaving the institution he or she probably was. Hounded, branded as "detdomers" (*detdomovtsy*), and assigned to the least desirable living quarters and jobs, many faced greater initial trials in schools and plants than the "normal" juveniles who entered with them.[55] As if their past had not been difficult enough, it clung to them as a notorious stain, throwing up one more obstacle to overcome.

Narkompros's concern led it to conduct surveys here and there to ascertain how youths fared after growing up largely in government hands. An investigation in 1929 of *detdom* "graduates" in approximately twenty factory-apprenticeship and other technical schools in the Moscow area determined that half the sample had lived in *detdoma* for seven to ten years, very much Lunacharskii's "state children." As the author of an article on the survey put it, "we are completely responsible for them." If so, the study's results represented grounds for neither euphoria nor despair—about the best Narkompros could reasonably expect. Only half the respondents felt that they had received adequate training in *detdoma*, but three-fourths indicated satisfaction with work in their current institutions. The average success rate hovered unimpressively between 50 and 55 percent, though school administrators evaluated students from *detdoma* as "no worse than children from the general population."[56] If this last assessment (which ran contrary to the impression of other officials just cited) were true throughout the country, Narkompros would deserve credit for a remarkable salvage operation.

Certainly, the sources do not lack for portraits of individuals who made a successful start in work or school after leaving institutions. Some returned to visit their *detdoma* and communes; others sent photographs and letters—all of which must have heartened staff members. When Anton Makarenko died, former inhabitants of his colony and commune came from around the country to pay their respects, no longer as delinquents but as engineers, journalists, students, and army officers. Veterans of the street also pursued careers as musicians, actors, teachers, economists, doctors, artists, athletes, skilled workers, and activists in the trade unions, Komsomol, and Party.[57] A few became well known in their fields within the Soviet Union, as the journalist Mikhail Leshchinskii discovered. In 1955 he met Anna Kurskaia, widow of the country's first procurator general and a participant in the effort to assist homeless youths thirty years before. Sometime after their introduction, she communicated to Leshchinskii her curiosity about the fate of these children, adding that too much time had likely passed now to pursue the matter successfully. Leshchinskii took up the challenge by writing a newspaper article that soon called forth responses from a number of former urchins. He then tried to contact them and eventually produced a book depicting the lives of several, including a major general in the Red Army and a conductor with the rank of People's Artist of the USSR.[58]

And yet, in the laborious process of tracking down a handful, Lesh-chinskii uncovered no records to show what became of the vast majority. Reports and resolutions at conferences occasionally tossed off such fig-ures as "many tens of thousands" of former waifs engaged in "socialist construction," and one article in 1930 mentioned, without reference to a source, "hundreds of thousands" helping to build socialism after time in *detdoma*.[59] But even assuming these totals to be accurate, they leave *millions* from the 1920s unaccounted for. Many perished, especially at the beginning of the period, but how many? Tens of thousands? Hun-dreds of thousands? Millions? A multitude doubtless slipped back into the criminal world as adults (including some who later attracted atten-tion in the dock at murder trials) or continued to drift elsewhere on the fringe of society. In all these areas, estimates differ little from guesses.[60] There appears no reason to question that "hundreds of thousands" from *detdoma* found themselves shoulder to shoulder with most of the pop-ulation, straining to fulfill the First Five-Year Plan's goals. A substantial number, together with a boy mentioned in Leshchinskii's book, must have added their names later to the country's long list of casualties from the Second World War.[61] According to scattered claims, youths also gained employment in the secret police, thereby exchanging the roles of defendant and inmate for those of guard, interrogator, and executioner. Hardened by their experiences in the street and alienated from the sur-rounding community, they purportedly carried out the security force's chilling commands without hesitation. Similar charges have recently de-scribed Romania's orphanages as recruiting grounds for the dreaded Securitate. The Soviet police had indeed long run some juvenile insti-tutions, providing ample opportunity to enlist residents; but the meager evidence available cannot suggest the extent of such levies.[62]

In any case, scathing criticism of *detdoma* at decade's end (and ear-lier) from educators, observers, and official bodies accentuates a judg-ment that teenagers routinely emerged from the institutions unqualified for respectable careers. Looking back in 1930, Krupskaia concluded that most *detdoma* "have not provided any sort of vocational training," and therefore "the *detdom* has not prepared [children] for life." From Siberia an author argued that "our *detdoma* have failed their exam," turning out "useless" adolescents, whom another pen labeled "junk." "In the final analysis," concluded an article in one of Narkompros's journals, "no type of educational facility has received so much criticism and, per-haps, contained so many shortcomings as the *detdom*."[63] Surely, if even a half or two thirds of the juveniles who departed institutions did so

prepared for productive work, reproach would not have flared so ve-
hemently. No doubt the demand for labor created by the First Five-Year
Plan absorbed thousands of these ill-trained youths. But it strains cre-
dulity, as it did in 1930, to conclude that nearly all overcame in this way
their schooling in the street and their years in dismal *detdoma*.

Criticism of *detdoma* helped spark a debate in Narkompros and its
publications over the institutions' future. The journal *Detskii dom* carried articles in 1929 arguing a variety of positions on such questions as:
Should the facilities be restricted to street children—and thus gradually
disappear along with homelessness—or should an ever larger number
of places be made available to youths from viable families? At a conference in June a Narkompros report urged discussion of the institutions'
role in the new society then under construction, in light of the great
disparity between the work of existing *detdoma* and the function originally envisioned for them.[64] Immediately following the Revolution,
many in the Party had viewed *detdoma* as sites for raising children of
the population in general—a means to provide them with a socialist
outlook rarely cultivated in traditional families. Instead, as the years
passed, homeless juveniles saturated the structures and precluded institutional nurturing for most other boys and girls. Not only that, severe
overcrowding prompted the transfer of some *out* of *detdoma* and into
peasant families—opposite to the direction desired in 1918. Among the
issues debated in 1929, then, stood the question of whether the institutions' initial mission could, or should, be restored.

One side in the dispute echoed sentiments of 1918, demanding that
detdoma be multiplied, not closed, after the elimination of homelessness.
The need to provide institutions for the working population's sons and
daughters mounted without pause, enthusiasts maintained, as the nation
accelerated its economic development. On a practical plane, sweeping
industrialization employed additional millions of parents, requiring
mass child care as never before. If nothing else, in other words, *detdoma*
could help working families fulfill the Five-Year Plan. To the ideologi-
cally minded, though, there *was* something else, aimed not at supporting
families but at supplanting them. The country's quickening pace increased the urgency of instilling socialist principles in youths soon to
reach adulthood in a society fundamentally different from that of their
parents. *Detdoma*, not the family hearth, advocates emphasized, could
provide this upbringing.[65]

A more powerful battery of voices opposed proliferation of the facilities. Some stressed the expense and ineffectiveness of *detdoma* and
called for their elimination. Others combined financial arguments with
observations on the population's low "cultural" level to reject as premature the transfer of numerous offspring from families to institutions.
Few people were ready for such a step, the authors contended, even if
the state could afford it. Moderates favored the preservation of *detdoma*
at roughly current number—and as institutions devoted primarily to the
destitute.[66] This was the road followed by the government as it entered
the 1930s. *Detdoma* and similar institutions did not face oblivion, but
they remained by and large the preserve of abandoned children and
other unfortunates. A swift expansion of the network to accommodate
the general population's progeny, while not rejected once and for all,
became a goal too remote for serious consideration.

There was no going back to 1918. Ten years after the Revolution, in
his greeting to the All-Russian Conference of *Detdom* Personnel, Lunacharskii characterized as "utopian" the initial hope of some comrades
that families would rapidly yield juveniles' upbringing to the state.[67] In
one respect, of course, this anticipation was anything but quixotic, for
civil war and famine, as if granting the wish in ghastly fashion, soon
shattered millions of households. But the aftermath bore slim resemblance to Bolshevik reverie. Instead, the government found itself
swamped by a multitude of youths it could not properly raise and who
obliterated the original mission of *detdoma*. Not even the hypothetical
absence of catastrophes in 1918–1922 restores plausibility to the Party's
original expectations, for without the privation of these years it seems
unlikely that many families would have desired to hand over their children to institutions. As it turned out, whatever the popular view of
detdoma in 1918, virtually no enthusiasm flickered for them among
citizens a decade later, because the facilities had become widely stig-
matized as shelters for society's dregs.[68] Only the desperate and the ideo-
logically zealous could want to place dependents in settings now more
commonly regarded as dens of sloth and depravity.

❖ ❖ ❖ ❖

In 1925 Viktor Shul'gin, director of what came to be known later as the
Marx-Engels Institute of Pedagogy, asserted that street children, by their
very nature, lived in constant struggle with bourgeois notions of property and order. "The *besprizornye* are objectively interested in the destruction of bourgeois society," he concluded, "and they are destroying,

undermining it."[69] Other Soviet commentators chose a different emphasis, regarding the poison of homelessness as toxic for socialism too. They might view capitalism as the problem's cause, and they all presumed a socialist government more inclined to assist the needy. But few considered their socialist aspirations unmenaced by the presence of abandoned juveniles. On the eighth anniversary of the October Revolution, President Mikhail Kalinin warned: "Both the government and our society must, with all their energy, set to saving the *besprizornye*. The situation here threatens grave dangers for the future if we are not able to eradicate promptly in youths the bad habits that a vagrant life imparts to them."[70]

Throughout the second half of the decade, officials and other authors repeated arguments offered in previous years regarding the danger at hand. Boys who are petty thieves today, ran a common refrain, will tomorrow be adults able to subsist only through crime. Even those who did not become full-time criminals would hardly emerge from the street's forge as champions of the new society that Bolshevik leaders prophesied. Concern also persisted throughout the 1920s that waifs would infect others with their language, behavior, and values. Viewed in this light, they not only sapped government resources in the short run, but threatened to corrupt a portion of the next generation—themselves and those susceptible to their influence—on whom the Party counted to remake the nation. Visible to all, their presence daily spotlighted serious problems still to be overcome before one could hail the victory of socialism.[71] Stanislav Kosior, a secretary of the Party Central Committee, took to the pages of both *Pravda* and *Izvestiia* to caution in 1928 that "juvenile *besprizornost'* remains a great evil in the country. Although its dimensions have diminished significantly, thousands of socially neglected children and adolescents on the streets of our cities stand in sharp contrast to the growing economic prosperity of the country and its rising cultural level."[72]

Kosior sought not to paint a picture of unrelieved pessimism. He combined the concern quoted above with an assessment that the government could eliminate the problem nearly completely "during the next year or two." Numerous officials, resolutions, and individual authors gave further voice to this confidence, maintaining that prosperity and enlightenment brought by "socialist construction" would soon expunge homelessness.[73] By 1930–1931, if decrees and other exhortations served as a guide, the blight faced welcome extinction. During the "third, decisive year of the Five-Year Plan," when so many corners were to be turned, the end of juvenile destitution ostensibly waited around one of them. "In 1931," trumpeted a slogan in one of Narkompros's journals, "not a single *besprizornyi* in the Soviet Union!"[74]

That year witnessed the release of the early Soviet sound film *Road to Life*, which portrayed the lives and eventual rehabilitation of several delinquents from the street. A Soviet reviewer welcomed the film, but with the words "better late than never" to underscore an observation that its subject had ceased to plague the country. Hence, the article concluded, "this film has become today a historical document that illuminates a stage through which we have now passed." The American educator John Dewey, who appears onscreen to introduce the feature, apparently reached much the same conclusion, for he assured audiences that "wild children" no longer inhabited the Soviet Union.[75] Many other enthusiastic pens joined in celebrating the accomplishment (variously claimed to be total or virtual), including that of Nikolai Semashko, chairman of the Children's Commission: "At last in 1931 Soviet society could state with pride that *besprizornost'* in the Russian Republic was liquidated in the main. Socialist construction was enriched with yet another historic achievement: the end of this sad inheritance from the years of famine, war, and ruin."[76]

The Three-Year Plan approved in 1927 bred similarly buoyant predictions of triumph. Amid the optimism, however, thoughtful observers regarded as unlikely the satisfaction of requirements essential to the plan's fulfillment.[77] For the project to succeed, local officials would have to obey instructions to replace adolescents discharged from *detdoma* with similar numbers of incoming residents, while providing additional beds for still more. At the same time, no new homeless urchins could surface. As it happened, these conditions were not met—and thus neither were the plan's goals for 1928/29, its final year.[78] Far fewer youths traversed cities and rails in 1929 than in 1921, but claims of the problem's demise rang false. *Pravda*, for example, reported in 1928 the absence of abandoned children in seventeen major regions, including the Northern Caucasus. This territory, long a gathering place for vagrants, could not possibly have been emptied so soon—a point supported by a recent Soviet account that included the Northern Caucasus in a list of areas (along with Moscow and Leningrad) on whose streets juveniles still lived in 1929.[79]

Nevertheless, had the corps of forsaken youths continued to thin during the early 1930s as it had in the late 1920s, the problem would have shrunk rapidly to negligible proportions—in line with announcements of the tragedy's elimination that resounded in 1930–1931. Perhaps some readers were puzzled, then, by a handful of articles and other sources that mentioned considerable numbers of street children shortly after the decade's turn. Most likely, few noticed these hints of trouble, for the documents remained widely scattered and sometimes unpublished.[80] In the new political climate, the government would no longer concede a swell of homeless youths, let alone permit detailed studies routinely conducted a few years before. With the country now allegedly speeding to socialism, there could not be another tide of abandoned juveniles. Then, too, the problem's origins differed in each era. A majority of the 1920s' orphans owed their distress to war, famine, and associated epidemics— none of which could be blamed primarily on the Soviet government. But how could a new army of the uprooted be explained in the first half of the 1930s without reference to collectivization, dekulakization, and the famine of 1933? Faced with this question, the Party chose not to acknowledge such traumatic consequences of its actions—and in the case of the famine denied the event itself. In contrast, when Hitler's invasion filled the country yet again with roving children, they were recognized openly and presented as products of fascist brutality.[81]

By shunning in the 1930s an honest assessment of juvenile destitution's scale, the government broke with the previous decade's practice. It did so as well by adopting a harsher view of young deviants, formerly declared victims of their environment. If a community on the verge of socialism could not generate mass homelessness and vice, how could it be faulted for those hooligans who endured to blemish an otherwise dazzling vista? Responsibility shifted to the culprits themselves, who were now regarded as criminals rather than victims of their surroundings. This reappraisal of juvenile delinquency corresponded to a change in Soviet criminology as a whole. Thereafter, as one scholar observed, "Soviet criminal law has stressed condemnation and disapproval of the crime and the criminal. Earlier jurists have been reprimanded for failing to understand the educative value of punishment."[82] As the sterner disposition gained prominence in the 1930s, police and courts pushed aside Narkompros's social workers and stepped forward to confront offenders. Streets were cleared more aggressively, and journals ceased promoting rehabilitation through "voluntary entry" and "open doors." A defector from the secret police even claimed that Stalin ordered the execution of waifs caught stealing or found infected with venereal diseases.[83]

While no confirmation of the executions has appeared, laws on delinquency did grow far more severe by the middle of the decade. A decree of April 7, 1935, specified that children as young as twelve, charged with such crimes as theft, rape, assault, and murder, bypass Narkompros's Juvenile Affairs Commissions for trial in regular courts as adults. The commissions, now roundly criticized for coddling offenders, were abolished a few months later.[84] Following the April 7 decree, a wave of arrests swept up teenagers between the ages of twelve and fifteen, mainly for petty theft. Once in official hands, they landed ever more frequently in labor colonies—not facilities of the sort run by Narkompros in the 1920s, but penal institutions administered by the Commissariat of Internal Affairs. In 1934 approximately 17 percent of minors charged with hooliganism entered these colonies; three years later the figure reached 65 percent.[85]

Meanwhile, juvenile homelessness soared. As a benchmark, consider a report from the Children's Commission listing a sum of seven to eight thousand stowaways plucked from the nation's rails and waterways in 1928/29. This total was dwarfed not only by those of a few years before, but also by quantities suggested in fragmentary data for 1930–1933. A single train-car receiver in Rostov-on-the-Don, for example, processed fully 600 to 800 youths per *month* in 1930/31. Over a six-month period beginning in March 1930, the receiver at Moscow's Kazan' Station took in 7,000 children. During a similar stretch, over 26,000 boys and girls packed train-car receivers throughout the Soviet Union. From April 1930 to April 1931, nearly 8,000 were gathered from the network of railroads and waterways around Leningrad, while an ODD document reported that the organization's members participated in removing 21,985 from seven railroad lines in 1933.[86] There is no reason to suppose that the tens of thousands of itinerant adolescents discovered on railways in the early 1930s had been there earlier, awaiting detection by more vigilant officials. The facts point instead to another cycle of refugees searching desperately, as in 1921–1922, for necessities of life no longer available in their villages.

If official sources shrouded the new eruption of indigence—and especially its link to government policies in the countryside—others reported the calamity without hesitation. Foreign residents and Soviet citizens who later departed for the West described crowds of hungry peasant children in the streets and around railway stations. No sooner had the nation weathered the previous decade's flood, an American journalist observed, than "new thousands of boys and girls, mere infants some of them seemed, roamed through the land. They were the children of kulak parents who had died or who preferred to leave their children to shift for themselves rather than to drag them into exile."[87] An anonymous contact of the émigré newspaper *Sotsialisticheskii vestnik* depicted youths abandoned during the famine of 1933 as sick, swollen beggars, nothing like the adroit, devious figures who had earlier shaped the popular image of *besprizornye*. Though the government systematically drove the newcomers out of Moscow, noted another article in the paper, they continued to arrive at a rate sufficient to fill cellars and other refuges in the capital.[88]

Some decrees and other official documents in the 1930s conceded a small number of street children, generated by such problems as lack of supervision, poorly functioning *detdoma* and schools, inadequate work by local officials and "society," and crumbling traditional families. Most often, the sources claimed that escapees from *detdoma*—that is, restless souls orphaned by difficult conditions no longer prevalent—made up the main contingent.[89] All these factors did yield homeless juveniles, but the total could not have compared with the number deprived of parental care by collectivization, dekulakization, and the famine of 1933.[90] On this point, Soviet documents and articles of the time remained largely silent. Brief references to "unorganized influxes" of people from rural areas and beleaguered kulak families expelling adolescent laborers only obscured the scope and nature of events that left untold millions desperate and alone once again.[91]

Throughout the 1920s, Soviet authors and officials responded indignantly to Western and émigré claims that the ragged children crowding the nation's streets stemmed chiefly from the Revolution and subsequent canons of the new order. They also scoffed at various foreign statements on the problem's extent and rejected allegations that the government treated urchins brutally.[92] In so doing, fervent or unscrupulous partisans strayed far from the facts, especially on the number of homeless, and ignored evidence published widely within their own borders. Rebuking a German newspaper in 1929, for instance, an ODD journal contended ludicrously that the country had never been overrun by millions or even hundreds of thousands of waifs. Soviet embarrassment over youths still on the street ten years after the Revolution also inspired such window dressing as mass roundups to cleanse Moscow temporarily before foreign guests arrived to attend decennial festivities.[93] In some cases, however, Western criticism swept too broadly, as in charges that an iron fist formed the essence of government policy in the 1920s. While local officials abused orphans here and there, the dismissal and occasional prosecution of personnel for such offenses better reflected the sentiments of Lunacharskii. Indeed, the treatment of delinquents *desired* by Narkompros surpassed the West in leniency. If actual conditions and achievements in Soviet children's facilities ranked below those of other European countries—which might be difficult to prove—one could not fairly attribute the Soviet showing to heartless motives in the capital or most institutions.

Finally, it is misleading to seize on the millions of abandoned children from the early 1920s and identify them as progeny of the Revolution and "communist" policies that followed. Though most (but by no means all) had lost their homes after 1917, primary blame does not lie necessarily with the Soviet government. The Bolsheviks deserve only half the onus for the Civil War, still less for the famine of 1921–1922. Nor does the imagination suggest an alternative government capable of eliminating the crush of rural overpopulation and poverty that continued to drive youths in smaller numbers to cities later in the decade. This is not to judge Lenin and his colleagues free of all responsibility. Besides the cruelty of the Civil War (alien to none of the major participants), measures adopted by the Party after the famine—certain aspects of the New Economic Policy and family law, for instance—contributed to the suffering. But the number flung inadvertently onto the streets by these decrees represented a small fraction of the amount deposited there earlier.

If nothing else we should avoid the mistake, made by some observers in the 1920s, of attributing all troubling phenomena in a state to the agenda of a new government one may find disturbing. In countries of very different political stripe today, combat and hunger have left myriad orphans living much like the *besprizornye* seventy years ago, and caution of new sorrow should current adversity escalate among the independent remnants of the Soviet Union. Beyond locales ravaged by war and famine, many other nations report flocks of boys and girls fending for themselves, as populations stream from impoverished villages to the shantytowns of Manila, Bombay, Nairobi, Mexico City, Rio de Janeiro, and other bulging cities. Childhope, an organization partially funded by UNICEF, has estimated that approximately one hundred million homeless youths now inhabit the planet.[94] By no means all are confined to war-torn, parched territories and the slums of developing lands. Governments of the United States, Great Britain, and other Western countries—far more experienced, wealthy, and secure than Third World states or the Soviet regime in 1921—have presided over expanding populations of street children in recent years. Estimates of the runaway, "throwaway," and otherwise abandoned adolescents living in New York City reach twenty thousand or higher, and the nation's total ranges over one million by some reckonings. "The growing phenomenon of homeless children is nothing short of a national disgrace," the American National Academy of Sciences concluded, "that must be treated with the urgency such a situation demands."[95]

Had this been foreseen by those most eager in the 1920s to associate homeless juveniles with Bolshevik rule, they might have hesitated with their charges. In any case, numerous Soviet officials, educators, and journalists deserve credit for publicizing the problem and struggling to overcome it. The concern they displayed for children's welfare rings true. But just as it served no useful purpose to link the youths' plight to a "communist" government, Soviet commentators did not further the campaign to save them by portraying their misfortune as an inheritance from "capitalist" society. Shul'gin, for example, dismissed contention that the root of the matter lay in war and famine. These afflictions sprung from the bourgeoisie's rule, he maintained, adding that, come war or peace, castoffs always thronged capitalism's harsh landscape. While many of Shul'gin's compatriots did not insist as narrowly on "capitalist" responsibility, their statements approached unanimity in asserting that social and economic development in the Soviet Union would purge conditions that drove human beings to the street.[96] In such accomplishments lay the appeal of socialism. How ironically tragic, then, that the very "socialist construction" billed as the means to overcome juvenile homelessness produced instead another wave in the 1930s. Here were orphans for whom the Soviet leadership bore full responsibility— and whom it refused even to acknowledge.

Notes

PREFACE

1. The plural word *besprizornye* may be used as either an adjective or a noun (as may *besprizornyi* in the singular). Some sources employ the variant noun form *besprizornik* (pl. *besprizorniki*). The condition of homelessness is conveyed by the word *besprizornost'*.

2. Anne O'Hare McCormick, *The Hammer and the Scythe* (New York, 1929), 198–199. For a sampling of comments by other observers on the ubiquity of *besprizornye* in the 1920s, see N. K. Krupskaia, *Pedagogicheskie sochineniia*, 11 vols. (Moscow, 1957–1963), 2:231; *Komsomol'skaia pravda*, 1925, no. 73 (August 21), p. 3; *Drug detei* (Khar'kov), 1925, no. 6: 5; no. 9: 17; *Pravda*, 1925, no. 255 (November 7), p. 2; Konstantin Paustovsky, *The Restless Years* (London, 1974), 46.

3. W. Averell Harriman, *America and Russia in a Changing World: A Half Century of Personal Observation* (Garden City, N.Y., 1971), 5.

4. S. V. Poznyshev, *Detskaia besprizornost' i mery bor'by s nei* (Moscow, 1926), 7; P. I. Liublinskii, *Bor'ba s prestupnost'iu v detskom i iunosheskom vozraste* (Moscow, 1923), 57, 178–179; E. K. Krasnushkin, G. M. Segal, and Ts. M. Feinberg, eds., *Nishchenstvo i besprizornost'* (Moscow, 1929), 129, 131–132; V. I. Kufaev, *Iunye pravonarushiteli* (Moscow, 1924), 215.

5. Some journalists in the 1920s began to refer caustically to inanimate objects, left to deteriorate through abandonment or neglect, as *besprizornye*—a *besprizornyi* factory, for example, or a *besprizornyi* telephone system. *Krasnaia gazeta* (Leningrad), 1926, no. 236 (October 13), p. 5; *Krasnaia gazeta* (Leningrad), evening ed., 1926, no. 154 (July 5), p. 3; *Molot* (Rostov-on-the-Don), 1925, no. 1206 (August 13), p. 3; 1926, no. 1557 (October 12), p. 3; *Rabochii krai* (Ivanovo-Voznesensk), 1924, no. 198 (August 31), p. 4.

6. L. M. Vasilevskii, *Besprizornost' i deti ulitsy*, 2d ed. (Khar'kov, 1925), 10–13; Maro [M. I. Levitina], *Besprizornye. Sotsiologiia. Byt. Praktika raboty* (Moscow, 1925), 47–49; *Bol'shaia sovetskaia entsiklopediia*, 65 vols. (Moscow, 1926–1947), 5:783 (for the quotation); Poznyshev, *Detskaia besprizornost'*, 8–9; Liublinskii, *Bor'ba*, 57–58; Kufaev, *Iunye pravonarushiteli* (1924), 219–220; Krasnushkin et al., *Nishchenstvo i besprizornost'*, 130; *Drug detei*, 1930, no. 4: 20.

7. Aleksandr I. Solzhenitsyn, *The Gulag Archipelago 1918–1956: An Experiment in Literary Investigation*, 3 vols. (New York, 1974–1978), 2:447.

8. *Besprizornye* receive the most attention in Jennie A. Stevens, "Children of the Revolution: Soviet Russia's Homeless Children (*Besprizorniki*) in the 1920s," *Russian History* 9, nos. 2–3 (1982): 242–264; Margaret K. Stolee, "Homeless Children in the USSR, 1917–1957," *Soviet Studies* 40 (January 1988): 64–83; Peter H. Juviler, "Contradictions of Revolution: Juvenile Crime and Rehabilitation," in *Bolshevik Culture*, ed. Abbott Gleason, Peter Kenez, and Richard Stites (Bloomington, Ind., 1985), 261–278; and Wendy Z. Goldman, "The 'Withering Away' and the Resurrection of the Soviet Family, 1917–1936" (Ph.D. diss., University of Pennsylvania, 1987).

9. Vladimir M. Zenzinov, *Deserted: The Story of the Children Abandoned in Soviet Russia* (London, 1931; reprint, Westport, Conn., 1975). The book was published originally (Paris, 1929) in Russian, with the title *Besprizornye*.

10. The dissertation (presented at Columbia Pacific University) has recently been published, unrevised; see René Bosewitz, *Waifdom in the Soviet Union: Features of the Sub-Culture and Re-Education* (Frankfurt am Main, 1988).

11. The long list of these works is left to the bibliography.

INTRODUCTION

1. John Boswell, *The Kindness of Strangers: The Abandonment of Children in Western Europe from Late Antiquity to the Renaissance* (New York, 1988), 112, 172.

2. For a brief survey of changes over the centuries in the tsarist government's response to *besprizornost'* and juvenile delinquency, see Krasnushkin et al., *Nishchenstvo i besprizornost'*, 116–122. For a bibliography of works published prior to 1913 on *besprizornost'* and juvenile delinquency, see M. N. Gernet, ed., *Deti-prestupniki* (Moscow, 1912), *prilozhenie* 3. For more on homeless children and juvenile delinquency in prerevolutionary Russia, see Joan Neuberger, "Crime and Culture: Hooliganism in St. Petersburg, 1900–1914" (Ph.D. diss., Stanford University, 1985); G. D. Ryndziunskii and T. M. Savinskaia, *Detskoe pravo. Pravovoe polozhenie detei v RSFSR*, 3d ed. (Moscow-Leningrad, 1932), 273–274; Liublinskii, *Bor'ba*, 46–50; Bernice Q. Madison, *Social Welfare in the Soviet Union* (Stanford, 1968), chap. 1; A. D. Kalinina, *Desiat' let raboty po bor'be s detskoi besprizornost'iu* (Moscow-Leningrad, 1928), 18–21; David L. Ransel, *Mothers of Misery: Child Abandonment in Russia* (Princeton, 1988).

3. Moshe Lewin, *The Making of the Soviet System: Essays in the Social History of Interwar Russia* (New York, 1985), 210.

4. *Tsentral'nyi gosudarstvennyi arkhiv RSFSR* [hereafter cited as TsGA RSFSR], f. 2306, o. 70, ed. khr. 2, l. 4; Vasilevskii, *Besprizornost'*, 5; *Shkola i*

zhizn' (Nizhnii Novgorod), 1927, no. 10: 54; *Pervyi vserossiiskii s"ezd deiatelei po okhrane detstva. 2–8 fevral'ia 1919 goda v Moskve* (Moscow, 1920), 67; E. M. Konius, *Puti razvitiia sovetskoi okhrany materinstva i mladenchestva 1917–1940* (Moscow, 1954), 141; Maro, *Besprizornye*, 66; *Pravo i zhizn'*, 1927, nos. 8–10: 28.

5. G. Iu. Manns, *Bor'ba s besprizornost'iu i prestupnost'iu nesovershenno-letnikh i ee ocherednye zadachi v sibirskom krae* (Irkutsk, 1927), 3; Vasilevskii, *Besprizornost'*, 5–6, 14; Liublinskii, *Bor'ba*, 58; *Profilakticheskaia meditsina* (Khar'kov), 1926, no. 12: 75; Records of American National Red Cross, 1917–1937, National Archives Gift Collection, Record Group 200 [hereafter cited as American Red Cross], box 866, file 948.08 ("Commission to Russia [First], Billings Report, Oct. 22, 1917"), Appendix to "Report of the Committee on Child Welfare," 28 August/10 September 1917 (for the quotation).

6. *Pravo i zhizn'*, 1925, nos. 9–10: 89.

7. V. G. Rudkin, "Prichiny massovoi detskoi besprizornosti v Belorussii i zakonomernosti ee likvidatsii (1917–1930 gg.)" (Minsk, 1983; MS. 14433 at INION AN SSSR, Moscow), 2; Vasilevskii, *Besprizornost'*, 7.

8. *Narodnoe prosveshchenie*, 1923, no. 6: 129; *Shkola i zhizn'* (Nizhnii Novgorod), 1927, no. 10: 54; *Drug detei*, 1927, nos. 8–9: 9; *Besprizornye*, comp. O. Kaidanova (Moscow, 1926), 40–42; Maro, *Besprizornye*, 110; Rud-kin, "Prichiny," 2; L. A. Vasilevskii and L. M. Vasilevskii, *Kniga o golode*, 3d ed. (Petrograd, 1922), 73; Manns, *Bor'ba*, 20.

9. For illustrations from autobiographical sketches of youths evacuated to Cheliabinsk during World War I, see O. Kaidanova, *Besprizornye deti. Praktika raboty opytnoi stantsii* (Leningrad, 1926), 50–51 (for Korneliuk's account), 55–57. While there is no reason to doubt Korneliuk's story—which describes the experiences of so many children—this and other autobiographical statements of *besprizornye* used as illustrations throughout the book must be read with cau-tion. Youths sometimes confused dates and sequences of events, exaggerated individual incidents, or forgot important details as time passed (problems by no means unique to the recollections of *besprizornye*). For a discussion of how *besprizornye* "remembered" their experiences, see *Pravo i zhizn'*, 1925, nos. 7–8: 86.

10. Anna Grinberg's book *Rasskazy besprizornykh o sebe* (Moscow, 1925) contains descriptions of the lives of nearly seventy *besprizornye*. Most of these children were evacuated from western Russia during World War I to eastern regions (often to Cheliabinsk province, though a number were sent to Samara). Some lost their parents during the evacuation process, but many others lived for a few years with at least one parent in the regions to which they had been evacuated—until the famine decimated their families, leaving them on their own. See also *Drug detei*, 1927, nos. 8–9: 9.

11. Kaidanova, *Besprizornye deti*, 60–61. When the orphans were evacuated from Cheliabinsk he lost track of his brother because the authorities would not transport those who were ill. The account ends with the information that the "author" has begun to attend school.

12. American Red Cross, box 868, file 948.08 ("South Russian Unit"); *Tsen-tral'nyi gosudarstvennyi arkhiv Oktiabr'skoi revoliutsii, vysshikh organov go-*

sudarstvennoi vlasti i organov gosudarstvennogo upravleniia SSSR [hereafter cited as TsGAOR), f. 5207, o. 1, ed. khr. 63, l. 81; Prosveshchenie (Krasnodar), 1921, nos. 3–4: 9; TsGA RSFSR, f. 2306, o. 13, ed. khr. 11, l. 39; Cheliabinskaia guberniia v period voennogo kommunizma (iiul' 1919—dekabr' 1920 gg.). Dokumenty i materialy (Cheliabinsk, 1960), 173; Maro, Besprizornye, 66–67; Vasilevskii, Besprizornost', 6–7; Detskaia defektivnost', prestupnost' i besprizornost'. Po materialam I vserossiiskogo s''ezda 24/VI–2/VII 1920 g. (Moscow, 1922), 19; Venerologiia i dermatologiia, 1926, no. 5: 836.

13. American Red Cross, box 916, file 987.08. The document is dated 8 April 1919.

14. Ibid., box 868, file 948.08 ("South Russian Unit"), "Speech of Major George H. Ryden at American Red Cross Headquarters, Paris, France, Dec. 6, 1920" (regarding Sevastopol'); ibid., "American Red Cross Activities: Relief Work in South Russia. February 1919 to January 18th, 1920" (for the quotation); ibid., "Com. to South Russia. Report of Kuban Unit" (regarding refugees in the Kuban').

15. Ibid., "Report of Mission to Ukraine and South Russia by Major George H. Ryden," November 1919; ibid., box 916, file 987.08, "Third Semi-Annual Report of the Siberian Commission. American Red Cross," 1 July–31 December 1919.

16. Tsentral'nyi gosudarstvennyi arkhiv literatury i iskusstva SSSR [hereafter cited as TsGALI], f. 332, o. 2, ed. khr. 41, l. 21; Vasilevskii, Besprizornost', 10, 13; Kaidanova, Besprizornye deti, 59, 62, 72; Vasilevskii and Vasilevskii, Kniga o golode, 73; Profilakticheskaia meditsina (Khar'kov), 1926, no. 12: 76, 78; American Red Cross, box 868, file 948.08 ("South Russian Unit"), "Report of Mission to Ukraine and South Russia by Major George H. Ryden," November 1919. A "white" newspaper, published in Rostov-on-the-Don before the Bolsheviks captured the city, described a shelter for orphans of soldiers killed fighting the "reds." The facility was said to be overflowing with children. See Vechernee vremia (Rostov-on-the-Don), 1919, no. 367 (September 20), p. 4.

17. M. Ia. Leshchinskii, Kto byl nichem . . . (Moscow, 1967), 77–80.

18. TsGALI, f. 332, o. 2, ed. khr. 41, ll. 1, 21; Leshchinskii, Kto byl nichem, 39; Grinberg, Rasskazy, 64–65; Drug detei (Khar'kov), 1927, nos. 7–8: 35.

19. American Red Cross, box 916, file 987.08, "Third Semi-Annual Report of the Siberian Commission. American Red Cross," 1 July–31 December 1919.

20. B. S. Utevskii, V bor'be s detskoi prestupnost'iu. Ocherki zhizni i byta moskovskogo trudovogo doma dlia nesovershennoletnikh pravonarushitelei (Moscow, 1927), 105.

21. American Red Cross, box 868, file 948.08 ("South Russian Unit"), "Report" from Novorossiisk, 2 December 1919. Some 1,100 children from Petrograd, stranded in colonies around the Urals, came under the care of the American Red Cross. Eventually, as the white forces retreated and fighting moved into the Urals, the Red Cross evacuated approximately 800 of the boys and girls to a colony near Vladivostok. Here the youths stayed until their return by sea to Petrograd, after the Civil War. Ibid., box 916, file 987.08, "The American Red Cross in Siberia"; this file contains dozens of other documents on the "Petrograd children."

22. *Narodnoe prosveshchenie*, 1923, no. 6: 129.

23. See for example *Cheliabinskaia guberniia v period voennogo kommunizma*, 204.

24. *Golod i deti na Ukraine. Po dannym sektsii pomoshchi golodaiushchim detiam pri tsentr. sov. zashchity detei na Ukraine i po drugim materialam*, comp. V. A. Arnautov (Khar'kov, 1922), 3–4; *Itogi bor'by s golodom v 1921–22 g.g. Sbornik statei i otchetov* (Moscow, 1922), 462–465; *Gor'kaia pravda o Povolzh'i i otchet tulgubpomgola* (Tula, 1922), 17; Kalinina, *Desiat' let*, 61; *Zaria Vostoka* (Tiflis), 1922, no. 41 (August 5), p. 1; A. N. Kogan, "Sistema meropriiatii partii i pravitel'stva po bor'be s golodom v Povolzh'e 1921–1922 gg.," *Istoricheskie zapiski* 48 (1954): 229. For more information and statistics on the famine, see Vasilevskii and Vasilevskii, *Kniga o golode*; and *Vestnik statistiki*, 1923, nos. 4–6: 87–113. *Itogi bor'by s golodom*, 486–499, contains a bibliography of works on the famine of 1921–1922, and the texts of forty-two government decrees pertaining to the famine may be found on pp. 403–428 (pp. 478–486 list works on earlier Russian famines). For a sampling of Western sources on the famine, see, along with titles listed in following notes, *An American Report on the Russian Famine* (New York, 1921); Harold H. Fisher, *The Famine in Soviet Russia, 1919–1923: The Operations of the American Relief Administration* (New York, 1927); Paxton Hibben, *Report on the Russian Famine* (New York, 1922); *Report on Economic Conditions in Russia with Special Reference to the Famine of 1921–1922 and the State of Agriculture* (Nancy-Paris-Strasbourg, 1922).

25. By all accounts, deaths during the famine (including those due to diseases such as scurvy, typhus, cholera, and malaria, to which the population in its weakened condition was especially susceptible) ran into the millions. Newspaper reports told of numerous villages stripped of most inhabitants, while estimates of the number of people "facing" death from starvation ranged from 23 million to 32 million. See *Meeting Report* of the Kennan Institute for Advanced Studies, vol. 8, no. 11 (for the figure of "at least five million"); Murray Feshbach, "The Soviet Union: Population Trends and Dilemmas," *Population Bulletin* 37 (August 1982): 7; Iu. A. Poliakov, *1921-i: pobeda nad golodom* (Moscow, 1975), 27; *Itogi bor'by s golodom*, 6; *Istoricheskie zapiski* 48 (1954): 228; *Golod i deti*, 33–34; *Krasnaia nov'*, 1922, no. 2: 324; *Gor'kaia pravda*, 44; *Bich naroda. Ocherki strashnoi deistvitel'nosti* (Kazan', 1922), 84–90; *Krasnoarmeets*, 1921, nos. 40–41: 20. Estimates of the number of *children* on the verge of death in the famine region clustered in the neighborhood of 6 million to 10 million. One investigation concluded that at least 30 percent of the children in the Volga provinces and the Crimea died of hunger and disease during the calamity. Another work added that a "huge number" of children died in southern Ukraine during the winter of 1921–1922, unrecorded by anyone. Figures available for May 1, 1922, covering most of the famine region, specify that out of a total of 10,177,000 children in the territory, 6,728,000 were starving—56 percent of whom were receiving aid in the form of food. *Itogi bor'by s golodom*, 32; *Narodnoe prosveshchenie*, 1922, no. 102: 6; *Golod i deti*, 38; S. S. Tizanov and M. S. Epshtein, eds., *Gosudarstvo i obshchestvennost' v bor'be s detskoi besprizornost'iu. (Sbornik statei i pravitel'stvennykh rasporiazhenii)* (Moscow-Len-

ingrad, 1927), 35; *Chto govoriat tsifry o golode?*, *vypusk* 2 (Moscow, 1922), 13. For information on the number of children dying or facing death in various areas inside the famine region, see TsGAOR, f. 5207, o. 1, ed. khr. 60, l. 131; ibid., ed. khr. 61, l. 52; *Profilakticheskaia meditsina* (Khar'kov), 1924, nos. 11–12: 149; *Gor'kaia pravda*, 25; *Golod i deti*, 44–45; *Na pomoshch'! Illiustrirovannyi zhurnal* (Samara, 1922), 2.

   26. *Bich naroda*, 79–80; *Besprizornye*, comp. Kaidanova, 32; Vasilevskii, *Besprizornost'*, 73; *Golod i deti*, 29–30; Philip Gibbs, *Since Then* (New York, 1930), 393–400; Armand Hammer, *The Quest of the Romanoff Treasure* (New York, 1932), 51.

   27. TsGAOR, f. 5207, o. 1, ed. khr. 60, l. 153; *Gor'kaia pravda*, 44, 46; *Golod i deti*, 28–29; *Put' prosveshcheniia* (Khar'kov), 1924, no. 3: 49.

   28. TsGAOR, f. 5207, o. 1, ed. khr. 61, l. 52; *Na fronte goloda, kniga* 2 (Samara, 1923), 205–206; *Krasnaia nov'*, 1923, no. 5: 205; *Gor'kaia pravda*, 39, 43, 49; *Besprizornye*, comp. Kaidanova, 31–32; *Bich naroda*, 79; *Golod i deti*, 28; *Vestnik prosveshcheniia*, 1922, no. 1: 16; Pitirim A. Sorokin, *Hunger as a Factor in Human Affairs* (Gainesville, Fla., 1975), 195–196; Gustav Krist, *Prisoner in the Forbidden Land* (London, 1938), 326, 333; P. C. Hiebert and Orie O. Miller, *Feeding the Hungry: Russian Famine, 1919–1925* (Scottdale, Penn., 1929), 188, 231. Decrees seeking to regulate and limit the flow of famine refugees were often impossible to enforce. For examples of such orders, see *Sobranie uzakonenii i rasporiazhenii rabochego i krest'ianskogo pravitel'stva* [hereafter cited as *SU*], 1921, no. 59, arts. 396 and 397. For a fictional account of a youth's journey from the famine region (Samara province) to Tashkent in search of grain, see *Asfal'tovyi kotel. Khudozhestvennye stranitsy iz zhizni besprizornykh*, comp. M. S. Zhivov (Moscow, 1926), 11–54.

   29. *Tvorcheskii put'* (Orenburg), 1923, no. 6: 3–5.

   30. TsGAOR, f. 5207, o. 1, ed. khr. 28, ll. 5, 7; ibid., ed. khr. 61, l. 55; Kaidanova, *Besprizornye deti*, 69; *Golod i deti*, 31–33; Kalinina, *Desiat' let*, 65, 70; *Gor'kaia pravda*, 44; *Krasnaia nov'*, 1923, no. 5: 205; *Derevenskaia pravda* (Petrograd), 1921, no. 147 (October 25), p. 1 (for the quotation); 1922, no. 21 (January 28), p. 2; Hiebert and Miller, *Feeding the Hungry*, 188; Krist, *Prisoner*, 331.

   31. TsGAOR, f. 5207, o. 1, ed. khr. 61, l. 51; *Biulleten' tsentral'noi komissii pomoshchi golodaiushchim VTsIK*, 1921, no. 2: 37; *Bich naroda*, 80; *Golod i deti*, 30–31; Kalinina, *Desiat' let*, 71; Vasilevskii and Vasilevskii, *Kniga o golode*, 77; *Gor'kaia pravda*, 46; *Izhevskaia pravda* (Izhevsk), 1922, no. 101 (May 19), p. 1.

   32. Hiebert and Miller, *Feeding the Hungry*, 241.

   33. Regarding cannibalism during the famine (including numerous specific instances), see *Krasnaia gazeta* (Petrograd), 1922, no. 100 (May 7), p. 2; *Derevenskaia pravda* (Petrograd), 1922, no. 9 (January 13), p. 1; Grinberg, *Rasskazy*, 75, 88; *Golod i deti*, 5, 36–37; *Gor'kaia pravda*, 45–46; Vasilevskii and Vasilevskii, *Kniga o golode*, 82, 175–176, 179–181; Kalinina, *Desiat' let*, 71; *Bich naroda*, 103; *Krasnaia nov'*, 1922, no. 2: 325; 1923, no. 5: 204; *Novyi put'* (Riga), 1922, no. 295 (January 26), p. 3; 1922, no. 319 (February 24), p. 3; Sorokin, *Hunger*, 111–112; *Pravo i zhizn'*, 1922, no. 1: 37; *Pravda*, 1922,

no. 17 (January 24), p. 4; Donald J. Raleigh, ed., *A Russian Civil War Diary: Alexis Babine in Saratov, 1917–1922* (Durham, N.C., 1988), 208–210; British Foreign Office Records of General Political Correspondence for Russia, 1906–1945 (F.O. 371) [hereafter cited as British Foreign Office], 1922, reel 1, vol. 8148, p. 117; 1922, reel 2, vol. 8150, pp. 3, 199; Harrison E. Salisbury, *Russia in Revolution, 1900–1930* (New York, 1978), 246–247 (for photographs of peasants who had been selling human flesh).

34. TsGAOR, f. 5207, o. 1, ed. khr. 60, ll. 131, 200; *Kommunistka*, 1922, no. 1: 12; *Posle goloda*, 1922, no. 1: 65; *Bich naroda*, 24, 60 (for reports from Kazan'); *Vestnik prosveshcheniia*, 1922, no. 1: 16; *Prosveshchenie* (Krasnodar), 1921–1922, no. 2: 127; *Narodnoe prosveshchenie* (Saratov), 1922, no. 3: 26; *Biulleten' tsentral'noi komissii pomoshchi golodaiushchim VTsIK*, 1921, no. 2: 37; *Pravo i zhizn'*, 1922, no. 1: 38.

35. Hammer, *The Quest*, 44. For a similar description of people of all ages begging for food at train stations, see Hiebert and Miller, *Feeding the Hungry*, 198.

36. M. Artamonov, *Deti ulitsy. Ocherki moskovskoi zhizni* (Moscow, 1925), 39 (regarding Moscow's *besprizornye* at the end of 1923); *Prosveshchenie* (Krasnodar), 1921–1922, no. 2: 127 (regarding the telegraph from Simbirsk province).

37. For a sampling of works that identify the famine as a major cause of *besprizornost'*, see E. S. Livshits, *Sotsial'nye korni besprizornosti* (Moscow, 1925), 65; *Vtoroi otchet voronezhskogo gubernskogo ekonomicheskogo soveshchaniia (1 oktiabria 1921 g.–1 oktiabria 1922 g.)* (Voronezh, 1922), 34; *Otchet o deiatel'nosti saratovskogo gubernskogo ispolnitel'nogo komiteta sovetov rabochikh, krest'ianskikh i krasnoarmeiskikh deputatov i saratovskogo gorodskogo soveta XII-go sozyva za 1923 goda* (Saratov, 1923), 56; *Statisticheskii spravochnik po narodnomu obrazovaniiu 1923 g., vypusk 1* (Pokrovsk, 1923), 13; *Prosveshchenie na Urale* (Sverdlovsk), 1927, no. 2: 60; Liublinskii, *Bor'ba*, 58; *Narodnoe prosveshchenie* (Odessa), 1922, nos. 6–10: 44; *Vestnik prosveshcheniia*, 1923, no. 4: 163; *Vozhatyi*, 1926, no. 6: 29; *Itogi bor'by s golodom*, 32; *Narodnoe prosveshchenie*, 1922, no. 102: 6; *Prosveshchenie* (Viatka), 1922, no. 1: 20; *Put' prosveshcheniia* (Khar'kov), 1924, no. 3: 148, 165. For individual cases of children orphaned by the famine, see *Nash trud* (Iaroslavl'), 1924, nos. 11–12: 30; P. N. Sokolov, *Besprizornye deti v g. Saratove. Rezul'taty odnodnevnoi perepiski 19 oktiabria 1924 g.* (Saratov, 1925), 27; Grinberg, *Rasskazy*, 57. Investigations of *besprizornye* a few years later very often turned up youths who had been cast out on the street during the famine. See for example *Venerologiia i dermatologiia*, 1926, no. 5: 836–837; *Profilakticheskaia meditsina* (Khar'kov), 1926, no. 12: 75, 78.

38. A recent Soviet work estimates that the famine produced two million orphans; see Poliakov, *1921-i: pobeda nad golodom*, 27.

39. *Itogi bor'by s golodom*, 34; Vasilevskii, *Besprizornost'*, 5 (for the figures from individual cities); *Prosveshchenie* (Krasnodar), 1921–1922, no. 2: 39; TsGAOR, f. 5207, o. 1, ed. khr. 60, l. 200; ibid., ed. khr. 43, l. 134; *Narodnoe prosveshchenie*, 1922, no. 102: 6.

40. *Derevenskaia pravda* (Petrograd), 1921, no. 147 (October 25), p. 3.

41. *Gor'kaia pravda*, 24; *Narodnoe prosveshchenie*, 1922, no. 105: 7; *Vserossiiskoe obsledovanie detskikh uchrezhdenii. Doklad NKRKI v komissiiu po uluchsheniiu zhizni detei pri VTsIK* (Moscow, 1921), 34. For indications of the large number of *besprizornye* in other regions at this time, see TsGAOR, f. 5207, o. 1, ed. khr. 43, l. 8; *Itogi bor'by s golodom*, 241; *Pomoshch' detiam. Sbornik statei po bor'be s besprizornost'iu i pomoshchi detiam na Ukraine v 1924 godu* (Khar'kov, 1924), 5; *Drug detei* (Khar'kov), 1926, no. 10: 4; *Shkola i zhizn'* (Nizhnii Novgorod), 1926, no. 11: 31.

42. TsGAOR, f. 5207, o. 1, ed. khr. 61, l. 70; *The Russian Famines, 1921–22, 1922–23. Summary Report, Commission on Russian Relief of the National Information Bureau, Inc.* (New York, [1923]), 18; Vasilevskii, *Besprizornost'*, 7; Vasilevskii and Vasilevskii, *Kniga o golode*, 74; *Gudok*, 1921, no. 373 (August 12), p. 1.

43. *Smolenskaia nov'* (Smolensk), 1922, no. 1: 5; Sokolov, *Besprizornye deti*, 26; Vasilevskii, *Besprizornost'*, 16; *Drug detei*, 1926, no. 2: 15–16; Grinberg, *Rasskazy*, 123–124; L. G. Glatman, *Pioner—na bor'bu s besprizornost'iu* (Moscow-Leningrad, 1926), 3–4, 8; Kaidanova, *Besprizornye deti*, 51–52; *Narodnoe prosveshchenie*, 1922, no. 102: 12; 1923, no. 6: 129; *Drug detei* (Khar'kov), 1927, nos. 9–10: 14; F. A. Mackenzie, *Russia Before Dawn* (London, 1923), 152 (for the quotation).

44. *Besprizornye*, comp. Kaidanova, 30–34.

45. TsGAOR, f. 5207, o. 1, ed. khr. 47, l. 10; ibid., ed. khr. 61, ll. 51–52; *Otchet krymskogo narodnogo komissariata po prosveshcheniiu vtoromu vsekrymskomu s"ezdu sovetov rabochikh, krest'ianskikh, krasnoarmeiskikh i voenmorskikh deputatov. (S oktiabria 1921 g. po oktiabr' 1922 g.)* (Simferopol', 1922), 18; Vasilevskii, *Besprizornost'*, 16; Vasilevskii and Vasilevskii, *Kniga o golode*, 77; *Kommunistka*, 1921, nos. 14–15: 4, 7; *Golod i deti*, 35; C. E. Bechhoffer Roberts, *Through Starving Russia* (London, 1921), 44; Kufaev, *Iunye pravonarushiteli* (1924), 225; *Profilakticheskaia meditsina* (Khar'kov), 1926, no. 12: 79; *Prosveshchenie* (Viatka), 1922, no. 1: 20; *Prosveshchenie* (Krasnodar), 1921–1922, nos. 3–4: 153; Walter Duranty, *Duranty Reports Russia* (New York, 1934), 24; Gibbs, *Since Then*, 391.

46. *Bich naroda*, 79; *Derevenskaia pravda* (Petrograd), 1922, no. 1 (January 1), p. 1; *Golod i deti*, 35–36; Vasilevskii and Vasilevskii, *Kniga o golode*, 77; *Pravda*, 1921, no. 204 (September 14), p. 1. Children themselves sometimes chose to leave homes that could no longer support them (whether encouraged in some way by adults is generally impossible to determine). See *Kommunistka*, 1921, nos. 14–15: 7; Grinberg, *Rasskazy*, 11; *Besprizornye*, comp. Kaidanova, 32–33.

47. *Krasnaia gazeta* (Petrograd), 1922, no. 102 (May 10), p. 5.

48. Anna J. Haines, "Children of Moscow," *Asia* 22 (March 1922): 218 (regarding the girl in Samara); Maro, *Besprizornye*, 110.

49. TsGAOR, f. 5207, o. 1, ed. khr. 47, l. 10; ibid., ed. khr. 61, l. 52; *Prosveshchenie* (Viatka), 1922, no. 1: 19–20; Vasilevskii and Vasilevskii, *Kniga o golode*, 75; Sokolov, *Besprizornye deti*, 26; *Otchet krymskogo narodnogo komissariata po prosveshcheniiu*, 18; *Pravda*, 1921, no. 168 (August 2), p. 1 (regarding the report from Samara); Duranty, *Duranty Reports*, 25; Frank Al-

fred Golder and Lincoln Hutchinson, *On the Trail of the Russian Famine* (Stanford, 1927), 44. On a far less massive scale, current economic distress in the former Soviet Union has been blamed for the swell of juveniles placed in orphanages; see *Moscow News*, 1991, nos. 34–35: 14.

50. Vasilevskii and Vasilevskii, *Kniga o golode*, 79.

51. *Voprosy prosveshcheniia* (Rostov-on-the-Don), 1926, no. 2: 42; Sokolov, *Besprizornye deti*, 22; *Drug detei* (Khar'kov), 1925, no. 5: 39; 1927, nos. 9–10: 24. See also *Drug detei*, 1929, no. 1: 10–12; *Ural'skii uchitel'* (Sverdlovsk), 1926, nos. 11–12: 31; *Voprosy prosveshcheniia* (Rostov-on-the-Don), 1926, nos. 8–9: 50; *Drug detei* (Khar'kov), 1926, no. 1: 2; *Komsomol'skaia pravda*, 1926, no. 157 (July 11), p. 5.

52. *Pravda*, 1925, no. 275 (December 2), p. 1.

53. Livshits, *Sotsial'nye korni*, 199; Tizanov and Epshtein, *Gosudarstvo i obshchestvennost'*, 40; *Detskii dom i bor'ba s besprizornost'iu* (Moscow, 1928), 8; S. S. Tizanov, V. L. Shveitser, and V. M. Vasil'eva, eds., *Detskaia besprizornost' i detskii dom. Sbornik statei i materialov II vserossiiskogo s"ezda SPON po voprosam detskoi besprizornosti, detskogo doma i pravovoi okhrany detei i podrostkov* (Moscow, 1926), 168–169; *Kommunistka*, 1926, no. 6: 10; *Vozhatyi*, 1926, no. 6: 29; *Ural'skii uchitel'* (Sverdlovsk), 1926, nos. 11–12: 31.

54. *Dvukhnedel'nik donskogo okruzhnogo otdela narodnogo obrazovaniia* (Rostov-on-the-Don), 1924, no. 2: 10; *Volna* (Arkhangel'sk), 1926, no. 28 (February 4), p. 2; *Krasnaia nov'*, 1932, no. 1: 46; Tizanov et al., *Detskaia besprizornost'*, 169, 179; *Drug detei*, 1926, no. 7: 3–4; Tizanov and Epshtein, *Gosudarstvo i obshchestvennost'*, 41; *Sovetskoe stroitel'stvo*, 1927, nos. 2–3: 152; G. D. Ryndziunskii, T. M. Savinskaia, and G. G. Cherkezov, *Pravovoe polozhenie detei v RSFSR*, 2d ed. (Moscow, 1927), 85. Regarding local surges of *besprizornost'* following poor harvests, see *Voprosy prosveshcheniia* (Rostov-on-the-Don), 1926, no. 2: 42; *Obzor raboty po bor'be s detskoi besprizornost'iu i beznadzornost'iu v RSFSR za 1929/30 god* (Moscow, 1930), 5; *Drug detei* (Khar'kov), 1925, no. 4: 3–4; *Vecherniaia moskva*, 1924, no. 200 (September 2), p. 3.

55. Krasnushkin et al., *Nishchenstvo i besprizornost'*, 156; Livshits, *Sotsial'nye korni*, 56; P. S. Gilev, *Detskaia besprizornost' i bor'ba s nei v Buriatii za poslednie piat' let* (Verkhneudinsk, 1928), 6–7; *Vozhatyi*, 1926, no. 6: 29; *Narodnoe prosveshchenie v RSFSR k 1927–28 uchebnomu godu. Otchet narkomprosa RSFSR za 1926/27 uchebnyi god* (Moscow-Leningrad, 1928), 54; *Drug detei*, 1928, no. 3: 2; no. 6: 16; Tizanov and Epshtein, *Gosudarstvo i obshchestvennost'*, 10, 34; *Zhizn' Buriatii* (Verkhneudinsk), 1929, no. 5: 71; N. K. Krupskaia, *Pedagogicheskie sochineniia*, 11 vols. (Moscow, 1957–1963), 2:231–232. Of course, other motives could also launch peasant youths toward the cities—a desire to begin or continue school, for example, or to satisfy curiosity about urban marvels reported by others. Regardless of motive, these peasants often found themselves before long in the ranks of the *besprizornye*. See S. S. Tizanov, V. M. Vasil'eva, and I. I. Daniushevskii, eds., *Pedagogika sovremennogo detskogo doma* (Moscow-Leningrad, 1927), 259; *Vozhatyi*, 1928, no. 12: 19; *Drug detei*, 1926, no. 7: 4.

56. Artamonov, *Deti ulitsy*, 6–7; *Drug detei* (Khar'kov), 1925, no. 9: 31–32; 1927, nos. 9–10: 5; *Narodnoe prosveshchenie*, 1926, no. 8: 69; *Drug detei*, 1927, no. 2: 18; 1928, no. 1: 12.

57. Regarding poverty, often aggravated by unemployment, as a cause of *besprizornost'*, see *Sbornik deistvuiushchikh uzakonenii i rasporiazhenii pravitel'stva Soiuza SSR i pravitel'stva R.S.F.S.R., postanovlenii detkomissii pri VTsIK i vedomstvennykh rasporiazhenii po bor'be s detskoi besprizornost'iu i ee preduprezhdeniiu, vypusk 2* (Moscow, 1929), 215–216; *Narodnoe prosveshchenie v RSFSR k 1927–28 uchebnomu godu*, 54; *Krasnaia nov'*, 1932, no. 1: 46; Tizanov and Epshtein, *Gosudarstvo i obshchestvennost'*, 32. Regarding the plight of single mothers as a source of *besprizornost'*, see Livshits, *Sotsial'nye korni*, 25; *Voprosy prosveshcheniia* (Rostov-on-the-Don), 1926, no. 2: 46–47.

58. Wendy Z. Goldman, "Working-Class Women and the 'Withering Away' of the Family: Popular Responses to Family Policy," in *Russia in the Era of NEP: Explorations in Soviet Society and Culture*, ed. Sheila Fitzpatrick, Alexander Rabinowitch, and Richard Stites (Bloomington, Ind., 1991), 129 (for the statistics); Kufaev, *Iunye pravonarushiteli* (1924), 141, 148.

59. *Vestnik prosveshcheniia*, 1923, no. 2: 75; *Narodnoe prosveshchenie v R.S.F.S.R. k 1924/25 uchebnomu godu. (Otchet narkomprosa RSFSR za 1923/24 g.)* (Moscow, 1925), 78; *Drug detei*, 1928, no. 3: 2; *Krasnaia nov'*, 1932, no. 1: 46; Vasilevskii, *Besprizornost'*, 7–8; Tizanov and Epshtein, *Gosudarstvo i obshchestvennost'*, 10; Maro, *Besprizornye*, 88; Richard Stites, *The Women's Liberation Movement in Russia: Feminism, Nihilism, and Bolshevism, 1860–1930* (Princeton, 1978), 366–369; V. I. Kufaev, *Iunye pravonarushiteli*, 2d ed. (Moscow, 1925), 314; *Drug detei* (Khar'kov), 1927, no. 3: 20–21; Madison, *Social Welfare*, 38.

60. TsGALI, f. 332, o. 2, ed. khr. 41, ll. 11, 18; ibid., o. 1, ed. khr. 55, l. 12; ibid., o. 2, ed. khr. 58, roll 2, ll. 63–67; Poznyshev, *Detskaia besprizornost'*, 49; *Drug detei*, 1925, no. 2: 21; B. O. Borovich, ed., *Kollektivy besprizornykh i ikh vozhaki* (Khar'kov, 1926), 45–46, 88–89; Tizanov and Epshtein, *Gosudarstvo i obshchestvennost'*, 10, 14; Grinberg, *Rasskazy*, 56; *Drug detei* (Khar'kov), 1925, no. 9: 18; *Profilakticheskaia meditsina* (Khar'kov), 1926, no. 12: 76; *Prosveshchenie Sibiri* (Novosibirsk), 1927, no. 5: 64; *Pravo i zhizn'*, 1925, no. 6: 78.

61. *Puti kommunisticheskogo prosveshcheniia* (Simferopol'), 1928, nos. 1–2: 36; *Drug detei*, 1930, no. 7: 7; *Prosveshchenie Sibiri* (Novosibirsk), 1929, no. 12: 12. The word *beznadzornyi*, denoting a youth largely unsupervised by parents or other adult guardians, gained widespread currency in the 1920s. One author referred to the condition of *beznadzornost'* as hidden (*skrytaia*) *besprizornost'*; see Borovich, *Kollektivy besprizornykh*, 44–45.

62. *Nash trud* (Iaroslavl'), 1925, no. 1: 25; *Drug detei* (Khar'kov), 1925, no. 9: 14; Kufaev, *Iunye pravonarushiteli* (1924), 174–175; Vasilevskii, *Besprizornost'*, 21, 45–46; Boris Sokolov, *Spasite detei! (O detiakh sovetskoi Rossii)* (Prague, 1921), 46.

63. Borovich, *Kollektivy besprizornykh*, 97; see also pp. 93–94.

64. *Volna* (Arkhangel'sk), 1926, no. 28 (February 4), p. 2; *Ural'skii uchitel'* (Sverdlovsk), 1926, nos. 11–12: 31; TsGALI, f. 332, o. 2, ed. khr. 20, l. 5; *Drug*

detei, 1928, no. 9: 12; *Vozhatyi*, 1926, no. 6: 29; A. D. Kalinina, ed., *Komsomol i besprizornost'* (Khar'kov, 1926), 33; *Voprosy prosveshcheniia* (Rostov-on-the-Don), 1926, no. 2: 48; Ryndziunskii and Savinskaia, *Detskoe pravo*, 244; Borovich, *Kollektivy besprizornykh*, 45; Maro, *Besprizornye*, 85–86; Sokolov, *Spasite detei!*, 46; Kufaev, *Iunye pravonarushiteli* (1924), 151–152, 164; *Prosveshchenie Sibiri* (Novosibirsk), 1927, no. 5: 63–64; *Pravo i zhizn'*, 1925, no. 6: 76.

65. P. I. Liublinskii, *Zakonodatel'naia okhrana truda detei i podrostkov* (Petrograd, 1923), 87, 91; Vasilevskii, *Besprizornost'*, 88–89; Krasnushkin et al., *Nishchenstvo i besprizornost'*, 144–145. Of course, smaller numbers of children joined the *besprizornye* for a variety of other reasons as well, including a thirst for adventure; see TsGALI, f. 332, o. 2, ed. khr. 39, l. 143; *Profilakticheskaia meditsina* (Khar'kov), 1926, no. 12: 78; Krasnushkin et al., *Nishchenstvo i besprizornost'*, 238; *Drug detei* (Khar'kov), 1925, no. 9: 14, 21–22; 1926, nos. 4–5: 15; Poznyshev, *Detskaia besprizornost'*, 35.

66. A. A. Gusak, "Komsomol Ukrainy—pomoshchnik kommunisticheskoi partii v bor'be s bezrabotitsei molodezhi kak odnim iz istochnikov besprizornosti (1921–1928 gg.)," in *Kommunisticheskaia partiia Ukrainy v bor'be za pod''em trudovoi i politicheskoi aktivnosti trudiashchikhsia, vypusk* 3 (Dnepropetrovsk, 1975), 174–175; *Bor'ba s besprizornost'iu. Materialy 1-i moskovskoi konferentsii po bor'be s besprizornost'iu 16–17 marta 1924 g.* (Moscow, 1924), 42; Vasilevskii, *Besprizornost'*, 19, 89; Tizanov et al., *Detskaia besprizornost'*, 169; *Narodnoe prosveshchenie v RSFSR k 1927–28 uchebnomu godu*, 54.

67. *Prosveshchenie na Urale* (Sverdlovsk), 1929, nos. 5–6: 89; *Venerologiia i dermatologiia*, 1926, no. 5: 837; *Krasnaia nov'*, 1932, no. 1: 39, 46; *Sbornik deistvuiushchikh uzakonenii i rasporiazhenii* (1929), 65.

68. *Narodnoe prosveshchenie v R.S.F.S.R. k 1925/26 uchebnomu godu. (Otchet narkomprosa RSFSR za 1924/25 g.)* (Moscow, 1926), 68; Tizanov et al., *Detskaia besprizornost'*, 168–169, 184–185.

69. A recent Soviet work places the number of *besprizornye* in the country by 1921 at 4.5 million; Rudkin, "Prichiny," 4–5. A Narkompros document preserved in the archives sets the number in 1922—in the Russian Republic alone—at 5 million; TsGA RSFSR, f. 2306, o. 70, ed. khr. 119, l. 32. In Ukraine at this time, according to a journal article, the number of "*besprizornye* and half-*besprizornye* children" reached 2 million; *Pravo i zhizn'*, 1927, nos. 8–10: 30. An official of the Children's Commission of the All-Russian Central Executive Committee presented a figure of "about six million children, left to the whims of fate—thrown out onto the street"; *Drug detei*, 1927, nos. 11–12: 1. Numerous sources offer an estimate of 7–7.5 million *besprizornye* during the famine years. See for example Gusak, "Komsomol Ukrainy," 173; Stites, *Women's Liberation Movement in Russia*, 366; *Bol'shaia sovetskaia entsiklopediia* 5:786; *Krasnaia nov'*, 1932, no. 1: 50. A meeting of the directors of provincial Narkompros offices declared that the number of "starving and dying children" during the famine (excluding Ukraine) reached 7.5 million, with another 6 million children in need of immediate assistance; Krasnushkin et al., *Nishchenstvo i besprizornost'*, 140. No doubt a large percentage of these children were, or soon became, *besprizornye*. A few years later, another author, describing the

vast extent of *besprizornost'* in the Russian Republic during the famine, cited
these same figures—with the comment that they are based on far-from-complete
data (and thus likely to be well below the actual totals); Gilev, *Detskaia besprizornost'*, 3.

70. *Voprosy prosveshcheniia* (Rostov-on-the-Don), 1926, no. 2: 49; *Krasnoiarskii rabochii* (Krasnoiarsk), 1925, no. 140 (June 23), p. 3; Gilev, *Detskaia
besprizornost'*, 6; *Bol'shaia sovetskaia entsiklopediia* 5:787; *Statisticheskii obzor narodnogo obrazovaniia v permskoi gubernii za 1922–23 god*, comp. B. N.
Ber-Gurevich (Okhansk, 1924), 127; *Statisticheskii obzor narodnogo obrazovaniia v permskom okruge, ural'skoi oblasti za 1923–24 uch. god* (Perm', 1924),
37; *Drug detei*, 1925, no. 2: 20; *Profilakticheskaia meditsina* (Khar'kov), 1926,
no. 12: 73; *Drug detei* (Khar'kov), 1927, nos. 9–10: 4; *Detskii dom*, 1929, no.
5: 19; Sokolov, *Besprizornye deti*, 19. Not surprisingly, the overwhelming majority of *besprizornye* sprang from working-class or peasant families. Workers
and peasants accounted for most of the Soviet population, of course, and were
at least as vulnerable as anyone else to the forces that created *besprizornye*.
Children's institutions around the country typically reported that 75–80 percent
of their charges came from such backgrounds. The actual percentage may even
have been higher, because in many institutions the social backgrounds of some
youths could not be determined. Most of the inhabitants of children's institutions had previously been *besprizornye*, and there appears no reason to doubt
that the reported figures accurately describe the social origins of *besprizornye*
in general. Nearly all of the remaining children in these institutions came from
families of handicraftsmen, traders, and office workers (*sluzhashchie*). See *Narodnoe prosveshchenie v RSFSR k 1927–28 uchebnomu godu*, 54; Livshits, *Sotsial'nye korni*, 28; *Voprosy prosveshcheniia* (Rostov-on-the-Don), 1926, no. 2:
41, 45; Tizanov et al., *Detskaia besprizornost'*, 169; *Bol'shaia sovetskaia entsiklopediia* 5:787; *Shkola i zhizn'* (Nizhnii Novgorod), 1926, no. 11: 33; *Severo-
Kavkazskii krai* (Rostov-on-the-Don), 1926, no. 5: 21; *Profilakticheskaia meditsina* (Khar'kov), 1926, no. 12: 74; *Krasnoiarskii rabochii* (Krasnoiarsk), 1925,
no. 140 (June 23), p. 3.

71. TsGA RSFSR, f. 1575, o. 6, ed. khr. 152, l. 1; *Put' prosveshcheniia*
(Khar'kov), 1924, no. 3: 32; Vasilevskii, *Besprizornost'*, 4–5; *Krasnaia nov'*,
1932, no. 1: 50; *Na putiakh k novoi shkole*, no. 3 (May 1923): 76; *Prosveshchenie* (Krasnodar), 1923, no. 1: 7. L. M. Vasilevskii writes that in the summer
of 1923 there were, "according to official figures, over two million *besprizornye*;
the actual figure was, of course, much higher." See L. M. Vasilevskii, *Detskaia
"prestupnost' " i detskii sud* (Tver', 1923), 128n.

72. *Drug detei*, 1927, nos. 4–5: 8; Krasnushkin et al., *Nishchenstvo i besprizornost'*, 140; Tizanov et al., *Detskaia besprizornost'*, 165–166; *Krasnaia
nov'*, 1932, no. 1: 50; *Komsomol'skaia pravda*, 1925, no. 73 (August 21), p. 3;
Izvestiia, 1924, no. 78 (April 4), p. 6.

73. The Children's Commission of the All-Russian Central Executive Committee reported (employing data sent in from the provinces) that in September
1925 there were 314,690 *besprizornye* in the Russian Republic (including autonomous republics). Narkompros estimates—some of which were admittedly

based on "incomplete" and "clearly underestimated" data—ranged from 150,000 to 300,000 *besprizornye* in the Russian Republic in 1925. For a representative sampling of figures for 1925, see Poznyshev, *Detskaia besprizornost'*, 11; Krasnushkin et al., *Nishchenstvo i besprizornost'*, 140–141; *Volna* (Arkhangel'sk), 1926, no. 9 (January 12), p. 2; *Krasnaia nov'*, 1932, no. 1: 50; *Sbornik deistvuiushchikh uzakonenii i rasporiazhenii* (1929), 70; Tizanov and Epshtein, *Gosudarstvo i obshchestvennost'*, 32, 41; *Drug detei*, 1928, no. 3: 2; *Narodnoe prosveshchenie v RSFSR k 1926/27 uchebnomu godu. Otchet narkomprosa RSFSR za 1925/26 uchebnyi god* (Moscow-Leningrad, 1927), 59. According to one author, there were approximately 335,000 *besprizornye* in the USSR in 1926: 300,000 in the Russian Republic; 23,000 in Ukraine; 6,000 in the Transcaucasian republics; 5,000 in Belorussia; and 1,000 in Turkmenistan; see *Drug detei* (Khar'kov), 1926, nos. 4–5: 25. Other estimates of the number of *besprizornye* in the Russian Republic in 1926 tended to cluster in the neighborhood of 250,000 to 300,000. A Narkompros document dated June 1, 1926, stated that "the absence of complete data hinders an accurate determination of the extent of *besprizornost'*, but the incomplete data at hand, clearly underestimated, indicate the presence of 300,000 children in need of aid in the Russian Republic, of which not less than 150,000 are absolute *besprizornye*"; see *Molot* (Rostov-on-the-Don), 1926, no. 1461 (June 19), p. 3; *Drug detei* (Khar'kov), 1926, no. 2: 28; Krasnushkin et al., *Nishchenstvo i besprizornost'*, 141 (for the quotation); Gilev, *Detskaia besprizornost'*, 3. The census of 1926 counted 75,000 *besprizornye*, but this figure is clearly far below the actual total; see *Detskii dom i bor'ba s besprizornost'iu*, 7; Krasnushkin et al., *Nishchenstvo i besprizornost'*, 141. According to an article published early in 1927, the Children's Commission estimated that there were still "over 100,000" *besprizornye* on the streets of the Russian Republic; *Vecherniaia moskva*, 1927, no. 42 (February 21), p. 2. At roughly the same time, Narkompros estimated the number of *besprizornye* in the Russian Republic to be 150,000; *Pravo i zhizn'*, 1927, nos. 8–10: 33.

74. For the figure of 200,000, see *Za sotsialisticheskuiu kul'turu* (Rostov-on-the-Don), 1930, no. 12: 24. For sources claiming that the number of *besprizornye* had dropped to under 10,000 by the early 1930s, see *Krasnaia nov'*, 1932, no. 1: 50; *SU*, 1932, no. 21, art. 106.

75. TsGA RSFSR, f. 2306, o. 69, ed. khr. 349, l. 27; Manns, *Bor'ba*, 7; *Drug detei*, 1928, no. 3: 2; *Vserossiiskoe obsledovanie*, 43. The U.S. Census Bureau faced a similarly impossible task counting America's homeless population in 1990; see *New York Times*, March 4, 1990.

76. Tizanov et al., *Detskaia besprizornost'*, 165; Poznyshev, *Detskaia besprizornost'*, 11.

77. *Molot* (Rostov-on-the-Don), 1926, no. 1389 (March 24), p. 4; Kufaev, *Iunye pravonarushiteli* (1925), 315; Krasnushkin et al., *Nishchenstvo i besprizornost'*, 140; Vasilevskii, *Besprizornost'*, 9–10.

78. *Krasnaia gazeta* (Leningrad), evening ed., 1926, no. 304 (December 19), p. 3; *Drug detei*, 1927, no. 1: 16; Manns, *Bor'ba*, 6–7; *Drug detei* (Khar'kov), 1927, no. 1: 4.

1. CHILDREN OF THE STREET

1. Tizanov and Epshtein, *Gosudarstvo i obshchestvennost'*, 32; Kufaev, *Iunye pravonarushiteli* (1925), 317, 319; Tizanov et al., *Detskaia besprizornost'*, 167–168.

2. *Nash trud* (Iaroslavl'), 1928, nos. 7–9: 41; *Voprosy prosveshcheniia* (Rostov-on-the-Don), 1926, nos. 3–4: 44; *Itogi bor'by s golodom*, 32; *Narodnoe prosveshchenie*, 1926, no. 8: 69; *Shkola i zhizn'* (Nizhnii Novgorod), 1925, nos. 9–10: 87–88; Livshits, *Sotsial'nye korni*, 6, 134; *Smolenskaia nov'* (Smolensk), 1922, nos. 7–8: 8.

3. TsGAOR, f. 5207, o. 1, ed. khr. 62, l. 22; *Otchet cherepovetskogo gubernskogo ispolnitel'nogo komiteta XII-mu gubernskomu s''ezdu sovetov za vremia s 15 dek. 1922 g. po 1-e dek. 1923 g.* (Cherepovets, [n.d.]), 99; *Drug detei*, 1925, no. 2: 20; 1928, no. 5: inside back cover; *Shkola i zhizn'* (Nizhnii Novgorod), 1925, nos. 9–10: 87; 1926, no. 11: 30; *Drug detei* (Khar'kov), 1927, nos. 9–10: 4; *Put' prosveshcheniia* (Khar'kov), 1924, no. 3: 44.

4. *Shkola i zhizn'* (Nizhnii Novgorod), 1926, no. 11: 30–31; 1929, no. 3: 78.

5. *Komsomol'skaia pravda*, 1927, no. 139 (June 23), p. 2; Tizanov et al., *Detskaia besprizornost'*, 167.

6. *Krasnaia nov'*, 1932, no. 1: 37–38 (for the quotation); TsGA RSFSR, f. 1575, o. 10, ed. khr. 190, l. 2; *Komsomol'skaia pravda*, 1925, no. 27 (June 26), p. 3; Vasilevskii, *Besprizornost'*, 9; Maro, *Besprizornye*, 108; *Drug detei* (Khar'kov), 1925, no. 6: 5; 1926, no. 3: 41; Artamonov, *Deti ulitsy*, 7, 29 (for the estimate); *Leningradskaia oblast'* (Leningrad), 1928, no. 4: 111. Petrograd (renamed Leningrad in 1924) did acquire a large population of homeless youths during the Civil War years, as evidenced by the number of boys and girls in children's homes administered by the Commissariat of Social Security. At the beginning of 1919, figures for the city and the surrounding province listed 25,173 residents in these facilities. By the end of the year the city's total reached 35,000. The source provides no sum for Petrograd province as a whole at this time, though the data make it clear that the large majority of the province's facilities for homeless children were concentrated in its capital city. In Moscow (excluding the surrounding province) the number of wards in these institutions rose from 4,078 to 15,000 over the same period. See TsGA RSFSR, f. 1575, o. 6, ed. khr. 4, ll. 1–2. The figures may also indicate that officials were quicker to open children's homes in Petrograd than in Moscow. In any case, by the early 1920s, Moscow clearly attracted more *besprizornye* than did Petrograd.

7. *Narodnoe prosveshchenie*, 1926, no. 8: 69; Kalinina, *Komsomol i besprizornost'*, 6; *Drug detei*, 1925, no. 2: 21; 1927, no. 2: 18; 1929, no. 2: 8; *Detskii dom*, 1929, nos. 8–9: 37; *Put' prosveshcheniia* (Khar'kov), 1924, no. 3: 43.

8. *Proletarskii sud*, 1923, no. 1: 25; Artamonov, *Deti ulitsy*, 29; *Narodnoe prosveshchenie*, 1926, no. 8: 68; *Drug detei*, 1925, no. 1: 2; 1927, no. 1: 22; *Vozhatyi*, 1926, no. 6: 29; *Komsomol'skaia pravda*, 1926, no. 158 (July 13), p. 3; 1927, no. 104 (May 11), p. 4. Some of the craftier, more experienced *besprizornye* arriving in Moscow pretended to be natives of the city, because Muscovite children often received priority in admittance to children's institutions; see *Vecherniaia moskva*, 1924, no. 200 (September 2), p. 3.

9. *Molot* (Rostov-on-the-Don), 1925, no. 1144 (May 30), p. 5; 1925, no. 1175 (July 7), p. 5; *Pravo i zhizn'*, 1925, nos. 2–3: 92–93; *Sbornik deistvuiushchikh uzakonenii i rasporiazhenii* (1929), 48; *Voprosy prosveshcheniia* (Rostov-on-the-Don), 1926, no. 2: 41; *Severo-Kavkazskii krai* (Rostov-on-the-Don), 1926, no. 5: 20 (for the estimate).

10. *Voprosy prosveshcheniia* (Rostov-on-the-Don), 1926, no. 2: 41; Tizanov et al., *Detskaia besprizornost'*, 167; *Severo-Kavkazskii krai* (Rostov-on-the-Don), 1926, no. 5: 20; *Drug detei*, 1926, no. 2: 15; *Molot* (Rostov-on-the-Don), 1926, no. 1563 (October 19), p. 5.

11. *Izvestiia*, 1926, no. 129 (June 6), p. 4.

12. *Prosveshchenie* (Krasnodar), 1921, nos. 3–4: 9; *Put' prosveshcheniia* (Khar'kov), 1924, no. 3: 148–149; Tizanov et al., *Detskaia besprizornost'*, 168; *Drug detei* (Khar'kov), 1926, nos. 6–7: 19, 29; nos. 8–9: 14, 19.

13. Tizanov et al., *Detskaia besprizornost'*, 151, 167–168; *Gor'kaia pravda*, 40; *Asfal'tovyi kotel*, 236–237; *Komsomol'skaia pravda*, 1925, no. 88 (September 8), p. 3; 1926, no. 268 (November 19), p. 2.

14. Sokolov, *Besprizornye deti*, 7; *Molot* (Rostov-on-the-Don), 1925, no. 1249 (October 2), p. 2; 1926, no. 1462 (June 20), p. 5; 1926, no. 1569 (October 26), p. 3; *Drug detei* (Khar'kov), 1925, no. 4: 20; Tizanov and Epshtein, *Gosudarstvo i obshchestvennost'*, 42.

15. *Puti kommunisticheskogo prosveshcheniia* (Simferopol'), 1928, nos. 1–2: 40; *Drug detei* (Khar'kov), 1926, nos. 6–7: 29; *Severo-Kavkazskii krai* (Rostov-on-the-Don), 1926, no. 5: 20; *Drug detei*, 1930, no. 1: 9; Borovich, *Kollektivy besprizornykh*, 72; *Komsomol'skaia pravda*, 1927, no. 139 (June 23), p. 2; *Voprosy prosveshcheniia na Severnom Kavkaze* (Rostov-on-the-Don), 1928, no. 6: 7; Andrée Viollis, *A Girl in Soviet Russia* (New York, 1929), 221–222; Marcella Bartlett, "Stepchildren of the Russian Revolution," *Asia* 26 (April 1926): 336.

16. TsGALI, f. 332, o. 2, ed. khr. 41, l. 30; *Prosveshchenie Sibiri* (Novosibirsk), 1928, no. 10: 52; *Detskii dom i bor'ba s besprizornost'iu*, 9; Livshits, *Sotsial'nye korni*, 142; *Detskii dom*, 1929, no. 5: 41; Vasilevskii, *Detskaia "prestupnost'*," 100; *Voprosy prosveshcheniia na Severnom Kavkaze* (Rostov-on-the-Don), 1927, no. 9: 9; Dorothy Thompson, *The New Russia* (New York, 1928), 251.

17. *Drug detei* (Khar'kov), 1925, no. 5: 39; 1926, no. 1: 38; no. 2: 47; *Prosveshchenie na transporte*, 1925, no. 1: 88; *Drug detei*, 1927, no. 2: 6; 1931, no. 10: 14; *Pravda*, 1924, no. 49 (February 29), p. 6; Hebe Spaull, *The Youth of Russia To-Day* (London, 1933), 61.

18. *Vozhatyi*, 1926, no. 6: 30 (for the estimate); Artamonov, *Deti ulitsy*, 14; Gilev, *Detskaia besprizornost'*, 21; *Prosveshchenie na transporte*, 1926, no. 10: 29; Liublinskii, *Bor'ba*, 81; *Drug detei* (Khar'kov), 1925, no. 6: 5; *Detskii dom*, 1929, no. 10: 17 (for the quotation); *Venerologiia i dermatologiia*, 1926, no. 5: 837. For descriptions of the travels of individual *besprizornye*, see TsGALI, f. 332, o. 2, ed. khr. 41, ll. 18–19; *Nash trud* (Iaroslavl'), 1924, nos. 11–12: 29–30; *Drug detei* (Khar'kov), 1926, no. 1: 11; Grinberg, *Rasskazy*, 11; *Drug detei*, 1926, no. 1: 27; *Detskii dom*, 1928, no. 3: 64.

19. *Komsomol'skaia pravda*, 1925, no. 88 (September 8), p. 3; *Izvestiia*, 1926, no. 129 (June 6), p. 4; Maro, *Besprizornye*, 107; *Drug detei*, 1927, nos.

6–7: 24; Livshits, *Sotsial'nye korni*, 142; Kufaev, *Iunye pravonarushiteli* (1924), 73–74; *Drug detei* (Khar'kov), 1925, no. 6: 3; *Krasnaia nov'*, 1932, no. 1: 43; *Pravo i zhizn'*, 1925, nos. 9–10: 93–94; Duranty, *Duranty Reports*, 17–18.

20. *Pravo i zhizn'*, 1925, nos. 9–10: 92–94.

21. See for example TsGALI, f. 332, o. 1, ed. khr. 55, l. 12; *Drug detei* (Khar'kov), 1926, no. 2: 27; nos. 4–5: 26; *Prosveshchenie na transporte*, 1926, no. 10: 29. For two literary descriptions of *besprizornye* riding the rails, see A. V. Kozhevnikov, *Stremka* (Moscow-Leningrad, 1926), 27–54; Viktor Gornyi, *Besprizornyi krug* (Leningrad, 1926), 18.

22. *Drug detei* (Khar'kov), 1927, no. 3: 38.

23. *Pravda*, 1924, no. 83 (April 11), p. 4; *Asfal'tovyi kotel*, 236; Glatman, *Pioner—na bor'bu*, 4; *Drug detei* (Khar'kov), 1925, no. 6: 30; no. 9: 22; *Komsomol'skaia pravda*, 1927, no. 139 (June 23), p. 2; *Drug detei*, 1926, no. 1: 27; 1927, nos. 6–7: 24; no. 10: 24; Victor Serge, *Russia Twenty Years After* (New York, 1937), 28; Langston Hughes, *I Wonder as I Wander* (New York, 1956), 155; Bernard Edelhertz, *The Russian Paradox: A First-Hand Study of Life Under the Soviets* (New York, 1930), 67–68.

24. *Drug detei* (Khar'kov), 1925, no. 6: 6.

25. *Drug detei*, 1926, no. 3: 22.

26. *Drug detei* (Khar'kov), 1925, no. 6: 6.

27. TsGALI, f. 332, o. 1, ed. khr. 55, l. 12; *Drug detei*, 1927, nos. 6–7: 24; no. 10: 24; Grinberg, *Rasskazy*, 46–47; *Izvestiia*, 1925, no. 210 (September 15), p. 6; *Drug detei* (Khar'kov), 1925, no. 6: 6; H. J. Greenwall, *Mirrors of Moscow* (London, 1929), 185; Bartlett, "Stepchildren," 335. In some instances, *besprizornye* attempted to purchase the silence of conductors by slipping stolen food into the latter's compartments; see *Asfal'tovyi kotel*, 236–237. *Besprizornye* aboard trains also suffered on occasion at the hands of adult vagrants; TsGALI, f. 332, o. 2, ed. khr. 41, ll. 19–20.

28. *Drug detei* (Khar'kov), 1925, no. 6: 6; *Vchera i segodnia. Al'manakh byvshikh pravonarushitelei i besprizornykh*, no. 1 (Moscow, 1931), 153–154 (a story by a former *besprizornyi*); *Drug detei*, 1927, nos. 6–7: 24; no. 10: 24; 1928, nos. 11–12: 13. For a literary account of the difficulties (including a policeman on duty inside the station, conductors checking tickets, fences blocking access to the tracks, an armed guard outside along the tracks, and a conductor on the station platform who knocked children off the outside of cars as trains headed out of the station) faced by a group of three *besprizornye* trying to slip onto a train in Moscow's Kursk Station, see Gornyi, *Besprizornyi krug*, 29–37.

29. Theodore Dreiser, *Dreiser Looks at Russia* (New York, 1928), 242–243.

30. *Puti kommunisticheskogo prosveshcheniia* (Simferopol'), 1926, no. 12: 72 (regarding the "orphan's winter"); *Komsomol'skaia pravda*, 1925, no. 73 (August 21), p. 3; Kozhevnikov, *Stremka*, 14; *Drug detei* (Khar'kov), 1925, no. 9: 31; *Venerologiia i dermatologiia*, 1926, no. 5: 837.

31. *Kommunistka*, 1921, nos. 14–15: 4; Sokolov, *Besprizornye deti*, 10–11; Rudkin, "Prichiny," 5; *Molot* (Rostov-on-the-Don), 1925, no. 1249 (October 2), p. 2; Borovich, *Kollektivy besprizornykh*, 68–69; *Drug detei* (Khar'kov), 1925, no. 2: 23; no. 9: 13; 1926, no. 1: 11; *Venerologiia i dermatologiia*, 1926,

no. 5: 837; *Nash trud* (Iaroslavl'), 1924, nos. 11–12: 32; Serge, *Russia*, 28; Thompson, *New Russia*, 246.

32. *Vecherniaia moskva*, 1927, no. 75 (April 4), p. 2; *Drug detei* (Khar'kov), 1927, no. 1: 4; nos. 5–6: 36; *Komsomol'skaia pravda*, 1925, no. 73 (August 21), p. 3; Borovich, *Kollektivy besprizornykh*, 108; *Na putiakh k novoi shkole*, 1924, nos. 7–8: 145.

33. *Detskii dom i bor'ba s besprizornost'iu*, 10; *Drug detei*, 1926, no. 2: 15; 1927, no. 1: 16; Vasilevskii, *Besprizornost'*, 19; *Drug detei* (Khar'kov), 1926, no. 2: 27 (for the quotation); 1927, no. 1: 5; L. G. Glatman, *Pionery i besprizornye* (Moscow-Leningrad, 1925), 23–24.

34. *Venerologiia i dermatologiia*, 1926, no. 5: 837; Livshits, *Sotsial'nye korni*, 136.

35. *Puti kommunisticheskogo prosveshcheniia* (Simferopol'), 1926, no. 12: 70; *Drug detei*, 1927, no. 1: 16; Maro, *Besprizornye*, 102–103; *Drug detei* (Khar'kov), 1926, no. 3: 23; *Deti posle goloda. Sbornik materialov* (Khar'kov, 1924), 58; *Pravda*, 1926, no. 292 (December 17), p. 6; K. Enik and V. Blok, *Iz trushchob na stroiku* (Moscow-Saratov, 1930), 16–17.

36. *Molot* (Rostov-on-the-Don), 1925, no. 1250 (October 3), p. 5; *Drug detei* (Khar'kov), 1926, no. 1: 8.

37. *Komsomol'skaia pravda*, 1925, no. 104 (September 25), p. 4 (regarding the group in Tashkent); Maro, *Besprizornye*, 103; *Drug detei* (Khar'kov), 1925, no. 1: 46–47; no. 9: 13; 1926, no. 1: 11; no. 3: 21; 1927, no. 1: 4, 7; no. 3: 23; Sokolov, *Besprizornye deti*, 11; George A. Burrell, *An American Engineer Looks at Russia* (Boston, 1932), 187–188.

38. *Venerologiia i dermatologiia*, 1926, no. 5: 837; *Krasnaia gazeta* (Leningrad), evening ed., 1926, no. 247 (October 20), p. 3; *Drug detei* (Khar'kov), 1926, no. 3: 28; 1927, no. 1: 5; *Shkola i zhizn'* (Nizhnii Novgorod), 1929, no. 3: 78; *Drug detei*, 1926, no. 3: 5; Sokolov, *Besprizornye deti*, 12–14; *Pravda*, 1924, no. 32 (February 9), p. 3; 1924, no. 49 (February 29), p. 6 (regarding the ruins in Odessa); 1926, no. 292 (December 17), p. 6 (regarding the building in Dnepropetrovsk); Duranty, *Duranty Reports*, 54.

39. *Molot* (Rostov-on-the-Don), 1925, no. 1250 (October 3), p. 5.

40. *Komsomol'skaia pravda*, 1925, no. 73 (August 21), p. 3; 1927, no. 132 (June 15), p. 4; *Drug detei*, 1926, no. 3: 16; 1927, no. 1: 16; *Vecherniaia moskva*, 1927, no. 75 (April 4), p. 2; *Drug detei* (Khar'kov), 1926, no. 2: 27; 1927, no. 1: 6–7; Artamonov, *Deti ulitsy*, 35; William J. Chase, *Workers, Society, and the Soviet State: Labor and Life in Moscow, 1918–1929* (Urbana, Ill., 1987), 195.

41. Vyacheslav Shishkov, *Children of the Street* (Royal Oak, Mich., 1979), 145–146.

42. *Vestnik prosveshcheniia*, 1925, no. 9: 90, 92–94; Glatman, *Pionery i besprizornye*, 22–23; *Drug detei*, 1925, no. 2: 15; 1928, no. 3: 15; Gornyi, *Besprizornyi krug*, 51 (for a literary account of a *besprizornyi* longing for one of these caldrons); *Drug detei* (Khar'kov), 1926, no. 1: 14; *Komsomol'skaia pravda*, 1925, no. 162 (December 4), p. 4; *Izvestiia*, 1927, no. 47 (February 26), p. 5; Duranty, *Duranty Reports*, 55; Serge, *Russia*, 29.

43. Leshchinskii, *Kto byl nichem*, 92; *Drug detei*, 1926, no. 3: 23; Enik and Blok, *Iz trushchob na stroiku*, 10.

44. *Nash trud* (Iaroslavl'), 1924, nos. 11–12: 32; Glatman, *Pionery i bes-prizornye*, 17; *Drug detei*, 1926, no. 3: 18; *Vecherniaia moskva*, 1924, no. 149 (July 2), p. 2.

45. *Molot* (Rostov-on-the-Don), 1925, no. 1250 (October 3), p. 5; *Drug detei* (Khar'kov), 1925, no. 1: 47; 1926, no. 3: 28; Arthur Feiler, *The Russian Experiment* (New York, 1930), 28.

46. *Profilakticheskaia meditsina* (Khar'kov), 1926, no. 4: 66; *Venerologiia i dermatologiia*, 1926, no. 5: 837; *Drug detei*, 1926, no. 4: 6; 1927, no. 2: 9; nos. 6–7: 32; *Vecherniaia moskva*, 1927, no. 29 (February 5), p. 2; Artamonov, *Deti ulitsy*, 55–56; *Drug detei* (Khar'kov), 1926, no. 3: 17, 23; *Krasnaia gazeta* (Leningrad), evening ed., 1926, no. 193 (August 20), p. 3; *Pravo i zhizn'*, 1925, nos. 9–10: 90; Chase, *Workers*, 193–194. For a description of *nochlezhnye doma* in St. Petersburg during the last decades of the prerevolutionary period, see James H. Bater, *St. Petersburg: Industrialization and Change* (Montreal, 1976), 337–342.

47. Some *nochlezhki* opened early during the winter so that people would not have to wait as long outdoors in the cold. In Saratov, according to an article written in 1927, people lacking warm clothing and shoes were allowed to remain inside the city's two *nochlezhki* during the day in cold weather. Presumably they had to continue paying the entry fee each evening and thus required some source of income. In general, lodgers were awakened and ordered out on the street sometime between six and eight o'clock in the morning. See *Vchera i segodnia*, 52–53; *Drug detei* (Khar'kov), 1926, no. 3: 23–24; 1927, no. 1: 8; *Krasnaia gazeta* (Leningrad), 1926, no. 301 (December 29), p. 5; *Saratovskii vestnik zdra-vookhraneniia* (Saratov), 1927, no. 5: 66.

48. *Put' prosveshcheniia* (Khar'kov), 1924, no. 3: 44–45; *Saratovskii vestnik zdravookhraneniia* (Saratov), 1927, no. 5: 66; *Krasnaia gazeta* (Leningrad), evening ed., 1926, no. 302 (December 17), p. 3; *Drug detei*, 1926, no. 3: 16; *Moskovskii meditsinskii zhurnal*, 1925, no. 10: 62; *Drug detei* (Khar'kov), 1926, no. 3: 24.

49. *Profilakticheskaia meditsina* (Khar'kov), 1926, no. 4: 62–63, 69; *Drug detei* (Khar'kov), 1926, no. 3: 24; *Krasnaia gazeta* (Leningrad), evening ed., 1926, no. 187 (July 13), p. 3.

50. *Saratovskii vestnik zdravookhraneniia* (Saratov), 1927, no. 5: 66–70; *Krasnaia gazeta* (Leningrad), 1926, no. 301 (December 29), p. 5; *Rabochaia moskva*, 1924, no. 108 (May 15), p. 6; *Profilakticheskaia meditsina* (Khar'kov), 1926, no. 4: 63, 67–68; *Krasnaia gazeta* (Leningrad), evening ed., 1926, no. 151 (July 1), p. 3; 1926, no. 157 (July 8), p. 3.

51. TsGA RSFSR, f. 1575, o. 6, ed. khr. 152, l. 6; *Prosveshchenie na trans-porte*, 1926, no. 10: 29; Kalinina, *Desiat' let*, 51–52; Kufaev, *Iunye pravona-rushiteli* (1924), 94–95; *Drug detei* (Khar'kov), 1925, no. 6: 7; 1926, nos. 4–5: 38; *Gudok*, 1924, no. 1358 (November 28), p. 4; *Drug detei*, 1926, no. 3: 16; no. 4: 6; *Prosveshchenie Sibiri* (Novosibirsk), 1927, no. 5: 56 (regarding the investigation of the station in Omsk).

52. *Sbornik deistvuiushchikh uzakonenii i rasporiazhenii* (1929), 138; *Pro-letarskii sud*, 1923, no. 4: 16; Glatman, *Pioner—na bor'bu*, 4, 22; *Drug detei* (Khar'kov), 1925, no. 9: 13. For two literary descriptions of helpless *besprizor-*

nye from the countryside just arrived in train stations, see Kozhevnikov, *Stremka*, 3–5, 55–65.

53. *Nash trud* (Iaroslavl'), 1924, nos. 11–12: 30; *Drug detei* (Khar'kov), 1925, no. 6: 3, 7–8; Borovich, *Kollektivy besprizornykh*, 73–74; *Sbornik deistvuiushchikh uzakonenii i rasporiazhenii* (1929), 138; Glatman, *Pionery i besprizornye*, 22.

54. *Drug detei* (Khar'kov), 1925, no. 2: 47; *Gudok*, 1924, no. 1358 (November 28), p. 4; Sokolov, *Besprizornye deti*, 17 (on the census of *besprizornye* in Saratov).

55. *Prosveshchenie Sibiri* (Novosibirsk), 1927, no. 5: 56–58.

56. *Na putiakh k novoi shkole*, 1924, nos. 7–8: 132; *Drug detei*, 1927, no. 1: 16; Livshits, *Sotsial'nye korni*, 135–136; *Drug detei* (Khar'kov), 1927, no. 1: 5–6 (for the description of the catacombs). For a literary description of a similar subterranean refuge, including competition among *besprizornye* for the choicest spots, see Kozhevnikov, *Stremka*, 15–16.

57. *Drug detei* (Khar'kov), 1925, no. 1: 35; Artamonov, *Deti ulitsy*, 34. For a drawing by a *besprizornyi* depicting a guard, armed with a rifle, evicting a *besprizornyi* from a train station, see *Drug detei* (Khar'kov), 1925, no. 9: 20.

58. *Venerologiia i dermatologiia*, 1926, no. 5: 837; *Prosveshchenie na transporte*, 1926, no. 10: 29; *Asfal'tovyi kotel*, 235; *Komsomol'skaia pravda*, 1926, no. 293 (December 18), p. 4 (regarding the census); *Detskii dom*, 1928, no. 1: 41; *Drug detei* (Khar'kov), 1926, no. 2: 27; *Na putiakh k novoi shkole*, 1924, nos. 7–8: 145.

59. Maro, *Besprizornye*, 103–104.

60. *Vestnik prosveshcheniia*, 1923, no. 2: 69; *Drug detei* (Khar'kov), 1926, no. 3: 17; Kufaev, *Iunye pravonarushiteli* (1924), 77–78.

61. TsGA RSFSR, f. 1575, o. 6, ed. khr. 152, l. 6; *Drug detei* (Khar'kov), 1925, no. 6: 7; Artamonov, *Deti ulitsy*, 32–33 (regarding the Zemlianyi Val); *Drug detei*, 1925, no. 1: 10; 1926, no. 2: 16; no. 4: 6 (regarding the survey at the Sukharevka); 1927, nos. 6–7: 25; *Vestnik prosveshcheniia*, 1925, no. 9: 92; Poznyshev, *Detskaia besprizornost'*, 49; Sokolov, *Spasite detei!* 43. For more on the Sukharevka and other markets, see Alan M. Ball, *Russia's Last Capitalists: The Nepmen, 1921–1929* (Berkeley, 1987), 94–96. The Khitrovka was closed in the second half of NEP; see *Rabochaia moskva*, 1924, no. 182 (August 13), p. 7; *Drug detei*, 1926, no. 3: 16; *Vchera i segodnia*, 126.

62. Poznyshev, *Detskaia besprizornost'*, 48; *Drug detei*, 1926, no. 2: 16; Leshchinskii, *Kto byl nichem*, 79; *Drug detei* (Khar'kov), 1925, no. 9: 13. For a story by a former *besprizornyi* describing a street child who spends most of his time at a bazaar, see *Vchera i segodnia*, 134–137.

63. *Na putiakh k novoi shkole*, 1924, nos. 10–12: 88; *Drug detei* (Khar'kov), 1925, no. 6: 31; 1927, nos. 9–10: 4; Borovich, *Kollektivy besprizornykh*, 43, 75; Maro, *Besprizornye*, 160.

64. Glatman, *Pioner—na bor'bu*, 8; Borovich, *Kollektivy besprizornykh*, 68, 74, 104–105; *Drug detei* (Khar'kov), 1925, no. 6: 30–31.

65. Borovich, *Kollektivy besprizornykh*, 59–62, 64, 68, 72, 80, 121; Krasnushkin et al., *Nishchenstvo i besprizornost'*, 227.

66. *Drug detei* (Khar'kov), 1925, no. 9: 12; *Izvestiia*, 1925, no. 201 (September 4), p. 5 (regarding Vasilii Riabov). Descriptions of the *besprizornye* sometimes noted antipathy between experienced young thieves and those, often new to the street, who practiced begging; see *Drug detei* (Khar'kov), 1925, no. 6: 32; 1926, no. 2: 22–23; nos. 8–9: 16; Livshits, *Sotsial'nye korni*, 134; Thompson, *New Russia*, 250; Alexander Wicksteed, *Life Under the Soviets* (London, 1928), 76. For a literary description of the treatment received by a neophyte *besprizornyi* at the hands of a group of veteran *besprizornye*, see *Vchera i segodnia*, 141–147.

67. The statement was made by Lieutenant-Colonel Alexander Gurov, head of the National Research Institute's department studying organized crime. In the same interview he observed: "For a long time we have been convincing ourselves that we have only one socialist culture. No other culture—or shall we call it subculture—can exist. We have been blinding ourselves. Let's face it. The criminal world has its own subculture. It is a powerful aspect in the system of reproducing professional crime. Just like any other professional group, this one has its own laws, traditions, slang"; *Literary Gazette International*, 1990, no. 2: 18–19.

68. *Vozhatyi*, 1926, no. 6: 11; *Drug detei* (Khar'kov), 1926, no. 3: 14; *Vestnik prosveshcheniia*, 1923, no. 2: 72 (regarding the investigation of the fourteen-year-old girl); Borovich, *Kollektivy besprizornykh*, 114–115; Maro, *Besprizornye*, 170.

69. *Deti posle goloda*, 61; *Vestnik prosveshcheniia*, 1927, no. 1: 8; Borovich, *Kollektivy besprizornykh*, 54–55; *Drug detei* (Khar'kov), 1926, no. 3: 14–15; Krasnushkin et al., *Nishchenstvo i besprizornost'*, 228.

70. M. S. Pogrebinskii, *Fabrika liudei* (Moscow, 1929), 3, 6–7, 11, 24, 27, 29; *Molot* (Rostov-on-the-Don), 1925, no. 1249 (October 2), p. 2; *Detskii dom*, 1928, no. 1: 44; *Drug detei* (Khar'kov), 1925, no. 2: 33; *Vchera i segodnia*, 45; *Drug detei*, 1925, no. 1: 9–10; *Vestnik prosveshcheniia*, 1925, no. 9: 90, 93. For additional examples (and definitions) of the slang employed by *besprizornye*, see *Put' prosveshcheniia* (Khar'kov), 1924, nos. 4–5: 238–239; Artamonov, *Deti ulitsy*, 15–16; Maro, *Besprizornye*, 170–172; *Vestnik prosveshcheniia*, 1925, no. 9: 90–94, 97–108; Krasnushkin et al., *Nishchenstvo i besprizornost'*, 206–207, 227; *Sobranie russkikh vorovskikh slovarei*, comp. V. Kozlovskii, 4 vols. (New York, 1983), 3:5–9, 11–16, 137–147.

71. M. N. Gernet, *Prestupnyi mir moskvy* (Moscow, 1924), 231, 241–242 (for the results of the study in 1924, including photographs of the tattoos on two residents of the Moscow Labor Home); Utevskii, *V bor'be*, 87 (regarding the later study at the Moscow Labor Home); *Drug detei* (Khar'kov), 1925, no. 9: 18; 1926, nos. 8–9: 18; Maro, *Besprizornye*, 177; Livshits, *Sotsial'nye korni*, 136; Leshchinskii, *Kto byl nichem*, 94; Juviler, "Contradictions," 270–271. Regarding tattoos in the criminal subculture of the former Soviet Union, see *Literary Gazette International*, 1990, no. 2: 19.

72. Borovich, *Kollektivy besprizornykh*, 98–99.

73. *Drug detei* (Khar'kov), 1926, no. 3: 14; 1927, nos. 9–10: 3; *Drug detei*, 1926, no. 2: 16; Feiler, *Russian Experiment*, 27.

74. Borovich, *Kollektivy besprizornykh*, 56–57; *Drug detei*, 1926, no. 2: 16; 1927, nos. 6–7: 24; *Drug detei* (Khar'kov), 1926, no. 3: 15; 1927, no. 2: 28; nos. 9–10: 3.

75. *Komsomol'skaia pravda*, 1925, no. 73 (August 21), 3; *Drug detei*, 1925, no. 1: 10; *Drug detei* (Khar'kov), 1925, no. 6: 8. For examples of other street names acquired by *besprizornye*, see *Puti kommunisticheskogo prosveshcheniia* (Simferopol'), 1926, no. 12: 71; Pogrebinskii, *Fabrika liudei*, 3, 6, 31; Utevskii, *V bor'be*, 76.

76. *Vecherniaia moskva*, 1924, no. 225 (October 1), p. 2; Borovich, *Kollektivy besprizornykh*, 60, 63, 75; Krasnushkin et al., *Nishchenstvo i besprizornost'*, 228–229.

77. For examples of such claims, see E. S. Livshits, *Detskaia besprizornost' i novye formy bor'by s neiu* (Moscow, 1924), 23; Livshits, *Sotsial'nye korni*, 134; Maro, *Besprizornye*, 163; Duranty, *Duranty Reports*, 54–55.

78. Krasnushkin et al., *Nishchenstvo i besprizornost'*, 232; *Drug detei* (Khar'kov), 1925, no. 6: 31–32; 1926, nos. 8–9: 17.

79. *Vozhatyi*, 1926, no. 6: 10; Livshits, *Sotsial'nye korni*, 136–137; *Drug detei* (Khar'kov), 1925, no. 6: 31; 1926, nos. 8–9: 16; Borovich, *Kollektivy besprizornykh*, 62–63, 114; Krasnushkin et al., *Nishchenstvo i besprizornost'*, 235–236; Utevskii, *V bor'be*, 86 (regarding the Moscow Labor Home).

80. *Drug detei*, 1925, no. 2: 13 (regarding the boy who fled to Moscow); Utevskii, *V bor'be*, 76.

81. *Drug detei* (Khar'kov), 1926, nos. 4–5: 11–12.

82. Glatman, *Pioner—na bor'bu*, 8; Livshits, *Sotsial'nye korni*, 134; *Na putiakh k novoi shkole*, 1925, no. 4: 148; V. L. Shveitser and S. M. Shabalov, eds., *Besprizornye v trudovykh kommunakh. Praktika raboty s trudnymi det'mi. Sbornik statei i materialov* (Moscow, 1926), 91; *Drug detei* (Khar'kov), 1925, no. 6: 31; 1927, no. 2: 28; nos. 9–10: 4; Borovich, *Kollektivy besprizornykh*, 15, 75–76, 116. According to one study, the authority of a *vozhak* was typically less absolute among a group of street children who still maintained occasional contact with parents, relatives, or other adult "guardians" than it was among a group of children who knew no other home but the street—perhaps because the latter were more dependent on the *vozhak* for protection and sustenance. See Borovich, *Kollektivy besprizornykh*, 60–61.

83. Livshits, *Sotsial'nye korni*, 134; Borovich, *Kollektivy besprizornykh*, 99, 115–116; *Na putiakh k novoi shkole*, 1924, nos. 7–8: 134.

84. Borovich, *Kollektivy besprizornykh*, 116–117. The presence of a *vozhak* in a children's institution often caused great difficulty for the staff, as we shall see in chapter 7. *Drug detei* (Khar'kov), 1927, no. 2: 29.

85. For Chainik's story, see *Pravda*, 1924, no. 51 (March 2), p. 5.

2. BEGGARS, PEDDLERS, AND PROSTITUTES

1. Roberts, *Through Starving Russia*, 62–63.

2. TsGAOR, f. 5207, o. 1, ed. khr. 61, l. 52 (describing adults as well as juveniles devouring garbage in a market in Saratov province during the Volga

famine); Artamonov, *Deti ulitsy*, 5; Borovich, *Kollektivy besprizornykh*, 68; Krasnushkin et al., *Nishchenstvo i besprizornost'*, 233.

3. Edelhertz, *The Russian Paradox*, 67. A diner in Moscow had the following experience: "One day I was taking a hurried lunch of sausages and sauerkraut in a small restaurant on the Loubiansky Prood whose clientele was evidently of the working class. I had eaten the sausages but I thought it best to leave the sauerkraut on the plate. I asked for the bill. A small boy, pale, emaciated, poorly clad, of about seven was going from table to table begging a few millions. . . .There was half a piece of black bread lying on the table. The boy's eyes feasted upon it. 'Please, sir, may I have that?' he implored. I watched him as he swallowed it almost without tasting it"; Richard Eaton, *Under the Red Flag* (New York, 1924), 42–43.

4. Enik and Blok, *Iz trushchob na stroiku*, 8.

5. Vasilevskii, *Besprizornost'*, 25; Liublinskii, *Bor'ba*, 83–84; Krasnushkin et al., *Nishchenstvo i besprizornost'*, 156; TsGAOR, f. 5207, o. 1, ed. khr. 43, l. 8; *Itogi bor'by s golodom*, 32; *Vestnik narodnogo prosveshcheniia* (Saratov), 1921, no. 1: 44. For a brief discussion of various types of begging in evidence prior to the Revolution, see Krasnushkin et al., *Nishchenstvo i besprizornost'*, 200–202.

6. TsGAOR, f. 5207, o. 1, ed. khr. 61, l. 52.

7. *Gor'kaia pravda*, 40; *Drug detei*, 1927, no. 2: 5; *Zaria Vostoka* (Tiflis), 1922, no. 18 (July 9), p. 2.

8. TsGA RSFSR, f. 1575, o. 6, ed. khr. 152, l. 6; Krasnushkin et al., *Nishchenstvo i besprizornost'*, 156; *Drug detei* (Khar'kov), 1926, nos. 8–9: 16; Vasilevskii, *Besprizornost'*, 25. A decree from the All-Russian Central Executive Committee, dated September 10, 1932, ordered the Moscow Oblast' Executive Committee and the Moscow Soviet to take decisive measures in the struggle with juvenile begging; *SU*, 1932, no. 73, art. 328. Turmoil produced by the collectivization and dekulakization campaigns insured this problem's persistence.

9. Gilev, *Detskaia besprizornost'*, 6; Sokolov, *Besprizornye deti*, 23; Krasnushkin et al., *Nishchenstvo i besprizornost'*, 170 (regarding the survey mentioned).

10. Livshits, *Sotsial'nye korni*, 133; *Drug detei* (Khar'kov), 1925, no. 6: 33; no. 9: 14; *Pravo i zhizn'*, 1926, nos. 6–7: 101–102; Utevskii, *V bor'be*, 104.

11. Krasnushkin et al., *Nishchenstvo i besprizornost'*, 183, 186–187, 200.

12. Gilev, *Detskaia besprizornost'*, 7; *Drug detei* (Khar'kov), 1926, no. 2: 22; Artamonov, *Deti ulitsy*, 5; *Zhizn' Buriatii* (Verkhneudinsk), 1929, no. 5: 72; Krasnushkin et al., *Nishchenstvo i besprizornost'*, 201, 204, 208–209; *Zaria Vostoka* (Tiflis), 1922, no. 59 (August 27), p. 4. Various categories of beggars acquired their own names on the street, for example: *skladchiki* (those who went from apartment to apartment soliciting alms), *mogil'shchiki* (those who begged at cemeteries), *bogomoly* (those who begged at churches), *okusyvaly* (those who begged at cafeterias, snack bars, taverns, and the like), *sedoki* or *sidni* (those who sat or stood in a single spot and begged for long periods of time), *beguny* (those who attached themselves to individual pedestrians and chased along after them, requesting alms), *strelki* (those who invented stories of temporary need

or misfortune to justify their appeals for money), *filony* (those who feigned physical ailments in order to win sympathy for their appeals), *zheleznodorozhniki* (those who begged in train cars and stations).

13. *Drug detei* (Khar'kov), 1926, nos. 8–9: 16; Krasnushkin et al., *Nishchenstvo i besprizornost'*, 205; *Komsomol'skaia pravda*, 1926, no. 209 (September 11), p. 3 (regarding the boy on the train); A. Marinov, "Gosudarstvennye deti," *Novyi mir*, 1974, no. 2: 204.

14. *Shkola i zhizn'* (Nizhnii Novgorod), 1929, no. 3: 78; *Komsomol'skaia pravda*, 1925, no. 73 (August 21), p. 3; Krasnushkin et al., *Nishchenstvo i besprizornost'*, 203–204; E. M. Newman, *Seeing Russia* (New York, 1928), 215.

15. Ilya Ehrenburg, *Memoirs: 1921–1941* (New York, 1966), 73.

16. Krasnushkin et al., *Nishchenstvo i besprizornost'*, 210.

17. Ibid., 211.

18. TsGAOR, f. 5207, o. 1, ed. khr. 67, l. 56; *Drug detei* (Khar'kov), 1926, no. 2: 22 (regarding the girl in the Sukharevka); *Narodnoe prosveshchenie*, 1922, no. 102 (May 14), p. 7; Krasnushkin et al., *Nishchenstvo i besprizornost'*, 203–205, 208; *Krasnaia nov'*, 1923, no. 5: 206 (regarding the Crimea).

19. Krasnushkin et al., *Nishchenstvo i besprizornost'*, 203–204, 208–209; *Pravda*, 1924, no. 49 (February 29), p. 6. For a literary account of three *besprizornye* (two boys and a girl) begging in this fashion, see Gornyi, *Besprizornyi krug*, 52. The boys instruct the girl to follow a pedestrian with outstretched hand until he gives her some money. Should he refuse, she must persist by complaining that she has no mother or father—and show some tears. Should the tears fail, they advise her to curse the man and return to try again with someone else.

20. TsGAOR, f. 5207, o. 1, ed. khr. 67, l. 56; Krasnushkin et al., *Nishchenstvo i besprizornost'*, 220.

21. Krasnushkin et al., *Nishchenstvo i besprizornost'*, 203–204, 208–209, 218, 221–222. For a literary description of such deceptions, see Shishkov, *Children*, 26.

22. Bartlett, "Stepchildren," 337 (for the quotation); Glatman, *Pioner—na bor'bu*, 8; *Drug detei*, 1925, no. 2: 15 (for the passenger's account); 1926, no. 2: 13.

23. *Nash trud* (Iaroslavl'), 1925, no. 1: 25; *Voprosy prosveshcheniia na Severnom Kavkaze* (Rostov-on-the-Don), 1927, no. 9: 9; *Drug detei*, 1928, no. 4: 13; *Komsomol'skaia pravda*, 1926, no. 209 (September 11), p. 3; *Detskaia besprizornost' (preduprezhdenie i bor'ba s nei)* (Moscow, 1923), 26–27 (regarding the "nightingale"); *Drug detei* (Khar'kov), 1926, nos. 6–7: 29; 1927, nos. 5–6: 35 (regarding the "future Shaliapin").

24. *Shkola i zhizn'* (Nizhnii Novgorod), 1929, no. 3: 78; Glatman, *Pionery i besprizornye*, 20; Krasnushkin et al., *Nishchenstvo i besprizornost'*, 215; *Drug detei*, 1926, no. 2: 13; *Pravo i zhizn'*, 1925, no. 6: 80.

25. Glatman, *Pionery i besprizornye*, 20; Maro, *Besprizornye*, 208–209; Paustovsky, *Restless Years*, 47.

26. *Drug detei* (Khar'kov), 1926, no. 3: 15; Maro, *Besprizornye*, 206–208.

27. *Molot* (Rostov-on-the-Don), 1925, no. 1249 (October 2), p. 2.

28. Maro, *Besprizornye*, 204–206, 217–219 (regarding prisons); *Detskii dom*, 1929, no. 2: 87 (regarding children's institutions).

29. *Drug detei* (Khar'kov), 1927, no. 1: 14.

30. Maro, *Besprizornye*, 202–203.

31. Ibid., 210–212, 215–216, 219–221; Shishkov, *Children*, 77.

32. Gilev, *Detskaia besprizornost'*, 7; *Drug detei*, 1926, no. 2: 13; Krasnushkin et al., *Nishchenstvo i besprizornost'*, 204, 208; *Drug detei* (Khar'kov), 1925, no. 6: 34. For a literary description of a *besprizornyi* who sings and juggles simultaneously as he begs at a provincial train station, see Kozhevnikov, *Stremka*, 38–42.

33. *Drug detei* (Khar'kov), 1926, nos. 8–9: 16; 1927, no. 1: 14.

34. Leshchinskii, *Kto byl nichem*, 80.

35. *Drug detei*, 1929, no. 9: inside back cover.

36. *Prosveshchenie Sibiri* (Novosibirsk), 1927, no. 5: 57; Vasilevskii, *Besprizornost'*, 3.

37. Hughes, *I Wonder*, 153; Edelhertz, *The Russian Paradox*, 66. For a literary account of this practice, see Shishkov, *Children*, 133. Vladimir Mayakovsky, too, referred to such a threat in his poem "Besprizorshchina"; see *Polnoe sobranie sochinenii*, vol. 7 (Moscow, 1958), 171.

38. Livshits, *Sotsial'nye korni*, 133–134; Maro, *Besprizornye*, 157; *Drug detei* (Khar'kov), 1926, no. 2: 22; Krasnushkin et al., *Nishchenstvo i besprizornost'*, 198; Vasilevskii, *Besprizornost'*, 25. For a literary account of a man (who pretends to be blind) begging in the Sukharevka together with a homeless girl, see Gornyi, *Besprizornyi krug*, 23–26. For a literary account of a begging team composed of a homeless boy and a blind man, see Shishkov, *Children*, 3–4.

39. *Vestnik prosveshcheniia*, 1925, no. 9: 92–93; *Drug detei*, 1926, no. 2: 13.

40. TsGA RSFSR, f. 1575, o. 6, ed. khr. 155, l. 9; *Na pomoshch' rebenku* (Petrograd-Moscow, 1923), 8; *Drug detei*, 1926, no. 3: 14; *Voprosy prosveshcheniia na Severnom Kavkaze* (Rostov-on-the-Don), 1927, no. 9: 11; *Prosveshchenie Sibiri* (Novosibirsk), 1929, no. 12: 15; *Drug detei* (Khar'kov), 1927, nos. 5–6: 36; *Na pomoshch' detiam. Obshchestvenno-literaturnyi i nauchnyi sbornik, posviashchennyi voprosam bor'by s detskoi besprizornost'iu* (Moscow, 1926), 5–6; Records of the Smolensk Oblast' of the All-Union Communist Party of the Soviet Union, 1917–1941, reel 15, WKP 124, p. 61.

41. Hughes, *I Wonder*, 153; *Pravo i zhizn'*, 1926, nos. 6–7: 101 (for the budget of the two boys); Krasnushkin et al., *Nishchenstvo i besprizornost'*, 217, 219. Another young beggar reported that he sometimes made eighty kopecks in a day—which he spent on food and gambling; see Bartlett, "Stepchildren," 337.

42. Concerning juvenile trade during War Communism, see *Detskaia defektivnost'*, 32–33; Liublinskii, *Zakonodatel'naia okhrana*, 82; Vasilevskii, *Besprizornost'*, 45–47; Alexander Berkman, *The Bolshevik Myth (Diary, 1920–1922)* (New York, 1925), 56–58, 82–83; Ball, *Russia's Last Capitalists*, 6–7 (regarding private trade in general during War Communism).

43. Vasilevskii, *Besprizornost'*, 45–47.

44. Liublinskii, *Zakonodatel'naia okhrana*, 83 (regarding the competition produced by NEP); *Itogi bor'by s golodom*, 32 (regarding the large number of

juvenile traders produced by the famine). Concerning the continued involvement of *besprizornye* in street trade after 1921, see TsGA RSFSR, f. 1575, o. 6, ed. khr. 152, l. 6; Artamonov, *Deti ulitsy*, 5; Maro, *Besprizornye*, 146; Poznyshev, *Detskaia besprizornost'*, 41.

45. Vasilevskii, *Besprizornost'*, 44.

46. For a description of established young entrepreneurs (in this case, *besprizornye* who carried loads for hire at markets) driving off newcomers attempting to find similar work, see *Drug detei* (Khar'kov), 1925, no. 9: 13.

47. Ibid., 1926, no. 2: 18.

48. *Drug detei*, 1926, no. 1: 27; *Drug detei* (Khar'kov), 1926, no. 2: 19.

49. *Drug detei* (Khar'kov), 1926, no. 2: 28; 1927, no. 1: 32; Greenwall, *Mirrors of Moscow*, 185.

50. *Prosveshchenie Sibiri* (Novosibirsk), 1927, no. 5: 65; Borovich, *Kollektivy besprizornykh*, 91, 106.

51. Vasilevskii, *Besprizornost'*, 50.

52. *Na putiakh k novoi shkole*, 1927, nos. 7–8: 103 (regarding Moscow); *Drug detei*, 1930, no. 7: 6; *Pravda*, 1924, no. 49 (February 29), p. 6; Thompson, *New Russia*, 250.

53. *Na putiakh k novoi shkole*, 1927, nos. 7–8: 105. Another source put the average earnings of these young vendors in the same neighborhood (1 to 1.2 rubles); *Drug detei*, 1928, no. 1: 11.

54. *Na putiakh k novoi shkole*, 1927, nos. 7–8: 103–105. For a similar description of the daily schedule of children selling newspapers in the streets, see *Drug detei*, 1928, no. 1: 11. For a description of a *besprizornyi* hawking papers at a Moscow train station (which also served as the youth's home), see *Drug detei*, 1926, no. 3: 22–23. He had to accumulate one ruble to get started as a newspaper vendor.

55. For a detailed description of *besprizornye* selling water in the Sukharevka, see *Drug detei* (Khar'kov), 1926, no. 2: 16, 19–20.

56. Borovich, *Kollektivy besprizornykh*, 91; Vasilevskii, *Besprizornost'*, 41; *Drug detei* (Khar'kov), 1926, no. 2: 17; *Drug detei*, 1930, no. 7: 6–7; *Izvestiia*, 1925, no. 210 (September 15), p. 6; *Pravda*, 1924, no. 32 (February 9), p. 3 (regarding Leningrad).

57. *Pravda*, 1924, no. 49 (February 29), p. 6.

58. Livshits, *Sotsial'nye korni*, 133; Vasilevskii, *Besprizornost'*, 41; *Drug detei* (Khar'kov), 1925, no. 9: 13; *Drug detei*, 1930, no. 7: 6. For a literary description of a *besprizornyi* hired by a group of adult street vendors to stand watch at a corner and warn of approaching policemen, see Kozhevnikov, *Stremka*, 6–13. At the end of each day, the traders paid the girl with a small amount of the various food products they had been offering for sale.

59. *Drug detei*, 1927, no. 2: 9.

60. Concerning the lack of statistics, see Ryndziunskii et al., *Pravovoe polozhenie* (1927), 88; *Drug detei* (Khar'kov), 1925, no. 9: 17. On the link between *besprizornost'* and juvenile prostitution, see *Profilakticheskaia meditsina* (Khar'kov), 1924, nos. 11–12: 166; 1925, no. 1: 44; *Moskovskii meditsinskii zhurnal*, 1924, no. 5: 117; L. M. Vasilevskii, *Prostitutsiia i rabochaia molodezh'* (Moscow, 1924), 21; *Drug detei* (Khar'kov), 1925, no. 9: 17–18; Manns,

Bor'ba, 23. Prostitutes were also encountered among *beznadzornye* children (those with parents or other adult guardians but left largely unsupervised); see *Drug detei* (Khar'kov), 1926, no. 2: 27. For descriptions of individual girls driven to *besprizornost'* and then to prostitution, see Sokolov, *Spasite detei!* 57; L. Fridland, *S raznykh storon. Prostitutsiia v SSSR* (Berlin, 1931), 125–129. In the slang of the street, *besprizornye* sometimes referred to a prostitute as a *chekanka* or a *biksa*; see *Put' prosveshcheniia* (Khar'kov), 1924, nos. 4–5: 239; *Vchera i segodnia*, 103.

61. These and similar reports are quoted in Sokolov, *Spasite detei!* 55–56, 59.

62. On juvenile prostitution resulting from *besprizornost'* produced by the famine, see *Vestnik narodnogo prosveshcheniia* (Saratov), 1921, no. 1: 44; *Vestnik prosveshcheniia* (Voronezh), 1921, no. 1: 54–55; *Itogi bor'by s golodom*, 32; *Moskovskii meditsinskii zhurnal*, 1924, no. 5: 117; *Kommunistka*, 1921, nos. 14–15: 4. For the editorial comment, see *Spasennye revoliutsiei. Bor'ba s besprizornost'iu v irkutskoi gubernii i okruge (1920–1931 gg.)* (Irkutsk, 1977), 32.

63. L. A. Vasilevskii and L. M. Vasilevskii, *Prostitutsiia i novaia Rossiia* (Tver', 1923), 69; *Gor'kaia pravda*, 42.

64. *Venerologiia i dermatologiia*, 1925, no. 2: 102; *Drug detei*, 1926, no. 4: 7; *Detskii dom i bor'ba s besprizornost'iu*, 35.

65. *Drug detei*, 1925, no. 1: 12–13 (this is a short story, written by a former *besprizornyi*, describing a young girl who finds herself alone on the street; she tries at first to support herself by begging but soon turns to prostitution); 1927, no. 2: 9; Vasilevskii, *Besprizornost'*, 70; *Drug detei* (Khar'kov), 1925, no. 9: 18; Maro, *Besprizornye*, 118, 147.

66. *Drug detei*, 1927, no. 2: 9; Maro, *Besprizornye*, 170; *Drug detei* (Khar'kov), 1927, no. 3: 22; Goldman, "The 'Withering Away' and the Resurrection," 154. Some *besprizornye*, of course, earned considerably less through prostitution; see for example *Nizhegorodskii sbornik zdravookhraneniia* (Nizhnii Novgorod), 1925, no. 1: 43. An interview with two seventeen-year-old prostitutes revealed that one made over one hundred rubles per month, the other no more than sixty. A thirty-year-old streetwalker divided prostitutes (adults and juveniles taken together) into three categories with regard to earnings: the most desperate took customers for as little as fifty kopecks, others charged in the neighborhood of three rubles, and some would not accept less than ten rubles. See *Pravo i zhizn'*, 1928, no. 1: 54–55.

67. For the studies mentioned, see Sokolov, *Spasite detei!* 55; *Detskii dom*, 1929, no. 10: 17. According to another author, the "overwhelming majority" of female *besprizornye* practiced prostitution (often together with thievery); *Drug detei* (Khar'kov), 1927, no. 3: 20, 22. See also Stites, *Women's Liberation Movement*, 373; *Drug detei* (Khar'kov), 1926, no. 10: 6; Chase, *Workers, Society, and the Soviet State*, 195.

68. *Drug detei* (Khar'kov), 1925, no. 9: 17, 19; see also no. 6: 8.

69. Vasilevskii, *Prostitutsiia i rabochaia molodezh'*, 21; *Profilakticheskaia meditsina* (Khar'kov), 1925, no. 1: 44; Gernet, *Prestupnyi mir*, 148; *Drug detei* (Khar'kov), 1925, no. 6: 8; no. 9: 17; Sokolov, *Spasite detei!* 55; *Molot* (Rostov-on-the-Don), 1925, no. 1144 (May 30), p. 5; Maro, *Besprizornye*, 397.

70. Sokolov, *Spasite detei!* 59.

71. *Drug detei*, 1927, no. 2: 9. See also Fridland, *S raznykh storon*, 125. Regarding the use of alcohol and cocaine by juvenile prostitutes, see *Moskovskii meditsinskii zhurnal*, 1924, no. 5: 117; Manns, *Bor'ba*, 24.

72. Vasilevskii, *Besprizornost'*, 59, 70, 73; Sokolov, *Spasite detei!* 59; Maro, *Besprizornye*, 155–156.

73. *Pravo i zhizn'*, 1928, no. 1: 56.

74. *Moskovskii meditsinskii zhurnal*, 1924, no. 5: 116–117; *Drug detei*, 1927, no. 2: 9; Sokolov, *Spasite detei!* 58–59.

75. *Pravo i zhizn'*, 1926, nos. 6–7: 103.

76. *Profilakticheskaia meditsina* (Khar'kov), 1925, no. 1: 42, 45; no. 11: 128; *Pravo i zhizn'*, 1928, no. 1: 54; *Drug detei* (Khar'kov), 1925, no. 9: 18–19; *Venerologiia i dermatologiia*, 1925, no. 1: 83; *Moskovskii meditsinskii zhurnal*, 1924, no. 5: 116–117; *Detskii dom*, 1928, no. 3: 54.

77. *Venerologiia i dermatologiia*, 1925, no. 1: 83; *Drug detei* (Khar'kov), 1925, no. 9: 19; 1927, no. 3: 22; *Voprosy prosveshcheniia* (Rostov-on-the-Don), 1926, nos. 8–9: 50; *Moskovskii meditsinskii zhurnal*, 1924, no. 5: 116–117; *Detskii dom*, 1928, no. 3: 55; TsGA RSFSR, f. 1575, o. 6, ed. khr. 152, l. 6; *Drug detei*, 1925, no. 1: 12–13; 1927, no. 2: 9; *Pravo i zhizn'*, 1928, no. 1: 53 (regarding the girl caught in the public bathroom).

78. Poznyshev, *Detskaia besprizornost'*, 41; *Detskii dom*, 1929, no. 5: 20; Manns, *Bor'ba*, 23; *Drug detei* (Khar'kov), 1927, no. 3: 23.

79. Vasilevskii, *Prostitutsiia i rabochaia molodezh'*, 23; Manns, *Bor'ba*, 23; *Detskii dom*, 1928, no. 3: 56.

80. *Drug detei* (Khar'kov), 1925, no. 9: 18. See also Sokolov, *Spasite detei!* 58; *Drug detei*, 1927, no. 2: 9.

81. *Detskii dom*, 1928, no. 3: 56; *Drug detei* (Khar'kov), 1925, no. 9: 18; TsGA RSFSR, f. 1575, o. 10, ed. khr. 177, l. 13; Maro, *Besprizornye*, 401. Anton Makarenko concluded on the basis of his work with *besprizornye* that a juvenile prostitute was more difficult to rehabilitate than other youths, no matter how long the latter had been corrupted by the street. Part of the problem for a former prostitute, he added, stemmed not from her experiences on the street but from the stigma attached to her by others in the institution; see A. S. Makarenko, *The Road to Life*, 2 vols. (Moscow, 1951; reprint, 1973), 2:399. For a description of the gradual progress reportedly made by an institution rehabilitating former juvenile prostitutes, see Maro, *Besprizornye*, 398–399.

82. For an example, see *Drug detei*, 1927, no. 2: 9.

83. Regarding the gender imbalance, some authors maintained that parents or other adult guardians typically devoted more care (or granted less independence) to girls. If meager family resources forced a decision to send a child out of the home—whether to engage in trade or begging, to leave the countryside and go to a city for the winter, or to depart altogether—the one chosen was usually a boy. Others argued that boys broke more quickly from a bleak family situation, such as grinding poverty or parental abuse, and viewed the prospect of life on the street with less intimidation. See *Drug detei* (Khar'kov), 1926, nos. 8–9: 14; 1927, no. 3: 19; nos. 9–10: 4, 34; *Voprosy prosveshcheniia* (Rostov-on-the-Don), 1926, no. 2: 44–45; *Narodnoe obrazovanie v R.S.F.S.R. (po dan-*

nym godovoi statisticheskoi otchetnosti mestnykh organov narodnogo komis-sariata po prosveshcheniiu na I/VI 1924 goda) (Moscow, 1925), 119; Livshits, *Sotsial'nye korni*, 28; Thompson, *New Russia*, 251–252; *Pravda*, 1927, no. 112 (May 20), p. 5. It may also be that welfare institutions admitted girls more willingly than boys, or at least retained them with greater success. According to figures for 1926, the Russian Republic's orphanages housed roughly equal numbers of girls and boys; *Narodnoe prosveshchenie*, 1927, no. 7: 13. Possibly, too, boys embraced more readily the various aggressive activities (see chapter 3) that promoted survival on their own.

3. FROM YOU I CAN EXPECT NO PITY

1. P. N. Sokolov, *Detskaia besprizornost' i detskaia prestupnost' i mery bor'by s etimi iavleniiami s sovremennoi tochki zreniia* (Saratov, 1924), 3 (for the first quotation); *Vestnik prosveshcheniia*, 1923, no. 4: 182 (for the second quotation); *Statisticheskii obzor narodnogo obrazovaniia v permskom okruge*, 39; *Prosveshchenie* (Krasnodar), 1921, nos. 3–4: 9; Manns, *Bor'ba*, 4; *Voprosy prosveshcheniia* (Rostov-on-the-Don), 1926, no. 2: 57; Tizanov and Epshtein, *Gosudarstvo i obshchestvennost'*, 40; Gilev, *Detskaia besprizornost'*, 21; *Molot* (Rostov-on-the-Don), 1925, no. 1190 (July 24), p. 4; 1925, no. 1201 (August 6), p. 3; *Na putiakh k novoi shkole*, no. 3 (May 1923): 173–174; *Prosveshchenie na Urale* (Sverdlovsk), 1927, no. 2: 61.

2. *Otchet o deiatel'nosti saratovskogo gubernskogo ispolnitel'nogo komiteta*, 56; *Severo-Kavkazskii krai* (Rostov-on-the-Don), 1924, no. 11: 205; "Otchet Riazgubono za ianvar'—sentiabr' 1922 goda," in *Otchet o deiatel'nosti riazanskogo gubispolkoma za vremia s X po XI gubernskii s''ezd sovetov rabochikh, krest'ianskikh i krasnoarmeiskikh deputatov* (Riazan', 1922), 5; *Molot* (Rostov-on-the-Don), 1925, no. 1173 (July 4), p. 5; 1925, no. 1223 (September 2), p. 5.

3. According to one estimate, the elimination of *besprizornost'* would have reduced juvenile delinquency "by at least 75 percent"; *Bich naroda*, 69. See also *Komsomol'skaia pravda*, 1925, no. 73 (August 21), p. 3 (the figure of 75 percent appears here as well); *Deti posle goloda*, 9; Kufaev, *Iunye pravonarushiteli* (1924), 225; G. M. Min'kovskii, "Osnovnye etapy razvitiia sovetskoi sistemy mer bor'by s prestupnost'iu nesovershennoletnikh," in *Voprosy bor'by s prestupnost'iu, vypusk 6* (1967), 45; Juviler, "Contradictions," 264. As the number of *besprizornye* dwindled with the passing years, their share of juvenile crime shrank to well under 50 percent; see V. I. Kufaev, *Iunye pravonarushiteli*, 3d ed. (Moscow, 1929), 5–7; *Drug detei* (Khar'kov), 1925, no. 2: 46; *Ural'skii uchitel'* (Sverdlovsk), 1926, nos. 11–12: 32; *Drug detei*, 1928, no. 9: 12–13; *Nash trud* (Iaroslavl'), 1928, nos. 7–9: 40; *Prosveshchenie na Urale* (Sverdlovsk), 1929, nos. 5–6: 93. Regarding the relationship between incorrigibility and time on the street, see Gernet, *Prestupnyi mir*, 214; *Administrativnyi vestnik*, 1926, no. 12: 37; *Nash trud* (Iaroslavl'), 1928, nos. 7–9: 42.

4. *Psikhiatriia, nevrologiia i eksperimental'naia psikhologiia* (Petrograd), 1922, *vypusk* 1, 102. Regarding the increase in juvenile crime during World War I, see also *Put' prosveshcheniia* (Khar'kov), 1924, no. 3: 33; Kufaev, *Iunye*

pravonarushiteli (1924), 91; Maro, *Besprizornye*, 63; *Pravo i zhizn'*, 1927, nos. 8–10: 28; American Red Cross, box 866, file 948.08 ("Commission to Russia [First], Billings Report, Oct. 22, 1917"), Appendix to "Report of the Committee on Child Welfare," August 28/September 10, 1917. The juvenile-crime rate had been rising even before World War I; see Juviler, "Contradictions," 262.

5. On the link between the famine and increasing juvenile crime (in the country as a whole and in various localities), see TsGAOR, f. 5207, o. 1, ed. khr. 43, l. 8; *Itogi bor'by s golodom*, 32; *Vestnik narodnogo prosveshcheniia* (Saratov), 1921, no. 1: 44; Kufaev, *Iunye pravonarushiteli* (1924), 93; *Vestnik prosveshcheniia* (Voronezh), 1921, no. 1: 54–55; *Otchet gorskogo ekonomicheskogo soveshchaniia za period aprel'–sentiabr' 1922 g.* (Vladikavkaz, 1923), 123; Vasilevskii and Vasilevskii, *Kniga o golode*, 77–78; *Pravo i zhizn'*, 1922, no. 1: 37.

6. Kufaev, *Iunye pravonarushiteli* (1924), 92–93; Livshits, *Sotsial'nye korni*, 65. In Petrograd, more remote from the famine region, somewhat fewer juveniles appeared before commissions in 1921 compared to 1920. But even here, the number of juvenile delinquents per hundred thousand children (ages seven to eighteen) increased marginally in 1921. See Maro, *Besprizornye*, 64; Kufaev, *Iunye pravonarushiteli* (1924), 93–94. For additional figures from numerous provinces on the increase in juvenile crime in 1921–22, see *Vlast' sovetov*, 1923, no. 5: 164; *Pravo i zhizn'*, 1925, nos. 2–3: 93 (data showing a smaller—77 percent—increase for Rostov-on-the-Don in 1921).

7. Vasilevskii, *Besprizornost'*, 36 (regarding the figures for the first quarters of 1920, 1921, and 1922); *Vlast' sovetov*, 1923, no. 5: 162–163. The second source also provides the following figures for the Russian Republic: 1920, 8 percent; 1921, 10 percent; 1922, 9 percent. For Petrograd: 1920, 13 percent; 1921, 10 percent; 1922, 10 percent.

8. Kufaev, *Iunye pravonarushiteli* (1924), 142–144.

9. For the data cited, see *Sovetskoe stroitel'stvo*, 1927, nos. 2–3: 162; *Voprosy prosveshcheniia* (Rostov-on-the-Don), 1926, no. 2: 57 (the period covered here was October 1924–June 1925). Of the orphans appearing before Moscow Juvenile Affairs Commissions in 1922, 63.6 percent of the boys and 70.2 percent of the girls were born outside Moscow province; see Kufaev, *Iunye pravonarushiteli* (1924), 144. The overwhelming majority of all reported juvenile offenses took place in cities; Manns, *Bor'ba*, 12; Maro, *Besprizornye*, 65; G. G. Magul'iano, "K voprosu o detskoi prestupnosti i merakh bor'by s nei za gody revoliutsii," in *Sbornik trudov professorov i prepodavatelei gosudarstvennogo irkutskogo universiteta. Fakul'tet obshchestvennykh nauk, vypusk 6* (Irkutsk, 1923), 180. To some extent this situation was due to the fact that transgressions often went unrecorded in the countryside. But the torrent of destitute children pouring into many cities during the famine suggests that this urban concentration of juvenile crime was based on more than just incomplete rural records.

10. See for example Gernet, *Prestupnyi mir*, 126, 213; Maro, *Besprizornye*, 114; Kufaev, *Iunye pravonarushiteli* (1924), 144–145; *Drug detei*, 1930, no. 5: 16. For percentages of full and half orphans (the latter classified as having one parent alive) among youths charged with various specific offenses, see Kufaev, *Iunye pravonarushiteli* (1924), 152–157. One ought not to rely too heavily on

such numbers, however, for it frequently proved difficult to determine with any confidence a child's family situation. Youths on the street for any length of time often had no idea whether their parents were still alive. Also, data on juvenile delinquents commonly do not specify whether a child was a *besprizornyi*. Youths listed as orphans were very likely, but not necessarily, *besprizornye*. Similarly, half orphans frequently, but not always, inhabited the street children's world. Thus, figures such as those quoted above, and those to follow, should be regarded cautiously as rough indicators. Among juveniles listed as having only one parent, that parent was three or four times more likely to be a mother, owing to heavy male war casualties and the abandonment of wives and lovers. For a variety of studies, see Maro, *Besprizornye*, 90; *Drug detei* (Khar'kov), 1926, no. 10: 6; Kufaev, *Iunye pravonarushiteli* (1924), 147; Liublinskii, *Bor'ba*, 64.

11. Quoted in Liublinskii, *Bor'ba*, 45.

12. *Severo-Kavkazskii krai* (Rostov-on-the-Don), 1924, no. 11: 206; Kufaev, *Iunye pravonarushiteli* (1924), 92, 95–96. Kufaev argues that expanded government assistance to children also played a part in reducing the number of cases before commissions. Worth noting too, in 1920 the threshold of legal adulthood was raised from age seventeen to eighteen. This likely accounted for some of the increase in cases heard by commissions in 1920 compared to 1919. See Kufaev, *Iunye pravonarushiteli* (1924), 91.

13. Min'kovskii, "Osnovnye etapy," 47; Maro, *Besprizornye*, 78; *Drug detei* (Khar'kov), 1925, no. 2: 46.

14. *Vchera i segodnia*, 128; Gilev, *Detskaia besprizornost'*, 7; *Drug detei*, 1926, no. 1: 27; Kufaev, *Iunye pravonarushiteli* (1924), 71–72, 75–76; *Drug detei* (Khar'kov), 1926, no. 3: 17; Gernet, *Prestupnyi mir*, 119. According to Juvenile Affairs Commission records in Moscow for 1922 and 1923, children most often stole items such as bread, herrings, sugar, cigarettes, fruit (sold by vendors in markets), and bags of produce; see V. I. Kufaev, "Iz opyta raboty komissii po delam nesovershennoletnikh v period 1918–1935 gg.," *Voprosy kriminalistiki*, 1964, no. 11: 96–97.

15. *Nash trud* (Iaroslavl'), 1925, no. 1: 27; Borovich, *Kollektivy besprizornykh*, 65–66; Kufaev, *Iunye pravonarushiteli* (1924), 72–73.

16. For the study, see Krasnushkin et al., *Nishchenstvo i besprizornost'*, 167, 189–190. See also Kufaev, *Iunye pravonarushiteli* (1924), 74–75.

17. See for example *Drug detei*, 1925, no. 2: 20. Regarding the considerable number of children who practiced both begging and stealing, see Krasnushkin et al., *Nishchenstvo i besprizornost'*, 163–164. Regarding the reference to boys (rather than girls) engaged in crime, Juvenile Affairs Commissions and other sources in all parts of the country reported with near unanimous consistency that boys accounted for 85–95 percent of juvenile crime. See TsGA RSFSR, f. 1575, o. 10, ed. khr. 190, l. 1; ibid., ed. khr. 193, l. 5; *Statisticheskii obzor narodnogo obrazovaniia v permskom okruge*, 39; *Drug detei* (Khar'kov), 1926, no. 10: 6; *Voprosy prosveshcheniia* (Rostov-on-the-Don), 1926, no. 2: 58; Manns, *Bor'ba*, 19; Tizanov et al., *Detskaia besprizornost'*, 141; Vasilevskii, *Besprizornost'*, 20; *Drug detei*, 1928, no. 10: inside back cover; Ryndziunskii and Savinskaia, *Detskoe pravo*, 257; Magul'iano, "K voprosu o detskoi pres-

tupnosti," 172–175; M. Popov, *Detskaia besprizornost' i patronirovanie* (Iva-novo-Voznesensk, 1929), 8.

18. Krasnushkin et al., *Nishchenstvo i besprizornost'*, 164, 181–183, 196–197; Livshits, *Sotsial'nye korni*, 134.

19. On the transition from begging to stealing, see Krasnushkin et al., *Nishchenstvo i besprizornost'*, 191–192, 194–196. On the transition from petty trade to stealing, see *Drug detei* (Khar'kov), 1926, no. 2: 20; Kufaev, *Iunye pravonarushiteli* (1924), 130; Krasnushkin et al., *Nishchenstvo i besprizornost'*, 196; Vasilevskii, *Besprizornost'*, 47–48.

20. For these and several other examples, see Krasnushkin et al., *Nishchenstvo i besprizornost'*, 206–207.

21. *Drug detei* (Khar'kov), 1925, no. 1: 34; *Drug detei*, 1926, no. 3: 21. Juvenile crime, an investigator declared in 1924, could be summed up almost entirely with three words: *krazhi* (thefts), *spekuliatsiia* ("speculation," mainly violations of laws on trading), and *khuliganstvo* ("hooliganism," various types of disorderly, antisocial behavior); see Kufaev, *Iunye pravonarushiteli* (1924), 115. *Krazhi* towered above the other two categories, typically accounting for 60–80 percent of the offenses that bulged the files of Juvenile Affairs Commissions; TsGA RSFSR, f. 1575, o. 10, ed. khr. 190, l. 1; Gernet, *Prestupnyi mir*, 211; *Severo-Kavkazskii krai* (Rostov-on-the-Don), 1924, no. 11: 207; *Narodnoe prosveshchenie v RSFSR 1927–28 god* (Moscow, 1929), 188–191; Kufaev, *Iunye pravonarushiteli* (1929), 7; Vasilevskii and Vasilevskii, *Kniga o golode*, 78; Maro, *Besprizornye*, 77; Gilev, *Detskaia besprizornost'*, 22; Ryndziunskii and Savinskaia, *Detskoe pravo*, 256–257; *Otchet o sostoianii narodnogo obrazovaniia v eniseiskoi gubernii IV-mu gubs"ezdu sovetov* (Krasnoiarsk, 1922), 17. Attacks against individuals (murders, beatings, and sexual assaults, for example) accounted for only about 7–9 percent of all juvenile crimes; Kufaev, *Iunye pravonarushiteli* (1929), 13. Indeed, from the end of 1917 to the mid-1930s (when the commissions were abolished), thefts made up 70–80 percent of the crimes committed by youths nine to seventeen years of age, according to Kufaev, "Iz opyta," 96. More specifically, in the Russian Republic, thefts amounted to 81 percent of all recorded juvenile crimes in 1922, down slightly to 76 percent in 1927, and 75.6 percent in 1932; ibid. Thefts accounted for most juvenile crime before and after this period as well. See Kufaev, *Iunye pravonarushiteli* (1924), 103–104 (regarding prerevolutionary Russia); Min'kovskii, "Osnovnye etapy," 60 (statistics for the year 1940). While thefts remained by far the most widespread juvenile crime throughout the period under consideration, changes in government policies and economic conditions altered somewhat the mix of juvenile offenses. During War Communism, for instance, enforcement of laws against private trade increased the percentage of children (and adults) arrested for "speculation." By 1921–1922, the share of all juvenile crimes accounted for by theft swelled considerably, doubtless reaching its peak for the decade. See *Psikhiatriia, nevrologiia i eksperimental'naia psikhologiia* (Petrograd), 1922, *vypusk* 1, 97, 99; Kufaev, *Iunye pravonarushiteli* (1924), 104–107; Liublinskii, *Bor'ba*, 45. This reflected both the immense quantity of desperate children produced by the famine and the substantial relaxation of the government's policy on private trade. By the middle of the 1920s, if the reports

of several Juvenile Affairs Commissions are an accurate guide, thefts probably
surrendered a small portion of their share of juvenile crime to other offenses,
notably "hooliganism." See *Na putiakh k novoi shkole*, 1926, no. 3: 20. Assuming this occurred, the shift probably stemmed in part from the decreasing
number of *besprizornye*. This is not to suggest that *besprizornye* refrained from
disruptive, antisocial behavior. The point is simply that a less deprived delinquent tended to commit fewer thefts relative to acts of "hooliganism" than did
a *besprizornyi*. Thus, as the number of street children declined, less destitute
children came to represent a larger proportion of young criminals, and "hooliganism" expanded slightly its share of juvenile crime.

   As one might suppose, juveniles committed a share of all thefts larger than
their percentage of the total criminal population. In the Russian Republic, for
example, 31 percent of the imprisoned population (adults and children) in 1923
had been convicted of simple theft. Among the juveniles alone in this group,
however, the figure jumped to 80 percent. See Gernet, *Prestupnyi mir*, 211. For
figures from Siberia showing that in 1923 and 1924 juveniles committed a larger
share of all property crimes than any other category of crime, see Manns, *Bor'ba*,
13.
   22. *Bich naroda*, 66; *Krasnaia nov'*, 1923, no. 5: 206.
   23. *Krasnaia nov'*, 1923, no. 5: 205–206. A literary account described similar *besprizornye*, known as "knockers": "This is how they work: one of them
hides in a dark passage while the other walks about the street like one waiting
for his girl. No sooner does some madam come along with a handbag than the
one in the street throws himself violently under her feet and knocks her down,
while the other leaps out of his hiding place and snatches the bag, and then both
dash off"; N. Ognyov [M. G. Rozanov], *The Diary of a Communist Schoolboy*
(New York, 1928; reprint, Westport, Conn., 1973), 54.
   24. TsGALI, f. 332, o. 2, ed. khr. 41, l. 2; *Drug detei* (Khar'kov), 1926, nos.
4–5: 11; *Vozhatyi*, 1926, no. 6: 11; *Drug detei*, 1926, no. 3: 21; Glatman,
Pionery i besprizornye, 17; Krasnushkin et al., *Nishchenstvo i besprizornost'*,
228; *Rabochaia moskva*, 1924, no. 130 (June 11), p. 7; Thompson, *New Russia*,
246; Wicksteed, *Life*, 76; Shishkov, *Children*, 9 (for a literary account of youths
robbing a woman in the street); *Komsomol'skaia pravda*, 1925, no. 73 (August
21), p. 3; 1926, no. 48 (February 27), p. 4; *Vecherniaia moskva*, 1927, no. 71
(March 30), p. 3. Regarding youths snatching money from people paying cab
fares, see *Na pomoshch' detiam. Obshchestvenno-literaturnyi i nauchnyi sbornik*, 5; Greenwall, *Mirrors*, 185. For a drawing by a *besprizornyi* depicting a
youth running off with a lady's purse that he has just stolen, see *Drug detei*
(Khar'kov), 1925, no. 9: 21.
   25. *Vozhatyi*, 1926, no. 6: 11; *Put' prosveshcheniia* (Khar'kov), 1924, nos.
4–5: 237; *Drug detei* (Khar'kov), 1925, no. 6: 33; Maro, *Besprizornye*, 169.
For a drawing by a *besprizornyi* showing a boy picking a person's pocket, see
figure 22.
   26. *Drug detei* (Khar'kov), 1926, no. 2: 21–22 (regarding the Sukharevka);
Izvestiia, 1926, no. 189 (August 19), p. 4 (regarding Sevastopol'). As one would
expect, many *besprizornye* specialized in stealing suitcases and baskets from
passengers in train stations. One boy reportedly possessed such a talent for

appearing harmless and winning people's trust that travelers occasionally asked him to watch their luggage while they stepped out to perform a task of some sort. Needless to say, they found neither luggage nor boy when they returned. See *Vozhatyi*, 1926, no. 6: 11. For another drawing by a *besprizornyi*, this time showing two passengers sitting overnight on a bench in a train station while three waifs steal their bags, see figure 21.

27. *Krasnaia nov'*, 1932, no. 1: 46–47; *Drug detei* (Khar'kov), 1925, no. 6: 34; Serge, *Russia*, 30.

28. *Drug detei* (Khar'kov), 1926, no. 2: 20.

29. *Drug detei*, 1926, no. 5: 18.

30. *Drug detei* (Khar'kov), 1926, no. 2: 20.

31. *Vozhatyi*, 1926, no. 6: 11; *Drug detei*, 1926, no. 3: 21; Glatman, *Pionery i besprizornye*, 17–18; *Drug detei* (Khar'kov), 1926, no. 10: 41; *Pravda*, 1923, no. 99 (May 6), p. 3; Ilya Ehrenburg, *First Years of Revolution: 1918–21* (London, 1962), 31; Utevskii, *V bor'be*, 36 (regarding the survey in the Moscow Labor Home). For two short stories written by former *besprizornye* describing street children caught stealing and then beaten, see *Drug detei* (Khar'kov), 1926, no. 10: 16; *Vchera i segodnia*, 182.

32. *Pravo i zhizn'*, 1925, nos. 9–10: 91.

33. *Krasnaia nov'*, 1923, no. 5: 205–206.

34. *Detskaia besprizornost'*, 26 (regarding the raids on Strastnoi Boulevard); *Vecherniaia moskva*, 1927, no. 26 (February 2), p. 4; *Drug detei*, 1926, no. 5: 18; no. 6: 21; Artamonov, *Deti ulitsy*, 34; *Pravda*, 1924, no. 49 (February 29), p. 6; Duranty, *Duranty Reports*, 54 (for the quotation); Thompson, *New Russia*, 245–246; Viollis, *A Girl*, 219; McCormick, *Hammer and Scythe*, 199. For a drawing by a *besprizornyi* showing three street children robbing a cigarette vendor, see figure 23. For a literary description of a *besprizornyi* stalking women selling bread in one of Khar'kov's bazaars, see Gornyi, *Besprizornyi krug*, 49.

35. Rudkin, "Prichiny," 5; Artamonov, *Deti ulitsy*, 34; *Drug detei* (Khar'kov), 1926, nos. 4–5: 11.

36. Borovich, *Kollektivy besprizornykh*, 110. For a description of a similar assault on a woman selling apples, see Greenwall, *Mirrors*, 184–185.

37. Livshits, *Sotsial'nye korni*, 134; *Drug detei* (Khar'kov), 1925, no. 6: 31; 1926, no. 2: 20; Maro, *Besprizornye*, 163; *Drug detei*, 1927, no. 2: 8. In contrast to this generalization, a former *besprizornyi* indicated that he had preferred to steal from apartments on his own: that way, he did not have to share his loot with anyone; see Poznyshev, *Detskaia besprizornost'*, 48.

38. Kufaev, *Iunye pravonarushiteli* (1924), 78.

39. *Komsomol'skaia pravda*, 1926, no. 48 (February 27), p. 4.

40. Borovich, *Kollektivy besprizornykh*, 110–112.

41. *Put' prosveshcheniia* (Khar'kov), 1924, nos. 4–5: 237; Maro, *Besprizornye*, 168–169; *Molot* (Rostov-on-the-Don), 1926, no. 1399 (April 4), p. 5; Leshchinskii, *Kto byl nichem*, 92.

42. *Drug detei*, 1926, no. 2: 16.

43. *Pravda*, 1924, no. 48 (February 28), p. 4.

44. TsGALI, f. 332, o. 1, ed. khr. 55, l. 12.

45. *Vozhatyi*, 1926, no. 6: 10–11; *Drug detei* (Khar'kov), 1925, no. 6: 33; 1927, nos. 9–10: 15; Poznyshev, *Detskaia besprizornost'*, 48–50; *Drug detei*, 1926, no. 3: 15; *Pravo i zhizn'*, 1925, nos. 9–10: 89. "Begging" of this sort also provided a thief opportunities to ascertain an apartment's contents and the owner's daily schedule. A youth in a labor commune explained to some of the other children how he used to enter apartments carrying a small milk can, intent on stealing. Whenever he was discovered unexpectedly, he claimed to be making the rounds selling milk. See Pogrebinskii, *Fabrika liudei*, 14. To be sure, the technique required a *besprizornyi* to find an open but unoccupied room before he could steal anything. This often took considerable doing, which may help explain why some youths—generally veteran *besprizornye*—preferred to accept the risks associated with breaking into dwellings at night.

46. *Pravo i zhizn'*, 1925, nos. 9–10: 89, 91.

47. *Molot* (Rostov-on-the-Don), 1926, no. 1562 (October 17), p. 5; *Vecherniaia moskva*, 1924, no. 188 (August 19), p. 4; 1927, no. 34 (February 11), p. 4; Borovich, *Kollektivy besprizornykh*, 109; *Put' prosveshcheniia* (Khar'kov), 1924, nos. 4–5: 237. For a story written by a former *besprizornyi* describing two waifs who break into a trader's storage facility, see *Drug detei*, 1926, no. 3: 5.

48. *Nash trud* (Iaroslavl'), 1924, nos. 11–12: 30; *Drug detei*, 1927, no. 2: 8.

49. Viollis, *A Girl*, 222 (for the quotation); Spaull, *Youth of Russia*, 61–62; *Put' prosveshcheniia* (Khar'kov), 1924, nos. 4–5: 237. For a drawing by a *besprizornyi* showing four youths stealing belongings from a train car, see figure 20.

50. *Gudok*, 1924, no. 1297 (September 16), p. 3; Artamonov, *Deti ulitsy*, 13.

51. *Profilakticheskaia meditsina* (Khar'kov), 1925, no. 1: 44; *Molot* (Rostov-on-the-Don), 1925, no. 1250 (October 3), p. 5; *Komsomol'skaia pravda*, 1925, no. 104 (September 25), p. 4; Sokolov, *Besprizornye deti*, 17; Glatman, *Pionery i besprizornye*, 18; *Krasnaia gazeta* (Leningrad), evening ed., 1926, no. 302 (December 17), p. 3. For a short story written by a former *besprizornyi* describing the experiences of a boy who runs away from his home in the countryside and eventually comes under the tutelage of an adult criminal, see *Vchera i segodnia*, 149.

52. *Venerologiia i dermatologiia*, 1926, no. 5: 838; Livshits, *Sotsial'nye korni*, 134; Borovich, *Kollektivy besprizornykh*, 98; *Drug detei*, 1926, no. 4: 6; Kalinina, *Komsomol i besprizornost'*, 17.

53. Enik and Blok, *Iz trushchob na stroiku*, 14–16; Rudkin, "Prichiny," 5; Borovich, *Kollektivy besprizornykh*, 73; *Asfal'tovyi kotel*, 100–102, 104–106; *Vecherniaia moskva*, 1927, no. 20 (January 26), p. 3.

54. *Volna* (Arkhangel'sk), 1926, no. 28 (February 4), p. 2; Maro, *Besprizornye*, 162; Leshchinskii, *Kto byl nichem*, 93.

55. *Drug detei*, 1929, no. 2: 9; Maro, *Besprizornye*, 162; *Voprosy prosveshcheniia* (Rostov-on-the-Don), 1926, nos. 8–9: 50; *Ezhenedel'nik sovetskoi iustitsii*, 1924, nos. 39–40: 923.

56. *Drug detei* (Khar'kov), 1926, no. 2: 21; Livshits, *Sotsial'nye korni*, 135; *Put' prosveshcheniia* (Khar'kov), 1924, nos. 4–5: 237–238; Maro, *Besprizornye*, 157; Anna J. Haines, *Health Work in Soviet Russia* (New York, 1928), 130.

57. Leshchinskii, *Kto byl nichem*, 93; Livshits, *Sotsial'nye korni*, 135. For a literary account of such an undertaking, see *Drug detei* (Khar'kov), 1925, no. 6: 20–24. Adult criminals knew that juveniles would receive much more lenient treatment if apprehended by the authorities—not to mention the fact that extensive participation of children in a crime might enable the adult planner to remain on the sidelines and thus escape detection altogether. See G. D. Ryndziunskii and T. M. Savinskaia, *Pravovoe polozhenie detei po zakonodatel'stvu R.S.F.S.R.* (Moscow, 1923), 56, 60; Ryndziunskii and Savinskaia, *Detskoe pravo*, 257; *Drug detei*, 1926, no. 2: 24–25; *Rabochaia moskva*, 1924, no. 160 (July 17), p. 7.

58. Utevskii, *V bor'be*, 114.

59. Sokolov, *Besprizornye deti*, 17; *Drug detei* (Khar'kov), 1925, no. 1: 38; no. 4: 34; 1926, no. 1: 10; no. 2: 16; no. 3: 23; 1927, nos. 9–10: 2; Livshits, *Sotsial'nye korni*, 136; *Vestnik prosveshcheniia*, 1925, no. 9: 92; *Drug detei*, 1926, no. 2: 15; *Izvestiia*, 1927, no. 47 (February 26), p. 5 (regarding the boy in Batum); Greenwall, *Mirrors*, 184; Thompson, *New Russia*, 245; Wicksteed, *Life*, 75; Spaull, *Youth of Russia*, 62; *Pravda*, 1924, no. 51 (March 2), p. 5 (regarding the youths in Narkompros's waiting room).

60. Paustovsky, *Restless Years*, 46.

61. *Pravda*, 1924, no. 37 (February 15), p. 4.

62. *Asfal'tovyi kotel*, 235–236; *Izvestiia*, 1925, no. 210 (September 15), p. 6; Borovich, *Kollektivy besprizornykh*, 106; *Drug detei* (Khar'kov), 1926, no. 1: 14; *Drug detei*, 1926, no. 2: 11; Krasnushkin et al., *Nishchenstvo i besprizornost'*, 190; Grinberg, *Rasskazy*, 71–72.

63. Bartlett, "Stepchildren," 334–335.

64. *Krasnaia gazeta* (Leningrad), 1926, no. 221 (September 25), p. 2; 1926, no. 222 (September 26), p. 3 (for the quotation); *Molot* (Rostov-on-the-Don), 1926, no. 1569 (October 26), p. 3; V. N. Tolmachev, ed., *Khuliganstvo i khuligany* (Moscow, 1929), 48–50; Borovich, *Kollektivy besprizornykh*, 125.

65. Ia. P. Bugaiskii, *Khuliganstvo kak sotsial'no-patologicheskoe iavlenie* (Moscow-Leningrad, 1927), 89; *Drug detei*, 1927, nos. 6–7: 36; *Vchera i segodnia*, 128–129.

66. Krasnushkin et al., *Nishchenstvo i besprizornost'*, 190; *Drug detei*, 1927, nos. 6–7: 36; Kufaev, *Iunye pravonarushiteli* (1929), 11–12 (regarding juvenile hooligans in general, not just *besprizornye*); *Drug detei* (Khar'kov), 1927, no. 3: 22; Viollis, *A Girl*, 219–220; Duranty, *Duranty Reports*, 55.

67. Vasilevskii, *Besprizornost'*, 67; *Na putiakh k novoi shkole*, 1927, nos. 7–8: 104, 107; *Drug detei* (Khar'kov), 1926, no. 2: 23; Utevskii, *V bor'be*, 82. For a drawing by a *besprizornyi* showing a group of street children playing cards, see *Drug detei* (Khar'kov), 1925, no. 9: 20.

68. *Drug detei* (Khar'kov), 1927, no. 2: 28.

69. Ibid., 1926, no. 1: 10; 1927, no. 2: 29.

70. *Komsomol'skaia pravda*, 1925, no. 104 (September 25), p. 4; *Prosveshchenie Sibiri* (Novosibirsk), 1927, no. 5: 57.

71. Utevskii, *V bor'be*, 86.

72. *Na putiakh k novoi shkole*, 1927, nos. 7–8: 104.

73. Borovich, *Kollektivy besprizornykh*, 107; *Prosveshchenie Sibiri* (Novosibirsk), 1927, no. 5: 57.

74. *Drug detei* (Khar'kov), 1927, no. 2: 29. In one interesting case involving three *besprizornye*, child A owed a debt to child B. B sold this debt to child C for a pack of cigarettes, leaving C with the right to collect the debt from A. See ibid., no. 1: 14.

75. Gilev, *Detskaia besprizornost'*, 23; *Na putiakh k novoi shkole*, 1927, nos. 7–8: 105; *Drug detei* (Khar'kov), 1926, no. 1: 12; Borovich, *Kollektivy besprizornykh*, 53–54, 59; Vasilevskii, *Besprizornost'*, 60.

76. *Prosveshchenie Sibiri* (Novosibirsk), 1927, no. 5: 65; Vasilevskii, *Besprizornost'*, 60; Gilev, *Detskaia besprizornost'*, 24. Vladimir Mayakovsky's poem about the *besprizornye* mentions their taste for the cinematic escapades of Douglas Fairbanks; see "Besprizorshchina," 171. In a fashion similar to more recent commentaries, Vasilevskii (*Besprizornost'*, 60) lamented the influence of movies on *besprizornye* and children in general: "It is well known what poisonous food, in a spiritual sense, the overwhelming majority of movies are. They weaken and dull an adolescent's will. They arouse in him premature sexual instincts with scenes that are at times simply pornographic. They portray virtue as merely the prosperity of the individual, exalting wealth at the expense of labor, and lowering the artistic taste of the child—accustoming him to lachrymose melodrama, passive sentimentalism, and coarse vulgar clowning."

77. Krasnushkin et al., *Nishchenstvo i besprizornost'*, 190; Gilev, *Detskaia besprizornost'*, 23; *Drug detei*, 1927, nos. 6–7: 36; *Na putiakh k novoi shkole*, 1926, no. 3: 20; *Drug detei* (Khar'kov), 1926, nos. 4–5: 20; Borovich, *Kollektivy besprizornykh*, 107.

78. *Moskovskii meditsinskii zhurnal*, 1925, no. 10: 60; *Deti posle goloda*, 59; Thompson, *New Russia*, 248.

79. *Venerologiia i dermatologiia*, 1926, no. 5: 838; *Prosveshchenie na transporte*, 1926, no. 11: 38; *Drug detei*, 1925, no. 2: 20; 1930, no. 5: 10 (for the quotation); Livshits, *Sotsial'nye korni*, 133; Utevskii, *V bor'be*, 82.

80. Gernet, *Prestupnyi mir*, 215; *Venerologiia i dermatologiia*, 1926, no. 5: 838; *Prosveshchenie na transporte*, 1926, no. 11: 38; Livshits, *Sotsial'nye korni*, 133; Utevskii, *V bor'be*, 38.

81. *Molot* (Rostov-on-the-Don), 1925, no. 1250 (October 3), p. 5; *Asfal'-tovyi kotel*, 236; Vasilevskii, *Besprizornost'*, 66; *Moskovskii meditsinskii zhurnal*, 1925, no. 10: 59–60, 62; Borovich, *Kollektivy besprizornykh*, 53. For a literary description of a *besprizornyi* who waits at a tram stop for cigarette butts discarded by passengers preparing to board, see Gornyi, *Besprizornyi krug*, 26.

82. *Moskovskii meditsinskii zhurnal*, 1925, no. 10: 59; *Vestnik prosveshcheniia*, 1923, no. 2: 68, 74; *Detskaia defektivnost'*, 19.

83. TsGA RSFSR, f. 2306, o. 13, ed. khr. 52, ll. 1, 13, 24, 34 (for samples of forms containing questions about cocaine use); *Na pomoshch' detiam* (Semipalatinsk, 1926), 3; Vasilevskii, *Besprizornost'*, 68; *Drug detei*, 1925, no. 2: 11; 1926, no. 2: 16; Maro, *Besprizornye*, 193–194; *Vestnik prosveshcheniia*, 1925, no. 9: 102–103; *Deti posle goloda*, 59; *Molot* (Rostov-on-the-Don), 1925, no. 1144 (May 30), p. 5; *Pravda*, 1924, no. 46 (February 26), p. 4; *Illiustrirovannaia Rossiia* (Paris), 1926, no. 47: 5; Bartlett, "Stepchildren," 338; Thompson, *New Russia*, 248; Wicksteed, *Life*, 76; Haines, *Health Work*, 130–131;

Shishkov, *Children*, 20, 36, 61, 65, 78, 120 (a literary portrayal of street children's desire for cocaine).

84. *Komsomol'skaia pravda*, 1925, no. 88 (September 8), p. 3; 1925, no. 104 (September 25), p. 4; Vasilevskii, *Besprizornost'*, 65; *Molot* (Rostov-on-the-Don), 1926, no. 1398 (April 3), p. 5; *Vestnik prosveshcheniia*, 1923, no. 2: 67, 69; *Drug detei*, 1926, no. 1: 19.

85. Vasilevskii, *Besprizornost'*, 69; *Drug detei* (Khar'kov), 1925, no. 6: 33; *Moskovskii meditsinskii zhurnal*, 1925, no. 10: 59.

86. Livshits, *Sotsial'nye korni*, 132–133; Gernet, *Prestupnyi mir*, 215; *Prosveshchenie na transporte*, 1926, no. 11: 38. For similar findings yielded by other studies, see Maro, *Besprizornye*, 190; *Drug detei*, 1925, no. 2: 20; *Vlast' sovetov*, 1923, nos. 1–2: 59; *Izvestiia*, 1924, no. 66 (March 21), p. 5. Another study at the Moscow Labor Home (probably conducted in 1924) listed 56 percent of the youths as *kokainisty*—25 percent of whom had used cocaine for a period ranging from four to six years; see Utevskii, *V bor'be*, 36–37.

87. Regarding the physical effects of cocaine on children, see *Drug detei*, 1926, no. 1: 19; no. 2: 16; *Moskovskii meditsinskii zhurnal*, 1925, no. 10: 60–61; *Vestnik prosveshcheniia*, 1923, no. 2: 72.

88. *Pravda*, 1926, no. 56 (March 9), p. 5. Valentinov claimed that in his case the cocaine made him appear younger than his sixteen years, perhaps because of the weight he lost.

89. *Moskovskii meditsinskii zhurnal*, 1925, no. 10: 60 (on the ease with which cocaine could be purchased in Moscow); 1926, no. 1: 47 (regarding the study of crime and cocaine; the article's title is "Kokainizm i prestupnost'," and the text covers pp. 46–55). A journal in Iaroslavl', while noting that cocaine use was not uncommon among *besprizornye* in Moscow and other large cities, concluded that "among our children [those in Iaroslavl' province], one does not encounter this often"; *Nash trud* (Iaroslavl'), 1928, nos. 7–9: 41. More research is required to establish the sources of cocaine consumed in the Soviet Union. In an article titled "Bor'ba s kokainizmom," a Soviet health official identified a factory in Germany that allegedly refined cocaine, which was later shipped to many European countries; see *Vecherniaia moskva*, 1924, no. 266 (November 20), p. 2. Another author pointed to what he considered a sizable flow of cocaine smuggled into the Soviet Union across its borders with Estonia and Latvia (though he presented no information as to how, or from where, the drug reached these borders); L. M. Vasilevskii, *Durmany (narkotiki)* (Moscow, 1924), 68–69.

90. *Na pomoshch' detiam. Obshchestvenno-literaturnyi i nauchnyi sbornik*, 44–47; *Vestnik prosveshcheniia*, 1923, no. 2: 72; *Put' prosveshcheniia* (Khar'kov), 1924, nos. 4–5: 238; Livshits, *Sotsial'nye korni*, 135. For a song describing a group of thieves waiting to purchase cocaine and urging a youth to try some, see Maro, *Besprizornye*, 211. For a literary description of a thief using cocaine to embolden his young accomplice (a ten-year-old *besprizornyi*), see *Drug detei* (Khar'kov), 1925, no. 6: 21.

91. Regarding thefts to support cocaine use, see Livshits, *Sotsial'nye korni*, 135; *Moskovskii meditsinskii zhurnal*, 1925, no. 10: 60; *Vestnik prosveshcheniia*, 1923, no. 2: 72.

92. Poznyshev, *Detskaia besprizornost'*, 49–50; Vasilevskii, *Besprizornost'*, 66–68; *Drug detei*, 1926, no. 1: 20; Enik and Blok, *Iz trushchob na stroiku*, 13; *Moskovskii meditsinskii zhurnal*, 1925, no. 10: 62; Walter Duranty, *I Write as I Please* (New York, 1935), 148. Regarding narcotics sales by Chinese and Koreans (in Moscow and Saratov), see *Rabochaia moskva*, 1924, no. 196 (August 30), p. 7; *Vecherniaia moskva*, 1924, no. 191 (August 22), p. 4; 1924, no. 253 (November 3), p. 4; *Drug detei* (Khar'kov), 1927, nos. 5–6: 35; Enik and Blok, *Iz trushchob na stroiku*, 14.

93. *Vestnik prosveshcheniia*, 1923, no. 2: 69 (regarding the rooms catering to juvenile cocaine users); *Vozhatyi*, 1925, nos. 13–14: 7 (regarding the den offering cocaine for stolen goods); *Na pomoshch' detiam. Obshchestvenno-literaturnyi i nauchnyi sbornik*, 48–49.

94. *Venerologiia i dermatologiia*, 1926, no. 5: 843–844 (regarding the *besprizornye* in Odessa); *Detskii dom*, 1929, no. 5: 20 (regarding the institute for girls); Gernet, *Prestupnyi mir*, 215; *Profilakticheskaia meditsina* (Khar'kov), 1925, no. 1: 44; no. 11: 128; Vasilevskii, *Besprizornost'*, 57–58; Maro, *Besprizornye*, 190; Tizanov et al., *Detskaia besprizornost'*, 105; *Detskaia defektivnost'*, 26–27. Regarding the frequency of masturbation among *besprizornye*, see *Venerologiia i dermatologiia*, 1926, no. 5: 841–842; *Deti posle goloda*, 59.

95. Vasilevskii, *Besprizornost'*, 58–59; *Drug detei* (Khar'kov), 1925, no. 9: 16; *Venerologiia i dermatologiia*, 1926, no. 5: 844; *Profilakticheskaia meditsina* (Khar'kov), 1925, no. 7: 95.

96. For several individual cases, see *Drug detei* (Khar'kov), 1927, no. 3: 21–23; *Profilakticheskaia meditsina* (Khar'kov), 1926, no. 12: 79.

97. *Detskaia defektivnost'*, 27. On a similar note, a Red Cross official observed: "There is considerable dysentery in the Petliura area and also a high percentage of venereal diseases in the army. According to one report large numbers of civilians [not necessarily homeless juveniles] have been infected with the latter by soldiers." American Red Cross, box 868, file 948.08, "Report of Mission to Ukraine and South Russia by Major George H. Ryden," November 1919.

98. Vasilevskii, *Besprizornost'*, 59 (regarding impersonal, casual sexual relations among *besprizornye*); *Drug detei*, 1927, no. 2: 5; *Profilakticheskaia meditsina* (Khar'kov), 1925, no. 1: 44; *Drug detei* (Khar'kov), 1925, no. 6: 8; Utevskii, *V bor'be*, 36 (regarding the study at the Moscow Labor Home). For a literary description of a seasoned *besprizornyi* who comes upon a girl new on the street and takes her "under his protection," see *Vchera i segodnia*, 44–45. She soon becomes his lover (or *shmara*, in the jargon of the street).

99. *Prosveshchenie na transporte*, 1926, no. 11: 39; Kufaev, *Iunye pravonarushiteli* (1929), 16; *Drug detei* (Khar'kov), 1925, no. 6: 31–32; Utevskii, *V bor'be*, 86. On occasion, younger boys raped by others received as nicknames diminutive versions of common girls' names, such as Tan'ka, Marus'ka, and Dun'ka.

100. For some individual and group examples, see *Nizhegorodskii sbornik zdravookhraneniia* (Nizhnii Novgorod), 1925, no. 1: 43; *Profilakticheskaia meditsina* (Khar'kov), 1926, no. 12: 79; *Molot* (Rostov-on-the-Don), 1925, no. 1250 (October 3), p. 5; *Prosveshchenie Sibiri* (Novosibirsk), 1927, no. 5: 56, 58.

101. *Venerologiia i dermatologiia*, 1926, no. 5: 845; *Komsomol'skaia pravda*, 1925, no. 88 (September 8), p. 3; *Profilakticheskaia meditsina* (Khar'kov), 1926, no. 12: 78; *Drug detei* (Khar'kov), 1925, no. 1: 37.

102. *Profilakticheskaia meditsina* (Khar'kov), 1925, no. 7: 95; no. 11: 128 (for the study of a thousand street girls); *Drug detei* (Khar'kov), 1925, no. 9: 18; 1927, no. 3: 21–22; Livshits, *Sotsial'nye korni*, 133; *Detskii dom*, 1928, no. 3: 55.

103. *Profilakticheskaia meditsina* (Khar'kov), 1924, nos. 11–12: 159; Sokolov, *Spasite detei!* 61–62. By no means all juveniles (including *besprizornye*) with syphilis received the infection from sexual contact; see *Profilakticheskaia meditsina* (Khar'kov), 1924, nos. 11–12: 153–155; 1925, no. 7: 95–96.

104. *Na putiakh k novoi shkole*, 1924, nos. 7–8: 46; *Drug detei* (Khar'kov), 1927, nos. 9–10: 24; *Prosveshchenie na transporte*, 1926, no. 11: 37; Borovich, *Kollektivy besprizornykh*, 80; Livshits, *Sotsial'nye korni*, 137. For more on the differences between veteran and neophyte *besprizornye*, see Tizanov et al., *Detskaia besprizornost'*, 83–84; Poznyshev, *Detskaia besprizornost'*, 35–42.

105. For examples of such assertions, see *Na putiakh k novoi shkole*, 1924, no. 3: 89–90; Livshits, *Detskaia besprizornost'*, 23. According to Agnes Smedley, writing from Moscow early in 1929, *besprizornye* "have a background that should produce literature and art. Life has taught most of them to be extremely inventive and courageous, and there is every reason to expect that they will carry these qualities over into other spheres of activity"; *The Nation* 128 (April 10, 1929): 437.

106. Juviler, "Contradictions," 274. Maxim Gorky concluded at an optimistic juncture: "I should say that life, an excellent though stern teacher, has made collectivists 'in spirit' out of these children [the *besprizornye* in one of Anton Makarenko's colonies]"; in Makarenko, *Road to Life* 1:11.

107. *Narodnoe prosveshchenie*, 1924, nos. 4–5: 164; Tizanov et al., *Detskaia besprizornost'*, 94; *Deti posle goloda*, 60, 62; Livshits, *Detskaia besprizornost'*, 23; Borovich, *Kollektivy besprizornykh*, 64–65; *Prosveshchenie na transporte*, 1926, no. 11: 38.

108. Artamonov, *Deti ulitsy*, 55; *Drug detei* (Khar'kov), 1926, no. 2: 25.

109. For some examples, see *Komsomol'skaia pravda*, 1925, no. 104 (September 25), p. 4; *Drug detei* (Khar'kov), 1927, no. 1: 6; Sokolov, *Besprizornye deti*, 29.

110. Gernet, *Prestupnyi mir*, 148 (for the prostitute's statement); *Pravo i zhizn'*, 1926, nos. 6–7: 102–103 (for the boy's statement); Borovich, *Kollektivy besprizornykh*, 75, 100, 108, 120; Shveitser and Shabalov, *Besprizornye*, 13; Maro, *Besprizornye*, 276; *Drug detei* (Khar'kov), 1925, no. 9: 17; *Vozhatyi*, 1926, no. 6: 11. For literary descriptions of *besprizornye* who preferred to live on the street, see Gornyi, *Besprizornyi krug*, 39; Shishkov, *Children*, 129.

111. *Shkola i zhizn'* (Nizhnii Novgorod), 1927, no. 10: 59; *Pravda*, 1924, no. 48 (February 28), p. 4; 1926, no. 20 (January 26), p. 3; Krasnushkin et al., *Nishchenstvo i besprizornost'*, 237–238; Sokolov, *Besprizornye deti*, 16–17; *Drug detei* (Khar'kov), 1925, no. 9: 18; 1926, no. 1: 10; nos. 8–9: 17; Borovich, *Kollektivy besprizornykh*, 119; *Drug detei*, 1929, no. 2: 9; *Komsomol'skaia pravda*, 1925, no. 104 (September 25), p. 4; Thompson, *New Russia*, 250.

112. Maro, *Besprizornye*, 209, 223.

113. *Drug detei*, 1927, no. 2: 5.

114. Kaidanova, *Besprizornye deti*, 20; *Vchera i segodnia*, 128–129; Livshits, *Sotsial'nye korni*, 136; Maro, *Besprizornye*, 163; Sokolov, *Besprizornye deti*, 1–2; Borovich, *Kollektivy besprizornykh*, 70, 121; Krasnushkin et al., *Nishchenstvo i besprizornost'*, 234; Thompson, *New Russia*, 247–248. For a literary description of this attitude, see Ilya Ehrenburg, *A Street in Moscow* (New York, 1932), 32–33.

115. *Izvestiia*, 1926, no. 129 (June 6), p. 4 (regarding the station near the Black Sea); *Illiustrirovannaia Rossiia* (Paris), 1930, no. 40: 11 (regarding the station near Saratov).

116. *Drug detei* (Khar'kov), 1925, no. 9: 16; Livshits, *Sotsial'nye korni*, 136; Maro, *Besprizornye*, 164; Kufaev, *Iunye pravonarushiteli* (1924), 74, 78; Poznyshev, *Detskaia besprizornost'*, 47–48; *Molot* (Rostov-on-the-Don), 1925, no. 1249 (October 2), p. 2 (for the song).

117. Sokolov, *Detskaia besprizornost'*, 26.

118. *Prosveshchenie Sibiri* (Novosibirsk), 1927, no. 5: 58.

119. *Drug detei*, 1926, no. 2: 13; 1931, no. 10: 14 (for the quotation); *Illiustrirovannaia Rossiia* (Paris), 1930, no. 40: 11; *Drug detei* (Khar'kov), 1925, no. 9: 19; Popov, *Detskaia besprizornost'*, 9.

120. *Pravo i zhizn'*, 1925, nos. 7–8: 86 (for the first quotation); Livshits, *Sotsial'nye korni*, 138–139 (for the second quotation and other material supporting the same point); Poznyshev, *Detskaia besprizornost'*, 50; Karl Borders, *Village Life Under the Soviets* (New York, 1927), 152–153.

4. CHILDREN OF THE STATE

1. For a sampling of these decrees, see *SU*, 1918, no. 68, art. 732; no. 70, art. 768; no. 81, art. 857; *SU*, 1919, no. 20, art. 238; no. 26, art. 296; no. 47, art. 463. See also L. A. Zhukova, "Deiatel'nost' Detkomissii VTsIK po okhrane zdorov'ia detei (1921–1938)," *Sovetskoe zdravookhranenie*, 1978, no. 2: 64; *Pravo i zhizn'*, 1927, nos. 8–10: 29; Goldman, "The 'Withering Away' and the Resurrection," 88. In some cases the authorized support was earmarked solely for urban areas or for children of working-class families, but even these less sweeping goals far exceeded the meager resources available. On government agencies' inability to obtain food and clothing for children in anything approaching adequate quantities, see Sheila Fitzpatrick, *The Commissariat of Enlightenment: Soviet Organization of Education and the Arts Under Lunacharsky, October 1917–1921* (Cambridge, 1970), 228–229; Liublinskii, *Bor'ba*, 45.

2. *SU*, 1921, no. 57, art. 358.

3. Ryndziunskii et al., *Pravovoe polozhenie* (1927), 96; Kalinina, *Desiat' let*, 96, 98; V. Diushen, ed., *Piat' let detskogo gorodka imeni III internatsionala* (Moscow, 1924), 5, 28; *Vserossiiskoe obsledovanie*, 45; Krupskaia, *Pedagogicheskie sochineniia* 2:158; *Pedagogicheskaia entsiklopediia*, 3 vols. (Moscow, 1927–1930), 2:354–355.

4. TsGA RSFSR, f. 1575, o. 6, ed. khr. 4, l. 128; *Pervyi vserossiiskii s"ezd*, 3–4, 7, 11–12; Fitzpatrick, *Commissariat of Enlightenment*, 227–228; Madison,

Social Welfare, 36; Krupskaia, *Pedagogicheskie sochineniia* 3:393; *Sotsial'noe vospitanie*, 1921, nos. 3–4: 58–62. A few years later, in 1926, Anatolii Luna-charskii told a meeting of personnel from children's institutions: "If we can overcome our poverty, I would say that the children's home is the best way of raising children—a genuine socialist upbringing, removing children from the family setting and its petty-bourgeois structure"; see Tizanov et al., *Pedagogika*, 11. Some proponents of this vision added that children's homes would emancipate women from child rearing, freeing them to pursue activities outside the home. For more on the "withering away" of the family, see Goldman, "The 'Withering Away' and the Resurrection," 40, 47.

5. N. I. Bukharin and E. A. Preobrazhenskii, *The ABC of Communism: A Popular Explanation of the Program of the Communist Party of Russia* (Ann Arbor, Mich., 1966), 234. In their chapter on religion, the authors added (p. 253): "One of the most important tasks of the proletarian State is to liberate children from the reactionary influence exercised by their parents. The really radical way of doing this is the social education of the children, carried to its logical conclusion." The 1918 Family Code prohibited the adoption of children by individual families, revealing the belief of early Soviet jurists that the state would be a better guardian of juveniles. See Goldman, "The 'Withering Away' and the Resurrection," 84.

6. Diushen, *Piat' let*, 28; Kalinina, *Desiat' let*, 96, 98; *Vserossiiskoe obsledovanie*, 45.

7. TsGA RSFSR, f. 2306, o. 13, ed. khr. 11, l. 38; Fitzpatrick, *Commissariat of Enlightenment*, 227; Krasnushkin et al., *Nishchenstvo i besprizornost'*, 126. The Commissariat of Social Security (*Narodnyi komissariat sotsial'nogo obespecheniia*) had been called *Narodnyi komissariat gosudarstvennogo prizreniia* (in some documents, *Narodnyi komissariat obshchestvennogo prizreniia* prior to the end of April 1918; see *SU*, 1918, no. 34, art. 453.

8. *SU*, 1918, no. 19, art. 287; no. 22, art. 321; Krasnushkin et al., *Nishchenstvo i besprizornost'*, 126; *Detskii dom*, comp. B. S. Utevskii (Moscow-Leningrad, 1932), 9.

9. Krasnushkin et al., *Nishchenstvo i besprizornost'*, 126–127.

10. *SU*, 1919, no. 25, art. 288; Fitzpatrick, *Commissariat of Enlightenment*, 227–228; *Detskii dom*, comp. Utevskii, 4.

11. *Krasnaia nov'*, 1923, no. 5: 206, 209–210; Margaret Kay Stolee, " 'A Generation Capable of Establishing Communism': Revolutionary Child Rearing in the Soviet Union, 1917–1928" (Ph.D. diss., Duke University, 1982), 52.

12. *SU*, 1921, no. 65, art. 497. For other illustrations of the division of responsibilities between the Commissariat of Health and Narkompros, see *SU*, 1919, no. 61, art. 564; Krasnushkin et al., *Nishchenstvo i besprizornost'*, 126–127.

13. Stolee, "Generation," 53. For more on abandoned babies, see *Sbornik deistvuiushchikh uzakonenii i rasporiazhenii* (1929), 94, 99–103; Artamonov, *Deti ulitsy*, 57; *Drug detei*, 1927, no. 1: 12; 1928, no. 4: 14–15; *Okhrana materinstva i mladenchestva*, 1926, no. 12: 28–29; *Drug detei* (Khar'kov), 1926, no. 2 (this issue contains a number of short articles on abandoned infants).

14. *Narodnoe prosveshchenie v R.S.F.S.R. k 1924/25 uchebnomu godu*, 3–4; Stolee, "Generation," 58–59. Roughly similar units took shape in the Nar-

kompros of Ukraine and other non-Russian republics. Regarding the earlier internal reorganizations of Narkompros and the titles of subsections whose responsibilities included the *besprizornye*, see Kalinina, *Desiat' let*, 36; Krasnushkin et al., *Nishchenstvo i besprizornost'*, 127; Liublinskii, *Bor'ba*, 183; *Detskaia besprizornost'*, 4.

15. TsGA RSFSR, f. 1575, o. 6, ed. khr. 156, l. 1; Krasnushkin et al., *Nishchenstvo i besprizornost'*, 127–129; *Detskaia besprizornost'*, 4; Liublinskii, *Bor'ba* , 183–184; Tizanov et al., *Detskaia besprizornost'*, 171. Along with Glavsotsvos, another unit in Narkompros—the State Scientific Council (*Gosudarstvennyi uchenyi sovet*)—maintained its own SPON subsection. This particular SPON, rather than working directly with street children, devoted itself mainly to studying the theory and practice of upbringing in an effort to develop methods for rehabilitating *besprizornye*. See TsGA RSFSR, f. 298, o. 1, ed. khr. 45, ll. 42, 82, 100.

16. TsGA RSFSR, f. 1575, o. 6, ed. khr. 101, l. 3; *Besprizornye*, comp. O. Kaidanova (Moscow, 1926), 60; Tizanov et al., *Detskaia besprizornost'*, 130, 170; *Narodnoe prosveshchenie v R.S.F.S.R. k 1924/25 uchebnomu godu*, 5–6. A similar structure prevailed in areas where the main administrative unit was the *oblast'* rather than the *guberniia*. Before long, most *uezd otdely narodnogo obrazovaniia* were merged with the *uezd*-level divisions of various other commissariats into a general *otdel* of the corresponding *uezd* Executive Committee.

17. Kalinina, *Desiat' let*, 81, 83; Krasnushkin et al., *Nishchenstvo i besprizornost'*, 143–144; *Komsomol'skaia pravda*, 1925, no. 27 (June 26), p. 3.

18. *SU*, 1919, no. 3, art. 32.

19. Vasilevskii, *Detskaia "prestupnost'*," 81; *Deti posle goloda*, 75–76.

20. See for example Kalinina, *Desiat' let*, 50; E. Vatova, "Bolshevskaia trudovaia kommuna i ee organizator," *Iunost'*, 1966, no. 3: 91. According to Lennard Gerson, "one of the few diversions Dzerzhinsky allowed himself" consisted of frequent drives to visit former *besprizornye* being raised in a commune sponsored by the secret police. "He once confided to Kursky, the Commissar of Justice: 'These dirty faces are my best friends. Among them I can find rest. How much talent would have been lost had we not picked them up!' "; Gerson, *The Secret Police in Lenin's Russia* (Philadelphia, 1976), 127.

21. Quoted in Fitzpatrick, *Commissariat of Enlightenment*, 230–231. For a Soviet account of this conversation, see Konius, *Puti razvitiia*, 146–148.

22. *SU*, 1921, no. 11, art. 75.

23. Regarding the Ukrainian Commission, see *Detskoe pravo sovetskikh respublik. Sbornik deistvuiushchego zakonodatel'stva o detiakh*, comp. M. P. Krichevskaia and I. I. Kuritskii (Khar'kov, 1927), 18–22; *Deti posle goloda*, 78–79; *Pomoshch' detiam*, 20–21. For instructions from the Children's Commission in Moscow to its provincial branches, see Records of the Smolensk Oblast' of the All-Union Communist Party of the Soviet Union, 1917–1941 [hereafter cited as Smolensk Archive], reel 46, WKP 422, p. 299.

24. For these and other unsuccessful challenges to the Children's Commission, see Fitzpatrick, *Commissariat of Enlightenment*, 230–236.

25. Kalinina, *Desiat' let*, 30–33; Goldman, "The 'Withering Away' and the Resurrection," 83.

26. Ehrenburg, *First Years of Revolution*, 84.

27. Liublinskii, *Bor'ba* , 191, 194. The name *priemnik* was a shortened form of *detskii priemnyi punkt* (children's receiving station).

28. *Drug detei* (Khar'kov), 1925, no. 2: 30; *Detskoe pravo*, comp. Krichevskaia and Kuritskii, 479–480; Liublinskii, *Bor'ba*, 191, 193; *Detskaia besprizornost'*, 36. In some areas, especially Ukraine, these institutions were known as collectors (*kollektory*).

29. TsGA RSFSR, f. 1575, o. 6, ed. khr. 141, l. 42; Liublinskii, *Bor'ba*, 191–193; *Detskaia besprizornost'*, 37; *Detskoe pravo*, comp. Krichevskaia and Kuritskii, 479.

30. TsGA RSFSR, f. 1575, o. 6, ed. khr. 141, ll. 42–43; Liublinskii, *Bor'ba*, 193; *Detskaia besprizornost'*, 37; *Detskoe pravo*, comp. Krichevskaia and Kuritskii, 479. During the course of the decade, as evident in the archival document just cited and explained in a following chapter, Narkompros increased the period of time that children were to be kept in receivers.

31. *SU*, 1921, no. 66, art. 506; TsGA RSFSR, f. 1575, o. 6, ed. khr. 141, ll. 42–43; *Detskoe pravo*, comp. Krichevskaia and Kuritskii, 479, 481; *Vestnik narodnogo prosveshcheniia* (Saratov), 1921, no. 1: 43.

32. TsGA RSFSR, f. 1575, o. 6, ed. khr. 141, l. 42; Liublinskii, *Bor'ba*, 194; *Detskaia besprizornost'*, 38; *Detskoe pravo*, comp. Krichevskaia and Kuritskii, 479; Min'kovskii, "Osnovnye etapy," 43.

33. TsGA RSFSR, f. 1575, o. 6, ed. khr. 141, ll. 48, 50–51; Liublinskii, *Bor'ba*, 194–196. Children presenting unusually complex problems could be sent for diagnosis to even more specialized and well-equipped institutions in major cities.

34. TsGA RSFSR, f. 1575, o. 6, ed. khr. 141, ll. 48–49, 53; Liublinskii, *Bor'ba*, 194.

35. V. I. Kufaev, "Iz opyta," 94; Liublinskii, *Bor'ba*, 194.

36. The charter described a *detdom* for school-age youths that did not operate its own school; TsGA RSFSR, f. 1575, o. 6, ed. khr. 4, l. 86. See also, regarding different types of *detdoma* for delinquents, Ryndziunskii and Savinskaia, *Pravovoe polozhenie* (1923), 55.

37. TsGA RSFSR, f. 1575, o. 6, ed. khr. 156, l. 3; ibid., ed. khr. 4, l. 86.

38. Ibid., ed. khr. 4, ll. 86–87.

39. Ibid., l. 86; *SU*, 1923, no. 28, art. 326; *SU*, 1924, no. 23, art. 222.

40. TsGA RSFSR, f. 1575, o. 6, ed. khr. 4, l. 86; *Pervyi vserossiiskii s"ezd*, 7.

41. *SU*, 1918, no. 16, art. 227; Ryndziunskii and Savinskaia, *Pravovoe polozhenie* (1923), 54.

42. Prior to March 1920, the commissions were headed by a representative from the Commissariat of Social Security, with the other two members coming from Narkompros and the Commissariat of Justice; *SU*, 1920, no. 68, art. 308; Ryndziunskii and Savinskaia, *Pravovoe polozhenie* (1923), 55. Children accused of minor offenses could have their cases resolved in a receiver or a *raspredelitel'*.

43. See for example V. I. Kufaev, *Pedagogicheskie mery bor'by s pravonarusheniiami nesovershennoletnikh* (Moscow, 1927), 47; *Nesovershennoletnie*

pravonarushiteli, comp. B. S. Utevskii (Moscow-Leningrad, 1932), 8. Prior to the Revolution, the lowest age for criminal liability had been ten years; see Juviler, "Contradictions," 263.

44. *Vestnik narodnogo prosveshcheniia* (Saratov), 1921, no. 1: 43; Liublinskii, *Bor'ba*, 194; Ryndziunskii and Savinskaia, *Detskoe pravo*, 250, 253; Vasilevskii, *Detskaia "prestupnost'*," 80, 85. The number of commissions actually established lagged far behind the goal.

45. *SU*, 1920, no. 13, art. 83; no. 68, art. 308; Ryndziunskii et al., *Pravovoe polozhenie* (1927), 82.

46. *SU*, 1920, no. 13, art. 83; no. 68, art. 308; *Nesovershennoletnie pravonarushiteli*, 9–10; Z. A. Astemirov, "Iz istorii razvitiia uchrezhdenii dlia nesovershennoletnikh pravonarushitelei v SSSR," in *Preduprezhdenie prestupnosti nesovershennoletnikh* (Moscow, 1965), 255–256. Regarding the handling of juveniles fourteen through seventeen years of age, see *SU*, 1919, no. 66, art. 590.

47. Astemirov, "Iz istorii," 256; TsGA RSFSR, f. 1575, o. 10, ed. khr. 177, ll. 1–4, 13–16; *Vestnik prosveshcheniia*, 1923, no. 2: 66. Commissions could also send youths to institutions operated by the Commissariat of Health, but these were not nearly as numerous.

48. *Detskaia defektivnost'*, 56, 68; TsGA RSFSR, f. 1575, o. 10, ed. khr. 177, ll. 3–4, 15. These sources also advocated the introduction of "self-government" (*samoupravlenie*) for "morally defective" youths, but added that the staff should take this step more cautiously than in a regular *detdom*; see *Detskaia defektivnost'*, 69; TsGA RSFSR, f. 1575, o. 10, ed. khr. 177, ll. 4, 14.

49. TsGA RSFSR, f. 1575, o. 10, ed. khr. 177, ll. 3–4, 14; *Detskaia defektivnost'*, 69; Livshits, *Sotsial'nye korni*, 102.

50. TsGA RSFSR, f. 1575, o. 10, ed. khr. 177, ll. 2, 13; *Detskaia defektivnost'*, 57, 68–69.

51. TsGA RSFSR, f. 1575, o. 10, ed. khr. 177, l. 2; *Detskaia defektivnost'*, 35, 56, 69.

52. TsGA RSFSR, f. 1575, o. 10, ed. khr. 177, ll. 6–9; *SU*, 1924, no. 86, art. 870; Astemirov, "Iz istorii," 256–257; Ryndziunskii and Savinskaia, *Pravovoe polozhenie* (1923), 60; Min'kovskii, "Osnovnye etapy," 46. This did not exhaust the list of institutions to which courts could sentence juveniles. Reformatories (*reformatorii*), sometimes short-lived, were opened in a handful of places as early as 1918. In at least some instances, they appear to have been intended to house offenders from seventeen to twenty-one years of age, though they also received younger delinquents. In addition, the Correctional Labor Code of the Russian Republic called in 1924 for the establishment, as an alternative to prison, of *trudovye doma* specifically for young lawbreakers of worker or peasant background. To qualify, a youth was supposed to be from sixteen to twenty years of age and not carry a record of habitual offenses. See Astemirov, "Iz istorii," 254–255, 257; *SU*, 1924, no. 86, art. 870. These institutions were not built in numbers large enough to handle a significant volume of *besprizornye*.

53. TsGA RSFSR, f. 2306, o. 69, ed. khr. 350, ll. 8–9; *SU*, 1924, no. 86, art. 870; Ryndziunskii and Savinskaia, *Pravovoe polozhenie* (1923), 61–62; *Sbornik deistvuiushchikh uzakonenii i rasporiazhenii* (1929), 124. For a detailed

set of guidelines on the operation of labor homes, published a few years later, see Ryndziunskii and Savinskaia, *Detskoe pravo*, 307–315.

54. Vasilevskii, *Detskaia "prestupnost',"* 156; Ryndziunskii and Savinskaia, *Pravovoe polozhenie* (1923), 61.

55. *SU*, 1924, no. 86, art. 870; Ryndziunskii and Savinskaia, *Pravovoe polozhenie* (1923), 62.

56. *SU*, 1921, no. 66, art. 506; Ryndziunskii et al., *Pravovoe polozhenie* (1927), 99; *Detskaia besprizornost'*, 24–25; Liublinskii, *Zakonodatel'naia okhrana*, 82; Liublinskii, *Bor'ba*, 184–186; *Otchet gorskogo ekonomicheskogo soveshchaniia za period ianvar'–mart 1922 g.* (Vladikavkaz, 1922), 255; *Pravo i zhizn'*, 1925, nos. 4–5: 95–96. In 1926 a new decree and subsequent elaboration from Narkompros spelled out the functions of the Children's Social Inspection in greater detail. See *SU*, 1926, no. 32, art. 248; Krasnushkin et al., *Nishchenstvo i besprizornost'*, 137–138; Tizanov and Epshtein, *Gosudarstvo i obshchestvennost'*, 27–31. For a description from the Ukrainian Narkompros of the responsibilities intended for its *Detskaia inspektsiia* (that is, its equivalent of the Children's Social Inspection), see *Detskoe pravo*, comp. Krichevskaia and Kuritskii, 443–444.

57. *SU*, 1921, no. 66, art. 506; Liublinskii, *Bor'ba*, 184; TsGA RSFSR, f. 1575, o. 6, ed. khr. 141, l. 43.

58. TsGA RSFSR, f. 2306, o. 13, ed. khr. 52, ll. 9–10, 28; Liublinskii, *Bor'ba*, 184–185, 188–190. For a description of the similar responsibilities of *obsledovateli-vospitateli* in Ukraine, see *Detskoe pravo*, comp. Krichevskaia and Kuritskii, 524–530.

59. *Vserossiiskoe obsledovanie*, 37, 41–42; *Detskaia defektivnost'*, 62.

60. TsGA RSFSR, f. 1575, o. 6, ed. khr. 4, l. 134.

61. For examples of such instructions and resolutions, see TsGAOR, f. 5207, o. 1, ed. khr. 6, ll. 15, 62; *Detskii dom*, comp. Utevskii, 7.

62. TsGAOR, f. 5207, o. 1, ed. khr. 41, l. 7; *Vserossiiskoe obsledovanie*, 33, 35.

63. TsGAOR, f. 5207, o. 1, ed. khr. 41, l. 10; ibid., ed. khr. 62, l. 23; ibid., ed. khr. 63, l. 21; *Vserossiiskoe obsledovanie*, 38. For a decree and a Party resolution condemning the appropriation (except in military emergencies) of buildings housing children's institutions, see *SU*, 1921, no. 64, art. 470; *Detskii dom*, comp. Utevskii, 7.

64. TsGAOR, f. 5207, o. 1, ed. khr. 43, ll. 8–9; ibid., ed. khr. 60, l. 131; ibid., ed. khr. 61, l. 70; *Kommunistka*, 1921, nos. 14–15: 7; Kalinina, *Desiat' let*, 80; *Krasnaia nov'*, 1923, no. 5: 206–207; *Golod i deti*, 38, 40; *Vestnik prosveshcheniia T.S.S.R.* (Kazan'), 1922, nos. 1–2: 26; *Prosveshchenie* (Viatka), 1922, no. 1: 19; British Foreign Office, 1922, reel 1, vol. 8148, p. 128. This, of course, does not belittle the energetic work of many officials and volunteers who succeeded in saving thousands of children. For an illustration of their accomplishments, see *Krasnaia nov'*, 1923, no. 5: 213. Unfortunately, thousands of other children in the region died all around them.

65. *Otchet gorskogo ekonomicheskogo soveshchaniia* (1923), 122; *Golod i deti*, 15; *Prosveshchenie* (Krasnodar), 1921–1922, no. 2: 127 (regarding Simbirsk province); *Pravda*, 1921, no. 204 (September 14), p. 1.

66. TsGA RSFSR, f. 1575, o. 6, ed. khr. 4, l. 83; *Otchet o sostoianii narod-nogo obrazovaniia v eniseiskoi gubernii*, 14–15; Diushen, *Piat' let*, 27; *Pros-veshchenie* (Viatka), 1922, no. 1: 20; *Obzor narodnogo khoziaistva tambovskoi gubernii oktiabr' 1921 g.–oktiabr' 1922 g.* (Tambov, 1922), 32; *Biulleten' tsen-tral'noi komissii pomoshchi golodaiushchim VTsIK*, 1921, no. 2: 40–41.

67. *Leningradskaia oblast'* (Leningrad), 1928, no. 4: 112; *Golod i deti*, 22.

68. TsGAOR, f. 5207, o. 1, ed. khr. 43, l. 67; ibid., ed. khr. 61, l. 114; *Na pomoshch' rebenku* (Petrograd-Moscow, 1923), 47; *Obzor narodnogo kho-ziaistva tambovskoi gubernii*, 32; *Detskii dom*, comp. Utevskii, 4; *Narodnoe prosveshchenie* (Kursk), 1921, no. 10: 52; *Shkola i zhizn'* (Nizhnii Novgorod), 1927, no. 10: 57–58; Vasilevskii, *Besprizornost'*, 81; *Kommunistka*, 1922, no. 1: 8; *Otchet vladimirskogo gubispolkoma i ego otdelov 14-mu gubernskomu s"ezdu sovetov (10 dekabria 1922 goda)* (Vladimir, 1922), 51, 55; *Otchet sov-etu truda i oborony za period 1/X 1921 g.–1/IV 1922 g.* (Kursk, 1922), 40. Educational institutions of all types, not just those for *besprizornye*, experienced this decline in numbers; see Stolee, "Generation," 67. A report from Vladikav-kaz also noted that NEP had encouraged the former owners of buildings and other property, confiscated earlier and put at the disposal of *detdoma*, to petition for the return of these items; TsGAOR, f. 5207, o. 1, ed. khr. 43, l. 67.

69. Kalinina, *Desiat' let*, 81–82.

70. TsGA RSFSR, f. 1575, o. 6, ed. khr. 4, l. 26; *Narodnoe prosveshchenie*, 1922, no. 102: 8; *Biulleten' saratovskogo gubotnaroba* (Saratov), 1921, nos. 2–3: 1. In separate operations, several hundred thousand adults and whole families were also evacuated from famine provinces. See *Itogi bor'by s golodom*, 468; *Bich naroda*, 94; *Na fronte goloda, kniga 1* (Samara, 1922), 37; *Vlast' sovetov*, 1922, nos. 1–2: 45–48; nos. 4–6: 34–37. The recent past had witnessed two other mass evacuations (though neither was focused on orphans and other homeless children), one to remove people from the front during World War I and the other during War Communism to transport children out of starving cities, including Moscow. (Some children were also evacuated from areas of military activity at this time.) For autobiographical sketches of children evacu-ated during World War I, see *Besprizornye*, comp. Kaidanova, 31; Kaidanova, *Besprizornye deti*, 60–61, 70. Regarding evacuations during War Communism, see Kalinina, *Desiat' let*, 30; *Pervyi vserossiiskii s"ezd*, 47; *Letnie kolonii. Sbor-nik, sostavlennyi otdelom reformy i otdelom edinoi shkoly narodnogo komis-sariata po prosveshcheniiu* (Moscow, 1919), 8; *Krasnaia gazeta* (Petrograd), 1919, no. 72 (April 1), p. 2; *Narodnoe prosveshchenie*, 1923, no. 6: 129.

71. TsGAOR, f. 5207, o. 1, ed. khr. 6, l. 54; ibid., ed. khr. 63, l. 42; TsGA RSFSR, f. 1575, o. 6, ed. khr. 4, ll. 22–23, 29; *Biulleten' saratovskogo gubot-naroba* (Saratov), 1921, nos. 2–3: 1; *Biulleten' tsentral'noi komissii pomoshchi golodaiushchim VTsIK*, 1921, no. 2: 46.

72. TsGAOR, f. 5207, o. 1, ed. khr. 28, l. 7; ibid., ed. khr. 60, l. 153; ibid., ed. khr. 61, l. 70; ibid., ed. khr. 65, l. 95; ibid., ed. khr. 67, l. 52; *Narodnoe prosveshchenie* (Saratov), 1922, no. 3: 26; *Biulleten' tsentral'noi komissii po-moshchi golodaiushchim VTsIK*, 1921, no. 2: 38–39.

73. TsGAOR, f. 5207, o. 1, ed. khr. 44, ll. 1–2; *Golod i deti*, 11.

74. *Itogi bor'by s golodom*, 468; *Narodnoe prosveshchenie*, 1923, no. 8: 25; *Spasennye revoliutsiei*, 32; Min'kovskii, "Osnovnye etapy," 40; *Biulleten' tsentral'noi komissii pomoshchi golodaiushchim VTsIK*, 1921, no. 2: 44; TsGAOR, f. 5207, o. 1, ed. khr. 13, l. 21; TsGA RSFSR, f. 1575, o. 6, ed. khr. 4, l. 21; *Chto govoriat tsifry*, 14. A. N. Kogan (citing *Sputnik kommunista*, no. 16 [1922]: 94) presents a figure of 121,018 children evacuated by June 1, 1922; see Kogan, "Sistema meropriiatii," 235. For reports from several regions suggesting that a majority of the evacuees were orphans or otherwise homeless, see *Otchet o deiatel'nosti saratovskogo gubernskogo ispolnitel'nogo komiteta*, 57; *Krasnaia nov'*, 1932, no. 1: 36; *Bich naroda*, 25; *Smolenskaia nov'* (Smolensk), 1922, no. 6: 12.

75. TsGAOR, f. 5207, o. 1, ed. khr. 13, ll. 10, 17; ibid., ed. khr. 23, l. 1; ibid., ed. khr. 33, l. 2; *Golod i deti*, 10; *Chto govoriat tsifry*, 15; *Biulleten' tsentral'noi komissii pomoshchi golodaiushchim VTsIK*, 1921, no. 2: 38; Konius, *Puti razvitiia*, 142–143; *Bich naroda*, 25; TsGA RSFSR, f. 1575, o. 6, ed. khr. 4, l. 21; TsGA RSFSR, f. 2306, o. 70, ed. khr. 2, l. 7; Grinberg, *Rasskazy*, 18; *Smolenskaia nov'* (Smolensk), 1922, no. 1: 5; *Gudok*, 1921, no. 398 (September 11), p. 1; *Novyi put'* (Riga), 1921, no. 145 (July 29), p. 3; *Derevenskaia pravda* (Petrograd), 1921, no. 120 (September 21), p. 3.

76. TsGAOR, f. 5207, o. 1, ed. khr. 4, ll. 1, 7; ibid., ed. khr. 65, l. 117; *Novyi put'* (Riga), 1921, no. 213 (October 16), p. 3; *Narodnoe prosveshchenie*, 1922, no. 102: 14–15; 1923, no. 8: 25–26; British Foreign Office, 1922, reel 1, vol. 8148, pp. 82–83 (reference to a group of 439 Russian children evacuated to Czechoslovakian foster families). Turkey apparently also offered to accept a group of orphans from the Volga region, though it is unclear whether the children were ever sent; see *Pravda Zakavkaz'ia* (Tiflis), 1922, no. 8 (May 11), p. 2. The British government balked at permitting entry to Volga children, citing the "risks to public health that would be involved even if the strictest precautions were observed"; British Foreign Office, 1922, reel 1, vol. 8149, p. 75 (for the quotation and reference to "a party of Russian boys" already admitted to France); 1922, reel 17, vol. 8205, pp. 115–127. An American Red Cross document noted that earlier, before the famine, Polish Red Cross officials expressed a desire to remove Polish orphans from Siberia and place them in Polish-American families; American Red Cross, box 916, file 987.08, "Weekly Report," May 18, 1920. This report does not indicate whether such a transfer took place.

77. *Gor'kaia pravda*, 24; *Biulleten' tsentral'noi komissii pomoshchi golodaiushchim VTsIK*, 1921, no. 2: 46; *Derevenskaia pravda* (Petrograd), 1922, no. 23: 2; *Itogi bor'by s golodom*, 468.

78. TsGAOR, f. 5207, o. 1, ed. khr. 23, l. 3; ibid., ed. khr. 53, ll. 22–23; ibid., ed. khr. 63, l. 105; *Biulleten' tsentral'noi komissii pomoshchi golodaiushchim VTsIK*, 1921, no. 2: 45; *Narodnoe prosveshchenie* (Saratov), 1922, no. 3: 25; *Bich naroda*, 25.

79. TsGAOR, f. 5207, o. 1, ed. khr. 13, l. 15; TsGA RSFSR, f. 1575, o. 6, ed. khr. 4, l. 29; *Narodnoe prosveshchenie* (Saratov), 1922, no. 3: 27. Instructions received in Kazan' indicated that youths of preschool age should not be evacuated, and these orders doubtless went to other famine regions as well; see

Vestnik prosveshcheniia T.S.S.R. (Kazan'), 1922, nos. 1–2: 25. Anna Grinberg's book *Rasskazy besprizornykh o sebe* contains many autobiographical sketches by children who underwent evacuation. For similar accounts, see Kaidanova, *Besprizornye deti*, 56–57.

80. TsGAOR, f. 5207, o. 1, ed. khr. 13, l. 11; ibid., ed. khr. 47, l. 18; *Narodnoe prosveshchenie* (Saratov), 1922, no. 3: 28. Sometimes the trains themselves did not arrive punctually to pick up children, in part because railroad officials could not always provide the trains called for in evacuation plans. When such problems arose, youths who had been assembled at stations often had to wait there many days. See TsGAOR, f. 5207, o. 1, ed. khr. 61, l. 117; *Biulleten' tsentral'noi komissii pomoshchi golodaiushchim VTsIK*, 1921, no. 2: 46. In some cases, especially regarding the transportation of children to Central Asia, rail lines were at times so clogged that evacuations had to be postponed temporarily; TsGAOR, f. 5207, o. 1, ed. khr. 4, l. 10.

81. *Narodnoe prosveshchenie* (Saratov), 1922, no. 3: 27–28.

82. TsGAOR, f. 5207, o. 1, ed. khr. 13, ll. 1, 18; ibid., ed. khr. 60, l. 199; ibid., ed. khr. 61, l. 88; *Na fronte goloda, kniga* 1, 37; Kaidanova, *Besprizornye deti*, 69; Kalinina, *Desiat' let*, 71; *Narodnoe prosveshchenie* (Saratov), 1922, no. 3: 26–28.

83. TsGAOR, f. 5207, o. 1, ed. khr. 41, ll. 33, 36; ibid., ed. khr. 63, l. 72; *Golod i deti*, 17, 20.

84. For these reports and similar ones from other areas (Volynsk province, Zhitomir, Petrograd, and Kostroma), see TsGAOR, f. 5207, o. 1, ed. khr. 41, l. 33; ibid., ed. khr. 53, ll. 3, 8; *Otchet vladimirskogo gubispolkoma*, 56; *Golod i deti*, 18–19; *Narodnoe prosveshchenie*, 1922, no. 102: 12.

85. TsGAOR, f. 5207, o. 1, ed. khr. 13, ll. 7, 16; *Smolenskaia nov'* (Smolensk), 1922, no. 1: 5. In many cities, local authorities did not make adequate preparations, even though they knew that trains would be dispatched to their jurisdictions. Here, children might languish for days in the rail depots of their destinations, packed in the cars, while officials sought places to put them. See TsGAOR, f. 5207, o. 1, ed. khr. 44, l. 28; ibid., ed. khr. 61, l. 88; ibid., ed. khr. 64, ll. 8, 12–14; *Narodnoe prosveshchenie* (Saratov), 1922, no. 3: 28. For a description of the efforts made by various officials in Kostroma to find satisfactory accommodations for five hundred children soon to be delivered from the town of Vol'sk, see TsGAOR, f. 5207, o. 1, ed. khr. 13, l. 9. Their quest proved difficult, though not completely hopeless.

86. *Gor'kaia pravda*, 31; *Smolenskaia nov'* (Smolensk), 1922, no. 1: 5; Gilev, *Detskaia besprizornost'*, 4; *Narodnoe prosveshchenie*, 1922, no. 102: 12; *Krasnaia nov'*, 1932, no. 1: 37. Some reports tell of children placed in well-supplied and well-run institutions. More often, however, the sources describe shortages and poor, sometimes appalling, sanitation. See TsGA RSFSR, f. 1575, o. 6, ed. khr. 4, l. 21; *Golod i deti*, 18–19; *Smolenskaia nov'* (Smolensk), 1922, nos. 7–8: 11; *Otchet vladimirskogo gubispolkoma*, 56. Regarding children placed in peasant families, see Gilev, *Detskaia besprizornost'*, 4; *Itogi bor'by s golodom*, 33; *Otchet vladimirskogo gubispolkoma*, 56; *Golod i deti*, 15; *Zaria Vostoka* (Tiflis), 1922, no. 15 (July 6), p. 2. Regarding efforts by the Women's Section of the Party in Smolensk province to convince the local population to

take young famine refugees into their homes, see Smolensk Archive, reel 46, WKP 421, p. 4. National minority children unable to speak Russian found themselves in difficult straits when assigned to Russian villages or *detdoma*; see TsGA RSFSR, f. 1575, o. 6, ed. khr. 4, l. 21; *Bich naroda*, 60–61; Vasilevskii, *Besprizornost'*, 16–17.

87. TsGAOR, f. 5207, o. 1, ed. khr. 63, l. 50; ibid., ed. khr. 64, l. 41; *Golod i deti*, 11; *Smolenskaia nov'* (Smolensk), 1922, no. 1: 5–6; *Biulleten' tsentral'noi komissii pomoshchi golodaiushchim VTsIK*, 1921, no. 2: 38; *Itogi bor'by s golodom*, 33; *Narodnoe prosveshchenie*, 1923, no. 8: 25; Gilev, *Detskaia besprizornost'*, 4; *Otchet kurskogo gubernskogo ispolnitel'nogo komiteta X-mu gubernskomu s"ezdu sovetov* (Kursk, 1922), 150.

88. TsGAOR, f. 5207, o. 1, ed. khr. 43, l. 17 (regarding the Kuban–Black Sea province); *Otchet o sostoianii narodnogo obrazovaniia v eniseiskoi gubernii*, 17. Regarding the arrival of young famine refugees on their own in other regions, see TsGAOR, f. 5207, o. 1, ed. khr. 43, l. 26; *Golod i deti*, 12–13; *Smolenskaia nov'* (Smolensk), 1922, no. 1: 6; *Otchet vladimirskogo gubispolkoma*, 56.

89. TsGAOR, f. 5207, o. 1, ed. khr. 67, l. 58; *Pravda Zakavkaz'ia* (Tiflis), 1922, no. 2 (May 4), p. 4. In 1920, even before the famine, officials in some regions deployed cordons to deflect *besprizornye* traveling south; see Kalinina, *Desiat' let*, 52. Kalinina, a Narkompros activist who had traveled in the south of Russia, reported that many of the children had grown wild and even savage, determined to break through the blockade in any way possible. See also British Foreign Office, 1922, reel 4, vol. 8160, p. 58.

90. TsGAOR, f. 5207, o. 1, ed. khr. 52, l. 62; ibid., ed. khr. 53, ll. 4, 8; *Besprizornye*, comp. Kaidanova, 36–37; *Golod i deti*, 18–19. Regarding provincial officials' unsuccessful appeals to Moscow for more assistance in supporting the evacuees, see TsGAOR, f. 5207, o. 1, ed. khr. 41, l. 33; *Kommunistka*, 1922, no. 1: 8.

91. TsGAOR, f. 5207, o. 1, ed. khr. 43, l. 122; *Smolenskaia nov'* (Smolensk), 1922, nos. 7–8: 11; *Otchet cherepovetskogo gubernskogo ispolnitel'nogo komiteta*, 101; *Deti posle goloda*, 93–94; *Pravda Zakavkaz'ia* (Tiflis), 1922, no. 23 (May 30), p. 2; *Otchet gorskogo ekonomicheskogo soveshchaniia* (1923), 122; *Obzor deiatel'nosti gubernskogo ispolnitel'nogo komiteta za 1923 god* (Novgorod, 1923), 79; *Otchet o deiatel'nosti tul'skogo gubernskogo ispolnitel'nogo komiteta sovetov rabochikh, krest'ianskikh i krasnoarmeiskikh deputatov za 1922–23 khoziaistvennyi god* (Tula, 1924), 201.

92. *Smolenskaia nov'* (Smolensk), 1922, nos. 7–8: 11; *Pomoshch' detiam*, 26; *Posle goloda*, 1922, no. 1: 65; *Spasennye revoliutsiei*, 47.

93. *Narodnoe prosveshchenie*, 1923, no. 8: 26; *Narodnoe prosveshchenie v R.S.F.S.R. k 1924/25 uchebnomu godu*, 80; *Detskoe pravo*, comp. Krichevskaia and Kuritskii, 461; Kalinina, *Desiat' let*, 78–79; *Izvestiia*, 1923, no. 73 (April 3), p. 4. Many evacuees who returned to their home regions and failed to find their parents or relatives appeared later in the streets of Moscow; see Kalinina, *Desiat' let*, 78; *Besprizornye*, comp. Kaidanova, 38; Grinberg, *Rasskazy*, 18. During the course of 1922–1923, approximately fifty thousand children were reevacuated in organized fashion to their home regions; *Narodnoe prosvesh-*

chenie, 1923, no. 8: 25–26; *Bor'ba s detskoi besprizornost'iu*, comp. B. S. Utev-skii (Moscow-Leningrad, 1932), 7. Little information exists on the subsequent handling of the remaining hundred thousand removed from the famine zone in 1921–1922. No doubt numerous youths, reevacuated without authorization or simply jettisoned to different provinces, failed to appear in government statistics. Some, especially orphans, remained for a time in the *detdoma* to which they had been evacuated originally. Others were absorbed by the surrounding population so completely that they forgot their home villages, native languages, and even their names. They found work or joined local street urchins. A few became "evacuation professionals" (*professionaly evakuatsii*). After accepting the cloth-ing, food, and tickets given to those transported back to their (alleged) home districts, they slipped off the trains when an opportunity arose. Before long, their trails led to another receiver or *detdom*, where they initiated the ploy again. See *Otchet cherepovetskogo gubernskogo ispolnitel'nogo komiteta*, 101; Vasi-levskii, *Besprizornost'*, 9; *Pravo i zhizn'*, 1926, nos. 6–7: 103; Gilev, *Detskaia besprizornost'*, 18; *Pravda*, 1924, no. 44 (February 23), p. 4; Grinberg, *Ras-skazy*, 14 (regarding the "evacuation professionals").

94. *Besprizornye*, comp. Kaidanova, 35–39. The boy reported satisfaction with the children's home in Moscow and mentioned that he was able to visit Anna from time to time in her institution.

95. *Narodnoe prosveshchenie*, 1923, no. 6: 130; *Detskii dom*, 1928, no. 3: 25; Liublinskii, *Bor'ba* , 183; *Drug detei*, 1927, no. 2: inside front cover. Ad-dress bureaus were also established in the provinces and other republics, though far below the quantity desired by Narkompros; see Vasilevskii, *Besprizornost'*, 17. Regarding the organization of address bureaus outside Moscow, see for example *Detskoe pravo*, comp. Krichevskaia and Kuritskii, 459–461; "Otchet Riazgubono za ianvar'–sentiabr' 1922 goda," in *Otchet o deiatel'nosti riazan-skogo gubispolkoma*, 5. Public campaigns to assist *besprizornye* sometimes in-cluded efforts to inform citizens that address bureaus would help them find lost children; see TsGA RSFSR, f. 1575, o. 6, ed. khr. 155, l. 10.

96. *Narodnoe prosveshchenie v R.S.F.S.R. k 1924/25 uchebnomu godu*, 92. For additional figures on the work of address bureaus in Moscow and the prov-inces, see *Narodnoe prosveshchenie*, 1923, no. 6: 131; Gilev, *Detskaia bespri-zornost'*, 18; *Statisticheskii obzor narodnogo obrazovaniia v permskom okruge*, 39; *Narodnoe prosveshchenie v RSFSR k 1927–28 uchebnomu godu*, 61; *Det-skii dom*, 1928, no. 3: 26.

97. *Drug detei* (Khar'kov), 1926, no. 1: 48; *Sbornik deistvuiushchikh uza-konenii i rasporiazhenii* (1929), 130, 132; *Izvestiia*, 1924, no. 82 (April 9), p. 6; *Detskii dom*, 1928, no. 3: 28 (regarding the lists placed periodically in Nar-kompros's weekly bulletin, *Ezhenedel'nik NKP*). For examples of these lists, see *Drug detei* (Khar'kov), 1925, no. 1: 51–52; no. 2: inside front and back covers; no. 5: inside front and back covers; no. 9: inside front and back covers. Parents were often looking for children who had disappeared years earlier. In addition to the lists cited above, see *Drug detei* (Khar'kov), 1925, no. 1: 21; no. 6: inside back cover; nos. 7–8: 67–68; 1926, no. 1: 48; *Drug detei*, 1929, no. 1: inside back cover. For a list of twelve youths, sought by relatives, who had been found in various children's institutions, see *Drug detei*, 1927, no. 1: inside front cover.

98. *Biulleten' saratovskogo gubotnaroba* (Saratov), 1921, nos. 2–3: 3; *Drug detei* (Khar'kov), 1925, no. 1: 22–23; *Narodnoe prosveshchenie* (Saratov), 1922, no. 3: 26; *Detskii dom*, 1928, no. 3: 26; *Narodnoe prosveshchenie*, 1923, no. 6: 131; Vasilevskii, *Detskaia "prestupnost'*," 131. The fact that only a small number of address bureaus were organized around the country contributed to the difficulty of locating lost children. See Liublinskii, *Bor'ba* , 184; *Narodnoe prosveshchenie*, 1923, no. 6: 130; Vasilevskii, *Detskaia "prestupnost'*," 130–131; *Shkola i zhizn'* (Nizhnii Novgorod), 1926, no. 11: 38; Smolensk Archive, reel 15, WKP 124, p. 61 (on the frequent escape of Tatar children evacuated to a colony in Smolensk province).

99. Krasnushkin et al., *Nishchenstvo i besprizornost'*, 165; *Drug detei* (Khar'kov), 1925, no. 1: 22; *Narodnoe prosveshchenie*, 1923, no. 6: 131; *Vecherniaia moskva*, 1927, no. 32 (February 9), p. 2. Infants found abandoned in railroad terminals were sometimes named after the stations; hence Sergei Iaroslavskii and Boris Kazanskii (after Moscow's Iaroslavl' and Kazan' stations). See *Drug detei*, 1928, no. 4: 14. The article in *Vecherniaia moskva* also mentioned a *detdom* resident whom the staff had named Likder, short for *Litsom k Derevne*, or Face to the Countryside, a common slogan of the time.

100. *Kommunistka*, 1921, nos. 14–15: 7; TsGAOR, f. 5207, o. 1, ed. khr. 61, l. 88. In a similar vein, the British cabinet, unenthusiastic about evacuating Volga orphans to Great Britain, heard through the Foreign Office in 1922 that the "same amount of money if spent in Russia would probably keep a much larger number of children alive without raising the grave hygienic and social difficulties involved in bringing them to England." See British Foreign Office, 1922, reel 17, vol. 8205, p. 120.

101. TsGA RSFSR, f. 2306, o. 1, ed. khr. 2100, l. 3; Vasilevskii, *Besprizornost'*, 9; *Pomoshch' detiam*, 26; *Detskoe pravo*, comp. Krichevskaia and Kuritskii, 461; *SU*, 1924, no. 57, art. 559; *Narodnoe prosveshchenie v R.S.F.S.R. k 1924/25 uchebnomu godu*, 80–81.

102. *Golod i deti*, 15, 41; *Narodnoe prosveshchenie*, 1922, no. 102: 6–8. For more information on the trains (known as *pitatel'nye poezda, vrachebnopitatel'nye poezda*, and *banno-pracheshnye poezda*) sent to famine regions to provide food, medical care, and other sanitary services, see TsGAOR, f. 5207, o. 1, ed. khr. 6, ll. 44, 46–47, 50; ibid., ed. khr. 60, l. 100; *Novyi put'* (Riga), 1921, no. 157 (August 12), p. 3; *Narodnoe prosveshchenie*, 1922, no. 102: 8; *Bich naroda*, 54–55; *Biulleten' tsentral'noi komissii pomoshchi golodaiushchim VTsIK*, 1921, no. 2: 41; Zhukova, "Deiatel'nost' Detkomissii," 65.

103. See for example *Krasnyi flot* (Petrograd), 1922, no. 1: 121–122; 1923, no. 8: 107; *Gudok*, 1921, no. 379 (August 19), p. 3; *Turkestanskaia pravda* (Tashkent), 1923, no. 14, (January 19), p. 3; *Golod, 1921–1922* (New York, [1922]), 89; *Novyi put'* (Riga), 1921, no. 180 (September 8), p. 3; 1921, no. 248 (November 29), p. 3.

104. Figures vary on the number of children supported by these institutions, in some cases because they pertain to different dates or regions (including or excluding Ukraine, for example). See Min'kovskii, "Osnovnye etapy," 40; *Posle goloda*, 1922, no. 1: 64–65; *Prosveshchenie* (Krasnodar), 1923, no. 1: 7; Kogan, "Sistema meropriiatii," 246; *Chto govoriat tsifry*, 20. According to *Posle go-*

Ioda, by the end of 1922 trade unions were maintaining 175,000 children, and the military an additional 39,000. For more on the efforts of factories, trade unions, military units, institutes, and other organizations to aid children during the famine years, see TsGAOR, f. 5207, o. 1, ed. khr. 43, l. 66; ibid., ed. khr. 61, l. 86; *Prosveshchenie* (Viatka), 1922, no. 1: 21; *Otchet vladimirskogo gubispolkoma*, 55–56; *Gor'kaia pravda*, 15; *Novyi put'* (Riga), 1921, no. 18 (February 22), p. 4; *Derevenskaia pravda* (Petrograd), 1921, no. 122 (September 23), p. 2; *Prosveshchenie na Urale* (Sverdlovsk), 1927, no. 2: 60; *Golod i deti*, 41; *Vestnik prosveshcheniia T.S.S.R.* (Kazan'), 1922, nos. 1–2: 113; *Otchet o sostoianii narodnogo obrazovaniia v eniseiskoi gubernii*, 15; *Otchet kurskogo gubernskogo ispolnitel'nogo komiteta*, 153; *Zaria Vostoka* (Tiflis), 1922, no. 67 (September 7), p. 3; *Itogi bor'by s golodom*, 232; *Smolenskaia nov'* (Smolensk), 1922, no. 1: 5; *Prosveshchenie na transporte*, 1922, no. 1: 14; no. 2: 7; Smolensk Archive, reel 25, WKP 207, p. 6; reel 31, WKP 274, p. 58.

105. For more on the activities of foreign relief organizations in Soviet Russia (especially the American Relief Administration) and resources contributed by foreigners to aid homeless children (during and after the famine), see TsGALI, f. 332, o. 2, ed. khr. 75, l. 60; TsGAOR, f. 5207, o. 1, ed. khr. 4, ll. 5–7; ibid., ed. khr. 47, l. 18; ibid., ed. khr. 49, ll. 3–4b; TsGA RSFSR, f. 298, o. 1, ed. khr. 45, l. 51; TsGA RSFSR, f. 1575, o. 6, ed. khr. 4, l. 98; ibid., o. 10, ed. khr. 178, l. 10; *SU*, 1921, no. 66, art. 500; *Vestnik statistiki*, 1923, nos. 4–6: 112; *Itogi bor'by s golodom*, 5, 35; *Otchet samarskogo gubernskogo ekonomicheskogo soveshchaniia. Vypusk II-i. Polugodie 1 oktiabria 1921 g.–1 aprelia 1922 g.* (Samara, 1922), 141; *Derevenskaia pravda* (Petrograd), 1921, no. 134 (October 8), p. 3; 1921, no. 147 (October 25), p. 3; *Bich naroda*, 58, 96; *Narodnoe prosveshchenie*, 1922, no. 102: 7; *Prosveshchenie na transporte*, 1922, no. 2: 24; *Prosveshchenie na Urale* (Sverdlovsk), 1927, no. 2: 60; *Gor'kaia pravda*, 25; Fisher, *Famine in Soviet Russia*; Benjamin M. Weissman, *Herbert Hoover and Famine Relief to Soviet Russia, 1921–1923* (Stanford, 1974); Hiebert and Miller, *Feeding the Hungry*; *Drug detei* (Khar'kov), 1925, nos. 7–8: 59; 1926, nos. 4–5: 38; 1927, no. 2: 43; 1926, no. 1: 44; British Foreign Office, 1922, reel 1, vols. 8147, 8148, 8149; 1922, reel 2, vols. 8150, 8151.

106. For these figures and information for other months, see *Itogi bor'by s golodom*, 32; Fisher, *Famine in Soviet Russia*, 557; *Narodnoe prosveshchenie*, 1922, no. 102: 6–8; *Posle goloda*, 1922, no. 1: 65. According to figures for July 1, 1922 (for the Volga basin, Crimea, and Ukraine), food was also distributed to 6.9 million adults (with foreign organizations accounting for 5.7 million and Soviet operations 1.2 million); see *Itogi bor'by s golodom*, 465. In following years, individuals and organizations from many countries contributed funds to maintain a small number of Soviet *detdoma*. Among the institutions supported by American aid were three named for John Reed, Eugene Debs, and Helen Keller; *Pravda*, 1923, no. 96 (May 3), p. 3. Earlier, during the Civil War, the American Red Cross administered homes for orphaned and abandoned children in diverse regions outside the Red Army's control. Regarding Siberia, see American Red Cross, box 916, file 987.08, "The American Red Cross in Siberia."

5. PRIMEVAL CHAOS

1. *Vestnik prosveshcheniia*, 1923, no. 4: 166; *Novyi put'* (Riga), 1921, no. 163 (August 19), p. 3. In practice, some institutions bearing the name observation-distribution point (usually abbreviated in Russian as *raspredelitel'*) were indistinguishable from receivers; see for example *Vestnik prosveshcheniia*, 1923, no. 4: 169.

2. *Vestnik prosveshcheniia*, 1922, no. 1: 16; *Krasnaia nov'*, 1932, no. 1: 36; *Na putiakh k novoi shkole*, 1924, nos. 7–8: 45.

3. Vasilevskii, *Besprizornost'*, 91. According to another source, the country contained 160 receivers and 50 *raspredeliteli* by January 1, 1922; Sokolov, *Detskaia besprizornost'*, 61.

4. Sokolov, *Detskaia besprizornost'*, 62; *Otchet o sostoianii narodnogo obrazovaniia v eniseiskoi gubernii*, 16–17; *Otchet ekonomicheskogo soveshchaniia avtonomnoi oblasti Komi na 1-e aprelia 1922 g.* (Viatka, 1922), 59; *Vserossiiskoe obsledovanie*, 11; *Otchet tambovskogo gubernskogo ekonomicheskogo soveshchaniia sovetu truda i oborony za period s 1 oktiabria 1921 g. po 1 aprelia 1922 g.* (Tambov, 1922), 162; *Krasnaia nov'*, 1923, no. 5: 207; *Bich naroda*, 79. Where receivers did not exist, children detained for delinquency often remained in police stations while their cases were under consideration; see M. F. Kirsanov, *Rukovodstvo po proizvodstvu del v mestnykh komissiiakh po delam o nesovershennoletnikh* (Moscow-Leningrad, 1927), 22.

5. *Krasnaia nov'*, 1923, no. 5: 207–208.

6. Golder and Hutchinson, *On the Trail*, 57, 70–71. See also A. Ruth Fry, *Three Visits to Russia, 1922–25* (London, 1942), 13.

7. TsGAOR, f. 5207, o. 1, ed. khr. 43, l. 64; *Gor'kaia pravda*, 47; *Krasnaia nov'*, 1923, no. 5: 207–208; *Bich naroda*, 79; *Besprizornye*, comp. O. Kaidanova (Moscow, 1926), 34.

8. For examples of receivers in Tambov province and Khar'kov disrupted by experienced *besprizornye*, see *Otchet tambovskogo gubernskogo ekonomicheskogo soveshchaniia*, 162–163; Maro, *Besprizornye*, 333. A few receivers were established exclusively for juvenile prostitutes or other "morally defective" youths of one gender or the other. See for example *Psikhiatriia, nevrologiia i eksperimental'naia psikhologiia* (Petrograd), 1922, *vypusk* 1, 97; Livshits, *Sotsial'nye korni*, 109–114; Vasilevskii and Vasilevskii, *Prostitutsiia i novaia Rossiia*, 77. Such specialized institutions, however, tended to be located in or near the largest cities. Most receivers around the country admitted a wide range of *besprizornye*, from the naive to the unscrupulous.

9. TsGALI, f. 332, o. 2, ed. khr. 41, l. 21; *Krasnaia nov'*, 1923, no. 5: 208; 1932, no. 1: 37; *Vchera i segodnia*, 132–134; Grinberg, *Rasskazy*, 24, 45–46, 83–85, 88.

10. Livshits, *Sotsial'nye korni*, 113; *Na putiakh k novoi shkole*, no. 3 (May 1923): 176–177; Grinberg, *Rasskazy*, 15, 55, 68; Kaidanova, *Besprizornye deti*, 6.

11. *Na putiakh k novoi shkole*, no. 3 (May 1923): 168; *Puti kommunisticheskogo prosveshcheniia* (Simferopol'), 1926, no. 12: 72; Grinberg, *Rasskazy*,

85–86; Livshits, *Sotsial'nye korni*, 113; *Vchera i segodnia*, 134; Kalinina, *Desiat' let*, 34.

12. TsGA RSFSR, f. 1575, o. 10, ed. khr. 178, l. 10; Vasilevskii, *Detskaia "prestupnost'*," 146; *Otchet tambovskogo gubernskogo ekonomicheskogo soveshchaniia*, 162–163; *Smolenskaia nov'* (Smolensk), 1922, nos. 7–8: 8; *Otchet cherepovetskogo gubernskogo ispolnitel'nogo komiteta*, 100.

13. This transformation eventually found sanction in guidelines published for receivers. For an example, which specified that children not be kept in a receiver for more than four *months*, see Ryndziunskii and Savinskaia, *Detskoe pravo*, 228–229.

14. A handful of institutions were reorganized in 1922–1923 as "experimental-model" facilities, intended from the beginning to hold children for an extended period of training before sending them on to *detdoma* or other destinations.

15. See for example *Na putiakh k novoi shkole*, no. 3 (May 1923): 168–179.

16. See for example *Kommunistka*, 1922, no. 1: 13; *Vestnik prosveshcheniia*, 1923, no. 4: 174.

17. For several examples of the different names borne by children's institutions, see Magul'iano, "K voprosu o detskoi prestupnosti," 214; *Otchet vladimirskogo gubispolkoma*, 55; *Na putiakh k novoi shkole*, no. 3 (May 1923): 80; Maro, *Besprizornye*, 367–380; Shveitser and Shabalov, *Besprizornye*, 29; Glatman, *Pionery i besprizornye*, 26–28; *Statisticheskii obzor narodnogo obrazovaniia v permskoi gubernii*, 141.

18. *Nash trud* (Iaroslavl'), 1924, no. 2: 15; Shveitser and Shabalov, *Besprizornye*, 18, 67; Makarenko, *Road to Life* 1:32–33; Glatman, *Pionery i besprizornye*, 26.

19. TsGA RSFSR, f. 1575, o. 6, ed. khr. 4, l. 137; Leshchinskii, *Kto byl nichem*, 5; *Prosveshchenie na transporte*, 1922, no. 2: 15; *Kommunistka*, 1922, nos. 10–11: 44; *Zaria Vostoka* (Tiflis), 1922, no. 77 (September 19), 4; *Novyi put'* (Riga), 1921, no. 68 (April 24), p. 3; Makarenko, *Road to Life* 1:68–73; Shveitser and Shabalov, *Besprizornye*, 29–30, 41; Kalinina, *Desiat' let*, 27–28, 38–39.

20. *Tvorcheskii put'* (Orenburg), 1923, no. 6: 10–11; *Novyi put'* (Riga), 1921, no. 34 (March 12), p. 3; 1921, no. 187 (September 16), p. 3; *Nash trud* (Iaroslavl'), 1923, no. 7: 59; *Detskii dom*, 1930, no. 4: 10. For a literary description of a *detdom* located in a convent, a corner of which remained occupied briefly by the nuns, see Lydia Seifulina, "The Lawbreakers," in *Flying Osip: Stories of New Russia* (Freeport, N.Y., 1925; reprint, 1970), 69–72.

21. *Vserossiiskoe obsledovanie*, 14, 22, 25, 28, 30, 33; American Red Cross, box 868, file 948.08, "Report of Mission to Ukraine and South Russia by Major George H. Ryden," November 1919. For the similar findings of another prefamine survey of *detdoma*, see Kalinina, *Desiat' let*, 53.

22. TsGAOR, f. 5207, o. 1, ed. khr. 28, l. 7; ibid., ed. khr. 43, ll. 3, 27; ibid., ed. khr. 61, l. 52; *Otchet krymskogo narodnogo komissariata po prosveshcheniiu*, 18; *Otchet sengileevskogo uezdnogo ispolnitel'nogo komiteta. Za vremia s 1-go iiulia 1921 goda po 5-e fevralia 1922 goda* (Sengilei, 1922), 146; *Derevenskaia pravda* (Petrograd), 1921, no. 118 (September 17), p. 2; 1921,

no. 120 (September 21), p. 3; 1921, no. 131 (October 5), p. 3; 1922, no. 21 (January 28), p. 2; *Prosveshchenie na Urale* (Sverdlovsk), 1927, no. 2: 60; *Novyi put'* (Riga), 1921, no. 250 (December 1), p. 3; 1922, no. 295 (January 26), p. 3; *Posle goloda*, 1922, no. 1: 64; *Otchet gorskogo ekonomicheskogo soveshchaniia* (1923), 122; *Vestnik prosveshcheniia T.S.S.R.* (Kazan'), 1922, nos. 1–2: 26.

23. Vasilevskii and Vasilevskii, *Kniga o golode*, 74–75. The *detdoma* of Samara province took in twenty to twenty-five children each day as early as May 1921. During the next two months the number rose to fifty to fifty-five youths each day, and it passed one hundred in August. See TsGA RSFSR, f. 1575, o. 6, ed. khr. 4, l. 66. For additional data showing sharp increases in the number of children in *detdoma* in several portions of the famine zone, see *Gor'kaia pravda*, 23; *Prosveshchenie* (Viatka), 1922, no. 1: 20; *Vestnik prosveshcheniia T.S.S.R.* (Kazan'), 1922, nos. 1–2: 25; *Statisticheskii spravochnik*, 13.

24. Walter Duranty, *I Write as I Please* (New York, 1935), 131. A visitor to Kazan' during the famine described one of the city's *detdoma* as follows: "The children arrived at this one at the rate of a hundred and sometimes two hundred a day, and although the director of this home was a man of order, with sound ideas on sanitation, so that the children were washed and disinfected on arrival, all this method was overwhelmed by the pressure of new arrivals and the lack of clothes. They were all crawling with lice from which typhus was carried. Nothing the man could do, with his assistants, could destroy that plague of vermin which was the curse and terror of Russian life at this time"; Gibbs, *Since Then*, 391–392.

25. TsGAOR, f. 5207, o. 1, ed. khr. 43, l. 27.

26. *Deti posle goloda*, 92.

27. *Vserossiiskoe obsledovanie*, 18–20, 22–24; Kalinina, *Desiat' let*, 40, 42; TsGAOR, f. 5207, o. 1, ed. khr. 52, l. 56; ibid., ed. khr. 61, ll. 57, 97; *Golod i deti*, 40–41; *Otchet gorskogo ekonomicheskogo soveshchaniia* (1923), 122; Roberts, *Through Starving Russia*, 40; *Smolenskaia nov'* (Smolensk), 1922, no. 3: 3; *Derevenskaia pravda* (Petrograd), 1921, no. 131 (October 5), p. 3; *Deti posle goloda*, 43; *Vestnik prosveshcheniia* (Kazan'), 1921, nos. 6–7: 186–187. Prior to 1921, *detdoma* in some Volga provinces were better provisioned than many in the central part of the country. During War Communism, children were even evacuated from Moscow, Petrograd, and certain other cities to some of the Volga districts. Needless to say, the famine ended this practice.

28. *Vserossiiskoe obsledovanie*, 34; Makarenko, *Road to Life* 1:50–52; Kalinina, *Desiat' let*, 56; *Biulleten' tsentral'noi komissii pomoshchi golodaiushchim VTsIK*, 1921, no. 2: 37; Pitirim A. Sorokin, *Leaves from a Russian Diary—and Thirty Years After* (Boston, 1950), 221–222.

29. TsGALI, f. 332, o. 1, ed. khr. 52, l. 4; TsGAOR, f. 5207, o. 1, ed. khr. 43, ll. 17, 27; ibid., ed. khr. 61, l. 97; *Vserossiiskoe obsledovanie*, 8, 14, 22; Makarenko, *Road to Life* 1:164–165; Shveitser and Shabalov, *Besprizornye*, 31; Kalinina, *Desiat' let*, 40, 53; *Turkestanskaia pravda* (Tashkent), 1923, no. 3 (January 4), p. 2; *Deti posle goloda*, 42; F. E. Dzerzhinskii, *Izbrannye proizvedeniia*, 3d ed., 2 vols. (Moscow, 1977), 1:321. Shortages of facilities, fuel,

textbooks, and the like also plagued regular public schools during these years; see Stolee, "Generation," 41–42. But *detdoma* were generally more vulnerable, because they had to feed, clothe, and house youths as well as provide training of some sort.

30. TsGALI, f. 332, o. 1, ed. khr. 52, l. 49. At a *detdom* in Odessa, the floor was torn out to serve as fuel for cooking meals; see Golder and Hutchinson, *On the Trail*, 214.

31. TsGAOR, f. 5207, o. 1, ed. khr. 43, l. 27; *Vserossiiskoe obsledovanie*, 13, 22; *Krasnaia nov'*, 1932, no. 1: 32; *Nash trud* (Iaroslavl'), 1924, nos. 11–12: 31.

32. *Vtoroi otchet voronezhskogo gubernskogo ekonomicheskogo soveshchaniia*, 33; *Otchet cherepovetskogo gubernskogo ispolnitel'nogo komiteta*, 101; TsGAOR, f. 5207, o. 1, ed. khr. 43, l. 27; *Vserossiiskoe obsledovanie*, 17, 19, 22, 28, 35; *Deti posle goloda*, 43; Kalinina, *Desiat' let*, 40; Makarenko, *Road to Life* 1:46–47; *Smolenskaia nov'* (Smolensk), 1922, nos. 7–8: 11; *Nash trud* (Iaroslavl'), 1924, no. 2: 16; *Vestnik prosveshcheniia T.S.S.R.* (Kazan'), 1922, nos. 1–2: 26.

33. *Spasennye revoliutsiei*, 27; *Nash trud* (Iaroslavl'), 1923, nos. 8–9: 57; *Vestnik prosveshcheniia T.S.S.R.* (Kazan'), 1922, nos. 1–2: 26; *Vserossiiskoe obsledovanie*, 31, 34, 36; Kalinina, *Desiat' let*, 54.

34. *Turkestanskaia pravda* (Tashkent), 1923, no. 30 (February 10), p. 4 (regarding Samarkand); TsGAOR, f. 5207, o. 1, ed. khr. 28, l. 7; *Vtoroi otchet voronezhskogo gubernskogo ekonomicheskogo soveshchaniia*, 33–34; *Vserossiiskoe obsledovanie*, 9, 14–15, 22; Kalinina, *Desiat' let*, 55; *Deti posle goloda*, 41; Maro, *Besprizornye*, 374; *Na fronte goloda, kniga 1*, 37 (regarding the revolutionary tribunal).

35. *Otchet krymskogo narodnogo komissariata po prosveshcheniiu*, 18; *Saratovskii vestnik zdravookhraneniia* (Saratov), 1926, no. 1: 24–28; TsGAOR, f. 5207, o. 1, ed. khr. 61, l. 97; Maro, *Besprizornye*, 374; *Otchet samarskogo gubernskogo ekonomicheskogo soveshchaniia*, 140; *Deti posle goloda*, 43–44; Makarenko, *Road to Life* 1:106, 149; *Novyi put'* (Riga), 1922, no. 302 (February 4), p. 3; *Vserossiiskoe obsledovanie*, 13–14, 21–22, 24, 30, 35; *Tvorcheskii put'* (Orenburg), 1923, no. 6: 10; *Na fronte goloda, kniga 1*, 36; Kalinina, *Desiat' let*, 54, 56; Fry, *Three Visits*, 13.

36. TsGAOR, f. 5207, o. 1, ed. khr. 60, l. 154; ibid., ed. khr. 61, l. 86; *Vestnik prosveshcheniia* (Kazan'), 1921, nos. 6–7: 188; *Vtoroi otchet voronezhskogo gubernskogo ekonomicheskogo soveshchaniia*, 33–34; *Otchet krymskogo narodnogo komissariata po prosveshcheniiu*, 18; Vasilevskii and Vasilevskii, *Kniga o golode*, 76; *Pravda Zakavkaz'ia* (Tiflis), 1922, no. 11 (May 14), p. 1; Mackenzie, *Russia Before Dawn*, 134 (regarding Buzuluk).

37. *Prosveshchenie* (Viatka), 1922, no. 2: 85; *Nash trud* (Iaroslavl'), 1924, nos. 11–12: 29–30; Vasilevskii and Vasilevskii, *Kniga o golode*, 77–78; Vasilevskii, *Detskaia "prestupnost'"*, 155; Makarenko, *Road to Life* 1:39, 52–55, 166–170, 200, 202–209; Livshits, *Sotsial'nye korni*, 124.

38. Makarenko, *Road to Life* 1:165–166.

39. TsGALI, f. 332, o. 1, ed. khr. 52, l. 42; *Sibirskii pedagogicheskii zhurnal* (Novo-Nikolaevsk), 1924, no. 3: 54; Artamonov, *Deti ulitsy*, 8; Livshits, *Sot-*

sial'nye korni, 116; Makarenko, *Road to Life* 1:98; Maro, *Besprizornye*, 260; Vasilevskii, *Detskaia "prestupnost'*," 153; *Turkestanskaia pravda* (Tashkent), 1923, no. 3 (January 4), p. 2.

40. For evidence of at least temporary demoralization among staff members at a number of institutions, see Livshits, *Sotsial'nye korni*, 116; Makarenko, *Road to Life* 1:38, 216–218; Maro, *Besprizornye*, 389.

41. *Vserossiiskoe obsledovanie*, 13, 37; *Na putiakh k novoi shkole*, 1923, no. 9: 41; Makarenko, *Road to Life* 1:40, 86, 88, 98–99, 127–129; Borovich, *Kollektivy besprizornykh*, 19–20, 24–27.

42. TsGALI, f. 332, o. 1, ed. khr. 52, ll. 1–2, 60, 169; Makarenko, *Road to Life* 1:29, 35–36, 247–248; *Detskaia defektivnost'*, 49.

43. *Sibirskii pedagogicheskii zhurnal* (Novo-Nikolaevsk), 1924, no. 3: 54; *Smolenskaia nov'* (Smolensk), 1922, nos. 7–8: 14; Kalinina, *Desiat' let*, 38; Makarenko, *Road to Life* 1:248–250; *Detskaia defektivnost'*, 49, 59; Liublinskii, *Bor'ba*, 50, 278. In addition, many teachers and administrators of *detdoma* were ignorant of, or unsympathetic toward, the pedagogic methods and goals developed by Narkompros. See Kalinina, *Desiat' let*, 42, 48–49; Fitzpatrick, *Commissariat of Enlightenment*, 229.

44. *Nash trud* (Iaroslavl'), 1923, nos. 8–9: 57–59; *Pravda Zakavkaz'ia* (Tiflis), 1922, no. 17 (May 21), p. 4; *Turkestanskaia pravda* (Tashkent), 1923, no. 14 (January 19), p. 3; *Zaria Vostoka* (Tiflis), 1922, no. 6 (June 25), p. 3; Kalinina, *Desiat' let*, 42–46; *Besprizornye*, comp. Kaidanova, 39; *Vserossiiskoe obsledovanie*, 36; *Sibirskii pedagogicheskii zhurnal* (Novo-Nikolaevsk), 1924, no. 3: 54–57; TsGALI, f. 332, o. 1, ed. khr. 52, ll. 2–3; Maro, *Besprizornye*, 350–364; Shveitser and Shabalov, *Besprizornye*, 41–43.

45. Diushen, *Piat' let*, 177–205. Regarding the organization and involvement of children—not always with great success—in the daily household chores, field work, and discipline of other *detdoma*, see Livshits, *Sotsial'nye korni*, 116; *Sibirskii pedagogicheskii zhurnal* (Novo-Nikolaevsk), 1923, no. 3: 104–106; *Vserossiiskoe obsledovanie*, 18; Kalinina, *Desiat' let*, 40; Maro, *Besprizornye*, 376–378; *Na putiakh k novoi shkole*, 1923, no. 9: 41; Makarenko, *Road to Life* 1:233–241; *Pravda Zakavkaz'ia* (Tiflis), 1922, no. 17 (May 21), p. 4; Shveitser and Shabalov, *Besprizornye*, 73. For examples of comparatively successful circles and clubs at a number of institutions, see Shveitser and Shabalov, *Besprizornye*, 73–74; *Sibirskii pedagogicheskii zhurnal* (Novo-Nikolaevsk), 1923, no. 3: 102–103; Makarenko, *Road to Life* 1:107–108; Maro, *Besprizornye*, 379; *Vestnik prosveshcheniia*, 1923, no. 2: 115.

46. TsGA RSFSR, f. 1575, o. 10, ed. khr. 190, l. 1; Kufaev, "Iz opyta," 90; *Drug detei* (Khar'kov), 1926, no. 10: 4; Tizanov et al., *Detskaia besprizornost'*, 137. For slightly different figures, including an estimate that the country required an additional two hundred commissions in 1922, see Sokolov, *Detskaia besprizornost'*, 61–62; Vasilevskii, *Besprizornost'*, 91. By 1928 the number of commissions reached the neighborhood of five hundred; Kufaev, "Iz opyta," 91.

47. *Psikhiatriia, nevrologiia i eksperimental'naia psikhologiia* (Petrograd), 1922, *vypusk* 1, 99; Liublinskii, *Bor'ba*, 51–52. According to another source, the following numbers of children appeared before commissions in Moscow and Petrograd/Leningrad in 1922, 1923, and 1924 respectively: Moscow—8,069,

5,937, 5,399; Petrograd/Leningrad—4,098, 3,065, 3,978; see Tizanov et al., *Detskaia besprizornost'*, 140. A third work presents the following figures for Moscow commissions: 13,877 youths in 1921, 6,784 in 1922, and 4,591 in 1925; Ryndziunskii et al., *Pravovoe polozhenie* (1927), 83n.1. One reason for the discrepancies may be that some authors present figures based on the number of cases *sent* to commissions, in contrast to the number of cases actually decided in any given year. Also, it is not always clear whether data include those children whose cases were passed on to the courts.

48. Liublinskii, *Bor'ba*, 51; Kufaev, *Iunye pravonarushiteli* (1924), 94; Tizanov et al., *Detskaia besprizornost'*, 139. For data on the number of cases handled by commissions in many different provinces, see Kufaev, *Iunye pravonarushiteli* (1924), 100–101; *Narodnoe obrazovanie v R.S.F.S.R.*, 126–159. A more recent work maintains that the number of children processed by commissions jumped to 75,100 in 1925—largely as a result of better record keeping by commissions and a more effective struggle against juvenile crime and hooliganism; see Min'kovskii, "Osnovnye etapy," 48.

49. Astemirov, "Iz istorii," 253; Ryndziunskii and Savinskaia, *Pravovoe polozhenie* (1923), 54–55; E. V. Boldyrev, *Mery preduprezhdeniia pravonarushenii nesovershennoletnikh v SSSR* (Moscow, 1964), 16; *SU*, 1920, no. 13, art. 83.

50. *SU*, 1922, no. 15, art. 153; no. 20/21, art. 230; Ryndziunskii et al., *Pravovoe polozhenie* (1927), 77, 80; Boldyrev, *Mery preduprezhdeniia*, 18–19.

51. Ryndziunskii and Savinskaia, *Pravovoe polozhenie* (1923), 56–57; Ryndziunskii et al., *Pravovoe polozhenie* (1927), 77.

52. TsGA RSFSR, f. 298, o. 1, ed. khr. 45, l. 23; *Detskaia besprizornost'*, 48–49; *SU*, 1923, no. 48, art. 479; Ryndziunskii et al., *Pravovoe polozhenie* (1927), 77.

53. TsGA RSFSR, f. 2306, o. 13, ed. khr. 11, l. 43; Ryndziunskii and Savinskaia, *Detskoe pravo*, 243; Liublinskii, *Bor'ba*, 181; Kalinina, *Desiat' let*, 34, 56; Vasilevskii, *Detskaia "prestupnost'*," 89–90.

54. TsGA RSFSR, f. 1575, o. 10, ed. khr. 178, l. 22; *Shkola i zhizn'* (Nizhnii Novgorod), 1925, nos. 9–10: 91; Krasnushkin et al., *Nishchenstvo i besprizornost'*, 135; *Narodnoe prosveshchenie v R.S.F.S.R. k 1924/25 uchebnomu godu*, 88–89.

55. Statistics in other sources covering the country as a whole are in line with those presented in table 2. Naturally, practices varied from city to city, depending on many factors, including the availability of children's institutions and social workers. Where, for instance, the number of *besprizornye* and other delinquents far exceeded the capacity of facilities for "difficult" youths, local commissions were more likely to handle cases with discussions, reprimands, or by sending the offenders to any available relatives. Some also responded by transferring a larger than average percentage of cases to the courts. For additional data on the measures adopted by commissions in the Russian Republic and individual cities (Moscow, Petrograd, Vladikavkaz, Tver', Simferopol', Barnaul, and Vitebsk), see Liublinskii, *Bor'ba*, 50–52; V. I. Kufaev, *Bor'ba s pravonarusheniiami nesovershennoletnikh* (Moscow, 1924), 18, 25–26; *Psikhiatriia, nevrologiia i eksperimental'naia psikhologiia* (Petrograd), 1922, *vypusk* 1,

100; *Otchet gorskogo ekonomicheskogo soveshchaniia* (1922), 255; *Otchet tverskogo gubernskogo ekonomicheskogo soveshchaniia sovetu truda i oborony. No. 1 (iiul'–sentiabr')* (Tver', 1921), 71; *Otchet krymskogo narodnogo komissariata po prosveshcheniiu*, 19; TsGA RSFSR, f. 1575, o. 6, ed. khr. 101, ll. 1, 7, 9, 11, 13, 21–25; ibid., ed. khr. 105, ll. 1–6, 9–14. During the remainder of the decade as well, commissions concluded between 40 and 50 percent of their cases with either a conversation/reprimand or the child's dispatch to relatives. For data (roughly similar to that in table 2) on measures adopted by commissions through 1929, see Ryndziunskii et al., *Pravovoe polozhenie* (1927), 84; *Narodnoe prosveshchenie v RSFSR 1927–28 god* (Moscow, 1929), 180–181; Kufaev, *Iunye pravonarushiteli* (1929), 28; Kufaev, "Iz opyta," 97.

56. *Vtoroi otchet irkutskogo gubernskogo ekonomicheskogo soveshchaniia (oktiabr' 1921 g.–mart 1922 g.)* (Irkutsk, 1922), 119; Vasilevskii, *Detskaia "prestupnost'*,*"* 121; *Otchet gorskogo ekonomicheskogo soveshchaniia* (1922), 255; *Vtoroi otchet tverskogo gubernskogo ekonomicheskogo soveshchaniia sovetu truda i oborony (oktiabr' 1921 g.–mart 1922 g.)* (Tver', 1922), 53; *Otchet cherepovetskogo gubernskogo ispolnitel'nogo komiteta*, 100; *Otchet stavropol'skogo gubekonomsoveshchaniia sovetu truda i oborony za aprel'–sentiabr' 1922 g.* (Stavropol', 1923), 34; Tizanov et al., *Detskaia besprizornost'*, 133; TsGA RSFSR, f. 1575, o. 10, ed. khr. 178, l. 11. The Children's Social Inspection was also far understaffed (or did not exist at all) in many parts of the country; see TsGA RSFSR, f. 1575, o. 6, ed. khr. 147, ll. 4, 6–7; *Otchet o sostoianii narodnogo obrazovaniia v eniseiskoi gubernii*, 17; Vasilevskii, *Besprizornost'*, 88; Liublinskii, *Bor'ba*, 187; *Vtoroi otchet voronezhskogo gubernskogo ekonomicheskogo soveshchaniia*, 34. The shortage of *obsledovateli-vospitateli* continued to hinder the work of commissions in the middle and later years of the decade; see TsGA RSFSR, f. 1575, o. 10, ed. khr. 190, l. 1; Kufaev, *Pedagogicheskie mery*, 34; Poznyshev, *Detskaia besprizornost'*, 75; *Narodnoe prosveshchenie v R.S.F.S.R. k 1925/26 uchebnomu godu*, 70; Tizanov et al., *Detskaia besprizornost'*, 132–133; *Shkola i zhizn'* (Nizhnii Novgorod), 1927, no. 11: 10.

57. TsGA RSFSR, f. 1575, o. 10, ed. khr. 193, l. 5; Vasilevskii, *Detskaia "prestupnost'*,*"* 79, 82–83; *Otchet o sostoianii narodnogo obrazovaniia v eniseiskoi gubernii*, 17; Tizanov et al., *Detskaia besprizornost'*, 138; *Ezhenedel'nik sovetskoi iustitsii*, 1925, nos. 44–45: 1366.

58. Province-level commissions met, on average, between two and eight times each month, while district-level commissions typically convened not more than four times a month. Regarding the frequency of commission meetings around the country, see TsGA RSFSR, f. 1575, o. 6, ed. khr. 101, ll. 1, 7, 9, 11, 13, 21–25; ibid., ed. khr. 105, ll. 1–6, 9–14; Tizanov et al., *Detskaia besprizornost'*, 138; *Otchet gorskogo ekonomicheskogo soveshchaniia* (1922), 255; Magul'iano, "K voprosu o detskoi prestupnosti," 209.

59. TsGA RSFSR, f. 1575, o. 10, ed. khr. 178, l. 3; *Vserossiiskoe obsledovanie*, 18, 32; Vasilevskii, *Besprizornost'*, 82.

60. *Otchet cherepovetskogo gubernskogo ispolnitel'nogo komiteta*, 100; *Smolenskaia nov'* (Smolensk), 1922, no. 6: 11; nos. 7–8: 32; *Kommunistka*,

1921, nos. 14–15: 7; Kalinina, *Desiat' let*, 34, 36; Vasilevskii, *Detskaia "prestupnost'*," 85, 88; Kufaev, "Iz opyta," 98.

61. Institutions of this sort occasionally bore the title of reformatory (*reformatoriia* or *reformatorium*), especially in Ukraine. See the previous chapter for more on the role envisioned for labor homes.

62. Liublinskii, *Bor'ba*, 52; TsGA RSFSR, f. 298, o. 1, ed. khr. 45, l. 23; Ryndziunskii and Savinskaia, *Pravovoe polozhenie* (1923), 61–62; Vasilevskii, *Detskaia "prestupnost'*," 156–157; Min'kovskii, "Osnovnye etapy," 46; Astemirov, "Iz istorii," 257–258; *Administrativnyi vestnik*, 1926, no. 12: 38. Data in some sources differ slightly. In the middle of the decade, for instance, one author lists six labor homes, with a total capacity of 858 youths, in or near Moscow, Nizhnii Novgorod, Petrograd, Saratov, Tomsk, and Verkhotur'e; Poznyshev, *Detskaia besprizornost'*, 113. Such differences should not obscure the conclusion that these institutions existed in minuscule numbers. On rare occasions, Juvenile Affairs Commissions themselves sent offenders directly to labor homes. See for example *Vtoroi otchet irkutskogo gubernskogo ekonomicheskogo soveshchaniia*, 119.

63. Ryndziunskii and Savinskaia, *Pravovoe polozhenie* (1923), 62–63; Liublinskii, *Bor'ba*, 52; Vasilevskii, *Detskaia "prestupnost'*," 156; Sokolov, *Spasite detei!* 52; *Vserossiiskoe obsledovanie*, 9; TsGAOR, f. 5207, o. 1, ed. khr. 63, l. 2; Maro, *Besprizornye*, 182; Juviler, "Contradictions," 272; Astemirov, "Iz istorii," 257. In Kursk province Juvenile Affairs Commissions, lacking facilities in which to hold children while preparing to hear their cases, sought to place some temporarily in prisons (in rooms supposedly free of exposure to adult inmates); see *Narodnoe prosveshchenie* (Kursk), 1922, nos. 3–4: 80. For an autobiographical sketch of a youth caught breaking into a house and sentenced (together with two young companions) to a year in prison, see TsGALI, f. 332, o. 1, ed. khr. 55, l. 12. In 1921, juveniles, including those in labor homes, accounted for 1.1 percent of the Russian Republic's total prison population, a share that rose to 1.4 percent in 1922. Data for Moscow province alone provide a figure of 7.9 percent in 1921. See *Detskaia besprizornost'*, 46; Ryndziunskii and Savinskaia, *Pravovoe polozhenie* (1923), 62; Manns, *Bor'ba*, 12.

64. Kufaev, *Bor'ba*, 11; *Vserossiiskoe obsledovanie*, 12; *Detskaia besprizornost'*, 48. Books, articles, and reports (presented at meetings devoted to the struggle with *besprizornost'* and delinquency) often condemned the placement of juveniles in regular prisons and urged that they be removed to an expanded network of labor homes and similar institutions. For a sampling, see TsGA RSFSR, f. 2306, o. 13, ed. khr. 11, ll. 42–43; Poznyshev, *Detskaia besprizornost'*, 131; *Detskaia defektivnost'*, 43. Juveniles were supposed to receive sentences at least one-third shorter than those imposed on adults imprisoned for similar crimes. For details on sentencing procedures for juvenile delinquents and information on the lengths of sentences, see Ryndziunskii and Savinskaia, *Pravovoe polozhenie* (1923), 58–59; Liublinskii, *Bor'ba*, 53; Gernet, *Prestupnyi mir*, 212.

65. Sokolov, *Detskaia besprizornost'*, 27; Vasilevskii, *Besprizornost'*, 30–31.

66. Livshits, *Sotsial'nye korni*, 187; Tizanov et al., *Detskaia besprizornost'*, 152; Vasilevskii, *Besprizornost'*, 30; Sokolov, *Detskaia besprizornost'*, 26;

Maro, *Besprizornye*, 178; *Molot* (Rostov-on-the-Don), 1925, no. 1144 (May 30), p. 5.

67. *Administrativnyi vestnik*, 1926, no. 12: 37–38; Maro, *Besprizornye*, 181, 183, 207 (for the verse). These considerations prompted Maro to argue (p. 230) that "the imprisonment of youth in Soviet Russia is a direct blow against the achievements of October." For an autobiographical sketch of a *besprizornyi* turned back onto the street after serving time in prison, see TsGALI, f. 332, o. 1, ed. khr. 55, l. 12. One author contended that the serious problem of juvenile crime in the middle of the decade could be explained in large part by the activities of numerous youths, imprisoned for lesser offenses in earlier years, who had now graduated back onto the street from prison academies of crime; see *Administrativnyi vestnik*, 1926, no. 12: 38.

68. *Vestnik prosveshchentsa* (Orenburg), 1926, no. 2: 23–24; *Gor'kaia pravda*, 24; *Biulleten' tsentral'noi komissii pomoshchi golodaiushchim VTsIK*, 1921, no. 2: 37; *Statisticheskii spravochnik*, 13.

69. TsGAOR, f. 5207, o. 1, ed. khr. 61, l. 97; *Golod i deti*, 39; *Prosveshchenie na transporte*, 1922, no. 2: 24; Krasnushkin et al., *Nishchenstvo i besprizornost'*, 144; *Vserossiiskoe obsledovanie*, 13, 24; *Na putiakh k novoi shkole*, 1924, nos. 7–8: 45; Tizanov et al., *Detskaia besprizornost'*, 183; Tizanov and Epshtein, *Gosudarstvo i obshchestvennost'*, 35–36; *Prosveshchenie na Urale* (Sverdlovsk), 1927, no. 2: 60. Narkompros itself, along with other agencies, instructed local administrators of children's institutions (who had little choice in any event) to shift their focus from providing an upbringing to saving as many lives as possible. *Biulleten' tsentral'noi komissii pomoshchi golodaiushchim VTsIK*, 1921, no. 2: 37; *Gor'kaia pravda*, 23; TsGAOR, f. 5207, o. 1, ed. khr. 47, l. 10.

70. *Vestnik prosveshcheniia*, 1923, no. 2: 76.

6. FLORISTS AND PROFESSORS

1. *Bor'ba s besprizornost'iu*, 3, 18; *Narodnoe prosveshchenie v R.S.F.S.R. k 1924/25 uchebnomu godu*, 78; *Narodnoe prosveshchenie v R.S.F.S.R. k 1925/26 uchebnomu godu*, 63; *Vestnik prosveshcheniia*, 1924, no. 12: 30; Sokolov, *Detskaia besprizornost'*, 4; *Na pomoshch' rebenku*, 20–21, 32–33; TsGA RSFSR, f. 1575, o. 6, ed. khr. 155, ll. 5, 9–10 (for the slogans); *Deti posle goloda*, 8–9 (for the first quotation), 103–104; Maiakovskii, "Besprizorshchina," 170.

2. TsGA RSFSR, f. 1575, o. 6, ed. khr. 155, ll. 5, 9 (for the slogan); Ia. R. Gailis, ed., *V pomoshch' perepodgotovke rabotnikov sotsial'nogo vospitaniia*, 2d ed. (Moscow, 1924), 92; *Deti posle goloda*, 52; *Na putiakh k novoi shkole*, no. 3 (May 1923): 76; *Na pomoshch' rebenku*, 8, 33; *Drug detei*, 1926, no. 2: 24.

3. TsGA RSFSR, f. 298, o. 1, ed. khr. 45, l. 93; TsGA RSFSR, f. 2306, o. 69, ed. khr. 51, l. 1; *Na putiakh k novoi shkole*, 1924, nos. 4–5: 186–187; nos. 7–8: 28, 42; Ryndziunskii et al., *Pravovoe polozhenie* (1927), 86; Tizanov et al., *Pedagogika*, 3–4; *Narodnoe prosveshchenie v R.S.F.S.R. k 1924/25 uchebnomu godu*, 79; Krupskaia, *Pedagogicheskie sochineniia* 3:122–123.

4. Livshits, *Sotsial'nye korni*, 115, 131; Vasilevskii, *Besprizornost'*, 84–85; *Na putiakh k novoi shkole*, no. 3 (May 1923): 59; 1923, no. 9: 41–54; 1924, nos. 4–5: 187.

5. Raymond A. Bauer, *The New Man in Soviet Psychology* (Cambridge, Mass., 1952), 38; Walter D. Connor, *Deviance in Soviet Society: Crime, Delinquency, and Alcoholism* (New York, 1972), 29–31.

6. *Na putiakh k novoi shkole*, 1924, no. 3: 91. *Pravda* ran a series of articles on the conference. For a brief description of the attack on the theory of "moral defectiveness," see *Pravda*, 1924, no. 64 (March 20), p. 4.

7. *Na putiakh k novoi shkole*, 1924, no. 3: 92; nos. 4–5: 187; 1925, no. 4: 141; *Bor'ba s besprizornost'iu*, 8, 43; Livshits, *Sotsial'nye korni*, 12–13, 99–100; Kalinina, *Desiat' let*, 89–90; *Krasnaia nov'*, 1932, no. 1: 39–42. By no means all who referred to *besprizornye* as "defective" meant to suggest that the youths became homeless and delinquent *because* of defects in their personalities. Numerous commentators who employed this terminology, especially in remarks before the controversy over "moral defectiveness" reached the boiling point in 1923–1924, assumed that *besprizornye* acquired their "defectiveness" from their environment *after* reaching the street. Some, including Lunacharskii in an address to the First All-Russian Congress of Participants in the Struggle with Juvenile Defectiveness, *Besprizornost'*, and Crime (in the summer of 1920), even maintained that if a "defective" child's environment were changed for the better, the "defectiveness" would disappear. Thus the term "moral defectiveness" did not always carry the meaning later claimed by its opponents. See *Detskaia defektivnost'*, 12–13. A number of authors sought middle ground, arguing that *both* a child's environment and his own predisposition (the proportions varied with the author) accounted for his antisocial acts. See for example Liublinskii, *Bor'ba*, 60–61; N. P. Grishakov, *Detskaia prestupnost' i bor'ba s neiu putem vospitaniia* (Orel, 1923), 15–16. For illustrations of the argument—vigorously rejected by the reformers—that many *besprizornye* were so poisoned by their experiences on the street that they could never be rehabilitated completely, see Sokolov, *Spasite detei!* 44 (a quotation from the Soviet newspaper *Trud*); Vasilevskii, *Besprizornost'*, 24. This view did not prevent Vasilevskii from voicing strong support (pp. 84–85) for those engaged in the assault on the theory of "moral defectiveness."

8. TsGA RSFSR, f. 2306, o. 69, ed. khr. 349, l. 3; *Bor'ba s besprizornost'iu*, 41–42 (for the Moscow conference's resolution); Kufaev, *Iunye pravonarushiteli* (1924), 135; Maro, *Besprizornye*, 6, 10, 226; Maro [M. I. Levitina], *Rabota s besprizornymi. Praktika novoi raboty v SSSR* (Khar'kov, 1924), 14–19; Livshits, *Detskaia besprizornost'*, 6–8; *Na putiakh k novoi shkole*, no. 3 (May 1923): 59, 174; 1924, no. 3: 89–90; *Vestnik prosveshcheniia*, 1924, nos. 4–6: 23; no. 9: 135–139. These beliefs also inspired claims that *besprizornye* had to be studied in their natural street habitat (rather than in clinics and other institutions) if one wished to understand them and their actions; see *Bor'ba s besprizornost'iu*, 43; Livshits, *Sotsial'nye korni*, 131; *Drug detei* (Khar'kov), 1926, no. 2: 16, 24; Borovich, *Kollektivy besprizornykh*, 42–43.

9. TsGA RSFSR, f. 1575, o. 6, ed. khr. 155, l. 9 (for the slogan); Poznyshev, *Detskaia besprizornost'*, 14; *Proletarskii sud*, 1923, no. 4: 15. Of course some

people, not only in Moscow but in the provinces as well, objected prior to 1923–1924 to the practice of labeling difficult children "defective" or criminal. For illustrations of such misgivings in the provinces, see *Prosveshchenie* (Riazan'), 1918, nos. 2–3: 87; *Izvestiia otdela narodnogo obrazovaniia* (Petrozavodsk), 1918, nos. 4–5: 121; *Vestnik prosveshcheniia i kommunisticheskoi kul'tury* (Tashkent), 1921, nos. 7–8: 7.

10. *Narodnoe prosveshchenie*, 1924, nos. 4–5: 164–166, 174–175; *Put' prosveshcheniia* (Khar'kov), 1924, no. 3: 53; *Bor'ba s besprizornost'iu*, 41; Livshits, *Sotsial'nye korni*, 143; *Na putiakh k novoi shkole*, 1924, no. 3: 89, 91; nos. 4–5: 188–189; nos. 7–8: 35, 46–47; Maro, *Besprizornye*, 42, 228; Kaidanova, *Besprizornye deti*, 20; Shveitser and Shabalov, *Besprizornye*, 6–7 (for the quotation).

11. *Na putiakh k novoi shkole*, 1924, no. 3: 88–89.

12. Livshits, *Detskaia besprizornost'*, 15–16 (includes quotation); Shveitser and Shabalov, *Besprizornye*, 6; Vasilevskii, *Besprizornost'*, 93.

13. *Na putiakh k novoi shkole*, no. 3 (May 1923): 67; 1924, nos. 4–5: 187; nos. 7–8: 39, 141; 1927, no. 2: 85; Shveitser and Shabalov, *Besprizornye*, 7, 18, 87–90; Livshits, *Sotsial'nye korni*, 102–103, 116; *Vserossiiskoe obsledovanie*, 15, 36; Sokolov, *Spasite detei!* 51. Personnel in some *detdoma* were quick to regard rude, peevish, and other difficult children as "defective" and transfer them out of the institutions; see *Na putiakh k novoi shkole*, no. 3 (May 1923): 78; 1924, nos. 7–8: 29. For an indication that agreement on proper disciplinary measures had not been reached during the middle years of the decade, see *Vestnik prosveshcheniia*, 1928, no. 3: 8. Anton Makarenko employed stricter discipline and punishment in his colony for *besprizornye* than many in Narkompros considered appropriate, which exposed him to frequent criticism and reprimands throughout the 1920s—until he left his Gorky colony at the end of the decade to administer a children's institution sponsored by the secret police. For more on the criticism leveled at Makarenko, and his own views on discipline, see *Voprosy izucheniia i vospitaniia lichnosti* (Leningrad), 1928, no. 2: 44–45; James Bowen, *Soviet Education: Anton Makarenko and the Years of Experiment* (Madison, Wis., 1962; reprint, 1965), 136, 202; Makarenko, *Road to Life* 1:41, 43–44, 157–158; 2:360. Regarding contemporary colonies for juvenile delinquents, see *Moscow News*, 1990, no. 30: 8–9; *Current Digest of the Soviet Press*, 1988, no. 9: 17–18; no. 51: 25.

14. Livshits, *Sotsial'nye korni*, 107–108, 114; Maro, *Besprizornye*, 229; *Na putiakh k novoi shkole*, 1925, no. 4: 139–140; 1927, no. 2: 81; *Put' prosveshcheniia* (Khar'kov), 1924, no. 3: 55.

15. TsGA RSFSR, f. 298, o. 2, ed. khr. 58, l. 10. A decree from the All-Russian Central Executive Committee and the Council of People's Commissars, issued in November 1925, permitted provincial officials to reserve a few spaces in *detdoma* for youths whose parents (workers, peasants, or officials) paid for their children's support in the institutions. These *platnye* spaces were not to exceed 10 percent of the number of free places in any *detdom*. See *SU*, 1925, no. 76, art. 589. It is not known how many *detdoma* adopted this practice, or how many parents sought to place their children in such facilities for an upbringing among *besprizornye*.

16. For a sampling of instructions on the proper operation of *detdoma*, see TsGA RSFSR, f. 298, o. 2, ed. khr. 58, ll. 10–12; Tizanov et al., *Pedagogika* (250 pages, issued by Glavsotsvos, on the organization and operation of *detdoma*); *Detskii dom*, comp. Utevskii, 13–14; *Prosveshchenie na transporte*, 1925, no. 9: 32–38; *Sibirskii pedagogicheskii zhurnal* (Novo-Nikolaevsk), 1925, no. 2: 24–42; *Voprosy prosveshcheniia* (Rostov-on-the-Don), 1926, nos. 6–7: 50–60. Conferences of *detdom* personnel were held in Moscow and the provinces to explain and discuss the "new methods of work"; see for example *Na putiakh k novoi shkole*, 1925, no. 3: 199; no. 4: 146.

 17. TsGA RSFSR, f. 298, o. 2, ed. khr. 58, l. 11; Ryndziunskii et al., *Pravovoe polozhenie* (1927), 86–87; Livshits, *Sotsial'nye korni*, 7; *Na putiakh k novoi shkole*, 1924, nos. 4–5: 189–190; nos. 7–8: 44; 1927, no. 2: 83; Shveitser and Shabalov, *Besprizornye*, 9.

18. *Narodnoe prosveshchenie v R.S.F.S.R. k 1925/26 uchebnomu godu*, 67; *Detskii dom*, comp. Utevskii, 14; Ryndziunskii et al., *Pravovoe polozhenie* (1927), 97; *Na putiakh k novoi shkole*, 1924, nos. 7–8: 43–44; Tizanov et al., *Detskaia besprizornost'*, 192; *Drug detei* (Khar'kov), 1926, no. 3: 32; *Shkola i zhizn'* (Nizhnii Novgorod), 1926, no. 11: 34. Other benefits said to follow from the transfer of schools out of *detdoma* included a reduction in the operating expenses of *detdoma* and access to better-equipped schools outside the institutions.

19. Tizanov et al., *Pedagogika*, 37–53; Tizanov et al., *Detskaia besprizornost'*, 184; *Na putiakh k novoi shkole*, 1924, nos. 7–8: 44; 1927, no. 2: 86; Smolensk Archive, reel 45, WKP 402, p. 17 (on reorganizing *detdoma* along Pioneer lines). For a detailed description of a summer excursion undertaken by children from a Saratov receiver to a camp in the countryside, see *Na putiakh k novoi shkole*, 1924, no. 9: 79–90. The receiver had come to resemble a *detdom* in that children remained there for extended periods. While at the camp, Pioneer and circle activity occupied a good deal of the youths' time.

20. TsGA RSFSR, f. 298, o. 1, ed. khr. 45, l. 94; *Na putiakh k novoi shkole*, 1927, no. 2: 81–82, 85–87; Shveitser and Shabalov, *Besprizornye*, 14, 136–137. Regarding Narkompros's desire for "self-government" in Soviet schools in general, see Stolee, "Generation," 110, 118, 176; Sheila Fitzpatrick, *Education and Social Mobility in the Soviet Union, 1921–1934* (Cambridge, 1979), 27; Bauer, *New Man*, 43. Teachers often ignored the policy or twisted it to enhance their control of the students; see Larry E. Holmes, "Soviet Schools: Policy Pursues Practice, 1921–1928," *Slavic Review* 48 (Summer 1989): 238.

21. TsGA RSFSR, f. 298, o. 1, ed. khr. 45, l. 93; *SU*, 1925, no. 48, art. 364; Kufaev, *Pedagogicheskie mery*, 135; Shveitser and Shabalov, *Besprizornye*, 15, 91, 118, 122; *Na putiakh k novoi shkole*, 1924, nos. 7–8: 43; Tizanov et al., *Detskaia besprizornost'*, 189. Training in workshops was to be coordinated with classroom education. Measuring, counting, and record keeping in a workshop, for example, were also opportunities for a child to develop skills taught in the classroom. For more information on the guidelines presented by reformers—including detailed plans of instruction for carpentry and leatherworking shops and a model daily schedule—see Shveitser and Shabalov, *Besprizornye*, 109–112, 118, 120, 146–165. A good deal of controversy was sparked by the

question of whether youths should receive any of the money realized by the sale of goods they produced. Wages and other payments were variously described as a corrupting influence on the children and a means to motivate them. For an array of views, see TsGA RSFSR, f. 2306, o. 69, ed. khr. 349, l. 15; *Na putiakh k novoi shkole*, 1926, nos. 5–6: 53; 1927, no. 2: 86; Makarenko, *Road to Life* 2:369–370; Shveitser and Shabalov, *Besprizornye*, 85–92, 108.

22. Bukharin and Preobrazhenskii, *ABC of Communism*, 237; Sheila Fitzpatrick, ed., *Cultural Revolution in Russia, 1928–1931* (Bloomington, Ind., 1984), 83–84; Bauer, *New Man*, 44–45; Bowen, *Soviet Education*, 31–32. For more on the new curriculum, known as the "complex method," see Stolee, "Generation," 152–155; Bowen, *Soviet Education*, 139–140; Fitzpatrick, *Education and Social Mobility*, 19–20; Holmes, "Soviet Schools," 235–236; *Shkola i zhizn'* (Nizhnii Novgorod), 1924, no. 9: 14–87. The reforms were often misunderstood, disliked, and/or ignored by teachers in the field; see Fitzpatrick, *Education and Social Mobility*, 20–21, 34–35; Holmes, "Soviet Schools," 237–240. The educational reforms desired by Narkompros in the early postrevolutionary years were largely reversed or abandoned at the decade's turn; Stolee, "Generation," 190; Fitzpatrick, *Cultural Revolution*, 99–104.

23. Quoted in Stolee, "Generation," 146.

24. Liublinskii, *Bor'ba*, 278–279; Kalinina, *Desiat' let*, 41; *Vserossiiskoe obsledovanie*, 10; *Otchet o sostoianii narodnogo obrazovaniia v eniseiskoi gubernii*, 16; Livshits, *Sotsial'nye korni*, 118; *Na putiakh k novoi shkole*, no. 3 (May 1923): 81; 1924, nos. 7–8: 43; Shveitser and Shabalov, *Besprizornye*, 15. Narkompros instructed local officials to combine petty workshops of individual *detdoma* into larger, better-equipped, regional workshops to which institutions throughout the area could send children for labor training; see Ryndziunskii et al., *Pravovoe polozhenie* (1927), 97. Little progress appears to have been made in this direction except in a few provinces where local budgets were comparatively robust; Tizanov et al., *Detskaia besprizornost'*, 190.

25. Livshits, *Sotsial'nye korni*, 102–197; *Na putiakh k novoi shkole*, 1925, no. 4: 141–142.

26. *Na putiakh k novoi shkole*, 1927, no. 2: 78; Livshits, *Sotsial'nye korni*, 13–14; Tizanov et al., *Pedagogika*, 21; Poznyshev, *Detskaia besprizornost'*, 114–115 (for the quotations); *Pravda*, 1927, no. 112 (May 20), p. 5. Nikolai Semashko, the commissar of health, argued that *besprizornye* should be rounded up and placed in special colonies with a "strict labor regime, guarantees against escape, and so on"; *Izvestiia*, 1925, no. 201 (September 4), p. 5. See also his article in *Izvestiia*, 1927, no. 109 (May 15), p. 5. For more on the continuing swirl of disagreement over these issues, see Juviler, "Contradictions," 271–273.

27. TsGA RSFSR, f. 298, o. 1, ed. khr. 45, l. 94; TsGA RSFSR, f. 2306, o. 69, ed. khr. 51, l. 1.

28. *Molot* (Rostov-on-the-Don), 1925, no. 1266 (October 22), p. 5; *Drug detei* (Khar'kov), 1925, no. 6: 30; Kaidanova, *Besprizornye deti*, 60; Livshits, *Sotsial'nye korni*, 167; *Prosveshchenie na Urale* (Sverdlovsk), 1927, no. 2: 61; Krasnushkin et al., *Nishchenstvo i besprizornost'*, 146. Shortly before the October Revolution, a Provisional Government ministry advocated the establishment of similar institutions; American Red Cross, box 866, file 948.08 ("Com-

mission to Russia [First], Billings Report, Oct. 22, 1917"), Appendix to "Report of the Committee on Child Welfare," August 28/September 10, 1917. A handful of *nochlezhki* for *besprizornye* appear to have functioned in the years immediately following the Revolution. See *Drug detei* (Khar'kov), 1925, no. 2: 22–26, for a description of a *nochlezhka* in Ekaterinoslav in 1918. In most cities, however, *nochlezhki* materialized in 1923–1924 as institutions new not only in name but also in purpose.

29. Tizanov et al., *Detskaia besprizornost'*, 175–176; Maro, *Besprizornye*, 390; *Drug detei*, 1926, no. 4: 7; *Na putiakh k novoi shkole*, 1926, no. 4: 70; no. 11: 67–68; 1927, no. 2: 78–79. Some authors referred to a *nochlezhka* as a *dom bez dverei* or a *dom otkrytykh dverei*; see for example *Na putiakh k novoi shkole*, 1924, nos. 7–8: 49; *Volna* (Arkhangel'sk), 1925, no. 272 (December 1), p. 4.

30. *Na putiakh k novoi shkole*, 1924, nos. 4–5: 156–159; 1925, no. 6: 83–84; 1926, no. 4: 68–71; no. 11: 67–76; 1927, no. 2: 79–80. A daytime division of a *nochlezhka* was usually known as a *dom dnevnogo prebyvaniia* or a *dnevnoi dom*.

31. *Drug detei* (Khar'kov), 1925, no. 6: 32–33 (for the study); *Na putiakh k novoi shkole*, 1924, nos. 7–8: 49; *Drug detei*, 1925, no. 2: 21.

32. *Moskovskii meditsinskii zhurnal*, 1925, no. 10: 59; *Drug detei* (Khar'kov), 1925, no. 2: 27–29; no. 6: 30, 33; 1927, no. 2: 29; Kaidanova, *Besprizornye deti*, 60; Livshits, *Sotsial'nye korni*, 138, 167; *Drug detei*, 1925, no. 2: 11; *Na putiakh k novoi shkole*, 1925, no. 6: 82–83; *Bor'ba s besprizornost'iu*, 32; *Pomoshch' detiam*, 30; *Sibirskii pedagogicheskii zhurnal* (Novo-Nikolaevsk), 1925, no. 2: 70.

33. Livshits, *Sotsial'nye korni*, 137.

34. For data from *nochlezhki* in Moscow and Odessa, see *Drug detei* (Khar'kov), 1925, no. 5: 43; *Drug detei*, 1926, no. 4: 5; Tizanov et al., *Detskaia besprizornost'*, 176. For a description of a *nochlezhka* that began operation in very poor condition but thereafter improved gradually, see *Sibirskii pedagogicheskii zhurnal* (Novo-Nikolaevsk), 1925, no. 2: 70–72. Of course the passage of time by no means eliminated all squalid *nochlezhki*. At the end of the decade a group of youths, intoxicated with alcohol and hashish, went on a rampage in a *nochlezhka*, beating several of the other inhabitants. When the police were called, the young hooligans barricaded themselves in a room and greeted their besiegers with bricks, sticks, and anything else at hand. See *Detskii dom*, 1929, no. 4: 73.

35. For more on playgrounds (*ploshchadki*), see L. I. Chulitskaia-Tikheeva, *Doshkol'nyi vozrast i ego osobennosti* (Moscow, 1923), 92; *Detskii dom*, 1928, no. 1: 42–44; no. 3: 17–22; Glatman, *Pionery i besprizornye*, 52–54, 58–59; Ryndziunskii et al., *Pravovoe polozhenie* (1927), 98; *Drug detei* (Khar'kov), 1926, no. 3: 41; *Besprizornye*, comp. Kaidanova, 51–57; TsGA RSFSR, f. 298, o. 1, ed. khr. 45, l. 94; *Drug detei*, 1926, no. 4: 3; *Rabochaia moskva*, 1924, no. 107 (May 14), p. 7. Clubs and cafeterias were also set up in some cities to entice *besprizornye* off the street temporarily; see Ryndziunskii et al., *Pravovoe polozhenie* (1927), 98; *Drug detei* (Khar'kov), 1925, no. 1: 34–36; no. 9: 49–50; TsGA RSFSR, f. 298, o. 1, ed. khr. 45, l. 94; *Na pomoshch' detiam. Ob-*

shchestvenno-literaturnyi i nauchnyi sbornik, 61; Maro, *Besprizornye*, 382–387.

36. Livshits, *Detskaia besprizornost'*, 22; *Detskii dom*, comp. Utevskii, 11–12; *Na putiakh k novoi shkole*, 1924, nos. 7–8: 133; *Krasnaia nov'*, 1932, no. 1: 42. A handful of children's institutions had taken the name *trudovaia kommuna* as early as 1918–1920, though this did not necessarily mean that they shared all the features intended for labor communes in 1924. For references to pre-NEP and even prerevolutionary forerunners of the mid-1920s' labor communes, see TsGA RSFSR, f. 1575, o. 6, ed. khr. 4, ll. 136–137; N. V. Shishova, "Sozdanie sistemy detskikh uchrezhdenii dlia spaseniia besprizornykh detei na Donu i Kubano-Chernomor'ia v period vosstanovleniia narodnogo khoziaistva" (Rostov-on-the-Don, 1986; MS. 25907 at INION AN SSSR, Moscow), 8; Juviler, "Contradictions," 266, 268. In some documents and articles, an institution may be identified as a *trudovaia kommuna* and elsewhere in the text labeled a colony (*koloniia*) or even a new type of *detdom*; see for example *Na putiakh k novoi shkole*, 1925, no. 4: 146, 150; *Detskii dom*, comp. Utevskii, 4–5.

37. Shveitser and Shabalov, *Besprizornye*, 47, 180–181; *Na putiakh k novoi shkole*, 1924, nos. 7–8: 132; nos. 10–12: 85–86, 92; 1925, no. 4: 147; 1927, no. 2: 80; Livshits, *Sotsial'nye korni*, 186–187; *Drug detei*, 1926, no. 4: 8; Ryndziunskii et al., *Pravovoe polozhenie* (1927), 88, 96–97. Narkompros's regulations on *trudovye kommuny*, issued in 1925, stipulated that communes admit youths from twelve to sixteen years of age. Some institutions accepted adolescents as old as eighteen. See TsGA RSFSR, f. 298, o. 2, ed. khr. 58, l. 1; *Detskii dom*, comp. Utevskii, 14–15; *Na putiakh k novoi shkole*, 1924, nos. 7–8: 143; TsGALI, f. 332, o. 1, ed. khr. 52, l. 185. For a brief description of a *trudovaia kommuna* intended for younger children, see *Na putiakh k novoi shkole*, 1925, no. 4: 146–147.

38. *Na putiakh k novoi shkole*, 1924, nos. 7–8: 133; nos. 10–12: 92; 1925, no. 4: 149; Shveitser and Shabalov, *Besprizornye*, 60, 176; Kufaev, *Pedagogicheskie mery*, 148.

39. *Na putiakh k novoi shkole*, 1924, nos. 7–8: 133–134; nos. 10–12: 87–88. The second article also describes the similar recruitment to another labor commune of a group of *besprizornye* living in a railroad car at Moscow's Kursk Station.

40. Ryndziunskii et al., *Pravovoe polozhenie* (1927), 86–87; *Na putiakh k novoi shkole*, 1924, nos. 10–12: 86; *Detskii dom*, comp. Utevskii, 15–16. One often encountered the term "self-organization" (*samoorganizatsiia*) used together with, or in place of, "self-government" (*samoupravlenie*). According to Narkompros's regulations on labor communes, the director of a commune could block any decision of the general assembly that he or she regarded as illegal or clearly inexpedient. Such impasses were to be resolved by the local Narkompros office.

41. *Detskii dom*, comp. Utevskii, 12, 14–15; *Na putiakh k novoi shkole*, 1924, nos. 7–8: 133, 146; nos. 10–12: 87, 89–90; Ryndziunskii et al., *Pravovoe polozhenie* (1927), 86–87, 97; Shveitser and Shabalov, *Besprizornye*, 62; TsGA RSFSR, f. 298, o. 2, ed. khr. 58, l. 10; TsGALI, f. 332, o. 1, ed. khr. 52, l. 185. Some communes sought to operate self-sufficiently, producing everything they

needed or purchasing necessities with money earned through sales of goods manufactured in their own workshops. Such efforts appear to have failed sooner or later. In 1925, Narkompros instructed that communes not be established with the intent of meeting all their own needs. Funds were to come from subsidies (generally via the state) as well as from income generated by the commune's own enterprises and wages paid to commune youths who worked outside the institution. See Kalinina, *Desiat' let*, 92–93; TsGA RSFSR, f. 2306, o. 69, ed. khr. 349, l. 15; *Detskii dom*, comp. Utevskii, 16. In some communes, youths received a portion of the money they earned in wages or from the sale of goods they produced. Practices differed as to the size of this share and the degree of freedom the members had in disposing of it. In at least one institution they were allowed to purchase tobacco. Narkompros instructed communes in 1925 to accumulate a portion of these earnings in accounts for youths to receive on their discharge from the facilities. See *Na putiakh k novoi shkole*, 1924, nos. 7–8: 136; nos. 10–12: 90; *Detskii dom*, comp. Utevskii, 15; Shveitser and Shabalov, *Besprizornye*, 62–63.

42. On the appearance of *trudovye kommuny* in 1923–1924, see Kalinina, *Desiat' let*, 92–94; Livshits, *Sotsial'nye korni*, 175; *Na putiakh k novoi shkole*, 1924, nos. 7–8: 143; nos. 10–12: 85; Shveitser and Shabalov, *Besprizornye*, 60, 176.

43. Regarding Narkompros's regulations for labor communes, see TsGA RSFSR, f. 298, o. 2, ed. khr. 58, ll. 1–2; *Detskii dom*, comp. Utevskii, 14–16.

44. Richard Stites, *Revolutionary Dreams: Utopian Vision and Experimental Life in the Russian Revolution* (Oxford, 1989), 205–222.

45. Astemirov, "Iz istorii," 259–260; *Nesovershennoletnie pravonarushiteli*, 17–18; Min'kovskii, "Osnovnye etapy," 46; Pogrebinskii, *Fabrika liudei*, 3–9; *Detskii dom*, 1928, no. 1: 41n.; Juviler, "Contradictions," 268–269; Gerson, *Secret Police*, 127 (for the "baby farm" comment and the figure of thirty-five OGPU communes by 1928). Gerson's statement that the first OGPU commune opened at Bolshevo in 1925 is contradicted by other Western and Soviet sources—including Juviler, Pogrebinskii, and Astemirov—who place the event in 1924. E. Vatova writes that the first juveniles arrived at the Bolshevo commune on August 18, 1924; see Vatova, "Bolshevskaia trudovaia kommuna," 92. For more on Makarenko's Dzerzhinskii Commune, see TsGALI, f. 332, o. 2, ed. khr. 1–78; Makarenko, *Road to Life* 2:411–453; Juviler, "Contradictions," 267. The Commissariat of Labor also operated some labor communes; see *Nesovershennoletnie pravonarushiteli*, 18; Ryndziunskii and Savinskaia, *Detskoe pravo*, 262.

46. For references to, and descriptions of, labor communes that appeared to be enjoying some success, see *Prosveshchenie Sibiri* (Novosibirsk), 1927, no. 5: 61–62; 1928, no. 9: 72–73; *Komsomol'skaia pravda*, 1926, no. 29 (February 5), p. 3; Shveitser and Shabalov, *Besprizornye*, 48, 61; *Detskii dom*, 1929, no. 5: 86; no. 6: 21–22; Livshits, *Sotsial'nye korni*, 187–188; *Drug detei*, 1927, no. 2: 8; Tizanov et al., *Detskaia besprizornost'*, 172–173; *Na putiakh k novoi shkole*, 1924, nos. 7–8: 138; nos. 10–12: 86, 90; 1925, no. 4: 150–153; 1927, no. 2: 81; Kufaev, *Pedagogicheskie mery*, 148; Ryndziunskii and Savinskaia, *Detskoe pravo*, 262; *Pravda*, 1927, no. 97 (May 1), p. 3; TsGALI, f. 332, o. 2,

ed. khr. 29, l. 18. For indications of success in establishing "self-government," see *Na pomoshch' detiam. Obshchestvenno-literaturnyi i nauchnyi sbornik*, 30–31; *Na putiakh k novoi shkole*, 1924, nos. 7–8: 134–135; 1925, no. 4: 148, 151; Shveitser and Shabalov, *Besprizornye*, 63–64. Regarding the largely successful efforts of several communes to dissuade their members from fleeing, see *Na putiakh k novoi shkole*, 1924, nos. 7–8: 136–137, 139; nos. 10–12: 91; 1925, no. 4: 147; Shveitser and Shabalov, *Besprizornye*, 48; Kufaev, *Pedagogicheskie mery*, 148.

47. *Na putiakh k novoi shkole*, 1924, nos. 7–8: 134, 139–141; 1925, no. 4: 149–150, 153; no. 6: 84; Livshits, *Sotsial'nye korni*, 149–150; Shveitser and Shabalov, *Besprizornye*, 66. Some communes were also plagued by inadequate facilities and schooling; see *Na putiakh k novoi shkole*, 1925, no. 4: 158. Makarenko's commune was among those that experienced difficulties from time to time. For one set of problems, see TsGALI, f. 332, o. 2, ed. khr. 29, l. 16.

48. *Vozhatyi*, 1925, nos. 5–6: 8; Livshits, *Sotsial'nye korni*, 195; *Na putiakh k novoi shkole*, 1924, nos. 10–12: 88; *Drug detei* (Khar'kov), 1925, no. 9: 48; *Drug detei*, 1926, no. 4: 8 (for the article mentioned).

49. Astemirov, "Iz istorii," 260–261; *Na putiakh k novoi shkole*, 1924, no. 4: 156.

50. TsGA RSFSR, f. 298, o. 2, ed. khr. 58, l. 72 (regarding the comment at the State Scientific Council meeting); Shveitser and Shabalov, *Besprizornye*, 177.

51. See for example Ryndziunskii et al., *Pravovoe polozhenie* (1927), 86–87; *Detskii dom*, comp. Utevskii, 12.

52. *Besprizornye*, comp. Kaidanova, 63 (for the statistics). Nadezhda Krupskaia, in a retrospective gaze at the 1920s, noted that "labor communes never became particularly numerous"; *Detskii dom*, comp. Utevskii, 5.

53. Regarding the government's need for assistance from society in this endeavor, see *Na pomoshch' rebenku*, 6; *Drug detei* (Khar'kov), 1925, no. 9: 44; *Deti posle goloda*, 52; Sokolov, *Detskaia besprizornost'*, 62; *Na putiakh k novoi shkole*, 1926, no. 3: 23; Liublinskii, *Bor'ba*, 197–198; *Molot* (Rostov-on-the-Don), 1925, no. 1216 (August 25), p. 5; 1925, no. 1175 (July 7), p. 5; Krasnushkin et al., *Nishchenstvo i besprizornost'*, 149n. Calls for the greater involvement of society in the struggle with *besprizornost'* continued throughout the decade. See *Drug detei*, 1927, nos. 8–9: 17; *Na putiakh k novoi shkole*, 1927, no. 12: 73; *Sbornik deistvuiushchikh uzakonenii i rasporiazhenii* (1929), 6, 40, 191, 214, 238.

54. On the decline in assistance from various organizations in 1923, compared to 1921–1922, see *Drug detei* (Khar'kov), 1925, no. 5: 39; *Drug detei*, 1927, nos. 11–12: 1–2; *Put' prosveshcheniia* (Khar'kov), 1924, no. 3: 168.

55. *Deti posle goloda*, 51–52; *Na putiakh k novoi shkole*, no. 3 (May 1923): 59.

56. For assertions of inadequate involvement on the part of the Pioneers, Komsomol, and other segments of society in work with *besprizornye*, see Shveitser and Shabalov, *Besprizornye*, 133; Maro, *Besprizornye*, 380; *Sbornik deistvuiushchikh uzakonenii i rasporiazhenii* (1929), 219; *Deti posle goloda*, 52; Tizanov et al., *Detskaia besprizornost'*, 178–179; Kalinina, *Komsomol i besprizornost'*, 22–23. For a collection of stories, poems, and essays designed to

acquaint the public with the lives of *besprizornye* and thereby motivate citizens to participate in assisting the youths, see *Asfal'tovyi kotel*, 3 in particular. The title page indicates that all proceeds from the sale of the book would go to aid *besprizornye*.

57. *Izvestiia*, 1926, no. 47 (February 26), p. 5 (for the challenge issued by the authors); *Pravda*, 1926, no. 169 (July 25), p. 5 (regarding the opening of the labor commune, named the *Trudovaia kommuna besprizornykh im. chitatelei "Pravdy"*). The fund-raising column in *Izvestiia* appeared frequently from mid-February 1926 well into 1927. Narkompros asked provincial executive committees to direct newspapers in their regions to conduct campaigns similar to the one in *Pravda*. See Tizanov and Epshtein, *Gosudarstvo i obshchestvennost'*, 34. Many other newspapers solicited contributions from their readers to aid *besprizornye*; see for example *Leningradskaia pravda*, 1926, no. 73 (March 31), p. 2; *Volna* (Arkhangel'sk), 1926, no. 25 (January 31), p. 4; 1926, no. 28, (February 4), p. 2; 1926, no. 31 (February 7), p. 4; 1926, no. 34 (February 11), p. 4; 1926, no. 54 (March 7), p. 4; and several subsequent issues. For one of the numerous announcements that donations rather than wreaths had been received following Dzerzhinskii's death in 1926, see *Pravda*, 1926, no. 206 (September 8), p. 6.

58. A "Week of the Child" ("*Nedelia rebenka*") was held in the Russian Republic as early as November 1920 to engage the public in aiding children already institutionalized and to collect provisions for other starving youths in Moscow, Petrograd, and elsewhere; see *SU*, 1920, no. 86, art. 431; Krasnushkin et al., *Nishchenstvo i besprizornost'*, 139; Kalinina, *Desiat' let*, 46–47; *Vserossiiskoe obsledovanie*, 4. Similar "weeks" were also staged in some localities during the famine, though their results often proved disappointing, especially in stricken regions where much of the population possessed little to contribute. See for example *Prosveshchenie* (Krasnodar), 1921–1922, nos. 3–4: 153; *Prosveshchenie* (Viatka), 1922, no. 1: 21. These campaigns became more frequent by 1923–1924, and now almost invariably bore titles referring to the *besprizornye*. They continued throughout the decade and into the next. See TsGA RSFSR, f. 1575, o. 6, ed. khr. 156, l. 7; *Turkestanskaia pravda* (Tashkent), 1923, no. 11 (January 16), p. 2; *Pravda*, 1923, no. 94 (April 29), p. 4; 1923, no. 96 (May 3), p. 3; 1923, no. 97 (May 4), p. 1; 1923, no. 98 (May 5), p. 4; 1923, no. 99 (May 6), p. 3; 1923, no. 100 (May 8), p. 3; *Obzor deiatel'nosti*, 79; *Deti posle goloda*, 97; *Molot* (Rostov-on-the-Don), 1925, no. 1223 (September 12), p. 5; *Vestnik prosveshchentsa* (Orenburg), 1926, nos. 11–12: 86; *Drug detei* (Khar'kov), 1926, no. 1: 44; *Komsomol'skaia pravda*, 1927, no. 104 (May 11), p. 4; *Detskii dom*, 1929, no. 7: 72; 1930, no. 4: 63–65; *Prosveshchenie Sibiri* (Novosibirsk), 1927, no. 3: 102; 1928, no. 10: 46–47; 1929, no. 12: 11; 1932, no. 8: 59.

59. TsGA RSFSR, f. 1575, o. 6, ed. khr. 145, ll. 2–3; ibid., ed. khr. 151, ll. 1–7; *Vozhatyi*, 1924, no. 1: 32; *Deti posle goloda*, 116–117, 122–139; Glatman, *Pionery i besprizornye*, 33; *Na pomoshch' detiam* (Semipalatinsk, 1926), 10; *Volna* (Arkhangel'sk), 1926, nos. 97–98, (April 30–May 1), p. 6; Konius, *Puti razvitiia*, 146; Dzerzhinskii, *Izbrannye proizvedeniia* 1:321.

60. TsGA RSFSR, f. 1575, o. 6, ed. khr. 146, ll. 1–14; ibid., ed. khr. 151, l. 7; *Na pomoshch' rebenku*, 3–4; *Deti posle goloda*, 116–120; *Volna* (Arkhan-

gel'sk), 1926, no. 96 (April 29), p. 2; 1926, nos. 97–98 (April 30–May 1), p. 6; 1926, no. 235 (October 13), p. 2; 1926, no. 302 (December 31), p. 4; Tizanov et al., *Pedagogika*, 242; *Sibirskii pedagogicheskii zhurnal* (Novo-Nikolaevsk), 1925, no. 2: 70. For approximately two dozen slogans prepared for use in the "Week of the *Besprizornyi* and Ill Child" (April 30–May 6, 1923), see TsGA RSFSR, f. 1575, o. 6, ed. khr. 155, ll. 9–10; *Na pomoshch' rebenku*, 51–52.

61. *Molot* (Rostov-on-the-Don), 1926, no. 1383 (March 16), p. 5; 1926, no. 1399 (April 4), p. 3; *Volna* (Arkhangel'sk), 1926, no. 28 (February 4), p. 2; 1926, no. 279 (December 4), p. 2; *Drug detei* (Khar'kov), 1926, no. 1: 43; *Vozhatyi*, 1924, no. 1: 32; Tizanov et al., *Pedagogika*, 243; Makarenko, *Road to Life* 2:431; *Sbornik deistvuiushchikh uzakonenii i rasporiazhenii* (1929), 50. Numerous issues of *Komsomol'skaia pravda* for October and November 1927 contain articles on *subbotniki* (extra days of work without pay) organized by Komsomol units in order to raise money to combat *besprizornost'*.

62. *Narodnoe prosveshchenie*, 1926, no. 8: 66; N. V. Shishova, "Rol' obshchestvennosti v preodolenii detskoi besprizornosti na severnom Kavkaze v 1920–1926 gg."(Rostov-on-the-Don, 1979; MS. 4764 at INION AN SSSR, Moscow), 13–14; TsGA RSFSR, f. 1575, o. 6, ed. khr. 152, l. 5; *Sbornik deistvuiushchikh uzakonenii i rasporiazhenii* (1929), 51, 215; Maro, *Besprizornye*, 375.

63. *Drug detei* (Khar'kov), 1927, nos. 9–10: 23.

64. *Detskii dom i bor'ba s besprizornost'iu*, 16.

65. TsGA RSFSR, f. 1575, o. 6, ed. khr. 147, ll. 4, 6–7; *Drug detei* (Khar'kov), 1925, no. 4: 19, 21; 1926, nos. 6–7: 18; Sokolov, *Besprizornye deti*, 5–6; Tizanov et al., *Detskaia besprizornost'*, 171–172; *Drug detei*, 1926, no. 4: 7; *Detskoe pravo*, comp. Krichevskaia and Kuritskii, 444; Kalinina, *Desiat' let*, 86–87; Liublinskii, *Bor'ba*, 187, 201; *Detskaia besprizornost'*, 10–11; *Besprizornye*, comp. Kaidanova, 61; *Statisticheskii obzor narodnogo obrazovaniia v permskom okruge*, 39. Krupskaia reported in 1926 that "over two thousand students from pedagogic institutions" were working as volunteers with *besprizornye*; Krupskaia, *Pedagogicheskie sochineniia* 2:241. "Volunteers" also helped Narkompros respond to *besprizornost'* prior to 1924; see for example *Pravda*, 1924, no. 55 (March 7), p. 5; *Pravo i zhizn'*, 1925, nos. 4–5: 95–96. For more on the inadequate number of children's social inspectors in many regions, see *Shkola i zhizn'* (Nizhnii Novgorod), 1927, no. 10: 58; Kirsanov, *Rukovodstvo*, 21–22; *Narodnoe prosveshchenie v RSFSR k 1926/27 uchebnomu godu*, 59; TsGA RSFSR, f. 2306, o. 69, ed. khr. 349, l. 25.

66. TsGA RSFSR, f. 2306, o. 69, ed. khr. 349, l. 5; *Drug detei* (Khar'kov), 1925, no. 4: 19; no. 5: 37; 1926, no. 2: 27; *Besprizornye*, comp. Kaidanova, 61; *Vozhatyi*, 1924, no. 1: 32; *Drug detei*, 1928, no. 4: inside back cover; Kalinina, *Desiat' let*, 87; Sokolov, *Besprizornye deti*, 6–9; *Volna* (Arkhangel'sk), 1926, no. 46 (February 26), p. 1; Kufaev, *Iunye pravonarushiteli* (1929), 29. "Volunteers" also worked with former *besprizornye* in institutions; see, for example, Makarenko, *Road to Life* 1:254; *Na putiakh k novoi shkole*, 1924, nos. 7–8: 137–138; no. 9: 83, 89; 1925, no. 4: 149; *Na pomoshch' detiam. Obshchestvenno-literaturnyi i nauchnyi sbornik*, 28.

67. *Drug detei* (Khar'kov), 1925, no. 9: 52; 1926, no. 2: 27; *Pravda*, 1926, no. 292 (December 17), p. 6. Some college students, Pioneers, and others working to establish contact with *besprizornye* reported that it was virtually impossible to gain the confidence of hardened youths who had been on their own for years. Instead, these *druzhinniki* focused their attention on younger, less seasoned children, trying to divert them to institutions before they became deeply embedded in the underworld. See *Vecherniaia moskva*, 1924, no. 225 (October 1), p. 2; *Vozhatyi*, 1928, no. 12: 19.

68. *Drug detei* (Khar'kov), 1926, no. 1: 8, 10–11; no. 2: 40; Kalinina, *Desiat' let*, 83; *Vecherniaia moskva*, 1927, no. 75 (April 4), p. 2; *Pravda*, 1926, no. 68 (March 25), p. 1; *Drug detei*, 1927, nos. 6–7: 32; *Krasnaia gazeta* (Leningrad), evening ed., 1926, no. 242 (October 14), p. 3; 1926, no. 247 (October 20), p. 3; 1926, no. 274 (November 19), p. 3; *Izvestiia*, 1926, no. 73 (March 31), p. 4; 1927, no. 77 (April 5), p. 6.

69. *Pravda*, 1926, no. 68 (March 25), p. 1.

70. *Komsomol'skaia pravda*, 1925, no. 88 (September 8), p. 3; 1926, no. 241 (October 19), p. 2; *Asfal'tovyi kotel*, 229–234; *Krasnaia nov'*, 1932, no. 1: 39; *Pravda*, 1926, no. 68 (March 25), p. 1; *Drug detei* (Khar'kov), 1926, no. 1: 8–9; no. 2: 25; no. 3: 28; nos. 8–9: 18; 1927, no. 1: 6–7; nos. 7–8: 43; *Vecherniaia moskva*, 1927, no. 75 (April 4), p. 2; Enik and Blok, *Iz trushchob na stroiku*, 23. For literary descriptions of militiamen conducting roundups (*oblavy*) of *besprizornye*, see *Vchera i segodnia*, 136, 160; Kozhevnikov, *Stremka*, 16–24.

71. *Komsomol'skaia pravda*, 1925, no. 88 (September 8), p. 3; *Vecherniaia moskva*, 1927, no. 75 (April 4), p. 2; TsGALI, f. 332, o. 1, ed. khr. 55, l. 12; *Drug detei* (Khar'kov), 1926, no. 1: 8–11; no. 2: 25; no. 3: 28; nos. 8–9: 18; 1927, no. 1: 6–7; nos. 9–10: 2–3; Borovich, *Kollektivy besprizornykh*, 42; Maro, *Besprizornye*, 333; *Prosveshchenie na Urale* (Sverdlovsk), 1929, nos. 5–6: 89; *Drug detei*, 1927, no. 2: 16; nos. 6–7: 32; Enik and Blok, *Iz trushchob na stroiku*, 23, 25. As late as 1927, *Pravda* reported that a recent roundup of *besprizornye* netted 450; *Pravda*, 1927, no. 81 (April 10), p. 5. Some of the accounts cited above also indicated that many of the children apprehended soon found opportunities to escape.

72. On the genesis of ODD (whose cells existed under slightly different names in various locations), see *Narodnoe prosveshchenie*, 1926, no. 8: 65; *Spasennye revoliutsiei*, 68; *Detskoe pravo*, comp. Krichevskaia and Kuritskii, 22–23. N. V. Shishova claims that Rostov-on-the-Don was the first city to follow Moscow's example in establishing an ODD chapter in December 1923; see Shishova, "Rol' obshchestvennosti," 5–6. For figures on the expansion of the ODD network in the 1920s, see *Drug detei*, 1925, no. 1: 5; Krasnushkin et al., *Nishchenstvo i besprizornost'*, 145–146; *Narodnoe prosveshchenie*, 1926, no. 8: 65; Tizanov et al., *Pedagogika*, 242; *Obzor raboty po bor'be s detskoi besprizornost'iu i beznadzornost'iu v RSFSR za 1927/28 g.* (Moscow, 1928), 39. By the beginning of the 1930s, ODD claimed two million members; see Ryndziunskii and Savinskaia, *Detskoe pravo*, 239.

73. For more on the structure of the ODD network, the fund-raising channels open to it, and other organizational details, see *Sbornik deistvuiushchikh*

uzakonenii i rasporiazhenii (1929), 43–44, 228–236; Tizanov and Epshtein, *Gosudarstvo i obshchestvennost'*, 15, 69–81; *Obshchestvo "Drug detei,"* comp. B. S. Utevskii (Moscow-Leningrad, 1932), 17–19, 27–30, 36; *Bor'ba s detskoi besprizornost'iu*, 72; *Na putiakh k novoi shkole*, 1925, no. 3: 205; *Drug detei* (Khar'kov), 1927, no. 2: 37; Gilev, *Detskaia besprizornost'*, 25; *Pomoshch' detiam*, 45; *Ural'skii uchitel'* (Sverdlovsk), 1926, nos. 11–12: 60–61.

74. For instructions on the proper tasks for ODD cells to undertake, see *Sbornik deistvuiushchikh uzakonenii i rasporiazhenii* (1929), 43–44, 124–125, 229–231, 234–235; Tizanov and Epshtein, *Gosudarstvo i obshchestvennost'*, 14, 69–70; *Pomoshch' detiam*, 44–47. On the actual activities of cells around the country, see *Drug detei* (Khar'kov), 1925, no. 4: 44; no. 9: 49; 1927, no. 1: 4; *Narodnoe prosveshchenie v R.S.F.S.R. k 1924/25 uchebnomu godu*, 82; *Drug detei*, 1926, no. 4: 3; 1927, nos. 6–7: 31–32; *Vestnik prosveshchentsa* (Orenburg), 1926, nos. 11–12: 86; *Ural'skii uchitel'* (Sverdlovsk), 1926, nos. 11–12: 60–61; *Prosveshchenie Sibiri* (Novosibirsk), 1927, no. 3: 102; *Volna* (Arkhangel'sk), 1926, no. 94 (April 27), p. 4; 1926, no. 241 (October 20), p. 2; *Krasnoiarskii rabochii* (Krasnoiarsk), 1925, no. 141 (June 24), p. 3. For samples of ODD publications on *besprizornost'*, see Sokolov, *Detskaia besprizornost'*; and journals titled *Drug detei*, published in a number of cities, including Moscow and Khar'kov. For information on the activities of ODD in the early 1930s, see TsGA RSFSR, f. 393, o. 1, ed. khr. 81, ll. 1–53; TsGA RSFSR, f. 393, o. 1, ed. khr. 201, ll. 1–110.

75. British Foreign Office, 1926, reel 3, vol. 11785, p. 78; Tizanov et al., *Pedagogika*, 255; *Sbornik deistvuiushchikh uzakonenii i rasporiazhenii* (1929), 215; Tizanov and Epshtein, *Gosudarstvo i obshchestvennost'*, 14–15; *Krasnoiarskii rabochii* (Krasnoiarsk), 1925, no. 141 (June 24), p. 3; *Ural'skii uchitel'* (Sverdlovsk), 1926, nos. 11–12: 60; *Volna* (Arkhangel'sk), 1925, no. 272 (December 1), p. 4; 1926, no. 169 (July 27), p. 4; *Molot* (Rostov-on-the-Don), 1926, no. 1462 (June 20), p. 5.

76. *Bor'ba s detskoi besprizornost'iu*, 66; *Sbornik deistvuiushchikh uzakonenii i rasporiazhenii* (1929), 190, 193, 196, 199, 238; Tizanov and Epshtein, *Gosudarstvo i obshchestvennost'*, 14–15; *Molot* (Rostov-on-the-Don), 1926, no. 1567 (October 23), p. 3. For more on various shortcomings of ODD, see Tizanov et al., *Pedagogika*, 255; Gilev, *Detskaia besprizornost'*, 25; TsGA RSFSR, f. 298, o. 2, ed. khr. 58, l. 43. Little assistance in the struggle with rural *besprizornost'* was available from Peasant Mutual Assistance Committees (*Krest'ianskie komitety obshchestvennoi vzaimopomoshchi*), another network of "voluntary organizations" based (where they existed at all) in the countryside. For more on Peasant Committees and rural *besprizornost'*, see *Narodnoe prosveshchenie*, 1926, no. 8: 66; Tizanov and Epshtein, *Gosudarstvo i obshchestvennost'*, 15, 42; Gilev, *Detskaia besprizornost'*, 21; Shishova, "Rol' obshchestvennosti," 14; *Na putiakh k novoi shkole*, 1927, no. 12: 73; *Molot* (Rostov-on-the-Don), 1925, no. 1150 (June 6), p. 1; 1926, no. 1454 (June 10), p. 2.

77. *Obshchestvo "Drug detei,"* 21; *SU*, 1932, no. 73, art. 328; *SU*, 1934, no. 23, art. 131 (for the All-Russian Central Executive Committee quotation); *Drug detei*, 1931, no. 7: 27 (for the film review).

78. *Zaria Vostoka* (Tiflis), 1922, no. 15 (July 6), p. 2; *Golod i deti*, 15; *Vserossiiskoe obsledovanie*, 37; Tizanov et al., *Detskaia besprizornost'*, 176 (for

the estimate of one hundred thousand); Ryndziunskii et al., *Pravovoe polozhenie* (1927), 63; *Otchet o sostoianii narodnogo obrazovaniia v eniseiskoi gubernii,* 17; *Otchet vladimirskogo gubispolkoma,* 56; *Smolenskaia nov'* (Smolensk), 1922, no. 1: 5; *New York Times,* March 23, 1923 (regarding the children adopted by the Kalinins).

79. TsGAOR, f. 5207, o. 1, ed. khr. 43, l. 66; American Red Cross, box 866, file 948.08 ("Commission to North Russia"), "Report on Investigation into Children's Summer Holiday Arrangements at Kholmogori," June 12, 1919; *Leningradskaia oblast'* (Leningrad), 1928, no. 4: 112; *Voprosy prosveshcheniia na Severnom Kavkaze* (Rostov-on-the-Don), 1928, no. 2: 41–42; Tizanov and Epshtein, *Gosudarstvo i obshchestvennost',* 17–18; Kalinina, *Desiat' let,* 52; Tizanov et al., *Detskaia besprizornost',* 166, 176 (for the "huge percentage" quotation), 181.

80. Regarding the diminished utilization of *patronirovanie* in 1923–1924 compared to 1921–1922, see *Narodnoe prosveshchenie v R.S.F.S.R. k 1924/25 uchebnomu godu,* 91.

81. TsGA RSFSR, f. 1575, o. 10, ed. khr. 178, l. 9; TsGA RSFSR, f. 2306, o. 69, ed. khr. 51, l. 1; *Shkola i zhizn'* (Nizhnii Novgorod), 1925, no. 4: 56; nos. 9–10: 88–89; 1926, nos. 6–7: 29–30; *Vestnik prosveshcheniia,* 1926, no. 1: 3; Gilev, *Detskaia besprizornost',* 13; Ryndziunskii et al., *Pravovoe polozhenie* (1927), 63; Tizanov and Epshtein, *Gosudarstvo i obshchestvennost',* 17, 49; *Volna* (Arkhangel'sk), 1926, no. 152 (July 7), p. 6; *Ural'skii uchitel'* (Sverdlovsk), 1925, nos. 5–6: 41. Regarding the survey of 1925 and its influence on *patronirovanie* decrees, see Ryndziunskii and Savinskaia, *Detskoe pravo,* 215–216.

82. For indications of misgivings at Narkompros meetings and on the part of some authors, see TsGA RSFSR, f. 298, o. 1, ed. khr. 45, ll. 22–23; *Ural'skii uchitel'* (Sverdlovsk), 1925, nos. 5–6: 42; *Detskii dom i bor'ba s besprizornost'iu,* 19.

83. On the premature application of *patronirovanie* by some local officials, see *Narodnoe prosveshchenie v R.S.F.S.R. k 1925/26 uchebnomu godu,* 68.

84. *Leningradskaia oblast'* (Leningrad), 1928, no. 4: 112; Tizanov and Epshtein, *Gosudarstvo i obshchestvennost',* 18, 49–50, 52; *Volna* (Arkhangel'sk), 1926, no. 152 (July 7), p. 6; *Kratkii sbornik zakonodatel'nykh materialov po bor'be s detskoi besprizornost'iu* (Voronezh, [1926]), 18. The basic *patronirovanie* decree for the Russian Republic was issued on April 5, 1926, by VTsIK and Sovnarkom; *SU,* 1926, no. 21, art. 168. Little over a month later (May 13, 1926) the Ukrainian TsIK and Sovnarkom issued a similar decree for Ukraine. For a side-by-side presentation of the two decrees, see *Detskoe pravo,* comp. Krichevskaia and Kuritskii, 466–469. A series of decrees and instructions appeared thereafter, especially in 1928, providing amendments and elaborations of the regulations issued in 1926. For instance, the decree of April 5, 1926, had limited to one the number of *detdom* children who could be placed in a single family, with local authorities authorized to raise this to two at their discretion. On May 21, 1928, VTsIK and Sovnarkom raised each of these limits by one; *SU,* 1928, no. 58, art. 429. For other rulings and orders, see *Sobranie zakonov i rasporiazhenii raboche-krest'ianskogo pravitel'stva Soiuza Sovetskikh Sotsi-*

alisticheskikh Respublik [hereafter cited as *SZ*], 1928, no. 24, art. 212; *SU*, 1928, no. 27, art. 196; *Sbornik deistvuiushchikh uzakonenii i rasporiazhenii* (1929), 49; *Leningradskaia oblast'* (Leningrad), 1928, no. 4: 116. Regarding the transfer of orphaned or abandoned infants and very young children (under four years of age) to private families for upbringing, see Ryndziunskii and Savinskaia, *Detskoe pravo*, 216–218; *Sbornik deistvuiushchikh uzakonenii i rasporiazhenii* (1929), 104–105; *Drug detei*, 1927, no. 1: 12.

85. *Kratkii sbornik zakonodatel'nykh materialov*, 19–20; *Sbornik uzakonenii i rasporiazhenii pravitel'stva Soiuza SSR i pravitel'stva RSFSR o meropriiatiakh po bor'be s detskoi besprizornost'iu i po ee preduprezhdeniiu* (Moscow, 1927), 14; *SU*, 1926, no. 21, art. 168; Tizanov and Epshtein, *Gosudarstvo i obshchestvennost'*, 62. In May 1926, Narkompros instructed its local officials that a youth be provided with a complete set of clothing and shoes before transfer to a peasant family. The child was also to be accorded priority in admission to school and, once enrolled, receive free books and supplies. See Tizanov and Epshtein, *Gosudarstvo i obshchestvennost'*, 50–51.

86. Tizanov and Epshtein, *Gosudarstvo i obshchestvennost'*, 18, 50–51, 53–54; *Kratkii sbornik zakonodatel'nykh materialov*, 18.

87. *SU*, 1926, no. 21, art. 168; *Sbornik uzakonenii i rasporiazhenii*, 37–40. Narkompros also instructed its local offices to draw up agreements with families that had taken in children prior to the decree, cited above, of April 5, 1926; see Tizanov and Epshtein, *Gosudarstvo i obshchestvennost'*, 53.

88. Tizanov and Epshtein, *Gosudarstvo i obshchestvennost'*, 30, 51–52, 54; *Ural'skii uchitel'* (Sverdlovsk), 1925, nos. 5–6: 42. Guardianship (*opeka*)—unlike *patronirovanie*, which was a voluntary agreement between an individual and Narkompros—represented an obligation that one could not refuse except in special circumstances. The actual responsibilities assumed by the adult in each case, however, sometimes differed very little. In general, *patronirovanie* was meant to apply first and foremost to *besprizornye*—in other words, destitute, abandoned children otherwise earmarked for institutions—while guardianship was meant to apply to a wider range of youths, including those with property and those only temporarily deprived of parental care. See *Vestnik prosveshcheniia*, 1926, no. 1: 4; Ryndziunskii et al., *Pravovoe polozhenie* (1927), 64; Ryndziunskii and Savinskaia, *Detskoe pravo*, 219. For more on guardianship of children, some of whom were former *besprizornye*, see *Sbornik deistvuiushchikh uzakonenii i rasporiazhenii* (1929), 147, 150–156, 158–167; *Detskii dom*, comp. Utevskii, 64; *Narodnoe prosveshchenie v RSFSR k 1926/27 uchebnomu godu*, 67; *Bol'shaia sovetskaia entsiklopediia* 5:789; *Sovetskoe stroitel'stvo*, 1927, nos. 2–3: 159; *Vestnik prosveshcheniia*, 1927, no. 11: 142.

89. Tizanov and Epshtein, *Gosudarstvo i obshchestvennost'*, 18, 47–48, 52.

90. For more details on these arrangements, see Shveitser and Shabalov, *Besprizornye*, 186–188; *Sbornik deistvuiushchikh uzakonenii i rasporiazhenii* (1929), 65–70, 91; *Volna* (Arkhangel'sk), 1926, no. 152 (July 7), p. 6. In 1928 and 1929 the government issued guidelines for placing homeless children in the families of urban workers. The terms of these *patronirovanie* measures were generally similar to those of laws previously discussed. See *SU*, 1928, no. 64, art. 462; Ryndziunskii and Savinskaia, *Detskoe pravo*, 223–225.

91. The figures for 1927 are "incomplete," so the actual increase over 1926 was doubtless even greater. For data on *patronirovanie* in the period 1925–1927, see *Na pomoshch' detiam. Obshchestvenno-literaturnyi i nauchnyi sbornik,* 16; *Narodnoe prosveshchenie v R.S.F.S.R. k 1925/26 uchebnomu godu,* 71; *Drug detei,* 1928, no. 4: 8; *Bol'shaia sovetskaia entsiklopediia* 5:789; *Narodnoe prosveshchenie v RSFSR k 1927–28 uchebnomu godu,* 60; Tizanov and Epshtein, *Gosudarstvo i obshchestvennost',* 6; *Detskii dom i bor'ba s besprizornost'iu,* 19; *Molot* (Rostov-on-the-Don), 1926, no. 1568 (October 24), p. 2. For data pertaining to individual cities and regions, see *Drug detei* (Khar'kov), 1925, no. 2: 45; 1927, no. 2: 44; nos. 5–6: 33; *Drug detei,* 1928, no. 2: 15; *Leningradskaia oblast'* (Leningrad), 1928, no. 4: 113.

92. Regarding the policy's sluggish progress and disappointing results in many regions, see *Shkola i zhizn'* (Nizhnii Novgorod), 1926, no. 11: 34; 1928, no. 12: 18–19; Tizanov et al., *Detskaia besprizornost',* 181; Gilev, *Detskaia besprizornost',* 14; *Detskoe pravo,* comp. Krichevskaia and Kuritskii, 470; *Drug detei,* 1927, nos. 8–9: 18; *Molot* (Rostov-on-the-Don), 1926, no. 1579 (November 6), p. 3.

93. One of Lunacharskii's adjutants, Moisei Epshtein, confirmed in 1927 that the government still relied on *detdoma* to raise most waifs. All other means (including *patronirovanie,* which he mentioned specifically) played a "comparatively modest role." Epshtein added that approximately 60 percent of all *besprizornye* were under the age of fourteen—and thus next to impossible to place in jobs or the families of peasants and craftsmen. See *Pravda,* 1927, no. 78 (April 7), p. 3.

94. *Leningradskaia oblast'* (Leningrad), 1928, no. 2: 103; no. 4: 113–115; *Detskii dom i bor'ba s besprizornost'iu,* 20; Tizanov and Epshtein, *Gosudarstvo i obshchestvennost',* 6–7; *Shkola i zhizn'* (Nizhnii Novgorod), 1926, no. 11: 36; *Severo-Kavkazskii krai* (Rostov-on-the-Don), 1926, no. 5: 27; *Vestnik prosveshchentsa* (Orenburg), 1926, nos. 7–8: 29. In certain provinces, children were discharged from *detdoma* and dumped in groups on district authorities, along with orders to place the youths with peasants by a certain date. When it proved impossible to find enough willing families, officials sometimes "attached" a child to several households—in other words, several families were made responsible collectively for the youth's support. Such assemblages of unwilling hosts, Narkompros complained, doomed children to poverty. No doubt many soon returned to the street. See *Detskoe pravo,* comp. Krichevskaia and Kuritskii, 470; *Komsomol'skaia pravda,* 1926, no. 109 (May 14), p. 4.

95. *Narodnoe prosveshchenie,* 1927, no. 7: 11; *Shkola i zhizn'* (Nizhnii Novgorod), 1928, no. 12: 18. Problems might also develop when peasants received city youths. The latter, unaccustomed to village life and work, often did not agonize long over a decision to head for urban terrain. See Tizanov and Epshtein, *Gosudarstvo i obshchestvennost',* 49; Ryndziunskii and Savinskaia, *Detskoe pravo,* 220.

96. *Vestnik prosveshcheniia,* 1926, no. 1: 3; 1927, no. 11: 141–142; *Drug detei* (Khar'kov), 1927, no. 2: 44; nos. 5–6: 32–33; *Na pomoshch' detiam. Obshchestvenno-literaturnyi i nauchnyi sbornik,* 17 (regarding the figure of 2 percent for Samara province); Krasnushkin et al., *Nishchenstvo i besprizornost',* 151; *Vozhatyi,* 1926, no. 6: 31.

97. Kalinina, *Komsomol i besprizornost'*, 19; *Vestnik prosveshcheniia*, 1929, no. 1: 164; *Vestnik prosveshchentsa* (Orenburg), 1926, nos. 7–8: 29; Tizanov and Epshtein, *Gosudarstvo i obshchestvennost'*, 49. Regarding the figures for Irkutsk, see *Drug detei* (Khar'kov), 1927, no. 2: 44; *Prosveshchenie Sibiri* (Novosibirsk), 1929, no. 11: 52. Some families, unable to support the children they had previously accepted, asked to return the youths to institutions. For an example, see TsGALI, f. 332, o. 2, ed. khr. 20, l. 5. When juveniles failed to flourish in host families, most sources blamed the families. Occasionally, however, an author placed principal responsibility on the children (said to be undisciplined) and their *detdoma*, which had allegedly failed to provide them with suitable labor habits. See for example *Prosveshchenie Sibiri* (Novosibirsk), 1927, no. 8: 55–56.

98. *Sovetskoe stroitel'stvo*, 1927, nos. 2–3: 167; *Detskii dom i bor'ba s besprizornost'iu*, 16; Tizanov et al., *Pedagogika*, 245; *Voprosy prosveshcheniia na Severnom Kavkaze* (Rostov-on-the-Don), 1928, no. 2: 42. On the shortage (or complete absence) of Narkompros's social workers in the countryside, see Tizanov et al., *Detskaia besprizornost'*, 170–171; Tizanov and Epshtein, *Gosudarstvo i obshchestvennost'*, 26.

99. *Drug detei*, 1929, no. 11: 8; *Vestnik prosveshcheniia*, 1929, no. 1: 165; Ryndziunskii and Savinskaia, *Detskoe pravo*, 222; *Prosveshchenie Sibiri* (Novosibirsk), 1928, no. 9: 74; 1929, no. 12: 11; *Detskii dom*, 1929, nos. 8–9: 106.

100. For contemporary statements and predictions on the declining role of *patronirovanie*, see *Detskii dom*, 1930, nos. 2–3: 7; Ryndziunskii and Savinskaia, *Detskoe pravo*, 218–219; *Drug detei*, 1929, no. 11: 8. For a *patronirovanie* decree from 1936, see *SU*, 1936, no. 9, art. 49. For the figure of 350,000 orphans placed in families at the end of the Second World War, see A. M. Sinitsin, "Zabota o beznadzornykh i besprizornykh detiakh v SSSR v gody velikoi otechestvennoi voiny," *Voprosy istorii*, 1969, no. 6: 28.

7. PROGRESS AND FRUSTRATION

1. Most of the money applied to the struggle with *besprizornost'* was allocated through Narkompros; see *Vozhatyi*, 1926, no. 6: 31.

2. TsGAOR, f. 5207, o. 1, ed. khr. 43, l. 45; *SU*, 1924, no. 44, art. 409; no. 54, art. 530; no. 72, art. 706; *SZ*, 1926, no. 42, art. 307; no. 56, art. 407; *SZ*, 1927, no. 25, art. 273; *SZ*, 1930, no. 60, art. 639; *Deti posle goloda*, 80–81; *Drug detei* (Khar'kov), 1926, no. 1: 44; *Molot* (Rostov-on-the-Don), 1925, no. 1266 (October 22), p. 5; 1925, no. 1270 (October 27), p. 4; Marinov, "Gosudarstvennye deti," 201.

3. *SU*, 1925, no. 8, art. 57; *SU*, 1927, no. 61, art. 422; *Sbornik deistvuiushchikh uzakonenii i rasporiazhenii* (1929), 220; Gilev, *Detskaia besprizornost'*, 8–9; *Drug detei* (Khar'kov), 1926, nos. 6–7: inside front cover; *Pomoshch' detiam*, 27–29; *Molot* (Rostov-on-the-Don), 1926, no. 1389 (March 24), p. 4. The Ukrainian Central Commission for the Assistance of Children expected income from businesses and investments to provide a quarter of its budget in 1925/26; see *Drug detei* (Khar'kov), 1926, nos. 6–7: 10. The Children's Commission, together with the postal authorities, issued special postage stamps bearing a

surcharge earmarked for the struggle with *besprizornost'*; *Drug detei* (Khar'kov), 1926, no. 10: 41. Some Children's Commissions published books not only to acquaint the public with the plight of *besprizornye* but also to raise money from the sales. For an example, see *Na pomoshch' detiam* (Semipala-tinsk, 1926). According to a source published in 1927, the Children's Commission in Moscow raised, on average, 2 million rubles per year. When combined with funds obtained by other Children's Commissions throughout the Russian Republic, the yearly total ranged between 8 and 8.5 million rubles. See Rynd-ziunskii et al., *Pravovoe polozhenie* (1927), 100. For criticism of inadequate or improper fund-raising activities of some provincial Children's Commissions, see *Sbornik deistvuiushchikh uzakonenii i rasporiazhenii* (1929), 184, 191–192, 195–196; *Bor'ba s detskoi besprizornost'iu*, 67; *Molot* (Rostov-on-the-Don), 1926, no. 1553 (October 7), p. 4.

4. Regarding tax breaks for shows and other entertainments sponsored by Children's Commissions, see *SU*, 1924, no. 51, art. 491; *SU*, 1927, no. 61, art. 423; *SZ*, 1926, no. 35, art. 253. Regarding tax breaks for business enterprises operated by Children's Commissions, see *SU*, 1927, no. 61, art. 423; *SU*, 1931, no. 8, art. 101; *SZ*, 1925, no. 41, art. 307; *SZ*, 1926, no. 56, art. 407; *Sbornik deistvuiushchikh uzakonenii i rasporiazhenii* (1929), 289. Undertakings of nu-merous agencies and organizations (in addition to Children's Commissions) in-volved in work with *besprizornye* also received tax relief. See for example *SZ*, 1924, no. 14, art. 140; *SZ*, 1928, no. 1, art. 4; *SU*, 1927, no. 78, art. 532; *Bor'ba s detskoi besprizornost'iu*, 126; Smolensk Archive, reel 2, WKP 18, pp. 26, 35. Narkompros agencies and Children's Commissions were also entitled to a 50 percent reduction in the price of train tickets purchased to send *bespri-zornye* back to their home regions; see *SZ*, 1926, no. 56, art. 407.

5. Regarding the Ukrainian Commission's budget planning for 1925/26, see *Drug detei* (Khar'kov), 1926, nos. 6–7: 10. For an announcement of the winning numbers and the prizes they carried (from two hundred to five thousand rubles) in a lottery sponsored by the Children's Commission, see *Izvestiia*, 1927, no. 55 (March 8), p. 7. Regarding gambling operations run by various Children's Commissions, see *Na putiakh k novoi shkole*, 1925, no. 3: 205; *Drug detei* (Khar'kov), 1926, nos. 6–7: 40; *Krasnoiarskii rabochii* (Krasnoiarsk), 1925, no. 141 (June 24), p. 3. As in any large fund-raising operation, some of the money raised by the network of Children's Commissions disappeared into the pockets of dishonest officials. For a description of one such scandal involving roughly twenty thousand rubles, see *Molot* (Rostov-on-the-Don), 1926, no. 1389 (March 24), p. 5. Following issues carried an account of the trial.

6. Regarding orders to close casinos, taverns, and the like operated by local Children's Commissions, see *Sbornik deistvuiushchikh uzakonenii i raspori-azhenii* (1929), 273–275, 296–297; *Prosveshchenie Sibiri* (Novosibirsk), 1928, no. 10: 47. For orders in 1928 to close all casinos, state and private, throughout the country, see *Sbornik deistvuiushchikh uzakonenii i rasporiazhenii* (1929), 294–295. Well before decade's end, the Children's Commission in Moscow not only condemned fund-raising through gambling establishments but also advised (in vain) its branches not to operate their own trading enterprises; see Smolensk Archive, reel 46, WKP 422, p. 299. Later instructions from Moscow, cited at the beginning of this note, relented on the issue of business ventures.

7. *SU*, 1924, no. 29/30, art. 271; *SZ*, 1924, no. 3, art. 33. The July decree was amended in September 1926, without changing its basic features; *SZ*, 1926, no. 61, art. 466. Newspapers sometimes published lists of individuals, groups, and organizations that made contributions to the Lenin Fund; see for example *Izvestiia*, 1924, no. 95 (April 24), p. 3. In January 1925, the All-Russian Central Executive Committee and the Council of People's Commissars issued a decree describing the Lenin Fund to be established in the Russian Republic. This fund was to contain twenty million rubles: ten million from the government of the Russian Republic and ten million from local Lenin Funds, donations, and other levies. In the republic and local funds, as in the national fund, only the interest was to be spent. See *SU*, 1925, no. 8, arts. 52, 53. According to one report, donations in the Russian Republic were disappointing, leaving the fund well short of its goal; Goldman, "The 'Withering Away' and the Resurrection," 112–113. For more on the All-Union and All-Russian Lenin Funds at the end of the decade and later, see *SZ*, 1928, no. 38, art. 347; *SU*, 1929, no. 33, art. 340; *SU*, 1932, no. 71, art. 319; Ryndziunskii and Savinskaia, *Detskoe pravo*, 226.

8. *Molot* (Rostov-on-the-Don), 1926, no. 1406 (April 13), p. 2; Tizanov et al., *Detskaia besprizornost'*, 185.

9. TsGALI, f. 332, o. 1, ed. khr. 52, l. 137; Tizanov et al., *Detskaia besprizornost'*, 184; *Bol'shaia sovetskaia entsiklopediia* 5:789; Poznyshev, *Detskaia besprizornost'*, 108; *Pravda*, 1926, no. 42 (February 20), p. 1 (regarding the local budgets' share of sixty million rubles).

10. *Detskii dom*, 1930, no. 4: 10; *Severo-Kavkazskii krai* (Rostov-on-the-Don), 1926, no. 5: 24; *Shkola i zhizn'* (Nizhnii Novgorod), 1925, nos. 9–10: 90; Tizanov et al., *Detskaia besprizornost'*, 180; Poznyshev, *Detskaia besprizornost'*, 109; Gilev, *Detskaia besprizornost'*, 1; *Bol'shaia sovetskaia entsiklopediia* 5:789; *Narodnoe prosveshchenie v R.S.F.S.R. k 1924/25 uchebnomu godu*, 84; *Spasennye revoliutsiei*, 51, 74; *Ural'skii uchitel'* (Sverdlovsk), 1925, nos. 5–6: 41.

11. *Narodnoe prosveshchenie v R.S.F.S.R. k 1924/25 uchebnomu godu*, 84; *Narodnoe prosveshchenie v RSFSR k 1926/27 uchebnomu godu*, 63; Tizanov and Epshtein, *Gosudarstvo i obshchestvennost'*, 7, 25, 37; Tizanov et al., *Pedagogika*, 17; Tizanov et al., *Detskaia besprizornost'*, 183–184; Krasnushkin et al., *Nishchenstvo i besprizornost'*, 145; *Spasennye revoliutsiei*, 56; N. V. Shishova, "Sovershenstvovanie raboty partiinykh, gosudarstvennykh i obshchestvennykh organizatsii Dona i Kubano-Chernomor'ia po likvidatsii detskoi besprizornosti v 1926–1929 gg." (Rostov-on-the-Don, 1982; MS. 9322 at INION AN SSSR, Moscow), 18; Gilev, *Detskaia besprizornost'*, 11; *Narodnoe prosveshchenie*, 1929, no. 1: 83; *Detskii dom i bor'ba s besprizornost'iu*, 10; *Vestnik prosveshcheniia*, 1929, no. 3: 28–29. When Anton Makarenko learned at the end of 1922 that responsibility for the support of his colony had been shifted to local officials, he complained: "For me this is synonymous with ruin"; see TsGALI, f. 332, o. 1, ed. khr. 52, l. 50. Regarding Moscow's understanding that something had to be done to make room in *detdoma* and receivers for *besprizornye* still on the street, see TsGA RSFSR, f. 1575, o. 6, ed. khr. 152, l. 6; *Drug detei* (Khar'kov), 1926, nos. 4–5: 37; Tizanov and Epshtein, *Gosudarstvo i obshchestvennost'*, 25, 33; *Volna* (Arkhangel'sk), 1926, no. 9 (January

12), p. 2. It appears likely that children's institutions remaining on the central state budget were generally in better material condition than facilities (including the majority of *detdoma*) transferred to local budgets. See, regarding institutions for "difficult" children, Shveitser and Shabalov, *Besprizornye*, 91. Inadequate local resources remained a problem in the struggle with *besprizornost'* throughout the decade; see *Prosveshchenie Sibiri* (Novosibirsk), 1927, no. 8: 56; *Sbornik deistvuiushchikh uzakonenii i rasporiazhenii* (1929), 197; *Prosveshchenie na Urale* (Sverdlovsk), 1928, nos. 7–8: 62; Enik and Blok, *Iz trushchob na stroiku*, 27–28.

12. Tizanov and Epshtein, *Gosudarstvo i obshchestvennost'*, 7, 25; *Krasnaia gazeta* (Leningrad), 1926, no. 301 (December 29), p. 2.

13. *Narodnoe prosveshchenie v R.S.F.S.R. k 1925/26 uchebnomu godu*, 65, 68; *Sbornik deistvuiushchikh uzakonenii i rasporiazhenii* (1929), 41, 69–70, 89–90, 191; *SU*, 1930, no. 59, art. 704; *SU*, 1932, no. 73, art. 328; *Detskii dom i bor'ba s besprizornost'iu*, 32; Tizanov et al., *Detskaia besprizornost'*, 185; *Detskii dom*, 1930, nos. 8–10: 51.

14. Tizanov and Epshtein, *Gosudarstvo i obshchestvennost'*, 7.

15. *Prosveshchenie na Urale* (Sverdlovsk), 1927, no. 2: 61; *Obzor raboty po bor'be s detskoi besprizornost'iu i beznadzornost'iu v RSFSR za 1929/30 god*, 9 (regarding the Crimean Republic); *Vestnik prosveshcheniia*, 1929, no. 3: 28 (regarding Moscow province).

16. *Komsomol'skaia pravda*, 1925, no. 73 (August 21), p. 3; Artamonov, *Deti ulitsy*, 37–38; Tizanov et al., *Pedagogika*, 17; Tizanov and Epshtein, *Gosudarstvo i obshchestvennost'*, 32–33; *Pedagogicheskaia entsiklopediia* (1927–1930), 2:355.

17. *Sbornik deistvuiushchikh uzakonenii i rasporiazhenii* (1929), 189, 197, 235, 247; *Sbornik deistvuiushchikh uzakonenii i rasporiazhenii pravitel'stva Soiuza SSR i pravitel'stva R.S.F.S.R., postanovlenii detkomissii pri VTsIK i vedomstvennykh rasporiazhenii po bor'be s detskoi besprizornost'iu i beznadzornost'iu, vypusk* 3 (Moscow, 1932), 16; *Molot* (Rostov-on-the-Don), 1925, no. 1190 (July 24), p. 5. Some local Children's Commissions duplicated the work of the region's Narkompros offices to such an extent that the former were operating their own *detdoma* rather than channeling funds to Narkompros for the task. On occasion, the blame for these improper parallel organizations belonged at least as much with poorly informed or overly enthusiastic provincial Children's Commission officials as it did with Narkompros personnel seeking to reduce their contingent of *detdoma*. See *Obzor raboty po bor'be s detskoi besprizornost'iu i beznadzornost'iu v RSFSR za 1927/28 g.*, 30; *Sbornik deistvuiushchikh uzakonenii i rasporiazhenii* (1929), 184; *Prosveshchenie Sibiri* (Novosibirsk), 1932, no. 9: 22–23; *Severo-Kavkazskii krai* (Rostov-on-the-Don), 1926, no. 5: 21–22.

18. For the example of Makarenko's labor colony, see TsGALI, f. 332, o. 1, ed. khr. 52, ll. 3–4.

19. *Krasnaia gazeta* (Leningrad), 1926, no. 301 (December 29), p. 2; *Molot* (Rostov-on-the-Don), 1925, no. 1175 (July 7), p. 5; 1925, no. 1201 (August 6), p. 3; Tizanov and Epshtein, *Gosudarstvo i obshchestvennost'*, 25; Tizanov et al., *Detskaia besprizornost'*, 187; *Voprosy prosveshcheniia* (Rostov-on-the-Don), 1926, no. 2: 42–43.

20. Regarding rural officials sending homeless children off to cities, see *Drug detei*, 1926, no. 1: 6; 1930, no. 1: 9; Gilev, *Detskaia besprizornost'*, 7; *Zhizn' Buriatii* (Verkhneudinsk), 1929, no. 5: 71. Regarding orders to cease the unauthorized transfers of *besprizornye*, see *Dvukhnedel'nik donskogo okruzhnogo otdela narodnogo obrazovaniia* (Rostov-on-the-Don), 1924, no. 1: 3; *Sbornik deistvuiushchikh uzakonenii i rasporiazhenii* (1929), 126–129. For the "get out of our sight" quotation (from an article in *Molot*), see *Administrativnyi vestnik*, 1926, no. 12: 36–37. For the transfer of eight hundred *besprizornye* to Georgia, see *Okhrana detstva*, 1931, nos. 2–3: 33–34.

21. For the numbers of receivers and observation-distribution points cited, see Min'kovskii, "Osnovnye etapy," 42–43. Figures from the Central Statistical Administration on the number of receivers and observation-distribution points (along with similar institutions called isolators—*izoliatory*) in the USSR ranged somewhat lower: 292 institutions and 22,317 children on January 1, 1924, with the totals dropping to 244 and 16,862 a year later. In the Russian Republic alone, the figures were 263 institutions and 19,905 children on January 1, 1924—down to 222 and 15,319 a year later. See Poznyshev, *Detskaia besprizornost'*, 107. For additional data (other calculations of the number of receivers in the Russian Republic and figures on receivers in various regions and cities), see *Narodnoe obrazovanie v R.S.F.S.R.*, 117, 160; Manns, *Bor'ba*, 9; Vasilevskii, *Besprizornost'*, 92; *Statisticheskii obzor narodnogo obrazovaniia v permskom okruge*, 40. Moscow contained three major receivers in the middle of the decade: (1) the *Priemno-nabliudatel'nyi punkt imeni Krylenko*, located on Malaia Pochtovaia Street (Baumanskii district) and thus dubbed the *Pochtovka*; (2) the Domnikovskii receiver; and (3) the *Priemno-nabliudatel'nyi punkt imeni Kalininoi*, formerly the Pokrovskii receiver and thus often referred to colloquially as the *Pokrovka*. See *Drug detei* (Khar'kov), 1925, no. 6: 30; 1926, no. 1: 15; Kalinina, *Desiat' let*, 72; *Drug detei*, 1927, nos. 6–7: 28.

22. For a description of a *besprizornyi* taken into custody by the police and then delivered directly to a *detdom*, see TsGALI, f. 332, o. 1, ed. khr. 55, l. 12. A journal reported in 1925 that Smolensk, "at present," has no receiver; children were sent straight from the street, through the Juvenile Affairs Commission, to "permanent" institutions. See *Na putiakh k novoi shkole*, 1925, no. 4: 144. A Moscow *nochlezhka* conducted its work under the slogan "From the streets and asphalt caldrons to the *nochlezhka*; from the *nochlezhka* to the labor commune." See *Drug detei*, 1926, no. 4: 7. In cities containing both *nochlezhki* and receivers, uninitiated newcomers to the streets were more likely to turn up in the latter than in the former; *Drug detei* (Khar'kov), 1925, no. 6: 33. In 1924, a total of 183 receivers in the Russian Republic (excluding autonomous regions) processed 67,000 children; Tizanov et al., *Detskaia besprizornost'*, 175. Narrowing the focus to Moscow's *Pokrovka*, 3,985 youths passed through the receiver in 1923/24; 3,189 in 1924/25; 3,911 in 1925/26; and 3,461 in 1927/28. See *Vestnik prosveshcheniia*, 1929, no. 3: 28.

23. Poznyshev, *Detskaia besprizornost'*, 75; *Prosveshchenie Sibiri* (Novosibirsk), 1929, no. 12: 9; Tizanov et al., *Detskaia besprizornost'*, 173, 175; *Detskii dom i bor'ba s besprizornost'iu*, 10; Kirsanov, *Rukovodstvo*, 25. The waning of the theory of "moral defectiveness" may also have contributed to the

metamorphosis of receivers. If staff members in a receiver regarded a *besprizor-nyi* as "morally defective"—and thus largely incurable—they likely saw little reason to provide education or labor training. See Tizanov et al., *Detskaia bes-prizornost'*, 174.

24. The focus here, of course, is on children dispatched officially, not those who ran away; see *Narodnoe obrazovanie v R.S.F.S.R.*, 123; *Volna* (Arkhan-gel'sk), 1926, no. 290 (December 17), p. 4; *Statisticheskii obzor narodnogo obrazovaniia v permskom okruge*, 40.

25. Tizanov et al., *Pedagogika*, 10.

26. *Obzor raboty po bor'be s detskoi besprizornost'iu i beznadzornost'iu v RSFSR za 1927/28 g.*, 12; *Drug detei* (Khar'kov), 1927, nos. 7–8: 31; Poznyshev, *Detskaia besprizornost'*, 108; Tizanov et al., *Detskaia besprizornost'*, 184; Gilev, *Detskaia besprizornost'*, 3. According to data from twenty-seven prov-inces of the Russian Republic, the number of *detdoma* increased from 583 in 1918 to 1,613 in 1919. A table listing the number of *detdoma* administered by the Commissariat of Social Security in over thirty provinces of the Russian Re-public showed a total of 1,279 institutions for January 1, 1919, and 1,734 six months later; TsGA RSFSR, f. 1575, o. 6, ed. khr. 4, ll. 1, 99. A report from the Children's Commission specified the following numbers of *detdoma* in the Russian Republic: 3,002 in 1924/25; 2,491 in 1925/26; 2,020 in 1926/27; 1,645 in 1927/28; and 1,524 in 1928/29; *Obzor raboty po bor'be s detskoi bespri-zornost'iu i beznadzornost'iu v RSFSR za 1929/30 god*, 8. For similar, but not identical, calculations of the Russian Republic's *detdom* network for various years in this period, see *Narodnoe prosveshchenie v RSFSR k 1926/27 ucheb-nomu godu*, 63; *Narodnoe prosveshchenie v RSFSR k 1927–28 uchebnomu godu*, 56; Kufaev, *Pedagogicheskie mery*, 138; Poznyshev, *Detskaia besprizor-nost'*, 107; *Drug detei*, 1927, nos. 6–7: 7; TsGA RSFSR, f. 1575, o. 6, ed. khr. 4, l. 94.

27. Regarding Ukraine, see *Put' prosveshcheniia* (Khar'kov), 1923, no. 4: 274; *Bol'shaia sovetskaia entsiklopediia* 5:788. The figure for 1925 includes a small number of receivers. According to another source, the number of *detdoma* for "normal" (that is, not "defective") children soared in Ukraine from 300 in the middle of 1919 to 1,750 at the beginning of 1922; *Profilakticheskaia med-itsina* (Khar'kov), 1923, nos. 1–2: 105. For the Soviet Union as a whole, see Poznyshev, *Detskaia besprizornost'*, 107; *Narodnoe obrazovanie v SSSR v 1926/27 uch. godu* (Moscow, 1927), 17. The Belorussian Republic supported thirty-nine children's institutions (including a few receivers) in the summer of 1925; Transcaucasia, eighty-six; and the Turkmen Republic, eleven. See *Bol'shaia sovetskaia entsiklopediia* 5:788.

28. *Obzor raboty po bor'be s detskoi besprizornost'iu i beznadzornost'iu v RSFSR za 1927/28 g.*, 12; *Obzor raboty po bor'be s detskoi besprizornost'iu i beznadzornost'iu v RSFSR za 1929/30 god*, 8; Tizanov et al., *Detskaia bespri-zornost'*, 183–184; Poznyshev, *Detskaia besprizornost'*, 108; Ryndziunskii et al., *Pravovoe polozhenie* (1927), 96; Gilev, *Detskaia besprizornost'*, 3; *Drug detei* (Khar'kov), 1926, no. 2: 28; *Detskii dom*, comp. Utevskii, 4. For similar, but not identical, statistics on the number of children in the Russian Republic's *detdoma*, see *Narodnoe prosveshchenie v RSFSR k 1927–28 uchebnomu godu*,

56; Min'kovskii, "Osnovnye etapy," 43; *Drug detei* (Khar'kov), 1927, nos. 7–8: 30; TsGA RSFSR, f. 1575, o. 6, ed. khr. 4, ll. 1, 99; *Drug detei*, 1927, nos. 4–5: 8; nos. 6–7: 7; Poznyshev, *Detskaia besprizornost'*, 107; *Detskii dom*, 1929, no. 2: 5; *Narodnoe prosveshchenie v RSFSR k 1926/27 uchebnomu godu*, 63; *Sbornik deistvuiushchikh uzakonenii i rasporiazhenii* (1929), 53. Early in 1922, the following provinces of the Russian Republic contained the largest numbers of children in *detdoma*: Petrograd (57,000 *detdom* residents), Samara (45,000), Moscow (44,000), the Don *oblast'* (25,000), Voronezh (24,000), Cheliabinsk (22,000), Tsaritsyn (20,000), Saratov (18,000), Tambov (18,000), Ekaterinburg (13,000), Tobol'sk (13,000), Perm' (12,000), Simbirsk (12,000). See TsGA RSFSR, f. 1575, o. 6, ed. khr. 4, l. 94.

29. Regarding Ukraine, see *Put' prosveshcheniia* (Khar'kov), 1923, no. 4: 274; *Bol'shaia sovetskaia entsiklopediia* 5:788. The figure for 1925 includes children in receivers. The following Ukrainian provinces contained the largest numbers of children in *detdoma* early in 1923: Ekaterinoslav (23,000 youths), Odessa (22,000), Donets (18,000), Kiev (11,000), Poltava (10,000), Khar'kov (8,000). Regarding the Soviet Union as a whole, see *Detskaia besprizornost'*, 53 (for the figure of 1,000,000); Poznyshev, *Detskaia besprizornost'*, 107; *Narodnoe obrazovanie v SSSR v 1926/27 uch. godu*, 17. Another source places the total number of children in the nation's *detdoma* at scarcely more than 450,000 in 1922; *Pedagogicheskaia entsiklopediia* (1927–1930), 2:385–386. This figure is doubtless unreliable, for it falls nearly 100,000 below the total reported in many other publications for the Russian Republic alone. In June 1925, children's institutions (including receivers) housed 5,829 youths in Transcaucasia; 4,395 in the Belorussian Republic; and 730 in the Turkmen Republic. See *Bol'shaia sovetskaia entsiklopediia* 5:788.

30. *Narodnoe prosveshchenie v R.S.F.S.R. k 1924/25 uchebnomu godu*, 82; *Narodnoe prosveshchenie v RSFSR k 1927–28 uchebnomu godu*, 57; Tizanov et al., *Detskaia besprizornost'*, 187; TsGA RSFSR, f. 1575, o. 10, ed. khr. 177, l. 11. For similar statistics from individual provinces and institutions, see *Vestnik prosveshcheniia*, 1923, no. 2: 116; "Otchet Riazgubono za ianvar'–sentiabr' 1922 goda," in *Otchet o deiatel'nosti riazanskogo gubispolkoma*, 3; TsGALI, f. 332, o. 1, ed. khr. 52, l. 39; ibid., ed. khr. 55, l. 17; *Krasnoiarskii rabochii* (Krasnoiarsk), 1925, no. 140 (June 23), p. 3; *Shkola i zhizn'* (Nizhnii Novgorod), 1926, no. 11: 33; *Prosveshchenie* (Penza), 1926, no. 7: 63; Shveitser and Shabalov, *Besprizornye*, 31, 45, 71; *Sibirskii pedagogicheskii zhurnal* (Novo-Nikolaevsk), 1924, no. 3: 55; *Ural'skii uchitel'* (Sverdlovsk), 1925, no. 2: 39; *Statisticheskii obzor narodnogo obrazovaniia v permskom okruge*, 37. Receivers, as one would expect, yielded much the same data. See for example *Drug detei* (Khar'kov), 1926, nos. 8–9: 14; *Narodnoe obrazovanie v R.S.F.S.R.*, 121; Kufaev, "Iz opyta," 94; Sokolov, *Besprizornye deti*, 21. By the middle of the decade, *detdoma* contained few children whose parents were both known to be alive. Youths of this sort still in institutions generally belonged to one of the following categories: (1) those whose parents paid to place them in *detdoma*; (2) those who had committed crimes and were sent to *detdoma* by Juvenile Affairs Commissions; (3) those whose parents had been deprived of their parental rights (owing to poor mental health or criminal activities, for example);

and (4) a few whose fathers were soldiers. See *Narodnoe prosveshchenie v RSFSR k 1927–28 uchebnomu godu*, 57. On occasion children reportedly claimed, falsely, to be orphans in order to gain admittance to *detdoma*; Artamonov, *Deti ulitsy*, 8.

Roughly 60 percent of the children in *detdoma* ranged between eight and fourteen years of age. Approximately three-fourths of the remaining 40 percent were fourteen or older, with the rest between four and eight. These figures varied a few percentage points depending on the year and the region. See *Bol'shaia sovetskaia entsiklopediia* 5:788; *Narodnoe prosveshchenie v RSFSR k 1927–28 uchebnomu godu*, 57; Tizanov et al., *Detskaia besprizornost'*, 187.

The overwhelming majority of *detdom* residents came from the peasantry and the urban working class—hardly a surprise. According to data from the middle of the decade, slightly over 50 percent of the inhabitants of *detdoma* in the Russian Republic were classified as children of peasants; roughly 25 percent were the offspring of workers; over 5 percent were the progeny of artisans; and the rest came from other social backgrounds. In Ukraine, almost exactly half the youths in *detdoma* came from peasant families, with another third labeled children of workers. For the Belorussian Republic the shares were 37 and 40 percent, respectively. See Tizanov et al., *Detskaia besprizornost'*, 186–187; *Bol'shaia sovetskaia entsiklopediia* 5:788. According to a Narkompros report for 1926/27, approximately 45 percent of the children in the Russian Republic's *detdoma* were of peasant background, and 35 percent were from workers' families; *Narodnoe prosveshchenie v RSFSR k 1927–28 uchebnomu godu*, 57. For figures from individual institutions (not all of which adhered to the pattern outlined above, of course), see Maro, *Besprizornye*, 373; Shveitser and Shabalov, *Besprizornye*, 45, 71; TsGALI, f. 332, o. 1, ed. khr. 55, l. 17.

31. Regarding the confusing variety of names, see *Narodnoe prosveshchenie*, 1927, no. 7: 11; *Prosveshchenie na transporte*, 1925, no. 1: 88; Stolee, "Generation," 127; Livshits, *Sotsial'nye korni*, 128–129 (regarding the institutions in Rostov and Saratov). Statistics also varied from source to source because of differences in time periods and territories covered.

32. Poznyshev, *Detskaia besprizornost'*, 106–107n.

33. For examples and brief descriptions of these categories of institutions, see *Put' prosveshcheniia* (Khar'kov), 1925, nos. 5–6: 111–119; Shishova, "Sozdanie," 10–11; *Vtoroi otchet voronezhskogo gubernskogo ekonomicheskogo soveshchaniia*, 34; Poznyshev, *Detskaia besprizornost'*, 106; Kufaev, *Pedagogicheskie mery*, 135–136; TsGA RSFSR, f. 298, o. 2, ed. khr. 58, l. 10. On the different types of Narkompros institutions intended for "difficult" (previously, "morally defective") children, see TsGA RSFSR, f. 1575, o. 10, ed. khr. 177, l. 11; *Detskii dom*, 1928, no. 3: 77–78; *Nesovershennoletnie pravonarushiteli*, 45–46. These institutions for "difficult" youths appear not to have reached even three hundred in number, certainly not in the Russian Republic. See *Narodnoe obrazovanie v R.S.F.S.R.*, 123–124; *Narodnoe prosveshchenie v RSFSR k 1927–28 uchebnomu godu*, 58; Stolee, "Generation," 130; Liublinskii, *Bor'ba*, 50; Ryndziunskii et al., *Pravovoe polozhenie* (1927), 86; Min'kovskii, "Osnovnye etapy," 45–46. Regarding the physically handicapped, Narkompros reported that on June 1, 1924, the Russian Republic contained twenty-three *detdoma* for

the blind (with a total of 846 children); thirty-three for deaf-mutes (1,549 children); and fifty-five for the mentally retarded (3,314 children); *Narodnoe prosveshchenie v R.S.F.S.R. k 1924/25 uchebnomu godu*, 88.

34. TsGALI, f. 332, o. 1, ed. khr. 52, l. 96; ibid., ed. khr. 53, l. 2; *Prosveshchenie na Urale* (Sverdlovsk), 1927, no. 2: 62; *Sbornik deistvuiushchikh uzakonenii i rasporiazhenii* (1929), 201; *Detskii dom*, 1929, no. 7: 30; Shveitser and Shabalov, *Besprizornye*, 16, 167; *Narodnoe prosveshchenie v R.S.F.S.R. k 1924/25 uchebnomu godu*, 85; *Prosveshchenie Sibiri* (Novosibirsk), 1926, no. 11: 97.

35. On the subject of confusion: documents occasionally employed first one name and then another (colony and labor commune, for instance, or *detdom* and colony) in reference to a single institution. See for example TsGA RSFSR, f. 1575, o. 10, ed. khr. 193, l. 6; *Na putiakh k novoi shkole*, 1924, nos. 7–8: 31; 1925, no. 4: 144, 146, 150.

36. *Besprizornye*, comp. Kaidanova, 63. See also *Narodnoe obrazovanie v R.S.F.S.R.*, 70–71, 80; Tizanov et al., *Detskaia besprizornost'*, 172. Agricultural colonies (including Makarenko's) were most prominent in Ukraine, but even here they did not approach the number of *detdoma*. At the beginning of 1925 the Russian Republic contained fewer than three hundred agricultural colonies (with just over twenty-two thousand children). See Poznyshev, *Detskaia besprizornost'*, 85–87.

37. *Drug detei*, 1926, no. 7: 1–2 (for the figure of 90 percent). Regarding institutions run by the Central Commission for the Assistance of Children and the commissariats of health and transportation, see *Drug detei* (Khar'kov), 1926, nos. 6–7: 8–9; *Deti posle goloda*, 90; *Golod i deti*, 39–40; *Prosveshchenie* (Krasnodar), 1923, no. 1: 7; Poznyshev, *Detskaia besprizornost'*, 112–113; Shveitser and Shabalov, *Besprizornye*, 14; *Drug detei*, 1926, no. 1: 20; *Put' prosveshcheniia* (Khar'kov), 1923, no. 4: 274; *Prosveshchenie na transporte*, 1922, no. 2: 23–24; 1925, no. 1: 87.

38. Regarding the point that most *detdom* children who attended school did so outside *detdoma*, see Tizanov et al., *Detskaia besprizornost'*, 191 (for the statistics); *Prosveshchenie Sibiri* (Novosibirsk), 1926, no. 11: 98; *Bol'shaia sovetskaia entsiklopediia* 5:788; Ryndziunskii et al., *Pravovoe polozhenie* (1927), 96; *Voprosy prosveshcheniia* (Rostov-on-the-Don), 1926, nos. 6–7: 54. At a *detdom* in Tobol'sk, younger children received instruction inside the institution, while older youths attended a regular school in the city—a practice followed by a number of other *detdoma* as well. See *Ural'skii uchitel'* (Sverdlovsk), 1925, no. 2: 39.

39. *Narodnoe prosveshchenie v R.S.F.S.R. k 1924/25 uchebnomu godu*, 86 (regarding the Narkompros report for 1923/24); *Narodnoe prosveshchenie*, 1926, no. 8: 68; *Voprosy prosveshcheniia* (Rostov-on-the-Don), 1926, nos. 6–7: 54; Tizanov et al., *Detskaia besprizornost'*, 195; *Narodnoe prosveshchenie v R.S.F.S.R. k 1925/26 uchebnomu godu*, 69; *Ural'skii uchitel'* (Sverdlovsk), 1925, no. 2: 39.

40. A Narkompros report for 1926/27 observed that the provision of schooling for *detdom* children had improved considerably; *Narodnoe prosveshchenie v RSFSR k 1927–28 uchebnomu godu*, 57. For criticism of the education pro-

vided by many *detdoma* (inadequate resources and/or improper pedagogy), see Shveitser and Shabalov, *Besprizornye*, 110, 123; *Ural'skii uchitel'* (Sverdlovsk), 1925, no. 2: 39; *Na putiakh k novoi shkole*, 1924, nos. 7–8: 38; *Voprosy prosveshcheniia* (Rostov-on-the-Don), 1926, nos. 6–7: 54; Tizanov et al., *Detskaia besprizornost'*, 191. The periodic sending of additional batches of children from the street to institutions throughout the school year disrupted education in *detdoma*. These new arrivals, even if they were not veterans of the underworld, rarely fit well when placed in courses already long under way. See for example Shveitser and Shabalov, *Besprizornye*, 54, 79.

41. *Sovetskoe stroitel'stvo*, 1927, nos. 2–3: 155. For more on the workshops operated by a variety of institutions, some quite successful, see TsGALI, f. 332, o. 2, ed. khr. 58, roll 5, ll. 46–47; *Drug detei* (Khar'kov), 1927, nos. 7–8: 42; Makarenko, *Road to Life* 2:396–397; *Na putiakh k novoi shkole*, 1926, nos. 5–6: 54; *Molot* (Rostov-on-the-Don), 1925, no. 1230 (September 10), p. 4; Shveitser and Shabalov, *Besprizornye*, 61–62, 81, 194–207; *Detskii dom*, comp. Utevskii, 38; *Sibirskii pedagogicheskii zhurnal* (Novo-Nikolaevsk), 1924, no. 3: 56–57.

42. For examples of workshops striving to fulfill orders from customers outside the institutions, see TsGALI, f. 332, o. 2, ed. khr. 57, roll 6, ll. 12–12a; *Na putiakh k novoi shkole*, 1925, no. 4: 148; Glatman, *Pionery i besprizornye*, 30; *Voprosy prosveshcheniia* (Rostov-on-the-Don), 1926, nos. 6–7: 42; Makarenko, *Road to Life* 1:8; Shveitser and Shabalov, *Besprizornye*, 55, 61; *Narodnoe prosveshchenie v RSFSR k 1926/27 uchebnomu godu*, 61–62. For two different methods of channeling a portion of a workshop's earnings to its young craftsmen, see Shveitser and Shabalov, *Besprizornye*, 81; *Na putiakh k novoi shkole*, 1926, nos. 5–6: 53–54.

43. *Na putiakh k novoi shkole*, 1926, nos. 5–6: 52; Shveitser and Shabalov, *Besprizornye*, 85–86.

44. TsGALI, f. 332, o. 2, ed. khr. 57, roll 4, ll. 14–15; ibid., ed. khr. 58, roll 1, ll. 30–32; *Narodnoe prosveshchenie v R.S.F.S.R. k 1924/25 uchebnomu godu*, 86; Poznyshev, *Detskaia besprizornost'*, 109; Tizanov et al., *Pedagogika*, 20; *Voprosy prosveshcheniia* (Rostov-on-the-Don), 1926, nos. 6–7: 42; Krasnushkin et al., *Nishchenstvo i besprizornost'*, 146; Tizanov et al., *Detskaia besprizornost'*, 183; Gilev, *Detskaia besprizornost'*, 13.

45. Tizanov and Epshtein, *Gosudarstvo i obshchestvennost'*, 36–37; Poznyshev, *Detskaia besprizornost'*, 109; *Sovetskoe stroitel'stvo*, 1927, nos. 2–3: 156; Tizanov et al., *Detskaia besprizornost'*, 190–191; *Narodnoe prosveshchenie v R.S.F.S.R. k 1925/26 uchebnomu godu*, 67–68; *Narodnoe prosveshchenie v RSFSR k 1926/27 uchebnomu godu*, 61; Tizanov et al., *Pedagogika*, 20; *Sbornik deistvuiushchikh uzakonenii i rasporiazhenii* (1929), 52–53; Shishova, "Sovershenstvovanie," 9; *Pedagogicheskaia entsiklopediia* (1927–1930), 2:361. Some of these sources state that in 1925/26 roughly 15 percent of all *detdom* residents (and 25 percent of those at least fourteen years of age) received training in workshops.

46. For an example of *besprizornye* from an urban *detdom* going out to work on a state farm in the summer, see *Vestnik prosveshcheniia*, 1924, nos. 2–3: 100–104.

47. Glatman, *Pionery i besprizornye*, 31; Shveitser and Shabalov, *Besprizornye*, 55; *Ural'skii uchitel'* (Sverdlovsk), 1925, no. 2: 39.

48. Shveitser and Shabalov, *Besprizornye*, 19, 35, 37, 55–56, 69–70; *Besprizornye*, comp. Kaidanova, 48; Makarenko, *Road to Life* 1:8; *Sibirskii pedagogicheskii zhurnal* (Novo-Nikolaevsk), 1924, no. 3: 57; *Na putiakh k novoi shkole*, 1925, no. 4: 148; *Molot* (Rostov-on-the-Don), 1926, no. 1416 (April 24), p. 3.

49. Shveitser and Shabalov, *Besprizornye*, 20, 56, 70–71; Makarenko, *Road to Life* 2:94; Maro, *Besprizornye*, 370.

50. *Voprosy prosveshcheniia* (Rostov-on-the-Don), 1926, nos. 6–7: 43; Tizanov et al., *Detskaia besprizornost'*, 190; *Narodnoe prosveshchenie v R.S.F.S.R. k 1924/25 uchebnomu godu*, 86.

51. For the daily schedules reportedly followed by a number of institutions, see Kaidanova, *Besprizornye deti*, 13–14; Shveitser and Shabalov, *Besprizornye*, 24; Glatman, *Pionery i besprizornye*, 33–34, 40.

52. For examples of many different circles and clubs, see TsGALI, f. 332, o. 2, ed. khr. 57, roll 3, l. 2; ibid., ed. khr. 58, roll 1, ll. 65–66; *Sibirskii pedagogicheskii zhurnal* (Novo-Nikolaevsk), 1924, no. 3: 56; Makarenko, *Road to Life* 2:397–398; Kaidanova, *Besprizornye deti*, 14; Shveitser and Shabalov, *Besprizornye*, 25, 27, 54–55, 80; *Ural'skii uchitel'* (Sverdlovsk), 1925, no. 2: 40; *Shkola i zhizn'* (Nizhnii Novgorod), 1926, no. 11: 51.

53. *Detskii dom*, 1928, no. 3: 47; *Voprosy prosveshcheniia* (Rostov-on-the-Don), 1926, nos. 6–7: 48.

54. TsGALI, f. 332, o. 2, ed. khr. 58, roll 4, ll. 13–14; Shveitser and Shabalov, *Besprizornye*, 25, 35, 77; *Sibirskii pedagogicheskii zhurnal* (Novo-Nikolaevsk), 1924, no. 3: 56; Utevskii, *V bor'be*, 54.

55. TsGALI, f. 332, o. 2, ed. khr. 57, roll 3, ll. 45, 48, 53; ibid., ed. khr. 57, roll 4, l. 5; ibid., ed. khr. 58, roll 4, ll. 57–59; Makarenko, *Road to Life* 2:45–62; Shveitser and Shabalov, *Besprizornye*, 25; Utevskii, *V bor'be*, 51; *Sibirskii pedagogicheskii zhurnal* (Novo-Nikolaevsk), 1924, no. 3: 56; *Na putiakh k novoi shkole*, 1925, no. 6: 82–96; *Rabochii krai* (Ivanovo-Voznesensk), 1924, no. 183 (August 13), p. 2.

56. *Na putiakh k novoi shkole*, 1925, no. 6: 89–90.

57. TsGALI holds several issues of two wall newspapers ("Sharoshka" and "Dzerzhinets") produced in Anton Makarenko's Dzerzhinskii Commune in 1930; TsGALI, f. 332, o. 2, ed. khr. 57 (for "Sharoshka") and ed. khr. 58 (for "Dzerzhinets"). At least for a time, the two papers regarded each other as rivals. See for example TsGALI, f. 332, o. 2, ed. khr. 57, roll 4, l. 19. For excerpts from the wall newspapers of other institutions, see Livshits, *Sotsial'nye korni*, 172; Utevskii, *V bor'be*, 98–99.

58. *Drug detei*, 1926, no. 7: 22–23; *Na pomoshch' detiam. Obshchestvenno-literaturnyi i nauchnyi sbornik*, 31; Makarenko, *Road to Life* 2:397; *Voprosy prosveshcheniia* (Rostov-on-the-Don), 1926, nos. 6–7: 48; Shveitser and Shabalov, *Besprizornye*, 23, 25, 80; *Shkola i zhizn'* (Nizhnii Novgorod), 1926, no. 11: 51; *Sibirskii pedagogicheskii zhurnal* (Novo-Nikolaevsk), 1924, no. 3: 56; *Ural'skii uchitel'* (Sverdlovsk), 1925, no. 2: 41.

59. *Voprosy prosveshcheniia* (Rostov-on-the-Don), 1926, nos. 6–7: 48. "Dzerzhinets," mentioned above, also acquired a more ponderous, political aura once it became the organ of the commune's Komsomol organization.

60. TsGA RSFSR, f. 1575, o. 10, ed. khr. 178, l. 12; *Sibirskii pedagogicheskii zhurnal* (Novo-Nikolaevsk), 1924, no. 3: 56; *Ural'skii uchitel'* (Sverd-

lovsk), 1925, no. 2: 40–41; Shveitser and Shabalov, *Besprizornye*, 23–25, 54; *Krasnoiarskii rabochii* (Krasnoiarsk), 1925, no. 140 (June 23), p. 3.

61. TsGALI, f. 332, o. 2, ed. khr. 58, roll 3, l. 16; Glatman, *Pionery i besprizornye*, 40; Shveitser and Shabalov, *Besprizornye*, 23, 64. The Komsomol and Pioneer cells in some *detdoma*, colonies, and communes worked under the guidance of Komsomol organizations and leaders based outside the institutions. If a facility did not have its own Komsomol cell, interested youths might attend meetings of Komsomol organizations nearby. See Shveitser and Shabalov, *Besprizornye*, 22–23, 51, 64, 75–76. Many Komsomol and Pioneer groups reportedly opposed establishing cells in institutions for "difficult" children. They regarded former *besprizornye*, long under the influence of the street, as undesirable candidates for membership in their organizations. See Shveitser and Shabalov, *Besprizornye*, 131.

62. *Narodnoe prosveshchenie v R.S.F.S.R. k 1924/25 uchebnomu godu*, 85; Tizanov et al., *Detskaia besprizornost'*, 192; Shveitser and Shabalov, *Besprizornye*, 128; Tizanov et al., *Pedagogika*, 19, 248; *Vozhatyi*, 1924, no. 1: 32.

63. For more on dormant, unenthusiastic, and otherwise disappointing Pioneer and Komsomol cells in children's institutions, see TsGALI, f. 332, o. 2, ed. khr. 58, roll 3, ll. 15–17, 25; *Voprosy prosveshcheniia* (Rostov-on-the-Don), 1926, nos. 6–7: 49; Tizanov et al., *Detskaia besprizornost'*, 193; Shveitser and Shabalov, *Besprizornye*, 25, 129–130, 132; *Nash trud* (Iaroslavl'), 1926, no. 7: 4; Smolensk Archive, reel 45, WKP 402, p. 41. A number of institutions had difficulty introducing Pioneer cells because some youths (especially street-hardened former *besprizornye*) scorned such organizations and taunted other children wearing the red neckerchief of the Pioneers. See *Detskii dom i bor'ba s besprizornost'iu*, 45–46; *Besprizornye*, comp. Kaidanova, 48. Tension also developed on occasion between the pedagogic staff of a *detdom* and the leaders of its Komsomol or Pioneer group (especially, one supposes, if these leaders were based outside the institution). Each side regarded the other as diverting the children from more important endeavors. See *Vozhatyi*, 1925, nos. 9–10: 28–29; no. 17: 31; *Narodnoe prosveshchenie v R.S.F.S.R. k 1924/25 uchebnomu godu*, 86. Regarding the more general rivalry between the Komsomol and Narkompros, see Stolee, "Generation," 160.

64. Technically, "self-service" (*samoobsluzhivanie*) meant an assumption by children of responsibility for daily chores (cleaning, cooking, tending animals, gathering water and firewood, and so on), while "self-government" (*samoupravlenie*) implied a higher level of responsibility: participation in making the decisions required to run an institution (including matters of discipline and utilization of resources).

65. The wall newspaper "Sharoshka" contains a detailed description of a general meeting at Makarenko's Dzerzhinskii commune; TsGALI, f. 332, o. 2, ed. khr. 57, roll 7, ll. 1–22. For material on general meetings (which went by a variety of names), elections, and the structure of *samoupravlenie* at a number of institutions, see Shveitser and Shabalov, *Besprizornye*, 21–22, 39, 49–50, 75; *Sibirskii pedagogicheskii zhurnal* (Novo-Nikolaevsk), 1924, no. 3: 55; TsGALI, f. 332, o. 2, ed. khr. 57, roll 6, ll. 30–36, 41–42; Diushen, *Piat' let*, 200.

66. TsGALI, f. 332, o. 1, ed. khr. 52, ll. 186–189; Kaidanova, *Besprizornye deti*, 38; Shveitser and Shabalov, *Besprizornye*, 26, 37, 39, 56; *Shkola i zhizn'* (Nizhnii Novgorod), 1926, no. 11: 50; *Ural'skii uchitel'* (Sverdlovsk), 1925, no. 2: 39–40; *Krasnoiarskii rabochii* (Krasnoiarsk), 1925, no. 140 (June 23), p. 3.

67. Regarding the institutions at Perm' and Tobol'sk, see Shveitser and Shabalov, *Besprizornye*, 24; *Ural'skii uchitel'* (Sverdlovsk), 1925, no. 2: 41–42. On children disciplined by their peers, see Makarenko, *Road to Life* 2:416–425; Glatman, *Pionery i besprizornye*, 29; Hans Siemsen, "Russia's Self-Educated Children," *Living Age* 340 (August 1931): 556. On staff members called to account before students, see Maro, *Besprizornye*, 254–255; *Detskii dom*, 1929, no. 1: 41. For another advanced form of "self-government" (here called *samoorganizatsiia*) at an institution in Viatka, see Shveitser and Shabalov, *Besprizornye*, 74–75.

68. Livshits, *Sotsial'nye korni*, 106; *Na putiakh k novoi shkole*, 1924, nos. 7–8: 42–43; Shveitser and Shabalov, *Besprizornye*, 135; *Prosveshchenie Sibiri* (Novosibirsk), 1926, no. 11: 98; Tizanov et al., *Detskaia besprizornost'*, 41–42; *Detskii dom*, 1928, no. 3: 46.

69. *Na pomoshch' detiam. Obshchestvenno-literaturnyi i nauchnyi sbornik*, 29; Glatman, *Pionery i besprizornye*, 35–36; *Krasnoiarskii rabochii* (Krasnoiarsk), 1925, no. 202 (September 5), p. 5.

70. TsGALI, f. 332, o. 1, ed. khr. 55, l. 12.

71. Pogrebinskii, *Fabrika liudei*, 30; Makarenko, *Road to Life* 2:249; *Detskii dom i bor'ba s besprizornost'iu*, 46–47; *Drug detei*, 1928, no. 5: 20; *Krasnoiarskii rabochii* (Krasnoiarsk), 1925, no. 201 (September 4), p. 3.

72. Regarding the abuse of newcomers, girls, and young children, see TsGALI, f. 332, o. 2, ed. khr. 58, roll 2, l. 68; *Drug detei*, 1928, no. 5: 20; *Put' prosveshcheniia* (Khar'kov), 1924, nos. 4–5: 236; Makarenko, *Road to Life* 2:245–246. On fighting among children in institutions, see *Na pomoshch' detiam. Obshchestvenno-literaturnyi i nauchnyi sbornik*, 29; Glatman, *Pionery i besprizornye*, 35–36; *Na putiakh k novoi shkole*, 1925, no. 4: 155.

73. *Na putiakh k novoi shkole*, 1925, no. 3: 202; no. 4: 148; no. 6: 88–89; *Detskii dom*, 1928, no. 3: 81–83; Makarenko, *Road to Life* 2:47–48, 72–73, 96, 102; Shveitser and Shabalov, *Besprizornye*, 23, 26, 30, 34–35, 39, 51–52, 54, 64, 77; Pogrebinskii, *Fabrika liudei*, 28–29. A number of institutions conducted anti-alcohol and anti-religion campaigns in their regions—efforts that doubtless failed to win the sympathy of the entire local population. See TsGALI, f. 332, o. 2, ed. khr. 58, roll 1, ll. 56, 58–59, 61, 63; Shveitser and Shabalov, *Besprizornye*, 53; *Drug detei* (Khar'kov), 1925, no. 5: 24; *Voprosy prosveshcheniia* (Rostov-on-the-Don), 1926, nos. 6–7: 49.

74. Regarding thefts from neighboring households and merchants, see TsGALI, f. 332, o. 2, ed. khr. 41, l. 22; *Nash trud* (Iaroslavl'), 1924, nos. 11–12: 29; *Shkola i zhizn'* (Nizhnii Novgorod), 1927, no. 4: 78; *Detskii dom*, 1929, no. 6: 24–25. Reversing occasionally the roles of predator and victim, local youths raided the gardens of some children's institutions; *Detskii dom*, 1929, no. 1: 40.

75. *Prosveshchenie Sibiri* (Novosibirsk), 1928, no. 3: 63; *Na pomoshch' detiam. Obshchestvenno-literaturnyi i nauchnyi sbornik*, 30; Livshits, *Sotsi-*

al'nye korni, 175; *Molot* (Rostov-on-the-Don), 1925, no. 1261 (October 16), p. 4; *Volna* (Arkhangel'sk), 1926, no. 28 (February 4), p. 4; *Krasnoiarskii rabochii* (Krasnoiarsk), 1925, no. 168 (July 25), p. 3 (regarding stones thrown at the statue of Lenin).

76. *Voprosy prosveshcheniia* (Rostov-on-the-Don), 1926, no. 2: 59. A report from Novocherkassk indicated in 1925 that "an especially large number of juvenile lawbreakers are to be found among adolescents in the city's *detdoma*"; *Molot* (Rostov-on-the-Don), 1925, no. 1200 (August 5), p. 4. Referring to Ukraine, an article reported that 5 percent of all cases coming before Juvenile Affairs Commissions in 1925 involved inhabitants of *detdoma*; *Drug detei* (Khar'kov), 1926, no. 10: 7.

77. *Krasnaia nov'*, 1932, no. 1: 39.

78. *Shkola i zhizn'* (Nizhnii Novgorod), 1926, no. 11: 31; *Detskii dom i bor'ba s besprizornost'iu*, 41; *Detskii dom*, 1929, no. 1: 17; no. 5: 3–4. Regarding gambling and the use of tobacco, alcohol, cocaine, and hashish in children's institutions, see TsGALI, f. 332, o. 1, ed. khr. 53, l. 2; ibid., ed. khr. 55, l. 12; ibid., o. 2, ed. khr. 57, roll 7, l. 43; *Put' prosveshcheniia* (Khar'kov), 1924, nos. 4–5: 235–236; Borovich, *Kollektivy besprizornykh*, 78; Kaidanova, *Besprizornye deti*, 24; *Na putiakh k novoi shkole*, 1924, nos. 7–8: 140; 1927, no. 2: 87; *Drug detei*, 1928, no. 5: 20.

79. British Foreign Office, 1926, reel 3, vol. 11785, p. 75; *Venerologiia i dermatologiia*, 1926, no. 5: 834; *Vestnik prosveshcheniia*, 1928, no. 3: 10; Panait Istrati, *Russia Unveiled* (London, 1931; reprint, Westport, Conn., 1975), 102; Shveitser and Shabalov, *Besprizornye*, 26–27, 69; *Drug detei*, 1928, no. 1: 17; no. 5: 20; *Prosveshchenie Sibiri* (Novosibirsk), 1928, no. 3: 58; *Detskii dom*, 1929, no. 5: 77–78.

80. TsGALI, f. 332, o. 1, ed. khr. 60, l. 3; *Vestnik prosveshcheniia*, 1925, no. 9: 89; *Krasnaia nov'*, 1932, no. 1: 39; Makarenko, *Road to Life* 2:209; *Detskii dom*, 1929, no. 5: 16–18; no. 6: 45; Shveitser and Shabalov, *Besprizornye*, 32, 36, 65, 167.

81. Livshits, *Sotsial'nye korni*, 141–142, 151–152; Borovich, *Kollektivy besprizornykh*, 22–24, 76–78, 119; TsGALI, f. 332, o. 1, ed. khr. 53, l. 2; Glatman, *Pionery i besprizornye*, 36; *Na putiakh k novoi shkole*, 1924, nos. 7–8: 140; nos. 10–12: 88; *Pravda*, 1926, no. 68 (March 25), p. 1. Gang leaders exercised a similar influence in some receivers as well; for an example, see *Na putiakh k novoi shkole*, 1925, no. 4: 154.

82. Makarenko, *Road to Life* 2:268.

83. *Detskii dom*, 1929, no. 7: 30; Livshits, *Sotsial'nye korni*, 151. For the approaches used by the staff at two institutions to break the grip of gang leaders, see *Na putiakh k novoi shkole*, 1925, no. 4: 148–149; Livshits, *Sotsial'nye korni*, 153.

84. *Na putiakh k novoi shkole*, 1924, nos. 7–8: 29–30; nos. 10–12: 88; Glatman, *Pionery i besprizornye*, 36–37; Shveitser and Shabalov, *Besprizornye*, 16, 21; TsGALI, f. 332, o. 2, ed. khr. 41, l. 2; ibid., ed. khr. 57, roll 4, l. 1.

85. Livshits, *Sotsial'nye korni*, 13; *Drug detei* (Khar'kov), 1926, nos. 6–7: 39; 1927, nos. 7–8: 43; *Na putiakh k novoi shkole*, 1924, nos. 7–8: 34, 38; *Voprosy prosveshcheniia* (Rostov-on-the-Don), 1926, no. 2: 27; Bowen, *Soviet*

Education, 8; TsGALI, f. 332, o. 1, ed. khr. 60, l. 10; Makarenko, *Road to Life* 1:219–220.

86. *Prosveshchenie Sibiri* (Novosibirsk), 1928, nos. 7–8: 99–100; *Volna* (Arkhangel'sk), 1926, no. 173 (July 31), p. 3; Livshits, *Sotsial'nye korni*, 103; *Krasnoiarskii rabochii* (Krasnoiarsk), 1925, no. 137 (June 19), p. 2; *Komsomol'skaia pravda*, 1927, no. 225 (October 2), p. 2; *Pravda*, 1927, no. 235 (October 14), p. 4 (regarding the *detdom* in Odessa); *Izvestiia*, 1928, no. 17 (January 20), p. 1; 1928, no. 152 (July 3), p. 4. Sometimes, beatings represented abuse (by drunken staff members, for example) more than punishment. An investigation of *detdoma* in Tula province discovered girls who had been raped by instructors. See *Pravda*, 1926, no. 113 (May 19), p. 4. Regarding the abuse of children by personnel at the *Pokrovka*, see *Komsomol'skaia pravda*, 1927, no. 196 (August 30), p. 4; 1927, no. 201 (September 4), p. 6; *Vestnik prosveshcheniia*, 1928, no. 3: 3, 5. In rare instances, mistreatment and poor conditions drove youths to mutiny and sack their facilities; *Pravda*, 1926, no. 113 (May 19), p. 4; Istrati, *Russia Unveiled*, 102–103.

87. Livshits, *Sotsial'nye korni*, 103–104; *Komsomol'skaia pravda*, 1927, no. 225 (October 2), p. 2 (regarding the *detdom* in Nikolaev); *Prosveshchenie Sibiri* (Novosibirsk), 1928, nos. 7–8: 100 (regarding the *detdom* in Barnaul); Makarenko, *Road to Life* 2:149.

88. *Drug detei* (Khar'kov), 1927, nos. 7–8: 42; Livshits, *Sotsial'nye korni*, 106.

89. Anton Makarenko, walking through a dormitory in a neglected children's colony not far from Khar'kov, asked a youth why there were no pillows. The lad replied:

" 'But here nobody even keeps a list of *people*, let alone pillows! Nobody! And nobody counts them. Nobody!'

'How can that be?'

'It's quite simple! Just like that! Do you think anybody has ever written down that Ilya Fonarenko lives here? Nobody has! Nobody even knows! And nobody knows me! And there's lots here like that—they live here, and then they go and live somewhere else, and then they come back here again' "; Makarenko, *Road to Life* 2:241. Regarding the flight of youths from strict-regime institutions, see *Vestnik prosveshcheniia*, 1925, no. 9: 90.

90. Utevskii, *V bor'be*, 88–89.

91. *Detskii dom i bor'ba s besprizornost'iu*, 11; *Na putiakh k novoi shkole*, 1924, nos. 7–8: 49; nos. 10–12: 85; *Drug detei* (Khar'kov), 1927, nos. 9–10: 5; *Krasnaia nov'*, 1932, no. 1: 44; Kalinina, *Komsomol i besprizornost'*, 8; V. I. Kufaev, *Shkola-kommuna imeni F. E. Dzerzhinskogo* (Moscow, 1938), 6.

92. Livshits, *Sotsial'nye korni*, 108 (regarding the figures for 1923/24); *Narodnoe prosveshchenie v RSFSR 1927–28 god*, 175; *Drug detei*, 1928, no. 3: 3 (for Lunacharskii's comments). According to Narkompros records, 18–20 percent of the children who entered receivers in 1923/24 later fled; see Ryndziunskii et al., *Pravovoe polozhenie* (1927), 87n.1; Tizanov et al., *Detskaia besprizornost'*, 174. Boys were much more likely to run away than girls; *Narodnoe obrazovanie v R.S.F.S.R.*, 122–123. Escapees accounted for 22 percent of all the youths leaving receivers in the Russian Republic during 1927; *Narodnoe prosveshchenie v RSFSR 1927–28 god*, 175.

93. TsGALI, f. 332, o. 2, ed. khr. 41, ll. 4–5; *Volna* (Arkhangel'sk), 1926, no. 173 (July 31), p. 3; *Molot* (Rostov-on-the-Don), 1925, no. 1250 (October 3), p. 5; Shveitser and Shabalov, *Besprizornye*, 91; *Drug detei*, 1928, no. 5: 20; *Detskii dom i bor'ba s besprizornost'iu*, 47; *Voprosy prosveshcheniia na Severnom Kavkaze* (Rostov-on-the-Don), 1928, no. 10: 23.

94. *Vozhatyi*, 1925, nos. 5–6: 7; Maro, *Besprizornye*, 108, 166; Shveitser and Shabalov, *Besprizornye*, 87; *Na putiakh k novoi shkole*, 1927, no. 2: 87; McCormick, *Hammer and Scythe*, 200; Hughes, *I Wonder*, 153; *Detskii dom i bor'ba s besprizornost'iu*, 47.

95. *Pravda*, 1924, no. 51 (March 2), p. 5. The article ends with Chainik's claim that he will now return to a Narkompros institution "forever." No doubt more than a few readers remained skeptical.

96. Tizanov et al., *Detskaia besprizornost'*, 100.

97. *Pravo i zhizn'*, 1925, nos. 7–8: 85–86.

98. In addition to the sources cited above, see (regarding the meager and unpredictable support provided *detdoma* by local officials) *Narodnoe prosveshchenie v R.S.F.S.R. k 1924/25 uchebnomu godu*, 85; *Detskii dom i bor'ba s besprizornost'iu*, 15; *Severo-Kavkazskii krai* (Rostov-on-the-Don), 1926, no. 5: 24; *Krasnoiarskii rabochii* (Krasnoiarsk), 1925, no. 144 (June 27), p. 3.

99. TsGA RSFSR, f. 1575, o. 10, ed. khr. 178, l. 20; *Molot* (Rostov-on-the-Don), 1925, no. 1196 (July 31), p. 3; 1925, no. 1269 (October 25), p. 4; *Statisticheskii obzor narodnogo obrazovaniia v permskom okruge*, 38; *Volna* (Arkhangel'sk), 1926, no. 152 (July 7), p. 6; *Krasnaia nov'*, 1932, no. 1: 38; *Narodnoe prosveshchenie v R.S.F.S.R. k 1924/25 uchebnomu godu*, 85; Tizanov et al., *Pedagogika*, 19 (for the figure of more than 40 percent of *detdom* children sleeping two or three to a bed). The problem of overcrowding in *detdoma* was apparently less severe in Leningrad than in Moscow and a number of other cities. Perhaps this was due in part to Leningrad's location on the country's periphery, which sheltered it to some extent from the currents of *besprizornye* that continued to stream to cities such as Moscow and Rostov-on-the-Don. However, other cities more remote, such as Arkhangel'sk, maintained overcrowded *detdoma*, so some credit for Leningrad's achievement should also be given to city officials. See Ryndziunskii et al., *Pravovoe polozhenie* (1927), 86.

100. TsGALI, f. 332, o. 2, ed. khr. 41, l. 17; TsGA RSFSR, f. 1575, o. 10, ed. khr. 178, l. 20; *Severo-Kavkazskii krai* (Rostov-on-the-Don), 1926, no. 5: 26; *Komsomol'skaia pravda*, 1927, no. 225 (October 2), p. 2; Shveitser and Shabalov, *Besprizornye*, 44, 68; *Voprosy prosveshcheniia* (Rostov-on-the-Don), 1926, no. 2: 34. Regarding poor sanitation, see TsGALI, f. 332, o. 2, ed. khr. 58, roll 1, ll. 84–92; *Severo-Kavkazskii krai* (Rostov-on-the-Don), 1926, no. 5: 26; Makarenko, *Road to Life* 2:191; *Okhrana zdorov'ia detei*, comp. N. N. Spasokukotskii (Moscow-Leningrad, 1932), 166. An article in the wall newspaper of Makarenko's labor commune grumbled that the amount of dirt in the bathroom would permit the opening of a Machine-Tractor Station there; TsGALI, f. 332, o. 2, ed. khr. 57, roll 8, l. 50. In Siberia, an investigation of several *detdoma* in Irkutsk, Tomsk, and Krasnoiarsk found most sleeping quarters saturated with the odor of urine, a distinction by no means unique to facilities in these cities; *Prosveshchenie Sibiri* (Novosibirsk), 1927, no. 8: 58–59. Similarly

distressing conditions obtained in many receivers. A factory worker sent a newspaper the following description of a receiver she visited in Rostov-on-the-Don: "Even as we approached Receiver No. 1, we saw on the threshold and stairs half-naked, trembling bodies, barely covered with rags. We walked up into the building, and there reigned such filth and stench that it was difficult to breathe. The windows were broken and it was cold inside. On the floor lay barefoot, undressed children in rags, with bluish faces. The children stood, lay on the floor, and sat by a stove that did not so much warm as smoke"; *Molot* (Rostov-on-the-Don), 1926, no. 1399 (April 4), p. 3. An investigation of several *detdoma* in Nizhnii Novgorod province found their sanitary condition "in general" to be acceptable in 1926, though, in some, food was still being stored on the floor; see *Shkola i zhizn'* (Nizhnii Novgorod), 1926, no. 11: 53.

101. Regarding the unsatisfactory or nonexistent medical care at many institutions, see *Vestnik prosveshchentsa* (Orenburg), 1926, no. 10: 69; *Okhrana zdorov'ia detei*, 167; Livshits, *Sotsial'nye korni*, 104; Shveitser and Shabalov, *Besprizornye*, 69; Tizanov et al., *Pedagogika*, 18; *Sbornik deistvuiushchikh uzakonenii i rasporiazhenii* (1929), 189.

102. *Puti kommunisticheskogo prosveshcheniia* (Simferopol'), 1928, nos. 1–2: 28; *Saratovskii vestnik zdravookhraneniia* (Saratov), 1926, no. 1: 74–78; Shveitser and Shabalov, *Besprizornye*, 69; *Komsomol'skaia pravda*, 1925, no. 29 (June 28), p. 2; Tizanov et al., *Detskaia besprizornost'*, 195; *Narodnoe prosveshchenie v R.S.F.S.R. k 1924/25 uchebnomu godu*, 85.

103. *Severo-Kavkazskii krai* (Rostov-on-the-Don), 1926, no. 5: 26 (regarding the *detdoma* in the Northern Caucasus); *Profilakticheskaia meditsina* (Khar'kov), 1926, no. 5: 29 (for the second investigation mentioned); *Drug detei* (Khar'kov), 1926, nos. 4–5: 10 (for the tuberculosis figures). An investigation in 1926 of 1,244 children housed in twenty-one *detdoma* in Penza province found 908 healthy and 336 in poor condition; see *Prosveshchenie* (Penza), 1926, no. 7: 63. In some institutions, of course, most children were in good health; see for example Shveitser and Shabalov, *Besprizornye*, 31.

104. Regarding the poor state of repair of many of the buildings utilized by children's institutions, see TsGALI, f. 332, o. 2, ed. khr. 41, ll. 4–5; *Severo-Kavkazskii krai* (Rostov-on-the-Don), 1926, no. 5: 26; Shveitser and Shabalov, *Besprizornye*, 57–58. Regarding the various types of buildings occupied by *detdoma*, see Tizanov et al., *Pedagogika*, 19 (for the statistics cited); Gilev, *Detskaia besprizornost'*, 12; *Shkola i zhizn'* (Nizhnii Novgorod), 1927, no. 10: 59; *Besprizornye*, comp. Kaidanova, 48; American Red Cross, box 916, file 987.08, "Chita Revisited."

105. *Detskii dom*, 1929, no. 6: 58; 1930, nos. 8–10: 51; *Detskii dom*, comp. Utevskii, 62; Tizanov et al., *Detskaia besprizornost'*, 186; *Okhrana detstva*, 1931, no. 7: 30 (regarding the incubator), 35; Tizanov et al., *Pedagogika*, 17; *Drug detei*, 1927, nos. 6–7: 7; *SU*, 1930, no. 59, art. 704; *Voprosy prosveshcheniia na Severnom Kavkaze* (Rostov-on-the-Don), 1927, no. 9: 10. Officials sometimes transferred *detdoma* out of their cities and towns for other reasons as well. These included a desire to remove *besprizornye* (those in *detdoma*, in this case) from the municipality and an effort to place financial responsibility for the institutions on the shoulders of other authorities. For voices condemning

the transfer of *detdoma*, and futile central-government efforts to restrict the practice, see *Detskii dom*, comp. Utevskii, 30, 62–63; *Detskii dom*, 1929, no. 1: 16; 1930, no. 6: 12; *Detskii dom i bor'ba s besprizornost'iu*, 32; Tizanov and Epshtein, *Gosudarstvo i obshchestvennost'*, 38; *Rezoliutsii 3-go vserossiiskogo s''ezda po okhrane detstva 25–30 maia 1930 g. i 1-go vserossiiskogo soveshchaniia po bor'be s detskoi besprizornost'iu i beznadzornost'iu 7-go dekabria 1930 g.* (Moscow, 1931), 16.

106. *Detskii dom i bor'ba s besprizornost'iu*, 48; *Na putiakh k novoi shkole*, 1925, no. 4: 157; Shveitser and Shabalov, *Besprizornye*, 87; Tizanov et al., *Detskaia besprizornost'*, 188.

107. *Narodnoe prosveshchenie*, 1926, no. 8: 67; *Detskii dom i bor'ba s besprizornost'iu*, 15; Krasnushkin et al., *Nishchenstvo i besprizornost'*, 151; *Na pomoshch' detiam. Obshchestvenno-literaturnyi i nauchnyi sbornik*, 28; Shveitser and Shabalov, *Besprizornye*, 18–19, 67, 106; Gilev, *Detskaia besprizornost'*, 10–11; *Molot* (Rostov-on-the-Don), 1926, no. 1569 (October 26), p. 3; *Sbornik deistvuiushchikh uzakonenii i rasporiazhenii* (1929), 201; Tizanov et al., *Detskaia besprizornost'*, 188; *Prosveshchenie na Urale* (Sverdlovsk), 1928, nos. 7–8: 65; *Voprosy prosveshcheniia* (Rostov-on-the-Don), 1926, nos. 6–7: 50–51; *Na putiakh k novoi shkole*, 1926, nos. 5–6: 51–52; 1927, no. 12: 71; *Drug detei* (Khar'kov), 1927, no. 3: 35; *Krasnoiarskii rabochii* (Krasnoiarsk), 1925, no. 168 (July 25), p. 3; *Narodnoe prosveshchenie v RSFSR k 1927–28 uchebnomu godu*, 57 (for the figures contained in the Narkompros report). For more on appeals and efforts to provide additional training for *detdom* personnel—a campaign that did not produce dramatic results across the country in the 1920s—see TsGA RSFSR, f. 298, o. 2, ed. khr. 58, l. 52; *Narodnoe prosveshchenie v R.S.F.S.R. k 1924/25 uchebnomu godu*, 83; *Sbornik deistvuiushchikh uzakonenii i rasporiazhenii* (1929), 41; Tizanov and Epshtein, *Gosudarstvo i obshchestvennost'*, 38; *Na putiakh k novoi shkole*, 1927, no. 12: 72. Regarding the low pay of instructors in *detdoma*, see *Voprosy prosveshcheniia* (Rostov-on-the-Don), 1926, nos. 6–7: 51; *Volna* (Arkhangel'sk), 1925, no. 182 (August 15), p. 5; *Severo-Kavkazskii krai* (Rostov-on-the-Don), 1926, no. 5: 27; *Voprosy prosveshcheniia na Severnom Kavkaze* (Rostov-on-the-Don), 1927, no. 9: 9; *Drug detei*, 1926, no. 1: 7; Tizanov et al., *Detskaia besprizornost'*, 188; *Detskii dom i bor'ba s besprizornost'iu*, 15; Shishova, "Sozdanie," 13.

108. *Detskii dom*, 1929, no. 6: 25.

109. Gilev, *Detskaia besprizornost'*, 10–11. Entries from teachers' diaries reveal some of the daily frustration they experienced working with *besprizornye* (and also some successes). For a number of these entries, see Livshits, *Sotsial'nye korni*, 143; Kaidanova, *Besprizornye deti*, 27–40.

110. Kufaev, *Shkola-kommuna*, 7–8; Livshits, *Sotsial'nye korni*, 140–141; Krasnushkin et al., *Nishchenstvo i besprizornost'*, 237; Maro, *Besprizornye*, 334–335; Shveitser and Shabalov, *Besprizornye*, 46; Kaidanova, *Besprizornye deti*, 23–24; *Drug detei* (Khar'kov), 1926, nos. 6–7: 24; *Detskii dom*, 1928, no. 3: 44; *Vozhatyi*, 1926, no. 2: 31.

111. *Pravo i zhizn'*, 1925, nos. 7–8: 86–88.

112. Ibid., nos. 9–10: 90–91.

113. TsGALI, f. 332, o. 2, ed. khr. 41, l. 17; *Asfal'tovyi kotel*, 258; *Prosveshchenie Sibiri* (Novosibirsk), 1928, no. 3: 60, 63; *Besprizornye*, comp. Kai-

danova, 48; *Drug detei*, 1928, no. 5: 20; *Ural'skii uchitel'* (Sverdlovsk), 1925, nos. 9–10: 39; Poznyshev, *Detskaia besprizornost'*, 50; Bartlett, "Stepchildren," 368; Utevskii, *V bor'be*, 23; British Foreign Office, 1926, reel 3, vol. 11785, p. 76. Youths also abused personnel in some receivers; see for example *Vestnik prosveshcheniia*, 1928, no. 3: 6; Kalinina, *Komsomol i besprizornost'*, 44.

114. *Krasnaia gazeta* (Leningrad), evening ed., 1926, no. 224 (September 24), p. 3.

115. Eventually, administrators gained control of the clinic by admitting only five youths, "taming" them, bringing in five more, and so on up to a limit of twenty-five; see British Foreign Office, 1926, reel 3, vol. 11785, pp. 72–73.

116. I have relied on extensive quotations from these articles—which appeared originally on December 8, 9, and 10, 1926, in *Rabochaia gazeta*—compiled and translated by the British Mission in Moscow. Ibid., pp. 74–78.

117. See for example *Narodnoe prosveshchenie v R.S.F.S.R. k 1924/25 uchebnomu godu*, 87; *Severo-Kavkazskii krai* (Rostov-on-the-Don), 1926, no. 5: 25; *Prosveshchenie na Urale* (Sverdlovsk), 1927, no. 2: 60–61; *Detskii dom i bor'ba s besprizornost'iu*, 14; Kalinina, *Desiat' let*, 99.

118. For reports and descriptions of comparatively successful institutions, see *Na putiakh k novoi shkole*, 1925, no. 4: 142–144; *Prosveshchenie Sibiri* (Novosibirsk), 1927, no. 9: 84–86; 1928, no. 3: 75; nos. 7–8: 102; Kaidanova, *Besprizornye deti*, 7–47; *Drug detei*, 1926, no. 1: 20–21; Shveitser and Shabalov, *Besprizornye*, 58, 71–72; *Voprosy prosveshcheniia* (Rostov-on-the-Don), 1926, no. 2: 22–28; Maro, *Besprizornye*, 259–260; Glatman, *Pionery i besprizornye*, 34–41; *Drug detei* (Khar'kov), 1925, no. 1: 48; no. 6: 25–27; *Krasnoiarskii rabochii* (Krasnoiarsk), 1925, no. 168 (July 25), p. 3; *Molot* (Rostov-on-the-Don), 1926, no. 1438 (May 22), p. 2; 1926, no. 1561 (October 16), p. 3; 1926, no. 1573 (October 30), p. 4.

119. *Detskii dom i bor'ba s besprizornost'iu*, 11, 13 (regarding the report to the All-Russian Conference of Detdom Personnel); Smolensk Archive, reel 45, WKP 402, p. 17; *Volna* (Arkhangel'sk), 1926, no. 28 (February 4), p. 2; *Na putiakh k novoi shkole*, 1925, no. 4: 141; Shveitser and Shabalov, *Besprizornye*, 16–17; Istrati, *Russia Unveiled*, 100–101.

120. TsGALI, f. 332, o. 2, ed. khr. 41, l. 3; *Voprosy prosveshcheniia* (Rostov-on-the-Don), 1926, no. 5: 34; Maro, *Besprizornye*, 262; *Prosveshchenie na transporte*, 1927, no. 6: 68; Poznyshev, *Detskaia besprizornost'*, 109; *Prosveshchenie Sibiri* (Novosibirsk), 1926, no. 11: 97; 1927, no. 8: 58–59.

121. Diushen, *Piat' let*, 5–31; *Otchet kurskogo gubernskogo ispolnitel'nogo komiteta*, 153–154; Shishova, "Sozdanie," 2, 4–5; *Statisticheskii obzor narodnogo obrazovaniia v permskoi gubernii*, 133; *Detskii dom*, 1930, nos. 8–10: 51; *Na pomoshch' detiam. Obshchestvenno-literaturnyi i nauchnyi sbornik*, 40; Tizanov et al., *Detskaia besprizornost'*, 185; *Drug detei*, 1927, nos. 8–9: 23; *Prosveshchenie na Urale* (Sverdlovsk), 1927, no. 2: 60; *Na putiakh k novoi shkole*, 1924, nos. 4–5: 91, 93; *Drug detei* (Khar'kov), 1925, no. 5: 21.

122. TsGALI, f. 332, o. 2, ed. khr. 41, l. 22; *Vestnik prosveshcheniia*, 1925, no. 11: 3; *Statisticheskii obzor narodnogo obrazovaniia v permskoi gubernii*, 112 of the *prilozhenie*; *Na pomoshch' detiam. Obshchestvenno-literaturnyi i nauchnyi sbornik*, 41; *Molot* (Rostov-on-the-Don), 1926, no. 1579 (November

6), p. 3; *Komsomol'skaia pravda*, 1928, no. 19 (January 22), p. 6. For two positive descriptions of *detskie gorodki*, see *Na pomoshch' detiam*. *Obshchestvenno-literaturnyi i nauchnyi sbornik*, 39–43 (despite the negative comment made on p. 41, just cited); and *Molot* (Rostov-on-the-Don), 1925, no. 1205 (August 12), p. 4. For a detailed look at the strengths and weaknesses of several *detskie gorodki*, see *Na putiakh k novoi shkole*, 1924, nos. 4–5: 90–109.

123. *Detskii dom i bor'ba s besprizornost'iu*, 13; Tizanov et al., *Detskaia besprizornost'*, 185–186; *Voprosy prosveshcheniia na Severnom Kavkaze* (Rostov-on-the-Don), 1929, no. 1: 58; *Detskii dom*, 1930, no. 4: 11; *Besprizornye*, comp. Kaidanova, 63 (for the statistics).

124. *Obzor raboty po bor'be s detskoi besprizornost'iu i beznadzornost'iu v RSFSR za 1927/28 g.*, 10–11, 13–14; *Detskii dom*, 1928, no. 3: 66; *Vestnik prosveshcheniia*, 1928, no. 3: 3 (for the article in the Moscow Narkompros journal). For other generally negative assessments of *detdoma* offered at this time, see *Drug detei*, 1928, no. 5: 13; *Sbornik deistvuiushchikh uzakonenii i rasporiazhenii* (1929), 188; *Komsomol'skaia pravda*, 1927, no. 208 (September 13), p. 4.

CONCLUSION

1. Tizanov and Epshtein, *Gosudarstvo i obshchestvennost'*, 1.

2. *Detskii dom i bor'ba s besprizornost'iu*, 8–9, 31–32. In the months thereafter, the Children's Commission issued numerous instructions to provincial authorities, calling on them to draw up plans for the elimination of *besprizornost'* in their territories. A directive of July 2, 1928, noted that the Children's Commission would process the local designs it received into a comprehensive, single plan; see *Sbornik deistvuiushchikh uzakonenii i rasporiazhenii* (1929), 178. *Detdoma*, too, were sometimes urged to devote more attention to planning in their operations; see for example *Detskii dom*, 1929, no. 7: 7–16.

3. The draft Three-Year Plan and the decree of June 20, 1927 that brought it into force are available in a number of sources. See for example *Trekhletnii plan bor'by s detskoi besprizornost'iu* (Moscow, 1927); *Sbornik deistvuiushchikh uzakonenii i rasporiazhenii* (1929), 20–39; *SU*, 1927, no. 65, art. 446 (just the decree of June 20). The plan called for the allocation of the following sums to carry out its provisions: 11,161,125 rubles in 1926/27; 21,036,125 in 1927/28; and 23,285,125 in 1928/29. Roughly 90 percent of this money was earmarked for Narkompros, with the commissariats of health and internal affairs sharing the rest.

4. *Trekhletnii plan*, 8; *Detskii dom i bor'ba s besprizornost'iu*, 25. Concern that more needed to be done to remove *besprizornye* from railroads and waterways appeared at other meetings as well. See *Sbornik deistvuiushchikh uzakonenii i rasporiazhenii* (1929), 134.

5. TsGA RSFSR, f. 393, o. 1, ed. khr. 81, l. 17; *Prosveshchenie na transporte*, 1926, no. 10: 30; *Drug detei* (Khar'kov), 1926, nos. 4–5: 26; *Sbornik deistvuiushchikh uzakonenii i rasporiazhenii* (1932), 77; *Detskii dom*, 1929, no. 10: 17; *Okhrana detstva*, 1931, no. 6: 25; nos. 9–10: 29; *Drug detei*, 1931, no. 8: 15; *Izvestiia*, 1926, no. 110 (May 15), p. 3 (for the figure of 24,000).

6. *Prosveshchenie na transporte*, 1926, no. 10: 29; Tizanov and Epshtein, *Gosudarstvo i obshchestvennost'*, 64; *Krasnaia gazeta* (Leningrad), evening ed., 1926, no. 189 (August 16), p. 3.

7. *Prosveshchenie na transporte*, 1926, no. 10: 29–30; no. 11: 107; Tizanov and Epshtein, *Gosudarstvo i obshchestvennost'*, 63–68; *Sbornik deistvuiush-chikh uzakonenii i rasporiazhenii* (1929), 144; Krasnushkin et al., *Nishchenstvo i besprizornost'*, 148–149n.; *Drug detei* (Khar'kov), 1927, no. 3: 38; *Bor'ba s detskoi besprizornost'iu*, 90; *Drug detei*, 1927, no. 3: 14. The Commissariat of Transportation's budget for 1926/27 allocated over ten times as much money for receivers along railroads as it did for receivers intended to hold *besprizornye* removed from waterways; see *Drug detei*, 1927, no. 2: 19. For a list of the locations of stationary receivers on twelve railroad lines and a list of the stations at which the special train cars (*teplushki*) made stops, see *Sbornik deistvuiush-chikh uzakonenii i rasporiazhenii* (1929), 140.

8. *Bor'ba s detskoi besprizornost'iu*, 89–90; Ryndziunskii and Savinskaia, *Detskoe pravo*, 232; *Drug detei* (Khar'kov), 1927, nos. 5–6: 38; *Detskii dom*, 1929, no. 10: 19–20; TsGALI, f. 332, o. 2, ed. khr. 20, ll. 39–40. Children were sometimes sent straight from a *teplushka* (also called a *vagon-priemnik*) to a *detdom* or other permanent institution.

9. *Prosveshchenie na transporte*, 1926, no. 11: 107 (regarding organizational problems); *Detskii dom*, 1929, no. 10: 16–18 (regarding the Armavir station); *Okhrana detstva*, 1931, nos. 2–3: 32.

10. *Drug detei*, 1927, no. 3: 14; *Bor'ba s detskoi besprizornost'iu*, 89–92; *Prosveshchenie na transporte*, 1926, no. 11: 107; 1928, nos. 4–5: 109; Tizanov and Epshtein, *Gosudarstvo i obshchestvennost'*, 65; *Okhrana detstva*, 1931, no. 5: 33; *Pravda*, 1927, no. 32 (February 9), p. 3. Even some Juvenile Affairs Commissions rejected delinquency cases originating in the nation's transportation network, complained a circular from Narkompros, which instructed local commissions to cease such recalcitrance; *Nesovershennoletnie pravonarushiteli*, 42.

11. A report from the Children's Commission listed twenty-four *vagony-priemniki* and fifteen stationary receivers in the Russian Republic in 1928/29; *Obzor raboty po bor'be s detskoi besprizornost'iu i beznadzornost'iu v RSFSR za 1929/30 god*, 24. Another source mentions forty *vagony-priemniki* under the administration of the Commissariat of Transportation in the early 1930s; Ryndziunskii and Savinskaia, *Detskoe pravo*, 231.

12. *Detskii dom*, 1929, nos. 8–9: 88; no. 10: 14–17; *Okhrana detstva*, 1931, nos. 2–3: 32; no. 6: 20, 25; *Drug detei* (Khar'kov), 1927, nos. 5–6: 38; nos. 9–10: 20 (regarding the Tikhonova-Pustyn' station); *Bor'ba s detskoi besprizor-nost'iu*, 30, 91, 93; *SU*, 1932, no. 73, art. 328; Ryndziunskii and Savinskaia, *Detskoe pravo*, 230–232; *Prosveshchenie na transporte*, 1929, nos. 11–12: 107; *Prosveshchenie na Urale* (Sverdlovsk), 1930, no. 12: 72.

13. *SU*, 1927, no. 65, art. 446; *Detskii dom i bor'ba s besprizornost'iu*, 36.

14. For examples of earlier concern on Narkompros's part regarding the need to aid children who might soon become *besprizornye*, see TsGA RSFSR, f. 2306, o. 69, ed. khr. 349, l. 3; *Na putiakh k novoi shkole*, 1926, no. 3: 103–109; no. 4: 80–84.

15. Regarding calls in 1927–1929 to alleviate *beznadzornost'* (as the condition of these neglected children was called), see *Sbornik deistvuiushchikh uzakonenii i rasporiazhenii* (1929), 5–6, 40, 169, 188–189, 191, 195, 197, 202, 237, 240; *SU*, 1927, no. 65, art. 446; *Detskii dom i bor'ba s besprizornost'iu*, 36–37; Tizanov and Epshtein, *Gosudarstvo i obshchestvennost'*, 11–14. Regarding demands for legal action against parents who neglected their children, see *Sbornik deistvuiushchikh uzakonenii i rasporiazhenii* (1929), 172–173. Parents (and other guardians) found guilty of inadequate supervision of their children faced more severe penalties in the 1930s; see for example *SU*, 1932, no. 73, art. 328; *SZ*, 1935, no. 32, art. 252.

16. For a sampling of these orders, see *SU*, 1928, no. 117, art. 734; *SU*, 1929, no. 56, art. 547; *SU*, 1930, no. 59, art. 704; *Sbornik deistvuiushchikh uzakonenii i rasporiazhenii* (1929), 47, 53–54; 174–175.

17. *Sbornik deistvuiushchikh uzakonenii i rasporiazhenii* (1932), 37–38. For the resolution of December 1930, see *Rezoliutsii 3-go vserossiiskogo s"ezda*, 53. For similar sentiments, see *Detskii dom*, comp. Utevskii, 25, 27; *Obshchestvo "Drug detei,"* 43. The All-Russian Central Executive Committee issued a decree in October 1931 that included a call for resettling some older adolescents, discharged from *detdoma*, in new construction projects around the country; *SU*, 1931, no. 61, art. 446.

18. For the original decree, see *SU*, 1928, no. 44, art. 331. For the edited version published in 1932, see *Nesovershennoletnie pravonarushiteli*, 53.

19. *SU*, 1929, no. 85/86, art. 842 (the decree on apprentice brigades); *SU*, 1930, no. 59, art. 704; *Detskii dom*, comp. Utevskii, 38–39, 42–44; *Nesovershennoletnie pravonarushiteli*, 55; *Bor'ba s detskoi besprizornost'iu*, 31, 45; Ryndziunskii and Savinskaia, *Detskoe pravo*, 236, 312, 314; *Detskii dom*, 1930, nos. 2–3: 5–6; no. 6: 14; *Prosveshchenie na Urale* (Sverdlovsk), 1930, nos. 1–2: 107. The same transformation gripped the country's handful of labor homes. In 1930–1931 they were attached to factories and restructured as factory-apprenticeship schools (*shkoly fabrichno-zavodskogo uchenichestva*, or FZU schools)—until their replacement in 1935 by other facilities for juvenile delinquents. For more on labor home–FZU schools, see Astemirov, "Iz istorii," 258–265; *Nesovershennoletnie pravonarushiteli*, 18–20, 55; Ryndziunskii and Savinskaia, *Detskoe pravo*, 310–312; *Sbornik deistvuiushchikh uzakonenii i rasporiazhenii* (1932), 53; *SU*, 1933, no. 48, art. 208. For a negative assessment of these institutions by a Soviet author, see Min'kovskii, "Osnovnye etapy," 52–53.

20. *Detskii dom*, 1930, nos. 2–3: 5–6; no. 6: 14; *Bor'ba s detskoi besprizornost'iu*, 45; *Detskii dom*, comp. Utevskii, 29; *Obshchestvo "Drug detei,"* 36; *Sbornik deistvuiushchikh uzakonenii i rasporiazhenii* (1932), 37–42.

21. *Bor'ba s detskoi besprizornost'iu*, 108–109. By the end of the decade, articles promoting the discharge of *detdom* youths to collective farms often included criticism of foster-care arrangements with individual peasant families. See for example *Prosveshchenie Sibiri* (Novosibirsk), 1929, no. 11: 50–52; *Detskii dom*, 1929, no. 1: 14.

22. Regarding "socialist competition" and "shock work," see *Sbornik deistvuiushchikh uzakonenii i rasporiazhenii* (1932), 29, 49; *Detskii dom*, comp.

Utevskii, 30; *Bor'ba s detskoi besprizornost'iu*, 47, 49; *Detskii dom*, 1929, no. 7: 4–6; *Prosveshchenie Sibiri* (Novosibirsk), 1929, nos. 7–8: 136; 1932, no. 8: 60–61; TsGALI, f. 332, o. 2, ed. khr. 7, ll. 20–21; ibid., ed. khr. 57, roll 1, l. 1; ibid., roll 3, l. 52; ibid., roll 6, ll. 37–38, 43–47; ibid., ed. khr. 58, roll 3, ll. 1–3; ibid., roll 4, ll. 3–6. Regarding "opportunism" and "wrecking," see ibid., ed. khr. 57, roll 4, l. 16; *Sbornik deistvuiushchikh uzakonenii i rasporiazhenii* (1932), 28; *Bor'ba s detskoi besprizornost'iu*, 44–45, 48; *Obshchestvo "Drug detei,"* 20; *Okhrana detstva*, 1931, no. 7: 3. In 1930 the wall newspapers of Anton Makarenko's labor commune condemned kulaks, extolled collectivization, and praised Stalin's direction of these campaigns in the countryside; see for example TsGALI, f. 332, o. 2, ed. khr. 57, roll 8, ll. 36, 45; ibid., ed. khr. 58, roll 3, ll. 4–8.

23. TsGA RSFSR, f. 393, o. 1, ed. khr. 81, l. 12; *Sbornik deistvuiushchikh uzakonenii i rasporiazhenii* (1932), 46–47; *Detskii dom*, 1929, no. 2: 85–86, 91–92; no. 5: 46; no. 6: 58–59; *Prosveshchenie Sibiri* (Novosibirsk), 1929, no. 12: 9; *Obzor raboty po bor'be s detskoi besprizornost'iu i beznadzornost'iu v RSFSR za 1929/30 god*, 10–11; *Khoziaistvo TsChO* (Voronezh), 1929, no. 3: 178.

24. *Sbornik deistvuiushchikh uzakonenii i rasporiazhenii* (1929), 92–93; *Sbornik deistvuiushchikh uzakonenii i rasporiazhenii* (1932), 75; *Khoziaistvo TsChO* (Voronezh), 1929, no. 3: 178; *Okhrana zdorov'ia detei*, 167–168; *Detskii dom*, 1929, no. 2: 85 (for the quotation). Laments also persisted over the lack of dedication and qualifications of numerous staff members; see *Prosveshchenie na Urale* (Sverdlovsk), 1929, no. 10: 74; 1930, no. 12: 74–75; *Za sotsialisticheskuiu kul'turu* (Rostov-on-the-Don), 1930, no. 12: 25; *Detskii dom*, 1929, no. 2: 93; 1930, no. 6: 12; *Khoziaistvo TsChO* (Voronezh), 1929, no. 3: 177; *Prosveshchenie Sibiri* (Novosibirsk), 1929, no. 12: 10; *SZ*, 1935, no. 32, art. 252. In addition to complaints about dedication and qualifications, the political atmosphere of this period also generated more frequent charges that some staff members were former tsarist officers or children of nobles and priests. See for example *Detskii dom*, 1929, no. 6: 25. The government issued several decrees ordering increased pay and benefits for *detdom* personnel—without producing dramatic improvement, at least through the early 1930s. For a sampling of these decrees, see *SU*, 1928, no. 42, art. 318; no. 54, art. 410; no. 55, art. 412; *SU*, 1933, no. 31, art. 111; *SZ*, 1933, no. 31, art. 185.

25. *Obzor raboty po bor'be s detskoi besprizornost'iu i beznadzornost'iu v RSFSR za 1929/30 god*, 13; *Prosveshchenie Sibiri* (Novosibirsk), 1929, no. 11: 74; *Sbornik deistvuiushchikh uzakonenii i rasporiazhenii* (1932), 80; *Khoziaistvo TsChO* (Voronezh), 1929, no. 3: 177; *SU*, 1934, no. 21, art. 124; *Prosveshchenie na Urale* (Sverdlovsk), 1930, no. 12: 74–75; *Detskii dom*, 1929, no. 2: 87; *Okhrana detstva*, 1931, no. 1: 38.

26. *Drug detei*, 1929, no. 11: 5; 1930, no. 5: 10; *Detskii dom*, 1929, no. 2: 93; no. 4: 75; no. 5: 42, 44–45; *Prosveshchenie Sibiri* (Novosibirsk), 1929, no. 12: 12. Occasionally, articles mentioned mass revolts of children in institutions; see for example *Detskii dom*, 1929, no. 2: 87; no. 4: 75.

27. TsGA RSFSR, f. 393, o. 1, ed. khr. 81, l. 17; *Detskii dom*, 1929, no. 2: 87; no. 5: 42–43; 1930, nos. 8–10: 52.

28. For examples of successful institutions, see *Detskii dom*, 1929, no. 1: 67; no. 2: 87–89; no. 5: 87; *Okhrana detstva*, 1931, no. 1: 38; *Prosveshchenie na transporte*, 1928, no. 6: 16; *Prosveshchenie Sibiri* (Novosibirsk), 1929, no. 11: 73.

29. For discharge figures, see *Sovetskoe stroitel'stvo*, 1927, nos. 2–3: 157; *Narodnoe prosveshchenie v RSFSR k 1927–28 uchebnomu godu*, 57; Tizanov and Epshtein, *Gosudarstvo i obshchestvennost'*, 6; *Narodnoe prosveshchenie v RSFSR k 1926/27 uchebnomu godu*, 62; *Detskii dom*, 1929, no. 2: 4; *Narodnoe prosveshchenie*, 1929, no. 1: 79; *Obzor raboty po bor'be s detskoi besprizornost'iu i beznadzornost'iu v RSFSR za 1929/30 god*, 16.

30. A considerably smaller number were discharged from *detdoma* into the army, often to special music-training units. See *SZ*, 1926, no. 56, art. 407; *Sbornik deistvuiushchikh uzakonenii i rasporiazhenii* (1929), 23; *Trekhletnii plan*, 6; Ryndziunskii and Savinskaia, *Detskoe pravo*, 236–237; *Detskii dom*, 1928, no. 3: 67; 1929, no. 5: 73–76; Gilev, *Detskaia besprizornost'*, 14; *Drug detei*, 1927, no. 1: 21; 1928, no. 2: 15; Thompson, *New Russia*, 252.

31. For the figures presented, see *Narodnoe prosveshchenie v RSFSR 1927–28 god*, 175. For additional information on the distribution of youths discharged from institutions, see TsGALI, f. 332, o. 1, ed. khr. 52, l. 144; ibid., o. 2, ed. khr. 29, l. 4; *Molot* (Rostov-on-the-Don), 1926, no. 1576 (November 3), p. 3; *Vestnik prosveshcheniia*, 1927, no. 11: 141–142; Kalinina, *Desiat' let*, 106; *Prosveshchenie na transporte*, 1928, no. 6: 15; Shveitser and Shabalov, *Besprizornye*, 45; *Detskii dom*, 1929, nos. 8–9: 94; *Prosveshchenie na Urale* (Sverdlovsk), 1927, no. 2: 61; *Shkola i zhizn'* (Nizhnii Novgorod), 1927, no. 10: 62; *Puti kommunisticheskogo prosveshcheniia* (Simferopol'), 1928, nos. 1–2: 35.

32. *Voprosy prosveshcheniia* (Rostov-on-the-Don), 1926, nos. 6–7: 42; *Detskii dom*, comp. Utevskii, 64; *Bol'shaia sovetskaia entsiklopediia* 5:789; *Molot* (Rostov-on-the-Don), 1926, no. 1455 (June 12), p. 3; 1926, no. 1553 (October 7), p. 5.

33. On high unemployment as a hindrance to placing youths from *detdoma* in the industrial sector, see *Narodnoe prosveshchenie v R.S.F.S.R. k 1924/25 uchebnomu godu*, 82; *Drug detei*, 1928, no. 6: 16; *Vestnik prosveshcheniia*, 1928, no. 3: 121.

34. The sample was composed of 8,486 youths discharged from *detdoma* in the Northern Caucasus, the Lower Volga region, the Kirghiz Republic, the Crimea, the Central Black-Earth region, the Nizhnii Novgorod region, and the Tatar Republic. See *Obzor raboty po bor'be s detskoi besprizornost'iu i beznadzornost'iu v RSFSR za 1929/30 god*, 16.

35. Vasilevskii, *Besprizornost'*, 89–90 (regarding the percentage of places reserved for all juveniles, not just those from *detdoma*); *Drug detei* (Khar'kov), 1926, nos. 4–5: 37 (on the decree from the All-Russian Central Executive Committee in 1923). Regarding provincial quotas of jobs to be reserved for youths from *detdoma*, see V. G. Rudkin, "Deiatel'nost' organov sovetskoi vlasti i obshchestvennykh organizatsii Belorussii po preduprezhdeniiu detskoi besprizornosti (1921–1930 gg.)" (Minsk, 1983; MS. 14431 at INION AN SSSR, Moscow), 8; *Sbornik deistvuiushchikh uzakonenii i rasporiazhenii* (1929), 58, 198,

202. For details on the registration of *detdom* youths at labor exchanges, see *Sbornik deistvuiushchikh uzakonenii i rasporiazhenii* (1929), 60–62.

36. *Vestnik prosveshcheniia*, 1928, no. 3: 121–122; Rudkin, "Deiatel'-nost'," 8; Fitzpatrick, *Education and Social Mobility*, 48. It appears that enterprises taking on juveniles as part of a quota were often required to provide housing and other support for them. A number of decrees specified that if a factory accepted a larger number of youths from *detdoma* than required by law, the *detdoma* had to continue to support those juveniles hired beyond the quota. See *Sbornik deistvuiushchikh uzakonenii i rasporiazhenii* (1929), 58, 66, 68.

37. Regarding places reserved in schools for youths from *detdoma* (including first-priority consideration for admission), see TsGALI, f. 332, o. 1, ed. khr. 52, l. 102; *Narodnoe prosveshchenie v R.S.F.S.R. k 1925/26 uchebnomu godu*, 67; *Molot* (Rostov-on-the-Don), 1925, no. 1230 (September 10), p. 5; *Detskii dom i bor'ba s besprizornost'iu*, 26; *Detskii dom*, comp. Utevskii, 50. For fragmentary data on the number of *detdom* children discharged to schools of various types in the years prior to the industrialization drive, see *Narodnoe prosveshchenie v R.S.F.S.R. k 1925/26 uchebnomu godu*, 68; *Shkola i zhizn'* (Nizhnii Novgorod), 1926, no. 11: 34; *Vestnik prosveshcheniia*, 1927, no. 11: 141–142; *Detskii dom*, 1929, no. 2: 4; no. 3: 10; *Sovetskoe stroitel'stvo*, 1927, nos. 2–3: 157.

38. On the expansion of factory-apprenticeship schools brought on by the industrialization drive, see *Obzor raboty po bor'be s detskoi besprizornost'iu i beznadzornost'iu v RSFSR za 1929/30 god*, 18. At the end of 1930, Narkompros ordered that all children over fourteen years of age in *detdoma* be transferred to factory-apprenticeship and other technical schools during the spring and fall enrollments of 1931—an order that could not possibly be implemented fully. See *Sbornik deistvuiushchikh uzakonenii i rasporiazhenii* (1932), 36. For more on factory-apprenticeship schools, see Fitzpatrick, *Education and Social Mobility*, 47–48.

39. *Narodnoe prosveshchenie v R.S.F.S.R. k 1924/25 uchebnomu godu*, 84; *Narodnoe prosveshchenie v RSFSR k 1926/27 uchebnomu godu*, 62; *Obzor raboty po bor'be s detskoi besprizornost'iu i beznadzornost'iu v RSFSR za 1927/28 g.*, 17.

40. The presence of "children" sixteen to eighteen and even twenty to twenty-one years of age naturally hindered the work of many institutions intended for younger inhabitants. See Enik and Blok, *Iz trushchob na stroiku*, 37 (regarding the *detdoma* in Saratov); *Drug detei*, 1928, no. 6: 16; Tizanov et al., *Detskaia besprizornost'*, 180; *Nash trud* (Iaroslavl'), 1926, no. 7: 6; *Drug detei* (Khar'kov), 1925, no. 9: 5; *Narodnoe prosveshchenie*, 1929, no. 1: 81; *Narodnoe prosveshchenie v R.S.F.S.R. k 1924/25 uchebnomu godu*, 84; *Prosveshchenie Sibiri* (Novosibirsk), 1927, no. 8: 55; 1929, no. 11: 74; *Khoziaistvo TsChO* (Voronezh), 1929, no. 3: 178; *Detskii dom*, 1929, nos. 8–9: 114; TsGALI, f. 332, o. 1, ed. khr. 53, ll. 2–3.

41. *Prosveshchenie na transporte*, 1928, no. 6: 14–16; *Narodnoe prosveshchenie v R.S.F.S.R. k 1924/25 uchebnomu godu*, 86; *Narodnoe prosveshchenie v RSFSR k 1927–28 uchebnomu godu*, 55; *Sbornik deistvuiushchikh uzakonenii i rasporiazhenii* (1929), 21, 69; *Na putiakh k novoi shkole*, 1924, nos. 7–8: 43;

Tizanov et al., *Detskaia besprizornost'*, 194; *Detskii dom i bor'ba s besprizornost'iu*, 33; *Prosveshchenie Sibiri* (Novosibirsk), 1929, no. 12: 10; *Khoziaistvo TsChO* (Voronezh), 1929, no. 3: 178; *Drug detei*, 1929, no. 11: 7; *Vestnik prosveshcheniia*, 1928, no. 3: 122; *Detskii dom*, 1929, no. 1: 16; no. 3: 51–52; nos. 8–9: 94.

42. TsGA RSFSR, f. 1575, o. 6, ed. khr. 4, l. 87; *Sbornik deistvuiushchikh uzakonenii i rasporiazhenii* (1932), 47–48; *Detskii dom*, comp. Utevskii, 18; Shveitser and Shabalov, *Besprizornye*, 45; *Detskii dom*, 1928, no. 3: 68–69.

43. For instructions from Narkompros to maintain contact with youths discharged from institutions, see TsGA RSFSR, f. 1575, o. 6, ed. khr. 4, l. 87; *Detskii dom*, comp. Utevskii, 18. For descriptions of efforts by institutions to support recently discharged members, see *Detskii dom*, 1929, no. 7: 61–63; no. 10: 44–45. For complaints that *detdoma* frequently maintained no ties with the youths they discharged, see *Detskii dom*, 1929, no. 7: 61; *Prosveshchenie na transporte*, 1928, no. 6: 16–17; *Prosveshchenie Sibiri* (Novosibirsk), 1932, no. 7: 62.

44. *Sbornik deistvuiushchikh uzakonenii i rasporiazhenii* (1929), 71–72 (p. 72 contains the Narkompros circular); *Sbornik deistvuiushchikh uzakonenii i rasporiazhenii* (1932), 23 (for the circular from the Children's Commission); *SU*, 1931, no. 61, art. 446.

45. *Obzor raboty po bor'be s detskoi besprizornost'iu i beznadzornost'iu v RSFSR za 1927/28 g.*, 17; *Sbornik deistvuiushchikh uzakonenii i rasporiazhenii* (1929), 71; *SU*, 1933, no. 7, art. 21.

46. *Drug detei* (Khar'kov), 1926, nos. 4–5: 28 (for the report from Vladimir); *Komsomol'skaia pravda*, 1927, no. 241 (October 21), p. 4 (for the report from Tula); *Prosveshchenie Sibiri* (Novosibirsk), 1932, no. 7: 60–61. Some cities contained special dormitories for adolescents, though not nearly enough to absorb the youths discharged from *detdoma*. For more on these dormitories, see Maro, *Besprizornye*, 403–415; *Detskii dom*, 1929, no. 7: 72; *Detskii dom*, comp. Utevskii, 18.

47. *Detskii dom*, 1929, no. 5: 95–96; *Detskii dom*, comp. Utevskii, 64.

48. Regarding the preference to be shown *detdom* "graduates" in the areas of housing and employment, see *SU*, 1930, no. 59, art. 704; *SU*, 1931, no. 61, art. 446; *SU*, 1932, no. 21, art. 106; *Sbornik deistvuiushchikh uzakonenii i rasporiazhenii* (1929), 215; *Sbornik deistvuiushchikh uzakonenii i rasporiazhenii* (1932), 69; *Bor'ba s detskoi besprizornost'iu*, 31; Tizanov and Epshtein, *Gosudarstvo i obshchestvennost'*, 25–26, 39; *Volna* (Arkhangel'sk), 1926, no. 73 (April 2), p. 4; *Molot* (Rostov-on-the-Don), 1926, no. 1563 (October 19), p. 5. For complaints that these instructions were often ignored, see Shveitser and Shabalov, *Besprizornye*, 58; *Rezoliutsii 3-go vserossiiskogo s"ezda*, 16; *Sbornik deistvuiushchikh uzakonenii i rasporiazhenii* (1932), 15–16.

49. *Prosveshchenie Sibiri* (Novosibirsk), 1929, no. 12: 13 (for the comment from Siberia); Tolmachev, *Khuliganstvo*, 52 (regarding the questioning of Leningrad students); Stites, *Women's Liberation Movement*, 334 (regarding the citizen urging ignition of *besprizornye*); Artamonov, *Deti ulitsy*, 17; *Drug detei* (Khar'kov), 1926, no. 1: 14; 1927, no. 1: 10; *Vestnik prosveshcheniia*, 1925, no. 9: 94; *Deti posle goloda*, 52; *Na putiakh k novoi shkole*, 1927, no. 2: 92;

Kalinina, *Komsomol i besprizornost'*, 18; *Drug detei*, 1926, no. 2: 13; 1927, no. 2: 5; 1931, no. 10: 14 (for the remark by the chairman of the Baku Children's Commission); *Komsomol'skaia pravda*, 1927, no. 196 (August 30), p. 4 (regarding the director of the Moscow receiver); *Profilakticheskaia meditsina* (Khar'kov), 1926, no. 12: 83; Popov, *Detskaia besprizornost'*, 9; *Illiustrirovannaia Rossiia* (Paris), 1930, no. 40: 11; *Volna* (Arkhangel'sk), 1926, no. 173 (July 31), p. 3. According to a British diplomatic report titled "Situation in the Soviet Union [in 1927]," *besprizornye* "are indeed a pest if not a menace to society; insolent, aggressive, incredibly filthy, wrapped in odious rags, familiar with most aspects of vice and crime, they prowl the streets and railways in predatory bands, often terrorising the people and holding at bay the police"; British Foreign Office, 1927, reel 8, vol. 12596, p. 182. Juvenile Affairs Commissions sometimes found it difficult to place youths requiring medical attention in clinics and hospitals because of the children's reputation as troublemakers; see Ryndziunskii et al., *Pravovoe polozhenie* (1927), 84. Gypsies encountered much of the same hostility from the population as did *besprizornye*; see *Drug detei*, 1927, nos. 6–7: 29–30. For literary accounts mentioning the revulsion and fear inspired in citizens by *besprizornye*, see Gornyi, *Besprizornyi krug*, 5; *Vchera i segodnia*, 155.

50. For reports of institutions said to have established amicable relations with people living nearby, see Glatman, *Pionery i besprizornye*, 33; Shveitser and Shabalov, *Besprizornye*, 61, 64; *Besprizornye*, comp. Kaidanova, 57; Pogrebinskii, *Fabrika liudei*, 27–28.

51. *Shkola i zhizn'* (Nizhnii Novgorod), 1928, no. 12: 19; *Prosveshchenie na Urale* (Sverdlovsk), 1930, no. 12: 74; *Narodnoe prosveshchenie*, 1927, no. 7: 14; *Voprosy prosveshcheniia* (Rostov-on-the-Don), 1926, no. 2: 28–29; Tizanov et al., *Pedagogika*, 20; *Prosveshchenie Sibiri* (Novosibirsk), 1927, no. 8: 54; 1929, no. 12: 13; Shveitser and Shabalov, *Besprizornye*, 68; *Detskii dom*, 1929, no. 4: 75; no. 7: 72; nos. 8–9: 27, 29; *Vestnik prosveshchentsa* (Orenburg), 1926, nos. 11–12: 14; *Pravda*, 1927, no. 78 (April 7), p. 3.

52. *Detskii dom*, 1929, no. 2: 87 (regarding the *detdom* in Tambov); *Na putiakh k novoi shkole*, 1924, no. 9: 89.

53. *Prosveshchenie na Urale* (Sverdlovsk), 1929, nos. 5–6: 92–93 (regarding the fire); *Drug detei*, 1928, nos. 11–12: 9.

54. *Pravda*, 1988, no. 26 (January 26), p. 6. For an article describing *detdoma* in the Kalinin region of the Russian Republic in 1989, see *Moscow News*, 1989, no. 37: 5. For a gloomy assessment of contemporary *detdoma* and boarding schools (together with an estimate that roughly three hundred thousand children currently live in these institutions), see *Moscow News*, 1991, nos. 34–35: 14.

55. On schools and economic enterprises displaying no desire to accept youths from *detdoma*, see *Vestnik prosveshcheniia*, 1928, no. 3: 122; *Prosveshchenie Sibiri* (Novosibirsk), 1928, no. 9: 74; *Detskii dom*, 1929, nos. 8–9: 27; *Sbornik deistvuiushchikh uzakonenii i rasporiazhenii* (1929), 67 (for the Narkompros quotation). For examples of complaints by teachers and administrators about thefts, hooliganism, and poor work on the part of *detdom* "graduates," see *Prosveshchenie na Urale* (Sverdlovsk), 1930, no. 12: 74; *Prosveshchenie*

Sibiri (Novosibirsk), 1932, no. 7: 61. Regarding discrimination, suspicion, and harassment faced by former inhabitants of *detdoma* while in school or at work— which drove some to run away—see *Detskii dom*, 1929, nos. 8–9: 94; *Prosveshchenie Sibiri* (Novosibirsk), 1932, no. 7: 61; *Drug detei*, 1928, no. 5: 8–9 (these pages also describe an instance in which a group of youths received good treatment); nos. 11–12: 9–10.

56. *Vestnik prosveshcheniia*, 1929, no. 6: 57–60, 63.

57. TsGALI, f. 332, o. 2, ed. khr. 75 (a photograph album from Makarenko's Dzerzhinskii Commune); *Detskii dom*, 1929, no. 2: 89; nos. 8–9: 108–109; no. 10: 44–45; *Narodnoe prosveshchenie v RSFSR k 1927–28 uchebnomu godu*, 57; *Drug detei*, 1929, no. 4: 10–11; Makarenko, *Road to Life* 2:446–447; Iu. B. Lukin, *A. S. Makarenko. Kritiko-biograficheskii ocherk* (Moscow, 1954), 181 (regarding Makarenko's funeral), 192–197; Maro, *Besprizornye*, 255–256; Astemirov, "Iz istorii," 260; Kalinina, *Desiat' let*, 44; Popov, *Detskaia besprizornost'*, 9; *Krasnaia nov'*, 1932, no. 1: 43–44; *Spasennye revoliutsiei*, 97; Marinov, "Gosudarstvennye deti," 200–226; Ella Winter, *Red Virtue: Human Relationships in the New Russia* (New York, 1933), 34; Hughes, *I Wonder*, 148; Vatova, "Bolshevskaia trudovaia kommuna," 92.

58. Leshchinskii, *Kto byl nichem*.

59. *Detskii dom*, comp. Utevskii, 24; *Detskii dom i bor'ba s besprizornost'iu*, 6; *Detskii dom*, 1930, no. 4: 5 (for the reference to hundreds of thousands of children); Zhukova, "Deiatel'nost' Detkomissii," 66.

60. Frederic Lilge speculates as follows: "It is probable that the greater number [of *besprizornye*] died of famine and epidemics, that others grew up into adult criminals, and only a small minority were rehabilitated. Many who were temporarily accommodated ran away either because of intolerable conditions in the overcrowded asylums, or because the directors were unable to discipline or accustom the children to work or study. Directors who, like Makarenko, succeeded were rare exceptions"; Lilge, *Anton Semyonovitch Makarenko: An Analysis of His Educational Ideas in the Context of Soviet Society* (Berkeley, 1958), 14. Regarding four *detdom* graduates convicted of murder, see British Foreign Office, 1927, reel 8, vol. 12596, p. 182.

61. For other references to former *besprizornye* who died fighting in World War II, see Lukin, *Makarenko*, 184; Marinov, "Gosudarstvennye deti," 222.

62. Regarding the recruitment of former *besprizornye* into the secret police, see William Reswick, *I Dreamt Revolution* (Chicago, 1952), 244–245; Gerson, *Secret Police*, 128; Robert Conquest, *The Harvest of Sorrow: Soviet Collectivization and the Terror-Famine* (New York, 1986), 293. Regarding claims that Romania's Securitate drew members from orphanages, see the *Milwaukee Journal*, March 5, 1990. Even if the police recruited nearly all the children in the institutions they administered during the period 1918–1930 (an assumption supported by no published evidence), the total would still represent a tiny fraction of all *besprizornye*.

63. For Krupskaia's comment, see *Detskii dom*, 1930, no. 4: 10. For the article from Siberia and the comment about "junk," see *Prosveshchenie Sibiri* (Novosibirsk), 1928, no. 3: 73; *Okhrana detstva*, 1931, no. 5: 26. For the last quotation, see *Narodnoe prosveshchenie*, 1929, no. 1: 83. At the end of 1929

the Siberian journal cited above asked rhetorically whether *detdoma* in the region were performing adequately, and then responded: "It must be said bluntly that the condition of *detdoma* is extremely unsatisfactory and that they are fulfilling the tasks before them very poorly"; *Prosveshchenie Sibiri* (Novosibirsk), 1929, no. 12: 9. The Workers' and Peasants' Inspectorate of the Urals observed that "the general condition of the mass of children's institutions in the region, with rare exceptions, continues to be difficult"; *Prosveshchenie na Urale* (Sverdlovsk), 1929, nos. 5–6: 91. A report for 1928–1929 from the Children's Commission, after noting that the performance of "some *detdoma*" had "markedly improved," added: "But along with this, Detkomissiia VTsIK considers itself obligated to emphasize categorically that the position of the majority of *detdoma* remains unsatisfactory"; *Obzor raboty po bor'be s detskoi besprizornost'iu i beznadzornost'iu v RSFSR za 1929/30 god*, 8. A resolution of the Third All-Russian Congress for the Protection of Children proclaimed in 1930 that the "overwhelming majority" of *detdoma* were in "unsatisfactory condition" and "require fundamental improvement" to produce young people "skilled and devoted to the task of socialist construction"; *Detskii dom*, comp. Utevskii, 25. Five years later a decree of the All-Union Sovnarkom and the Party Secretariat found little improvement, stating that "the majority of *detdoma* are unsatisfactory both economically and educationally"; *SZ*, 1935, no. 32, art. 252. For other predominantly negative assessments of *detdoma* at this time, see TsGA RSFSR, f. 393, o. 1, ed. khr. 81, l. 12; *SU*, 1934, no. 21, art. 124; *Rezoliutsii 3-go vserossiiskogo s"ezda*, 13, 16; *Detskii dom*, 1930, no. 6: 12; *Prosveshchenie na Urale* (Sverdlovsk), 1930, no. 12: 74–75; *Bor'ba s detskoi besprizornost'iu*, 28, 65; *Prosveshchenie Sibiri* (Novosibirsk), 1927, no. 8: 55; 1932, no. 7: 60; no. 9: 23–24; Enik and Blok, *Iz trushchob na stroiku*, 33–34; *Drug detei*, 1928, nos. 11–12: 9–10; *Sbornik deistvuiushchikh uzakonenii i rasporiazhenii* (1929), 52; *Sovetskaia iustitsiia*, 1930, no. 7/8: 20. The government frequently ordered provincial officials to increase spending and other efforts to improve the condition of *detdoma* at the end of the decade (as it had previously). See for example *SU*, 1929, no. 56, art. 547; *Sbornik deistvuiushchikh uzakonenii i rasporiazhenii* (1929), 198, 237; *Sbornik deistvuiushchikh uzakonenii i rasporiazhenii* (1932), 16. A similarly large number of complaints asserted that these orders were not implemented; see *Detskii dom*, 1929, no. 2: 5; *Bor'ba s detskoi besprizornost'iu*, 44; *SU*, 1930, no. 59, art. 704; *Sbornik deistvuiushchikh uzakonenii i rasporiazhenii* (1932), 58.

    64. In addition to issues of *Detskii dom* from 1929 (nos. 2 and 3 in particular), see *Narodnoe prosveshchenie*, 1929, no. 1: 84–85; *Vestnik prosveshcheniia*, 1929, no. 3: 28. Regarding the Narkompros report, see *Detskii dom*, 1929, nos. 8–9: 24.

    65. *Detskii dom*, 1929, no. 2: 12; nos. 8–9: 25–26, 28, 32; 1930, no. 4: 3–4, 6–7; no. 5: 57; *Obzor raboty po bor'be s detskoi besprizornost'iu i beznadzornost'iu v RSFSR za 1929/30 god*, 9; John Dunstan, "Soviet Boarding Education: Its Rise and Progress," in *Home, School, and Leisure in the Soviet Union*, ed. Jenny Brine, Maureen Perrie, and Andrew Sutton (London, 1980), 114.

    66. For a sampling of these views, see *Detskii dom*, 1929, no. 2: 13–14; no. 3: 11; 1930, no. 6: 3–4; *Narodnoe prosveshchenie*, 1929, no. 1: 85; *Rezoliutsii 3-go vserossiiskogo s"ezda*, 19.

67. *Detskii dom i bor'ba s besprizornost'iu,* 27.

68. For thoughts on how the flooding of *detdoma* with *besprizornye* transformed the nature of these institutions, see *Narodnoe prosveshchenie,* 1929, no. 1: 83–84; *Detskii dom,* 1929, no. 2: 20; 1930, no. 4: 9–10; Krupskaia, *Pedagogicheskie sochineniia* 3:393; Smolensk Archive, reel 45, WKP 402, p. 1.

69. Livshits, *Sotsial'nye korni,* 4.

70. *Pravda,* 1925, no. 255 (November 7), p. 2.

71. *Administrativnyi vestnik,* 1926, no. 12: 37; Poznyshev, *Detskaia besprizornost',* 4; Vasilevskii, *Besprizornost',* 56–57; *Vestnik prosveshcheniia,* 1927, no. 1: 8–9; *Prosveshchenie Sibiri* (Novosibirsk), 1929, no. 12: 14; *Vozhatyi,* 1926, no. 6: 29; *Puti kommunisticheskogo prosveshcheniia* (Simferopol'), 1928, nos. 1–2: 39; Tizanov and Epshtein, *Gosudarstvo i obshchestvennost',* 35; Gilev, *Detskaia besprizornost',* 1; Tizanov et al., *Detskaia besprizornost',* 164; *Detskii dom i bor'ba s besprizornost'iu,* 7.

72. *Pravda,* 1928, no. 81 (April 5), p. 4; *Izvestiia,* 1928, no. 81 (April 5), p. 5.

73. *Sbornik deistvuiushchikh uzakonenii i rasporiazhenii* (1929), 5 (another source containing Kosior's article); *Komsomol'skaia pravda,* 1927, no. 222 (September 29), p. 4; *Spasennye revoliutsiei,* 94; *Bor'ba s detskoi besprizornost'iu,* 44–45, 47; *Narodnoe prosveshchenie,* 1929, no. 1: 79; *Sbornik deistvuiushchikh uzakonenii i rasporiazhenii* (1932), 77.

74. *Prosveshchenie na Urale* (Sverdlovsk), 1930, no. 12: 71; *Obshchestvo "Drug detei,"* 20, 43; *Sbornik deistvuiushchikh uzakonenii i rasporiazhenii* (1932), 3; *Okhrana detstva,* 1931, no. 1: 12; no. 5: 45 (for the slogan quoted). The period 1930–1931 was not the first time such slogans and instructions had appeared. Back in 1924, for example, the Ukrainian Council of People's Commissars and Central Executive Committee issued the slogan: "Not a Single *Besprizornyi* by the Winter of 1925!'"; *Pomoshch' detiam,* 33. In July 1928, Narkompros issued a circular stating: "The coming year must be the year of the complete liquidation of street *besprizornost'* so that encountering *besprizornye* on the street will not be considered mundane, as it has been up to now, but rather completely abnormal"; *Bor'ba s detskoi besprizornost'iu,* 54.

75. *Drug detei,* 1931, no. 7: 27 (for the review); Bowen, *Soviet Education,* 5 (for Dewey's remarks). Much of the filming took place in the OGPU labor commune at Bolshevo.

76. *Bor'ba s detskoi besprizornost'iu,* 10 (for the statement by Semashko). For other claims that *besprizornost'* had all but disappeared by 1931 (earlier in some cases) from various regions, see *Pravda,* 1928, no. 166 (July 19), p. 6; *Sbornik deistvuiushchikh uzakonenii i rasporiazhenii* (1929), 195; *Detskii dom,* 1930, no. 4: 64; *SU,* 1932, no. 21, art. 106; *Krasnaia nov',* 1932, no. 1: 50; Min'kovskii, "Osnovnye etapy," 49; Rudkin, "Prichiny," 14–15.

77. For a sampling of both optimistic and guarded assessments of the plan, see *Drug detei,* 1928, no. 8: 1; *Detskii dom i bor'ba s besprizornost'iu,* 21; *Narodnoe prosveshchenie,* 1927, no. 7: 10; *Sovetskoe stroitel'stvo,* 1927, nos. 2–3: 166.

78. This was acknowledged openly in some sources. In July 1929, for example, the Council of People's Commissars stated that reports from Narkom-

pros and the Children's Commission made it clear that the goals for 1927/28 had not been fulfilled; *Bor'ba s detskoi besprizornost'iu*, 29. A book published in 1930 contained a section titled "The Three-Year Plan Has Not Been Fulfilled"; see Enik and Blok, *Iz trushchob na stroiku*, 30, 51.

79. *Pravda*, 1928, no. 166 (July 19), p. 6; Shishova, "Sovershenstvovanie," 23–24. To be sure, the number of *besprizornye* had dropped sharply in Rostov-on-the-Don compared to levels of a few years before. A Western observer recalled: "When I first visited the bustling city of Rostov-on-the-Don, several years ago, it was a huge rendezvous of the byezprizorni. They surrounded the station in a veritable cordon; the traveler had to keep his hand on his pocket every minute to forestall the attentions of these precocious young pickpockets. Revisiting Rostov in 1928, I was impressed by the absence of the waifs on the streets"; William Henry Chamberlin, *Soviet Russia: A Living Record and a History* (Boston, 1935), 53. According to a Siberian journal in 1929, *besprizornost'* had diminished significantly in the region compared to its scale at the beginning of the decade, "but we are still far from the liquidation of this extremely grave phenomenon"; *Prosveshchenie Sibiri* (Novosibirsk), 1929, no. 12: 9. Agnes Smedley wrote from Moscow at the beginning of 1929: "The number [of *besprizornye*] in Moscow has noticeably decreased, but they are still to be met in every part of the city"; *The Nation* 128 (April 10, 1929): 436.

80. In addition to sources cited below, see TsGA RSFSR, f. 393, o. 1, ed. khr. 81, l. 12; ibid., ed. khr. 201, ll. 23–24; *SU*, 1932, no. 73, art. 328; *Sbornik deistvuiushchikh uzakonenii i rasporiazhenii* (1932), 23; Enik and Blok, *Iz trushchob na stroiku*, 31; Ryndziunskii and Savinskaia, *Detskoe pravo*, 4; *Okhrana detstva*, 1931, no. 1: 18; *Drug detei*, 1930, nos. 8–9: 6.

81. For an example of the blind spot regarding *besprizornye* in the 1930s, see *Pedagogicheskaia entsiklopediia*, 4 vols. (Moscow, 1964–1968), 1:191–195. This article discusses *besprizornye* of the 1920s and mentions that "many children lost their parents" during World War II; but there is not the slightest hint that another wave of *besprizornost'* occurred in between. Concerning *besprizornost'* during World War II, see Stolee, "Homeless Children," 76–78; Min'kovskii, "Osnovnye etapy," 60–63; Madison, *Social Welfare*, 45; Victor Kravchenko, *I Chose Freedom* (New York, 1946), 381, 407, 451. By 1945, the Soviet Union reportedly contained roughly 6,000 *detdoma* (housing some 600,000 children). This exceeded by over 4,300 the number of *detdoma* in the country at the beginning of 1940. See Sinitsin, "Zabota," 29.

82. Goldman, "The 'Withering Away' and the Resurrection," 365; Bauer, *New Man*, 39–40 (for the quotation and other material on this point).

83. An American historian writes: "The measures against street *besprizornost* grew harsher throughout the thirties, finally culminating in a policy that relied on harsh punitive sanctions and strong parental control"; Goldman, "The 'Withering Away' and the Resurrection," 366. See also Freda Utley, *The Dream We Lost* (New York, 1940), 110–111. Alexander Orlov, who defected in 1938, wrote regarding the alleged execution order: "I learned that as far back as 1932, when hundreds of thousands of stray children, driven by hunger, had jammed the railway stations and big cities, Stalin issued orders to shoot secretly those children who were plundering and stealing food from railway cars in transit and

also children who had contracted venereal diseases. As a result of those mass shootings and other administrative measures the problem of the stray children was 'solved' in the true Stalinist spirit by the summer of 1934"; Orlov, *The Secret History of Stalin's Crimes* (New York, 1953), 39–40. If this claim is accurate, it would not be the only time that police have waged campaigns of execution against street children. For reports from Guatemala and Brazil, see the *New York Times*, October 14, 1990; November 13, 1990; October 21, 1991; November 4, 1992. According to the fourth article, "a report this month by the São Paulo chapter of Brazil's Bar Association said the military police and death squads paid by shantytown shopkeepers killed most of the nearly 1,000 street children slain here in 1990."

84. Min'kovskii, "Osnovnye etapy," 53, 57–58; Boldyrev, *Mery predu-prezhdeniia*, 26–27; Bauer, *New Man*, 41; Stolee, "Homeless Children," 74; *SU*, 1936, no. 1, art. 1. It is interesting to compare the interpretations of the two Soviet scholars cited above regarding Moscow's new hard line on juvenile crime. Boldyrev argues that the April 7 decree reflected the general tendency of the time to increase judicial repression in the struggle with crime: "This was a result of the harmful influence of Stalin's cult of personality and his mistaken belief that strengthening judicial punishments would liquidate crime in the country." In contrast, Min'kovskii displays sympathy for the stern measures adopted in the 1930s. For the text of the April 7 decree, see the front page of the following day's *Pravda* or *SZ*, 1935, no. 19, art. 155. Years before 1935, even in the 1920s, some courts treated juveniles with a severity then illegal—accepting cases of defendants under sixteen, for example, or punishing young offenders beyond prescribed limits. See Ryndziunskii and Savinskaia, *Detskoe pravo*, 263; *Ne-sovershennoletnie pravonarushiteli*, 25–27, 57.

85. Goldman, "The 'Withering Away' and the Resurrection," 368–369; Sto-lee, "Homeless Children," 73–74 (for the statistics); Astemirov, "Iz istorii," 264–266 (for details on the types of juvenile institutions operated by the Commissariat of Internal Affairs in the 1930s).

86. *Obzor raboty po bor'be s detskoi besprizornost'iu i beznadzornost'iu v RSFSR za 1929/30 god*, 24 (for the report from the Children's Commission); *Drug detei*, 1931, no. 8: 15; no. 11: 22 (regarding the *vagon-priemnik* at Rostov-on-the-Don); Ryndziunskii and Savinskaia, *Detskoe pravo*, 232 (regarding the *vagon-priemnik* at Kazan' Station and the total for the Soviet Union during this period); *Okhrana detstva*, 1931, no. 6: 22 (regarding the transportation network around Leningrad); nos. 9–10: 29; TsGA RSFSR, f. 393, o. 1, ed. khr. 201, l. 17 (for the ODD document); *Za sotsialisticheskuiu kul'turu* (Rostov-on-the-Don), 1930, no. 12: 24.

87. Eugene Lyons, *Assignment in Utopia* (New York, 1937), 281. See also Allan Monkhouse, *Moscow, 1911–1933* (London, 1933), 213, 231; Serge, *Russia*, 28; Kravchenko, *I Chose Freedom*, 63; Orlov, *Secret History*, 39; Bauer, *New Man*, 41–42; Fred E. Beal, *Proletarian Journey* (New York, 1937), 311–312. André Gide, during a visit to the Soviet Union in 1936, "hoped there would be no more *besprizornis* for me to see. But there are plenty of them at Sebastopol [*sic*], and I was told that there are even more at Odessa"; Gide, *Back from the U.S.S.R.* (London, 1937), 118.

88. *Sotsialisticheskii vestnik* (Paris), 1933, no. 12: 15; no. 24: 15; see also no. 8: 16; no. 18: 16.

89. *Sbornik deistvuiushchikh uzakonenii i rasporiazhenii* (1932), 4, 34; *SZ*, 1935, no. 32, art. 252; *Bor'ba s detskoi besprizornost'iu*, 45–46, 48; *Spasennye revoliutsiei*, 94; Enik and Blok, *Iz trushchob na stroiku*, 19; Obshchestvo *"Drug detei,"* 36; *Okhrana detstva*, 1931, no. 1: 10; nos. 9–10: 5. The author of one article rejected the contention that collectivization and dekulakization were producing a new flood of *besprizornye*; see *Okhrana detstva*, 1931, no. 1: 19. If this contention came from a specific source, such as an émigré publication, the author did not reveal it.

90. Regarding collectivization, dekulakization, and the famine of 1933 as causes of *besprizornost'*, see Stolee, "Homeless Children," 72, 76; Conquest, *Harvest of Sorrow*, 284, 286–293, 296.

91. See for example *Prosveshchenie Sibiri* (Novosibirsk), 1932, no. 9: 22; *Detskii dom*, 1930, no. 4: 7; no. 6: 12; Krupskaia, *Pedagogicheskie sochineniia*, 4:255.

92. TsGA RSFSR, f. 2306, o. 70, ed. khr. 119, l. 32; Popov, *Detskaia besprizornost'*, 12–13; *Bor'ba s besprizornost'iu*, 8–9; Kalinina, *Desiat' let*, 11; *Drug detei*, 1927, nos. 4–5: 6–10; *Detskii dom i bor'ba s besprizornost'iu*, 24; *Deti posle goloda*, 54, 57; *Narodnoe prosveshchenie*, 1924, nos. 4–5: 162; Krupskaia, *Pedagogicheskie sochineniia*, 11:264–266; Obshchestvo *"Drug detei,"* 4–5. According to an American Red Cross report, when the Bolsheviks occupied Odessa temporarily during the Civil War, "they took children from the orphanages and placed them in luxurious villas only to contaminate their minds with 'free love' ideas"; American Red Cross, box 868, file 948.08, "Report of Mission to Ukraine and South Russia by Major George H. Ryden," November 1919. For a sampling of published Western and émigré reports on *besprizornost'* in the USSR, see "The 'Wild' Children of Russia," *The Nation* 128 (April 10, 1929): 436–437; "Russia's Wild Waifs," *Literary Digest* 88 (February 6, 1926): 34; "Russia's 'Wolf Packs' of Homeless Children," *Literary Digest* 88 (March 13, 1926): 71–75; "The Chaos of Free Love in Russia," *Literary Digest* 94 (August 6, 1927): 31–32; "Russia Still Scourged by Vagabond Children," *Literary Digest* 103 (December 14, 1929): 16; Zenzinov, *Deserted*; Sokolov, *Spasite detei!* By no means all these Western accounts place primary blame for the problem on the policies of the Soviet government.

93. *Drug detei*, 1929, no. 7: 6; British Foreign Office, 1927, reel 8, vol. 12596, pp. 181–182, 234.

94. For the figure of one hundred million, see "City of Lost Boys," *Life* 11 (June 1988): 73. Three years earlier, an article in a UNESCO journal estimated the world's population of street children "at not less than seventy million—and numbers are rising rapidly"; Merrick Fall, "Streets Apart," *UNESCO Courier* 38 (June 1985): 25. For more on street children around the world, see the *New York Times*, May 11, 1987; July 10, 1987; July 13, 1987; October 16, 1988; November 4, 1988; October 14, 1990; December 23, 1990; January 2, 1991; *New York Times Magazine*, January 6, 1991; *World Watch* 2 (July–August 1989): 36–38 (for a figure of "40 million children who spend the majority of their days and nights living and working on the streets of the world's poorest

cities"); *Sports Illustrated* 67 (21 December 1987): 95; Lourdes G. Balanon, "Street Children: Strategies for Action," *Child Welfare* 68 (March–April 1989): 159–160; *World Press Review*, 38 (August 1991): 54.

95. Some estimates of the number of homeless children in America reach as high as three million when they include youths living with parents in shelters and welfare hotels (as opposed to focusing solely on juveniles living alone on the street). For a variety of estimates, both for New York City and the nation, see Patricia Hersch, "Coming of Age on City Streets," *Psychology Today* 22 (January 1988): 31; *New York Times*, February 3, 1987; May 5, 1987; September 20, 1988; *New York Times Magazine*, October 2, 1988, p. 31. Regarding the report of the National Academy of Sciences, see the *New York Times*, September 20, 1988. For additional sources on juvenile homelessness in America, see Mario M. Cuomo, *1933/1983—Never Again: A Report to the National Governor's Association Task Force on the Homeless* (Portland, Maine, 1983); Robert M. Hayes, "Homeless Children," in *Caring for America's Children*, ed. Frank J. Macchiarola and Alan Gartner (New York, 1989), 58–69; U.S. Congress, Senate, Committee on the Judiciary, Subcommittee on the Constitution, *Homeless Youth: The Saga of "Pushouts" and "Throwaways" in America*, 96th Cong., 2d sess., 1980 (pp. 89–97 contain a bibliography of works on homeless youths). Regarding Great Britain, an article in the *Economist* reported that "about 50,000 unemployed teenagers are now homeless in London. Once they would have stayed in bed-and-breakfast lodgings, their rents met from welfare benefits. Then, in 1985, the government tightened its social security regulations. Its aim was to force teenagers to return to their parental homes. Few have done so"; "Street-wise, Street-foolish," *The Economist* 305 (December 26, 1987): 57.

96. For a sampling of these opinions, see Livshits, *Sotsial'nye korni*, 3–5 (for Shul'gin's views), 36, 199–200; Livshits, *Detskaia besprizornost'*, 8; *Drug detei*, 1931, no. 7: 27; Krupskaia, *Pedagogicheskie sochineniia* 3:716–717. Z. I. Lilina, a Narkompros official and wife of Zinoviev, wrote: "Deserted children form a heritage of capitalist society; they are the harvest sewn by that society and the phenomenon accompanies capitalism inevitably in its every development"; quoted in Zenzinov, *Deserted*, 77. In 1935, M. S. Epshtein, deputy people's commissar of education, "compared the care by our Party and its leaders for children with the horrifying status of children in the capitalist countries. The falling number of schools, the tremendous growth of homelessness—that is characteristic of all capitalist countries"; quoted in Conquest, *Harvest of Sorrow*, 290.

Select Bibliography

ARCHIVES

British Foreign Office Records of General Political Correspondence for Russia, 1906–1945 (F.O. 371)

Records of American National Red Cross, 1917–1934. National Archives Gifts Collection. Record Group 200.

Records of the Smolensk Oblast' of the All-Union Communist Party of the Soviet Union, 1917–1941 [Smolensk Archive]

Tsentral'nyi gosudarstvennyi arkhiv literatury i iskusstva SSSR [TsGALI]

    Fond 332 (A. S. Makarenko)

Tsentral'nyi gosudarstvennyi arkhiv Oktiabr'skoi revoliutsii, vysshikh organov gosudarstvennoi vlasti i organov gosudarstvennogo upravleniia SSSR [TsGAOR]

    Fond 5207 (*Detkomissiia pri VTsIK*)

Tsentral'nyi gosudarstvennyi arkhiv RSFSR [TsGA RSFSR]

    Fond 298 (*Gosudarstvennyi Uchenyi Sovet*)

    Fond 393 (*Obshchestvo "Drug Detei"*)

    Fond 1575 (*Glavsotsvos*)

    Fond 2306 (*Narkompros*)

PERIODICALS

The city of publication is Moscow unless otherwise indicated. In cases where a periodical's title varied over the life span listed after each entry, only those variants actually consulted—and found to contain material on the *besprizornye*—are included here. If no final year of publication is provided, the periodical appeared at least until 1960.

Administrativnyi vestnik, 1925–1930
Biulleten' gosplana RSFSR, 1925–1929
Biulleten' narodnogo komissariata zdravookhraneniia, 1922–1935
Biulleten' saratovskogo gubotnaroba (Saratov), 1921–1922
Biulleten' tsentral'noi komissii pomoshchi golodaiushchim VTsIK, 1921
Derevenskaia pravda (Petrograd), 1918–1922
Detskii dom, 1928–1931 (also cited under the title *Okhrana detstva*, 1931)
Drug detei (Khar'kov), 1925–1933
Drug detei, 1925–1933
Dvukhnedel'nik donskogo okruzhnogo otdela narodnogo obrazovaniia
    (Rostov-on-the-Don), 1924–1926
Ezhenedel'nik sovetskoi iustitsii (see *Sovetskaia iustitsiia*)
Gudok, 1917–
Illiustrirovannaia Rossiia (Paris), 1924–1939
Iskusstvo i deti, 1927–1932
Iugo-Vostok (see *Severo-Kavkazskii krai*)
Izhevskaia pravda (Izhevsk), 1917–
Izvestiia, 1917–
Izvestiia otdela narodnogo obrazovaniia (see *Narodnoe obrazovanie olonet-
    skoi gubernii*)
Khoziaistvo TsChO (Voronezh), 1928–1937
Kommunistka, 1920–1930
Komsomol'skaia pravda, 1925–
Krasnaia gazeta (Petrograd/Leningrad), 1918–1939
Krasnaia gazeta, evening edition (Petrograd/Leningrad), 1922–1936
Krasnaia nov', 1921–1942
Krasnoarmeets, 1919–
Krasnoiarskii rabochii (Krasnoiarsk), 1917–1918, 1920–
Krasnyi flot (Petrograd/Leningrad), 1922–1928
Leningradskaia oblast' (Leningrad), 1928–1929
Molot (Rostov-on-the-Don), 1917–1918, 1920–
Moskovskii meditsinskii zhurnal, 1921–1931
Na putiakh k novoi shkole, 1922–1933
Narodnoe obrazovanie olonetskoi gubernii (Petrozavodsk), 1918–1919 (also
    cited under the title *Izvestiia otdela narodnogo obrazovaniia*, 1918)
Narodnoe prosveshchenie (Kursk), 1921–1922
Narodnoe prosveshchenie, 1918–1930
Narodnoe prosveshchenie (Odessa), 1921–1922
Narodnoe prosveshchenie (Saratov) 1921–1922 (also cited under the title
    Vestnik narodnogo prosveshcheniia, 1921)
Narodnyi uchitel', 1924–1935
Nash trud (Iaroslavl'), 1922–1929
Nizhegorodskii prosveshchenets (Nizhnii Novgorod/Gor'kii), 1929–1935
Nizhegorodskii sbornik zdravookhraneniia (Nizhnii Novgorod), 1925–1928
Novaia zhizn' (Petrograd), 1917–1918
Novyi put' (Riga), 1921–1922
Okhrana detstva (see *Detskii dom*)

Okhrana materinstva i mladenchestva, 1926–41
Posle goloda, 1922–1923
Pravda, 1917–
Pravda Zakavkaz'ia (see *Zaria Vostoka*)
Pravo i zhizn', 1922–1928
Profilakticheskaia meditsina (Khar'kov), 1922–1937
Proletarskii sud, 1922–1928
Prosveshchenie (Krasnodar), 1921–1923
Prosveshchenie (Penza), 1926
Prosveshchenie (Riazan'), 1918–1919
Prosveshchenie (Viatka), 1922
Prosveshchenie na transporte, 1922–1930
Prosveshchenie na Urale (see *Ural'skii uchitel'*)
Prosveshchenie Sibiri (Novo-Nikolaevsk/Novosibirsk), 1923–1935 (also cited
    under the title *Sibirskii pedagogicheskii zhurnal,* 1923–1925)
Psikhiatriia, nevrologiia i eksperimental'naia psikhologiia (Petrograd), 1922–
    1923
Put' prosveshcheniia (Khar'kov), 1922–1935; (Kiev), 1936–1941
Puti kommunisticheskogo prosveshcheniia (Simferopol'), 1925–1928
Rabochaia moskva, 1921–
Rabochii krai (Ivanovo-Voznesensk), 1917–
Saratovskii vestnik zdravookhraneniia (Saratov), 1920–1931
Severo-Kavkazskii krai (Rostov-on-the-Don), 1922–1935 (also cited under the
    title *Iugo-Vostok,* 1922–1924)
Shkola i zhizn' (Nizhnii Novgorod), 1923–1929
Sibirskii pedagogicheskii zhurnal (see *Prosveshchenie Sibiri*)
Smolenskaia nov' (Smolensk), 1922–1923
Sobranie uzakonenii i rasporiazhenii rabochego i krest'ianskogo pravitel'stva
    [SU], 1917–1949
*Sobranie zakonov i rasporiazhenii raboche-krest'ianskogo pravitel'stva Soiuza
    Sovetskikh Sotsialisticheskikh Respublik* [SZ], 1924–1949
Sotsialisticheskii vestnik (Berlin, Paris, New York), 1921–1965
Sotsial'noe vospitanie, 1921
Sovetskaia iustitsiia, 1922– (also cited under the title *Ezhenedel'nik sovetskoi
    iustitsii,* 1922–1929)
Sovetskoe stroitel'stvo, 1926–1937
Trud, 1921–
Turkestanskaia pravda (Tashkent), 1922–
Tvorcheskii put' (Orenburg), 1923
Ural'skii uchitel' (Sverdlovsk), 1925–1935 (also cited under the title *Prosvesh-
    chenie na Urale,* 1927–1931)
Vechernee vremia (Rostov-on-the-Don), 1918–1920
Vecherniaia moskva, 1923–
Venerologiia i dermatologiia, 1924–
Vestnik narodnogo prosveshcheniia (see *Narodnoe prosveshchenie*)
Vestnik prosveshcheniia (Kazan'), 1921–1924 (also cited under the title *Vest-
    nik prosveshcheniia T.S.S.R.,* 1922)

Vestnik prosveshcheniia, 1922–1929
Vestnik prosveshcheniia (Voronezh), 1921
Vestnik prosveshcheniia i kommunisticheskoi kul'tury (Tashkent), 1920–1921
Vestnik prosveshcheniia T.S.S.R. (see *Vestnik prosveshcheniia*)
Vestnik prosveshchentsa (Orenburg), 1925–1928
Vestnik statistiki, 1919–
Vlast' sovetov, 1917–1938
Volna (Arkhangel'sk), 1920–
Voprosy izucheniia i vospitaniia lichnosti (Petrograd/Leningrad), 1919–1932
Voprosy prosveshcheniia (see *Voprosy prosveshcheniia na Severnom Kavkaze*)
Voprosy prosveshcheniia na Severnom Kavkaze (Rostov-on-the-Don), 1926–
  1934 (also cited under the titles *Voprosy prosveshcheniia,* 1926, and *Za
  sotsialisticheskuiu kul'turu,* 1930–1934)
Vozhatyi, 1924–
Za sotsialisticheskuiu kul'turu (see *Voprosy prosveshcheniia na Severnom
  Kavkaze*)
Zaria Vostoka (Tiflis), 1922– (also cited under the title *Pravda Zakavkaz'ia,*
  1922)
Zhizn' Buriatii (Verkhneudinsk), 1924–1931

OTHER PUBLISHED SOURCES

An American Report on the Russian Famine. New York, 1921.
Artamonov, M. *Deti ulitsy. Ocherki moskovskoi zhizni.* Moscow, 1925.
Asfal'tovyi kotel. Khudozhestvennye stranitsy iz zhizni besprizornykh. Com-
  piled by M. S. Zhivov. Moscow, 1926.
Astemirov, Z. A. "Iz istorii razvitiia uchrezhdenii dlia nesovershennoletnikh
  pravonarushitelei v SSSR." In *Preduprezhdenie prestupnosti nesovershen-
  noletnikh,* 253–269. Moscow, 1965.
Balanon, Lourdes G. "Street Children: Strategies for Action." *Child Welfare*
  68 (March–April 1989): 159–166.
Ball, Alan M. *Russia's Last Capitalists: The Nepmen, 1921–1929.* Berkeley,
  1987.
Bartlett, Marcella. "Stepchildren of the Russian Revolution." *Asia* 26 (April
  1926): 334–338, 367–369.
Bater, James H. *St. Petersburg: Industrialization and Change.* Montreal, 1976.
Bauer, Raymond A. *The New Man in Soviet Psychology.* Cambridge, Mass.,
  1952.
Beal, Fred E. *Proletarian Journey.* New York, 1937.
Berkman, Alexander. *The Bolshevik Myth (Diary, 1920–1922).* New York,
  1925.
Besprizornye. Compiled by O. Kaidanova. Moscow, 1926.
Bich naroda. Ocherki strashnoi deistvitel'nosti. Kazan', 1922.
Boldyrev, E. V. *Mery preduprezhdeniia pravonarushenii nesovershennoletnikh
  v SSSR.* Moscow, 1964.
Bol'shaia sovetskaia entsiklopediia. 65 vols. Moscow, 1926–1947.

Bor'ba s besprizornost'iu. Materialy 1-i moskovskoi konferentsii po bor'be s besprizornost'iu 16–17 marta 1924 g. Moscow, 1924.

Bor'ba s detskoi besprizornost'iu. Compiled by B. S. Utevskii. Moscow-Leningrad, 1932.

Borders, Karl. *Village Life Under the Soviets.* New York, 1927.

Borovich, B. O., ed. *Kollektivy besprizornykh i ikh vozhaki.* Khar'kov, 1926.

Bosewitz, René. *Waifdom in the Soviet Union: Features of the Sub-Culture and Re-Education.* Frankfurt am Main, 1988.

Boswell, John. *The Kindness of Strangers: The Abandonment of Children in Western Europe from Late Antiquity to the Renaissance.* New York, 1988.

Bowen, James. *Soviet Education: Anton Makarenko and the Years of Experiment.* Madison, Wis., 1962; reprint, 1965.

Bugaiskii, Ia. P. *Khuliganstvo kak sotsial'no-patologicheskoe iavlenie.* Moscow-Leningrad, 1927.

Bukharin, N. I., and E. A. Preobrazhenskii. *The ABC of Communism: A Popular Explanation of the Program of the Communist Party of Russia.* Ann Arbor, Mich., 1966.

Burrell, George A. *An American Engineer Looks at Russia.* Boston, 1932.

Chamberlin, William Henry. *Soviet Russia: A Living Record and a History.* Boston, 1935.

Chase, William J. *Workers, Society, and the Soviet State: Labor and Life in Moscow, 1918–1929.* Urbana, Ill., 1987.

Cheliabinskaia guberniia v period voennogo kommunizma (iiul' 1919–dekabr' 1920 gg.). Dokumenty i materialy. Cheliabinsk, 1960.

Chto govoriat tsifry o golode?. Vypusk 2. Moscow, 1922.

Chulitskaia-Tikheeva, L. I. *Doshkol'nyi vozrast i ego osobennosti.* Moscow, 1923.

"City of Lost Boys." *Life* 11 (June 1988): 73–78.

Connor, Walter D. *Deviance in Soviet Society: Crime, Delinquency, and Alcoholism.* New York, 1972.

Conquest, Robert. *The Harvest of Sorrow: Soviet Collectivization and the Terror-Famine.* New York, 1986.

Cuomo, Mario M. *1933/1983—Never Again: A Report to the National Governor's Association Task Force on the Homeless.* Portland, Maine, 1983.

Deti posle goloda. Sbornik materialov. Khar'kov, 1924.

Detskaia besprizornost' (preduprezhdenie i bor'ba s nei). Moscow, 1923.

Detskaia defektivnost', prestupnost' i besprizornost'. Po materialam I vserossiiskogo s"ezda 24/VI–2/VII 1920 g. Moscow, 1922.

Detskii dom. Compiled by B. S. Utevskii. Moscow-Leningrad, 1932.

Detskii dom i bor'ba s besprizornost'iu. Moscow, 1928.

Detskoe pravo sovetskikh respublik. Sbornik deistvuiushchego zakonodatel'stva o detiakh. Compiled by M. P. Krichevskaia and I. I. Kuritskii. Khar'kov, 1927.

Diushen, V., ed. *Piat' let detskogo gorodka imeni III internatsionala.* Moscow, 1924.

Dreiser, Theodore. *Dreiser Looks at Russia.* New York, 1928.

Dunstan, John. "Soviet Boarding Education: Its Rise and Progress." In *Home, School, and Leisure in the Soviet Union*, edited by Jenny Brine, Maureen Perrie, and Andrew Sutton, 110–141. London, 1980.

Duranty, Walter. *Duranty Reports Russia*. New York, 1934.

———. *I Write as I Please*. New York, 1935.

Dzerzhinskii, F. E. *Izbrannye proizvedeniia*. 3d ed. 2 vols. Moscow, 1977.

Eaton, Richard. *Under the Red Flag*. New York, 1924.

Edelhertz, Bernard. *The Russian Paradox: A First-Hand Study of Life Under the Soviets*. New York, 1930.

Ehrenburg, Ilya. *First Years of Revolution: 1918–21*. London, 1962.

———. *Memoirs: 1921–1941*. New York, 1966.

———. *A Street in Moscow*. New York, 1932.

Enik, K., and V. Blok. *Iz trushchob na stroiku*. Moscow-Saratov, 1930.

Fall, Merrick. "Streets Apart." *UNESCO Courier* 38 (June 1985): 25–27.

Feiler, Arthur. *The Russian Experiment*. New York, 1930.

Fisher, Harold H. *The Famine in Soviet Russia, 1919–1923: The Operations of the American Relief Administration*. New York, 1927.

Fitzpatrick, Sheila. *The Commissariat of Enlightenment: Soviet Organization of Education and the Arts Under Lunacharsky, October 1917–1921*. Cambridge, 1970.

———, ed. *Cultural Revolution in Russia, 1928–1931*. Bloomington, Ind., 1984.

———. *Education and Social Mobility in the Soviet Union, 1921–1934*. Cambridge, 1979.

Fridland, L. *S raznykh storon. Prostitutsiia v SSSR*. Berlin, 1931.

Fry, A. Ruth. *Three Visits to Russia, 1922–25*. London, 1942.

Gailis, Ia. R., ed. *V pomoshch' perepodgotovke rabotnikov sotsial'nogo vospitaniia*. 2d ed. Moscow, 1924.

Gernet, M. N., ed. *Deti-prestupniki*. Moscow, 1912.

———. *Prestupnyi mir moskvy*. Moscow, 1924.

Gerson, Lennard D. *The Secret Police in Lenin's Russia*. Philadelphia, 1976.

Gibbs, Philip. *Since Then*. New York, 1930.

Gide, André. *Back from the U.S.S.R.* London, 1937.

Gilev, P. S. *Detskaia besprizornost' i bor'ba s nei v Buriatii za poslednie piat' let*. Verkhneudinsk, 1928.

Glatman, L. G. *Pioner—na bor'bu s besprizornost'iu*. Moscow-Leningrad, 1926.

———. *Pionery i besprizornye*. Moscow-Leningrad, 1925.

Golder, Frank Alfred, and Lincoln Hutchinson. *On the Trail of the Russian Famine*. Stanford, 1927.

Goldman, Wendy Z. "The 'Withering Away' and the Resurrection of the Soviet Family, 1917–1936." Ph.D. diss., University of Pennsylvania, 1987.

———. "Working-Class Women and the 'Withering Away' of the Family: Popular Responses to Family Policy." In *Russia in the Era of NEP: Explorations in Soviet Society and Culture*, edited by Sheila Fitzpatrick, Alexander Rabinowitch, and Richard Stites, 125–143. Bloomington, Ind., 1991.

*Golod i deti na Ukraine. Po dannym sektsii pomoshchi golodaiushchim de-
tiam pri tsentr. sov. zashchity detei na Ukraine i po drugim materialam.*
Compiled by V. A. Arnautov. Khar'kov, 1922.
Golod, 1921–1922. New York, [1922].
Gor'kaia pravda o Povolzh'i i otchet tulgubpomgola. Tula, 1922.
Gornyi, Viktor. *Besprizornyi krug.* Leningrad, 1926.
Greenwall, H. J. *Mirrors of Moscow.* London, 1929.
Grinberg, Anna, ed. *Rasskazy besprizornykh o sebe.* Moscow, 1925.
Grishakov, N. P. *Detskaia prestupnost' i bor'ba s neiu putem vospitaniia.*
Orel, 1923.
Gusak, A. A. "Komsomol Ukrainy—pomoshchnik kommunisticheskoi partii v
bor'be s bezrabotitsei molodezhi kak odnim iz istochnikov besprizornosti
(1921–1928 gg.)." In *Kommunisticheskaia partiia Ukrainy v bor'be za
pod"em trudovoi i politicheskoi aktivnosti trudiashchikhsia, vypusk 3,*
173–183. Dnepropetrovsk, 1975.
Haines, Anna J. "Children of Moscow." *Asia* 22 (March 1922): 214–218.
———. *Health Work in Soviet Russia.* New York, 1928.
Hammer, Armand. *The Quest of the Romanoff Treasure.* New York, 1932.
Harriman, W. Averell. *America and Russia in a Changing World: A Half
Century of Personal Observation.* Garden City, N.Y., 1971.
Hayes, Robert M. "Homeless Children." In *Caring for America's Children,*
edited by Frank J. Macchiarola and Alan Gartner, 58–69. New York, 1989.
Hersch, Patricia. "Coming of Age on City Streets." *Psychology Today* 22
(January 1988): 28–37.
Hibben, Paxton. *Report on the Russian Famine.* New York, 1922.
Hiebert, P. C., and Orie O. Miller. *Feeding the Hungry: Russian Famine,
1919–1925.* Scottdale, Penn., 1929.
Holmes, Larry E. "Soviet Schools: Policy Pursues Practice, 1921–1928."
Slavic Review 48 (Summer 1989): 234–253.
Hughes, Langston. *I Wonder as I Wander.* New York, 1956.
Istrati, Panait. *Russia Unveiled.* London, 1931; reprint, Westport, Conn., 1975.
Itogi bor'by s golodom v 1921–22 g.g. Sbornik statei i otchetov. Moscow, 1922.
Juviler, Peter H. "Contradictions of Revolution: Juvenile Crime and Rehabili-
tation." In *Bolshevik Culture,* edited by Abbott Gleason, Peter Kenez, and
Richard Stites, 261–278. Bloomington, Ind., 1985.
Kaidanova, O. *Besprizornye deti. Praktika raboty opytnoi stantsii.* Leningrad,
1926.
Kalinina, A. D. *Desiat' let raboty po bor'be s detskoi besprizornost'iu.*
Moscow-Leningrad, 1928.
———, ed. *Komsomol i besprizornost'.* Khar'kov, 1926.
Kirsanov, M. F. *Rukovodstvo po proizvodstvu del v mestnykh komissiiakh po
delam o nesovershennoletnikh.* Moscow-Leningrad, 1927.
Kogan, A. N. "Sistema meropriiatii partii i pravitel'stva po bor'be s golodom
v Povolzh'e 1921–1922 gg." *Istoricheskie zapiski* 48 (1954): 228–247.
Konius, E. M. *Puti razvitiia sovetskoi okhrany materinstva i mladenchestva
1917–1940.* Moscow, 1954.
Kozhevnikov, A. V. *Stremka.* Moscow-Leningrad, 1926.

Krasnushkin, E. K., G. M. Segal, and Ts. M. Feinberg, eds. *Nishchenstvo i besprizornost'*. Moscow, 1929.

Kratkii sbornik zakonodatel'nykh materialov po bor'be s detskoi besprizornost'iu. Voronezh, [1926].

Kravchenko, Victor. *I Chose Freedom*. New York, 1946.

Krist, Gustav. *Prisoner in the Forbidden Land*. London, 1938.

Krupskaia, N. K. *Pedagogicheskie sochineniia*. 11 vols. Moscow, 1957–1963.

Kufaev, V. I. *Bor'ba s pravonarusheniiami nesovershennoletnikh*. Moscow, 1924.

———. *Iunye pravonarushiteli*. Moscow, 1924.

———. *Iunye pravonarushiteli*. 2d ed. Moscow, 1925.

———. *Iunye pravonarushiteli*. 3d ed. Moscow, 1929.

———. "Iz opyta raboty komissii po delam nesovershennoletnikh v period 1918–1935 gg." *Voprosy kriminalistiki*, 1964, no. 11: 89–109.

———. *Pedagogicheskie mery bor'by s pravonarusheniiami nesovershennoletnikh*. Moscow, 1927.

———. *Shkola-kommuna imeni F. E. Dzerzhinskogo*. Moscow, 1938.

Leshchinskii, M. Ia. *Kto byl nichem* . . . . Moscow, 1967.

Letnie kolonii. Sbornik, sostavlennyi otdelom reformy i otdelom edinoi shkoly narodnogo komissariata po prosveshcheniiu. Moscow, 1919.

Lewin, Moshe. *The Making of the Soviet System: Essays in the Social History of Interwar Russia*. New York, 1985.

Lilge, Frederic. *Anton Semyonovitch Makarenko: An Analysis of His Educational Ideas in the Context of Soviet Society*. Berkeley, 1958.

Liublinskii, P. I. *Bor'ba s prestupnost'iu v detskom i iunosheskom vozraste*. Moscow, 1923.

———. *Zakonodatel'naia okhrana truda detei i podrostkov*. Petrograd, 1923.

Livshits, E. S. *Detskaia besprizornost' i novye formy bor'by s neiu*. Moscow, 1924.

———. *Sotsial'nye korni besprizornosti*. Moscow, 1925.

Lukin, Iu. B. *A. S. Makarenko. Kritiko-biograficheskii ocherk*. Moscow, 1954.

Lyons, Eugene. *Assignment in Utopia*. New York, 1937.

McCormick, Anne O'Hare. *The Hammer and the Scythe*. New York, 1929.

Mackenzie, F. A. *Russia Before Dawn*. London, 1923.

Madison, Bernice Q. *Social Welfare in the Soviet Union*. Stanford, 1968.

Magul'iano, G. G. "K voprosu o detskoi prestupnosti i merakh bor'by s nei za gody revoliutsii." In *Sbornik trudov professorov i prepodavatelei gosudarstvennogo irkutskogo universiteta. Fakul'tet obshchestvennykh nauk, vypusk 6*, 167–221. Irkutsk, 1923.

Maiakovskii, Vladimir. "Besprizorshchina." In *Polnoe sobranie sochinenii*, 7:170–172. Moscow, 1958.

Makarenko, A. S. *The Road to Life*. 2 vols. Moscow, 1951; reprint, 1973.

Manns, G. Iu. *Bor'ba s besprizornost'iu i prestupnost'iu nesovershennoletnikh i ee ocherednye zadachi v sibirskom krae*. Irkutsk, 1927.

Marinov, A. "Gosudarstvennye deti." *Novyi mir*, 1974, no. 2: 200–226.

Maro [M. I. Levitina]. *Besprizornye. Sotsiologiia. Byt. Praktika raboty*. Moscow, 1925.

———. *Rabota s besprizornymi. Praktika novoi raboty v SSSR*. Khar'kov, 1924.

Min'kovskii, G. M. "Osnovnye etapy razvitiia sovetskoi sistemy mer bor'by s prestupnost'iu nesovershennoletnikh." In *Voprosy bor'by s prestupnost'iu, vypusk 6*, 37–74. Moscow, 1967.

Monkhouse, Allan. *Moscow, 1911–1933*. London, 1933.

Na fronte goloda. Knigi 1 and 2. Samara, 1922–1923.

Na pomoshch' detiam. Semipalatinsk, 1926.

Na pomoshch' detiam. Obshchestvenno-literaturnyi i nauchnyi sbornik, posviashchennyi voprosam bor'by s detskoi besprizornost'iu. Moscow, 1926.

Na pomoshch'! Illiustrirovannyi zhurnal. Samara, 1922.

Na pomoshch' rebenku. Petrograd-Moscow, 1923.

Narodnoe obrazovanie v R.S.F.S.R. (po dannym godovoi statisticheskoi otchetnosti mestnykh organov narodnogo komissariata po prosveshcheniiu na I/VI 1924 goda). Moscow, 1925.

Narodnoe obrazovanie v SSSR v 1926/27 uch. godu. Moscow, 1927.

Narodnoe prosveshchenie v R.S.F.S.R. k 1924/25 uchebnomu godu. (Otchet narkomprosa RSFSR za 1923/24 g.). Moscow, 1925.

Narodnoe prosveshchenie v R.S.F.S.R. k 1925/26 uchebnomu godu. (Otchet narkomprosa RSFSR za 1924/25 g.). Moscow, 1926.

Narodnoe prosveshchenie v RSFSR k 1927–28 uchebnomu godu. Otchet narkomprosa RSFSR za 1926/27 uchebnyi god. Moscow-Leningrad, 1928.

Narodnoe prosveshchenie v RSFSR k 1926/27 uchebnomu godu. Otchet narkomprosa RSFSR za 1925/26 uchebnyi god. Moscow-Leningrad, 1927.

Narodnoe prosveshchenie v RSFSR 1927–28 god. Moscow, 1929.

Nesovershennoletnie pravonarushiteli. Compiled by B. S. Utevskii. Moscow-Leningrad, 1932.

Neuberger, Joan. "Crime and Culture: Hooliganism in St. Petersburg, 1900–1914." Ph.D. diss., Stanford University, 1985.

Newman, E. M. *Seeing Russia*. New York, 1928.

Obshchestvo "Drug detei". Compiled by B. S. Utevskii. Moscow-Leningrad, 1932.

Obzor deiatel'nosti gubernskogo ispolnitel'nogo komiteta za 1923 god. Novgorod, 1923.

Obzor narodnogo khoziaistva tambovskoi gubernii oktiabr' 1921 g.,-oktiabr' 1922 g. Tambov, 1922.

Obzor raboty po bor'be s detskoi besprizornost'iu i beznadzornost'iu v RSFSR za 1927/28 g. Moscow, 1928.

Obzor raboty po bor'be s detskoi besprizornost'iu i beznadzornost'iu v RSFSR za 1929/30 god. Moscow, 1930.

Ognyov, N. [M. G. Rozanov]. *The Diary of a Communist Schoolboy*. New York, 1928; reprint, Westport, Conn., 1973.

Okhrana zdorov'ia detei. Compiled by N. N. Spasokukotskii. Moscow-Leningrad, 1932.

Orlov, Alexander. *The Secret History of Stalin's Crimes*. New York, 1953.

Otchet cherepovetskogo gubernskogo ispolnitel'nogo komiteta XII-mu gubernskomu s"ezdu sovetov za vremia s 15 dek. 1922 g. po 1-e dek. 1923 g. Cherepovets, [n.d.].

Otchet ekonomicheskogo soveshchaniia avtonomnoi oblasti Komi na 1-e aprelia 1922 g. Viatka, 1922.

Otchet gorskogo ekonomicheskogo soveshchaniia za period aprel'–sentiabr' 1922 g. Vladikavkaz, 1923.

Otchet gorskogo ekonomicheskogo soveshchaniia za period ianvar'–mart 1922 g. Vladikavkaz, 1922.

Otchet krymskogo narodnogo komissariata po prosveshcheniiu vtoromu vsekrymskomu s"ezdu sovetov rabochikh, krest'ianskikh, krasnoarmeiskikh i voenmorskikh deputatov. (S oktiabria 1921 g. po oktiabr' 1922 g.). Simferopol', 1922.

Otchet kurskogo gubernskogo ispolnitel'nogo komiteta X-mu gubernskomu s"ezdu sovetov. Kursk, 1922.

Otchet o deiatel'nosti riazanskogo gubispolkoma za vremia s X po XI gubernskii s"ezd sovetov rabochikh, krest'ianskikh i krasnoarmeiskikh deputatov. Riazan', 1922.

Otchet o deiatel'nosti saratovskogo gubernskogo ispolnitel'nogo komiteta sovetov rabochikh, krest'ianskikh i krasnoarmeiskikh deputatov i saratovskogo gorodskogo soveta XII-go sozyva za 1923 goda. Saratov, 1923.

Otchet o deiatel'nosti tul'skogo gubernskogo ispolnitel'nogo komiteta sovetov rabochikh, krest'ianskikh i krasnoarmeiskikh deputatov za 1922–23 khoziaistvennyi god. Tula, 1924.

Otchet o sostoianii narodnogo obrazovaniia v eniseiskoi gubernii IV-mu gubs"ezdu sovetov. Krasnoiarsk, 1922.

Otchet samarskogo gubernskogo ekonomicheskogo soveshchaniia. Vypusk II-i. Polugodie 1 oktiabria 1921 g.–1 aprelia 1922 g. Samara, 1922.

Otchet sengileevskogo uezdnogo ispolnitel'nogo komiteta. Za vremia s 1-go iiulia 1921 goda po 5-e fevralia 1922 goda. Sengilei, 1922.

Otchet sovetu truda i oborony za period 1/X 1921 g.–1/IV 1922 g. Kursk, 1922.

Otchet stavropol'skogo gubekonomsoveshchaniia sovetu truda i oborony za aprel'–sentiabr' 1922 g. Stavropol', 1923.

Otchet tambovskogo gubernskogo ekonomicheskogo soveshchaniia sovetu truda i oborony za period s 1 oktiabria 1921 g. po 1 aprelia 1922 g. Tambov, 1922.

Otchet tverskogo gubernskogo ekonomicheskogo soveshchaniia sovetu truda i oborony. No. 1 (iiul'–sentiabr'). Tver', 1921.

Otchet vladimirskogo gubispolkoma i ego otdelov 14-mu gubernskomu s"ezdu sovetov (10 dekabria 1922 goda). Vladimir, 1922.

Paustovsky, Konstantin. *The Restless Years.* London, 1974.

Pedagogicheskaia entsiklopediia. 3 vols. Moscow, 1927–1930.

Pedagogicheskaia entsiklopediia. 4 vols. Moscow, 1964–1968.

Pervyi vserossiiskii s"ezd deiatelei po okhrane detstva. 2–8 fevral'ia 1919 goda v Moskve. Moscow, 1920.

Pogrebinskii, M. S. *Fabrika liudei.* Moscow, 1929.

Poliakov, Iu. A. *1921-i: pobeda nad golodom.* Moscow, 1975.

Pomoshch' detiam. Sbornik statei po bor'be s besprizornost'iu i pomoshchi detiam na Ukraine v 1924 godu. Khar'kov, 1924.

Popov, M. *Detskaia besprizornost' i patronirovanie.* Ivanovo-Voznesensk, 1929.

Poznyshev, S. V. *Detskaia besprizornost' i mery bor'by s nei.* Moscow, 1926.

Raleigh, Donald J., ed. *A Russian Civil War Diary: Alexis Babine in Saratov, 1917–1922.* Durham, N.C., 1988.

Ransel, David L. *Mothers of Misery: Child Abandonment in Russia.* Princeton, 1988.

Report on Economic Conditions in Russia with Special Reference to the Famine of 1921–1922 and the State of Agriculture. Nancy-Paris-Strasbourg, 1922.

Reswick, William. *I Dreamt Revolution.* Chicago, 1952.

Rezoliutsii 3-go vserossiiskogo s"ezda po okhrane detstva 25–30 maia 1930 g. i 1-go vserossiiskogo soveshchaniia po bor'be s detskoi besprizornost'iu i beznadzornost'iu 7-go dekabria 1930 g. Moscow, 1931.

Roberts, C. E. Bechhoffer. *Through Starving Russia.* London, 1921.

Rudkin, V. G. "Deiatel'nost' organov sovetskoi vlasti i obshchestvennykh organizatsii Belorussii po preduprezhdeniiu detskoi besprizornosti (1921–1930 gg.)." Minsk, 1983. MS. 14431 at INION AN SSSR, Moscow.

———. "Prichiny massovoi detskoi besprizornosti v Belorussii i zakonomernosti ee likvidatsii (1917–1930 gg.)." Minsk, 1983. MS. 14433 at INION AN SSSR, Moscow.

The Russian Famines, 1921–22, 1922–23. Summary Report, Commission on Russian Relief of the National Information Bureau, Inc. New York, [1923].

Ryndziunskii, G. D., and T. M. Savinskaia. *Detskoe pravo. Pravovoe polozhenie detei v RSFSR.* 3d ed. Moscow-Leningrad, 1932.

———. *Pravovoe polozhenie detei po zakonodatel'stvu R.S.F.S.R.* Moscow, 1923.

Ryndziunskii, G. D., T. M. Savinskaia, and G. G. Cherkezov. *Pravovoe polozhenie detei v RSFSR.* 2d ed. Moscow, 1927.

Salisbury, Harrison E. *Russia in Revolution, 1900–1930.* New York, 1978.

Sbornik deistvuiushchikh uzakonenii i rasporiazhenii pravitel'stva Soiuza SSR i pravitel'stva R.S.F.S.R., postanovlenii detkomissii pri VTsIK i vedomstvennykh rasporiazhenii po bor'be s detskoi besprizornost'iu i beznadzornost'iu. Vypusk 3. Moscow, 1932.

Sbornik deistvuiushchikh uzakonenii i rasporiazhenii pravitel'stva Soiuza SSR i pravitel'stva R.S.F.S.R., postanovlenii detkomissii pri VTsIK i vedomstvennykh rasporiazhenii po bor'be s detskoi besprizornost'iu i ee preduprezhdeniiu. Vypusk 2. Moscow, 1929.

Sbornik uzakonenii i rasporiazhenii pravitel'stva Soiuza SSR i pravitel'stva RSFSR o meropriiatiakh po bor'be s detskoi besprizornost'iu i po ee preduprezhdeniiu. Moscow, 1927.

Seifulina, Lydia. "The Lawbreakers." In *Flying Osip: Stories of New Russia.* Freeport, N.Y., 1925; reprint, 1970.

Serge, Victor. *Russia Twenty Years After.* New York, 1937.

Shishkov, Vyacheslav. *Children of the Street.* Royal Oak, Mich., 1979.

Shishova, N. V. "Rol' obshchestvennosti v preodolenii detskoi besprizornosti na severnom Kavkaze v 1920–1926 gg." Rostov-on-the-Don, 1979. MS. 4764 at INION AN SSSR, Moscow.

———. "Sovershenstvovanie raboty partiinykh, gosudarstvennykh i obshchestvennykh organizatsii Dona i Kubano-Chernomor'ia po likvidatsii detskoi besprizornosti v 1926–1929 gg." Rostov-on-the-Don, 1982. MS. 9322 at INION AN SSSR, Moscow.

———. "Sozdanie sistemy detskikh uchrezhdenii dlia spaseniia besprizornykh detei na Donu i Kubano-Chernomor'ia v period vosstanovleniia narodnogo khoziaistva." Rostov-on-the-Don, 1986. MS. 25907 at INION AN SSSR, Moscow.

Shveitser, V. L., and S. M. Shabalov, eds. *Besprizornye v trudovykh kommunakh. Praktika raboty s trudnymi det'mi. Sbornik statei i materialov*. Moscow, 1926.

Siemsen, Hans. "Russia's Self-Educated Children." *Living Age* 340 (August 1931): 555–559.

Sinitsin, A. M. "Zabota o beznadzornykh i besprizornykh detiakh v SSSR v gody velikoi otechestvennoi voiny." *Voprosy istorii*, 1969, no. 6: 20–29.

Snabzhenie detei. Compiled by N. K. Zamkov and B. S. Utevskii. Moscow-Leningrad, 1932.

Sobranie russkikh vorovskikh slovarei. Compiled by V. Kozlovskii. 4 vols. New York, 1983.

Sokolov, Boris. *Spasite detei! (O detiakh sovetskoi Rossii)*. Prague, 1921.

Sokolov, P. N. *Besprizornye deti v g. Saratove. Rezul'taty odnodnevnoi perepiski 19 oktiabria 1924 g*. Saratov, 1925.

———. *Detskaia besprizornost' i detskaia prestupnost' i mery bor'by s etimi iavleniiami s sovremennoi tochki zreniia*. Saratov, 1924.

Solzhenitsyn, Aleksandr I. *The Gulag Archipelago 1918–1956: An Experiment in Literary Investigation*. 3 vols. New York, 1974–1978.

Sorokin, Pitirim A. *Hunger as a Factor in Human Affairs*. Gainesville, Fla., 1975.

———. *Leaves from a Russian Diary—and Thirty Years After*. Boston, 1950.

Spasennye revoliutsiei. Bor'ba s besprizornost'iu v irkutskoi gubernii i okruge (1920–1931 gg.). Irkutsk, 1977.

Spaull, Hebe. *The Youth of Russia To-Day*. London, 1933.

Statisticheskii obzor narodnogo obrazovaniia v permskoi gubernii za 1922–23 god. Compiled by B. N. Ber-Gurevich. Okhansk, 1924.

Statisticheskii obzor narodnogo obrazovaniia v permskom okruge, ural'skoi oblasti za 1923–24 uch. god. Perm', 1924.

Statisticheskii spravochnik po narodnomu obrazovaniiu 1923 g. Vypusk 1. Pokrovsk, 1923.

Stevens, Jennie A. "Children of the Revolution: Soviet Russia's Homeless Children (*Besprizorniki*) in the 1920s." *Russian History* 9, nos. 2–3 (1982): 242–264.

Stites, Richard. *Revolutionary Dreams: Utopian Vision and Experimental Life in the Russian Revolution*. Oxford, 1989.

———. *The Women's Liberation Movement in Russia: Feminism, Nihilism, and Bolshevism, 1860–1930*. Princeton, 1978.

Stolee, Margaret Kay. " 'A Generation Capable of Establishing Communism': Revolutionary Child Rearing in the Soviet Union, 1917–1928." Ph.D. diss., Duke University, 1982.

———. "Homeless Children in the USSR, 1917–1957." *Soviet Studies* 40 (January 1988): 64–83.

"Street-wise, Street-foolish." *The Economist* 305 (December 26, 1987): 57.

Thompson, Dorothy. *The New Russia*. New York, 1928.

Tizanov, S. S., and M. S. Epshtein, eds. *Gosudarstvo i obshchestvennost' v bor'be s detskoi besprizornost'iu. (Sbornik statei i pravitel'stvennykh rasporiazhenii)*. Moscow-Leningrad, 1927.

Tizanov, S. S., V. L. Shveitser, and V. M. Vasil'eva, eds. *Detskaia besprizornost' i detskii dom. Sbornik statei i materialov II vserossiiskogo s"ezda SPON po voprosam detskoi besprizornosti, detskogo doma i pravovoi okhrany detei i podrostkov*. Moscow, 1926.

Tizanov, S. S., V. M. Vasil'eva, and I. I. Daniushevskii, eds. *Pedagogika sovremennogo detskogo doma*. Moscow-Leningrad, 1927.

Tolmachev, V. N., ed. *Khuliganstvo i khuligany*. Moscow, 1929.

Trekhletnii plan bor'by s detskoi besprizornost'iu. Moscow, 1927.

U.S. Congress. Senate. Committee on the Judiciary. Subcommittee on the Constitution. *Homeless Youth: The Saga of "Pushouts" and "Throwaways" in America*. 96th Cong., 2d sess., 1980.

Utevskii, B. S. *V bor'be s detskoi prestupnost'iu. Ocherki zhizni i byta moskovskogo trudovogo doma dlia nesovershennoletnikh pravonarushitelei*. Moscow, 1927.

Utley, Freda. *The Dream We Lost*. New York, 1940.

Vasilevskii, L. A., and L. M. Vasilevskii. *Kniga o golode*. 3d ed. Petrograd, 1922.

———. *Prostitutsiia i novaia Rossiia*. Tver', 1923.

Vasilevskii, L. M. *Besprizornost' i deti ulitsy*. 2d ed. Khar'kov, 1925.

———. *Detskaia "prestupnost' " i detskii sud*. Tver', 1923.

———. *Durmany (narkotiki)*. Moscow, 1924.

———. *Prostitutsiia i rabochaia molodezh'*. Moscow, 1924.

Vatova, E. "Bolshevskaia trudovaia kommuna i ee organizator." *Iunost'*, 1966, no. 3: 91–93.

Vchera i segodnia. Al'manakh byvshikh pravonarushitelei i besprizornykh. No. 1. Moscow, 1931.

Viollis, Andrée. *A Girl in Soviet Russia*. New York, 1929.

Vserossiiskoe obsledovanie detskikh uchrezhdenii. Doklad NKRKI v komissiiu po uluchsheniiu zhizni detei pri VTsIK. Moscow, 1921.

Vtoroi otchet irkutskogo gubernskogo ekonomicheskogo soveshchaniia (oktiabr' 1921 g.–mart 1922 g.). Irkutsk, 1922.

Vtoroi otchet tverskogo gubernskogo ekonomicheskogo soveshchaniia sovetu truda i oborony (oktiabr' 1921 g.–mart 1922 g.). Tver', 1922.

Vtoroi otchet voronezhskogo gubernskogo ekonomicheskogo soveshchaniia (1 oktiabria 1921 g.–1 oktiabria 1922 g.). Voronezh, 1922.

Weissman, Benjamin M. *Herbert Hoover and Famine Relief to Soviet Russia, 1921–1923*. Stanford, 1974.

Wicksteed, Alexander. *Life Under the Soviets*. London, 1928.

Winter, Ella. *Red Virtue: Human Relationships in the New Russia*. New York, 1933.

Zenzinov, Vladimir M. *Deserted: The Story of the Children Abandoned in Soviet Russia*. London, 1931; reprint, Westport, Conn., 1975.

Zhukova, L. A. "Deiatel'nost' Detkomissii VTsIK po okhrane zdorov'ia detei (1921–1938)." *Sovetskoe zdravookhranenie*, 1978, no. 2: 64–66.

Photo Credits

1–3. Records of American National Red Cross, 1917–1934. National Archives Gifts Collection, Record Group 200, box 916, file 987.08.

4–6. *Asia* 26 (April 1926): 334 (figs. 4 and 6), 337 (fig. 5).

7. *Drug detei* (Khar'kov), 1926, nos. 8–9: 45.

8. *Illiustrirovannaia Rossiia* (Paris), 1927, no. 3.

9. *Illiustrirovannaia Rossiia* (Paris), 1924, no. 1: 11.

10. K. Enik and V. Blok, *Iz trushchob na stroiku* (Moscow-Saratov, 1930), 17.

11. *Drug detei* (Khar'kov), 1926, no. 1: 8.

12. M. Ia. Leshchinskii, *Kto byl nichem . . .* (Moscow, 1967), 65.

13. *Drug detei* (Khar'kov), 1926, no. 1: 9.

14. E. M. Newman, *Seeing Russia* (New York, 1928), 42.

15. Enik and Blok, *Iz trushchob na stroiku*, 15.

16–17. *Drug detei* (Khar'kov), 1925, no. 6: 5, 6.

18–19. *Illiustrirovannaia Rossiia* (Paris), 1924, no. 1: 11, 10.

20–24. *Drug detei* (Khar'kov), 1925, no. 9: 20–23 (figs. 20–23); no. 6: 7 (fig. 24).

25. *Asia* 26 (April 1926): 335.

26. Nadezhda Azhgikhina, *All Children Are Our Children* (Moscow, 1988), 16.

27. B. S. Utevskii, *V bor'be s detskoi prestupnost'iu. Ocherki zhizni i byta moskovskogo trudovogo doma dlia nesovershennoletnikh pravonarushitelei* (Moscow, 1927), 87.

28. *Drug detei* (Khar'kov), 1926, no. 10: 46.

29. E. M. Konius, *Puti razvitiia sovetskoi okhrany materinstva i mlad-enchestva 1917–1940* (Moscow, 1954), 143.

30. Leshchinskii, *Kto byl nichem . . .* , 17.

31. *Izvestiia*, 1926, no. 39 (February 17), p. 3.

32. Leshchinskii, *Kto byl nichem . . .* , 67.

33–34. *Drug detei* (Khar'kov), 1926, no. 2: 24 (fig. 33); no. 1: 10 (fig. 34).

35. Frank Alfred Golder and Lincoln Hutchinson, *On the Trail of the Russian Famine* (Stanford, 1927), facing p. 19.

36. *Illiustrirovannaia Rossiia* (Paris), 1929, no. 24: 7.

37. P. C. Hiebert and Orie O. Miller, *Feeding the Hungry: Russian Famine, 1919–1925* (Scottdale, Penn., 1929), between pp. 224 and 225.

38. *Illiustrirovannaia Rossiia* (Paris), 1929, no. 24: cover.

39–40. Leshchinskii, *Kto byl nichem . . .* , 23, 111.

41. *Illiustrirovannaia Rossiia* (Paris), 1929, no. 16: 7.

42. *Illiustrirovannaia Rossiia* (Paris), 1926, no. 47: 5.

43. V. L. Shveitser and S. M. Shabalov, eds., *Besprizornye v trudovykh kommunakh. Praktika raboty s trudnymi det'mi. Sbornik statei i materialov* (Moscow, 1926), 59.

44–50. TsGALI, f. 332, o. 2, ed. khr. 72, ll. 7–8 (figs. 44–45); ed. khr. 74, ll. 69, 60 (figs. 46–47); ed. khr. 72, ll. 37, 2 (figs. 48–49); ed. khr. 74, l. 246 (fig. 50).

Index

Compositor:	Impressions, A Division of Edwards Brothers, Inc.
Text:	10/13 Sabon
Display:	Sabon
Printer:	Edwards Brothers, Inc.
Binder:	Edwards Brothers, Inc.